Open Minds to Equality

A SOURCEBOOK OF LEARNING ACTIVITIES TO AFFIRM DIVERSITY AND PROMOTE EQUITY

Second Edition

Nancy Schniedewind

State University of New York—New Paltz

Ellen Davidson

Simmons College

Allyn and Bacon
Boston London Toronto Sydney Tokyo Singapore

Credits
Series editor: Frances Helland
Series editorial assistant: Kris Lamarre
Marketing manager: Kathy Hunter
Advertising manager: Anne Morrison
Manufacturing buyer: Suzanne Lareau

Copyright © 1998, 1983 by Allyn & Bacon
A Viacom Company
Needham Heights, MA 02194

Internet: www.abacon.com
American Online: keyword: College Online

Library of Congress Cataloging-in-Publication Data

Schniedewind, Nancy, [date]–
    Open minds to equality : a sourcebook of learning activities to
affirm diversity and promote equity / Nancy Schniedewind, Ellen
Davidson.—2nd ed.
       p.   cm.
    Includes bibliographical references.
    ISBN 0–205–16109–X (pb)
    1. Equality—Study and teaching.   2. Prejudices—Study and
teaching.   3. Cooperativeness—Study and teaching.   I. Davidson,
Ellen.   II. Title.
    HM146.S26   1998
    305′.071—dc21   97–26994
                                                                         CIP

Printed in the United States of America
10 9 8 7 6 5 4 3 2 1   01 00 99 98 97

This book is dedicated to

Grace Douglass Schniedewind
and *William Schniedewind*

Adelaide Heyman Davidson,
Henry Alexander Davidson,
and *Ella Yohalem Heyman*

whose nurturance, courage, values,
and love inspired the vision of this book.

The Authors

Nancy Schniedewind is Professor of Educational Studies at the State University of New York, New Paltz, New York, where she teaches in a Masters Program in Humanistic Education. She also works with educators in professional development programs on diversity education in various school districts. She and Ellen Davidson have also written *Cooperative Learning, Cooperative Lives: Learning Activities for Building a Peaceful World*.

Ellen Davidson teaches education at Simmons and Wheelock Colleges in Boston and in a professional development program at Education Development Center in Newton, MA. She also works with schools to investigate and understand diversity issues, writes geography and history curricula, and helps teachers explore their teaching of mathematics.

Contents

Acknowledgments

Open Minds to Equality is truly a cooperative endeavor. The energy and hard work of many people are reflected in its pages!

Teachers with expertise in multicultural education, in public schools, private schools and universities, provided very helpful feedback. We are grateful for the suggestions of Lee Bell, Beverly Braxton, Karen Cathers, Catherine Menconari, José Salgado, and Sonia Nieto. We particularly appreciate the assurance offered by Karen Cathers and her fourth grade students that even the most challenging of these lessons are both accessible to, and meaningful for, young people. Nancy Braus of Everybody's Kids Books, Gail Pettiford Willet of Savanna Books and Edgar Rodriguez gave very helpful suggestions for the bibliography.

We appreciate the dedication and perseverance of our research assistants, Ann Farrell, Kate Mahar, Nina Malerba, and Sherri Ponzi. Gale McGovern edited the initial chapters with care. We have kept much of the art work from the first edition. Then thirteen-year-old Noelle Porter contributed the youthful pictures that may capture the spirit of some of your students.

Laurie Prendergast contributed her talent, skills and expertise in many ways throughout this project. In the original edition, she drew the wonderfully detailed characters that reflect the diversity of persons whose lives this book addresses. She has added new drawings to this edition as well. For this revision, Laurie also did extensive, comprehensive, and tedious work on the bibliography for which we are very grateful. Finally Laurie's insights, critiques and suggestions have helped us clarify and complicate our thinking and have made the lessons richer.

Nancy owes special thanks to people whose ideas and energy inspired her work in this book. They include friends, colleagues and students in the Humanistic Education Program and Women's Studies Program at S.U.N.Y.–New Paltz. She appreciates the support of the Dean of the School of Education at S.U.N.Y.–New Paltz as well as faculty members there. She values the commitment of those educators she has worked with in long-term professional development programs in anti-bias education, particularly those in two New York school districts—New Paltz and Shoreham-Wading River. Their teaching has demonstrated that young people truly want to open their minds to equality. Thanks to Jesse and Daniel for keeping life lively, full of drama and good humor. Her very special thanks go to David Porter for sharing his keen intellect and unfailing social vision, and for his ongoing support.

Ellen owes special thanks to the many people who support, challenge and collaborate with her in her work. They include colleagues and students at both Simmons and Wheelock Colleges in Boston, her housemates at Tkanye, and the women in *Hopeful Travelers: White Women Challenging Racism*. Thanks to Hannah and Aviva for their good energy, total enjoyment of diversity, full-hearted belief that the world can be fair, and frequent challenging of the status quo. And especially to Jim Hammerman for his hard questions, his constant support and encouragement in big ideas and little ones, and his theoretical and practical suggestions in multiple areas of this project.

Nancy Schniedewind
Ellen Davidson

Introduction

We have a dream. We envision classrooms and schools that are communities where students and teachers feel secure and cared about and where all forms of diversity are respected and appreciated. Here people don't feel afraid or threatened by those different from themselves, rather they feel stimulated by new discoveries about diversity that they regularly make. These are democratic classrooms and schools where all students are treated fairly and have equitable access to resources and opportunities. We envision a similar society and believe that as students and teachers we have the potential to contribute to the creation of that society.

Given all that the media tell us is wrong with students, teachers and schools, and given teachers' daily struggles with the difficulty of our jobs, such a vision may seem idealistic. Yet there are myriads of classrooms and schools in which pieces of this vision are realities every day. Through the activities in *Open Minds to Equality* we can put more and more of that vision into practice.

This challenge is far from easy. Many adults today fear the changes in our society, are alienated from their work and mourn the loss of community. It's comforting to seek ideas and organizations that provide certainty and simple answers. People perceived as "other" are easily blamed, just as ideas that challenge a person's coherent world view are easily feared. Young people imbibe the ideas and feelings of the adults and culture around them. To open their minds and hearts to equality necessitates our building classrooms and schools in which change is empowering, where work is meaningful and where community is genuine. Then young people, teachers, parents, can know, through lived experience, that alternatives are possible to what society offers people today.

In such classroom and school communities differences are named and appreciated. It takes hard intellectual and emotional work on the part of teachers and students to struggle with the ideas and feelings that keep us apart. Yet we know that elementary and middle school students can understand difficult issues that relate to equality and inequality, discrimination, power relations and social justice. They need adults to provide safe space, language and opportunities to talk about their lives, struggles and visions. *Open Minds to Equality* offers a sequenced process, skills and activities to empower students to understand and change their lives and the world around them.

OUR APPROACH TO EDUCATING FOR EQUALITY

We believe that for young people to truly appreciate diversity and understand democracy, our classrooms need to become places where students experience equality as part of their daily lives. They explore how different forms of discrimination such as racism and sexism affect them and their peers, as well as consider how to change them.

At the same time, young people can learn about the ways in which discrimination affects people different from themselves and how inequality is perpetuated societally. They can discover how people work together to promote social justice. Students' experience in an egalitarian classroom enables them to envision what a truly just society could be. Such a vision is essential to maintain direction, energy and hope as we collectively work for change.

Both classroom content and process are important for teaching to affirm diversity and promote equity. *Open Minds to Equality* explores many of the different forms of discrimination that inhibit equity. Young people as well as adults are affected by discrimination based on race, gender, class, age, physical/emotional/learning ability, sexual orientation, language and religion, among others. These forms of difference, rather than being seen as the source of richness, creativity and collective potential, are often used to maintain inequality. Through activities in this book students will learn how this happens and also explore actions that could, instead, foster social justice.

The content of the lessons also encourages students to be critical: to raise critical questions, explore different sources of information and various points of view, and to consider how knowledge can be constructed to maintain inequality. Lessons raise issues in ways that get students thinking, rather than putting them on the defensive. In turn, activities encourage students to do the same when talking about these issues with others.

The lessons in *Open Minds to Equality* reflect a classroom process that is experiential, participatory, cooperative and democratic. Students explore their own experience as a source of learning about equality. If, for example, they are studying racism, they think about ways racism has affected their lives. In this way their learning is personally meaningful. It is also participatory: students work with others to share experiences, investigate problems, answer questions and act for change.

Since competition maintains inequality and cooperation fosters equity, classroom norms are cooperative. Students are taught skills for communication, cooperation and interpersonal understanding. The class may engage in a community meeting to solve a common problem. While only some lessons reflect a carefully structured cooperative learning format, most encourage students to cooperate with each other to learn. Finally, the learning process is democratic in that all voices and ideas are encouraged and differences are dealt with by listening, talking and opening our minds and hearts to each other. We will describe in more detail our approach to educating for equality in Chapter Two.

A SEQUENTIAL PROCESS FOR CREATING INCLUSIVE CLASSROOMS AND SCHOOLS

From our teaching and research we have developed a sequential process for creating inclusive classrooms and schools, a process through which people gain greater understanding about personal and institutional inequality and develop the skills and commitment to foster change. The sequence of this book follows that process. Since dealing with diversity integrates both cognitive and affective learning, it is important to follow this sequential process, a process which engages

people with the issues in a nonthreatening way rather than alienating them.

Step A. Create an Inclusive, Trusting Community Where Students Appreciate Diversity in the Classroom

Initially, a supportive, caring environment is needed for students to feel safe enough to examine their attitudes and to explore ideas that may challenge preconceived notions. It takes very intentional work on the part of a teacher to create that environment. Students need to be taught skills for working together, just as they are taught reading or math skills. Chapter Three, "Building Trust and Communication," and Chapter Four, "Developing Skills for Creative Cooperation," contain activities that develop trust, as well as skills in cooperation, decision-making, listening, critical thinking, interviewing and group work. When students feel secure, accepted and respected by their teacher and peers, they will be most honest and willing to take risks to learn.

Step B. Enable Students to Empathize with Others' Life Experiences and Explore Why and How Inequality Based on Difference Exists

Students need an opportunity to explore their own social identities and then to empathize with the life experiences of people different from themselves, something lessons in Chapter Five, "Expanding Our Vistas: Our Lives to Others' Lives," provide for. Words and language to name, define and discuss inequality and its consequences are essential to students' growing awareness. In Chapter Six, "New Words: New Eyes for Seeing," students define and recognize prejudice, stereotypes and the "isms." In Chapter Seven, "Discrimination: Prices and Choices," they learn about the effects both individual and institutional inequality have on the lives and opportunities of people in various social groups. Here they also explore some of the complex dynamics of a system of oppression.

Step C. Help Students Examine Discrimination in the Institutions in Their Lives and See How It Has Affected Them

Once students understand these ideas they can apply them directly to their own lives. Chapter Eight, "Investigating Your Environment," and Chapter Nine, "More Environmental Influences and Their Effects," use the family, school and community as a laboratory for students to investigate how inequality is institutionalized. Students develop a critical awareness of the institutions they're a part of and discover the ways in which prejudice and the isms affect them daily.

Step D. Empower Students to Envision and Create Changes to Foster Greater Equality

By now, students have the knowledge and motivation to act for change. Chapter Ten, "Things Can Be Different," shows students realistic ways people have fostered equality in the past and continue to do so. The final chapter, "We Can Make Changes!", contains resources and activities that enable students to change unequal situations and promote social justice. Students who have identified sexism in their reading books, for example, write and illustrate alternative stories. This activity encourages them to act against sexism and develops their skills in creative writing and art. So often we hear, "You just can't change things." Through activities that point out what others have done to foster social justice and through their own initiative, students gain self-confidence, personal power and experience in collective responsibility and action.

Thus the activities in *Open Minds to Equality* help students progress developmentally and sequentially in their understanding of inequality and in their ability to foster change. This same sequenced process can be applied to learners of all ages, including ourselves, as we work to affirm diversity and promote equity in our personal and professional lives. Even though there are key ideas, themes and information that we expect students will learn, students in different schools and communities will have different experiences doing the activities. We encourage you to be flexible in adapting the lessons to your classroom and community context.

USING THIS BOOK

While *Open Minds to Equality* is geared for upper elementary and middle school students, it is also very appropriate for high school students as well. In fact, primary, high school and college teachers have used the first edition of this book with great enthusiasm and success. These teachers often need to adapt lessons to the level of their students.

There are many ways to integrate *Open Minds to Equality* into your teaching. What is most important is that you teach chapters, and chapter sections within them, sequentially. Given that, you can choose learning activities appropriate for your students within the sequential chapters. Your choices may depend on the needs of your students, areas you believe are important to emphasize, school and community variables, the subject matter focus of a lesson, your curriculum or the difficulty of the concepts.

First read through this Introduction, Chapter One and Two and the introduction to the other chapters; then skim through the lessons. This will give you a feeling for the progression of objectives and ideas in the book. Teachers in elementary schools who have students all day should find it possible to do one or two activities from a chapter section every week or two. If chosen carefully, these can reinforce the cognitive skills you are already teaching. Many middle and high school teachers can similarly integrate lessons into their curriculum, particularly in social studies, language arts/reading/ English, health, or home and career skills. The book is also very useful for special units or courses in multicultural education, human relations and diversity awareness. For example, in one high school, students in a Peer Leadership elective experienced lessons in *Open Minds to Equality* and then taught them to students in classes in the district's elementary school.

While *Open Minds to Equality* is written to be used in the classroom, there are other ways teachers can use the book. Many middle schools have advisory or home base. By giving careful attention to the time frame and modifying lessons or teaching them over several days, teachers can make *Open Minds to Equality* the focus of their advisory for a year. In fact, if the goal of an entire school is to encourage appreciation of diversity, this could be the program for all advisories. Similarly, these activities can be the focus of extracurricular multicultural clubs in schools and the programs of Ys, youth groups, camps and other organizations.

This second edition is different from the first in several ways that will affect its use. The first edition focused primarily on four forms of diversity—race, gender, class and age. In this edition we have expanded the range of diversity covered to include religion, physical and mental ability, sexual orientation and language. We hope teachers will address them all. You may choose to emphasize particular aspects of diversity given the composition of your class and community and the needs of your students.

This new edition of *Open Minds to Equality* also includes more complex and sophisticated lessons. In fact, many of the new lessons are thought-provoking and challenging for adults as well as young people. These lessons *are* doable for young people whose teachers have been addressing multicultural issues with them over time. They would be inappropriate for teachers and young people just beginning to deal with diversity. The content of most activities is accessible to students from upper elementary grades upward, although a few are more appropriate for those in middle school. Therefore choose lessons with an eye to their complexity and age-appropriateness.

The varying complexity of the lessons allows for *Open Minds to Equality* to be used across grade levels in a single school. If teachers in one grade teach the more basic concepts and lessons one year, still following the sequential process, other teachers in the next grade can build on those learnings and teach more sophisticated ideas and lessons in the next year. In this way ongoing awareness of issues of equality can be developed over time.

A Resource Section at the end of the book includes many ways you can integrate lessons from *Open Minds to Equality* into your standard curriculum, particularly in social studies, reading, language arts, math and art. The activities in this book are designed not as an appendage to your regular curriculum, but as a resource that can fit into it.

It's important to remember that *Open Minds to Equality* is an egalitarian approach to teaching and learning, not merely a series of lessons. You can infuse much of what you typically do in the classroom with the spirit of this book. For example, you can give students spelling sentences that include the names and experiences of people from various cultural backgrounds. You can make sure that math problems include low-income people. When you line students up, you can have lines based on creative variables like sock color rather than gender. Such an ongoing approach in your classroom reflects a personal and professional commitment to equality.

TEACHER LEARNING

We hope that this book will be a rich source of learning for you as well. We learn immeasurably as we write it and try lessons, so we expect you'll do the same. We've interspersed intriguing "boxes" of information and challenging ideas for teachers throughout the book. We hope the Background Reading for Teachers section in the Bibliography will spur you to read further.

If possible, try to teach *Open Minds to Equality* with support. Perhaps a colleague in your school will use it with you and you can give each other feedback, ideas and support. When a number of teachers in a school or school district use *Open Minds to Equality*, we urge that you ask your district for staff development opportunities on teaching for diversity that will heighten teachers' own personal awareness and critical consciousness of multicultural issues. This, followed by periodic support groups or sessions where teachers can share successes, problems and concerns, is valuable for working through the challenging task of teaching about diversity.

In the process of using *Open Minds to Equality* you may come to realize you've been unintentionally reinforcing inequality in your teaching or life. Try to see this awareness as positive, in that only when a problem becomes visible can it be rectified. For example, only when a white teacher becomes aware that to talk about issues of race as a "black problem" is to avoid personal responsibility for white racism, can that teacher gain a new perspective from which to confront racism.

It is this kind of growth that we hope you'll look forward to in this book. Such learning is not always easy, but it is hopeful. Implicitly and explicitly we've been taught prejudice, and we've been socialized not to examine and challenge institutional practices that support inequality. This is not our fault. Once aware of those behaviors and practices, however, it becomes our responsibility to change them.

Change, not guilt, is the intent of *Open Minds to Equality*. Guilt is paralyzing. If we wallow in it, we don't do anything to change things. We encourage you to be aware of the messages you give yourself as you read this book. Instead of becoming guilty or defensive, try telling yourself, "I'm glad I'm aware of this; now I can change it!" That's a powerful statement—a step to becoming an ever more effective teacher.

Ideally, making changes in your classroom will increase your involvement in efforts to make changes in your school, your community, and the broader society. Such activity is important not only because of your own desire to promote social justice, but for the opportunities it can open to your students. Linking students with community activists and involving students with issues beyond the school can be empowering. It also reinforces the reality that social change is a collective process, often bringing diverse groups of people together to work toward common goals.

OUR VISION

As teachers advocating personal and social change through education, we distinguish between long and short-term goals. We share a vision of an equitable society where personal and institutional discrimination based on any form of difference has been eliminated and where people cooperate toward goals that benefit all. While we know that this vision is far from realized, it is important for us to know what we are striving toward. We formulate short-term goals, those small day-to-day changes that are building-blocks toward the future. *Open Minds to Equality* provides ideas and activities to achieve such short-term goals. The consequences of these efforts contribute to the broader vision of a just and equal society. We're encouraged that you're joining us.

Chapter

1

Recognizing Roadblocks to Equality

As teachers in a pluralistic society we encounter an exciting challenge every time we enter the classroom. We interact with diverse young people with whom we strive to create a classroom community where all can learn together in an equitable, challenging and happy way. The lessons we teach students about living in this diverse community, as well as the knowledge and skills gained from academic subjects, prepare them for life in our democratic society. What we do affects not only our classroom but our nation's future as well.

Open Minds to Equality: A Sourcebook of Learning Activities to Affirm Diversity and Promote Equity will help you meet this challenge. For us equality implies the following:

- All people are truly valued and treated fairly.
- People from diverse social groups are respected.
- Social structures—from our classrooms to our communities to the broader society—are democratic and provide all people equitable opportunities.

When we use the word equality in this book, we don't mean mere sameness; we mean that which is equitable and just. Given the privilege that some people have and the discrimination others endure in our society, that which is the same is not always fair.

In classrooms that foster equality, teachers help students respect diversity. Educators work with stu-

dents and colleagues to change practices and curricula that prevent all students from learning to their full potential. Democratic classroom practices that foster respect and fairness are the norm. Students are involved in learning activities and problem solving processes that give them responsibility and power; that raise their awareness of the ways in which difference is used to maintain inequality; and that enable them to create changes that foster equity. Concurrently academic learning increases significantly as well.

Equality in our communities and society means that members of all social groups have respect and equitable opportunities. All people have access to the goods and power of the society—meaningful work at a fair wage, health care, decent housing, food, opportunities for personal development, and decision-making power in what affects their lives. People act for the common good. When discrimination impedes equality, people take action to foster social justice. *Open Minds to Equality* is a resource to help teachers make their classrooms and schools learning laboratories for equality.

Teaching for equality involves challenging many forms of bias that are commonplace in schools and society. *Open Minds to Equality* focuses particularly on discrimination based on race, gender, class and age. It addresses to a lesser degree physical/mental ability, religion, sexual orientation, language and those individualistic, competitive behaviors that deny some students basic human dignity.

The questions posed and information offered in Chapter One will help you reflect on how these forms of inequality may exist in your classroom and school. Subsequent lessons provide you and your students more detailed understandings about them. For the most part, we discuss various forms of inequality separately for the sake of initial clarity. In reality, they are very much woven together in people's individual lives as well as interconnected in a societal system of oppression. As you read, do so with an eye to the effects of the interrelationships of these forms of oppression on your life, the lives of your students and your community.

We try to use language that members of particular social groups prefer. While there is seldom unanimity within a group, there is often some agreement. For example, many blacks descended from African peoples want to be called African American. When there is less consensus within a group we use several terms, such as American Indian and Native American. These preferences may change over time.

RACISM

What is racism, and how is it different from prejudice? "Prejudice" is a negative personal behavior that discriminates against individuals. "Racism" is a belief that human beings have distinctive characteristics and that one race has a right to more power and resources than another: often policies, systems of government or societies are based on such beliefs. When power is added to prejudice, it becomes racism. For example, if a white child calls a black child a demeaning name, she exhibits prejudice. When, however, the policies and norms of a school system, school or teacher sanction (by action or inaction) such name-calling, this is racism.

While people can experience discrimination because of race or ethnicity, when we discuss racism in this book we mean oppression based on skin color. For us ethnicity has to do with historical, geographical and/or cultural roots of a person or group. In some approaches to multicultural education, culture and ethnicity are focussed on without attention to racism. This ignores the importance of how racial difference is used to maintain inequality. People with the same ethnic backgrounds may have very different experiences because of their race. For example, a light-skinned Latina from Cuba typically experiences less racism than a dark-skinned Latina from Puerto Rico.

We use the term "people of color" to refer to African Americans, Caribbean Americans, Asian Americans and Pacific Islanders, some Latino/as, and Native Americans, among others. Even within any one of these broadly defined racial groups there are significant differences in history, culture, and peoples' experience of oppression. Ethnicity often differs too; for example, Asian Americans can be of Japanese, Chinese or Filipino descent, among others. Despite these varied cultural and ethnic backgrounds, people of color experience racism in the United States because of their race.

Similarly white people, though of varied ethnic backgrounds, experience privilege because they are Caucasian. European Americans have had different experiences with discrimination because of their ethnic-

ity and the historical period in which they immigrated to the United States. For example, people from northern Europe typically faced less discrimination than those from southern or eastern Europe. Nevertheless, the socially constructed idea of race, designating specific groups with innate differences and defining whites as superior to other races, has provided advantages to whites whatever their ethnicity. The fact that whites haven't had to deal with racial discrimination, as people of color have, has provided whites opportunities and privileges because of race. While some lessons in *Open Minds to Equality* address ethnicity, when discussing racism we examine white racism and its effects on people of color.

Take a look at your school. How racially diverse are the administrators and teachers? Check the bulletin boards. How diverse are those faces? If you are in a school that enrolls children of color who are predominantly from one group, are portrayals of other children of color visible? Do a survey of your texts and supplementary books. What percentage deals with people of color? What roles do they play? Do the pictures show people with European features tinted black or brown? What holidays does the school celebrate and what cultures do they represent? Do you incorporate perspectives of people of color into your lessons?

Your school doesn't have to be integrated to be accountable for racism. In fact, children develop their racial attitudes not only from contact with people of other races but from the prevailing attitudes about them. If, in a predominantly white school, people of color and their cultures are omitted from reading materials and discussions, and aren't seen on bulletin boards, it isn't hard for students to conclude that people of color are not very important. In fact, if you teach in a predominantly white school, you might ask, "Why is it so white?"

In a racially mixed school, you might ask additional questions. To the extent there is ability grouping or tracking, is there a pattern of white students in the advanced groups and students of color in the lower tracks? Do some teachers make different interventions if a white child falls behind than if an African-American or Latino/a child does? If there is bussing in your district, does everybody get bussed or do some students get to stay in the neighborhood school? Is there a correlation between disciplinary actions and the race of the young people? Do racially diverse groups of parents and community members participate in educational decision-making, for example evaluating books for racial bias? Are the cultural values of children of color integral to school norms? Have teachers sought out new knowledge about the cultures of people of color in order to better understand their students' lives?

Racism in schools and society affects both children of color and white students. You have probably seen its effects. Racism may cause some children of color to act out in aggressive ways or withdraw and give up entirely. In other children, it may negatively affect their self-concepts and cause them to lower their educational goals. Sometimes well-intentioned teachers may encourage this. A Latino student reported that in his school when he and other Latino/a students he knew did poorly on a test, teachers asked them if they wanted to move into an easier class. Teachers didn't do that for white students he knew who tested similarly.

Because of discrimination in standardized testing, tracking and institutional norms, many children of color are denied their full potential for learning. A dou-ble standard on the part of the school system or the teacher has a powerful effect on children of color. An overly harsh, punitive standard creates fear and anger. One that is overly lenient—sometimes the result of a teacher's fear of confronting children of color in an honest, firm and supportive way—is equally harmful. Students are cheated of the expectation of meeting academic and behavioral standards. The message they receive in the first case is that teachers are unfair and really don't care about them. In the second, since they're not expected to achieve and abide by the school rules, they may come to believe that they're not capable of achievement and they won't face consequences for misbehavior. Their potential for learning and prosocial behavior diminishes.

Because of the unequal educational opportunities afforded most children of color, so well documented in Jonathan Kozol's *Savage Inequalities*, they often enter a teacher's class underprepared. This can be true for children of any race, particularly those living in poor communities. More teacher time and special learning opportunities are needed for these students to upgrade their knowledge and skills. If the teacher and school communicate the expectation that all children can and are expected to achieve, and if programs are available to students whose skills have been negatively affected by unequal opportunities, children of color within this group will be more successful in school. It is important that these programs assume the competence of the learners by designing them as enrichment programs, rather than remedial programs. If, however, the low educational expectations of poor children of color that many policy makers hold remain in place, children in urban schools will continue to get only the "basics" needed for entry level jobs. At the same time, students in predominantly white suburban schools get more expansive programs that focus on college preparation.

White children, who are privileged by racism in many ways, are negatively affected as well. These children can develop a distorted view of themselves, others and society. For those living in relatively segregated communities, their world is a white enclave that often reinforces stereotypes of people of color, denying them the enriching experience of learning and living with people of other races. Their chances for open communication in the future are diminished. Many textbooks, films and library books reinforce the message of the broader culture—that white is normal and therefore "right." The unconscious assumption that what is white is normal can affect white children's perceptions, values and interactions with others throughout life. They can develop paternalistic attitudes toward people of color and low expectations of their abilities. Further, if these young people perceive a double standard in teacher and administrator behavior favoring whites, their sense of superiority is reinforced. If teachers or administrators are lenient toward students of color, white students can harbor resentment and anger that permanently affects their impressions and actions.

Thus racism takes its toll on everyone. *All* children lose an opportunity to work together cooperatively and learn from the richness of others' experiences, world views, and lives. They lose out on valuable friendships and a much fuller education.

Racism Hurts White Children

Cultural racism as expressed in educational materials limits the development of white children.... it provides them with a false sense of their own self-esteem. Their self-esteem is not based on real things but on the alleged inferiority of someone else. And it frequently gives them a sense that they are owed something because they are white.

Dr. Alvin Poussaint, in *Bulletin*,
Council on Interracial Books for Children, Vol. 7, No. 1

SEXISM

"Sexism" is the belief that females and males have distinctive characteristics and that one gender has the right to more power and resources than the other; it is policies and practices based on those beliefs. As with racism and other forms of oppression, sexism is different from prejudice in that it is reinforced by power. When a female student in a math class is having difficulty figuring out a problem and a male student says, "Girls can't do math," he is exhibiting prejudice. However, when a teacher takes no action to deal with a pattern of males dominating the discussion in math class, or when a school district doesn't provide information or staff development about curricular and pedagogical approaches that confront some girls' beliefs of math incompetence, they are reinforcing sexism. School systems and teachers have the power to enforce and legitimize prejudice based on gender.

Because of efforts to promote gender equity in education, many teachers are conscious of sexism in school. Even as attitudes and awareness change, it takes much hard work to change behaviors. Think about the most recent class or school plays. How were women portrayed? If people from another culture were to view those plays, how would they describe the female gender in our culture? What do teachers do when boys make fun of girls in stereotypical ways? To do or say nothing is to sanction their behavior and words. Do teachers allow boys to call each other sissies or say "You're acting like a girl"? This reinforces aggressive gender socialization of males in our culture, misogyny and prejudice about gay youth or men. Have students been taught about sexual harassment so they understand what kinds of behaviors at their age are examples of sexual harassment and therefore not allowed in school?

Do teachers assign chores according to traditional gender roles? Do girls as well as boys move furniture? Have you noticed what books girls and boys choose to read? For example, do boys seldom choose to read library books about women or girls? Are they encouraged to do so? Are girls' papers expected to be neater than boys? Are girls encouraged to aspire to all occupations, including traditionally male occupations like scientist or carpenter? Are boys encouraged into alternative roles like nurse, dietitian or secretary? Are guest speakers with nontraditional jobs invited to the school? Have teachers actively encouraged fathers to help with class projects or bake something for the holiday party? Have there been changes in classroom schedules or procedures to make this possible?

You can see some of the effects of sexism on the behaviors of both boys and girls. Girls tend to be less sure of themselves than boys in activities that call for assertive behavior. They often use traditionally "feminine" behavior because of the positive attention they get from males. For example, if a girl is a captain of a team, she'll often pick boys first because, in the words of a fifth-grade girl, "Then they'll like you better." Girls may choose to wear clothes or shoes that are bad for their physical development and posture, or that prohibit active body movement because "that's the style" and they want to be "popular."

LOOK CINDERELLA...MAYBE YOU SHOULD SKIP THE BALL,
AND JOIN A CONSCIOUSNESS RAISING GROUP INSTEAD.

Girls' Self-Esteem Slide

In their comprehensive book *Failing at Fairness: How America's Schools Cheat Girls,* David and Myra Sadker present their research on what happens to girls' self-esteem in middle school. Among their findings are:

- Boys feel that "they can do things," while girls' belief in themselves falls.
- Teachers tend to jump in and help girls rather than supporting them in figuring things out themselves.
- Many girls lose the courage to express their honest thoughts and feelings; e.g., they might raise their hands halfway up and then pull them down.
- Bright girls play down their intelligence in order to be accepted.

Although they benefit from sexism, boys also pay a heavy price. Boys develop a sense of entitlement in school: they feel they have the right to the best library table, so they take it. You can also observe boys feeling the pressure to meet the image of the strong, tough male and giving up a willingness to show their emotions, be supportive of others and be tender or thoughtful to their friends, especially after grade four. When boys call each other sissies or chastise each other for "acting like a girl," they not only hurt others but inhibit gentle parts of themselves. Many boys feel inhibited from playing with dolls or stuffed animals when they're young. Do you see boys making pretty things in art, or is a robot or rocket a more familiar image? Do your textbooks show men only in adventurous roles or as athletes, limiting the role models depicted for boys? While it's okay for girls to dance together, boys wouldn't dare. Inhibiting the development of caring and warm behaviors in boys, sexism sets up other ex-

pectations—that boys like sports, be competitive, be ready to fight, and not be like girls.

The attitudes and behaviors that sexism produces in children take a heavy, long-range toll on both genders. By about the fourth grade, relationships between boys and girls tend to become antagonistic or of the boyfriend-girlfriend type. The potential for experiencing the fullness of equal friendships with young people of the opposite sex—building blocks for healthy adult relationships—is often relinquished. Girls often show low self-concepts and dependency traits which are disadvantages in personal and later career development. The early pressure for boys to compete, to be rational and to achieve at all costs produces behavior patterns that lead to stress-related diseases and premature death in adult men. Masculine conditioning and the power it confers have social implications as well, contributing to the acceptance of aggression and violence as solutions to problems, from the local to the international level. Teacher intervention in the classroom, however, can change many of these patterns.

Reading for Teachers

- In *Gender Play: Girls and Boys in School,* Barrie Thorne examines the social interaction of girls and boys in elementary school, especially in relation to gender socialization and the use of power.
- The voices of adolescent girls tell of the effects of sexism on their lives, spirit and self esteem in Mary Pipher's book, *Reviving Ophelia: Saving the Selves of Adolescent Girls.*
- In *Boys Will Be Boys: Breaking the Link Between Masculinity and Violence,* Myriam Miedzian looks particularly at how boys are drawn to the masculine mystique by the superiority promised by their socialization.

EXAMINING YOUR CLASSROOM FOR RACISM AND SEXISM

After twelve years of grade school and years of college, it's natural that our methods mimic those of our teachers. As a result, some of these methods may inadvertently be racist or sexist. Go through an average day in your classroom and ask yourself: Do you unconsciously segregate students by race or gender at any time of the day? Do you have them line up by gender? Have you seated students of the same race or gender together or allowed them to sit together by choice on a permanent basis? Do you ever set up academic or other contests with "boys against girls"? All these practices reinforce the idea that males and females, or white students and students of color, are, in fact, different.

Think about the language you use in your classroom. Do you call any of your students "dear" or "honey"? What terms do you use to refer to students of color? The word "boy", however innocently intended, has negative connotations for older black male students. Do you refer to "their" attitudes and feelings (Latino/as, women, Asian Americans and so on) as a group rather than as individuals? This can be a subtle form of stereotyping. Have you adopted nonsexist vocabulary? Do you say "human beings" rather than "mankind," for example?

Do you talk more with one group during discussions or let students of one race or gender take over? Do you allow for the fact that cultural or institutional sexism or racism may have done a job on such students before they even got to your classroom and intentional efforts to equalize participation may be necessary? Ask yourself, for example, "How am I intervening in the classroom process to encourage girls' voices and help boys learn to listen and share discussion time?"

What you don't say can be especially powerful. Not using a student's name or ignoring a group of students of one race or gender is a quick way to destroy self-worth. If another student or teacher is demeaning a student do you take action of some sort to try to effect change? Ignoring such words as "bitch," "nigga," "wimp," is very destructive.

How you group students can have a racist or sexist implication. If you group them by achievement or skill level, a practice we urge you to rethink, and the group working slowest or fastest is made up of students of one gender or race, a message is transmitted. Reexamine any grouping processes, however thoughtful your criteria, for racist or sexist outcomes.

Is your treatment of students consistent and fair? Is it fair to discipline Marie for speaking in what, for her, is a "normal" tone and never to reprimand Tom for using the same tone? To what extent do you try to rid yourself of preconceived expectations of student potential and give all students comparable feedback on their written work? Do you comment more on the form of girls' work and the content of males', or lower your expectations of African-American students' writing? Since these are things some teachers do unconsciously, have you worked with a colleague to observe each other's teaching to help pinpoint unintended bias?

Have you examined your curriculum for bias, not only in terms of representation of people of various racial and gender backgrounds, but in terms of what content is covered and what perspectives are presented? Do students assume from their texts, for example, that the European-based names are *the* names for the constellations and not know that this might not be the way a Caribbean-American student in the class learned to name the stars? Do you ask students to ask about their books, "From whose perspective is this written and what group(s) of people does it serve?"

Where Are the Women?

In *Failing at Fairness: How American Schools Cheat Girls*, Myra and David Sadker report results of 1992 research on textbooks, in which they found females underrepresented. Textbooks from Macmillan and D. C. Heath had twice as many boys and men as women and girls. In some readers that ratio was three to one. In Heath's 1992 sixth grade text, *Exploring Our World, Past and Present*, only eleven female names were mentioned and not a single American adult woman was included. In the entire 631 pages of a textbook covering the history of the world, only seven pages related to women, either as famous individuals or as a general group.

The impact of a male curriculum is reflected in student knowledge. When the Sadkers walked into classrooms at all levels and asked students to name twenty famous American women from history who weren't athletes or entertainers few students could meet the challenge. Many couldn't name ten or even five. Some wrote down names like Betty Crocker and Aunt Jemima in an attempt to name famous females.

These are all places for us to begin to examine our own classrooms for potential changes to foster greater race and gender equity. Include students, colleagues and parents in your explorations as well!

TYPES OF RACISM AND SEXISM

Most educators are fair, humane people who care about the welfare of their students. Most of us are not intentionally racist or sexist. Often, however, the institutional practices of our schools or classrooms are racist and sexist, and we unwittingly reinforce them. As you read about the ways of thinking about racism and sexism described here, be aware that they can be applied to the other forms of discrimination discussed later in the chapter as well.

Individual racism and sexism are different from their institutional forms. Individual racism and sexism are those racist or sexist beliefs that are expressed in individual acts. An example is the teacher who calls a black male student "boy" with knowledge of the racist history of that term. In these cases people with more power than others are reinforcing racist or sexist beliefs. Another example is that of the media specialist who teaches only males to run the audio-visual equipment. Most of us try to avoid such acts.

More difficult to avoid, because they are more difficult to see, are institutional racism and sexism—racist and sexist behaviors that stem from social, economic, and political institutions. Some policies and practices of schools fit into this category. For example, financing public education by the property tax reinforces inequality. A typical wealthy, predominantly white suburb draws upon a larger tax base in proportion to its student population than a city of many poor people, predominantly of color. Even if the poor district taxes itself at a higher rate than the wealthy district, it is likely to end up with less money for each child in its schools. Look at the percentage of women who are superintendents of schools in your area. If that percentage is tiny, as it is in most areas of the country, you can readily see institutional sexism close to home. In fact, in 1995 seven percent of school superintendents in the United States were women.

Another important distinction among types of racism and sexism concerns intentionality. Conscious racism and sexism are acts which stem from thought-out racist or sexist attitudes. For example, if, after becoming aware that a textbook distorts the images or contributions of people of color, a teacher still uses the book without providing opportunities for students to investigate its bias, that is an example of conscious racism. Similarly, conscious sexism occurs when a teacher articulates a double standard for the behavior of girls and boys by saying, "Boys will be boys." This behavior may thwart independence in girls and allow boys to get away with aggressive behaviors that give them permission to be macho or "cool" in ways that hurt others.

> ### Examples of Institutional Racism and Sexism in Schools
>
> 1. **School Boards**
>   Some 93.95 percent of this country's school board members are white, 3.2 percent are black, 1.5 percent are Latino/a, 0.8 percent are Native American, 0.2 percent are Asian American and 0.5 percent are from other ethnic groups.
>
>   Two thirds of school board members have family incomes over $50,000 and 65.2 percent are male.
>
>   These data were reported in the January 1993 issue of the *American School Board Journal*. The statistics do not differ significantly from fifteen years ago, when the journal first began surveying American school boards.
>
> 2. **Administration**
>   The following percentages of school administrators are female. Note the decline in higher levels of administration.
>
>   - 44.2% of elementary school principals
>   - 21.4% of junior high school principals
>   - 14.5% of high school principals
>
>   National Association of Secondary School Principals, 1994

While most of us avoid such behavior, many of us unwittingly practice unconscious racism or sexism. These are acts which give advantages to whites or males over people of color or females regardless of conscious motivation. We may act with the best intentions, but if the results give unfair advantages to males or whites, our actions are sexist or racist. For example, a criterion for advancement to administrative and supervisory positions is years of service. The intent of this criterion is to get experienced people into these jobs. However, if a school district only began hiring Puerto Rican teachers ten years ago, the result of the criterion is to give advantages to whites, who have not been previously discriminated against in hiring.

While most schools have changed from gender-segregated physical education programs, boys still typically get more experience and motivation to play basketball because of opportunities in recreation programs, support from male role models, and cultural messages. In a mixed sixth grade basketball class the girls often don't do as well as the boys, not because of lack of innate ability but because of less experience and motivation. If the boys make an issue of the girls' limited skills and the physical education teacher continues to teach without comment, she exhibits unconscious sexism. While her intentions of playing gender-integrated sports are positive, the results may be sexist. Instead, she might ask students why girls typically have less experience playing basketball than boys. She could make teasing unacceptable and structure the class in such a way as to allow skilled students to help the less-skilled ones in constructive, cooperative ways. This is the humanistic educator's goal—making sure the methods and materials used in the classroom promote fairness. It is a challenging task.

Institutional Racism and Sexism in Society

Schools are one of many institutions that reinforce inequality. Institutional discrimination in housing, employment and health care affects the lives of your students and their families, especially if these are low-income or single-parent families. As educators we need to work in collaboration with others and challenge all forms of inequality if we intend to provide opportunity and hope for all our students.

- In 1992, the U.S. Department of Housing and Urban Development found that 59% of African Americans faced discrimination when buying a home; 56% when renting an apartment; and 36% when applying for a job.

    Emerge magazine, February 1992, p. 9

- Despite three decades of affirmative action, "glass ceilings" and "concrete walls" still block women and minority groups from the top management ranks of American industry, a bipartisan Federal commission reported in March, 1995. White men, while constituting about 29% of the workforce, hold about 95 of every 100 senior management positions. White women have had greater success moving into middle management. White women hold 40% of those jobs, black women hold 5% and black men 4%. The report identified the barriers to advancement principally as the fears and prejudices of white male executives on the lower rungs of the corporate ladder. Hearings around the country revealed that many of these white men view their female and minority counterparts not in terms of their merit but in terms of their color and sex.

    At the same time the Equal Employment Opportunity Commission, the main Federal agency that investigates complaints of bias in employment, has a backlog of more than 90,000 cases.

    The New York Times, March 16, 1995, p. 22

CLASSISM

Class has to do with a person's position in society that is based on money, power and access to resources and opportunities. "Classism" is the differential treatment of groups of people because of their class background and the reinforcement of those differences through the cultural values and practices of institutions, such as schools. Classism systematically assumes and enforces the legitimacy, power and values of people of the middle and upper economic classes.

We don't talk much in the United States about class differences because of the prevailing myth of upward mobility. This claims that if you work hard you can make it; if you don't succeed, it's your fault and you deserve a lower class position. Moving from a poor or low-income background to a high class status has been possible for a small minority of people in the United States. It is these people who are held up to legitimize this Horatio Alger mythology.

However, institutional practices and cultural values in U.S. society actively maintain a relatively fixed class structure. Many poor and working class people are locked into their positions not by lack of motivation, inventiveness or hard work, but by policies of institutions and lack of opportunities, factors beyond their individual control. Schools are one institution that advantage children with class privilege and disadvantage those without. For example, Johnathan Kozol documents in *Savage Inequalities* that the best public schools in the US spend over $15,500 per pupil and have class sizes of about 15. The worst public schools spend under $3,000 and have over 60 students per class. In addition, economic inequality has increased significantly since the early 1980s in the United States, widening the gap between rich and poor and squeezing the shrinking middle class.

These questions may help you examine how class barriers to equality may be manifested in your school. Does the staff in your school have different academic and behavioral expectations of children, based on their class background? This is usually unintentional and very hard to notice. For example, do they assume that some will eventually go to college and others won't? Such expectations are often subtly communicated to students and affect their own expectations. Do teachers ask students to talk about vacations and trips, assuming that all children have these experiences? Do they use examples of expensive consumer products in their lessons, reinforcing the idea that "normal" people have the money and desire to buy them?

The Results of Economic Inequality

The percentage of children living in poverty in the U.S. is more than double that of other major industrialized countries, according to a 1992 report by the United Nations Children's Fund. Slightly more than 20% of U.S. children live in families with incomes below the poverty level. Comparable figures were 9.3 for Canada, 4.6 for France, 2.8 for West Germany and 1.6 for Sweden.

Reported in *Rethinking Schools*, May–June 1992

More American children lived in poverty in 1992 than in any other year since 1956, although our Gross National Product doubled during the same period.

Wasting America's Future
Children's Defense Fund, 1994

Are parents expected to provide extra money for school items? Do students have to pay for gym equipment or special trips? If students are tracked into reading or other academic groups, which income level class do most students in the lower groups or tracks come from? If there are special programs for the gifted, which socioeconomic class background do most of these students come from? Are there certain low income families in your school who are labeled, stereotyped and made into outcasts?

What messages about class are given in the textbooks and children's literature teachers use? What income level are the people who are portrayed? Look at the messages in the stories in your books. If people work hard, do they always succeed? What message does this give to a child whose parents are struggling very hard and not making it? Examine biographies in particular for this Horatio Alger theme since, by their nature, biographies describe people who have become prominent and don't address the lives of those who worked equally hard but did not. Do texts and stories implicitly blame poor people for their situation, or do they help children understand how some people have unequal opportunities because of their class background? Do texts focus on "famous people," usually those of privileged class status, or are the accomplishments and hard work of poor and working-class people given equal focus and respect?

You can probably recognize the effects of classism on poor and low-income students in your school. Because some of these children don't have the symbols of status that are "in" among students, they may be joked about, put down or ignored. In some schools students give teachers presents at Christmas and Chanukah. You may know of instances where students have resorted to stealing in order to be "just like everybody else." As they get older, students may find it harder to cross class lines in social interactions, either in school or in the community. Lower-socioeconomic-class students may be embarrassed to mix with more privileged students because of where their families live and who their friends are.

Expectations Matter

In a classic study by Robert Rosenthal and Lenore Jacobsen, described in their book *Pygmalion in the Classroom*, teachers were told that their class was tested and found to be "late bloomers" and would be expected to achieve exceptionally well that year. Indeed they did! However the "late-bloomers" were in fact a random sample of students with no special characteristics. Teachers' expectations affected their teaching and student learning.

In a detailed three-year study, Ray Rist found that in the initial year of school, teachers' expectations about academic potential were based almost totally on racial and socioeconomic facts about the child. These viewpoints affected student achievement and subsequent teachers' expectations.

Harvard Education Review, September 1970

Students from families with relatively little money may buy the most prized, expensive symbols of status—sneakers, X-brand jeans—in order to feel a positive identity and a sense of belonging. The sacrifices they make and the lengths to which they may go to purchase these items speak to the power of classism in our society. Because of the inequitable system for funding public education, schools serving low-income and poor students often have fewer resources, and inferior buildings. Sometimes teachers have become demoralized. Because of this, students often sense that education for them isn't that important and they lose confidence and hope.

Class differences also affect learning. Given that many low-income parents are struggling to get by and may not have had access to a good education themselves, they are less able to give their children academic help at home, provide many books in the home, pay for expensive trips or afford camps or extracurricular opportunities. Their children may come to school with fewer skills affirmed by the school and less self-confidence than their middle-class counterparts—an unequal start to academic equality. The skills that these children and their parents have and could contribute to school life aren't always valued. Finally, the prevailing portrait of higher-income people as "normal," bright and successful, evident in many texts and children's books and in the media, can lower other children's self-expectations, self-confidence and motivation. Young people usually don't see these as inhibitors to academic success and tend to blame themselves for being "dumb" if they don't do as well as others in school.

The effects of classism are evident in the behavior and attitudes of middle- and upper-class children as well. Privileged students may develop a conscious or unconscious sense of superiority by name-calling or merely through mental comparison. Privileged children may acquire either a lack of empathy for others or an equally destructive feeling of pity that motivates paternalistic behavior. They feel comfortable in school and other institutions, which they believe exist to help and support them, and from which they expect returns. They often have a history of family success in school, so they too expect to be successful. Students, parents and teachers usually don't see how their class advantage contributes to their academic success. They learn to take much for granted.

The effects of the attitudes and behaviors that classism fosters can be life-long. Children of all classes develop stereotypes of each other and a lack of respect, caring and communication. Although most do not consciously think about class, many develop a feeling that "this is my place in life." Lower-income children may be reinforced in their sense of inferiority of self-hate. They may either feel hostile toward more privileged people or emulate them while degrading themselves. Some come to accept their position and rationalize that they "deserve" this because they're "not good enough." In school such beliefs lower their academic expectations and impede learning. As adults they can project feelings of inadequacy, resentment and/or anger onto people different from themselves or onto institutions, like government, perceived to be supporting these "oth-

ers." For example, some low-income white people can project negative feelings about themselves onto people of color and onto programs like affirmative action that they perceive to support "them" against "us," exemplifying connections between classism and racism.

The effect on more privileged children can be equally strong. They can become accustomed to putting others down, either verbally or mentally, maintaining a false sense of their own superiority. They come to assume they are "normal Americans" and that because they have money, opportunities and the respect that goes with them, they are somehow better than others. They take for granted the choices they have in school and in life and assume that others have comparable choices; this makes it very hard for them to empathize with groups of people who don't have their access to resources and opportunities. Most don't see how their privileges are integrally connected to others' lack of them.

Our job is twofold. It is to foster in students greater awareness of attitudes, policies and practices that reinforce class stratification, and help them see alternatives to this form of inequality. It is also to encourage mutual understanding between students of all classes and to help them see the benefits to all of collaborative action to foster change.

The High Costs of Child Poverty

If we do not care about the healthy development of other people's children because it is right or implicit in America's deepest professed values about ensuring a fair playing field for every citizen, then perhaps we will care because it is in our self-interest and our national interest to care.

We conservatively estimate that future losses to the economy stemming from the effects of just one year of child poverty for 14.6 million children reach as high as $177 billion.

Wasting America's Future: The Children's Defense Fund Report on the Costs of Child Poverty, 1994

AGEISM

Age is another category used to label people and to re-inforce social inequality. "Ageism" is any attitude, action or institutional structure that subordinates a person or group because of age, or any assignment of roles in society on the basis of age. Ageism affects both old people and young people. Typically in this society young people and older people are dis-advantaged, while mid-life adults benefit from both greater acceptance and access to goods and power.

Stereotypes about both young people and old people help maintain this inequality. They are often seen as not capable of taking responsibility for themselves or able to make wise decisions because of their age. They are often denied access to opportunities, power or autonomy because of age rather than ability or maturity. While many old people do lose some of their physical and mental capabilities, others tend to generalize that if they can't do some things for themselves, they can't do anything.

It is often because of society's neglect of the needs of older people and youth, through inadequate health care, recreational opportunities, housing and income, that their powerlessness is reinforced. Employers sometimes use ageism to retire higher paid older workers with seniority and replace them with younger, lower paid workers. The speed of change in society has also strengthened inequality. In many cultures older people's wisdom was appreciated and revered. In modern U.S. society, change comes so quickly that much of what older people can contribute is no longer considered relevant or meaningful.

Attitudes about both old age and youth are shaped and reinforced in school. Are students given opportunities to develop positive attitudes toward older people? Do teachers intervene when students tell jokes that make fun of old people? Check your books and texts. How are older people characterized? Are they stereotyped as incompetent, listless and helpless? Are they even present at all? What do these books imply as the source of older people's powerlessness—themselves or society? Are students given the tools and opportunities to examine the media and our culture for biases against the elderly? Have they examined social policies and laws for their impact on old people?

Are old persons sought out to be involved in your school as aides, foster grandparents and so forth? Many welcome involvement with children, and children get more adult attention. Have invitations to school concerts and plays been sent to grandparents and retired persons in the community? Have older people who are involved in activist groups like the Gray Panthers been invited to your school to talk about projects to help

eliminate discrimination toward elderly people? Since some older people have physical limitations, has your school made necessary changes to make it accessible to old people? Is parking available near the building, for example?

Are older people interviewed for projects and invited to share their historical perspective on history and issues? Has the awareness of students been raised, for example, by writing an essay on the important part some older person has played in their lives? Have students explored the situation of older people in the school community? What facilities and jobs are open to them, what discrimination do they face, and how is class status or race connected to their problems? Can they assist the school and/or the school them?

Do students get an opportunity to do any community service in nursing homes or senior centers, where they can not only give something of themselves but learn more about the lives and struggles of older persons? Is this community service on an ongoing basis and not just a "one-shot deal?" Have there been opportunities for students to take action to foster changes that would positively affect old people?

What You Can Do to Help Stamp out Ageism

- Quit complimenting people on how young they look
- Promote intergenerational job sharing, part-time hours and no hiring or retirement according to a plan based on chronological age
- Criticize your local news media when a headline or cartoon is offensive
- Fight ageism with knowledge and a willingness to approach every person, regardless of age, as an individual with unique strengths, weaknesses, options and opportunities

"Ageism: What Is It? How Can We Avoid It?"
Gray Panthers, Washington, D.C.

Does youth face ageism in your school? In literature and other materials are young people presented as competent, able to take responsibility, solve problems and create change? Are they taught skills and then given more and more responsibility for decision-making in classrooms and schools? Are young people encouraged to organize programs and discussions about their concerns? Are they on committees with adults that make decisions about the school? Does your school have programs like peer leadership and peer mediation where students take responsibility for helping their age-mates solve problems and develop student-led activities? Are students treated with respect by adults who are willing to listen to and negotiate problems with young people?

Does your school address bias based on age that might exist among the students themselves? Do older students harass younger ones in the halls, in the lunchroom or on buses? Are educational and problem-solving strategies developed to deal with this discrimination? Are there inter-age activities and programs that encourage students to work in positive ways with students of other ages? All these efforts can contribute to making your school a place where students develop respect for people of all ages and appreciation for the discrimination some face because of age.

Ageism in Children's Literature

Numerous studies document that the elderly do not get a fair shake in children's literature. Research on age and ageism in children's literature found very few older characters in it; when portrayed, they usually did not have a major role and were not readily noticeable characters. Cumulative portrayals of older people showed them as unimportant, unexciting, inarticulate, flat, unidimensional, unimaginative, noncreative, and boring. Three adjectives were consistently used to describe older people: old, sad, poor. Meaningful, realistic, positive characterization of older people were rare.

Education Digest, 12/93

HETEROSEXISM

"Heterosexism" is the belief and practices that classify people based on sexual orientation. It gives legitimacy and privilege to heterosexuals, and it targets and disadvantages lesbians, gay men and bisexuals. The heterosexism in our society fosters homophobia, the fear and hatred of homosexuality which is grounded in prejudice and stereotyping. Heterosexism, like racism and sexism, is reinforced in school and hurts everybody.

Look at your classroom and school for evidence of heterosexism. It's as important to notice who isn't visible as who is. Is there any evidence in books, on bulletin boards, in classroom discussions, that there are all kinds of families and that some children have lesbian and gay parents. Since at least 6 million children in the U.S. have lesbian and gay parents, to omit reference to these families encourages their children to be afraid to

talk about their families and come to believe there's something wrong with them. Are authors, historical figures and contemporary persons who are lesbian, gay or bisexual acknowledged as such—e.g., Walt Whitman, Martina Navratilova, James Baldwin? Are issues related to sexual orientation discussed, when age-appropriate, in current events, such as gays in the military or custody cases? Such discussion legitimizes the reality that gay men, lesbians and bisexuals are part of our population. Heterosexism is maintained when lesbians and gay men have to stay "in the closet"—not be honest about who they are—for fear of losing jobs, children, friends, or relatives. Schools can become places where it's safe to "come out of the closet" and for all people to be accepted for who they are.

Why Discuss Lesbian and Gay Issues with Children?

All children need to feel safe in schools and to have their personal experience validated. Teachers do not necessarily know which children in their classes have a gay, lesbian, or bisexual parent, aunt, uncle, cousin, grandparent or other significant person in their lives; which children have friends whose parents are gay; or which children will grow up to be gay themselves. All children need to have the existence of gay people recognized, and to be taught that all people, regardless of sexual orientation, are entitled to respect.

Lesbian and Gay Parents Association
San Francisco, Ca. 1995

Do children use heterosexist put-downs like "faggot," "lezzie," "queer" and "homo?" Even if young children don't really know what they mean, they know these words are a way to hurt people. Do teachers intervene and not only stop the name-calling but discuss with children different kinds of families and different kinds of relationships? Remember, discussing gay and lesbian family members doesn't mean talking about sex; rather it means talking about love, acceptance and diversity. When students study sex education they will discuss sexuality. Do administrators work with staff and staff work with students to learn how to interrupt the language of hate and foster respect for all regardless of sexual orientation? Are lesbians and gay men included when adults are invited to your school to speak about their lives, work and families in age-appropriate ways? Ridding schools of homophobia and making them safe is, after all, an equity issue.

How does heterosexism affect students from lesbian or gay families? How does it influence students who feel that they themselves may be or may become homosexual or bisexual? For these young people school can be a very painful and frightening place. Young people often assume that because a child's parents are gay or lesbian, the child is also, an assumption that can hurt a child. Life in school can be very painful for young people who are gay or are identified as having homosexual family members or friends. The harassment, taunting and name-calling they face produces fear and anxiety, making school feel unsafe and often making learning difficult. This emotional distress can be life-threatening. The 1989 Report of the Secretary's Task Force on Youth Suicide (U.S. Department of Health and Human Services) reported that since 1960 there has been a 200 percent increase in teen suicides, one third of them related to stress about young people's sexual orientation.

Heterosexism also hurts young people who don't have lesbian or gay family members or who don't believe they are lesbian or gay. Heterosexism breeds homophobia, which creates fear of lesbians and gay men in particular, and, more broadly, fear of difference. Young people who are homophobic may become adults who accept violence against homosexuals. Heterosexism makes it harder for young people to appreciate the parts of themselves that don't conform to gender stereotypes. For example, boys may not play the violin, become gymnasts or risk showing vulnerability for fear of being called gay. An obsession with sports captures more boys than might be the case if proving one's heterosexual masculinity were not a constant concern. Heterosexism makes it hard for young people to express genuine warmth for friends of the same gender. For young people who are not sure of their sexual orientation, heterosexism hinders them from coming to terms with their sexual identity, whatever it may be, in a safe, comfortable way. It adds stress and confusion to the already difficult process of growing up.

It's important, and often difficult, to address heterosexism in our schools. It's important because this is a social justice issue that's part of any broad effort to make school safe for all children and to promote respect for diversity. It's difficult because people may mistakenly think that making lesbians and gay men visible in school is teaching about sexual acts, or that it will turn straight children gay. Even teachers who personally feel uncomfortable with homosexuality have realized that making bisexual, gay and lesbian people visible is important for creating both inclusive, caring schools and a just society. How we address this will depend, in part, on what is developmentally appropriate for the children we work with and the level of education and sensitivity of school staff and the community.

LINGUICISM

Language is yet another way to categorize people and reinforce their dominant or subordinate status. Tove Skutnabb-Kangas has proposed the term "linguicism" to refer to discrimination based particularly on language. Language oppression, often tied to discrimination based on race, ethnicity and class, has become more visible to educators in recent years as varied groups of immigrant children with limited English proficiency enter school. Linguicism thwarts equality to the extent that these students are not provided an education in a language they understand and in schools that respect their linguistic and cultural backgrounds.

Linguicism

Linguicism refers to those ideologies and structures which are used to legitimate and re-create an unequal division of power and resources between groups that are defined on the basis of language. For more detail about this term see "Multilingualism and Education of Minority Children" in *Minority Education: From Shame to Struggle*, edited by Tove Skutnabb-Kangas and Jim Cummins.

Linguicism often reinforces the dominant culture and prevailing power relationships. In some situations students with limited English proficiency are encouraged to give up their mother tongue, when in fact, the more they improve in their native language, the better they will learn English. Sometimes in the same school English-speaking students are encouraged to learn a second language and become bilingual when Spanish-speaking children, for example, must give up their language, learn English and lose their bilingualism. Such a situation not only presents a double standard but perpetuates power imbalances among groups of people in our society.

Linguicism and the Social Environment

A bilingual child's cognitive development can be enhanced or hindered by the school environment and social value placed on her/his native language. If the dominant language and the child's language are equally valued, a bilingual experience will increase the child's cognitive functioning, promoting greater creativity, problem solving ability, and verbal flexibility among other abilities. This is called "additive bilinguality." If the mother tongue is devalued in the environment the child's cognitive development may be delayed and the child will underachieve in school. This "subtractive bilinguality" occurs when a minority child who has a socially devalued language is schooled through a more prestigious language in which s/he has limited proficiency.

Josiane Hamers and Michel Blanc
Bilinguality and Bilingualism

How well does your school handle language differences? To what extent is the language and culture of students who speak English as their first language considered superior to students whose first language is not English? Is a bilingual student's first language seen as an asset to the classroom and school or a detriment? Are bilingual students encouraged to use their language and teach it to their peers? Is there a difference in the tone of teacher interaction with those students who speak English and those who do not? Is Black English, sometimes called African American Language, appreciated as a distinct language that is legitimate for some types of writing in school?

Is the language and culture of students and parents whose first language is not English respected and included in all aspects of school life? Are signs and posters in the different languages represented in your school? Are parents involved through programs like home-school reading projects and bilingual events at school? If you have bilingual programs in your district, has the district considered two-way bilingual programs? Some schools have these highly effective programs which bring language majority and language minority students together in one setting where each group learns in the other's language for half of their instructional time together. Do you avoid types of instruction where students with English as a second language are constantly corrected? Instead do you use instruction that encourages their speaking and writing in expressive ways to make meaning of their experiences and to generate knowledge? Are parents given a choice about the kind of program they want for their child?

Linguicism has an impact both on students whose second language is English and on language-dominant students. Academic achievement of limited-English-proficiency students is negatively affected when their language and culture isn't used for some instruction or represented in school. They can experience isolation, alienation and inferiority when their language and culture are not validated in the school. High drop-out rates ultimately result. Students can come to devalue their own language and stop using it, even in situations where it would be appropriate.

Language-majority students can come to believe that their language and culture are superior if they experience it as the norm. They miss out on opportunities to learn other languages through experience with their peers. They miss out on friendships with students whose first language isn't English. In our increasingly global community they will pay a price for ethnocentric ideas about the primacy of English and for limited understanding of different languages and cultures.

ANTI-SEMITISM AND OTHER RELIGIOUS OPPRESSION

In a nation to which many immigrants came seeking religious freedom, it is painful to know that religion is commonly used to separate groups of people and to maintain inequities. Historically in the U.S. many have been persecuted for their religious beliefs. Sometimes even some groups of Christians have discriminated against others groups of Christians. Since the historic roots of anti-Semitism in Anglo-European culture are long-lasting and deep, we pay particular attention to anti-Semitism. Discrimination against other religious faiths—such as Islam, Hinduism, Native American beliefs—and people of no religious faith, is evident today as well. It reinforces inequality in our society by giving advantages to people who are Christian and disadvantaging people who are not.

Does your school explicitly or implicitly assume Christianity as the religious norm? If any religious holidays are commemorated in school, what are they? Remember that Santa Claus and Christmas trees are connected with a religious holiday. If there are young people of varied religious backgrounds, or who aren't members of any faith, how are their beliefs, feelings and rights respected? Is the school policy of giving days off for religious holidays consistent for the different religions represented in your school? How are decisions made about days on which school should be closed? Do the criteria respect a variety of religions and are people of different faiths consulted?

Do students learn about the most meaningful holy days when studying various religions, like Yom Kippur for Jews, or those which typically coincide with Christian holidays, like Hanukkah? Do teachers respond as clearly and directly to students' anti-Semitic or anti-Muslim bigotry as they do to racist slurs? Do students study about anti-Semitism and other forms of religious oppression? When they discuss spirituality does it take in the traditions of a wide variety of peoples and cultures?

As with other forms of oppression, anti-Semitism and other forms of religious discrimination hurt both those groups that are targeted and those that are privileged. Knowing well the history of anti-Semitism, Jewish children can become anxious and alienated in an environment that excludes their beliefs and culture. It's painful for them to take the brunt of other students' anti-Semitism, as when a penny is thrown in front of them with the taunt "Grab it, Jews." Often they feel invisible given the pervasiveness of Christian culture in school.

Many gentiles grow to believe in the rightness of their religion and the superiority of their culture. Their limited exposure to the ideas and traditions of other faiths keeps them from seeing the many spiritual beliefs that are held in common and keeps them divided from, rather than connected with, others.

ABLEISM

"Ableism" is a form of oppression that provides advantages to people without learning, emotional and physical disabilities and dis-advantages those with these disabilities. There is a wide range of disabilities that people live with. Physical disabilities range from deafness or blindness, a crippling disease like rheumatoid arthritis to paralysis. Learning disabilities or emotional disorders can include language disorders, problems with memory, reading disorders, attention deficit disorders, social skills deficit and problems expressing emotions appropriately, among others. Sometimes a person experiences a combination of disabilities, such as a young person with cerebral palsy who may have both physical and learning disabilities. Stereotyping and institutional practices combine to classify and limit people with disabilities.

How well has your school addressed the effects of ableism? To what extent do students label children with disabilities "retard," "dumb" or "spastic," and what do teachers do about it? To what extent has the student population been educated about the types of disabilities others live with and ways to be supportive of their peers? Are young people helped to see that students with disabilities also have abilities? Are they helped to structure games and activities in such a way as to use all students' abilities? Do teachers intervene so students don't isolate those with difficult learning or emotional problems? Do they work to help the class learn ways to constructively respond to a peer's difficult behavior or learning patterns?

Are students asked to read about people with disabilities to understand what they have and can achieve?

Do teachers modify pedagogical and curricular approaches to meet the needs of students with disabilities? Has the school district provided the professional development needed for teachers to create inclusive classrooms that meet these varying needs? Are extra staff provided to ensure the success of inclusive classrooms?

Ableism powerfully affects young people with disabilities. To the extent that children with disabilities are stereotyped or isolated, they can lose confidence in themselves, blame themselves and sometimes take out their frustrations on peers with similar disabilities. If learning activities and games are consistently structured competitively rather than cooperatively, students with disabilities can experience patterns of losing, reinforcing their low self worth. A teacher's stereotypes about students with disabilities have powerful impacts. If s/he believes that a blind person always needs help, that leads to dependence. If s/he assumes that a student with cerebral palsy has little to communicate, s/he may not find ways to listen and thereby reinforce that student's isolation.

To the extent that ableist attitudes and practices aren't dealt with in school, students without disabilities can harbor stereotypes and ungrounded fears about people with disabilities. They won't have information with which to understand, support and build relationships with others who are challenged. They are cut off from the examples of their peers as a source of empathy and courage, capacities that could help them face difficulties of their own. They may develop a false sense of their own invulnerability, something that is transient since most of us will grow old and some of us will face unexpected disabilities due to accident or illness. They restrict the development of their skills and emotional sensitivities for helping people who struggle with adversity. They lose out on rewarding friendships in which they could recognize the gifts and strengths of their disabled peers. In these ways students without disabilities are limited too.

How Many People Are Limited in Physical Function?

More than 20% (37.3 million) of noninstitutionalized U.S. residents are limited in the ability to perform selected physical functions. Some people have more than one limitation. Examples include: having one's speech understood; hearing normal conversation; seeing words and letters in newsprint; getting into and out of bed; etc. More than one-third of functionally limited people have a severe limitation.

Chartbook on Disability in the U.S.
National Institute on Disability and
Rehabilitation Research, 1989

COMPETITIVE INDIVIDUALISM

Competition maintains the system of inequality in both schools and society. Supporting competitive systems is the ideology of competitive individualism—the notion that an individual's success or failure in life depends solely on her or his own efforts and merits, and that each person has an equal chance to compete and succeed. This discounts the powerful influence of race, gender, class, or any other aspects of a person's social identity, on a person's chances for opportunity and success. Competitive individualism places the blame for failure squarely on people rather than on social institutions that privilege some people at the expense of others. The message is clear: both winners and losers deserve what they get. Individualism is very different from individuality, which is the growth of each person's unique and full characteristics. Competitive individualism, in fact, hinders the growth of individuality in many people.

Cooperation, on the other hand, demonstrates that it is through interdependence that people can most effectively learn and develop their competence while supporting the similar growth of others. Further, by working cooperatively people can change those conditions that maintain inequality. Since most teachers' goals are to have all students learn, let's take a closer look at your school to explore the effects of competition and competitive individualism.

Competition, Bias and Inequality

Competitiveness and individualism are tied in with the racial question. If one is very competitive and needs to feel superior, one is more open to prejudice and scape-goatism. If there were less competitiveness and individualism in our society, there would be less need for scape-goating and for feeling threatened by other people's achievement.

Dr. Alvin Poussaint, in *Bulletin*,
Council on Interracial Books for Children, Vol. 6, No. 1

Roderic Gorney, in his book *The Human Agenda*, demonstrated a significant correlation between competition in a culture and the presence of sharply delineated "have" and "have-not" groups. On whatever grounds competition might be defended, equity simply cannot be considered one of its benefits.

Alfie Kohn
No Contest: The Case Against Competition, p. 73

COACH, THE TEAM WOULD LIKE TO RAP WITH YOU
ON THE DESTRUCTIVENESS OF COMPETITION.

Do students in your school bicker, name-call and put each other down? Are put-downs so common that they've become part of the school culture so that students stop thinking about their effect? Often the need to put others down comes from a desire to boost one's own self-esteem. Such belittling of others is not "human nature" but is often a result of people's struggle to maintain self-worth in a competitively structured social system, whether classroom, school or society. Do students cheat? Cheating often arises from a competitive setting where students fear losing or not being good enough. Take a look at textbooks, curricula and library books. Do they reinforce competitive individualism by assuming that if you work hard you're bound to get ahead? Do they subtly blame people for their poverty, status or lack of success? Does your school track students, relegating lower-tracked students to classes in which they quickly learn to give up hope for themselves?

Is yours, on the other hand, a cooperative school where people work together so everyone can succeed? Do teachers structure learning activities so that students work in cooperative groups and take responsibility not only for their own learning but for others' as well? Has the district provided professional development to help teachers make heterogeneous cooperative groups challenging and accessible for students at all ability levels? Are classroom behavior problems or schoolwide problems framed as collective problems in which everyone can contribute to the solution? Do children learn cooperative sports and games as well as competitive ones?

Do people try to make schoolwide events cooperative? The science fair is an apt example. Typically science fairs are competitive, with awards often going to the students whose parents were able to give them the most support. Have teachers considered cooperative alternatives? For example, they can brainstorm with students to define a community problem and work cooperatively as classes to do the investigation and scientific work needed to contribute to the solution of that problem. In this case all students build competence and confidence in their scientific abilities while working cooperatively and purposefully with, not against, their peers.

How does competitive individualism affect students? In general, young people often develop antagonistic feelings toward each other when competing for grades, teacher attention or peer approval. Mistrust is inevitable, and the possibility for friendships with all students is discouraged. Students are constantly comparing themselves to others, rather than working to do their best. This is reflected in a sixth-grade student's comment that is typical of much student thinking: "A good answer may not be good enough. It has to be better than someone else's." Empathy is discouraged and young people develop a "me-them" or "us-them" mentality that inhibits interpersonal and intergroup understanding and collaboration.

> ### *Myths about the Value of Competition*
>
> In his excellent book *No Contest: The Case Against Competition*, Alfie Kohn argues that we have been socialized to believe in what he has shown to be myths regarding the positive effects of competition. Among those myths are:
>
> 1. Competition is inevitable; it's part of human nature.
> 2. Competition builds character.
> 3. Competition keeps productivity high and is necessary for excellence.
> 4. Recreation requires competition.
>
> Many teachers reading this book as part of professional development work in cooperative learning have found it very challenging, with far-reaching implications for their educational practice. We encourage you to read it!

Competition reinforces the negative self-expectations of students who don't usually win. Failure isn't fun, and if it happens too often some students tend to give up and drop out, cheat or act aggressively and defensively. These overt behaviors are easy to notice in students, but with other students the effects of competition are more subtle and harder to identify. If the culture, texts and teachers tell students that anyone can make it if they try, and don't acknowledge how inequality makes that tough or impossible for some people, students can easily blame themselves for their failure. For example, a student with a learning disability that isn't being addressed may come to believe he's stupid. Or he may project his pain on others as a way of bolstering his own sense of competence. He may, for example, harass an academically talented student on the basketball court for that student's limited athletic skills. Typically girls and many students of color prefer cooperatively structured environments, so to the extent that success in our classrooms and schools is defined competitively these students are dis-advantaged.

Students who tend to succeed also pay a price. Often "winners" feel intense pressure to be number one and feel good about themselves only if they are "the best." This often creates high levels of anxiety and stress. In competitive structures difference is something to be used to put others down and to elevate oneself in the hierarchy. These students may verbally or mentally make negative judgments about others whom they see as "losers," distancing themselves from students with whom they have many other things in common or from whom they can learn. They may be unwilling to share and consider the needs of others, contributing to their own self-centeredness and indifference. They may come to believe that their "success" is rooted in their own innate abilities, not understanding how their privilege contributed to their success. For example, suburban, middle-class white students may believe themselves to be brighter than the black and Latino students bussed into their school district from the city if they've always come out on top academically and never examined all the advantages they came to school with relative to their urban peers.

Competition and Our Society

Often politicians chide educators to improve the schools so the United States can maintain its number-one position in the world. In his telling book *We're Number One: Where American Stands and Falls in the New World Order*, Andrew Shapiro compares the United States to the nineteen major industrial nations in the areas of health care, education, the economy and so forth. Among his findings are:

- The United States is number one in billionaires—and number one in children living in poverty.
- The United States is number one in highest-paid athletes, but last in teachers' salaries.
- The United States is on top in the ratio of CEO pay to that of the average manufacturing worker, 25:1. The next highest is France at 16:1; Japan stands at 11:1 and Germany at 10:1.
- We're last, however, in paid vacation days, at 10.8. Spain offers the most at 32, closely followed by the Netherlands, Norway and Germany.

The long-term effects of competitive individualism confront us daily. Lack of motivation, drug abuse and disregard for others are evident among young people who feel themselves to be losers. As one young woman remarked, "If no one cares about me, why should I care about them?" Some "winners" feel such pressure to be superior that they pay a price in stress. Some commit suicide. Other winners become self-centered, justifying their success with a rationale of individualism, and feel no responsibility for the situation of others. Another effect is young people's lack of experience and skills to look at a problem and work cooperatively toward creative, effective solutions that benefit all people. We miss out on the power of synergy—the coming together of many unique persons to create a whole greater than the sum of the individual parts.

Restructuring our classrooms and schools to make them more cooperative, working with students to help them become aware of the effects of competition on them, and helping them explore more cooperative alternatives can help reverse these patterns. While some of the activities in *Open Minds to Equality* are structured cooperatively, a full range of cooperatively structured activities that also enable students to become more conscious of the effects of competition and cooperation on their lives, school, community, nation and world are available in our book *Cooperative Learning, Cooperative Lives: A Sourcebook of Learning Activities for Building a Peaceful World*.

The effects of all the forms of inequities discussed above are woven in different ways into the fabric of our individual lives and the life of our nation. They create a system of oppression which, while always changing, is also pervasive. By understanding the effects of oppression on our lives and others' lives we can use our diverse strengths to work with each other to create more equitable classrooms, schools and society.

Democracy for the 21st Century

Today this nation's people is more diverse than ever. If there is to be democracy in the 21st century, it must be a multiracial/multicultural democracy. Unless democracy is conceptualized such that all groups are included, democracy loses its meaning. And if a democracy which includes all of America's people is to be fostered and prefigured in this nation's educational system, then multicultural education must be at the heart, and not on the margins, of all discussions about education in this country. In this situation, multicultural education becomes not a matter of simply adding new material to the school curriculum, but of fundamentally re-visioning the relationship of schooling to a democratic society.

Theresa Perry and James Fraser
Freedom's Plow, p. 3, 1993

Chapter

2

Teaching for Equality

Teaching for equality challenges us to think in new ways about teaching and learning, the relationship of schools to society and strategies for creating change. Initially in this chapter we describe the model underlying *Open Minds to Equality* that will help you both address issues of diversity in the lives of your individual students and make broader changes in your classroom, school and community. Since schools and society are integrally related, we examine how current social realities, particularly increasing economic inequality, affect our efforts. Lastly we explore some feelings and issues that may emerge for you as a teacher as you work to open minds and hearts to equality.

A. A HUMANISTIC, SOCIAL JUSTICE APPROACH FOR TEACHING ABOUT EQUALITY

Open Minds to Equality is based on a model that recognizes the importance of both personal and social change. People working for a better society will be more successful with self-knowledge and interper-

sonal skills. Similarly, the more knowledge they have of both systems that maintain inequality and strategies for collective action, the more effectively they can change discriminatory institutions. Our approach emphasizes the importance of knowledge and skills for both personal and social change. It offers personally reflective perspectives and experiential skills from humanistic education. These are integrated with socially-conscious perspectives and skills for critical analysis from social justice education. The four components central to a humanistic, social justice approach for teaching about equality are outlined in the diagram on page 25.[1]

By supporting the development of your students' self-worth, competence and the belief that they can make a difference, you can bolster your students' *personal power*. By teaching students to encourage and care for each other in the class, you can foster a feeling of *group support* among them. Within such a supportive classroom community students feel safe to act as individuals to promote equality. For example, by standing up for themselves or sticking up for someone else hurt by bias, they feel empowered to take action that fosters *personal change*.

You can foster students' *critical awareness* through activities that increase their understanding of the ways in which difference is used to advantage some groups of people and dis-advantage others. Students then can be supported to *take action* to foster *social change* to challenge inequality. Whether such change affects their school (e.g., changing the unwritten rules about who gets to use the basketball courts at recess) or the broader society (e.g., writing to textbook publishers to encourage revisions in biased books), students will be contributing to social justice.

You can foster such change through intentional instructional activities, either those in *Open Minds to Equality* or those you develop yourself. Since *Open Minds to Equality* reflects this model, practical ideas for applying it to your teaching are described below.

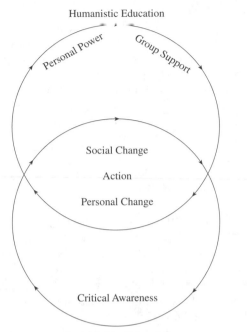

Humanistic Education

Personal Power

Group Support

Social Change

Action

Personal Change

Critical Awareness

Social Justice Education

1. Humanistic Education: Personal Empowerment and Community Building

Open Minds to Equality reflects a humanistic approach to education that provides teachers with ideas and skills to help students strengthen their personal power and to build a supportive classroom community. It is based on the belief that young people learn most effectively when they are engaged in activities that not only stretch their intellect but deepen their feelings as well. It assumes we need to teach students skills for self-reflection, working together and critical thinking. Since it is based on the belief that students learn from the *process* of classroom interaction as well as the *content* of the curriculum, attention is given to both.

A trusting classroom community is the foundation for both opening minds to equality and for strong academic learning. At the beginning of the year engage in experiences in which class members get to know each other as individuals, and include yourself in the process! Select activities in which students will feel emotionally safe. If you have students share with partners or in small groups first, then they feel more comfortable and are then more willing to participate in discussion with the whole class. Also, the content of the classroom discussion will be richer because students have already been stimulated by each other's ideas.

Together with your class, brainstorm ground rules for how people want to interact during the year, especially when discussing issues of diversity. Typically students agree to norms like the following: a) Encour-
age each student's participation; b) Listen to each other without interrupting; c) Put ups, not put downs; d) Disagree with others in a kind way: focus on their ideas and not on them as persons; e) No gossip; keep confidential personal experiences that anyone shares. Post the ground rules as a reminder of your shared contract. Students may want to modify them as the year progresses.

Respect

Fourth grade teacher Karen Cathers describes her process of setting norms and thinking about values at the beginning of the school year.

In the beginning of the year I ask the children, "What kind of classroom do you want?" They say, "I want a classroom where everybody is nice to one another. I want a class where I can learn . . . ." Somewhere in the discussion someone will use the word respect. I jump on it and say, "Respect. That sounds like a word we could use." . . .

We talk about what respect means and generally come up with a definition that is close to the one I like. "Respect means everyone feels safe—safe in their head and in their heart and in their body." If you're not feeling safe in your body because someone is running and you might get pushed up against a table and hit your head, then you're not being respected. You're not feeling safe: therefore, we don't run in the room. Do we need to write "Don't run in the room"? No, just "Respect." It encompasses everything.

"A Cooperative Classroom"
Cooperative Learning magazine, Vol. 14, No. 2

Teach skills for democratic classroom interaction—listening, sharing feelings, giving feedback, cooperation and conflict resolution—just as you would reading or math skills. Lessons in chapters 3 and 4 offer activities for doing this. Students who get a strong foundation in these social skills at the beginning of the year can use and build on them throughout the year and in future years both in and outside of school.

Introduce community meetings early and use them regularly for planning and problem-solving. Hold meetings once a week. Select topics from a list generated by the students. As students learn the process, they can take responsibility for facilitating the meetings. This democratic process is particularly helpful in dealing with diversity issues. (See Chapter 4 for a lesson on facilitating community meetings.)

To maintain democratic classroom procedures throughout the year, ask students to respond to "processing questions" after completing a lesson. Processing questions help them reflect on their group interaction; how well they worked together and what they could do differently next time. For example: "To what extent did you encourage all group members' participation in the activity? Is there anything you could do differently next time to be more encouraging of others?" Vary the format for their responses, as time allows. For example, in their small groups have students write a short response to a processing question, share their comments, and jot down a plan for improvement to be turned in to you. Or ask students to respond orally in their small groups; then in the whole class elicit examples of effective interaction and areas for change. Since processing questions are the source of very significant learning, we urge you to leave plenty of time to discuss them. In addition, students will work much more efficiently in groups throughout the year.

Well-sequenced discussion questions that help students reflect on what they learned from the content of an activity are important parts of any lesson dealing with diversity. Many discussion questions in *Open Minds to Equality* reflect the following sequence, originally conceived by Terry Borton:

WHAT: Share your feelings and experience of the learning activity.

SO WHAT: Analyze and critically reflect on that experience.

NOW WHAT: Connect these insights to broader equity issues and actions

To maintain a supportive classroom community, encourage all students' ideas and points of view. Set clear limits regarding biased statements directed at others in the classroom. If, for example, you have set classroom norms at the beginning of the year, most likely "respect for others" would be among them. Since any biased statement targeting another student would be violating those norms, you or another student would respond immediately. You can provide information that corrects misinformation. Ask the student for examples or specifics if s/he is making a generalization. If you have students with diverse points of view, ask, "How do others feel about that?" or "Are others' experiences the same or different?" Share your experiences. You can then follow up with lessons from *Open Minds to Equality* that would address the underlying biases and encourage students to think in new ways and see alternative perspectives.

As you can see, a humanistic approach values students' own lives as content for discussing issues of diversity. Experiential activities, such as role plays and simulations, are also used. These help students get into the shoes of people different from themselves or experience the dynamics of broader social realities that affect themselves and others. Throughout the lessons in *Open Minds to Equality* we ask students to relate what they are learning to their own lives. With the sense of personal power and group support that comes from a humanistically oriented classroom, students are more ready to address discrimination and act to foster change.

2. Social Justice Education: Critical Awareness of Inequality

Education that aims to promote social justice provides background about the causes of inequality. It also offers ideas to foster fair and equitable schools, communities and society. It addresses a variety of forms of discrimination—those based on race, gender, class, age, physical ability, learning ability, sexual orientation, religion and language, among others. It examines the ways some individuals and social groups benefit from inequality while others are hurt. It stimulates awareness, ideas and skills for change. We can think about concepts of social justice in terms of our own lives as well as teach them to our students.

Important to developing critical awareness is understanding the connections between peoples' personal lives and institutional inequality. Each of us has a social identity which reflects various aspects of human diversity. For example, race is one aspect of a person's social identity. It might be black, white, Native American, Asian American, biracial or racially mixed, and so forth. Some aspects of our social identity are typically constant, such as race and gender. Some, like class, religion and language, may change over our lifetimes. Others, like age, are guaranteed to change.

Inequality in our society advantages some of us as members of certain social groups and dis-advantages others. (We use this word not to imply any innate inferiority, but to mean that discrimination takes away from subordinated groups advantages that dominant groups have.) For example, upper income people receive benefits and others are hurt by institutional class inequality, such as tax policies that allow wealthy people to pay a lower proportion of their income in taxes than poor, working class and middle class people.

Even when people experience discrimination, their social group memberships can be a source of pride. Many American Indians, for example, maintain a positive group identity, taking pride in being Cherokee, Sioux, Mohawk and so forth, and resist the cultural stereotypes of themselves. The history of resistance to anti-Semitism by previous generations is a source of strength to many Jews. Our social group memberships can often be both painful and affirming.

Given the many aspects of each of our social identities, most of us experience some benefits and pay some prices because of institutional inequality. While an affluent African-American male will benefit from class and gender privilege, he will still face discrimination because of his race. However limited by gender bias an able-bodied woman may be in our society, she still has her sight, an advantage that a blind woman doesn't have.

In *Open Minds to Equality* we explore the particularities of various types of discrimination as well as examine similarities in the way they are perpetuated. Their historical contexts distinguish various forms of discrimination. African Americans, for example, suffer from the legacy of slavery and over two hundred years of racism in the United States. Some immigrant groups of color have voluntarily come to the United States to seek a better life. While experiencing discrimination based on race, they avoid the cumulative effects of historic oppression that African Americans face.

At the same time, different forms of discrimination share similarities. They are perpetuated by stereotypes we are socialized to believe and maintained through accepted norms and practices of institutions. Just as the advertising industry, for example, perpetuates sexism by objectifying women's bodies and presenting an idealized image of female beauty, it reinforces heterosexism by portraying relationships as heterosexual; lesbians and gay men are invisible.

These forms of discrimination combine to create a powerful system of oppression spread throughout social institutions. Since they are interrelated, all must be dealt with to create a truly democratic society. While it would be liberating for a Jewish woman to experience an end to anti-Semitism, would her life be fully fair if she still had to face the ongoing burdens of sexism? How effective would it be to try to change racism alone, when often it is class-based inequality that fuels racist practices?

The similarity in the dynamics of oppression on members of different social groups opens up the possibility for empathy and common understanding. While a white man with a physical disability hasn't experienced racism, he may be able to empathize with a person of color if he makes the connection with his discriminatory experiences rooted in ableism. We can help students make these kinds of connections in our classrooms and schools.

These dynamics are depicted in the Filter of Oppression diagram reproduced here from a lesson in Chapter Seven. While not encompassing all types of oppression that people and groups experience, it does depict the following: racism; sexism; classism; ageism; ableism; heterosexism; linguicism and anti-Semitism/other forms of religious oppression. The metaphorical flower can represent either: an individual person, with various aspects of her social identity; or our society, composed of diverse social groups. In a system of oppression, a person receives privileges or pays prices

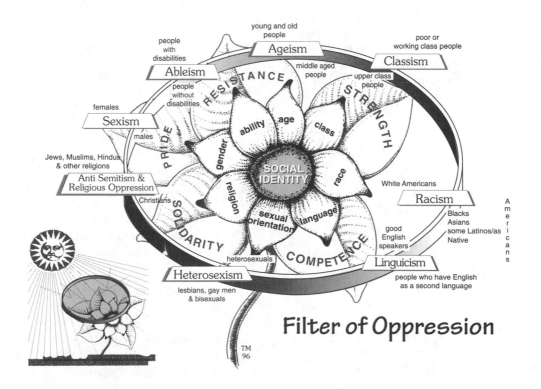

Filter of Oppression

based on aspects of her/his social identity. Thinking nationally, social groups are similarly affected. Oppression acts like a filter, allowing sun to nourish some petals of the flower and keeps them from others, affecting the overall health of the flower. The goal of social justice education is to eliminate the filter of oppression so all parts of the flower flourish.

Social justice education also acknowledges the strength that can come from aspects of an individual's social identity, or social group, that are targets of oppression. On the metaphorical flower the sepals can boost the drooping petals. This represents the pride, strength, competence, resistance and solidarity that individuals and social groups can develop even when they are oppressed and with which they can resist discrimination.

Oppression hurts us all—the privileged and disadvantaged—although to different degrees. While women are hurt most by sexism, many men suffer too. Some men lose touch with their feelings, miss out on equal and intimate relationships, and never develop personality qualities and skills that are stereotyped as feminine because of sexist norms and values. Oppression is maintained when members of both dominant and subordinate groups accept their roles without questioning them. We can challenge it when we understand how the system works and when privileged groups become allies with dis-advantaged groups in working together for change.[2]

None of us invented oppression, but once we become aware of it we have a responsibility to work to change it. This can be an energizing and hopeful endeavor! The lessons in *Open Minds to Equality* introduce young people to issues of inequality in an accessible, carefully sequenced, supportive way. Through these lessons students learn to think critically about their lives, what they read and what they see in the media. Our experience, and that of teachers who have used this book, shows that young people have great potential for understanding these issues if introduced to them in meaningful ways.

Our social group memberships have influenced our perspectives. When we make this explicit, students can become more reflective about the sources of their own ideas as well. For example, a teacher explained to her class that because she was white she'd always thought positively about westward expansion and therefore had never before introduced an American Indian's viewpoint of that experience. As we become more aware of how our views reflect our positions in society we'll be able to listen to each other more sensitively.

Once conscious of the dynamics of oppression you and your students can become more critically aware of the ways in which inequality is sustained by the many institutions in our society and explore how various myths maintain the status quo. For example in *Open Minds to Equality* students examine how schools, the media, families, and workplaces, among others, can reinforce practices and values that give unequal power and resources to different groups of people. This awareness stimulates action for change.

Listening with Open Hearts and Minds

The dilemma is . . . in addressing the more fundamental issue of power, of whose voice gets to be heard in determining what is best for poor children and children of color, both sides do need to be able to listen, and I contend that is those with the most power, those in the majority, who must take the greater responsibility for initiating the process. To do so takes a very special kind of listening, listening that requires not only open eyes and ears, but open hearts and minds. We do not really see through our eyes or hear through our ears, but through our beliefs. To put our beliefs on hold is to cease to exist as ourselves for a moment—and that is not easy. It is painful as well, because it means turning yourself inside out, giving up your own sense of who you are, and being willing to see yourself in the unflattering light of another's angry gaze. It is not easy, but it is the only way to learn what it might feel like to be someone else and the only way to start the dialogue.

Lisa Delpit, "The Harvard Educational Review"
Vol. 58 #3, 1988, pp. 296–7

Education for social justice is multicultural education and more. Some teachers think of multicultural education as teaching about the traditions, holidays and foods of diverse cultural groups. While valuable, this approach to multicultural education often emphasizes habits of a culture and not deeper issues like values and belief systems. Furthermore, it doesn't deal with the ways in which difference is used to maintain social inequality. A social justice approach encourages teachers and young people to go beyond teaching about culture and to apply the democratic value of fairness to everyone's life and to promote equality for all.

3. Integrating Humanistic and Social Justice Education

When you integrate humanistic and social justice education in your classroom, students will gain understandings and skills for self-reflection and positive interpersonal interaction, as well as become critical thinkers. Personal and social change occurs concurrently as students take personal actions to foster equality and work together to make changes in their school and community. A fifth grade class offers an example of how the process of integrating personal and social change is ongoing. At the beginning of the school year their teacher used activities from Chapters Three and Four to develop students' listening, group process, and problem solving skills, all strengthening their personal power and group support. Throughout the year they engaged in lessons to raise their critical awareness about inequality from Chapters Five through Nine.

Then students started noticing stereotypes and bias in the books they were reading to second graders in a cross-grade project. Individual students spoke out about the bias they saw in books. As a group they developed criteria for equitable books, reviewed the books they were using, and began choosing books that portrayed all people fairly. Their teacher supported these actions with lessons from Chapters Ten and Eleven that strengthened their skills for change. By acting to foster personal and social change students reinforced their sense of personal power and group solidarity. They then taught second graders how to look for stereotypes in books and created more fair versions with them. This process became ongoing.

The activities in *Open Minds to Equality* reflect this humanistic, social justice approach to multicultural education and are organized following the sequential process for teaching about diversity presented in the Introduction. This approach and sequence can also be the framework to which you apply your own resources and ideas tailored specifically to your students, curriculum and community.

Educating to Affirm Diversity and Promote Equity

Christine Sleeter and Carl Grant have delineated five different approaches to multicultural education.[3] A humanistic, social justice approach combines key elements of three of these. It focuses on building respectful feelings and cooperative interpersonal skills among students, characteristic of a human relations approach. It promotes cultural pluralism and social structural equality, similar to a multicultural education model. It is visionary and prepares students to work actively toward social equality, typical of their multicultural social transformation approach. All elements are vital for educating to affirm diversity and promote equity.

B. THE CONNECTIONS: OUR CLASSROOMS, SCHOOLS, AND THE BROADER SOCIETY

1. Societal Challenges to Equity

Our work in classrooms and schools is not done in a vacuum. We are very much affected by the culture and politics of the broader society. We can better understand the dynamics of the inequality described above both by being politically aware and by participating in collective efforts to change them.

When *Open Minds to Equality* was first published in 1983, young people came into our classrooms from a society that was more accepting of efforts to foster equality. Today bigotry is more socially condoned. Popular talk show hosts encourage divisiveness and the language of hate. Powerful interests have organized to push back the gains that women, people of color, and other oppressed groups had made in the 1960s and 1970s. More fearful and less hopeful, many people concerned with their own survival don't see the connections between themselves and people different from them who may be similarly oppressed. When we better understand the sources of these dynamics, we can address them more effectively.

Increasing economic inequality in the U.S. is a very significant challenge to the promise of all forms of equality. Since the first edition of *Open Minds to Equality* was published, the economic situation of the average person in the United States has worsened. At the same time, class inequality is typically one of the forms of oppression least talked about in schools. We may have gone to a workshop or taken a course on dealing with racism or sexism in education, but how often have we been offered a workshop on class inequality? We may distance ourselves from looking at issues of class because they seem overwhelming. Critical analysis of economic inequality is typically omitted from the mainstream media. Also those of us who benefit from our class status have choices about what we do with our money and resources that we may not want to examine. Yet becoming more critically conscious of the dynamics of economic inequality and its connections to racism and sexism and other forms of inequality is central to any hope for social justice.

The real wage—what the average worker's paycheck actually buys after taking inflation into account—peaked in 1973 and has been declining ever since for the average person in the United States. Income inequality has increased, and the number of millionaires has grown along with the number of poor people. Economist Richard McIntyre explains that for the past twenty years we actually have been experiencing a "silent depression," with the standard of living declining for most people, but for different groups of people at different times during this period.[4]

Economics for the Layperson

Particularly accessible and helpful books that relate issues of economic inequality concretely to our daily lives with humor and good cartoons to boot are:

Chaos or Community: Seeking Solutions, Not Scapegoats for Bad Economics by Holly Sklar

The New Field Guide to the U.S. Economy by Nancy Folbre and the Center for Popular Economics

---

The statistics are staggering. The richest 1 percent of the population now owns 37 percent of the wealth, more wealth than that owned by the bottom 90 percent of the people all together. The CEOs of the Fortune 500 corporations earn 157 times more than their average worker. Twenty percent of our children live in poverty. Five million children go hungry. About two million Americans lack permanent shelter.[5] Economic studies show that social mobility has not risen for most Americans and has diminished for many, particularly for the poor and for young people.[6]

Economic inequality breeds violence. Violence is not just rough or injurious physical actions, but damage that is done to people when they are denied dignity, power and opportunities to live a fulfilling life. While many bemoan the violence in American society, economic inequity is itself structural violence, violence that is done to people by economic policies of corporate and political leaders and carried out through laws and institutional policies. Sometimes those most destitute respond to the structural violence of hunger, joblessness, and poverty with individual acts of violence when their lives have become overwhelmingly painful and hopeless. Changing institutionalized economic inequality is essential for creating a more nonviolent and just society.

The Wrong Target

The attack on affirmative action is an expression of the anger and frustration felt by large numbers of overwrought and underemployed white men. Their anxiety is understandable, but affirmative action is not their enemy . . . . These men are caught up in the treacherous world of technological innovation, economic globalization and unrestrained corporate greed. Buffeted by forces that seem beyond their control (forces that are affecting everybody, not just white men), they listen to the demagogues. "It's the blacks doing this to you. It's the women. They're getting your piece of the pie. Otherwise you'd be O.K."

Bob Herbert, *The New York Times*
April 5, 1995

Many Americans are rightfully angry about their declining economic situations. The problem is that rather than direct this anger at its source—corporate and government policies that increase economic inequality—many take out their frustrations on others in similar or worse economic straits, often those who are perceived as different or "other." Class inequality can fuel racism, sexism, anti-Semitism, homophobia and other forms of discrimination.

While targeting other oppressed groups may provide an emotional release, an alternative analysis points to a different source of the problem. For example, a report on discrimination commissioned by the Labor Department found very little evidence of employment discrimination against white men. A high proportion (71 percent) of so-called reverse discrimination claims brought by white men were without merit.[7] While often poor people on welfare are blamed as the cause of "average American's" declining economic status, most welfare does not go to poor people. Virtually every part of American society receives some "welfare," as indicated in the box below. In fact, Congress finances more than 125 programs that subsidize private businesses at a net cost of about $85 billion per year. Add tax breaks and the price tag exceeds $100 billion a year—or half the annual federal deficit.[8]

Alternatives to class inequality that would provide greater economic justice would also reduce other forms of inequality. Most Americans don't hear of alternatives that are proposed because the media, itself corporately controlled, seldom reports them. The congressional Black Caucus and Progressive Caucus, for example, annually submit a Common Sense Budget to Congress that would cut the military budget and invest in jobs, housing, education, health care and so forth. This would change where a U.S. citizen's tax dollar goes, including the 49% (1997) that goes to the military.[9]

Many Americans Get Welfare: Why Are the Poor Targeted?

- By allowing taxpayers to deduct interest payments on home mortgages, the federal government gives an annual $41 billion subsidy to homeowners who are mainly middle class and wealthy. 85% of the subsidy is for taxpayers earning above $50,000.
- The federal government provides an annual $39 billion subsidy to agribusiness, compared to $15 million for AFDC (welfare). In 1991 the USDA gave Gallo wines $5.1 million to promote wines, M&M $1.1 million to promote candy bars and McDonald's $465,000 to promote chicken nuggets.
- The federal government spends $900 billion a year on entitlement programs—Social Security, veterans benefits, housing tax breaks, civil service pensions, food stamps, etc. Four hundred billion dollars goes to households with incomes over $30,000 and $200 billion of that goes to households with incomes over $50,000.

Hunger Action Network,
Albany, N.Y., December 1995

© Kirk Anderson. Reprinted with permission.

The Progressive Congressional Caucus: Examples of 1996 Proposals

- The Job Creation and Invest in America Act: Create 2 million jobs in two years to upgrade the nation's infrastructure and clean up the environment; funded by increased taxes on corporations and the wealthy.
- The National Economic Security Act: Cut defense spending to more fully meet domestic needs.
- The Equal Justice Before the Law Act: Tighten the consequences for corporate and white-collar crime; restore collective bargaining for working people and cut corporate welfare
- The Take Back Our Congress Act: Legislate campaign and lobbying reform with some public financing of elections to curb the influence of wealthy special interests.

If more citizens knew of these economic alternatives that would provide most Americans more economic equity, their energy could go into working for them rather than into blaming people different from themselves for their situation. Then diverse groups of people could work collaboratively for the common good. In 1993 in Rhode Island, for example, teachers worked with other unions, women's organizations, environmental groups and organizations representing poor people to pass a surcharge on incomes over $100,000. The revenue from this increased income tax on the top 10 percent of earners went into the general fund of the state.

Why not work together for a "maximum wage," for example? Sam Pizzigati, a labor journalist, suggests this idea of "salary caps." While that may sound far-fetched, years ago the idea of a minimum wage did too. Today we take it for granted.[10] There have been periods of greater economic equity in the U.S. In 1943, U.S. workers who made the equivalent of at least $1 million in modern dollars paid 78 percent of their total incomes in federal income taxes. This percentage has decreased ever since. In 1990 the richest 1 percent paid 21.5 percent in federal income taxes.

One of our biggest challenges in dealing with all forms of inequality is to keep a vision of the common good guided by principles of fairness. John Rawls, an American philosopher, contends that a society is fair if its level of inequality appears acceptable to a hypothetical individual who is about to join the society and who does not know if the inequality would work for or against him. In other words, the individual would not know what place he would hold in that society. We can apply such a measure of fairness not only to our society, but to other forms of social organization as well, such as classrooms and schools.

How Fair Is It?

Students who learned to ask questions like those in "How Fair is Our School?" might become the kind of adults who ask questions like those in "How Fair is Our Society?"

"How Fair Is Our School?"
- "Is our athletic program fair?" knowing I might enter the program as a girl as well as a boy; or
- "Is our urban school district structured fairly if I knew I might have an equal chance of going to the crowded inner city school as well as the magnet school on the outer edge of the city?"

"How Fair Is Our Society?"
- "Is our society fair if I knew I would as likely enter it as a homeless person than as a middle class person"?
- "Is our society fair if I knew that I might enter it and not have health insurance so my serious health problems would not be treated?

And then all might more readily ask, "What can we do to make it fair?"

---

2. Teachers, Students, and the Power to Change

Our schools can help students envision how our communities and society might be organized to be more fair for all. We can begin by creating such communities in our classrooms. Using their own life experiences, the theory and ideas from *Open Minds to Equality,* and challenges that face their school and community, students can learn about forms of inequality and alternatives to this. They can discover our nation's powerful tradition of collective action for social change.

As you use these activities, set high goals for yourself and your students. Expect that students will learn. When all students feel respected, a basic precondition for learning is met. Help young people who experience discrimination decrease the degree to which they internalize inferiority that schools and society can instill in them. Expect that all children, including those who are privileged, can understand causes of inequality and make changes.

Dealing honestly with young people about diversity issues can be frightening. Our fears are common and natural. If you have just begun to explore some of these issues yourself, it is unsettling to think about being responsible for discussing them with young people. It can help to let go of your expectations of having all the answers and try to trust the *process*. As long as you maintain firm guidelines for respectful communication, letting young people speak about their lives usually results in meaningful learning for everyone, including yourself. Learning about diversity is life long for each of us; the more we open ourselves to the process the more we learn.

We encourage you to begin where you are and do what you can. People are often afraid to take risks, imagining catastrophic results. While sometimes we do experience negative consequences for our actions, often our fears aren't borne out in reality. Think about the context of your particular situation when deciding on change strategies. Look for allies among other educators, parents and community members. While change is long and hard, we often have more power and flexibility than we think—especially when working together!

It has been our experience that activities in *Open Minds to Equality* can be taught in most school districts. That is not to say that you shouldn't be prepared for resistance. Some school personnel, board members and parents, either out of ignorance or because their value systems or political perspectives don't encourage considering diverse points of view, oppose teaching toward equality. Your dedication to giving all students a meaningful education and to confronting bias will be important in meeting this resistance. Speak clearly about the role of public schools in a democracy. Public schools must protect the rights of everyone; bias or discrimination toward any person because of their social identity or toward any social group is incompatible with American values of justice and equality.

We also recognize that what we do in schools alone won't change society. By practicing democracy on a small scale students: a) experientially understand what democracy is; b) develop insights about what democracy can be when practiced on a broader scale; c) become knowledgeable about the sources of inequality and approaches to change; d) act to create those changes. These are important first steps.

In addition to educating students, we can all be involved in broader efforts to foster social equality. Along with our colleagues, students, parents and administrators, we can examine our schools for practices and policies that may maintain discrimination, such as tracking and hiring practices, and work to change them. We can become involved in community-based projects and national organizations committed to social justice and share these efforts with our students.

While you won't use all these lessons with your students, we hope that you read them all; you'll gain valuable information yourself about addressing inequality. Look for examples in your life and your school that relate to the issues raised. Talk to your colleagues about them. As you become more conscious of examples of discrimination in your school we expect you'll feel motivated to work with others to change these.

Alternative and diverse sources of information can support your developing critical consciousness. Books like Howard Zinn's *A People's History of the United States,* journals for teachers such as *Rethinking Schools* and periodicals such as *Extra* from Fairness and Accuracy in Reporting keep us thinking. They also introduce us to perspectives and ideas not typically available in the mainstream media, ideas that are important to share with students. The Bibliography provides a wide range of choices in the "Background Reading for Teachers" and "Periodicals" sections.

It is energizing to know that there are numerous educators and people from all walks of life working together—as colleagues, union members, participants in national organizations—to change all forms of inequality in their schools, communities and nation. We are particularly fortunate as educators to be in a profession where, as part of our job, we can help shape a more just future.

In this book we aren't providing a bag of tricks for promoting equality. We do offer activities and ideas toward that end. Your honesty, critical thinking, commitment, collegiality and individual and collective action are what ultimately will ensure not only a democratic classroom but an egalitarian society as well. Carry on!

Becoming Fleas for Justice

Sojourner Truth could not stand injustice; she was an early feminist and she constantly fought against slavery; she couldn't read or write but she knew right from wrong. One day when it was terribly unpopular after the civil war to be speaking out against slavery, Sojourner Truth stood up and made one of her fiery speeches. A man stood up in the audience and heckled her, "Old woman you think your talk does any good? Why I don't care anymore for it than for a flea bite." "Maybe not," Sojourner snapped back at him, 'the Lord willing, I'll keep you scratching . . . .'

You dedicate yourselves to becoming fleas for justice.

Marian Wright Edelman
Children's Defense Fund

ENDNOTES

1. For more details on this model see, Lee Bell and Nancy Schniedewind, "Reflective Minds, Intentional Hearts: Joining Humanistic Education and Critical Theory," *Journal of Education,* Vol. 169, No. 2, 1987, pp. 55–77.

2. See Maurianne Adams, Lee Bell and Patricia Griffin, *Teaching for Diversity and Social Justice,* Routledge, N.Y. 1997 for more information on social justice education as geared to adults. Also see the work of Bailey Jackson, School of Education, University of Massachusetts, Amherst relating to anti-oppression education.

3. Christine Sleeter and Carol Grant. *Making Choices for Multicultural Education,* Merrill Publishing Company, N.Y., 1994.

4. Richard McIntyre, "Understanding the Hate Campaign," *New York Teacher,* June 12, 1995.

5. Bernard Sanders, "Whither American Democracy?" *The Los Angeles Times,* January 16, 1994.

6. Keith Bradsher, "America's Opportunity Gap," *The New York Times,* June 4, 1995.

7. Alfred Blumrosen, "Daily Labor Report," U.S. Department of Labor, March 23, 1995.

8. Stephen Moore, "How to Slash Corporate Welfare," *The New York Times,* April 5, 1995.

9. "Where Your Income Tax Money Really Goes," fiscal year 1997. War Resisters League, New York, N.Y. This differs from the government's tax budget pie, because the chart depicted on income tax returns buries the expenses of past military spending—26 percent in 1997—in nonmilitary parts of its pie. The government's pie also includes trust funds (such as Social Security) which are raised and spent separately from income taxes. This makes the human needs portion of the budget seem larger and the military portion smaller in the government's presentation.

10. Sam Pizzigati, "Salary Caps for Everyone!" *The New York Times,* August 8, 1994.

Building Trust and Communication

Egalitarian classrooms don't emerge overnight! They're the result of a great deal of hard work on the part of teachers and students. Just as a gardener prepares the soil for seeds and potential growth, so an educator must prepare students for working democratically. This chapter provides activities that teach basic skills which we feel are vital to a supportive classroom environment where students feel free to question, let down their defenses, and learn.

Such a supportive, caring environment is needed for students to feel safe enough to examine their attitudes and explore ideas that may challenge preconceived notions. It takes very intentional work on your part to create that environment. This works well if done intensively at the beginning of a school year. Engage students in activities to get them to know each other on a personal level. Help them work together to set classroom norms that will support learning and respect for each other. Subsequently, processes for problem-solving, like conflict resolution and community meetings, can be taught.

Explain to your students why these interactive skills are important. We often say something like this to students or people with whom we work: "We're in this class together this year to learn many things. You'll improve your reading and math, and become more aware and knowledgeable in social studies and science . . . . We're also here to learn about ourselves and each other. Everyone in this class is as valuable and special as anyone else and we'll be working together as a group in cooperative ways. *How* we do things is as important as *what* we do. Therefore we'll be taking time to practice listening to each other, working in groups, and using cooperative skills." Explain that these skills are applicable to many life-situations and once students learn them they will be able to use them at home, in groups, and in future work.

Sometimes teachers assume that if they place students in groups they will automatically work together well. Working cooperatively in a group is a skill, just as learning to ride a bike or learning to read. By teaching students cooperative skills—such as listening, affirming others, including others, disagreeing respectfully—students can gradually learn a repertoire of skills that will enable them to collaborate effectively in a group.

The activities in this chapter are sequential. Students initially learn simple skills and move on to more complex ones. They begin with lessons with a low level of risk and progress to more challenging activities. First, it's important that students get acquainted with each other and learn about their peers' lives and interests. This is a basis for trust and further communication.

Activities that teach students to listen to each other are followed by those that enable them to understand and improve their group process skills. These activities let students step back from the group, think about how well the group is working together, and pinpoint areas for change. Essential to successful group work is teaching students to identify and share feelings and to give each other feedback. With these skills, students can communicate honestly and change dysfunctional individual or group behavior.

The value of the activities in this chapter is brought out in the discussion. *Processing questions* are those questions you ask after an activity is over. These enable students to look back on the activity and draw learnings from it. Some questions refer to the task—*what* students did; others refer to the process—*how* students worked together. As a rule of thumb, ask questions about the task first, then go on to questions about the process. Be sure to ask both types, and to allow plenty of time for them at the end of an activity. They are extremely important for improving student learning, communication, and cooperation.

Don't be discouraged if activities don't go well at first, since it takes time and practice to develop new skills. Keep on teaching activities, processing them thoroughly, and reinforcing the skills in all aspects of your classroom procedures. Your efforts will be worth it, for not only will students have skills they can use throughout life, but you will have laid the groundwork for trust and communication for this school year and subsequent ones as well.

The content of Chapters 3 and 4 does not always address itself to issues of equality. It is often difficult for students to concentrate on new process skills and on challenging content at the same time. Therefore we have chosen some non-threatening topics for the activities that teach listening, group process and feedback skills. Once your students have practiced these skills, you can use them again and again with lessons throughout the book.

Section A   Getting Acquainted

NAME GAME

OBJECTIVES   To have students learn the names of the other children in the class at the beginning of the
school year.
To validate what children do well.

IMPLEMENTATION   Gather children in a circle. Ask children to think of something they like to do or are good
at. Give some examples—"I'm good at singing." "I'm good at making friends," "I like to
read."

Ask children to turn what they're good at or like to do into an "ing" word and to preface their name with that word—for example, singing Bob, making-friends Daryl, reading
Jennifer.

One child introduces himself by saying, "My name is ____ and I like to/am good at
____." The student on his left introduces herself and then repeats the name and gives "ing"
word of the person before her—for example, dancing Mel. This process continues, as each
person introduces himself and then repeats the names and "ing" words of several students
before him (about 3, depending on your group).

Urge the children to concentrate hard. Also remind them it's not a memory test, and
if they forget that's perfectly okay. To make this activity easier and more fun, you might
have students briefly act out their "ing" word—or give creative clues—if someone is stuck.
In this way the responsibility is on the group for everyone's success.

DISCUSSION   1. What did you learn about someone you didn't know before?
2. How hard or easy was it for you to think of something you're good at?
3. How would we feel if more of us told each other the things we think they're good at?
4. How did members of the group help each other remember names and "ing" words?

Cooperative People Machines

Divide students into groups of five to eight. Tell each group to think of a machine which
they will act out, without words, using all their members as parts. Allow about ten minutes for planning and rehearsal time in groups. Gather together as a class. Each group
in turn acts out its machine and other class members guess what it is. Ask students to
talk with their group members about the group process. How well did they work together?
What would they do differently next time?

CONCENTRIC CIRCLES

OBJECTIVES   To have students get to know each other at the beginning of the school year.
To encourage students to share information about themselves with others, that can foster
communication.
To begin to think about experiences in which inequality or discrimination has affected
them.

IMPLEMENTATION Divide the class into two groups. Have one half of the class move their chairs into a central area and form a circle facing out. Or have children sit on the floor in that same formation. Ask the other half of the class to form an outer circle, facing in. In this way each person has a partner.

Tell the students that you will give them a question to talk about with their partners. (See examples at the end of this lesson.) Each person has about a minute to respond. Give a signal at the minute mark so the other child gets enough time. Then say, "People on the outside circle, please each move one chair to your right." The inner circle stays stationary. Now each person has a new partner. Give them a new question to which they can respond.

Continue having students in the outer circle rotate to new partners as many times as seems appropriate or until they have come back to their original positions.

DISCUSSION
1. How did you like talking with your classmates?
2. Think of a person you talked with who you felt was really listening to you. Without naming that person, share some things that person did to make you feel listened to.
3. What's some new or surprising information that you learned about someone in your class?
4. Some of the experiences you talked about were about being treated unfairly or unequally. How does that feel? What can we do to change those situations?

Sample Questions Note that there are different types of questions—those that are relatively unthreatening, and those that focus on feelings or experiences of inequality.

1. Tell your partner what you like to do in your spare time.
2. If you could have one wish granted, what would it be?
3. Describe an experience where you didn't get to do something you wanted to do because of your age.
4. Describe something you did recently to help another person.
5. Tell your partner about a time where you were treated unfairly by someone else.
6. How are you like and unlike your father, mother, or an important adult in your life.
7. Describe a time you couldn't get to do something because you were a girl/boy.
8. If you could pass a law to make the world a better place to live in, what law would you pass?
9. Describe an experience you were part of, or know about, where you or someone you know was discriminated against because of race.
10. Describe something that someone did with or for you recently that made you feel good.

PEOPLE SCAVENGER HUNT

OBJECTIVES To have students find out more about all members of their classroom community
To encourage students to interact with a wide variety of people
To encourage appreciation of particular skills and traits

MATERIALS Copies of "Worksheet: Scavenger Hunt: Information Planning" and "Worksheet: Human Beans Board," pp. 51 and 52; pencils; individual bags with 25 beans or chips in each; an envelope with slips of paper, one for each student or adult in the classroom.

IMPLEMENTATION   Ask students about their previous experiences with scavenger hunts. If these are all to do with finding objects, explain that on this hunt they will be finding people, namely their classmates and anyone else in the classroom community.

There are two versions to this activity. In one version simply hand each participant a "Worksheet: Human Beans Board." Each participant is to try for a complete *Board* with one name in each space and with no name used more than once. In the alternative version pass out both the "Worksheet: Scavenger Hunt: Information Planning" and the "Worksheet: Human Beans Board." The goal is the same, but participants can use the "Worksheet: Scavenger Hunt: Information Planning" to help them gather information for filling out their "Worksheet: Human Beans Boards." In this manner they can strategize, perhaps figuring out which questions are hardest to complete and thus finding folks for those first, or getting each participant down several places on the "Worksheet: Scavenger Hunt: Information Planning" so that they can then make choices for their "Worksheet: Human Beans Boards," or deciding which squares are in more critical locations to fill and thus being sure to get those.

You may need to make modified versions of these for your particular class. It is helpful to have the same number of spaces as there are members of the class community. If the numbers don't work out right, go for more spaces rather than fewer. You may also want to make alternative versions of the boards, with the same questions on each but with varied locations so that not all participants have the same boards.

When participants have completed their "Worksheet: Human Beans Boards" have them return to their seats. Hand out a bag of beans or chips to each participant.

Pick a name out of the envelope. Ask that person to stand. All players who have that person's name on their "Worksheet: Human Beans Board" may cover it. Continue until all players each have a row.

DISCUSSION   1. What did you learn that you didn't know before about the members of our classroom community?
2. How might you use that information in ways that will be satisfying? Helpful for our class?

GOING FURTHER   Make a bar graph of all of the answers on the "Scavenger Hunt: Information Planning Worksheet." Which answers appeared frequently? rarely? What theories do you have about this? How can you check them out?

COMMONALITIES

OBJECTIVES   To find that, in spite of whatever differences we have, we have something in common with every other person.
To find specific commonalities with each member of the class community.
To think of ways to further develop these commonalities.
To develop a sense of community.

MATERIALS   Paper and pencils; bulletin board space; yarn; cards with names of each classroom member; stapler; address labels

IMPLEMENTATION   Begin by having all classroom members circulate around the room having conversations in pairs. Each pair must find one characteristic they have in common. This could be a favorite kind of music, something they really like about school, a common heroine, etc. As soon as they find this, each participant moves on to a new conversation. It is helpful if you say that no one person can use the same commonality with more than one other person. For example if Manuel and Natasha find they both love roller blading and then Maylan asks Natasha if she loves roller blading, Natasha would need to say something like, "Yes I do, but Manuel and I have already listed that, let's find something else." Pairs record their commonalities on paper.

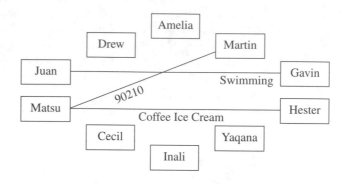

This experience is more powerful in building a sense of community in your classroom if you create a bulletin board with the results. Use a bulletin board at least 3 feet by 4 feet for a class of approximately 25. Two possible ideas are as follows.

Have classroom members put their names on cards and arrange these in a circular or oval shape. Then participants can draw lines between their names and the names of each other person. They write each commonality along the appropriate line.

Or participants can record their commonalities on computer address labels where they write both their names across the top half of the label and across the bottom half they write the characteristic they had in common. See drawing below for an example of a sheet of computer labels where a student named Hannah has recorded some of her commonalities. The bulletin board is set up like the example above except that names are connected to each other with separate pieces of yarn. While this is time consuming, the results are very satisfying and feel genuinely like a web.

Students then take each of their labels and fold them over the appropriate piece of yarn, connecting their name with the appropriate friend, with the commonality showing. See illustration below for how Hannah affixed her commonality with Dylan to the correct piece of yarn.

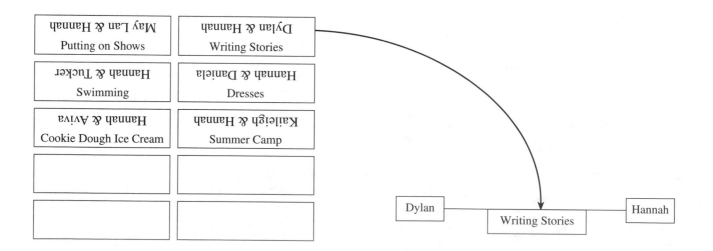

DISCUSSION

1. Did this activity get easier? or harder? or both easier and harder as you went on? Why?
2. Did you find any surprises? What were those? Think about what might have caused them.
3. Are you planning to follow up on any of the uncovered commonalities? What might you now do with a classroom member that you hadn't thought of before?
4. How can we use the information we gathered as we think about our year together?

GOING FURTHER

1. Finding out how many pieces of yarn you need (i.e. how many separate conversations took place) is a good math problem. Have students work in pairs or small groups on this. There are many possible good ways to solve this problem. Some students may work with a smaller case first, others may make a diagram, others may make a chart, still others may do something else. This is an excellent opportunity to affirm diversity and emphasize that one right way does not exist.
2. The commonalities piece of this activity could be a good one to do at a classroom breakfast or Open House. This is a wonderful way for parents from different backgrounds to find that they have much in common.

A Commonalities Bulletin Board

I do this activity to begin the school year in elementary school, college and graduate school classrooms. If you are using the web version, it is helpful to have several people working on setting up the initial bulletin board. In a primary classroom you may want to solicit the help of a student teacher, parent, or upper grade student.

—Ellen

Section B   *Developing Listening Skills*

I FEEL GOOD ABOUT MYSELF

OBJECTIVES

To have students identify and share positive points about their own personalities and skills and learn about those of classmates.
To give students the opportunity to hear about their own good traits from two other people.
To create a supportive classroom feeling.

IMPLEMENTATION

Explain to students that this is an "affirmation" activity, one which helps them feel good about themselves. They will have the opportunity to share their positive feelings about themselves and then listen to these said back. Divide students into pairs. Try to pair those who do *not* know each other well. Give students in the class three minutes to think of ways they like themselves and of skills they have. You can give a range of examples such as: things you're good at like bike-riding, cooking, carpentry; things you do well as a person, such as helping your friends when they're in trouble, doing chores for neighbors, not criticizing people; and personality traits, such as being fair, cooperative, understanding of others' feelings, not being mean to people. Have younger children make a list so they can remember. Help students who have trouble thinking of words.

When you tell them to begin, one person in each pair spends three or fewer minutes telling her partner three or four of these positives. The listeners may not talk except to give the speakers one-word reminders not to put themselves down in any way or qualify what they say! For example, it is okay to say, "I am a good guitar teacher because I was just recently a student myself and can remember how hard it is to begin." It is *not* okay to say, "I am a good guitar teacher but only for very beginning kids because I'm not really a very advanced player." If the second part of that second sentence is true simply leave it out. In the activity students only look at what they do well and how they help others. If the speaker runs out of things to say, both sit quietly until the time is up. At the end of the time, switch roles.

Each pair now gets together with another pair. Then each person in the group of four introduces her partner to the other two people. She tells the other two as many good things about her partner as she can remember. All four get a turn to do this.

DISCUSSION

1. How did it feel to talk about yourself?
2. To what extent did you have trouble thinking of enough to say?
3. To what extent did you feel you were bragging? Did you feel bad about doing that?
4. When you were listening, was it hard not to interrupt? Why or why not?
5. How did it feel to listen to your partner tell the other two about you? Was it easier or harder than the original talking?
6. How hard was it to remember what your partner had said about himself?
7. What did you learn about yourself in this activity? about your partner?
8. What is one thing you can do in the next few days with what you learned?

GOING FURTHER

Sometimes a re-do of this activity, with different partners, is helpful later in the year if class atmosphere is less supportive than you wish. Sometimes even a reluctant or hostile group can do this well and come out with significantly changed feelings.

LISTENING-CHECKING

OBJECTIVES

To learn a communication skill, "listening-checking," that will improve group discussion and empathizing skills.

To encourage students to hear what others are saying, rather than spend all their energies formulating their next contributions to a discussion.

To help students realize that often we don't express ourselves clearly and others misinterpret, or that we may be expressing ourselves well, but others may be mishearing.

IMPLEMENTATION

This is an excellent way to build class discussion skills. It works best with a controversial topic where students are giving opinions and supporting those with facts.

Use a topic where interpretation and understanding of what others are saying is necessary. Here are a few suggestions. If you were making an advice booklet for parents what would you put in it? What are some effective ways you have handled put-downs from other students? What are some of the things you would like about being another race, another gender? What should parents or teachers do when you hit another student (or swear at another student)? What are some of the ways to better get to know people different from yourself-different race, neighborhood, age, other gender?

Explain that after the first person speaks, the next person is to re-phrase what the first speaker said. This must be done in the second speaker's own words accurately enough so that the first speaker is satisfied that she was understood. If the second person cannot do that, then the first should re-say what she said until the second can re-phrase it correctly. The second speaker then makes her own contribution. The third speaker must re-phrase that before giving his contribution. Discussion proceeds in this manner. Before any student can join in the discussion, she must re-phrase the previous speaker's contribution.

This is awkward and time-consuming. However, it helps students concentrate on other people and greatly reduces people's tendencies to think through what they want to say while others are talking.

You certainly wouldn't want to do this every time you have a discussion. You might want to do it near the beginning of the year, when working on these methods, and then again later if poor listening is a problem.

GOING FURTHER   This is an activity that you could suggest families try at home. After one of the authors did it with a Girl Scout troop, several girls, on their own initiative, tried it with their families. The author got some very positive feedback from parents.

"Listening-Checking" is a skill. It can be used throughout the year, as needed.

Cooperative Energizer: Group Juggle

Needed: Three balls of different sizes.

Gather students into a circle. Ask if anyone knows how to juggle. If so, have that student give an example. Tell students that they will learn to juggle as a group.

Begin by calling one student's name and tossing the ball to her. Tell the students they must remember two things—who they received the ball from and who they threw the ball to—because they will continue to receive balls from that person and throw balls to that same person. The student who has the ball calls another name and throws it to that student, and so on.

For the first round, and the first round alone, have students raise their hands once they have thrown the ball. Others must throw to a person whose hand isn't up. In this way all students become a part of the pattern.

Once one ball has reached everyone in the group, the group's basic pattern has been established. Practice until students know it well. Now, start the first ball again, in the same sequence, but add a second ball, and then a third, so all three balls are being thrown in the group's pattern at the same time.

Discuss what helped or hindered the group's success. Often students need to focus on the cooperative nature of catching a ball—it is both the responsibility of the thrower and receiver for someone to make a catch. Discuss what students did to *help* their partner catch the ball. Ask students what they can do to make the juggle even more effective. Try juggling several more times to see if the group can get all balls around without dropping any!

ADJECTIVE ATTRIBUTES

OBJECTIVES   To learn a process for checking and improving listening skills that can be used throughout the year.
To build positive self-concept.
To learn new vocabulary and practice creative writing.

MATERIALS   Index cards; magic markers.

Develop a "Worksheet: Listening" with these questions listed, with spaces for student responses, down a single page. 1.a. Who listened to you? b. What made you think so? 2.a. How well did you listen to others? b. How would they know that? 3.a. Was anyone easy to listen to? b. What makes them easy to listen to? 4. One way I will improve my listening next time I work in a group will be to:

IMPLEMENTATION   Tell the class they should try to listen better to each other in this activity. Go over the "Worksheet: Listening" with them. Tell them they will fill it out at the end of the lesson. Tell students they will work together in groups to select positive adjectives that describe each other. They will help each other learn new words, have a chance to talk about positive qualities they see in each other, and practice careful listening.

On the board, make a list of adjectives that *positively* describe others. Here are suggestions: friendly, helpful, competent, athletic, tolerant, hard-working, kind, honest, strong. Add others relevant to your grade level. Define them together.

Divide students into heterogeneous groups of three or four. Students write down the adjectives and definitions of difficult words. They check others' work to make sure each student has correct words and definitions.

Then students choose an adjective that describes each member of their group. They do this by focusing on one group member at a time. He must sit quietly while the others agree on an adjective and the reason for their choice. Continue for all students. Remind students that all discussion regarding people must be positive. Monitor groups to catch any put-downs.

Next, each group has fifteen minutes to write a very short story in which each person in the group shows the quality described by the positive adjective the group picked for him. Groups read the stories to each other. Other groups try to guess the adjective the group chose for each person.

Have the students write their adjectives on a 3 × 5 card with a magic marker. They tape the card to their desks or chairs as a reminder of the positive quality their peers see in them.

The final, and very important, step in this activity is to have each student fill out the Worksheet.

DISCUSSION   Task (The content of the activity).
1. How did you feel about the adjective your group chose for you? Would you have chosen that one or another adjective for yourself?
2. How hard or easy was it to decide on an adjective for another person? Why?

Process (How people work together—in this case, listen).
3. Discuss all four questions on the Worksheet in some depth.

Keep the emphasis positive by focusing on what they learned about listening and how they can improve. Tell students they'll be using the Worksheet throughout the year as a way to check their improvement in listening. Return their Worksheet to them after you check them. Next time they do a group activity have them look at their answer to number 4 and work hard at that goal.

Listen!

Use the "Worksheet: Listening" throughout the year with any academic lesson that involves listening. Watch student improvement!

Section C *Building Group Process Skills*

THE EQUAL SCHOOL

OBJECTIVES To have students heighten their awareness of group process by use of a group process observation form.
To have students think about what makes schools just and equal.

MATERIALS Copies of "Worksheet: Our Group," p. 53, one per student; paper and pencils.

IMPLEMENTATION Divide students into heterogeneous groups of four. Make sure students of different genders and races are mixed within the groups, where possible.

Explain to students that there are two important areas to notice about working in a group—the task and the process.

TASK—*What* the group is trying to accomplish or complete (for example, make a social studies map, draw a mural).

PROCESS—*How* the group is working together (for example, how well students are helping each other, the amount of listening).

Reiterate to students that the task—the goals they are working toward—and the process—their group interaction—are equally important. Tell them they will have an opportunity to practice doing a task and to evaluate their group behavior.

Tell students that they are to work together to plan and then develop a mural that reflects the diversity within their community. First they will work cooperatively in small groups and then cooperatively as a class to put the sections of the mural together.

Each group will be responsible for one area or place in the community—e.g., library, supermarket, park, laundromat, etc. In that place students are to show the variety of people who use that area—e.g., people of all ages, genders, physical abilities, etc. Before breaking into groups decide together on the size of the mural and scale.

In groups students work together to plan their section of the mural. What will be in it? Who will draw/paint what? Next, students will draw/paint their section of the mural. When all segments are complete, assemble the class mural.

After completing the task, and before discussion, ask each student to check questions 1 through 4 on the Worksheet. Collect their Worksheets and make a quick composite tally for each group. Put a hypothetical group tally on the board and ask students what they could learn about that group from the tally. In this example, one person felt left out and students didn't ask each other for their ideas too often.

Example:

1. How much did I contribute to the group?   1 ✓   2 ✓   3 ✓✓
2. How well did I listen to the ideas of others?   1 ___ 2 ✓✓ 3 ✓
3. How much did I ask other people for their ideas? 1 ✓✓ 2 ✓✓ 3 ___

Now distribute the tally sheets to each group. Ask students to study their tally and see what they can learn about their group. Finally return individual Worksheets and have each student answer the last question.

Good Team Work

DISCUSSION "First, let's talk about the *task* of your group."

1. Who are some of the different types of people we see when we look at the diversity of people in our community.
2. What issues or problems did you face when deciding who should be represented in your picture?
3. Are any types of people missing from our mural? How can we support diversity in our community?

"Now let's talk about the *process*."

1. What did your group learn from the tally sheet?
2. How can you tell if group members are listening to each other?
3. How can you improve your group behavior next time you work in a group?

GOING FURTHER Use the Worksheet again, on academic as well as other tasks, until students become familiar with looking at the process of groups.

Resources for Helping Students Work in Groups

If you need support for helping students to develop interpersonal skills and to work more effectively in groups see:

Chapters 3 and 4 of *Cooperative Learning, Cooperative Lives: Learning Activities for Building a Peaceful World*. Nancy Schniedewind and Ellen Davidson

Chapter 6 of *Circles of Learning* by David and Roger Johnson, and Edythe Johnson Holubec.

Both of these books are excellent resources for gaining basic skills for implementing cooperative groups in your classroom, more structured groups that assure that all students work interdependently toward common goals and are accountable for their learning.

GUM DROP INVENTIONS

OBJECTIVES
To become aware of the roles students can play in groups.
To recognize the role a student usually plays in a group, and to try out an alternative to that role.
To give students the opportunity to work collectively.
To challenge students to think of a priority in our nation's problems.

MATERIALS Coffee stirrers, cut in half; about 150 small gumdrops; copies of "Worksheet: Roles People Play in Groups," p. 55.

IMPLEMENTATION Pass out the Worksheet and discuss it with the class. Have students give examples of times they have played one of the roles mentioned. Ask them to think about what role they typically play, what role they want to play today and then fill in the worksheet. Share a few responses.

Divide students into heterogeneous groups of five. Give each group 20 to 40 coffee stirrers and about 30 gumdrops. Tell them that they have five minutes to discuss, within groups, an invention which would help make our country a better place to live in. During the five minutes they should decide on the type of invention, how it works, and how they can build a model of it with stirrers and gumdrops. They may look at the materials during this time but not touch them. Explain that once they start building they may not talk at all, so they should reach whatever decisions they can before they begin.

After five minutes, announce that there is no talking and groups may begin building. While the groups are working, circulate around the room. When all the groups are finished, talk together, but keep groups near their own projects.

Going to the first group, ask others to guess what the invention is and how it works. If no one guesses, the group which created it can give hints. Finally, the group members describe their invention in detail. Continue around the room for all the inventions. Then go on to the group discussion, which follows the pattern of beginning with questions about the task and continuing with questions about the process.

DISCUSSION
1. Think of a word that you feel describes your invention.
2. How did what you built differ from your plan?
3. What roles did you play in the group?
4. What did you do so other people could recognize that role?
5. What role did others think you were playing? What did you do to give them that idea?
6. How did you feel playing the role you did?
7. How did the roles group members played affect how well you created your invention?
8. What happened if there were too many negative roles? How is this like other groups you are in? How can this be changed?
9. Did you learn anything new doing this activity? If so, what?
10. How will you use what you learned in other groups this week?

GOING FURTHER Assign students roles to play in other group activities to give them an experience of an alternative. They can learn that they're not "stuck" in roles they typically take on.

WHO'S DOING THE TALKING?

OBJECTIVE To make students more conscious of the role they play in group discussions and to encourage them to make more critical decisions about that.

MATERIALS Ball of yarn; two bags of dry beans or peas.

IMPLEMENTATION Explain to students that often when we get very involved in a discussion we lose our awareness of how much we are contributing, or not contributing. Often some people do almost all the talking while others are silent or nearly silent. Sometimes a dialogue will take place between two people while other group members are excluded. The following activities help focus awareness of these issues. (They are probably *not* ones that you will want to use regularly, but only when the need arises.) For some discussion topics, see "No Interrupting," p. 59.

Method One. Students sit in a circle. The first speaker starts with a ball of yarn, tying the end loosely around her wrist. When she is done talking, she gently throws the ball of yarn to the next speaker. After that person is finished, he winds it once loosely around his wrist and throws it onward. In this way students can keep track of the pattern of a discussion. After the discussion, and before rewinding the yarn, discuss the questions listed below.

Method Two. Students sit in a fairly tight circle. Give each student ten or more dried beans or peas. Place a large container, such as a garbage can, in the center of the circle. Each time someone talks he must throw one of his beans into the container. When a student uses up all his beans he may not participate any more in that discussion. Again be sure to process this at the end when some students still have left-over beans.

DISCUSSION

1. What did you discover about your group participation? What could you have predicted?
2. Do you think you behaved any differently in these activities than you would otherwise in a group discussion? Why or why not? Are those differences ones which please you?
3. Were some people not participating in the discussion? Think of reasons which have to do with their choices and the choices of other class members. How is this helpful? harmful?
4. Were some people participating a great deal? What causes this to happen? How is this helpful? harmful?
5. Look at the yarn. Are there some people who always responded to the same people? Are there some people who got responses from a variety of people? Think back on these people and what they said and try to come up with reasons.
6. Did having to give up beans make you more cautious about what you said, more reluctant to speak? As the discussion came to a close, how did you feel if you had many beans left?
7. What could you do differently the next time you have a class discussion because of what you learned today?

FOLLOW-UP "Fantasy Problem-Solving," p. 68.

LOVE AND FRIENDSHIP FOR THOSE OF US WHO CANNOT HEAR...

Section D   *Sharing Feelings and Giving Feedback*

COLOR ME LOVABLE AND CAPABLE

OBJECTIVES   To increase and share positive feelings about one's self.
To become more sensitive to one's own feelings and those of others.

MATERIALS   Paper and crayons.

IMPLEMENTATION   Tell children that we can help ourselves, like ourselves, and help others like themselves, by what we say and do. Tell them the phrase IALAC stands for "I Am Lovable and Capable."

Step One. Read our short adaptation of Sidney Simon's *I Am Lovable and Capable*. See the IALAC story, pp. 54.

Before telling the story to your students write IALAC in very big letters on a piece of paper. Hold this up in front of you as you tell the story. At each point where Josh's IALAC is chipped away (marked * in our adaptation) rip a piece of the IALAC sign. By the end of the story there should be nothing left.

In discussing the story with your students the following questions can be starters: How would you feel if you were Joshua? What do people do to you that tears away at your IALAC? What has someone done to you to increase your IALAC? Only discuss briefly, as the rest of this activity allows students to go into more detail.

Step Two. Divide students into heterogeneous groups of about three or four and distribute materials. Have each student make wide letters spelling IALAC on their papers. Their letters should be open, so that they can color them in.

Tell students there are many ways we can increase IALAC. For example, through the things we say and do to others; the things others say and do to us; and the things we do or say to ourselves. You may want to solicit examples.

Students tell each other how their IALAC—their feeling of being lovable and capable—was boosted recently, in any of the three ways listed above. One student starts and they proceed around the circle, telling of an experience and coloring in a letter. Continue around the circle five times until all students have told of five experiences and colored their IALAC signs. Hang these around the room or on their chairs or desks.

DISCUSSION   1. What did you learn about yourself?
2. What did you learn about someone else?
3. How can you build up a friend's IALAC?
4. How can someone increase your IALAC?

GOING FURTHER   Remind students about their IALAC as you proceed through the year. Return to this activity periodically to build up positive individual and group feeling.

FEELING MESSAGES

OBJECTIVES   To practice sharing feelings.
To practice giving feedback in the form of "feeling messages."

MATERIALS   Oak tag; marker.

IMPLEMENTATION Introduce "feeling messages" to the class: "When people work in groups, it helps to let others know how they are feeling about what's happening. This is true when things go well and when they go badly. One way to give feedback is through 'feeling messages' or 'I-messages'."

Write the format for a feeling message on oaktag.

Name, _____ "When you _____, I feel _____, because _____.
                              [behavior]   [feeling]   [explanation]

Examples: "Omar, when you helped me understand the math problem, I felt thankful, because I had been very confused." "Lizzie, when you asked me to play soccer, I felt accepted because sometimes no one asks me to play."

Explain to students that by using feeling messages we can tell other people how particular behaviors of theirs make us feel. The feelings can be positive or negative. Feeling messages don't label the whole person as bad or good, they only point to specific behavior. Only if a person knows how he affects you, does he know either to continue or change his behavior. (See Thomas Gordon's *Parent Effectiveness Training* for a full discussion of "I-messages.")

Brainstorm a list of feeling words. Put them on oaktag and post in the class. Have students write down two or three feeling messages for the teacher or other students in the class. Ask students to share one of their feeling messages with a partner and check for correct format. They correct their work as needed. (Tell them to avoid sharing a negative feeling message about another person.) Ask a few students to share theirs with the class in order to reinforce the correct format.

Ask each student to pick one feeling message they would like to share with the person they wrote it for. Tell them to go to that person and give him the message. Sit down as a class and talk about how they felt giving and receiving feeling messages.

DISCUSSION 1. How did you feel giving your feeling message?
2. If you received a message, how did it feel?
3. Why is it sometimes hard to give feeling messages?
4. How could giving and receiving feeling messages help us get along better in our class? At home? On the playground?
5. Think of one more feeling message you would like to give today. Find a good time to do it and tomorrow we'll talk about how it went.

GOING FURTHER Leave the oaktag with the list of feelings, feeling message format, and examples up in the classroom. Remind students to use feeling messages often. Model them yourself. Periodically give the class time to write these messages to each other as a way to reinforce good feelings or helpful behavior, or as a way of working through tense or highly charged situations.

Create a mail box in your classroom for "Feeling Messages." Have a stack of blank forms next to it. Allow students to fill in slips when they wish and have these delivered at the end of the day. Be sure they know they can send messages to you too. Allow time for discussion after students give and receive messages.

speaks another language fluently (what language?) _____

has taught a sport to someone else (what sport?) _____

knows how to cook a food from an ethnicity that is not her/his own (what ethnicity?)_____

is friends with an elderly person _____

has been successful in doing something cooperatively (give example) _____

has made a new friend recently _____

has worked on something s/he believes in (what work?) _____

has learned a new skill in the last six months (what skill?) _____

loves science _____

has helped someone out recently (give example)_____

reads books about people from other cultures _____

rides a bike as a means of transportation_____

looks things up when interesting questions arise in a discussion _____

has more than two siblings _____

knows the words to a song s/he'd love to teach this class (what song?)_____

likes doing secret favors that stay anonymous (give example)_____

felt proud recently (give example) _____

was born in another country (what country?) _____

repaired something that was broken_____

has regular responsibilities in her/his family (give example) _____

stuck up for a person being "put down" _____

is good at something that isn't typical of her/his gender (give example)_____

felt happy recently (give example) _____

has taught someone something in last month (give example) _____

knows a game from another country (what game?) _____

has learned a new skill in the last six months	has taught someone something in last month	reads books about people from other cultures	is good at something that isn't typical of her/his gender	felt proud recently
knows the words to a song s/he'd love to teach this class	knows how to cook a food from an ethnicity that is not her/his own	stuck up for a person being "put down"	likes doing secret favors that stay anonymous	has worked on something s/he believes in
has been successful in doing something cooperatively	loves science	rides a bike as a means of transportation	has made a new friend recently	was born in another country
has more than two siblings	felt happy recently	has taught a sport to someone else	looks things up when interesting questions arise in a discussion	has regular responsibilities in her/his family
speaks another language fluently	is friends with an elderly person	knows a game from another country	repaired something that was broken	has helped someone out recently

Let's see how well your group worked together! Answer each question by putting a circle around a number.

	none, not well	somewhat	a lot, very well
Example: How well do I play kickball?	1	2	3

Try these:

	none, not well	somewhat	a lot, very well
1. How much did I contribute to the group?	1	2	3
2. How well did I listen to the ideas of other people?	1	2	3
3. How much did I ask other people for their ideas?	1	2	3
4. How well did our group work together?	1	2	3

Look at your answers.

Write down one thing you'll try to do better when you work in a group next time.

THE IALAC STORY

All people are born with a big IALAC—a feeling that "I Am Lovable and Capable." Sadly, as we grow up, other people and events in life chip away at our IALAC. I'll tell you about a day in the life of Joshua, so you'll see how this happens. He is a ten-year-old boy, who's perhaps very much like you.

On this particular day, Joshua was awakened by his father who was yelling, "Joshua, you overslept again. What's the matter with you? Hurry or you'll be late for school."* Nevertheless, Joshua said to himself, "I'll hurry and will be ready on time."

Joshua got dressed and tried to get in the bathroom. His older brother had the door locked and wouldn't let him in. "You can wait your turn, squirt, I was here first."* Josh waited, and waited, and waited . . . .

Joshua had been looking forward to his yummy, crispy, crackling cereal. As he entered the kitchen his mother remarked, "My, Josh, you certainly are the poke of our family."* He hung his head, sat down, and there was a bowl of mushy, soggy cereal.*

Not to be discouraged, Joshua gathered his homework and started walking quickly toward his bus stop. He was very proud of his science homework. It had taken a lot of time and research. He was eager to show it to Ms. Vega, his teacher. As Joshua was heading toward the bus stop, a huge gust of wind blew up behind him and his science papers flew into the air and landed in a puddle! He tried to gather his wet papers, but they were completely soaked.*

Josh was so discouraged! He'd just have to explain things to Ms. Vega. He started quickly toward the bus stop. With only two blocks left to walk, he looked up and saw the bus pulling slowly away.*

Josh had to walk the rest of the way to school. As he walked in the door of the school, the principal, Ms. Johnson, stopped him. "Joshua, you should be ashamed of yourself—twenty minutes late. I want you in my office during recess."*

By this time Josh was feeling so low! He got to his classroom and began doing his work. Then Ms. Vega said, "And now students, please take out your science homework." Joshua slowly raised his hand and said, "Ms. Vega, I know you might not believe this, but as I was walking to school a huge gust of wind . . . ."

Ms. Vega straightened up and said in a loud, stern voice, "Students, if you don't do your homework please do not make up ridiculous stories and excuses. I want people to tell the truth in class." She gave Joshua a very serious look.*

Joshua had very little IALAC left. As he walked to lunch he said to himself, "Well at least a good lunch will make me feel better." As he carried his tray across the lunchroom, someone tripped him. Crash, down everything fell. All the kids laughed at him.*

---

*Adapted from "I Am Lovable and Capable" by Sidney Simon.

HELPFUL

1. **idea-giver**

   gives helpful ideas to the group

   I'VE GOT AN IDEA!

2. **idea-seeker**

   asks other people for their ideas

   HEY JILL, WHAT'S YOUR IDEA?

3. **friendly helper**

   is friendly to people and thinks
   of other people's feelings

   TYRONE, WE MISSED YOU IN THE GROUP LAST WEEK!

4. **peace-keeper**

   tries to help people who disagree or
   fight to understand each other

   WHY ARE YOU TWO ARGUING?

5. **organizer**

   encourages people to get the job done

   WE'D BETTER GET BUSY IF WE'RE GOING TO FINISH!

6. **supporter**

   tells people things he likes about them

   I LIKE YOUR PLAN, LATISHA!

NOT HELPFUL

1. **boss**

   acts like a "know-it-all"

   DO WHAT I SAY!

2. **do-nothing**

   sits to the side and doesn't help

   I'M NOT GOING TO DO THAT!

3. **talker**

   talks and talks and talks and talks

   YAP YAP YAP YAP

4. **dart-thrower**

   makes fun of other people and their ideas

   OH THAT'S A STUPID IDEA!
   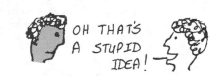

Questions:

1. Which do you usually play in a group?_____

2. Which role will you try to play today?_____

Developing Skills for Creative Cooperation

Cooperation is an underlying value in a democratic classroom. In such a classroom students learn to support each other academically and emotionally, rather than to compete with each other. The words "we" and "our" are commonly heard, as in: "*we* can do it," *our* classroom, "*we* met our class goal for spelling words" and "how can *we* solve this problem?" It takes intentional work on our parts to foster such a spirit of cooperation in the classroom.

Similarly it takes ongoing, intentional effort to teach students skills for working together cooperatively. Sometimes we expect students to have the tools for productive collaboration at their fingertips. This, however, isn't usually the case. Explicitly and implicitly our culture teaches competitive values and skills, and much less often cooperative ones. This chapter provides lessons that give students important tools for interdependent learning.

The first lessons provide opportunities for students to see that several heads are usually better than one, and that each group member has positive contributions to make. Skills in not interrupting, helping, and coming to consensus are introduced. Interviewing skills, needed in many data-gathering activities throughout the year, are taught. It's when people work cooperatively that the most creative problem-solving and divergent thinking results. The final lessons in the chapter give students experience with brainstorming, creative controversy, and role-play.

Some lessons in *Open Minds to Equality* are structured cooperatively. In these lessons students work together in a group on a common task and are accountable to the group. Each person succeeds if, and only if, the group succeeds. Cooperatively structured learning enhances not only students' responsibility for themselves, but for their peers.

While only some lessons are designed in a carefully structured cooperative learning format, most expect students to work together in groups. We encourage you to apply basic principles of cooperative learning to these lessons and actually structure them cooperatively to make them most efficient and democratic. David and Roger Johnson's *Circles of Learning* and our *Cooperative Learning, Cooperative Lives* are very useful resource books on cooperative learning. Whether you have students work in groups or structure more tight cooperative learning formats, tasks should be divided equitably, students taught skills for working together, and time set aside for students to talk about how well they worked together and how they might improve.

Many lessons ask you to set up heterogeneous groups; groups that mix students according to a wide range of diversity such as race, gender, learning ability and personality. Also add other forms of diversity as you specifically address them in a lesson. For example, if a lesson is on anti-Semitism, make groups heterogeneous by religion as well, if possible.

As you go through the chapter, continue to remind students that they can learn as much, or more, by working together as by working alone, and that they can learn as much from other people as from books. Help them understand that learning is a many-faceted experience.

In this chapter, as in Chapter 3, the content does not always directly focus on issues of equality. Students are still learning process skills with some nonthreatening topics, so they will have had practice with those skills when they study discrimination. But if students are learning those skills, your classroom process will already be reflecting more equality!

Vietnamese Saying

In hell people starve because their hands are chained to six-feet-long chopsticks, too long to bring rice to their mouths.
Heaven is the same—only there, people feed each other.

Women in Vietnam by Arlene Eisen

Section A *Learning Cooperative Skills*

BRAINSTORMING

OBJECTIVES To teach students a skill in drawing information out of themselves and sharing it with others.
To encourage more creative thinking and generation of ideas.
To show students how others' ideas can help them come up with more ideas of their own—and how a combination of ideas from many people can often be more exciting than any single one.

MATERIALS Chart paper; magic markers.

IMPLEMENTATION　Explain to the students that brainstorming is a method that is helpful in getting people to think creatively and in getting many solutions to a problem. Often hearing others' ideas helps get one thinking better. Discuss the rules of brainstorming, below, then post in front of the room. Remind students to follow them during the lessons.

1. All ideas are accepted—everything gets written down.
2. No one comments (positively or negatively) on anyone else's ideas.
3. Say anything that comes to mind, even if it seems silly.
4. Think about what others have suggested and use those ideas to get your brain moving along new lines.

Divide into heterogeneous groups of four students. Each group needs several pieces of chart paper and a recorder. If ideas come too fast for one person to write, have two recorders. Printing should be big enough so everyone can read it while brainstorming is going on.

Brainstorming Task One. Each small group must come to agreement on a name for this product: sneakers that are fluorescent green, have neon shoelaces and flashing lights. After ten minutes call "time" and have each group share the title it created.

Brainstorming Task Two. Students come up with composite solutions for how to do a task. Tell each group that often the process for picking teams in gym class or on the playground isn't helpful because some people are always picked first and others last. Come up with new ways of picking teams that would be fun and make everyone feel good! After five minutes have groups share their ideas.

Brainstorming Task Three. Students come up with a problem-solution of a more subjective nature. Tell them: "You told your best friend that you think your parents are getting a divorce. You explained clearly that this was confidential and not to be told to anyone. A few days later you discover that your friend has told everyone. What are you going to say to your friend? What are you going to do?" After ten minutes have all groups share their ideas.

DISCUSSION
1. Was it difficult not to compliment or criticize other ideas? Why do you think this is a rule of brainstorming?
2. In what ways was each of the three tasks easy or hard?
3. Which task did you find easiest? hardest? Why?
4. In what ways did brainstorming as a group help you come up with a solution that you wouldn't have thought of on your own?
5. How could brainstorming be used in some of our regular classes? Think of something we did in any subject last week that might have been helped by using brainstorming. Explain how.
6. Are there any other rules we should set up as a class when we use brainstorming in the future?

GOING FURTHER　Many other lessons in this book use brainstorming. If your students need further practice in this technique, before you use it as a crucial part of the content of other lessons, try some additional topics.

Cooperation for Survival

Microbiologists agree that the extraordinarily rapid development of penicillin was possible only because groups of scientists in many countries were impelled to rise above all questions of national pride or personal scientific credit and pool their efforts to make this efficient antibiotic available for wounded soldiers in the field.

From *Stress Without Distress,* by Hans Selye

THE BEAN JAR

OBJECTIVE To examine how the involvement of different numbers of people in decision-making affects accuracy.

MATERIALS A jar filled with beans. You must know the number of beans in the jar. For 3rd–4th grade use around 100 beans, 5th–6th about 175, and more for older students.

IMPLEMENTATION Set the jar of beans in a place where all children can see it. Have each student estimate the number of beans in the jar. Record the estimates.

Have children form partnerships and repeat the process. Record the estimates. Do the same for groups of four. Encourage children to discuss their reasoning with their group members as they make their group estimates. Have the quartets pick another foursome and record estimates.

Tell the children the number of beans in the jar and have them compare it with their various estimates.

DISCUSSION
1. How did sharing ideas with others and cooperating in a group affect how close you came to guessing the right number?
2. Why did the number of members in the group affect your accuracy?
3. How did you feel during each decision-making process—alone, with partners, with groups?
4. How can you apply what you learned today to other decision-making situations?

NO INTERRUPTING

OBJECTIVES To give students a method to eliminate interrupting each other when having a group discussion.
To eliminate hand-raising while others are talking.

MATERIALS A rolled up clean sock.

IMPLEMENTATION Tell students they will learn a method to promote better group discussion techniques. List some problems in group discussions on the board. For example, "No one really listens to anyone else," or, "People always cut each other off." Then list reasons for these. Students may realize that often people don't mean to be rude, but interrupt because they want to be sure to get a turn. Understanding that, and knowing that methods can be developed to cope with it is helpful in instituting a new approach.

Explain the following method. In the group discussion, the first person to speak will be handed a rolled up sock. While he is speaking he holds the sock in his hand on his lap. During that time none of the other students may say anything or raise their hands. When the speaker is finished, he holds up the sock in front of him. This is the signal for other people to raise their hands if they wish to speak. The speaker then throws the sock to someone with a raised hand. If that person is going to speak directly on the topic, she does so; everyone else must put hands down until she holds up the sock as the signal that she is done speaking. If, however, she is going to go off on any kind of tangent from what the previous speaker said, she must say so and give anyone who wants to speak more directly to the original point a chance to go first. In that case, when that person is done, the sock comes back to her before going onward. No one may say anything when not holding the sock except for the facilitator who may make "points of order," such as reminding people not to interrupt or not to repeat what has already been said. No one may raise a hand except when the sock is being held up.

Here are some suggestions for topics:

1. A classroom project, such as a luncheon for the parents and children, that the whole class could work on cooperatively.
2. A local issue that involves race, gender, or age discrimination—such as unequal funding for girls' athletics or funding for public health nurses for homebound older persons.
3. A problem relevant to your students and their age group, such as teasing and put-downs.

GOING FURTHER   You can use this as a model whenever you do a whole-class discussion. Once students master the technique it is automatic, not distracting, and an excellent way to encourage more considerate group practice. Often it is helpful even when working in small groups, especially with a high-energy topic.

HELPFUL HINTS FOR HELPING

OBJECTIVE   To practice some "do's and don'ts" of helping other students in a cooperative group.

MATERIALS   Large poster board or piece of newsprint for chart; copies of "Worksheet: Do's and Don'ts of Helping," p. 75, two per student.

IMPLEMENTATION   To simplify this activity it is broken down into three days. Schedule it in any way that works best for you.

Day One   *A) Making the Chart, "Do's and Don'ts of Helping."* With the whole class together, students think of a time that someone was teaching them on a one-to-one basis or in a small group setting. They close their eyes and picture that experience as clearly as possible in their minds. Allow a minute or two. Ask them to think of the ways that that person's interaction with them helped or hindered their learning the new skill or information.

They open their eyes and list these helpful and unhelpful behaviors on the board in two categories: "Do" and "Don't." Add items yourself.

When the list is complete, select the most important items from each category and put them on a large poster. It probably will be a variation of the chart on the next page, depending on your grade level.

B) Learning Style. Explain that different people learn in different ways. Give some examples. Sue, a fourth-grader, learns spelling best by writing the letters in the air. John likes

Do	Don't
1. *Give Praise.* ("Great, I think you're catching on!")	1. *Tell the answers.* ("Listen, here's the answer.")
2. *Have the learner explain the information to you.* ("I think you've got it! Now teach it back to me.")	2. *Give put-downs or embarrass the learner.* ("Do you mean you don't understand how to do this?")
3. *Try varied ways of going over the same skill.* ("Fine, you know this multiplication table. Now I'll give you problems with multiplication in them.")	3. *Pressure.* ("Hurry up! What's taking you so long?")
4. *Find relevant examples.* ("Write a sentence using these vocabulary words to describe a person you know.")	4. *Ignore a person who doesn't understand something.* ("Jim doesn't get this. We've got to hurry and finish the project. though.")
5. *Quit while you're ahead.* ("You've got it! Now let's continue solving the group task.")	5. *Pile on too much information.* ("You learned it, but there's a lot more you're behind on. Now listen to this. . . .")
6. *Find the person's learning style and use it.* ("You learn your spelling best when you write the letters in the air.")	

to spell his vocabulary words out loud in order to reinforce them. Ask students to name some of the strategies they have used to help themselves learn. Discuss them together. Each person completes these statements: "I learn well when. . . ." "I learn well by. . . ." Remind the students that when they are helping each other, they are to use the learning style that works best for the person with whom they are working.

Day Two   **A) *Practicing Helping Skills.*** Students work in trios to practice the "Do's and Don'ts of Helping." They number off. During the first stage of the activity #1 helps #2, and #3 observes. Person #2 receives five "hard-but-intriguing" vocabulary words that she helps person #1 to learn. (Examples include: ambivalent, mediate, mutuality, collaborate, assimilate, cultural, affirm, precedent, interdependence, symbolic, grapple, inadvertently, liabilities, anonymous.) Remind helpers to try to use the "Do's" of helping and to avoid the "Don'ts." The observer receives a dittoed copy of the "Do's and Don'ts" in the form of a checklist. (Use Worksheet, p. 75 if applicable, or make up your own based on the list your class generated.) Each time the helper manifests one of the behaviors, the observer makes a mark on the checklist. When person #2 has mastered the words, rotate so that #2 teaches #3 and #1 observes. Lastly, #3 teaches #1 and #2 observes. Each new process-observer gets a new checklist.

B) *Processing.* When finished, process the activity. Remind students that this was a practice session and the use of the checklist was to help them see the strengths and weaknesses of their helping skills, not to judge anyone. Also point out that since process-observing is a new skill for students, it wasn't expected that the checklist would be 100 percent accurate. This activity was to give practice to observers too! Don't worry about omissions or errors.

One at a time, students share information from the checklist with others in their group. The observer makes comments about what the helper did particularly well and in what area improvement is needed.

Come together as a class and discuss students' experiences in doing and processing this activity.

Day Three   *Story.* Students return to their original groups of three and use the new words to write a story together. Tell students to plan a way for all group members to participate equally in the story writing. Tell them you will ask anyone in the group to explain how they did that. Allow thirty minutes. Come back together and read the stories to the class.

GOING FURTHER   During future cooperative academic activities in which some members have higher skill levels than others, assign a process-observer to use the checklist for helping.

Set as one of the main criteria upon which the activity will be evaluated students' scores for helping. In this way the use of helping skills and the accomplishment of the task are equally important to group success.

HAVE YOU GOT A GAME THAT DEVELOPS
SHARING AND COOPERATION ?

ZEBULON'S FALL

OBJECTIVES   To encourage the use of consensus.
To help children realize that pooling their information can often help them make more accurate decisions than if each child works independently.

MATERIALS   Copies of "Worksheet: Zebulon's Fall," p. 76, 25 percent more copies than there are students in the class; paper and pencils; library books on first aid.

IMPLEMENTATION   Go over the Consensus Guidelines listed on the next page and posted in your classroom. Distribute copies of the Worksheet. Students work individually to fill out Worksheets. Collect those.

Divide students into heterogeneous groups of four students. *Note:* in this case "heterogeneous" means mixed in terms of their knowledge about first aid—reading and writing levels are irrelevant. In fact, this is a good chance for some of your students with good health-care information and poor academic skills to be leaders and extra-helpful group members.

Consensus Guidelines

Consensus is a way of working together as a group to reach a decision with which everyone is comfortable. It is informal discussion involving talking things through, understanding what other people are saying and feeling, and trying to work out decisions that are acceptable to everyone. Everyone must be part of the decision and satisfied with it. When a decision is reached the group shapes it and puts it into words that everyone understands.

Here are some helpful attitudes in consensus:

Unity—trying to come up with things the whole group can go along with.
Cooperation—understanding that the needs, feelings, and ideas of everyone are important.
Openness—checking our own beliefs regularly and changing them if new ideas make us feel different.
Diversity—bringing out disagreements and seeing value and truth in what everyone says.
Creativity—coming up with new ideas.
Patience—working until we find something acceptable to everyone.
Respect—recognizing that everyone has rights, whether they agree with us or not.

Give each group a clean Worksheet. Each group must try to reach consensus on the items. When they're done, collect the sheets. If a group can't reach consensus, it should present the different points of view.

Score the individually-done Worksheets and the group Worksheets. (The correct answers are given on p. 64.) Usually the group ones will be better than any individual one since students have combined their knowledge. Hand back both group and individual sheets. Discuss the content and then the process.

DISCUSSION

1. How did you feel doing the Worksheet by yourself?
2. How much did you think you knew?
3. How did you feel when working with the group?
4. Did you think your group was getting better answers than you did individually? Than any of you did individually?
5. How was your group process? Did some people talk too much? Too little? Did everyone listen?
6. Looking at the class as a whole, how well did people do individually compared to the group scores? Why do you think that's the case?

GOING FURTHER

Students interested in content may want to look up more information.

Students may want to make up their own quiz sheets for their classmates to do individually and then in small groups. Many social studies and science content topics lend themselves to this.

Are More Heads Better Than One?

Here is a fine exercise to convince students that more heads are better than one! Show a film or read a story that has a complicated multi-step ending. Don't read or show the ending. Have students first predict it on their own. Then have them work in small groups to do so. Then read or show the actual ending and compare individual with small-group predictions.

Answer Sheet for Zebulon's Fall

1. No. Poking in the wound might cause more injury. The wound will be cleaned with antibiotics in the hospital.
2. No. If nothing else is done until help arrives, serious bleeding could lead to shock, coma, and perhaps even death. Proper first aid treatment will also lessen pain.
3. Yes, do this second. Direct pressure over the wound site is the best method to stop the bleeding.
4. Yes, do this fourth. Using traction to hold the leg steady while straightening it lessens pain, reduces the chance of making the injury worse and allows splinting.
5. No. Unnecessary motion by Zeb will make the injury worse.
6. No. Zeb will have to have surgery. Fluid in the stomach may be vomited and go into the lungs when Zeb is placed under general anesthesia.
7. Yes, do this first. One person should go to call for help, and then wait until it arrives to lead the rescuers to the victim.
8. Yes, do this fifth. Splinting a broken bone stops motion so the injury won't get worse; it also reduces pain.
9. Yes, do this sixth. Preserving body heat is one way of preventing shock.
10. No. Zeb would be unable to stand because of his injury, and would most likely fall again, causing further injuries. His confidence can be restored after his fracture has completely healed.
11. No. It is better to let trained personnel move the victim; they will most likely have special equipment to permit them to do so without hurting Zeb more.
12. Yes, do this third. Comforting Zeb, letting him know that help is on the way, and finding out what his injuries are, all help to calm him (which reduces shock). Also Zeb might have other injuries that are not as obvious but which may be serious.
13. No. Tourniquets are used ONLY after all other methods to control bleeding (direct pressure, elevation) have failed.

Section B *Practicing Interviewing*

INTRIGUING INTERVIEWS

OBJECTIVES To practice interviewing skills.
To learn more about people in the class.

MATERIALS Paper and pencils.

IMPLEMENTATION Have students write down three questions they would like to ask another person in order to get to know him better. Encourage students to ask unusual questions. Rather than, "Where do you live?" ask questions like, "If you could be granted one wish, what would it be?"; "What's one thing you've done that you're proud of?"; "Where in the world would you most like to visit?"

Students mill around the room. Each finds another student to speak with, and asks one question. The other person asks one in return. Students write down the name of the person interviewed and a summary of how that person answered the question. When finished with one person, they move on to another, with another question.

Remind students to ask their questions clearly and write enough of a summary to be able to remember their interviewee's answer.

When students have had an opportunity to interview three or four people, come back into the large group and sit in a circle. Begin with one student. Call out her name. Ask everyone who interviewed her to share the question they asked and what they learned about her. Go on to the next student and continue until everyone has had a chance to be highlighted.

DISCUSSION

1. What new and intriguing things did you learn about your classmates?
2. How hard or easy was it to interview your classmates?
3. What did you learn about doing a good interview? What could you do in the future to improve your interviewing skills?
4. How did you like being interviewed? What could the interviewer have said or done to make you feel more comfortable or talk more?

Cooperative Energizer: Attribute-Linking

In this fast, lively energizer, students move around the room quickly from one group to another.

You will call out an attribute and students must quickly move around the room to find all other children with the same attribute. For example, if you call "birthday month," students call out their birthday month and move around to form a group with all others with the same month. When students are finally in their groups ask each group to say its month, one at a time. Then name a new attribute and have students form new groups.

Other possible attributes include place of birth, (provide some general categories) color of socks, how many generations your family has been in this country, favorite subject in school, hobby or pastime, birth order in their family.

This is a fun and fast way to enable students to find out what they have in common with each other.

Compliments of *The Philadelphia Affective Education Project*

"HELLO, I'D LIKE TO KNOW . . ."

OBJECTIVES

To help students learn to interview peers and adults in a way that is interesting and comfortable for all participating.

To help students become skillful enough in interviewing so that it is a useful means of gathering information.

MATERIALS

Paper and pencils; a resource person for one session; copies of "Worksheet: Guidelines for a Successful Interview," p. 77.

IMPLEMENTATION

Explain to students that interviews are ways of getting information and learning about other people. Sometimes they are done alone, sometimes as part of other research. Background research is often needed for a successful interview.

Day One

Post a large copy of the Worksheet. You can simplify it for younger grades. Go over it in class. Students brainstorm topic areas appropriate for interviewing the teacher. Encourage questions around issues of equality and inequality—for example, how being female or male, white or a person of color affected your childhood. Then they divide into groups of four or five. Each group picks a topic and brainstorms a list of relevant questions. The group then decides on four or five questions and puts them in a sensible order. One group then begins to ask questions while the other students observe and fill in the Worksheet. After members of the first group have asked their questions, they evaluate themselves. Other students help them with their evaluations. Continue until each group has had a turn. During these interviews the teacher should be a cooperative interviewee.

Day Two   Brainstorm more topic areas. Next, tell students that not all interviewees are relaxed and cooperative. The class then brainstorms a list of the various kinds of personality styles an interviewee might have—hostile, verbose, friendly, confused, and so on. Write each personality style on a slip of paper.

Students then divide into heterogeneous groups of three or four; each group picks a topic area and brainstorms questions within that area. When they are ready, the teacher draws a slip of paper and uses that personality style as the first group asks him questions. Evaluate before going on. The teacher draws another slip for the second interview and proceed until all groups have had their turns. Discuss what they learned. Pinpoint strategies for working with difficult interviewees.

Day Three   Quickly review what has been learned about interviewing. Add to the Guidelines, if desired. Students divide into pairs. Each person interviews his partner for ten minutes on any topics he chooses. You can suggest topics relating to equality and inequality. Then they switch roles for another ten minutes. Following that, in pairs, students give feedback to each other on how they felt.

Pairs now combine with other pairs to make groups of four. The groups list what they learned about interviewing. For example, "I learned to ask simple questions before asking anything hard," or, "I learned not to tell my interviewee that I thought something he said was bad." As a whole class, discuss what has been learned and techniques for improvement.

Topics Relating to Equality

1. What are the problems/good things about being male/female?
2. What are the advantages/disadvantages of being white/a person of color?
3. What are the positive and negative aspects of being young?
4. What are times in your life you've been taken advantage of? What are times you've stood up for other people who were being taken advantage of?

Homework. As a class, decide on the category of person to be interviewed—for example, previous teachers, parents, children over five and under ten. Agree on an interview topic. In pairs, students make out a list of initial questions. The interviews are done after school. One student asks the questions of the interviewee while the other takes notes. Then they find a second interviewee and switch roles. Evaluate the next day.

Day Four   Students are now ready to interview an outside expert. This should be a person who can speak about issues relating to equality—for example, someone doing a job that is not sex-role typical; someone who has recently been discriminated against because of age; someone who has just contributed in some way which is pro-equality. Use the format from Day One for students to brainstorm topics, then specific questions, then the order of questions.

As a class, agree how the interview will be conducted. Will everyone get a turn? Will you set up an order beforehand? Are people allowed to use questions as they think of them or only the set ones? Conduct the interview, in the ways that you have decided. If possible, evaluate afterwards with the guest speaker; if not, evaluate on your own as a class.

DISCUSSION

1. How hard was it to think of topics? Was this harder with your teacher? Your student partner? Your homework interviewee? The expert resource person?
2. How did your actual interview questions compare to your projected ones? In what ways was it helpful to have a list ahead of time? Is there a way you could make that kind of list even more helpful?
3. How comfortable was the interviewee? If comfortable, what did you do to help create that? If not comfortable, what could you do differently another time?
4. What did you learn in content? Are there ways you could learn more content?
5. What did you learn about interviewing? What advice can you now give yourself for future interviewing?

GOING FURTHER

Interviewing is used in many lessons in *Open Minds to Equality*. It can also be an excellent part of your curriculum for all other subject areas.

Everybody Gets a Turn

A strategy to:

Develop equal participation in group discussion.
Encourage students to observe and change the pattern of participation.
Improve listening skills.

During a discussion, explain that no one may speak a second time until each member of the group has spoken once. *Variation:* Students may speak a second time if it is to encourage another student to participate. For example, "Juanita, what do you think about this?"

We suggest you use this activity with care because sometimes it puts too much pressure on some quiet students. One safe way to try it is in smaller groups that tend to be less threatening to reserved students.

Also, pick a topic about which everyone *does* have something to contribute—for example, where we should go for a class trip, a suggestion for change in classroom procedure, and so on.

FOLLOW-UP

"... And How Do They Feel About That" (p. 222); "Please Buy Me One," p. 244; "On the Horns of a Dilemma," p. 248; "Stop, Don't Take It for Granted," p. 271; "The Children's Place," p. 282; "Removing Those Hurdles," p. 340.

Section C   *Encouraging Creative Thinking and Problem-Solving*

FANTASY PROBLEM-SOLVING

OBJECTIVES   To free students' thinking.
To help them evolve more creative, divergent solutions to problems.

MATERIALS   Chart paper; markers; clock with a second-hand or a timer.

An Example of Fantasy Problem-Solving

1—Brainstorm on Problem Ideas
There's a boy in our class who is two years older than the rest of us who gets teased a lot.
A few of the same kids keep failing all the spelling tests.
On class trips some kids have lots of spending money and some have none.
Two kids in the class speak only Spanish and no one else tries to talk with them.
The librarian keeps giving us "girl" books for girls and "boy" books for boys.

2—Pick one problem and brainstorm fantasy solutions for it
Problem: On class trips some kids have lots of spending money and some have none.
Plant money seeds in our window boxes.
Ask the principal for money for the kids who don't have it.
Do trips where there is no way to spend money.
Sell stuff for money.
Put all the money kids bring in a bag and split it evenly.

3—Develop one fantasy idea
Idea Chosen: Sell stuff for money.
Sell our younger brothers and sisters.
Auction the teachers off to the kids.
Sell wishes.
Sell tickets to adults to ride on the school buses on weekends.

4—Pick one idea (or a combination of ideas) and brainstorm practical steps for it.
Idea: Sell wishes and split the money earned equally.
Create a wishing well out of a carton and paint it.
Make a sign for different kinds of wishes and the prices for each.
Make a magician costume. Take turns wearing it in well.
Have people throw in money with a written down wish.
Get together as a class and figure out how to carry out each wish.
Split all the money for the next class trip.

IMPLEMENTATION   Explain to students that they will learn a problem-solving technique where they get to use their imaginations, starting out with seemingly "silly" solutions to problems and making those practical.

Make a copy on chart paper of the Sample Fantasy Problem-Solving, above. Discuss with the class. Then have class brainstorm for several minutes on either classroom problems or community problems. After you have a list of eight to twelve items, stop. Then have the class as a whole pick one of those problems to discuss. Write the chosen problem on the top of another sheet of chart paper.

Now brainstorm, again as a whole class, on fantasy solutions for this problem. The single requirement is that the students may give only ideas they think are impossible to implement. These include science fiction solutions or those that necessitate wishing on stars. This approach is partly to loosen thinking and partly because often a fantasy solution can become a real one. Go on until you have ten or fifteen ideas.

Take a clean sheet of chart paper and have students pick one of the fantasy solutions. Either the class can pick one in a consensus manner, or the student who originally suggested the problem can pick one he particularly likes.

Next, brainstorm on practical ways to develop this fantasy solution. As you start those, some of the "practical" ways may also be fanciful, but usually some realistic possibilities will emerge. Be careful to allow yourself and your students to see as "realistic" some ideas that you might reject initially.

Then, on a final sheet of chart paper, pick one of these ideas and develop very specific practical steps for how to carry it out. Finally, try the idea.

DISCUSSION
1. How did you feel giving fantasy solutions? Did you see any point in it? Was it fun?
2. Can you see the practical value in these? What happens when we only let ourselves see sensible solutions? What is to be gained from fantasy ones?
3. Think of a problem other than the one used. Can you, on your own, think of both practical and fantasy solutions? Can you combine those into something that might work? What is the advantage of doing this as a group? on your own?

GOING FURTHER
Use this technique when you have a real problem in the classroom that needs solving.

WE ALL OWN THE PROBLEM

OBJECTIVES
To help students realize that they can generate constructive ideas for the solution of both their own problems and those of their peers.
To help students learn that group problem-solving is often more effective than isolated independent problem-solving.
To give students practice in "walking in another person's shoes."

MATERIALS
Scrap paper; pencils; clock with a second-hand or a timer.

IMPLEMENTATION
Instruct each student to anonymously write on scrap paper a brief answer to the following question: "What is a way that you are, or might be, treated unfairly in school by your peers?" Then have them fold the paper in quarters.

Divide students into groups of six. Students within a group put their slips of paper in a container and mix them up. Students draw a slip. If anyone gets her own, they all go back in and get reshuffled.

When all students have a slip, they read these silently and spend a minute thinking about the problem and possible solutions. Each group chooses a first speaker. That person reads aloud the problem on her sheet to others within the small group. She must *own* the problem, reading it as though it is her own. Then she spends a minute talking about how she is going to deal with the problem, again in the first person. After a minute call "Time." The group has two minutes to discuss the problem and give other ideas, before moving on to the person sitting on the original speaker's right. Continue in this manner until all problems have been discussed. Be careful to call "Time" promptly, and to see that groups move on.

DISCUSSION

1. What was it like to hear your problem read by someone else as though it were that person's problem?
2. What was it like to have to talk about a problem as if it were your own, when it wasn't?
3. Did your group members have similar problems?
4. Did you get any good ideas on your own problem? On others'?
5. What ideas that the speaker didn't think of came up during the two minutes of group discussion on a problem? Why do you think some new ideas came up in that way?
6. What are some advantages of this technique? Of having your problem be anonymous? What are some disadvantages?
7. How could we use this method at other times in our classroom?

GOING FURTHER

This activity can be used during the year when there is a particular issue involving the class, or in connection with problems of racism, sexism or class bias. Anonymity allows for more openness than your students may have when having to "own" their own problems.

In using this approach with your students in connection with specific topics you might want to try: "What is one way racism (sexism, class bias) has affected you personally and how did you handle it?" "What is a worry you have about being an adult female (male)?" "What is a concern you have about an elderly person in your family or neighborhood?"

Class Achievement Goal

Set a class achievement goal in an academic area to encourage students to work together as a group.

For example, set the goal that the class will get 95 percent of the words on the weekly spelling test correct. At the beginning of the week set up small peer-tutoring groups in which students help each other learn the words. They study at home and later in the week the groups meet to test and further help each other. The small group is working to see that *everybody* can spell all the words!

Have students decide on a special kind of pictorial chart on which they can record their weekly progress as a class. Ellen's class used a rocket ship. A flower with petals that gets fully or partially filled in is another of many possibilities. Have a group of students make the pictorial chart.

At the end of the week, students take a quiz, and after correcting papers, record their class score on the chart. They work in subsequent weeks to improve it. Students are achieving *as a class*!

ROLE-PLAY GUIDELINES AND TECHNIQUES

OBJECTIVE

To help students learn skills for good role-playing.

MATERIALS

Clock with a second-hand or a timer.

IMPLEMENTATION

Role-plays are designed to help students see the choices they have in situations and to show them that they do not have to continue in past patterns. They encourage creative problem-solving and enable students to experiment with solutions. Take notes during role-plays. Write down any crucial moments, body-language, strategies used, quotations, changes in tone of voice. Caution the rest of the class not to laugh, cheer, boo or clap during a role-play, since these behaviors are distracting.

Role-playing can be threatening to many students. Others will participate eagerly but sometimes not thoughtfully. "Facing Lines" and "Group Decisions" are preliminary activities for role-playing. You will stand a better chance of having more participation and better involvement, if you use these, or other warm-ups, first.

"Facing Lines" This involves only brief action and creates less self-consciousness than role-playing because no one is watching. The activity encourages a variety of solutions to the same problem and forces people to think and act quickly. Students can observe their own and others' body-language.

Ask for two rows of partners facing each other. Use the whole length of your room. Designate one line "X" and the other "Y." Read the scenario to the students. Then allow thirty seconds for all students to stand quietly and think about their roles and get in character. When you say "Begin," students start talking with their partners. They may physically act out the scene as long as they stay more or less in the long line. They continue until you say "Time," which should be about two minutes later. They must then freeze in place.

Scene One. Line X is Robin. Line Y is Leslie. Leslie asks to use an old school paper of Robin's as Leslie's own work. Although Leslie is a good friend of Robin's, Robin is generally against cheating.

Scene Two. Line X is Tracy. Line Y is Toby. Tracy has just teased Toby because Toby speaks English with a heavy Chinese accent.

Scene Three. Line X is Lee. Line Y is Terry. Lee tells Terry that Lee doesn't want to spend the weekend at Terry's house because Terry lives only with Terry's eighty-five-year-old grandfather.

DISCUSSION
1. How did it feel when you were in each role? Which made you most comfortable? most uncomfortable? Why? In which scene were you playing a part with which you could identify?
2. What happened in each scene? Share your solutions to the problems. As a class compare solutions. Were there many different ones?
3. In what ways were the responses you tried successful? Unsuccessful?
4. What kinds of behavior in your partner were helpful in coming to resolution? What kinds of behavior turned you off? Why? What suggestions do you have for yourself of what you might have done differently in each, or some of, the scenes? How about for your partner?

"Group Decisions" This requires people to think quickly in stressful situations and with a time-pressure. As a small group they must reach agreement. Conflicts often necessitate such quick thinking. Several possible solutions usually come up in different groups; thus, divergent problem-solving is encouraged. Because acting per se is not involved, students who are uncomfortable "on stage" often participate more.

Divide students into groups of three or, if necessary, four. Read the first situation to the class. Then allow thirty seconds of quiet thinking time. Then each group has one or two minutes to talk together and reach a decision of what it will do. Students are playing themselves—they are to decide what they would do if the three of them were actually in the situation. After you call "Time," have each group share its decision with the class.

Situation One. You* are on a school trip. You get separated from the group and cannot find them. You see a truant officer questioning another group of kids. He'll be over to your group in one minute.

_____
*In all cases, "you" means the three students.

Situation Two. You are in the classroom at recess. The principal comes in with a new girl for your class. Serena uses crutches and has metal braces on both legs. Instead of her right arm and hand, she has a plastic arm with a metal hook at the end.

Situation Three. Your class has been planning a trip to a local fair. All of you would be able to bring a few dollars each. It is the day before the fair and you realize that several kids in your class won't have any money to bring along.

DISCUSSION

1. How did you feel in each situation? Which were easy? Which were hard?
2. In which decisions could your group reach consensus? In which could they not? Why? In what sorts of real-life situations do you have to reach decisions quickly? In what kinds can you wait?
3. What types of group behavior were helpful? harmful? What suggestions can you give yourself for functioning in a group that must decide something quickly?
4. What are some values that are important in making the decisions in these situations?

Traditional Role-Play

This activity is a more standard role-play. When using role-play, give the characters names not belonging to anyone in your class. After the role-play ends, have participating students stay where they are in the scene. Using character names, ask each in turn how she is feeling. After each person answers she then returns to a regular class seat. Then ask the students, now back to their real names, how they feel as themselves. When discussing the role-play, it is important to direct questions in either character names or real names—depending on what you are asking. Ask the students who participated if the problem was resolved. If they reached a resolution did the characters feel satisfied? Ask the discussion questions below after each role play.

Role-Play One. Pat, twelve years old, and Devin, seven years old, are in the grocery store. Devin is staring at a woman in a wheelchair ahead of them on line.

Role-Play Two. Eduardo has been at his friend Mark's house. Mark's father gets home from marketing and finds Eduardo and Mark playing. Mark's father calls Mark aside and says he doesn't want Eduardo at their house because Eduardo is Puerto Rican.

Role-Play Three. Tillie finds spelling difficult. Everytime she writes a story she asks her classmates for help with many words. Today she is just asking, "How do you spell 'please'?" Jayral and Gilbert begin, as is typical for them, to tease her. Nereida is a quiet student who is often teased herself. In this case, however, she feels it is necessary to come to Tillie's defense.

Do this role-play a second time leaving Tillie, Jayral, and Gilbert the same. This time, though, Nereida is a popular, outgoing student who never gets teased.

Role-Play Four. The setting is a baseball field and Carlene, who almost always strikes out, steps up to the plate. Immediately the in-field, consisting of Anselmo, Josh, and Airin, begin heckling Carlene with, "Hey, no batter, no batter," and, "Easy out, easy out," and, "Carlene can't hit nothin' but air."

In the second role-play the in-field is heckling a batter, but this time it is Maura who is known all over school as one of the very best batters.

DISCUSSION

1. In what ways did the actors make choices that resolved the problems?
2. What choices did they make that made problems greater?
3. Give some specific examples of what people said or did that was helpful, that you might want to try in similar circumstances.
4. What other ideas can you think of that might work well? In what ways is it sometimes easier to think of more ideas when you are not directly in a situation? Thinking about that, how can role-plays help you to learn new behaviors for your own life?

5. How could we use role-plays to help us solve some of our own classroom problems? How could we use them to learn about other people and their problems?

6. Are there any new guidelines we have to establish to make role-plays work better in this class?

GOING FURTHER If you decide to use role-plays as a way of understanding classroom conflict, there are some suggestions that can help. Try to isolate the conflict, understand its basis, and then create a role-play that speaks to the same issue, but is different enough so that students don't say, "Oh, this one is about Samantha. . . ." Try to put students in a variety of roles.

FOLLOW-UP "If Only We Had More Money," p. 87; "Seeing Eyes Glasses," p. 91; "M. and S. Auto Repair," p. 107; "Health or Home," p. 122; "Assignment Research Paper," p. 167; "What if It Hurts," p. 251; "Say It So They'll Hear It," p. 314; "Relearning about Native Americans," p. 322.

Guidelines for Role-Play

1. Set the scene for both the actors and the audience, to make sure everyone knows what is going on.
2. Make sure the actors know their roles very clearly (conducting an interview of the actors is a good way to do this and help them get into their roles).
3. Give the audience something(s) to look for as they watch the role-play.
4. If side coaching is necessary, break in and do it obviously, so everyone knows what is going on.
5. If the scene is not coming to its own resolution, make it do so. Say something like, "Take two minutes now for a resolution."
6. After role-play is finished, ask a sharp, focusing question to get discussion going and students focusing on the significance of what they say.

From *The Philadelphia Affective Education Project*

COMMUNITY MEETINGS*

OBJECTIVE To teach students the process for holding community meetings.

IMPLEMENTATION Talk with students about community meetings, a process for planning and problem solving that they will use throughout the school year. Post the steps for a Community Meeting on posterboard and go over them with the students.

COMMUNITY MEETING STEPS
1. A student or students propose a plan or describe a problem.
2. Students brainstorm ideas or solutions.
3. Students choose one to try.
4. Students implement the idea or solution, assess it, and revise if necessary.

At the beginning of the year the teacher is the facilitator, but later on students can learn to facilitate. During the meeting students must raise their hands and each person speaks in turn. There is no interrupting. Facilitators must strictly enforce that guideline.

In step one, when a problem is being discussed, the facilitator makes sure that stu-

---

*This lesson is based on the work of Karen Cathers, Lenape School, New Paltz, N.Y.

dents share their feelings. Allow a limited time for step one. After ideas have been brainstormed in step two, there is often one solution with the most energy or enthusiasm that students want to try. While typically a vote isn't needed, it can be used. When, however, what the majority wants is problematic for those who are outvoted, it is important to try to come to consensus. A consensus solution is one that everyone can go along with even if it's not their first choice. At the end of step three, students can discuss what it will mean for their solution to be "working" so later they'll be able to assess its success.

Because students have an investment in the solution, it often works. If after a trial run, the solution isn't working, students return to a new community meeting to decide on revisions or another solution. Depending on the problem, this can be done anywhere from a couple of days after the first community meeting to a week later.

Hold community meetings at the same time every week. Usually about twenty minutes is needed, although some difficult problems may need a longer period of time. Don't change the day and time because students count on them. If an emergency situation arises, a special community meeting can be scheduled (see box below). Students come to learn that *they* can solve problems in a democratic way.

Try a first community meeting. Begin with a plan for the first few meetings, rather than a problem, because it makes it easier for students to learn the process. For the future, post a "Community Meeting Topics" sheet in the room. During the week students list potential topics, and at the time of the community meeting, choose one. Once students have selected the topic, follow the steps. Make sure all students who wish to speak have a turn and that a few don't dominate. To help students keep track of this, you can give each a few tokens. Once a student speaks, she places a token in front of her so the facilitator is aware of those who have had a turn. Discuss with students the importance of using respectful tones. After community meetings hold a short discussion about the process.

DISCUSSION

1. How did you feel about our first community meeting?
2. What went well? What could we improve?
3. For anyone who didn't participate today, what would help you feel comfortable to participate in our next community meeting?
4. How is this way of making plans or solving problems different from other ways these are dealt with in school?
5. What might be some benefits to using community meetings during the year?

Students Use a Community Meeting to Deal with Racism

This meeting focused on a playground incident. A student in another class was making a racist remark all around the playground. It was now a classroom problem because everyone came in from recess very upset about it. They felt like something had to be done. We had an emergency community meeting. We went through the same steps; here's the problem, what are some solutions? The solution that they liked the best was to send two representatives, one African American child and one white child, to speak to this person in the hall and tell him how they felt—that they were hurt by it and the whole classroom was hurt by it. They told him about the community meeting and how they were representing the entire class.

I felt it was important to make the assumption that the child was ignorant of the offensive nature of his remarks. They spoke from that point of view. We left it this way. "Now that you understand this, let's hope it solves the problem." Apparently it did. We couldn't have gone on with whatever lesson we were involved in because everyone was so upset. We dealt with it through the community meeting process; then we could go on.

Karen Cathers, 4th grade teacher

Make a check each time the person you are observing shows one of the behaviors below.

Do's

1. Gives praise. _____

2. Has the learner explain the information back to the helper. _____

3. Tries a variety of ways for going over the same skill. _____

4. Finds relevant examples. _____

5. Quits while ahead. _____

6. Uses helpee's learning style. _____

7. _____ _____ _____

8. _____ _____ _____

Don'ts

1. Tells the answer. _____

2. Gives put-downs or embarrasses the learner. _____

3. Pressures the learner. _____

4. Ignores the person being helped if she doesn't understand. _____

5. Piles on too much information. _____

6. _____

7. _____ _____ _____

8. _____ _____ _____

It is a late fall afternoon. On their way home from school, a group of six seventh-graders stop to play ball in an area several minutes' walk from the street. After a while, Zebulon climbs up to the top of an old wall. He shows his friends how he can hop along the wall on one leg. Suddenly he falls to the ground. His friends see Zebulon lying on his back with his left leg tucked under his right one. The bone on his left shin is sticking out through the skin. The wound is bleeding. Zebulon is screaming and complaining about the pain.

Which of the following should the friends do?

1. _____ Poke in the wound to get the dirt out.

2. _____ Send one friend for help while the other four comfort Zeb; do nothing else.

3. _____ Wrap a T-shirt or jacket tightly around the wound to stop the bleeding.

4. _____ Have one friend lift Zeb's right leg, while another puts her hands on Zeb's ankle and pulls gently to straighten out the left leg.

5. _____ Help Zeb to his feet and support him while he hops to the street.

6. _____ Give Zeb a soda to drink since he complains he's thirsty.

7. _____ Send one friend for help.

8. _____ Take two strong sticks and use belts to tie sticks onto Zeb's left leg so it won't move.

9. _____ Put friends' jackets on Zeb to keep him warm.

10. _____ Cooperatively lift Zeb back up to the top of the wall so he won't develop a fear of heights.

11. _____ Carry Zeb out to the streets so that his injured leg does not move.

12. _____ Have one friend ask Zeb, "What hurts?" and talk quietly to comfort him.

13. _____ Tie a belt tightly around the top of Zeb's left thigh to stop bleeding.

Now number your "Yes" choices in the order you think they should be done.

1. Create a safe atmosphere. _____

2. Begin with some door-opener, "at ease" type of questions. _____

3. Go from general questions to specific ones. _____

4. Mix intellectual with emotional questions. (Don't start the emotional ones until at least half-way into the interview.) _____

5. Make eye-contact with the respondent. _____

6. Give the respondent the right to refuse to answer questions without having to explain why. _____

7. Don't fire questions too fast. _____

8. Keep questions short and simple. _____

9. Ask open-ended questions. _____

10. Don't debate questions with the respondent. (You're there to listen, not give your opinions.) _____

11. Write down key words to help remember what the respondent said. _____

12. At the end, ask the respondent if there is anything else to be added. _____

13. Thank the respondent. _____

14. Write up the interview as soon as possible. _____

Chapter
5

Expanding Our Vistas: Our Lives to Others' Lives

To appreciate diversity in a multicultural society means that we acknowledge and appreciate both the similarities and differences we share with others. Sometimes this can be difficult. Some of us are quick to focus on the similarities we see in human beings and ignore the very real differences in people's lives that arise from aspects of our social identities—such as race, gender or class. Others of us are quick to look only for the differences between ourselves and people of other social groups, overlooking the similarities in our lives, especially in our experiences of discrimination.

The activities in this chapter will help students understand and experience ways in which they are similar to and connected with other people, and ways in which their life-situations and opportunities are different. It is difficult for all of us—adults and children alike—to step outside our own lives and examine our perceptions and behaviors as observers. It's also hard to get inside others' shoes to understand how others view the world and experience reality. That's why your thoughtfulness, sensitivity, and willingness to risk stepping outside your own experience will be so important for student learning in this chapter, and in *Open Minds to Equality* as a whole.

The first section of this chapter is entitled, "New Perspectives to See the World." Many of us grow up with a very ethnocentric world view, assuming that our life-experiences are "typical," when this is usually far from true. Activities in this chapter will enable students to see how their perceptions of reality shape their ideas, values, and behaviors. Further, it will expand their vistas and help them understand that when they see only part of a picture, their perceptions may be inaccurate.

An apt metaphor to explain this is to say that all of us grow up with a pair of blinders on our eyes. Our particular life-experiences, values, and opportunities are those blinders. The purpose of Section A is to help students see that they might be wearing blinders. The goal of the chapter as a whole is to help students take those blinders off so they can see a bigger picture and legitimize the many points of view and life-experiences that are not their own. Often it's when we take off our blinders that we can most creatively solve problems and work in cooperation with diverse groups of people.

Activities in Section B, "Sharing Who We Are," enable students to learn more about their own families' ethnic and cultural backgrounds and share those with their classmates. Activities also allow students to look at the various aspects of their own social identity—race, gender, religion, class and so forth—to understand that each person has many diverse characteristics. Students can then explore the various similarities and differences they share with their classmates.

Section C, "Others' Shoes: Others' Views" is comprised of activities that will increase students' abilities to get into other peoples' shoes and empathize with their feelings and life-situations. They will see those things they have in common with people different from themselves and better understand and appreciate the very real differences.

Lessons help students examine how differences in people are used to hurt them, and to think about the ways they might inadvertently be contributing to that process. Particular emphasis is placed on race, gender, and class, although age, religion, sexual orientation and physical/learning abilities are also introduced. These topics will be discussed in more detail in Chapter Six. Other lessons help students feel the effects of competitive individualism, as compared to cooperation.

The lessons in this section aim to help children *feel* the feelings of those hurt by differences and inequality. Upcoming chapters of this book will help them move a step further and *name* and *analyze* the processes at work.

Section A   New Perspectives to See the World

IT'S ALL IN HOW YOU LOOK AT THINGS

OBJECTIVES To have students realize that their own perspective is not necessarily the only way to see the world.
To help them realize that there may be advantages in multiple viewpoints.

MATERIALS Copies of "Worksheet: Phantom Tollbooth," p. 93; paper and pencils.

IMPLEMENTATION Distribute copies of the Worksheet to all students. Have them meet in pairs, being sure that one student in each pair is capable of reading the Worksheet. Students can take turns reading aloud to each other.

When they have read the Worksheet, each pair takes a piece of paper and divides it vertically in half. At the top of one half they write, "Advantages of growing upward" and at the top of the other side, "Advantages of growing downward." Then using the ideas from the Worksheet, plus their own, they list as much as they can in each column.

Pairs get together with one or two other pairs to form groups. Each group picks, or is assigned, one or more of the following tasks:

1. Draw a picture of a specific scene from your point of view. Then draw it from the point of view of someone your age in the land where people grow downward.
2. Act out a scene taking place in the land where people grow downward. Show some of the problems they might have and also some of the advantages. Act out the same scene from our point of view.
3. Hold a debate or discussion between Milo and the boy in the story. In addition to what the story says, be sure to point out any other advantages you can see—from both points of view.
4. Suppose we could choose and sometimes be in the land we're in, and sometimes be in one where we start with our heads at the top. When would you choose each? Write some journal entries for a week in your life, each time saying whether you were in our land or in the land in the story. Tell about what you are doing and why you made the choices you made.

The following day in class you can stretch students' perspectives further by having them open themselves up to other differences that might exist in a fantasy world. Students get into new heterogeneous groups of three to five. Each group comes up with a different fantasy world—a world where everyone looked identical, for example, or one where people grew younger instead of older, or one where there was no such thing as money. Then the group does one of the above four tasks, using our world as one alternative and their new world as the other. When completed, share with the whole class.

DISCUSSION

1. What did you think when you first read the passage from *The Phantom Tollbooth?* Explain.
2. Do you think that kind of world could really exist? Why or why not?
3. Would you ever *really* want to live in a world like that? Explain.
4. What was it like to design another type of world? Did you have trouble thinking of ideas? Making a group decision?
5. In what ways can looking at the world from such very different points of view make it easier for you to understand other people better and learn about equality?
6. In what ways are you "locked into" your point of view, such that you sometimes are not as open as you might be to someone else's way of seeing the world? Give three or four examples of when that was harmful and explain something you could do about it.

GOING FURTHER

Students may want to finish *The Phantom Tollbooth.* They could design their own lessons on point of view using another chapter in the book, since there are many suitable ones.

Stop!

Are you remembering to have students process their group work? If not, look back to Chapter 3. Don't forget that the process skills students learned can be used with many activities throughout the year.

WHAT'S IN THE PICTURE?

OBJECTIVES

To enable students to see how easy it is to make assumptions when only seeing part of the whole.

To help students understand that their perspectives about other people and the world may be only partial pictures, limited by their life-experiences.

To encourage students to look for the "whole picture" when examining issues of equality and inequality.

MATERIALS

Copies of pictures 1-A and 1-B, 2-A and 2-B, p. 94 for all students.

IMPLEMENTATION

Examine the pictures yourself before you begin the lesson. Pictures 1-A and 2-A each represent the central portion of a larger scene. Picture 1-A portrays a woman pouring from a measuring cup. The larger scene, 1-B shows her as a chemist in a laboratory. Picture 2-A shows a black woman holding back a white girl. Picture 2-B places them at a busy street corner, where the woman is trying to keep the girl from being hit by a car.

Divide students into heterogeneous groups. Be sure they're mixed by race and gender, if possible. Give each student a copy of pictures 1-A and 2-A. Have students look at picture 1-A and write down the answer to these questions. 1. How do you feel about this picture? 2. Describe what you think is happening here. Repeat for picture 2-A.

Now ask students to discuss their feelings in their groups. Ask them to compare their ideas about what's going on in the two pictures. Have a recorder in each group take notes on the different ideas. Then, without having students move their desks, discuss their feelings and ideas as a whole class.

Now tell students they will work silently again. Give each a picture of 1-B. Have them look at it and write down the answer to this question. Have your feelings changed now? If so, how? why? Repeat for 2-B. Then have them share their feelings in the small group. Finally come together as a whole class for discussion.

DISCUSSION
1. What was the difference in your feelings about the pictures when you saw part of the picture compared to the whole picture? Why was this so?
2. What assumptions did you make when you saw part of the picture alone?
3. When in real life have you only seen part of a "picture," or looked at a situation from one point of view, and later changed your mind when you saw the "whole picture"?

Tell students that because we grow up with limited experiences, we often see only "part of the picture." Sometimes we don't even know we're doing this. Explain that learning to see situations from others' points of view helps us perceive larger pictures. End by saying that in exploring issues of equality and inequality this year, this point is very important. For that reason, you will be asking them to remember this exercise as they deal with lessons and ideas about fairness and equality throughout the year.

THE NINE DOT PROBLEM

OBJECTIVES
To show students that sometimes they must step outside usual limits in order to solve problems creatively.
To understand that we unconsciously limit our perspectives and alternatives.

MATERIALS
Pencils and paper.

IMPLEMENTATION
Draw nine dots on the board as indicated below. Have students copy the same configuration onto their papers. Their task is to try to connect all nine dots with four straight lines without taking their pencils off the paper. Give them several minutes to work at it. They might try in pairs. If no one gets it, give clues like, "You might have to go outside the dots."

When a student solves the problem, have her go to the board and connect the dots.

DISCUSSION
1. Why is it that most of us didn't think of going outside the boundaries to solve the problem?
2. When in your life have you found new alternatives by looking at a situation from an expanded perspective?

Tell the students that in this unit they will be asked to step outside their own perspectives and look at the lives of others from a new viewpoint. Explain to them that most people grow up thinking that the way they see the world is the way everyone else does, but in fact that's not so. We'll be learning to see the world from many different points of view.

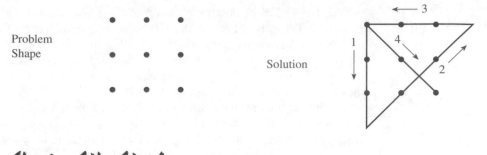

Problem
Shape

Solution

Section B: Sharing Who We Are

WHO ARE WE?

OBJECTIVES

To have students learn more about their own family ethnic backgrounds and culture.

To help students understand that we ALL have family cultural backgrounds even if our families have been in this country for generations.

To help students understand the role and impact of ethnicity for those who come from both monocultural and mixed ethnic backgrounds.

To have students find commonalities and differences in the experiences of their families and those of others.

MATERIALS

Newsprint; markers; paper and pencil; tape recorders if possible; construction paper; bulletin board space.

IMPLEMENTATION

As a whole class, discuss with students what they currently know about their family ethnic/cultural backgrounds. There may well be a variety of responses with some students knowing a great deal and some students knowing very little. Record what they know on newsprint. Depending on the make-up of your class it may be that some students have complex issues around this question. For example some adopted children who are a different race from their parents know a great deal about their birth parents' ethnicity while others know very little. Some families actively focus on their cultural backgrounds while others intentionally do not.

Review with students Chapter 4, Section B, "Practicing Interviewing." If you haven't done any of these lessons you may want to do one now before doing this lesson. In heterogeneous groups of five or six students, label one piece of newsprint *what we want to know about our ethnic backgrounds,* and another piece *questions we can ask to find out.* Students first brainstorm what they want to know and then, using that list as reference, brainstorm the kinds of questions that would get them this information. Discuss these as a class and compile a list of question ideas for all students to have as a resource for their interviews. Make copies and distribute to students.

Students go home and individually interview parents, grandparents, aunts and uncles, or any other knowledgeable relatives. In some cases it may be appropriate to interview older neighbors, members of cultural or religious groups, or others with relevant expertise. Students write up their interviews in essay form. They post these on a classroom bulletin board. They may also want to display photos, drawings, or family artifacts. Be sure to have available multicultural drawing supplies and paper so students can accurately portray their own and their families' skin color. Allow time for students to read each others' essays and look at any displays.

DISCUSSION

1. What did you learn about your own ethnic identity? What was particularly interesting?
2. Did you learn anything that surprised you? What made this surprising?
3. What commonalities did you find with other students from similar ethnic backgrounds?

4. What differences did you find with other students from similar ethnic backgrounds?
5. What commonalities did you find with other students with ethnic backgrounds different from your own?
6. What was this activity like for students whose parents and ancestors represent only one or two ethnicities? For students who have ancestors from a large range of cultures?

FOLLOW-UP   Students may be interested in doing more substantial displays about their own backgrounds. These open possible discussions for an open house or parents' night or as an exchange with another classroom.

Ethnic Identity

Sometimes people think of ethnic/cultural identity as racial identity. Race has more to do with skin color while ethnicity has to do with geographic, historical, and cultural roots of our families. For example, this can be a problem when using the term African American for all black people in this country. Black people from the Caribbean have a different cultural background than African Americans and usually don't identify with that label, nor with many aspects of African American culture. In the same way, Latino people from Chile will have many customs that are very different from those from Mexico or those from the Dominican Republic.

European American students may think they "don't have an ethnic background." It is important that these students realize that their ancestors had customs, values, stories, and so forth that are an important part of who they are. Through this activity, and discussion in your classroom, students can gain a greater understanding of the impact of ethnic identity within racial groups. Students may also find it interesting to read *Who Am I?* by Aylette Jenness from the Boston Children's Museum series *Multicultural Celebrations*. In this story a white boy works to understand his ethnic identity.

WE ARE EACH OF MANY TRAITS

OBJECTIVES   To help students see themselves as a combination of many of their social identities.
To have students identify themselves in terms of their own race, gender, class, abilities and religion as well as any other identities that are important to them in their own lives.
To have students see their similarities and differences with their classmates.

MATERIALS   Construction paper of assorted colors; tape or stapler; space on bulletin board.

IMPLEMENTATION   Discuss with students how we are each a combination of many of our social identities. (To refresh your thinking, see Chapter 2, pp. 26–28.) These may include as many of the following as students know and understand and feel they can share: race, gender, age range, socio-economic class, language(s) spoken, ability/disability, and religion. Sometimes it is a combination that is most apparent to us, other times a particular identity or two stands out.

You may want to use yourself as an example. Perhaps you are male, heterosexual, young adult, middle-class, native Russian speaking, and Jewish. Talk with children about times when you are particularly aware of some of these identities and other times when you don't notice one or more of them. Encourage students to share relevant and age-appropriate information about themselves. Be clear students may choose not to share pieces of information they wish to keep private.

Have students list those aspects of their own social identities they feel comfortable sharing. Students may also include other categories in addition to the ones listed above, if they wish. For example, if ethnicity is important in your students' backgrounds, they may want to add that as well. Students then informally discuss these lists in partners or small groups.

Tell students they will be making flowers out of construction paper. Each petal will represent one aspect of their social identity that they want to share. Allow students to select construction paper in colors they wish for their flower petals. Students create their own flowers with each identity on a separate petal. All flowers can then be posted on a bulletin board.

As the year goes on, students may wish to add additional identities or perhaps to modify some of theirs as they understand more about these issues.

DISCUSSION
1. Which of these identities was easiest for you to name? Why?
2. Did you have some identities that were confusing to you? Why?
3. Were there any identities in which you weren't sure about your answer? Why?
4. Did you have any identities that you could identify but you chose not to share? What makes some of these ones we don't want to share?
5. In what ways are you a combination of these identities? Give some examples
6. When does one of your identities stand out for you particularly?
7. Are some of your identities ones that don't seem to you to be very important in defining who you are? Why?

FOLLOW UP "The Filter of Oppression," p. 180.

Section C Others' Shoes: Others' Views

IF I WERE . . . .

OBJECTIVES
To have students appreciate their library book reading as an opportunity to empathize with another person in a life situation different from their own.
To have them see what they have in common with other people as well as positively appreciate differences.

MATERIALS
Copies of "Worksheet: If I Were . . . ," p. 95; paper; pencils; drawing materials; a selection of children's books. For historical fiction, we suggest: *Roll of Thunder, Hear My Cry,* by Mildred Taylor; *Nothing to Fear* by Jackie Koller; *Letters from Rifka* by Karen Hesse; *Letters from a Slave Girl: The Story of Harriet Jacobs* by Mary Lyons; and *Radical Red* by James Duffy. For contemporary fiction we suggest: *Felita* (younger readers) or *Nilda* (older readers) by Nicholosa Mohr; *Children of the River* by Linda Crew; and *Lark in the Morning* by Nancy Garden.

IMPLEMENTATION
Ask each student to pick any fiction book that she is reading, or has recently finished. Distribute the Worksheets and have each student do one or more of the tasks listed, or cut up sections and distribute individual task cards.

This lesson can be done independently or in reading groups. For sharing results, you may want to use a bulletin board or small discussion groups.

DISCUSSION
1. How did these lessons help you look at your book differently?
2. How did they help you look at the world differently?
3. What are some advantages in being able to do this?
4. What positive difference would it make for you and others to see the world through the eyes of people of different cultures, races, and backgrounds?
5. What difference would it make in the world if we were all better at doing this? Give some examples.

GOING FURTHER   Make these task cards a part of your regular choices for book reports. Create some more of your own, or have students create them, following the same sorts of themes.

FOLLOW-UP   "Here's What Some People Did," p. 270.

A GIRL ON OUR TEAM!

OBJECTIVES   To encourage understanding of what it feels like to be teased and put down because of your gender.
To help students learn to be supportive of equal opportunities and diversity in participation in activities.

MATERIALS   Copies of "Worksheet: Rebekah's Journal," p. 96; paper for additional entries; pencils.

IMPLEMENTATION   Hand out copies of the Worksheet to all students. Have them staple on additional sheets of the same size to create something like a notebook.

"MAIL-CARRIER"

Students can read the Worksheet to themselves or work in small groups if the reading is hard. Explain any difficult vocabulary to the class. Assign students to write several additional entries. They can write a few at once, or one a day.

After each student has written several new entries, divide the class into groups of three or four and share journal entries in the small groups. Gather for discussion. Then as a class, brainstorm on what you would like to see happen. Agree on one idea. Then assign several more journal entries, the first being a description of what happened, and the other continuing in any way each student desires. (Save these for another lesson on Rebekah on pp. 318–319.)

DISCUSSION
1. How did Rebekah feel? Explain why she felt that way.
2. How would you feel if the same thing happened to you?
3. Why did Rebekah keep trying?
4. What would you do? Explain your decision.
5. What different things did the other children on the team do? What do you think of their choices?

THAT'S WHAT YOU BROUGHT FOR LUNCH?

OBJECTIVES   To help students understand what it feels like to be made fun of because of racial or ethnic background.
To help students realize that people from different racial or ethnic backgrounds are people with whom they have many things in common.

MATERIALS   Copies of "Worksheet: Consuela's and Marita's Lunch," p. 97, one for each student. Make copies of "Worksheet: A Time I Felt Different," one for each pair. List these questions with space for students to respond. 1. List some of Consuela's and Marita's feelings. 2. What caused them to feel that way? Give two examples. 3. Brainstorm times when each of you has felt different and has been teased. List the examples. 4. Pick one of those times and work together to write a description of what it was like. 5. Think about what some other kids could have done to make you feel better. Write down some ideas.

IMPLEMENTATION   Divide students into pairs. Hand out "Worksheet: Consuela's and Marita's Lunch" to each student and have them either read silently, or aloud. (Be sure someone in each pair can read the worksheet comfortably.)

After students have finished reading, ask if there are any questions or difficult vocabulary words. Then direct each pair to write a lunchroom dialogue. This can be done in one of two ways, depending on the level of English mechanics of your class. If they can write conversation, in standard form with quotation marks, that is better language arts practice. If they are not yet at that level, they can use drama format.

Each pair brainstorms ideas for a one- or two-page dialogue of how they think the lunchroom conversation might go. One student dictates a sentence, the other writes. The paper is switched and the student dictating checks the writing. Next the second student dictates and the first writes. Continue for the whole dialogue. Move among groups to assist those having trouble getting started. Then gather as a class and have each pair read its dialogue aloud. At the end, go through the discussion questions.

Students then get back into their pairs. This time each pair writes a dialogue about how they would like to see the conversation go in a way that would make it *supportive*, or even more supportive, *for all the children.* Again, these are read aloud and discussed.

On the following day students work in groups to either illustrate their new conversations, or to copy them over in comic strip format with the dialogue in balloons. Then pairs go on to Worksheet, "A Time I Felt Different." When these are completed, they are shared with the entire class and discussed.

DISCUSSION
1. Why did Consuela and Marita get teased? How do you think they felt?
2. Consuela and Marita are Chicanas—Mexican Americans. In what ways are people of different races or cultures teased because of their ethnic background?
3. What are some reasons that we tease people who are "different?"
4. How do you feel when you are teased?
5. In what ways did your group have the other children react to Consuela and Marita? Do these things happen in your school? In what ways?
6. What new solutions did you make up in the second set of conversations? How can you make those more likely to happen in your school?
7. How can you help yourself not to tease people who do things differently from the way you do?
8. How can we help each other not to do that?

GOING FURTHER   If parents of children in your class, or your school, cook food of various ethnic groups (for example, German, Mexican, Jewish, Jamaican) have them come in and do so with you. If not, use cookbooks that teach about food of different cultures. See Bibliography for ideas. Have students create a classroom cookbook to distribute or to sell as a fund-raiser for class events.

Involve Parents

Are you wondering about parental responses to activities in *Open Minds to Equality?* Why not:

- Write a letter to parents describing the expected academic gains, new learning opportunities, and increased self-confidence that will result for all students from these activities.
- Invite parents into your class to participate in lessons. Urge them to ask questions. Encourage their involvement.

FALLING BEHIND

OBJECTIVES   To understand the feelings of someone who is left out because of competitive individualism.
To help children think through creative solutions to problems of conflicting needs.

IMPLEMENTATION   Tell students you are going to describe a situation that takes place in a class like theirs. They should try to understand the feelings of these two students. They are going to have to make a decision. This is the situation:

> Norman has been out of school sick for a week and he just came back. This is not his first absence this year—he's been sick again and again. Norman is getting behind in his work. He's scared that he might not catch up.
>
> Norman found out that the class is having a big unit test on multiplying and dividing fractions. He decides he will ask his friend, Essie, to spend her study period and lunchtime recess reviewing the math with him before the test. His teacher told him she wants him to take the test today. Norman is worried that he won't pass. He hopes Essie will help him.
>
> Essie has a report due in social studies at 2:30. She has a little more work to do on it. She's trying for an A. Essie works hard and likes to get good grades. The teacher said that for each day the report is late that grade will be lowered a full grade. For example, what would have been an A will be a B.
>
> Norman asks Essie to help him—just when she is about to put the finishing touches on her social studies report. To help Norman might mean she won't get an A. She wants an A very badly.

Divide students into heterogeneous pairs, each with paper and pencil. Ask students to get into Norman's shoes and write a response to: (1) I feel . . . . (2) Essie, what I'd like you to do is . . . . Have students trade worksheets with their partner and read what Norman says. Ask students to get into Essie's shoes and decide if you will help Norman. Write responses to: (1) I feel . . . . (2) What I will do is . . . . Have students trade papers once more. Read what Essie says. Get into Norman's shoes. Write response to: (1) Now I feel . . . .

DISCUSSION
1. How did you feel as Norman before Essie's decision?
2. How did you feel as Norman after her decision?
3. Was the decision you came up with as Essie based on what was best for you or best for Norman?
4. What were some solutions that met both people's needs?
5. When were some times you have felt left out, when others were thinking only of themselves? Give examples.
6. When were some times you had to decide between helping someone else or helping yourself? Give examples.
7. What are some things we can do to help ourselves be more cooperative—to make choices that involve working with others?

IF ONLY WE HAD MORE MONEY

OBJECTIVES   To help students understand what it feels like to be left out because of class background.
To help students realize how economic differences in families effect social interactions.

IMPLEMENTATION These are role-plays. Be sure you have done some work on role-playing from the lesson on p. 70. Choose one or both situations to role-play.

Role-Play One—Out for a Soda. There are four students in this role-play: Gwen, Amanda, Ashley, and Lloyd. Ashley comes from a home with very little money. The other three all get allowances of approximately $3 a week, which they are allowed to spend in any way they wish. The scene takes place right outside the building one day after school. Amanda has suggested to the other three that they all go out for a soda to continue working on their group social studies project. Gwen, Lloyd, and Amanda have been out for sodas together before. This is the first time they have done a school project with Ashley. They enjoy her and want to include her in their activities. All four children normally walk home.

Role-Play Two—The Budding Artist. Tom, Ramon, Lois, and Gloria are friends. They're very excited about the new after-school program in drama, cooperatives games, and art that is about to begin at their school. Gloria is an excellent artist and Ramon and Lois have been trying to convince her all week to sign up for the after-school program. This would help her in her goal of being an artist. Tom knows Gloria can't sign up because she has to go home to baby-sit for her younger brothers and sisters, Gloria has been avoiding the issue by saying, "Oh, I'm not interested in the after-school program." She doesn't admit she has to baby-sit. All four friends are now together. This is the last day to sign up.

DISCUSSION
1. How do you think Ashley felt? Explain.
2. Have you ever felt that way? When? What did you do?
3. What did you think of the ways Ashley handled the situation in the role-play? Can you think of anything else she could have done or said?
4. What do you think of what the other children said or did? Are there any other more creative ways they could have handled the situation?

Repeat discussion questions 1 through 4, substituting Gloria for Ashley.

5. Are there other times in your own lives when there have been problems for you or children who come from families with little money? Give examples.
6. How do you feel in these situations, when you don't have enough money to do what others are doing? What would you like others to do or say?

GOING FURTHER Now set up role plays of these same situations and have students develop creative strategies for dealing with class differences in these, and other, social interactions.

Ms Meg   **by bulbul**

MORE IS NOT ALWAYS BETTER, ROGER.

LEFT OUT

OBJECTIVES To encourage understanding of what it's like to feel excluded based on difference in religion, family structure, physical ability, learning ability, or language difference.
To consider what a friend might do in these situations.

MATERIALS One piece of paper and pencil per group, "Worksheet: Left Out," pp. 98–99, cut up into sections, enough for one situation per group.

IMPLEMENTATION Discuss with students examples of the many kinds of differences that cause people to be excluded by others. Add some the students omit. Explain that today we will focus on five of those—physical disability, family structure, religion, learning ability and language difference.

Discuss these briefly with the students. Ask any student volunteers who are comfortable doing so to share how they, their friends or relatives may sometimes be perceived as different because of any of the five areas above. You may also want to share examples from your life or lives of your friends and relatives.

A Cooperative Learning Strategy for Equal Participation

The implementation of the following part of the lesson uses a highly structured cooperative learning procedure that encourages equal participation of all students. Students number off 1, 2, 3, 4. Different parts of the task are assigned to students with different numbers. At first read, it may seem overly complex. However once students are used to this type of procedure, it can be used easily again and again. It is an effective way of keeping one or two students from dominating a group and necessitates that more reticent students participate. Make appropriate modifications for students with special needs.

Divide students into heterogeneous groups of four. Give each group one of the "Exclusion Situations" (e.g., Luis' Situation) from the Worksheet. The following steps of the task may be posted or handed out as a worksheet.

1. Read the "Exclusion Situation"—student 3.
2. By passing a piece of paper around from person to person, the group lists as many feeling words as possible to describe how the excluded person might feel.
   - Student 1 suggests a word, student 2 writes it down.
   - Student 2 says a word, student 3 writes it down.
   - Continue around group similarly until suggestions are exhausted.
   - Give spelling help as requested.
3. Group members try to agree on five or six of the most appropriate feeling words for their situation.
   - Student 4 fills them in on the Worksheet. All check for spelling.
4. Students discuss what kind of difference is the basis for exclusion.
   - Student 4 writes that on the Worksheet.
5. Read the "As a Friend" section of the Worksheet—Student 1.
6. Group members take a minute of silence to think about what they'd do.
   - Go around the group with each giving her idea beginning with student 3.
   - When each person has contributed an idea, group members discuss what approach might be most effective and why.
   - Student 2 writes that on the Worksheet.

Prepare board space titled "Laura's Situation," "Jamila's Situation," "Luis' Situation," "Derek's Situation," and "Rosa's Situation." At the same time, ask group members to huddle to make sure each member can explain the "exclusion situation" in her own words and explain what they decided they would do as a friend, and why. When all groups are finished, ask student 2 from each group to come to the appropriate section of the board and write a list of all his group's feeling words. (There may be lists from several groups in each section.)

After the words are listed, call on student 4 in a group that read about Laura to explain "Laura's Situation" to the class, and student 2 of all groups with "Laura's Situation" to read their words and explain why they circled the ones they did. Continue similarly for Luis, Jamila, Rosa, and Derek.

DISCUSSION   (Keep students in groups of four during discussion.)

1. What kind of difference was used to exclude each person?
2. What do you notice about the feeling words on the board under each person's name? Are they similar? How so? Are they different? How so? Discussion also might focus on how, when people feel conflicted, they can experience different feelings at the same time. Also, since we're not inside another person, we can never be sure of how any other person feels.

    Ask students to briefly reconvene with their groups. Even when people are unlike each other, they can experience the same feelings because of others' responses to differences, whatever the differences are. Ask students to think of a time when they felt excluded because of religion, family structure, physical ability, or any other difference. Invite them to share their situations with each other.
3. To what extent did your experience of being excluded because of difference generate similar feelings among your group members? Different feelings?

    Taking each situation separately, ask student 1 to share her group's idea about what she would do as a friend, and why.
4. What commonalities are there in the steps the group suggested a friend might take? What are the differences?
5. What have you ever done in your life as a friend of someone who has been excluded for being different? What did you learn from that?

"Family Structures"

Since this chapter aims to help students empathize with feelings of those hurt because of difference, and not to name and analyze the differences themselves, we discuss family structures here. In "Laura's Situation" it is possible, but not explicit, that Laura's mother and the woman she lives with are lesbians. If your students raise issues about gay or lesbian families, you may chose to explain that you will teach about stereotypes and discrimination toward lesbian and gay people soon and defer extended discussion until then. If, however, students exhibit significant misinformation, bias, or interest, suggesting that this topic should be addressed now, or if you feel ready to address it now, go to Chapter 6 and see lesson "Females/Males: The Way We're Supposed to Be" p. 111.

> ### Teaching about Class
>
> Societal values and institutions bombard Americans with the message that if you're poor it's your own fault and that those who prosper have *only* themselves to thank. Your students from poor or low-income families have most likely internalized this message and feel ashamed and inferior, but they may or may not admit it.
>
> Your students from higher-income families have most likely internalized this message and feel self-righteous and superior, and they may or may not admit it. It's tough to talk about economic differences because these feelings get activated!
>
> What can you do:
>
> Reiterate again and again that many times it's not people's fault that they have little money. They often haven't had an fair chance.
>
> Remind students in ways they can understand, that "not having money" is a relative term. When middle-class students talk about "not having enough money," help them see how that statement feels to a person who *really* doesn't have enough money to live on.

SEEING-EYE GLASSES*

OBJECTIVES   To enable students to understand how a point of view effects how one acts in a situation.
To help students understand the choices people have in life regarding individualism and cooperation.
To help students experience the feelings resulting from individualism compared to cooperation.

MATERIALS   Copies of "Worksheet: Concetta's Choice," p. 100, one per student; pairs of sunglasses and frames of old eye glasses (ask students to bring these from home the day before).

IMPLEMENTATION   Tell students that they are going to get to wear some very special glasses—"seeing-eye glasses." Each pair of glasses enables them to see the world in a different way.

Part One.   Assign students to heterogeneous groups of three. Explain the following situation to them.

> In Bill's family everyone takes turns cooking dinner. Each person has a night to cook. Tonight is Sam's turn. Sam is Bill's older brother. Sam calls Bill on the phone and says he's working on a play at school and will be late. He asks Bill to cook for him.

Have ready different sets of glasses—angry glasses, empathic glasses, creative glasses, fussy glasses, and so on. Define words and feelings as needed. Use actual sunglasses or old eye glass frames. You should role model the difference in glasses by putting them on and speaking briefly. For practice, have one group come to the front of the room and role-play the situation. One person is Bill, one Sam, and one the observer.

Begin the role-play with the phone ringing. Give Bill one of the four pairs of glasses and have him respond to Sam. Correct any misinterpretations. Have them have a dialogue with each other for about thirty seconds. Then give Bill a different set of glasses and have them continue. The observer is instructed to watch for changes. Next have students switch roles and give the new Bill yet another set of glasses. Continue the process until all have played each role and tried on at least a couple of pairs of glasses each.

Now that class members have the idea, let each small group of three do this, or a similar, role-play. Students change roles as above. After they're finished, talk together about the experience.

---

*Adapted from an activity in *Toward a Humanistic Education,* by Mario Fantini and Gerald Weinstein.

DISCUSSION

1. How did the kind of glasses you wore affect how you saw the situation?
2. How did your perspective change as you changed glasses?
3. When you were the observer, how did you see other people change when they switched glasses? What else did you notice?
4. In which glasses did people think mostly of themselves? In which did they think of others?
5. In real life when we look at a situation only from one point of view, it's like wearing only one pair of glasses. When has this happened recently in your life? Watch for this during the day. Why not try another pair of glasses!

Part Two. Have students read "Worksheet: Concetta's Choice." Explain that for this role-play there are two types of seeing-eye glasses—"me first glasses" and "we first glasses." When you wear "me first glasses" you are thinking about only what's best for yourself. When you wear "we first glasses" you are thinking of what's best for *you and other people;* your friend's need or wishes are as important as your own.

Students form pairs. One person is Concetta and the other the observer. Concetta is at home, trying to decide what she's going to say to her boss tomorrow. Concetta puts on the "me first glasses" and begins "thinking aloud." At thirty seconds call "time" and have Concetta put on the "we first glasses." Again, she thinks aloud. The observer watches for the change in her point of view. Have her switch two more times and then ask students to reverse roles.

Finally, with glasses off, give pairs a minute to come up with their suggestions for a good solution.

DISCUSSION

1. How did you feel with the "me first glasses" on? With the "we first" on?
2. When you were the observer, what did you note as the difference in Concetta when she was wearing different glasses?
3. What solution did you come up with regarding Concetta's choice?
4. When in real life have you gotten ahead at the expense of someone else? How do you feel about that?
5. When in real life have you had to choose between what was best for you as an individual and what was best for the entire group? What thinking went into your choice?
6. If we want *everybody* in our class to feel happy and successful, which glasses will help make that happen?

GOING FURTHER

The "seeing-eye glasses" technique can be used throughout the year in a variety of ways to help students see things from different points of view.

bülbül © 74

"I said it's all in how you look at things," repeated the voice.

Milo turned around and found himself staring at two very neatly polished brown shoes, for standing directly in front of him (if you can use the word "standing" for anyone suspended in mid-air) was another boy just about his age, whose feet were easily three feet off the ground.

"How do you manage to stand up there?" asked Milo, for this was the subject which most interested him.

"I was about to ask you a similar question," answered the boy, "for you must be much older than you look to be standing on the ground."

"What do you mean?" Milo asked.

"Well," said the boy, "in my family everyone is born in the air, with his head at exactly the height it's going to be when he's an adult, and then we all grow toward the ground. When we're fully grown up or, as you can see, grown down, our feet finally touch. Of course there are a few of us whose feet never reach the ground no matter how old we get, but I suppose it's the same in every family."

"You certainly must be very old to have reached the ground already."

"Oh no," said Milo seriously. "In my family we all start on the ground and grow up, and we never know how far until we actually get there."

"What a silly system." The boy laughed. "Then your head keeps changing its height and you always see things in a different way? Why, when you're fifteen things won't look at all the way they did when you were ten, and at twenty everything will change again."

"I suppose so," replied Milo, for he had never really thought about the matter.

"We always see things from the same angle," the boy continued. "It's much less trouble that way. Besides, it makes more sense to grow down and not up. When you're very young, you can never hurt yourself falling down if you're in mid-air, and you certainly can't get into trouble for scuffing up your shoes or marking the floor if there's nothing to scuff them on and the floor is three feet away."

"That's very true," thought Tock, who wondered how the dogs in the family liked the arrangement.

From *The Phantom Tollbooth*,
by Norton Juster, pp. 102–106.

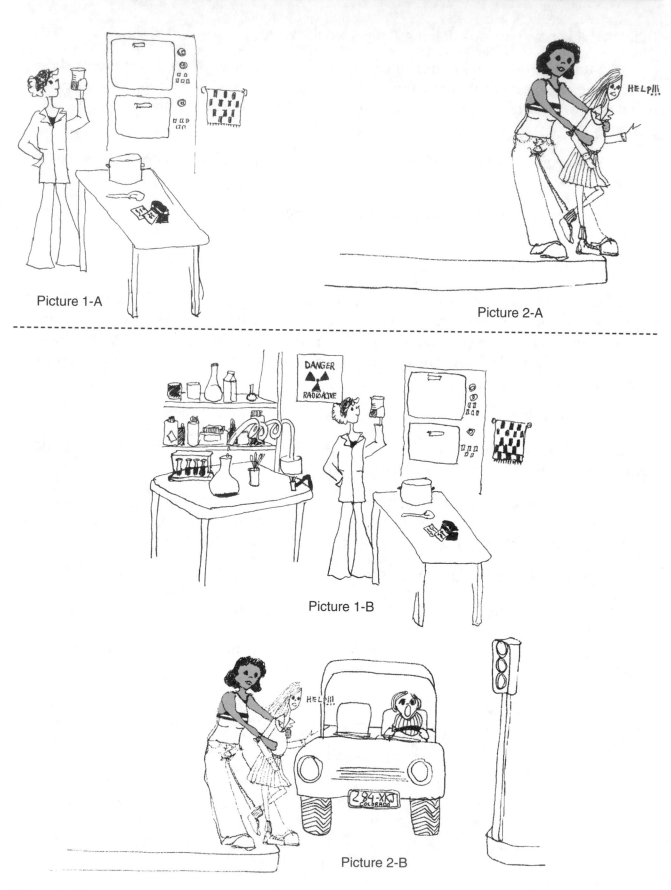

Picture 1-A

Picture 2-A

Picture 1-B

Picture 2-B

Pretend you are a character in the book. Write about a day in your life which is not already described in the story. Give your thoughts and feelings, not just what you do.

_____

Pretend you are a character in the book. Write a sequel about some time in your life taking place after the book ends. Give your thoughts and feelings, not just what you do.

_____

Take one scene in the book. Describe it three times, from points of view of three different people in the story, explaining how each would see it. Illustrate those.

_____

Be yourself. Write a letter to a character in the story. Then write a letter from that character back to you. Write a correspondence back and forth with at least four letters in it.

_____

What do you and one of the characters in the book have in common? List five adjectives that describe both of you. List five skills you both have. List two problems you both have. List three things you would like to do together if that person visited you. List five words that you and that character would both use to describe your families or your schools.

_____

Pick a character in your book. What are some ways you would like to be like that person that aren't true for you now?

September 15

Dear Diary,

I'm so glad I got you for my birthday. The most exciting thing happened today. I got the best birthday present. You're a good present, but I got another one that is maybe a little better. Our town finally realized that they have to let girls on the town soccer teams. Finally I get to play on a real team. What a perfect present for my eleventh birthday.

My father said he would take me down to sign up tomorrow after school. I can't wait.

Oh, I also got a great new long skirt for folk dancing and the best book of mystery stories!!

Love,
Rebekah

September 16

Dear Diary,

You're not going to believe this. I sure didn't! My dad and I went to sign up for soccer. Well, this real big man with no smile on his face just stared at me. Finally he said, "You mean her?" Then he looked at my brother, Scott, and said, "Doesn't he want to play? What kind of family you got, Mister?"

Scott just laughed. He can't understand why I want to play on a town team. He likes playing soccer with me in our yard, but he'd much rather be building stuff on his clubhouse up in the woods, than be going to practice all the time.

My dad said he meant me and the man signed me up. But we knew it was just because he had to and that he was going to make it as hard as possible.

Aren't some people mean?

Love,
Rebekah

September 17

Dear Diary,

I can't write too much today since Dad and I are making egg-rolls for dinner and that takes a long time. I had my first soccer practice this afternoon. I'm not one of the best kids on the team, but I'm not one of the worst either. It's a good thing Norbert had practiced with me a lot before he moved away. It's bad enough how much the boys tease me as it is. The coach is just as bad.

They all say, "Why does she got to get to play?" and, "I never would have signed up if I knew I'd be playing with a girl."

I wonder if they'd be nicer to me if I was better than they all are. Maybe they'd be even meaner.

Love,
Rebekah

September 20

Dear Diary,

I'm sorry I haven't written for three days. Life hasn't been much fun.

The second day we had soccer practice the boys were just as mean. One of them purposely kicked me at least ten times. The coach asked me if I wouldn't be happier mending uniforms. Mending uniforms, he's got to be kidding!

Then we didn't have practice one day, and would you believe I was actually glad? Well, today's practice wasn't much better. I'm playing okay and I'm getting better at passing. It really helps to be able to play with a whole team. But if no one will include me, what kind of team game is it?

Tonight I'm staying over with Tammy. We're going to try out a new chocolate cake recipe. But what should I do about soccer?

Love,
Rebekah

It was the third week of school. At lunchtime the children got in their usual two lines. One line was for children who bought lunch. The other line was for those who brought lunch from home. Consuela, a fifth-grader, had her lunch in a bag from home. She stood at the back of the line so she could leave the line quickly: She always joined her sister, Marita, when the fourth-graders came in to eat.

Consuela and Marita's family had moved to town in August. Their parents were both working on one of the citrus farms. The girls felt funny in their new school, which was almost all white. Most of the other girls wore jeans to school, but they wore cotton dresses. Their English didn't sound like the other students'. The worst time of the day was lunch. Everyone else who brought lunch seemed to have peanut butter and jelly or bologna sandwiches. The first day Consuela had wanted to sit with the other fifth-graders. Her parents had told her to try to be friendly. She had sat down and taken out her tortillas. Right away three of the other kids in her class started laughing. They laughed and laughed. Then they started saying that she had a strange lunch and they would never eat anything like that.

That first afternoon Consuela and Marita told their parents about lunch at school. They didn't want to be teased every day, but they liked tortillas. They also liked doing something the way they were used to. It felt safe and reminded them of home.

After that day they sat at a table away from the other students. That way they could have their tortillas and not be teased. But they could never quite enjoy it. They felt ashamed that they had a lunch other kids thought was strange. They wanted to make new friends and worried about what the other kids thought.

Now it was late September. This day, right after Consuela and Marita sat down, two of Consuela's classmates, Heather and Deborah, sat down with them.

Now write the conversation that took place among the four girls and anyone else who came over.

Luis' Situation

Luis learned that his friend, Barbara, was planning a birthday party for Saturday. He waited to get an invitation, but never did. Luis heard that since part of the birthday party was roller-skating, Barbara didn't invite Luis because he couldn't go skating in his wheel chair.

Brainstorm 5 or 6 feeling words to describe how Luis might have felt and why.

What kind of difference was used to exclude Luis?

As a Friend

You are Luis' friend and know that Luis wishes people would talk to him more about his handicap and ask him whether or not he wants to be involved in different events. What might you do now?

Laura's Situation

Laura invited six girls from her Girl Scout Troop who are working together on an activity to her house on Saturday to finish the project. Only two are coming. Laura overheard some of the other girls say that their parents wouldn't let them go because Laura's mother lives with another woman.

Brainstorm 5 or 6 feeling words to describe how Laura might have felt and why.

What kind of difference was used to exclude Laura?

As a Friend

You are a friend of Laura's and have been to her house many times. You know that her mother and the woman she lives with are kind, responsible women. They're lots of fun to be with. Your parents have often said that Laura has a terrific mom. What could you do now?

Jamila's Situation

It's December and Jamila's teacher has the class sing secular (not religious) Christmas songs. Some have been Deck the Halls, O Christmas Tree, Jolly Old St. Nicholas. Everyone in her class knows the songs and sings with enthusiasm. Jamila is Muslim and doesn't celebrate Christmas.

Brainstorm 5 or 6 feeling words to describe how Jamila might feel and why.

What kind of difference kept Jamila excluded?

As a Friend

You are a friend of Jamila and know that she wishes that people would not assume that everyone is Christian and celebrates Christmas. She doesn't feel comfortable singing songs about Christmas, but if she doesn't she feels isolated. You know Jamila feels hurt that holidays important to her religion, Islam, are never even mentioned. What might you do now?

Derek's Situation

At your school's afterschool program students were doing skits. The teacher said he would give out short scripts for groups of students to read aloud. Then they would present them. When kids were forming groups you heard Paul say, "Let's not let Derek be in our group, he's so stupid, he can't even read the script." You know Derek heard him.

Brainstorm 5 or 6 feeling words to describe how Derek might have felt and why.

What kind of difference did Paul focus on to exclude Derek?

As a Friend

You are a friend of Derek's and know he has a reading disorder. Derek's not stupid at all, in fact he's very smart. He's fantastic at scientific experiments, at fixing things and electronics, to mention a few. It's just that his kind of mind has trouble with word sounds. What might you do now?

Rosa's Situation

The art teacher came into your class and spoke with your teacher in a place where you and Ming could hear them. The art teacher asked your teacher to send her five students who like to paint and who could work together well to make a special mural for the front of the school. During the conversation your teacher said, "Rosa likes art, but I won't send her because her English is so bad."

Brainstorm 5 or 6 feeling words to describe how Rosa might have felt and why.

What kind of difference kept Rosa excluded?

As a Friend

You are a friend of Rosa's and know that while Rosa is still learning English, she can be understood. If other students ask her to say a word again or help her learn a word she doesn't know, it's easy to work with her in a group. She's a great artist and would add so much to the mural. What could you do now?

Concetta is a worker in a fast-food restaurant. She works with ten other teenagers. Concetta is earning money to help support her younger brothers and sisters. She feels good that she can work to help the family out.

Working at the restaurant has been getting worse because the manager has made several new rules lately. One is that if a worker drops any food she must pay for it herself. One worker slipped on a wet floor and dropped a huge pile of hamburgers—it cost him $40.

Another new rule is that workers must do the clean up. The manager used to hire another person to do this job. Many of the workers, however, cannot stay later because they have school the next day.

Concetta and the other workers are very upset about the new rules. They are all very careful, but once in a while accidents do happen. The leaky dishwasher—which the manager hasn't fixed—makes the floors very wet. One slip can cost them two days' pay. Many workers can't possibly stay late to clean up, but the manager has said, "Well that's your problem. You *must* be here or lose your job."

The workers have decided to go to the manager as a group and tell him they'll all quit if he won't sit down with them and find ways to work out these problems. They feel if they all stick together they can succeed. After all, he can't run a restaurant without experienced workers!

The day before the meeting, the manager called Concetta into his office. He said, "Concetta, you're such a good worker, I'd like to make you my assistant. I'll give you a raise and you won't have to pay for any dropped food. Also you won't have to stay late. What do you say? Of course, if you want the job, you'll have to convince all the other workers to stop all their complaining about the new rules. Let me know tomorrow."

Chapter

6

New Words: New Perspectives

Most young people have been hurt by prejudice and discrimination and observed others being hurt as well. As students get into the shoes of others who have faced bias, as they did in lessons in Chapter Five, they often become more conscious of these incidents in their daily lives. Often this can be both painful and confusing. Young people need language to talk about what they and others have experienced. Activities in this chapter provide students the words to name and talk about situations of inequality. This empowers young people to reflect on these experiences and then potentially to change them.

In "Prejudice and Stereotypes," students learn to recognize and examine these two types of attitudes and behaviors. They will pinpoint experiences in their own lives when prejudice and stereotypes have been involved, and will identify the accompanying feelings. Through the stories and accounts of other people, many of them their own age, they will understand the feelings of people who are negatively stereotyped on the basis of their age, language, race, class, religion, gender, sexual orientation or ability. They will explore ways in which *all* people are hurt by prejudice and stereotypes, both those on the receiving and those on the giving ends. It is intended that students will develop an awareness that stereotypes are learned and that they therefore can be changed.

Section B, the "Isms," contains lessons that take students a step further in their understanding of inequality—that is, to a knowledge of institutionalized discrimination. The term "ism" is used throughout the book. Sometimes a word with an "ism"—racism or ageism, for example—threatens people. This can be handled if you and your students deal with the words with open minds. All "ism" implies is that a form of inequality is institutionalized. Using an "ism" word is to take institutional norms, practices, and power relationships into account. It is an accurate and inclusive description of inequality. Help your students understand the isms without being scared by them!

Prejudice and stereotyping are sometimes practiced by individuals. They can also be practiced by institutions—the school, family, workplace, government—and it is then that they become "isms." We can ask children to share examples of prejudice and stereotyping that are practiced by individuals. An example might be that John called Tyrone a racist name. Then we can ask children to think of examples of ways in which they have experienced or seen discrimination practiced by institutions. An example might be a child being the target of a pattern of racist name-calling and, after complaints by the child and parent, the school failing to take action to stop it. This would be an example of racism.

Thus, an "ism" is a discriminating behavior practiced in a consistent pattern, often through the policies of institutions. A way to help students understand this is to use the following equation. "Ism = prejudice + power." Ask students to offer examples from their own lives of individual prejudice and institutional discrimination as you discuss the activities in this chapter with them.

The lessons are planned so that students can experience the feelings of people affected by "isms" and understand how their options and opportunities in life are negatively affected. By allowing enough time for students to respond to the discussion questions in Section B, and by keeping the discussion focused, students can learn to pinpoint the ways in which policies and practices of institutions reinforce such inequality. Explain that the situations described in particular case studies in the lessons are typical for *many* people in the United States today.

As you can tell, your role in this section is especially important! While the lessons will enable students to recognize institutional and cultural discrimination and see its effects, your leadership in the discussion can help students make broader connections to our society. The ways in which the "isms" divide people who otherwise might have common interests, and the ways they serve to maintain the status quo, can be discussed with some students, particularly those in the upper grades. Again, it's important to encourage students to discuss how we *all* lose out by the effects of the "isms."

In introducing students to ways that various forms of difference are used to maintain inequality, we examine heterosexism. As we discussed in Chapter 1, this is both an important and difficult form of discrimination to deal with. Emphasize to adults that the purpose of educating young people about heterosexism and homophobia is to make schools safe and fair for all students and to build respect for all forms of human diversity. Whatever our own personal feelings about homosexuality, our society *is* comprised of lesbians, gay men and bisexuals, just as it is of people of color, people of various religions, people with disabilities and so forth. Acknowledging their lives and contributions in ways that are developmentally appropriate, is not "encouraging homosexuality," but validating the reality of those children with lesbian and gay families and friends or those young people who are/may be homosexual. Reinforce the point that teaching about homophobia is teaching about families and relationships, not teaching about sexuality.

You want to feel comfortable dealing with the various ideas and issues in *Open Minds to Equality*. Of all the forms of diversity represented in the book, teachers probably get the least professional development time given to teaching about heterosexism and homophobia. Encourage your school district to offer such workshops/educational programs, or seek them from other groups. We need opportunities to reflect on our feelings and values, to gain accurate information, and to learn about age-appropriate approaches in order to feel competent to educate students about heterosexism and homophobia.

If you are uncomfortable saying the words lesbian, gay or bisexual, you may want to practice with a supportive friend or colleague and discuss your feelings as well. Students need to hear those words and know what they mean, in age-appropriate language. You may find it helpful to invite a guest to your class to provide information and answer students' questions. Team teach one of the lessons in the book that deals with homophobia with a supportive colleague. The more you read with young people books about alternative families, discuss current events related to these issues that are appropriate for your students, and talk about the ordinary lives of lesbian and gay people, the more comfortable and skilled you'll become in dealing with this equity issue in your classroom.

If you can make time to do more reading about institutional discrimination, you will feel the excitement of new learning along with your students! Some fine books are listed in the box below; there are many more in the bibliography.

Useful Reading for Educators about Institutional Discrimination

Non-fiction
Savage Inequalities: Children in America's Schools, Jonathan Kozol
Failing at Fairness: How American Schools Cheat Girls, Myra and David Sadker
Backlash: The Undeclared War Against Feminism, Susan Faludi
The Hidden Injuries of Class, Richard Sennett and Jonathan Cobb
Equality, William Ryan
Why Survive? Being Old in America, Robert Butler

Fiction
When reading these novels, look for ways in which forms of social inequality—such as racism, class bias, sexism—affect the characters. When we avoid "blaming the victim," the effects of institutional discrimination on the life experiences and choices of individuals become clear.

Daughter of the Earth, Agnes Smedley
The Bluest Eye, Toni Morrison
Betsey Brown, Ntozake Shange

Children Can Understand Injustice in Our Society

It's important to teach terminology that deals with current issues and problems, words like stereotyping, bias, sexual bias, harassment, victimization, inequality. Children do understand these issues, but they may not have the words for them. This gives them an opportunity to articulate what they understand on a very intuitive level. Children understand injustice in our society. They see it all the time, and what I try to do is give them the vocabulary so that they can discuss it, then we have some very sophisticated discussions . . .

Karen Cathers
fourth grade teacher

Section A   *Prejudice and Stereotypes*

WHAT ARE THEY?–PREJUDICE AND STEREOTYPES

OBJECTIVES   To define prejudice and stereotypes.
To have students think of times when prejudice and stereotyping affected them and to identify the feelings involved.
To have students explore the similarities and differences between different people's experiences of prejudice and stereotyping.

MATERIALS   Chart of definitions (next page), paper, pencils. Make one copy per student of "Worksheet: When It Happened to Me." List these questions down a page with room for student responses. 1. Describe a time when you were the victim of prejudice or stereotyping. 2. How did you feel during this experience? 3. How did you respond in this incident? 4. How do you feel about your response? 5. Was this an unusual or surprising incident for you? The type of thing that happens occasionally? The type of thing that happens frequently?

IMPLEMENTATION Remind students that this year you are all working together to try to create a classroom based on equality. You may want to do a quick review here with the students sharing equality success stories from the year so far. Explain to students that they will now be exploring ways that inequality gets reinforced. Tell them they will begin by examining prejudice and stereotypes.

Post the definitions, from the box below, of prejudice and stereotypes. You may also wish to pass out copies to students. Discuss these definitions with the whole class. Ask the students to share examples from their own lives. Be sure that some of these examples look at times they were *victims* of prejudice or stereotyping.

Now ask students to think of one specific time that they were the victim of prejudice or stereotyping. Have them fill in the worksheet, "When It Happened to Me" on their own. Then have the students find partners and read their accounts to each other. Ask them to talk particularly about their feelings and about how common or uncommon this type of experience has been for them.

Come together in a large group to share accounts and find commonalities and differences.

DISCUSSION
1. What are some feelings you had when you were stereotyped or felt prejudice directed at you?
2. Are your feelings similar to others in our class? How?
3. Are your feelings different from others in our class? How?
4. Look back at your responses on the worksheet. How do you feel about those?
5. Why do people show prejudice or stereotype others? How can we help ourselves and others to examine our beliefs and attitudes and the way we act?
6. How is it a different experience for people to face prejudice constantly because of their race or disability, for example, from someone who only experiences this once in a while?

How Often Are You a Victim?

It may be useful to discuss Question #5 on the worksheet with students before they begin their own writing. You may want to generate some group examples for each of these three possibilities. For example it is *unusual* for children to expect their low income classmates to do better in school than their middle class classmates *Occasionally* boys get teased about running for class secretary (but rarely about running for president or treasurer.) *Frequently* students thought by others to be lesbian or gay are teased and called names.

Definitions

Prejudice. An opinion about a person or group of people formed without knowledge, or with limited knowledge. For example:
Joey says, "I don't like Puerto Ricans!"
Joey has never met a Puerto Rican. He is prejudiced against Puerto Ricans.
Stereotype. A general viewpoint about a group of people. For example:
Stereotype—Girls are lousy basketball players.
Fact—Many girls are excellent basketball players.
Stereotype—Older people are sick and helpless.
Fact—Many older people are healthy and independent. Others have illnesses and need support.
Stereotype—Historically Native Americans were savage and wild.
Fact—Many Native American nations were peace-loving and only fought whites when their land was being invaded.

NO GRANDMOTHERS WANTED

OBJECTIVES To have students recognize a stereotype based on age.
To have students realize how stereotypes of people are harmful to those who have the stereotype, to those who are stereotyped, and to others who are part of the situation.
To encourage an awareness that stereotypes are learned and can be unlearned.

MATERIALS Copies of "Worksheet: No Grandmothers Wanted," p. 132; paper and pencils.

IMPLEMENTATION Divide students into groups of four. Give each student a copy of the Worksheet. If possible, have some students work in the hallway so that groups can rehearse without too much interference. Each group assigns parts for the skit. They read aloud the script as written, write their own endings, and rehearse those.

Come back together. Each group acts out its script. After all the groups are done, discuss the issues. Pick one script, or a combination, to present to another class.

DISCUSSION
1. What was Ms. Yung's stereotype about older people?
2. What reasons do you think there might be for Ms. Yung having that stereotype? How do you think we learn stereotypes?
3. Why did Angela suggest her grandmother for the hike? Why didn't Angela have the same stereotype about older people that Ms. Yung had?
4. How do you feel about the different endings to the script our class made up? Did the endings address the stereotype?
5. What can you do when you see someone acting in a certain way because of a stereotype she has?
6. Think back about some decisions you or someone else made because of some stereotype? Where did you get that stereotype? What can you do to unlearn it?
7. What would the class have lost out on if Ms. Yung's stereotype wasn't challenged?

Gardening across the Ages

Young and old join each other in the Penn South housing development in New York City to garden together. Children are individually paired with adults over the age of 60 to share garden plots. They learn from each other, share tools and labor, harvest vegetables and flowers and, in many case, become family.

RENEE RAMOS

OBJECTIVES To have students recognize stereotypes based on race, in this case those of Asian Americans.
To have students compare the stereotype to the actual situation of a person, in this case an Asian American student.

MATERIALS Copies of "Worksheet: Renee Ramos," p. 133, one per student. Type a "Worksheet: Group Questions—Renee Ramos," copy one per group (see Implementation for questions).

IMPLEMENTATION This is a cooperative group project. Students work together as a group and hand in one assignment per group. Divide students into heterogeneous groups of four. Make sure that a strong reader is in each of the groups.

As a group, ask students to brainstorm words that describe Asian American people. You might ask them to think about what Filipino/a, Chinese, Japanese, or other Asian people their age are like. If you have Asian American children in your class or if you are an Asian American teacher, ask students not to think of the particular people in the room, but of Asian Americans in general. After about five minutes have someone from each group read off that group's words or descriptions. Put these on the board.

Now, in small groups, have students read the story of Renee Ramos, a Filipina American. Assign the weakest reader in each group the paragraphs numbered 4 and the strongest those numbered 3 and those numbered 1 and 2 to the others. Students read their paragraphs to themselves first. Tell them to ask for help from others if they don't know the words. Then students read the account aloud.

Together, they decide on the answers to the Worksheet, "Group Questions: Renee Ramos," that include the following questions.

1. Choose at least four words to describe Renee Ramos.
2. Renee has told about her experiences through her eyes. From this description, what prejudices and stereotypes do some people have about Renee?
3. How do these prejudices and stereotypes hurt those who hold them?
4. What are some ways Renee feels that people treat her because she is Asian American?
5. How does Renee feel about being Asian American?
6. What description do you think some of the other children might give about this situation?

They fill out and hand in one Worksheet for the group. When discussing the questions below, remind students that no one story or person gives us enough information to draw conclusions about a group, but different lives help us understand the variety within particular groups of people.

DISCUSSION
1. First, discuss responses to the five questions on the Worksheet.
2. What negative stereotypes do some people have of other people of color—blacks, Latino/as, American Indians? How do these stereotypes affect people?
3. How does your understanding of Renee Ramos compare to the words your groups came up with about Asian Americans? How are they the same? How are they different? Why do you think this is?
4. How do we learn stereotypes? What can we do about them?
5. What do we lose out on when we stereotype people?

GOING FURTHER
Have students watch for examples of stereotyping of people of color in books, advertising, or on TV.
Encourage them to read books that have authentic portrayals of people of color. (See bibliography.)

LIZZIE GETS OLD CLOTHES

OBJECTIVES
To have students recognize stereotypes based on class bias.
To understand how someone who is poor might feel when faced with class bias.
To understand how "trying to do something nice" without truly understanding someone else's situation isn't always beneficial.

MATERIALS
Make a copy of "Worksheet: Lizzie Gets Old Clothes," p. 134, and copy enough for one set per pair. (See Implementation below.)

IMPLEMENTATION Tell students that they will be working in pairs to read a story aloud to each other. Mix students from different class backgrounds when possible.

Have students work together to fill out one "Worksheet: Lizzie Gets Old Clothes" that contains the following questions:

1. This story ends with these words: "If Carita and Tina had come over to me right then, I'd . . ." Write a paragraph to describe one idea you have about what Lizzie might have done.
2. List three or four feelings Lizzie had.
3. What are one or two stereotypes the other students had about Lizzie?
4. The other children are prejudiced toward Lizzie because she is poor. How do they show this prejudice?
5. Now that you've been doing these lessons you might respond differently. If you had been a classmate of Lizzie's, what would you have done? Said to her? Said to the other children? Can you think of more than one alternative? Pick one you'd like to write about below.

Encourage them to discuss their answers first and try to come to agreement before writing. Tell them to alternate writing down the answers to questions, and have the student not writing check the other's spelling and punctuation.

DISCUSSION
1. Begin the discussion by asking students for responses to questions 2 through 4 on their Worksheets.
2. How did you finish the story? Let's hear some examples.
3. When you have been hurt by prejudice or stereotypes, do you sometimes "not show it"? How do you do this? Why do you do this?
4. How did you answer question 5?
5. What can you do in your life when people act in hurtful ways toward others because of prejudices or stereotypes?
6. Sometimes people try to make themselves feel better about themselves by putting other people down because they are different. What are ways to feel good about yourself without using prejudice and stereotypes?
7. What did the children at school lose out on by stereotyping Lizzie? What do we lose out on in real life by stereotyping other people?

GOING FURTHER An excellent book to read with a reading group, or aloud to your class, is *The Hundred Dresses* by Eleanor Estes. This story, about a child from a poor family who is teased for wearing hand-me-down dresses, does an excellent job raising issues about cross class friendships and about teasing.

M. AND S. AUTO REPAIR

OBJECTIVES To have students recognize stereotypes based on gender.
To understand the feelings of persons who experience prejudice and discrimination because of stereotypes based on gender.

MATERIALS Copies of "Worksheet: M. and S. Auto Repair," p.135x, one per student. Make Role Cards for Marcie and Jim, one per pair (see next page).

IMPLEMENTATION Have students read "Worksheet: M. and S. Auto Repair" and answer the questions at the end. Discuss the Worksheet questions together as a class. (If your students are inexperienced with role-play, see "Role-Play Techniques," p. 70.)

Now tell students that we'll do a role-play. Tell the students that five months after the scenario in the Worksheet have gone by. After much hard work and fighting opposition to their idea from many people, Marcie and Sonia have opened the M. and S. Auto Repair Shop.

Ask two students to do a sample role-play in the front of the class. Remind students they must *become* the person whose role they are playing. Even if they don't agree with the role, they should get into the feelings. Make Role Cards to read:

Marcie

You are very confident in your abilities at auto repair. You successfully fixed at least 400 cars when you worked in your past job. You received very few complaints. In fact, your boss told you that you're one of the most skilled auto repair workers that he ever employed.

In the role-play, try to convince the customer to leave his car at M. and S. for you

---

Jim

You read about a new garage that is opening in town, M. and S. Auto Repair. You're so pleased, since mechanics at the other shops have never successfully fixed your car. You called and made an appointment to leave the car. When you walk in, you see a woman. You're shocked. You don't want a woman repairing your car.

In the role-play, try to find a way to get out of leaving your car at M. and S. Auto Repair.

Give the Role Card for Marcie to a volunteer and Role Card for Jim to another volunteer. After they've read it, check with them privately to make sure they understand their roles well. Tell the students that since this is a sample, you will interrupt after two minutes even though the role play may not be over.

Now divide all the students into pairs, give each child a role, and begin role-playing simultaneously. After about three or four minutes stop them. Have students exchange roles.

DISCUSSION

1. Describe your feelings playing Marcie.
2. Describe your feelings playing Jim.
3. In the end did Jim leave his car or not? What arguments influenced his decision?
4. What are other stereotypes some people have about women? Let's list them on the board. How do these stereotypes hurt women?
5. What can *we* do to counteract stereotypes that hurt people because of their gender?

FROM FEATHERS TO FACTS

OBJECTIVES

To have students recognize stereotypes based on race, in this case of American Indians. To help students understand how stereotypes of American Indians do not reflect either historical or current reality, and are harmful.

To help students understand how stereotypes in general are harmful both to those who have them and those who are stereotyped.

MATERIALS   Paper; pencils; drawing supplies.

IMPLEMENTATION   Try to read *Unlearning "Indian" Stereotypes* (curriculum and filmstrip) published by the Council on Interracial Books for Children before doing this lesson. It will give you valuable information and ideas about teaching about American Indians. While out of print, it is often available in college libraries and curriculum centers or school curriculum libraries. A valuable resource currently in print is *Through Indian Eyes: Native Experience in Books for Children* by Beverly Slapin and Doris Seale from New Society Publishers. Encourage your librarian to order it for your school.

Students work individually. Each student draws a picture of an American Indian in a setting in the United States today. This can be a school, or town, as long as a child the age of your students is included. Each student should write a short story about this child. Collect and post these.

Divide students into groups of four. Have each group divide a piece of paper into three columns entitled "Us," "Them," and "Both." In the first column they are to list characteristics of themselves (what they like to do, eat, play; how they feel; what they believe, and so on). In the second column they should list the same sorts of characteristics of American Indian children their age. In the third column they should list characteristics they think are true of themselves and of American Indian children.

Gather together as a class. Have students take turns calling out notations from their lists. Make a common list on chart-paper for all three columns. Post this with the drawings and pictures. (Save drawings for lesson in Chapter 11.)

After discussion, if possible, show the filmstrip "Unlearning 'Indian' Stereotypes."

DISCUSSION   If you have Indian children in your class be sure to reframe these questions to be inclusive.

1. What are some of the ways many of you pictured American Indians? What did you think they looked like? In what ways are any of these stereotypes?
2. Did you imagine American Indian children doing different things from what you do? If so, where did you get these ideas?
3. How would you feel if you were an American Indian child and you saw the pictures and stories in this classroom? Explain.
4. In what ways are our stereotypes about American Indians damaging to them?
5. In what ways are our stereotypes of American Indians harmful to those who stereotype?

GOING FURTHER   Have students collect materials that perpetuate stereotypes about American Indians. (For example, packaging for foods and games, athletic team mascots, greeting cards, school worksheet.) Look for times when parts of Indian life—e.g., headresses—are used when they have nothing to do with Native Americans themselves. Have them analyze them. Save for lessons in Chapter 11.

Have students look through library books and social studies textbooks that teach about American Indians. Have them analyze those that "teach" stereotypes.

FOLLOW-UP   "Relearning about Native Americans," p. 322; "Say It So They'll Hear It," p. 314.

Respect Native Culture

There is nothing harmful in children dressing up to play clowns, cowboys, or pilots. These are roles that can be taken on by people of any racial, religious or national group. But being a Native American is not a role. Native people are human beings with diverse cultures and distinctive national identities. . . .

When books show children doing "Indian" dances (or teachers have students do "Indian" dances) it is often insulting to Native cultures, and is frequently sacrilegious. Just as books and schools would not have children play at High Mass or Yom Kippur services, respect should be given to Native American religious ceremonies.

From *Unlearning "Indian" Stereotypes*

Sources of Information about Indians

As a children's librarian, it is my obligation to see that the collection contains balance, that the Children's Room be a place where all children will feel welcome, and comfortable. As a Native woman, it doesn't seem to me a lot to ask that the books written about Indians be honest, if nothing else. This is not so simple as it sounds. Very few non-Native writers have bothered to acquire the knowledge to produce meaningful work about our history, culture and lives—although this ignorance does not stop them from doing the books and getting published . . . In fact, Indians are the only Americans whose history has been set down almost exclusively by those who are not members of the group about which they are writing.

Doris Seale
Through Indian Eyes, 1992

DON'T JUDGE ME SO FAST

OBJECTIVES To have students recognize stereotypes based on physical ability, language fluency, and religion.
To have students understand why these stereotypes are harmful to all concerned.

MATERIALS Six copies of each script of "Worksheet: Don't Judge Me So Fast" (1a, 1b, 1c), pp. 136–138.

IMPLEMENTATION Do this lesson after you have done "What Are They?—Prejudice and Stereotypes." Review with students the definitions of "prejudice" and "stereotype." Explain that in this lesson students will be exploring stereotypes related to three groups of Americans: (1) those with physical disabilities, in this case a child with cerebral palsy who cannot walk and cannot speak clearly, (2) those whose native language is not English, in this case a Spanish speaking child and (3) those who are not Christian, in this case a Jewish child. Explain that they will be participating in skits to explore these stereotypes.

Step One. This lesson has three skits with six characters in each. You may need to modify these, or have one of the skits done by more than one group, depending on the number of students in your class. There are six parts for each script. Each group works cooperatively to rehearse its skit and to write the ending.

Step Two. After groups have rehearsed their skits and written the last few lines, have them gather as a class. Write the following on the board. Title it "Skit Analysis Form." Focus of skit: _____ 1. What stereotypes were presented in this skit? 2. In what ways are these stereotypes bad for the "victim" of the stereotypes? 3. In what ways are these stereotypes bad for others who hold the stereotypes? Have students have available 4 sheets of paper. Explain that students are to fill out responses to the "Skit Analysis Form" after each skit.

Step Three. Have students in Skit #1a perform their skit. Then have all students, including those who were in the skit, fill out one copy of "Skit Analysis Form."

Step Four. Continue in this manner for the other two skits.

Step Five. Have students share and discuss their "Skit Analysis Forms" with a partner.

Step Six. After all three skits have been performed, hold a discussion with the entire class. See questions below.

DISCUSSION
1. For each skit have students name all the stereotypes that were portrayed.
2. How did your group decide on the ending for your skit?
3. What do you think about the endings for each of the skits?
4. What were some similar themes you noticed that were carried through in these skits?
5. How might the characters in each skit have come to believe the stereotypes they held?
6. What other ways do you know about that people develop stereotypes?
7. If some characters in the skits hadn't "learned" these stereotypes, how have they avoided that?
8. What other examples do you know of people managing to resist believing stereotypes even when those around them believe these?
9. How are stereotypes harmful to ALL who hold them?

FEMALES AND MALES: HOW WE'RE "SUPPOSED" TO BE?

OBJECTIVES To have students recognize prejudice and stereotypes based on sexual orientation.
To help students understand the feelings of people who experience prejudice and discrimination because of stereotypes based on sexual orientation.
To help students understand the relationship between rigid, traditional gender roles and homophobia, and the subsequent effect on students' choices and actions.

MATERIALS "Worksheet—Josh and Jenna," one per pair, p. 139.

IMPLEMENTATION

Part A Tell students we will begin this lesson by thinking about the stereotypes in our society about appropriate behavior for girls and boys. While these stereotypes aren't truths and while we may not believe many of them, messages from the media, our friends, and parents can reinforce these messages.

Ask students to brainstorm stereotypes about boys. Make a list on newsprint or the board with one side titled "should" and the other "should not." What should boys/men like to do, what should they be like, how should they act? Do the same for shouldn't. Next brainstorm a similar list for girls. (Remove list after lesson to preclude misunderstanding by others.)

DISCUSSION 1. How do you, your friends, or adults you know fit these stereotypes? How are they different from these stereotypes?

2. How do these stereotypes of the ways females and males "should" or "shouldn't" be, influence some people your age? What do these stereotypes encourage? Discourage?

Part B Tell students they will be reading about the experiences of two people their age who, in some ways, challenged societal stereotypes of how males and females should act. Ask students to try to empathize with these young people. Ask them to be attentive to ways they challenged stereotypes, and in turn, how they were stereotyped.

Assign students to heterogeneous pairs. Give one the role of Josh and the other Jenna. Tell them they are to read their roles and be ready to share: 1. information about themselves in their roles; and 2. the incident of prejudice they experienced.

While they share this, their partner will be using active listening. Go over active listening guidelines listed below with students if this is new to them and model it with a simple example.

Active Listening Guidelines

1. Put yourself in the other person's place to understand what the person is saying and how he feels.
2. Show understanding and acceptance by nonverbal behaviors: tone of voice, eye contact, facial expressions and so forth.
3. Restate the person's most important thoughts and feelings.
4. Do not offer your thoughts and feelings.

When they are finished, keep students in pairs. Ask the following questions one at a time. Have students respond to their partner. For the first questions have Josh go first, for the second Jenna etc. After students have had a chance to talk briefly with each other about a question, call on a student to share her response with the class. Then open it up for a brief class discussion. Go on to question #2 and continue accordingly.

1. What was it like to actively listen to your partner? What was hard about it? What was easy?
2. How did it feel to have someone actively listen to you? Why was that?
3. How did Josh fit socially accepted male roles? How did he challenge the stereotypes?
4. In what ways did Jenna fit socially accepted female roles? How did she challenge the stereotypes?
5. When you were playing the role of Josh, how did you feel about yourself? How did you feel when you were called "faggot"? Why?
6. When you were playing the role of Jenna, how did you feel about yourself? How did you feel when you were called "lesbian"? Why?
7. How was Josh stereotyped? Why?
8. How was Jenna stereotyped? Why?

Now break up the pairs and come together for a class discussion. Talk about any of the questions above that need more discussion. Then address the following questions.

Discussing Sexual Orientation

It's important to help young people understand that lesbians and gay men live the same kinds of lives that everybody else does. The one difference is that lesbians and gay men love people of the same, rather than opposite, sex. They have jobs, homes, and often families, like others. If age-appropriate, also point out that lesbians and gay men have no more interest in sex than other people. Discuss any other stereotypes that students may have (see subsequent box).

In this lesson students are using the words "lesbian" and "faggot" as put-downs. The word "faggot" is always a put-down, and not an acceptable word in any context. The word "lesbian" is not a pejorative word unless it is being used for the purpose of putting someone down. Otherwise it is a polite and acceptable word for a woman who is homosexual.

1. Why would someone call Josh a "faggot"? Why does going against a socially accepted male role make someone like Josh the target of prejudice?
2. Why would someone call Jenna a lesbian? Why does going against a socially accepted female role in her school make someone like Jenna the target of prejudice?
3. How does stereotyping others who challenge typical roles for boys and girls serve the name-callers?
4. Why are some people afraid of being labeled lesbian or gay? What stereotypes about lesbians and gay men feed people's fears? What are the myths that underlie these stereotypes?
5. How does the fear of being called lesbian or gay limit the choices some girls and boys make about what they do or how they act? What could be done to change that?
6. Why are some young people who feel they might be lesbian or gay often afraid to talk with others about this? What could be done to change that?

Stereotypes about Lesbians and Gay Men

- Lesbians and gay men try to convert other people to be gay.
  (Although homosexual "seduction" does occur, it is far less common than heterosexual "seduction.")
- Gay men and lesbians take sexual advantage of children.
  (Most incidents of sexual molestation of children are committed by adult heterosexual males on minor females. Studies show 90% of reported incidents involve men the child knows—father, step-father, uncles, and family friends.)
- Lesbians and gay men chose to be gay and could change and be heterosexual if they wanted to.
  (Psychologists do not consider sexual orientation for most people a conscious choice that can be voluntarily changed.)
- Gay men and lesbians are much more interested in sex than heterosexuals.
  (Gay men, lesbians, and bisexual people have the same range of sexual activity—from none to a lot—as heterosexuals do.)
- Gay men have high voices and limp wrists. Lesbians have short hair and stocky bodies.
  (The vast majority of lesbians and gay men cannot be identified by appearance.)
- Lesbians and gay men do things different from most people of their gender—e.g., men are dancers, women work in the trades.
  (People who are lesbians, gay and bisexual work in all types of jobs.)

Data from: American Psychological Association, National Gay Task Force, Massachusetts Safe Schools Program for Gay and Lesbian Students, Massachusetts Department of Education.

Through the discussion help students separate gender roles from sexual orientation. Help them see that there are many heterosexual men, for example, who like dancing just as there are gay men. Pro football players often take ballet lessons and are fine dancers. Also help students separate issues of same-gender friendship and sexual relationships. Showing affection for those of the same gender is often an important part of friendship. This is especially easy to see in some other cultures. For example, heterosexual French males commonly hold hands or hug in public, whether they are heterosexual or homosexual.

Depending on the kinds of issues that are raised by this lesson, it may be wise to go on to the follow-up lesson that looks at institutional discrimination based on sexual preference and defines, and helps young people understand, heterosexism and homophobia. That lesson, "Separation," is in the next section of this chapter, 6B.

FOLLOW-UP Use the lesson "Put-Downs" on page 352 that helps students examine the source of put downs and their effects on people.

WE ALL LOSE

OBJECTIVE To have students recognize how stereotypes and prejudice have negative effects on everyone concerned.

MATERIALS Copies of Situation Cards, p. 140, one set per group (cut and mounted); paper; pencils; pens; eight 3 × 5 cards per group.

IMPLEMENTATION Divide students into heterogeneous groups of three or four. Give each group copies of the Situation Cards and paper and pencils, four 3 × 5 cards and pens. Review definitions of prejudice and stereotypes and go over several cards as a whole class to give students the idea.

Students read cards aloud in their small groups. For each one, they discuss: (1) what stereotype of prejudice it shows; (2) why they think people might have that stereotype; and (3) what harm it causes. Allow enough time for thinking through these questions. The students may need your support, and perhaps some resource books, to seriously consider these questions. After they have worked through their cards, each group picks four cards that especially intrigue them. Members fill out 3 × 5 cards with the following information on them: a. Card Number; b. Stereotype or Prejudice; c. Harm caused by stereotype or prejudice to *each* person in the situation. Come together as a class for the discussion questions.

After discussion, have group members take the other four 3 × 5 cards and create new cards describing situations that sometimes happen in their school or lives. In that way they will have to pick a stereotype or a type of prejudice and think it through clearly.

Share these with the whole class, perhaps having each group pass its stack on to another group. Finally, as a group, discuss the new cards.

DISCUSSION 1. How did the person stereotyped lose in the situations? Discuss one at a time.
2. How did the person stereotyping lose out?
3. Why do you think people hold some of the stereotypes on the cards?
4. What can you do to unlearn these stereotypes and to help yourself not to learn more?

GOING FURTHER Use these cards as part of a board game. Just add "lose a turn," "go back a space," or "take another turn," at the end of the card. Students can create a regular pathway game board. The theme should be connected with equality. This stack of cards can form the basis for the "luck" cards.

FOLLOW-UP   "From Fear to Power," p. 315.

Those Who Stereotype Are Hurt Too

Throughout the activities in this section, "Prejudice and Stereotypes," it's important to emphasize how those of us who stereotype are also hurt. We often lose out on important learnings, experiences, and friendships.

For example:

- The class could have lost out on a hike because of ageist stereotyping.
- Kids lose out on Renee's friendship as well as lots of learning about Filipina culture.
- Kids lose out on Lizzie's company and a chance to face and potentially change their own false sense of superiority.
- The residents of North Jefferson might lose out on a fine auto repair shop—and girls of the town lose out on non-traditional role models.
- We lose out on a knowledge and appreciation of the American Indian culture and therefore the opportunity to learn from it.

ANALYZING STEREOTYPES: WHAT'S BEHIND THE LABELS?

OBJECTIVES   Students will think about stereotypes they hold, including ones they don't generally acknowledge.

Students will understand historical and societal contexts for these stereotypes.

Students will better understand that even if a characteristic is more common for some groups than others, that doesn't mean that it will be true for any particular individual in the group.

Students will learn how to counter these stereotypes with reality.

Students will examine how any stereotype can be a problem for both the holders and the recipients of the stereotypes.

MATERIALS   Newsprint; markers; paper; pencils; reference books. Type "Worksheet: Analyzing Stereotypes" and make copies, 1 per group of four. (See #3 below.)

IMPLEMENTATION   Be sure to do the lesson, "What Are They?—Prejudice and Stereotypes," p. 103, before doing this lesson.

Many of us know of, or hold, beliefs that portray whole groups of people in positive or negative ways. Some of these stereotypes that show people in positive ways might be "black people have a good sense of rhythm," "lesbians are good at sports," "girls are good at taking care of people when they're upset," or "Asians and Jews are smart in school." Some stereotypes that portray people in negative ways might be "girls aren't good at fixing things," "Irish people drink a lot," "Jews take advantage of people in business," or "boys don't talk about their feelings." Sometimes these stereotypes are based on what we have read or heard or seen in the media.

Stereotypes that portray whole groups of people, whether in positive or negative ways, can be damaging to individuals. They can be damaging to those who hold them and to those who are stereotyped. If we think only men can be good dentists we may miss out on choosing the best dentist for ourselves. If we think only boys can be good soccer players we may miss out on trying a sport we might enjoy.

In order to discourage students from holding stereotypes, we sometimes tell them that these stereotypes are "wrong" or "not true." This lessons uses a different approach. In it students are asked to directly name any stereotypes that they hold themselves, or that they have heard from others. After naming them, students work to uncover the origins of these so they can examine them more closely and understand them better. They then work to sort out what may be "true" in these stereotypes and how, even with those pieces of truth, these do not hold for all, or most, members of any group.

(A) As a whole class review the definition of a stereotype. If you wish, use the examples above as a reference. Tell students that, in this lesson, they will be examining stereotypes that portray people in positive ways and others that portray people in negative ways, and investigating origins of many of these.

Generate a brainstormed list of stereotypes about groups. Remember this is a brainstorm list, so don't censor it. Although it may be difficult, we encourage you to keep the brainstorming going without discussion. If you don't spontaneously get a list that has stereotypes which portray groups in both positive and negative ways, you may need to encourage whichever type is missing. If you need some ideas to get the students going, you may want to try some of the examples we've given at the beginning of this lesson.

Often stereotypes are based on an over generalization of historical information. See the box on the next page for a more detailed exploration of the stereotype "Black men are good basketball players." It is important for students to understand that a stereotype *can be based in reality while not being true for most people*. Understanding the origins for stereotypes and realistically understanding the data of what is true, helps us deal with them effectively.

(B) Divide students into groups of four. Each group will investigate one stereotype. In order to be sure that all students get a choice that interests them, begin by asking each group to choose three or four possible stereotypes they would like to investigate and to list those in priority order. They can choose from the brainstorm list, or come up with another stereotype that interests them. Go around the room giving each group the chance to name the stereotype they wish to investigate. If a stereotype that interests them has already been chosen, they must then choose a different one from their priority list.

(C) Students work in small groups to complete the Worksheet: "Analyzing Stereotypes." List these questions down worksheet page, leaving room for student responses.

1. Name your chosen stereotype.
2. Brainstorm your best guesses of why people have this stereotype. Think about how they learned this stereotype. Consider the impact of television, advertising, books, magazines, school materials. List as many sources as you can think of here.
3. What pieces of this stereotype are true?
4. Why are these pieces true? What are some of the social, economic, historical, geographic or other factors that have contributed to the truth of the stereotype?
5. What are the exaggerations and inaccuracies in the stereotype?
6. How and why have those pieces come into being?

When they are done with their worksheets, each group creates a poster to share the information they learned in their investigation. These posters include the phrase that names the stereotype, and the information on their "Worksheet: Analyzing Stereotypes." Posters should convey this information in visually appealing and easy to understand ways.

(D) Students share their posters by giving mini oral reports.

DISCUSSION

1. What was it like to think of stereotypes about groups of people? How did this make you feel?
2. What was it like to name, or investigate, stereotypes that portray a group in a positive way compared to naming or investigating ones that do so in a negative light?
3. Why do we develop stereotypes about groups of people?
4. Stereotypes are usually based on some historical information. What happens to this information when it causes us to develop a stereotype about a whole group?
5. How are these stereotypes helpful for the holders? For those being described?
6. What can we do to give ourselves more accurate and fuller pictures of people?
7. What can we do to help others counter stereotypes that they hold?

Sample Worksheet: Analyzing Stereotypes

1. Name your chosen stereotype.
   Black men are good basketball players.

2. Brainstorm on your best guesses of why people have this stereotype. You may begin by thinking about how they learned this stereotype. You may want to consider the impact of television, advertising of all sorts, books, magazines, school materials. List as many sources as you can think of here.
   When you watch basketball on TV you see mostly black male players.
   When you walk around your neighborhood you see black men playing basketball.
   Sports magazines have black men basketball players in them.
   The kids at my school who are best at basketball are boys and are black.

3. What pieces of this stereotype are true?
   Professional basketball teams are all male.
   Professional basketball teams are 75% black.

4. Why are these pieces true? What are some of the social, economic, historical, geographic or other factors that have contributed to the truth of the stereotype?
   Professional sports teams have historically been all male.
   Many black people today live in urban areas, basketball doesn't need much room to play.
   Many black people in the U.S. don't have much money. Basketball doesn't take expensive equipment.
   Black men have been kept out of many other professions.

5. What are the exaggerations and inaccuracies in the stereotype?
   Even though 75% of professional basketball players are black men, very few black men become professional basketball players.
   Some black men are not athletic at all.
   Many women are fine basketball players.
   Many men of other colors are fine basketball players.

6. How and why have those pieces come into being?
   Maybe white people have liked thinking of black people as athletes as that may be less threatening than giving black people equal access to all professions.
   Black boys have needed an area for hope and for role models and basketball has provided this.
   Black men athletes advertise products on TV.

Section B   The "Isms"

WHAT ARE THEY?—THE "ISMS"

OBJECTIVES   To define the words racism, sexism, classism, and ageism.
                   To understand how prejudice, when reinforced by institutional power, becomes an "ism."

MATERIALS   A large "ISM Chart," p. 141; Copies of "Worksheet: Find the ISM," pp. 142; "Worksheet:
                   Find the Ism—Supplement," if desired, p. 143, one for every two students.

IMPLEMENTATION This lesson introduces students to racism, sexism, classism and ageism. The same dynamic
                    of institutional discrimination applies to other forms of diversity—religion, sexual orien-
                    tation, language and physical ability, among others. There is a lesson on each of these forms
                    of discrimination later in this chapter. You may choose to address these latter forms of dis-
                    crimination in this lesson. If so, fully complete the "ISM chart" and both pages of "Work-
                    sheet: Find the Ism." You may choose to do the full lessons first and then add these forms
                    of discrimination to your "ISM Chart."

                    Explain to the students that when prejudice and stereotypes are practiced by people with
                    more power than others or by institutions—like schools, families, government, businesses—
                    their effect is very great. Also, prejudice and stereotypes become more powerful when
                    imbedded in cultural attitudes and values. In these cases, people or institutions practice dis-
                    crimination—they treat people or groups of people differently because of their age, race, gen-
                    der, or class. The practice of such discrimination is summarized by using an "ism" word.

                    Post the ISM Chart and discuss each "ism" separately. (Change the key words on the
                    chart as appropriate.) In discussing the "isms" and the examples, explain that because
                    norms and procedures of *institutions* or prevailing attitudes and values in society reinforce
                    "isms" they are much more powerful than prejudice and stereotypes. In addition, exam-
                    ples of "isms" are harder to spot because they are often "hidden" in institutions. Explain
                    that victims of "isms" subtly learn that they are not as good or important as others, whereas
                    those who benefit from the "isms" learn that they are normal, right, or important. While
                    in real life we can be affected by many isms at once, for purposes of learning, they are dealt
                    with separately in this lesson.

                    Have students work in heterogeneous pairs. Give each pair a copy of the Worksheet.
                    One person reads the first situation aloud. Together they decide on answers and one per-
                    son writes them in. They continue this procedure with other situations, deciding together
                    who will read and write. Join as a class for discussion.

To Review

A *prejudice* is an *opinion* about a person or group of people formed without knowledge,
    or with limited knowledge.
A *stereotype* is a *general* viewpoint about a whole group of people.
Isms are prejudice and stereotypes enforced by people with more power than others, by
    institutions, and by cultural attitudes and values.
Prejudice + Power = Isms.

DISCUSSION   1. What are the "isms" in the situations on the Worksheet?
                 2. What feelings do people have who are victims of "isms"?
                 3. What feelings might people have who benefit from "isms"?
                 4. Are there examples of "isms" in your life like those in the stories? What are they?

Isms in the Media

In 1968 the Kerner Commission on civil disorders decided that the nearly all-white media was a problem, and recommended that the professional staff of news operations should be integrated. But at the top of most news organizations today, at least 95 percent of decisions are made by white males.

"Extra", July/August 1992, p. 12

ME, MYSELF, AND I

OBJECTIVES   To define competitive individualism.
                   To give students practice recognizing it.

MATERIALS   Paper; pencils; copies of "Worksheet: Ms. Lopez's Class (1)," p. 144, one per pair. (Worksheet: Ms. Lopez's Class (2), p. 145, is optional.)

IMPLEMENTATION   *Part One.* Tell students they will be discussing the concept of "competitive individualism." This may be a new idea for some students; for others it may be a new vocabulary word for a familiar, but maybe not discussed, idea. Define the term. Encourage students to share experiences they may have had with competitive individualism. Then give out "Worksheet: Ms. Lopez's Class (1)" to students and have them work in pairs to complete it. As a class, discuss their responses. Then, if you wish, give out part 2 of that Worksheet for them to read with their partners. Discuss any points raised on the Worksheet that weren't already mentioned.

Me or We?

Part Two. Divide students into groups of four. Each person describes one or two situations in which she thinks she'd be the winner if she and her group were to compete against each other. Examples: "I could ski farthest down a hill without falling"; "I could bake the most tasty fried chicken"; "I could speak the most words in Spanish." Each person then writes a sentence explaining how much time she has spent on these activities in the past, or how much experience she has had. For example: "My older sister takes me skiing in the mountains two or three times a year." Or, "I practice skiing, when it snows, at the recreation department hill in our town."

Students share their situations with their group and agree on one situation for each person in which they all expect that that person would win. Join together in the class for discussion.

Me-First-Ism

The term, "me-first-ism" is an easy way to describe individualism. Try this with students in younger grades.

DISCUSSION
1. What situations did people think of in which they expect they'd be a winner?
2. How much time and practice had been spent on these activities? How did that compare to the amount of experience of others?
3. What effect does the amount of encouragement and help you've had in something have on your feelings of "winning" in that?

4. How do your feelings about winning change if you have had the same opportunity as other people, compared to if you have had more or less opportunity than others?
5. When you've "lost" in a competition where you didn't have a fair chance, how did you feel?
6. Give some examples of times when you've shared your knowledge and skills with others. How did this feel for you?
7. Give some examples of times when others have shared their knowledge and skills with you? How did this feel for you?
8. What are ways in this class that we can share knowledge and skills with each other?

Individualism or Individuality?!

Don't confuse these two! *Individualism* is very different from *individuality*, which is the development of the unique and full potential of each human being. Individualism is a belief that people should look out for themselves first before thinking of other people. Individualism assumes that competitive structures are fair.

Individualism in society *hinders* the growth of individuality in many people. When competing with others, people often focus on winning or excelling in comparison to others and the motivation to experiment and be creative is constrained. A cooperative structure provides the support and safety in which the creative individuality of each person can be stimulated by bouncing off the ideas of others.

For a fuller and provocative discussion of this point see Alfie Kohn's book *No Contest: The Case Against Competition.*

LETTER FROM SALLY

OBJECTIVE To have students understand classism and the situation and feelings of people whose life-experiences and opportunities are affected by their class background.

MATERIALS Copies of "Worksheet: Letter from Sally," p. 146; paper and pencils.

IMPLEMENTATION Have students read the Worksheet. Go over difficult vocabulary words first, if necessary. Then ask students to write a letter in response to Sally as if they are Theresa. Tell them to answer the two questions at the end of Sally's letter.

When completed, discuss Sally's situation as a class, and share some of the response letters.

DISCUSSION
1. What are some of the feelings you would guess you might have if you were Sally? Describe the reason you'd feel that way.
2. Sally may not be able to achieve her goal because she doesn't have enough money. Many times people have to give up things because they don't have the money. What might some of those things be?
3. How do you feel about Sally thinking about giving up her hopes of becoming a doctor because of lack of money?
4. How should programs to train future doctors select students? To what extent should the amount of money a person has matter?
5. Who remembers our definition of "classism"? How is Sally's case an example of classism?
6. How do all Americans lose out by this kind of classism?

Explain that we will talk more about the effect of class on people's lives as we go through the year. You'd like them to remember their feelings when they got into Sally's shoes.

FOLLOW-UP "Yes, You Can Be a Doctor," p. 283.

Children Affected by Economic Inequality: Look for Their Strength!!

Poverty forces children to fight a many-front war simultaneously, often without the armors of stable families, adequate health care and schooling, or safe and nurturing communities. It is a miracle that the great majority of poor children stay in school, do not commit crimes, and strive to be productive citizens in a society that guarantees them a prison bed if they fail (for over $30,000 a year) but refuses to provide them a Head Start (for less than $3,800 a year) or a summer job (for less than $1,400) to help them succeed.

Marion Wright Edelman, *Wasting America's Future*, The Children's Defense Fund, 1994

WHO WILL TAKE CARE OF JAMIL?

OBJECTIVES To better understand sexism and the situation and feelings of those people whose life and opportunities are affected by sexism.
To better understand how institutional policies and practices reinforce sexism.

MATERIALS "Worksheet: Who Will Take Care of Jamil?" p. 147, one copy per pair. Type a second worksheet, "Questions to Consider," and copy one per pair. (See Implementation for questions.)

IMPLEMENTATION Tell students that they will read a story about a woman and her family that is an example of sexism. Ask students if they remember the definition of sexism. If necessary go over it with them. Then ask students if they have experienced, or if they know of anyone who has experienced, sexism. Encourage them to share a few stories. Ask them to think about these experiences as they learn more about Marva in this story.

Divide students into partners of mixed ability level. Pass out "Worksheet: Who Will Take Care of Jamil?" and have students read either silently or aloud to each other. In preparation for their newspaper story, students then work in partners to complete "Worksheet: Questions to Consider" which contains the following questions.

1. How do you think Marva felt?
2. How did Tyrone, Tyrone's co-workers, and his boss support sexism?
3. How did the college Marva goes to support sexism?
4. How does the idea that women should have the chief responsibility for caring for children support sexism?
5. What could the E.B.M. Company and Marva's college do to change these sexist practices?
6. How is the Williams' problem like that of other men and women?
7. What do others in the community lose out on by the lack of good day-care?

Next they outline their points for the article. Then have two sets of partners join together to share outlines. Each pair gives new information or suggestions that might improve the other's outline.

Then, in original pairs, students write the newspaper article. They may want to brainstorm together on all their important ideas. One student can take notes on these ideas. They then compose the article together, either with one student doing all the physical writing down of their article, or with the students alternating paragraphs for this scribe role. They then go over what they have written for information, story structure, spelling, and punctuation.

When articles are completed, have several pairs read theirs to the class.

DISCUSSION   Use the questions at the end of "Worksheet: Questions to Consider." Help students focus on the ways the institutions in this account (business and college) and also traditional family roles reinforce sexism and limit women from achieving their full potential.

Progress Made

Hewitt Associates, a national benefits consulting firm, surveyed 1,034 employers, most with 1,000 or more workers. They found that nearly 8 out of 10 U.S. employers now offer some sort of child-care help. This includes: 6 out of 10 companies providing some version of a flexible work schedule such as flextime, part-time work, job sharing. Ninety-four percent of the companies surveyed said they provided plans so employers could pay for child care with pretax dollars. Forty percent offer resources and referrals for child care.

Problems Remain

Unfortunately the number of companies sponsoring day care has remained steady at only 9% since the beginning of the 1990s. In addition, 31 states in the U.S. have lengthy waiting lists for openings in child care centers. Financial aid is available in only 25% of all child care programs and only 10% of all families using child care centers receive financial assistance, thus keeping these programs out of the reach of poor families. (Children's Defense Fund, 1994 Yearbook)

HEALTH OR HOME?

OBJECTIVE   To have students better understand ageism and the situation and feelings of people whose life-experiences and opportunities are affected by their age.

MATERIALS   Copies of "Worksheet: Can We Have our House?", p. 148, one per pair. Make Role Cards—Ted and Juanita Lund, one each per pair (see Implementation).

IMPLEMENTATION   Tell students that they will be reading about two older people, Juanita and Ted Lund.

Divide students into pairs. Mix the reading levels. Students read Worksheets with their partners.

Then tell them that they are going to role-play with their partner. One person will be Ted and the other Juanita. They will get more information about Ted and Juanita soon. Tell students that the purpose of the role-play is *not to solve the Lund's problem*. It is to *understand how they would feel* as Ted or Juanita. They might come up with plans for what they could do, but they don't have to. The main thing is to understand their feelings.

Give one student in each pair role-information for Ted and the other that for Juanita.

Ted Lund

You are very discouraged. You are also angry that the hospital bills are so high and insurance doesn't cover all the costs of your increasing health needs as you get older. You get very upset to think of leaving your house and garden.

With a sad heart, you feel that the best plan is to move.

Juanita Lund

You are very angry. You and Ted have worked very hard during your lives. Now one major illness may take away your house. You think it's wrong that hospital bills are so high and insurance doesn't cover all the costs of the greater health needs of older people.

You also feel it's unfair that you couldn't get a job because of your age. With a job you could have worked and paid more of the bills. You don't want to move. You want to use what's in the bank now to pay the bills. You also want to join the Gray Panthers, a group that fights for rights and resources for older people. Maybe by working together changes can be made in job discrimination and inadequate health care coverage.

They read silently. When students are ready, remind them that they are no longer themselves, but either Ted or Juanita. Tell them they are sitting together to talk about their feelings. After that they might try to decide what to do, but that is not necessary. They have five minutes for their conversation.

After the role-play students write down the feelings they had playing the role they did. They come together as a class for discussion.

You try being serene on $420 a month.

DISCUSSION

1. What were your feelings playing the role of Ted or Juanita Lund? Why did you feel this way?
2. What do *you* feel about the situation the Lunds are in?
3. What were some ways the Lunds were discriminated against because of their age?
4. Who remembers what "ageism" is and can define it for us? How is this account an example of ageism?
5. How did the stereotypes in the policies of the employers reinforce ageism?
6. How do we all lose out by practices that reinforce ageism?
7. What people do you know of—friends, relatives, people you've read about—who face similar situations as the Lunds because of ageism?
8. Did doing the role-play help you come up with any thoughts or ideas about what could be done?

Gran & Gramps

Aging in the U.S.

What Is Ageism?

Ageism is any attitude, action or institutional structure which subordinates a person or group because of age *OR* any assignment of roles in society on the basis of age. Ageism is usually practiced against older people, but it is also practiced against young people. Ageism can be individual, cultural or institutional *AND* it can be intentional or unintentional.

Examples of Ageism
- *Individual:* "She's too old to wear jeans," or "My grandfather is too old to understand me."
- *Cultural:* "You can't teach an old dog new tricks," or "There's no fool like an old fool."
- *Institutional:* Compulsory retirement. Also, the expectation that older people will be volunteers rather than paid employees.

Ageism intersects with the racism, sexism, and classism many people have experienced throughout their lives to create poverty in old age.
- In 1990 more than 20% of people over 64 were poor or near poor.
- The average retired male received $735 a month in Social Security benefits in 1993. The average retired female received $526.
- The Social Security average monthly benefit in real dollars for retired workers dropped in the last decade: in 1980 –$717, in 1993 –$674.
- In 1993 half of older men had incomes of less than $15,000. Half of older women had incomes of less than $8,600.

If the U.S. spent 15% less on the defense budget each year, we could abolish poverty.

Gray Panthers, 1996

LILLIE'S DILEMMA

OBJECTIVES To better understand racism and the situation and feelings of those people whose life-opportunities are affected by racism.
To learn how institutional policies and practices enforce racism.
To help students see the situation and feelings of people whose life-experiences are affected simultaneously by their race, class, and gender.

MATERIALS Copies of "Worksheet: Lillie's Dilemma," p. 149, one per pair. Type a Worksheet, "Questions to Consider" and make one copy for each pair. List these questions with space between for student responses.

1. What are three feelings Carolyn might have felt? Why might she have felt that way?
2. If you were Lillie, what might you be feeling? What might you say to your mother?
3. How was the landlord racist? How did he use racism to hurt Lillie's family?

IMPLEMENTATION Tell students that they are about to read a story based in fact. Divide students into pairs. Pass out a Worksheet to each pair. Have them read aloud to each other. Pair up students of different reading levels, so one can help the other. When possible, mix partners racially since students of color may bring their particular insights about racism to the activity. Once they have finished the story, they talk about the questions, decide on the best responses, and fill those in on the Worksheet, "Questions to Consider." Then come together as a class to discuss their responses.

DISCUSSION

1. Discuss the three questions on the Worksheet.
2. How could the landlord use the power of institutions—school, the housing office, government—against Carolyn?
3. The landlord called Carolyn a troublemaker. Why are people who speak up for their rights sometimes called troublemakers?
4. Carolyn was a poor black woman. How did discrimination based on race, gender, and class work together to affect her?

Tell students that people can use prejudice to hurt individual people, as when the landlord called Lillie a name. They can also use the power of institutions, like schools, government and housing, to hurt people as well. When they do this, we find an "*ism*." The landlord threatened to use his influence, connections and power to deny Carolyn a job; this was an example of institutional discrimination based on racism, sexism and classism.

Double Jeopardy

The impact of "double jeopardy" (the joint impact of racism and sexism) is indicated in these statistics about wages. Below are median annual earnings for all full time workers in 1993.

White men—$33,776	White women—$23,482
Black men—$24,105	Black women $20,304

U.S. Census Bureau

The "Isms" Hurt Us All

Remind students that we *all* lose out from institutional discrimination based on race, gender, class, and age. For example:

- Americans lose out on committed bright doctors—like Sally Garcia could be—because of class discrimination.
- We lose out on the talent, wisdom, and experience of older Americans, like Juanita Lund, because of ageism.
- Marva Williams's community and employer lose out on her skills in math, and Jamil and other children lose out on the nurturing of their fathers, because of sexism.
- Carolyn Raley's community loses out on a competent black teacher who could provide anti-racist education through content and example.

ALL KINDS OF BODIES AND ALL KINDS OF MINDS

OBJECTIVE

To have students understand ableism and the situation and feelings of people whose life-experiences and opportunities are affected by limited physical or learning abilities

MATERIALS "Worksheets: An Interview with Bobby," p. 150, and "Worksheet: An Interview with Aunt Sonia," p. 131—enough of each for half your class.

IMPLEMENTATION Tell students they will be reading interviews with two people, one who has a physical disability and one who has a learning disorder.

Divide students into groups of four, and then pair them within the fours. Assign one person in each pair to be a, the other b. In each pair place an able reader and give that student the role of Aunt Sonia or Bobby. The less able reader should be the interviewer.

"I believe... "

Have pairs read their interviews out loud to each other. Then they prepare to share what they learned with the other pair within their group. If any class members are non-readers, include a preparation period in which the reader reads the interview questions out loud to the non-reader in advance. Either member of the pair should be able to share Worksheet results. You might write these on the board.

1. Describe the person interviewed.
2. Describe the type of disability the person has and how the person feels about that.
3. Share examples of ways the person has faced discrimination from institutional practices—like school practices and policies.
4. In Bobby's case, the school practices were changed to accommodate his disability. Explain how that was done.

When each member of each pair can respond, pairs form back together in their group of four. Tell students which person to focus on first—e.g. Bobby. Then call out either a or b and ask that person to share information about question 1 with the other pair. If it was a, for example, then b will share information related to question 2, a does 3 and b ends with 4. Then repeat the process for Sonia.

Come together as a class to discuss these interviews and the issues they raise.

1. What are your feelings and ideas as you think about the school experiences Bobby had?
2. How did the institutional practices of the classroom limit Bobby because of his learning disorder?
3. What are your feelings and thoughts about Sonia's experience in college?
4. What are the ways the college's policies limited Sonia's chance to pursue her education like other students?
5. What could be done to change that in Sonia's case?
6. Do any of us, or people we know, have physical disabilities? What discrimination have we, or they, faced?
7. What are other kinds of learning disorders beside attention deficits? Do any of us, or people we know, have learning disorders? What discrimination have we, or they, faced?
8. What changes have been made to help provide improved opportunities for people with physical disabilities and learning disorders? What ones still need to be made?

GOING FURTHER Ask people with physical disabilities or learning differences to come to the class and speak about their experiences. If there are students in your class or school with particular disabilities, have other students learn more about those disabilities and talk with those students about their experiences with discrimination. Students can plan together to make any possible changes in the school that would be supportive of those students.

Resources to Learn More about Different Abilities

All Kinds of Minds: A Young Students' Book About Learning Abilities and Learning Disorders by Dr. Mel Levine is an accessible and positive book written from the point of view of young people who have learning disorders. It can sensitize all students, with or without learning difficulties, to the different kinds of minds we all have and to the strengths and difficulties young people face when their minds work differently.

American Sign Language, like any other language, has its own grammar, syntax and idioms. Useful children's books on ASL include: Mary Beth Sullivan's *A Show of Hands: Say It in Sign Language* and Lou Ann Walker's *Hand, Heart, and Mind*. These books can help readers better understand the conflict between *oralism* which proposes that deaf people learn to speak standard English, lip read, and use hearing aids and *manualism* which supports ASL as the primary or exclusive language of deaf people.

SEPARATION

OBJECTIVE To understand heterosexism and homophobia and the situations and feelings of people whose life experience and opportunities are affected by societal discrimination based on sexual orientation.

MATERIALS "Script—Grandfather's Tape," Parts One and Two, p. 152, put on audio tape, if possible.

IMPLEMENTATION Review with student stereotypes of lesbians and gay men they discussed in the lesson "Females and Males: How We're 'Supposed' to Be?" Post definitions of heterosexism and homophobia. Read aloud and discuss with students.

Definitions of Heterosexism and Homophobia

Heterosexism—Discrimination against people because of their sexual orientation. That is discrimination against people because they are in love with people of the same gender (men with other men, women with other women) and choose to be part of same-gender couples rather than mixed-gender couples.
Homophobia—Fear of people who are lesbian, gay or bisexual because of their sexual orientation.

In advance, make an audio tape of Omar's grandfather using the script (p. 152) with an adult male voice. Divide students into pairs mixed by gender. Tell students they will be learning about a boy, Omar, whose life has been hurt by heterosexism.

Omar loved his grandfather a lot. But Omar couldn't see his grandfather often. For the past few months they had been communicating by audio tape recordings. By the time you finish listening to the whole tape, you'll understand why.

Play Grandfather's Tape, Part One. Then tell students they will work in pairs to write Omar's response. Later it will be taped, if possible. Omar wants to be sure to do a few things.

1. Share his feelings with his grandfather.
2. Since he has been studying about discrimination in school, he wants to show his grandfather he understands the ways that his grandfather has been discriminated against because he's gay.
3. Include other things his grandfather will enjoy hearing about.

Students write a response. They check to make sure all three items are included and that ideas of each student in the pair are included. Then play Grandfather's Tape: Part Two. Discuss any concepts children might not understand, such as child custody agreements. Again students write a response. They check for the three parts and for inclusion of the ideas of both students.

Try to arrange for students to tape their scripts by sharing whatever tape recorders can be made available. Even though Omar is a male, partners share the taping. When finished, sets of pairs play their tapes for each other. You and the students might choose several tapes to play for the whole class.

Discussing Heterosexism with Students

Be sensitive to the values of your community. It is usually wise to discuss heterosexism as one form of discrimination among many and to put it under an umbrella of diversities that are important to educate students about. It is often advisable to focus on issues of discrimination and equity and not engage students' questions that specifically relate to sex, by explaining that those questions are most appropriately discussed in sex education classes and with their families.

DISCUSSION

1. How did you feel about the situation of Omar and his grandfather at the beginning of the activity? How did your feelings change, if they did, over the course of doing the activity? Why?
2. How did your tape, or tapes of others you listened to, show how heterosexism affected the life of Omar and his grandfather? What institutions reinforced heterosexism?
3. How do you see heterosexism or homophobia affecting people you know or know about?
4. What can be done to change heterosexism and homophobia?
5. What have you learned that's important to you from this lesson? How can you share that with others?

Heterosexual Privilege

If you are a heterosexual person there are some privileges you may not notice that you have. . . .
- The right to health insurance through your spouse/partner's employer.
- The right to not feel compelled to disprove the myths of your own heterosexuality.
- The right to not fear that your sexuality may affect the custody of your child, the job you want, the house you would like to buy, or the way you are treated by others.
- The right to be legal guardian in the event of a disabling accident or illness of your partner.
- The right to visit your partner or spouse when hospitalized.
- The right to be seen as a whole person, rather than be judged solely by your sexual orientation.

GROWING UP JEWISH IN THE U.S. TODAY

OBJECTIVES   To have students better understand anti-Semitism and the effects it has on the lives of in-dividual people.
To have students understand how institutional policies reinforce anti-Semitism, sometimes consciously and sometimes through lack of information or awareness.

MATERIALS   Copies of "Worksheet #1: Growing Up Jewish in the U.S. Today—Aliza and Amber's Cor-respondence," pp. 153–155, one per student. Type a "Worksheet #2: Growing Up Jewish in the U.S. Today—Discussion Questions"; make one per group of three. (See Implementation for questions.)

IMPLEMENTATION   Divide students into groups of three. Give each student one set of "Worksheet #1." Each student reads aloud one pair of letters to her group. After each pair is read, students dis-cuss the contents of the letters to be sure they understand what is being said. On a sepa-rate paper they list any questions that puzzle them.
After they are finished reading the letters students in each trio work collaboratively on the "Worksheet #2," which lists these questions:

1. Anti-Semitism is discrimination against Jewish people. List examples of anti-Semitism in this set of letters.
2. Sometimes people who are Jewish think of the United States as a Christian country even though there is no official religion here. Find examples in these letters that help you understand why people might feel this way. Also list any other examples your group can think of.
3. List other examples of anti-Semitism that Aliza and Amber don't mention in their letters.
4. Write down any questions you have or any things that still puzzle you.

Gather as a whole class for a discussion.

DISCUSSION   1. Discuss Worksheet questions together.
2. How might you find out the answers to the Worksheet questions that still puzzle you? How can you help each other answer these? How could adults help you? What can we do as a class to pursue these?
3. How do institutional policies in the U.S. discriminate against Jewish people?
4. What changes have been made to lessen this discrimination? What changes still need to be made?

LET'S TALK ABOUT TALK

OBJECTIVES   To better understand linguicism (language discrimination) and the impact that has on all peoples.

To learn how institutions reinforce discrimination.

To consider the impact language patterns and language fluency has on how we communicate.

MATERIALS   Paper and pencils; "Worksheet: Let's Talk About Talk," pp. 156–158, 2 copies of each Long Character Description, 4 or 6 copies of each Short Character Description.

IMPLEMENTATION   Begin with a class discussion on language discrimination. Have students ever experienced discrimination because of the way they talk? Have they ever witnessed such discrimination? Participated in it? Record student answers on newsprint so you can refer to these in the final discussion. Explain to students that, in this lesson, they will be exploring a number of different ways that children in this country experience institutional discrimination because of language fluency or language patterns.

This lesson has three main characters: Sarita, Bing, and Ililani. Divide students into six groups, so that each character is the focus in two groups. Give one member of each group a "Long Character Description" of their focal character. Give the other members of the group each a "Short Character Description."

Allow the six students with the "Long Character Descriptions" time to read these. Have the two children playing each character get together and talk about their character. While this is happening the other children work in their character groups, each group consisting of two or three children who have read the same "Short Character Description." They discuss the following questions: If you could get a chance to speak with your character, what would you ask? What would help you understand her or his experience better?

The students with the "Long Character Descriptions" then join the appropriate character groups. Each character group writes a dialogue between their focal character and the classmates listed at the end of the "Short Character Descriptions." The student in each group who received the "Long Character Description" becomes the focal character and the others become the classmates. They ask questions to try to understand the character's experience of language discrimination. Each dialogue needs to include: (a) the classmates' trying to understand both the general issue and (b) at least one specific situation where the focal character was discriminated against because of language-related issues.

Each group reads its dialogue aloud to the whole class. Class discussion compares the similarities and differences between the two groups that did each character and between characters. Talk about Discussion Questions.

1. What questions did you learn were good questions for understanding your focal character's experiences?
2. What were the similarities between the two scenes of the same character? Between different characters? What might cause these similarities? What were the differences between the two versions of each character? Between characters? What might cause these differences?
3. What was easy about understanding the experiences of your character? What was difficult?
4. What are some questions you still have about your focal character that the person in that role couldn't help to answer? How can we find out more about these situations?
5. How did the institutional practices of the classroom limit the opportunities that each of these students had for learning the most they could learn?
6. How did individuals, teachers and students, contribute to this discrimination?

Each group now works to address a discrimination situation that came up in their dialogue. They write a paragraph about how the character and a few friends might address the issue raised.

Groups post these and read them aloud. The whole class discusses the issues raised. See Discussion Questions.

DISCUSSION

1. What are the similarities and differences in the ways you chose to address the issues?
2. In what ways were these beneficial for addressing the problems raised? In what ways were they not?
3. What are some advantages of speaking more than one language as in Bing's case, or speaking more than one dialect of English as in Sarita's? How could schools acknowledge these advantages rather than see them as liabilities?
4. What can you learn from those students who have language patterns and language abilities different from yours?
5. Look back at the list you made at the beginning of this lesson. Now compare your own experiences to those of the children in these scenarios. What similarities and differences are there in your situation and those of these characters?

GOING FURTHER

1. Students could investigate language programs in their community. These may include: two-way bilingual programs, ESL (English as a Second Language) programs, TBE (Transitional Bilingual Education) programs or others. If possible they may want to get in touch with students in these programs to learn more about their experiences.
2. Students may want to find out if there are LEP (Limited English Proficiency) students in their school system. They could work together, perhaps in pairs, to help each other. The LEP students could learn more English. The English fluent students could learn more about the experience of being in an American school without fluent English and could also begin to learn another language.

Bilingual Programs

Some districts now have two-way bilingual programs. In these programs students fluent only in English have the opportunity to develop fluency in another language and those students fluent in the other language have the opportunity to become fluent in English. These programs are focused on English and one other language that is the language of origin for half the students. Students begin in kindergarten in mixed classes with some of the students native speakers of English and others native speakers of the other language. Structures for these programs vary in terms of how students have the opportunity to receive instruction in both languages. In any case students receive instruction in mixed groups and in all subjects in both languages so that, by the time they reach upper elementary grades, they are able to read, write and speak both languages and able to do school work, such as science or mathematics, in both languages.

Ms. Yung: Last night did any of you ask your parents if they could go on our class hike? Remember we need five parents in order to be allowed to go.

Eduardo: I tried to get my dad to take the day off but he didn't think his boss would let him.

Tessy: After both my parents said no, I called Janet, Heidi, and Mark and none of their parents could come either. I even asked my aunt, but she's got her computer class that day.

Ms. Yung: We certainly have a problem. I'd hate to see us cancel the hike.

Angela: My mom's working that day, but my grandma can come. She said she'd be really happy to.

Ms. Yung: That was really nice of you Angela, but this is going to be a hard hike. You can tell your grandma that we appreciate her offer, but really I don't think it's a hike that grandmas could do.

Angela: You said we really need more grown-ups and Grandma would be fine. She likes hiking.

Ms. Yung: Later this year, Angela, we're going to do a baking project for our unit on colonial America. Why don't you see if your grandma would like to help us then?

Angela: My grandma does like to bake and she's good. I bet she'd come then and also come on our hike—especially if she likes the class.

Ms. Yung: No, Angela, I meant the baking instead of the hike. Hiking isn't what grandmas do. Tell her how kind it is, but we'll keep trying to find parents.

Tessy: Ms. Yung, I was at Angela's last week and her grandma. . . .

Renee is a Filipina-American. Because the Philippines was a Spanish colony for almost three hundred years, Renee, like many other Filipino/as, has a Spanish surname. In 1849, the Spanish governor of the Philippines handed down an order which decreed what family names Filipino/as should bear. Many of the approved names were, of course, Spanish. In the U.S., this has caused confusion. Instead of being properly identified as Asian Americans, many Filipino/as are mistakenly categorized as Hispanic.

My name is Renee Ramos. I have six people in my family—Ramona, Abba, Anna, my mother and father. I am the oldest of the children. My mother does housework for people. She relies on me to help with the family chores, including baby-sitting my sisters and brother.

I am in the fifth grade. I go to Longfellow Elementary School in Berkeley. I like going to Longfellow because of my friends. When I play with people, I play with people who I think are nice to play with. They could be black, white, or Asian. I think the only thing that makes a friend is the personality and not the color.

There are some things I dislike about Longfellow. There are people who tease me about the food that I bring to school and because I am Asian; they act as if these things are bad. But I'm not ashamed of what they say because I know what I am, and I'm proud of it!. Sometimes I say to them, "I am proud I am," and other times I keep it to myself. I feel better keeping it to myself because I know not to be ashamed when people say that.

One thing about my family is, we never leave anybody out in what we do. If we were in trouble, we would help each other.

My mother usually stays home and keeps house. She is very responsible as a mother. She is happy when we are. I try to make her have the least trouble with my sisters and brother. She is always helpful with our personal problems and I take advice from her.

My father likes to talk. He fights for the rights of working people. He goes to union meetings which concern the liberation of farm workers and equal opportunities for jobs and homes for Asians, blacks, and Chicanos. I agree with him in every way.

There are both negative and positive things that happen because I'm an Asian American. A negative thing is that people stereotype Asians by saying, "All Asians are quiet and they can't do this or that." A positive thing is that when the class is talking about Asians, I can share my experiences with the class. Once on a school bus a black girl told her friend to sit by me and the other girl said, "I don't want to sit by that Chinese or Japanese girl."

"I WISH EVERYONE WOULD SEE ASIANS AS PEOPLE."

From *Asian American Women* by Yolanda Yokota and Linda Wing, pp. 83–84.

Most of the other kids in my class seem to like school. They know each other. I love learning about new things, but I feel so different.

When we go around the class and tell what our fathers and mothers do, they say salesman, doctor, nurse, teacher, computer programmer. When I say farm workers, some kids laugh and whisper.

That makes me so mad. My parents work very hard as farm workers. The problem is they can only work five months of the year—the time of picking. They try and try to work during the other seven months, but people always say, "We don't have any jobs." They don't want to move the family all year to follow the crops, because then I couldn't stay in one school.

I feel left out a lot. I hear the other kids talk about parties. No one ever invites me.

But the biggest problem is clothes. Some kids have so many different outfits—they act so important about it. When some of them talk about clothes, they glance at me from the corner of their eyes.

One day my teacher asked me to stay in by myself at recess. She said quietly, "Lizzie, I see you've been wearing the same clothes to school every day this week. Don't you have anything else?"

I stared down at the floor. I was wearing my only school clothes—a pair of jeans and a red and white striped T-shirt. I'd been given them by my older cousin. My mother tried to make them look nice. She washed them every other day and patched the places that were torn. I guess they were so old that nothing could make them look good anymore. My mother also made sure I took a bath every day, so even if my clothes were old, I was clean.

I didn't say anything. The teacher asked me again, "Are those your only clothes, dear? I just want to help."

I nodded my head. She kept on talking. "I have a good idea. I'll ask the other girls if they have any outgrown clothes school clothes they could give you. I'm sure you'll feel much better that way."

I couldn't answer. I bit my lip and kept looking down. The teacher told me I could go out to play. I walked out as quickly as I could. I felt so angry and embarrassed! The teacher will tell the other kids to bring in clothes for "poor Lizzie."

It would be okay if the girls were usually nice to me and let me be their friend. Then they might *want* to share their friendship and clothes. This way, though . . . I wanted to hide and never come back to school.

Three days later, my teacher asked me to see her after school. I looked down at my red and white shirt and knew what was happening. She gave me two brown paper grocery bags with folded up clothes in them. "Thank you, Ms. Smyth," I said, trying hard to smile.

The next day I wore one of the outfits—green corduroy pants and a flowered blouse. At recess that day I heard Carita whispering to Tina, "That's my old blouse Lizzie has on. I bet she'll get it all dirty and smelly. I'm sure glad I don't have to sit next to her."

Tina whispered back, "I feel bad for her. She must have lazy parents if they don't even buy her clothes for school."

If Carita and Tina had come over to me right then, I'd . . .

134

Marcie and Sonia are two women in their middle twenties who live in the town of North Jefferson. Both graduated from high school with a strong background in science, math, and auto mechanics. Since then they have worked in Bob Miller's auto repair shop. By now they have had seven years experience on the job. They have excellent reputations as auto mechanics.

Marcie and Sonia have all the skills they need to open their own shop, M. and S. Auto Repair. The women have saved the money they need to get their business going.

Sonia called the owner of a local garage to ask if it was for rent. The garage-owner said, "Sure, lady. Have your husband come over any time. I'm eager to rent."

Sonia went to the garage-owner later that afternoon. He said, "Where's your husband?" When she told him she wanted to rent it for herself he laughed in her face. "What? *You* want to rent the garage! What a joke."

"I'm not married. I'm an auto mechanic and here is my down payment."

"Look, lady, I'm not renting this to you. I'll lose money. You'll never be able to pay your rent. Nobody in this town will come to a garage run by women. Give up your pie-in-the-sky idea."

1. Describe how you might feel if you were Sonia.

2. How does the garage-owner show prejudice toward Sonia?

3. What are the stereotypes about women that the garage-owner has?

4. How do these stereotypes hurt Marcie and Sonia?

5. How will these stereotypes hurt the residents of North Jefferson?

Skit Focus: Physical Disability

Setting: It is October. Third through fifth grade children are at recess on the playground.

Characters:

Jasmine—9 years old, has cerebral palsy, needs to use a wheelchair, difficult for others to understand her spoken language

Roneisha, José, Matthew, Susanna, James—all "typically developing" 8, 9, and 10 year olds.

Skit:

José: Let's play some basketball. I brought my new ball today.

Susanna: Great idea! I'm all set. *(She runs to the blacktop that has the basketball net.)*

Roneisha: Hey, wait for me. I want to push Jasmine's wheelchair over with us.

Matthew: Great idea, maybe she can be the referee.

Susanna: How could she do that, I bet she doesn't even know the rules.

Roneisha: Sure she knows the rules. We watch basketball on TV a bunch.

James: But we won't be able to understand her even if she does tell us something.

Susanna: And she won't be able to move herself out of the way if the ball is coming at her.

Roneisha: Stop talking about Jasmine as though she can't hear. She hears fine. Jasmine, do you want to come over to our basketball game?

Jasmine: Yes.

José: How come she can understand us, when we can hardly ever understand her?

James: This is dumb. We're wasting recess time discussing this. And it's gonna slow us down to have to try to understand what she's saying.

Matthew: Don't you guys get it? Jasmine can hear fine. And she can think fine. And she wants to come to our game. Jasmine, do you know the rules of basketball?

Jasmine: Yes, I love basketball.

Roneisha: So, what are we waiting for, let's give her a chance.

José: Matthew, I think I want to understand about Jasmine. Recess is a half hour. We can spend a few more minutes trying to figure this out.

Susanna: Well, I'm going to find some people who are more fun. I don't want to spend my recess just talking when I could be playing. And playing with people who can move around and think and who you can understand.

Roneisha: Jasmine thinks really well. Once you learn to understand her you can have great conversations. It's just hard at first.

José: Well then, how come she acts, you know, sort of, you know, retarded?

Roneisha: It's just that you're not used to trying to understand someone whose speech is different. She can't control the way her body moves so that looks funny to you.

Matthew: If you pay attention and really listen to Jasmine, you can ask her questions and you'll realize that she's plenty smart.

Write the rest of this skit with whatever you think happens next.

Skit Focus: Language Differences

Setting: It is February. Fourth grade children are in the classroom at indoor recess.

Characters:

Maireid, Hajah, Erica, André and Margarita—all fourth graders, all of whom speak fluent English, and Jorge, a Salvadoran boy who has been in the United States for 10 months. He speaks fluent Spanish and somewhat limited English.

Skit:

The skit begins with Maireid, Hajah and Erica talking.

Maireid: I have a great idea. Let's write a play for the talent show.

Hajah: Let's ask Erica and André to join us. Erica's really good at mime and André's really funny when he imitates voices.

Maireid: Maybe we should ask Margarita too. Everyone loves her dancing.

Maireid and Hajah go and ask Erica, André and Margarita. They all say "yes."

Erica: What should our play be about? Should we act out a movie?

Hajah: I think it'd be more fun to make something up. And I want it to be funny.

Margarita: Maybe we could do something from one of the stories we've written in school.

André: How about something about the teachers in this school?

Maireid: Don't you think they'd get mad?

André: Not if we really were funny.

Margarita: Maybe we should see if Jorge wants to join us too. He's got a great imagination and he's really expressive.

Maireid: But it's so hard to talk with him.

André: We'd end up having to explain everything THREE times!

Erica: Margarita, how can you tell he's got a great imagination? He never says anything.

Margarita: Sure he does. You have to give him space. And take time to listen.

Hajah: But we'd never get done on time. It's easier to have it just be us. We all speak the same.

Margarita: I still think it's worth a try. I think you'll really like him and we'll end up with a better skit.

Maireid: He's over there playing *Myst* on the computer. Maybe we should go talk with him and see if we can understand anything.

André: Sure it's worth a try.

The whole group goes over to Jorge at the computer.

Write the rest of the skit about what happens once they start talking with Jorge.

Skit Focus: Anti–Semitism

Setting: It is March. A group of fifth and sixth graders are walking to school.

Characters:

Ernethia, Bob, Alfredo, Priscilla, Josh and Will

Skit:

Bob: I can't wait. Baseball will be starting soon.

Priscilla: Yeah. It's less than a month. This year there's going to be some mixed teams of girls and boys.

Alfredo: I think that's great. I know some of the boys didn't like the idea when it was discussed this fall, but I bet they'll be fine once we start playing.

Ernethia: I hope it doesn't have to be that all the girls have to be real hotshots in order to be accepted.

Bob: Nah. You just have to want to play. Our league isn't really a competitive one.

Will: Hey, stop, look at that money on the ground. I bet Josh will go after it.

Josh: Huh? Why? I deliver newspapers and I get an allowance. I don't need that money.

Will: But Jews always want money. That's what my uncle says.

Josh: Not me. And when I need money I earn it, just like any of you.

Ernethia: But don't Jews always want more money. And don't they want to be richer than other people?

Priscilla: What are you talking about? What does religion have to do with money?

Bob: Think about what we learn in history and in religion. Jews were money lenders. That's because they liked money.

Will: And Jews came to this country poor, but got rich in just one generation. That's different from what other groups did.

Alfredo: I bet there are lots of reasons for that. We need to understand more. It's dumb to believe something just because someone told it to you.

Josh: My family isn't rich. And we don't try to be rich. My parents have regular kinds of jobs. And my sister and I both deliver newspapers so we earn a little more. But it's not so we'll be rich, it's so we'll have a little spending money and it helps our parents out.

Ernethia: So if it isn't true that Jews always go after getting more money, why are we taught that? People don't just make stuff like that up, do they?

Continue this conversation as you think it might have happened.

Josh

You are a sixth grade boy and like some of the same things your friends do, but like different things too. You are really into computers and play computer games with your friends whenever you have a chance. You like making models, especially cars.

Ever since you were young, you've loved dancing. You've been taking both tap and ballet and are excellent at each. This is how you stay in shape. You aren't too interested in sports and play only when kids really need an extra player. You don't like clothes with sports teams on them and prefer to wear clothes that express your personality.

Today when your class was waiting for physical education to start, your friend Todd asked you to come to his house after school. You said you were busy, but he kept asking you what you were doing. You didn't want to tell him, but finally to make him stop bugging you you told him you had a dance class.

Unfortunately a few other students heard you and snickered, "faggot." You were really hurt and humiliated to be picked on like that. You have a right to your interests. You feel like you never want to come back this school.

Jenna

You're a sixth grade girl. In some ways you are like other girls in your grade, and in some ways you're not. You love music and play the flute. You also love kids and earn extra money by babysitting. You and your cousin have a babysitting service that's been very successful.

You enjoy hanging out with the boys in your grade more than girls because they play football, basketball or baseball after school. You play with them as much as they'll let you. You really don't care about dating boys, though. You don't call up boys, give them presents or talk about boys all the time the way some girls in your grade do. You think that's a waste of time. Your special interests, like music, are more important to you.

Today after school when you were waiting for the bus a group of girls next to you were talking about boys. One said to another, "Jenna never gets excited talking about boys. I bet she's a lesbian." Another girl looked at you and said, "Hi there, lesbian."

You felt very embarrassed and angry when they did that. What's wrong with having your own interests. You're glad you're not "boy crazy" like they are. Sometimes you wish you could just move away.

1. Joe gets hit in the eye with a baseball. He starts to cry. The other guys begin to make fun of him. You feel bad for him, but chime in with the other guys and say, "Don't be a sissy."

2. You want to build a pen for your dog. The only person around tall enough to help you is Ramona. You say, "I need a boy to help me." You don't get help and the dog runs away.

3. Some Latino students ask you to join their group to do a math project. You think they're not so smart, so you join another group. Their group gets an A, yours doesn't.

4. You are a fine dancer, and would like to take up ballet. You're afraid the other guys will make fun of you. You give up your plan, lots of good exercise, and a possible career.

5. You fall and think you've broken your ankle. A black woman who is a doctor offers to look at it. You don't trust her so you refuse. You end up lying there in pain for hour before someone else comes to help you.

6. Joan's family doesn't have much money. They live in a different neighborhood than you. She invites you to her birthday party. You don't go because you think her house will be messy and dirty. You miss a great time and a clean house.

7. You missed the bus and need a ride to school. Ms. Mendez is 82. She offered to drive you. You think she'll drive off the road. You kill your feet walking the four miles to school.

8. Your younger sister keeps calling her friend a "wild Indian." She shoots him again and again with a toy gun. You don't challenge her.

9. You don't invite Richard to your birthday party because he is blind. You love drama and plan to play a version of charades at your birthday. You figure he can't play if he can't see. You miss finding out how creative and funny he is.

10. You think the chess club advisor is a lesbian. You really like playing chess but don't join the club because you don't want to travel with her. You lose out on improving your chess game and having the fun of playing with the club.

11. A new family, the Epsteins, moves in near you. They don't decorate for Christmas or Easter. Your parents tell you that's because they're Jewish. Not doing anything for your favorite holidays seems strange to you. You think you have nothing in common with them and don't include them when you organize the neighborhood talent show. You miss finding out that Mrs. Epstein does jazz dance and Mr. Epstein juggles.

12. A few of the African American kids in your class speak really differently when they talk with each other than when they talk in class. Their out of class talk sounds odd to you and makes you think you can't be friends with them. You don't try. You miss out on some possible new friends and on learning about Black English.

_____ People are seen and treated differently because of _____.
A, B, C, D, E, F, or G

_____ is/are viewed as better or more important than others and has/have more power in
2

society. In our society those people are _____. Values and practices of institutions
3

(schools, families, churches, media, etc.) support these inequalities.

KEY WORDS (Fill in according to "ism" being discussed.)

A: *Racism* 1) skin color; 2) one race; 3) whites.
B: *Sexism* 1) being male or female; 2) one sex; 3) males.
C: *Classism* 1) the amount of money a person/family has; 2) some classes; 3) upper-class and middle-class.
D: *Ageism* 1) age; 2) certain ages; 3) adults (not elderly).
E. *Heterosexism* 1) the gender of who they love; 2) one sexual orientation; 3) heterosexuals.
F. *Ableism* 1) physical, mental, and emotional abilities; 2) those fully abled; 3) people with no physical, mental or emotional disability.
G. *Anti-semitism* 1) religion; 2) one religious group; 3) Christians.
H. *Linguicism* 1) how they speak; 2) those who speak a particular language or a particular way; 3) those whose English is fluent and unaccented.

EXAMPLES

Racism: Jean walks through her school and notices there is only one picture of a person of color on the bulletin boards. The school bulletin boards show racism.
Sexism: Laurie wants to be on a baseball team. Applications were only given to boys. Laurie calls the recreation department and she's told girls should sign up for the girls' softball league. The recreation department reinforces sexism.
Classism: Dominick looks through his social studies book and realizes that most of the people who are described as "important" are people with prestige and money. Few working-class or poor people are emphasized, even though their hard work built the nation. The textbook publishing company encourages classism.
Ageism: For a school project, Lamar did a study of television shows and found that only three percent of the characters were over sixty years old, even though in real life in this country over fifteen percent of the people are over sixty. Lamar concluded that the television industry reinforces ageism.
Heterosexism: Arij is doing a project on messages in advertising. She notices that all the ads that show teenagers or young adults dating show males and females as couples. None show people of the same gender in relationships. The advertising companies support heterosexism.
Ableism: Miguel brought a friend to church with him. His friend needs a wheelchair. Miguel and his mother had to pull the wheelchair up several steps to get it into the church because there was no door that was accessible. Miguel's church maintains ableism.
Anti-Semitism: Gary's mother is directing a children's play for their community arts program. Children of many religions are in the play, including Jews. She organized the dress rehearsal on Rosh Hashanah, the religious holiday marking the Jewish New Year. The community arts program reinforces anti-Semitism.
Linguicism: Margarita's family moved to a new state for a better job for her father. When they got there they discovered that it is a state that has an "English only law". This meant that Margarita would get less support in bilingual education than she needed in school. The legal system there sustains linguicism.

1. Jobs are divided in the Wright family. Susan must do the dishes and vacuum the rug. She doesn't like these jobs! Peter's jobs are to mow the lawn and weed the garden. Peter likes getting exercise while doing his jobs. Susan would like to have some of Peter's jobs, but her parents say she must learn "women's work."

   Susan probably feels _____.

   Peter might feel_____.

   The Wright parents encourage _____.

2. Laverne did a survey of her school library books. She found that most characters over sixty were described as old, ill, and helpless, or as active grandparents eagerly involved in projects. Laverne's own grandparents are alert and energetic *and* also face many health problems that often come with old age.

   Laverne probably feels_____.

   Her grandparents might feel _____.

   Children's book publishing companies reinforce _____.

3. Ralph's father works in a factory. He is a hard worker and hardly ever misses a day of work. He makes $8 an hour, or $320 a week. This comes out to $16,000 a year. Ralph is an excellent student and would like to become a doctor. His family can't afford it. Even scholarships can't cover the $160,000 or more needed to get medical training.

   Ralph probably feels_____.

   Colleges and medical schools support_____.

4. Myra and Dwayne are excited because today they are going to the store to buy a board game. They walk up and down the aisles and notice that there are only four black children on any of the game boxes.

   Dwayne is black. He might feel _____.

   Myra is white. She might feel_____.

   Toy companies reinforce _____.

5. Students in Hannah's dancing school need to earn money to buy costumes for their dance recital. The dance teacher announces that all dance students will be expected to sell Christmas cards to raise money. Hannah is Jewish.

Hannah probably feels_____.

Hannah's dancing school promotes_____.

6. Rosa was adopted by Gina and Carolyn, so Rosa has two mothers. She knows other children, too, with either two mothers or two fathers. When Rosa was filling out her camp application there was a space for "Mother" and another for "Father."

Rosa might have felt_____.

The camp maintains _____.

7. Gilberto loves reading. Since Gilberto is blind he needs to read books in braille. He went to the library to get books, but they didn't have any books in braille.

Gilberto might have felt _____.

The library reinforces _____.

8. Soo Nam's family recently immigrated to the U.S. and lives in a community where there is a large population of Koreans. When he was admitted to the community hospital none of the signs or the paperwork that he had to fill out were in Korean.

Soo Nam might have felt_____.

The hospital supports _____.

Definitions

Individualism—A belief that people should look out for themselves first before thinking of other people.

Competition—People work against each other to get something for themselves. There is a winner who is rewarded.

Add individualism and competition and stir:

Competitive individualism—A belief that competition is fair and that each person has an equal chance to succeed or win in a situation. The individualist may feel:

—If I win it's because of how good I am.
—I must compete with others and win in order to feel successful.
—I must feel better than others in order to feel good about myself.

Ms. Lopez's Class

Most boys in Ms. Lopez's class have had lots more experience playing basketball than most girls before they started playing basketball together in physical education class in Davidson School. Many fathers, older siblings or male friends would encourage boys to learn basketball at a young age. Boys practice after school. Boys have many more role models than girls in the media as well.

The boys in Ms. Lopez's sixth-grade class make more baskets than the girls and in general have more basketball skills. In gym class, the boys make negative comments about the girls. They say such things as, "Boys are naturally better ball players. We always knew girls are lousy athletes." The boys call the girls names like "spastic" and "clumsy." Some boys say, "You girls have an equal chance to get points and you don't—that proves boys are the greatest athletes."

Questions

1. Can you tell how the story is an example of competitive individualism? Discuss it with your partner and write down a few ideas.

2. How could you change the story so it wasn't an example of competitive individualism? Write down a few changes.

Explanation

Here's how the story is an example of competitive individualism!

Competitive Individualism: The boys say everyone had an equal chance to succeed.

Reality: Everyone didn't have an equal chance. The boys had three years of practice and skill-building.

Competitive Individualism: The boys pretend they make baskets because they're naturally better than girls.

Reality: Most girls haven't played as much before and haven't been encouraged by society or parents to think they can be good. If girls had equal training and encouragement, many *could* be as good.

Competitive Individualism: The boys feel good about themselves and put the girls down because they get more points than the girls.

Reality: Their feeling of success is not deserved—they had a head start. They put the girls down to make themselves feel good.

Alternative

Here's what could happen to change the story so it wouldn't be an example of competitive individualism.

The teacher would pair up those players who were already skilled in basketball—mostly, but not only, boys—with those students less skilled—mostly, but not only, girls—to practice basketball skills and strategies together. Boys could offer helpful pointers.

Boys would play for a while with a disadvantage in order to make it a fair game. For example they could only use their opposite hand from the one they were used to. Boys would feel good about themselves for helping others to learn. They would feel pleased when girls got baskets too. Girls would feel competent in their new skills and pleased with their friends' support. This would be an example of *cooperation*, which is an alternative to individualism.

Questions

1. What are your thoughts and feelings about this alternative?

2. How would you make such an alternative work?

Below is a letter from Sally to her friend Theresa. Sally is graduating from high school.

Dear Theresa,

I've missed you so much since you've moved away. I'm very sad and discouraged this week. I need a friend to talk to. I wish you were closer by!!

Since you left, Dad got sick and had to quit his job. He probably won't ever be able to go back to work as a salesman. There was no insurance plan in the small company he worked at. All he gets is $640 a month from the government. He's in the hospital and may be there for a long time.

I've told you how much I want to be a doctor. I worked so hard in high school to get good grades. I got a scholarship to an excellent college with a pre-med program, but it covers only part of the cost.

This year I've been helping Mom raise the four younger kids. Her job as a secretary only pays $320 a week. She doesn't get home until 5:30. I'm here after school with them until then.

It's impossible for Mom to pay the rent, buy clothes, and feed the family on her small salary and Dad's monthly check. I'm going to have to give up my idea of college and becoming a doctor and get a full-time job.

Do you know how disappointed and angry I am?! It's not right that I work so hard in school and then have to give up my plan to be a doctor because our family doesn't have enough money. Why should college and medical school be so expensive? Another student just like me, but with parents who make more money, will become a doctor. I won't.

Theresa, do you understand how I feel? Do you think it's fair that people with more money have more chances to become what they want to be?

Please write back!

                                        Your friend,
                                        Sally

Marva and Tyrone Williams are the parents of a three-year-old child, Jamil. Tyrone works as a salesman for a local business, the E.B.M. Company. Marva had stayed home to take care of Jamil.

Before Jamil was born, Marva worked as a secretary. She didn't like the typing too much, but she started to learn about computers. She caught on quickly. Her employer told her she'd be great in that area of work.

When Jamil was two, Marva decided she wanted to return to school to study math and computers. She was nervous about it, but she wanted to try. The local college used radio and newspaper ads to tell women to come back to school.

Last fall Marva decided to take one course. The class met from 4:00 to 6:00. She asked if Tyrone could get off work an hour early a few days a week to take care of Jamil.

Tyrone asked his boss if he could come to work an hour early in the morning. Then he would get off from work an hour sooner in the afternoon to take care of Jamil. His boss looked surprised. "Is babysitting more important than your job?" Tyrone explained he would still work the same number of hours, just different ones. Finally the boss agreed.

Other workers laughed at Tyrone when he'd leave at 3:30. "Off to mind the kid! You won't get ahead in the world like that!" Sometimes his boss would tell Tyrone to stay at a meeting even if it went past 3:30. This would make Marva late for school.

Tyrone was angry at his business. It was supposed to be an "equal opportunity employer." But it didn't help a father change his hours for child-care. Tyrone liked taking care of Jamil very much. Yet he was afraid he would be kept back from advancing in the company for leaving work at 3:30. At the end of her course he told Marva he wouldn't rearrange his schedule again.

Marva had done very well in school and she decided that she would go all day the next term. When she went to enroll Jamil in the college's day-care center, she found out it was full. There was only room for twenty-five children and there was a waiting list of fifty! She was angry! "How can you have ads to tell women to come to school when there's not enough day-care?"

Marva decided to look at day-care centers in her town. There were only three. One was full, one was poor in quality, and the other was too expensive.

Marva was very angry. Messages on TV, radio, and in magazines told women that they could go to school, get a job, and become active in the world. They never said what she had learned: "But don't try it if you have a child."

Marva decided to write an article for the newspaper on how sexism affects parents. If you were Marva, what might you say in that article?

Ted and Juanita Lund face a decision. You will soon understand how difficult their decision is.

Ted is sixty-nine and Juanita is seventy years old. Ted used to work as a gardener. He knows a great deal about plants, flowers, and trees. He loved his work. His only regret was that he was paid so little. Juanita worked as a clerk in an office. She found the work boring, yet she was pleased that she could help support the family.

Ted and Juanita saved their money so they could buy the house they now live in. Over the past twenty-five years, Juanita and Ted have made furniture and decorations for the inside of the house so it feels like "home." Their garden is outstanding. Both work hour after hour in their yard. The beautiful flowers and flowering bushes are admired by all who pass by. The Lunds get much pleasure out of their garden!

Juanita had to retire from her full-time job at age sixty-five. Then she tried to get a part-time job working with people. She was tired of working with files and was eager to work with children. She applied for many jobs. She was always told, "We only hire people who already have had jobs working with children. Besides, we want someone who can work with us for many years." Juanita didn't feel old. Now she had the time to do something she always wanted to do—and she couldn't find a job.

Juanita was angry she couldn't get a job for another reason—they needed the money. It was too hard to live on the small Social Security check they got each month. Prices for food and clothes kept going up. By budgeting their money *very* carefully, they were able to pay their bills. Nothing was left.

Six months ago, Ted had a major operation. He was in the hospital for a month. Now he is getting better at home. He still has to take a lot of medicine and visit the doctor often.

The bills for Ted's medical care were very high. His insurance paid for some of it, but there are still a lot of bills that the Lunds have to pay themselves. They don't have that much money in the bank.

Juanita and Ted are faced with a painful decision. Should they sell their house to have more money in the bank to use to pay their bills and for future expenses? Then they could pay for things their insurance didn't cover, like Ted's physical therapy. They could move into apartments for the elderly. Yet this is their home. Ted and Juanita get very sad when they think of leaving the house that they put so much work into. The greatest joy in their life still comes from working in their garden.

Lillie is eleven years old, the oldest of five children. Lillie lives with her mother and three sisters and brother in a rural county in Maryland. Her father left the family when she was eight.

Lillie's mother, Carolyn Raley, loves her children very much. She's going to college in order to become a teacher. It's not easy to raise a family and be a student in college. Carolyn has worked hard, though, and will graduate in a month. She hopes to join the small number of black women teachers in the county. Until a few years ago, the school system hadn't hired any black teachers.

Since Lillie's father left, the family has been on welfare. Carolyn and her children don't like to be on welfare. However, this is the only way they can survive. Carolyn is very happy that soon she'll be a teacher so *she* can support her family.

There is only one set of apartments in this county that low-income people can afford. This is where Lillie and her family live. About half the people living there are black. The landlord doesn't take care of the apartments. When their water pipe broke, the landlord didn't have it repaired for four days. Lillie's family was without water the whole time. Carolyn's many phone calls to him made no difference. Furthermore, the landlord doesn't like black people. When Lillie met him once and asked him to make repairs, he replied, "Waiting a few days won't hurt your type of people, kid."

Last week the heat was off for three days. Carolyn called the landlord. When nothing happened she called the county housing office. Someone said, "We'll talk to your landlord"—but still no heat. Carolyn was furious. Her children were freezing and nothing was being done.

Carolyn decided to organize a rent strike. This meant that none of the people living in the apartments would pay their rent until the landlord promised that he would make repairs on time. Since the other people in the apartments had problems with no heat and no water, they were all willing to work together in the rent strike. Carolyn was so hopeful. "Now, maybe we can have a decent place to live after all. The landlord will certainly change his ways now!"

The day before the rent strike was to start, Carolyn came to Lillie's room. She looked very upset. "The landlord just called me on the phone. He said, 'You're a rotten colored troublemaker. If you don't call off this rent strike, I'll make sure you never get a teaching job in this county. Never!'"

Lillie, I'm so angry and confused. I want to stand up for our rights. We deserve to have good housing since we pay our rent. Everyone is so determined to finally stand up to the landlord. I don't want to let them down. But, Lillie, I so much want to be a teacher! Worst of all, the landlord is good friends with the superintendent of schools and the head of the county housing office. They all stick together and have so much power in the county. Lillie, how do you feel about this?

Mr. Wilson's class is making a class booklet on "Institutional Discrimination: How It Affects People We Know." Each student will interview one person affected by discrimination and all the interviews will be compiled into a class booklet. Below is Rose's interview with her brother, Bobby.

Rose: Tell us a little about yourself, Bobby.

Bobby: I'm ten years old. I'm a kid who likes to have a lot of fun. I have great ideas and I love to imagine fantastic inventions, tell creative stories and play practical jokes.

Rose: Tell us what happened to you in school, Bobby.

Bobby: Last year I was in a class where I got into a lot of trouble. My teacher had us sit at our desks and work for long periods of time. That was really hard for me. I had to get up and move around and I got yelled at when I did. My teacher put my desk next to the window. It was so tempting to look out, then my mind would wander and I couldn't answer any question. My teacher would get upset with me—and I'd feel dumb again.

I got in trouble with Carmen, who sat next to me. I had a lot of difficulty sitting still and my arms and legs kept wanting to move. Sometimes they'd hit Carmen, by accident. I'd get punished. Finally, we never did much of my favorite subject—creative writing. We had to write about real life—I like to use my imagination. When I asked my teacher if I could do more creative writing she said I had to do better on my other work first.

Rose: I know it was a hard year because I remember you never wanted to go to school. You felt like you were being discriminated against.

Bobby: Yes!! Also I felt like I was the most bad and stupid kid around!

Rose: Later you found out that you really were being hurt by the normal practices of that classroom. How did you find out?

Bobby: Finally Mom took me to a pediatrician and I got a very complete check up. It included some tests that were like puzzles and games that helped Dr. Valdez understand my way of learning and thinking. Dr. Valdez told Mom that I was very smart, but I had a learning disorder called an attention deficit. That meant I had trouble paying attention and concentrating.

Rose: Didn't she say too that it's hard for kids with attention deficit to sit still and listen?

Bobby: Right! That's why my body kept moving—and hitting Carmen. Also we are distractible—that means we pay attention to little things, like the fly outside the window. Dr. Valdez told me that an attention deficit is something I was probably born with and some of my problems were not my fault.

Rose: What's happening now that you know this?

Bobby: I'm changing some things I can change. Also my school is changing a lot so that instead of hurting me as an ADD kid, it will help me. This year I'm in a regular class where we work in groups and I can move around a lot more. My teacher put my seat right in the front of the room where I look at her and won't be distracted as much. Whenever she sees me go on a mind trip, she taps me on the shoulder so I tune in again.

Rose: Don't you do lots of creative drawing and writing now?

Bobby: Yes. I like that a lot. Now I feel much better about school—and I'm starting to like myself too!

Mr. Wilson's class is making a class booklet on "Institutional Discrimination: How it Affects People We Know." Each student will interview one person affected by discrimination and all the interviews will be compiled into a class booklet. Below is Nydia's interview with her Aunt Sonia.

Nydia: Tell us a little about yourself, Aunt Sonia.

Sonia: I'm 35 years old. I'm married and have two children. I work at a group home for people with disabilities. I'm deaf and communicate with many people using American Sign Language.

Nydia: That's why I can interview you—because we have Molly here who uses sign language to interpret what you say to me.

Sonia: Yes, and that's why you can understand my ideas. American Sign Language has grammar that is different from standard English, the kind of English you learn in school. I need interpreters except when I'm communicating with people who know American Sign Language themselves.

Nydia: Aunt Sonia, were you always deaf?

Sonia: Yes, I was born without hearing.

Nydia: We've been studying ableism in school. We're learning that our society offers advantages to people who are physically able and that sometimes institutions discriminate against people with disabilities. Have you faced this?

Sonia: Yes, I have. For example when I was younger I couldn't go to many events with my friends, plays for example, because there was no interpreter. More recently I couldn't go to some talks and lectures at my college and in the community for the same reason.

Nydia: Are you facing discrimination now in your life?

Sonia: Yes I am. Here is the situation. I want to go back to college to get my Master's degree so I can be more effective in my job. Thanks to the Americans with Disabilities Act, which is a federal law, there are many sources of support to people with disabilities that there weren't when I was growing up.

Nydia: What are some of those?

Sonia: For example, the college must provide me a sign language interpreter for my courses. This is so important to me.

Nydia: So you can get your Masters Degree?

Sonia: Well, we'll see. I need to learn to write much more clearly in standard English. My first language is American Sign Language and it's very hard to translate my thinking and writing into standard English. I need tutoring help to do that.

Nydia: Won't the college give you a tutor?

Sonia: Yes, but none of the tutors knows American Sign Language, so you can imagine it's very difficult to get the help I need. The college does not have to pay for an interpreter for my tutoring sessions. As you know, I can't afford to pay for one either! So I'm feeling stuck! I want to go on with my education like other people can, and being deaf makes it much harder.

Nydia: Good luck, Aunt Sonia! I'm going to find out if there are classes for people my age to learn American Sign Language. If there are, I'll start learning it soon. Then I might be able to help out too.

GRANDFATHER'S TAPE: PART ONE

I've been so sad ever since we've had to talk by tape. I've also been thinking a lot about my life and our lives since your parents got divorced and I haven't been allowed to see you.

You'll remember that when you were six I explained to you that I was gay. I told you that your grandmother and I were married and we had a daughter, your mother. I realized, however, that though I liked your grandmother and other women very much, I felt more attracted to men. Your grandmother and I decided it was best to get a divorce, hard as that was.

A couple of years later I fell in love with Peter. He was a teacher too. The hardest thing about our lives was being "in the closet." This meant that we had to hide the fact that we were gay. Otherwise it would have been possible to lose our jobs. We wouldn't be accepted in our church. Peter and I didn't live together for fear of being "discovered." We were afraid of losing the acceptance of some friends. As you can imagine, this was a very hard way to live.

Omar, you have always been wonderful! We had such good times playing ball, going to the park, and just talking. You accepted Peter as another grandfather. Thanks, Omar, for being a special grandson. Love, Grandfather.

GRANDFATHER'S TAPE: PART TWO

Thanks for your tape. It was great to hear from you! I admire your courage. You've been through a lot for a 10 year old.

While I felt sad when your mother and father got divorced last year, I never imagined it would bring such pain to you and me. I have never been angrier in my life as when I learned that your father tried to convince the judge that I was a bad influence on you because I was gay. As part of the child custody agreement he didn't want me to have any time with you. Even though the court didn't give him that, he almost got what he wanted. Three weekends a year is too little time for a grandson and grandfather to see each other, especially when we live 15 miles away from each other! I remember how we both cried when we heard about the judge's decision.

Your idea for making tapes so we can at least hear each others' voices and talk as long as we want was a great one. Hearing one of your tapes makes my day! Take care, Omar. Love, Grandfather.

September 1

Dear Amber,

I'm so excited to be writing to you this year. It was fun to see each other this summer. It's hard to be cousins and really know each other when we live 500 miles apart. I liked all that swimming and the games we played and I also liked the talking we did. I've been thinking about the stuff we were saying about my being Jewish and your being Black (and a little Jewish too.) We got home from vacation and in our mail we found the public school calendar for this year. It turns out school starts on Yom Kippur. That's the holiest day of the Jewish year. It is a day we always stay together as a family. Usually we go to services for part of the day. Do you? It's the day we talk about the whole last year, what we liked and what we felt bad about, and we figure out how we want to act this next year. My parents fast all day and then we have a family "break fast" dinner at night.

So it looks like I'm going to miss THE FIRST DAY of school. I hate that. It's the day kids will figure out their seats, get new books, and decide on class rules. Only a few other kids will be out; I think school will start as if it weren't an important holiday for some of us. Why can't they start school one day earlier or one day later?

Guess what, I'm getting to take gymnastics this year. I'm so excited. Rachel and Felita will both be in my class. I wanted to take last year but it's through the public recreation program in Alvy and last year, they didn't let kids from other cities take it. And Monroe doesn't offer gymnastics in public classes. Lucky for me, this year Alvy started more classes and is letting out of town kids in their classes.

Love,
Aliza

September 20

Dear Aliza,

This is fun. Maybe we can see each other sometime this winter and not just over the summer. My parents are talking about inviting your whole family to visit us in Washington over February vacation. Your parents would probably really like it. They could take you and Sara sightseeing and we could make up plays like we did over the summer.

I really do know what you mean about starting school on Yom Kippur. Our school calendar had that one year. There were some phone calls and complaints from people in town, even some Christian people wrote to the newspaper to say they thought it was wrong. Since the Jewish calendar is different from the regular one, Jewish holidays don't come at the same time every year so I think people forget if it hasn't been a problem for a few years. Anyway, all those letters last time made a difference and this year they started school two days earlier. It means the Jewish kids still missed school on Yom Kippur, but at least it wasn't the first day, so it wasn't so bad.

You're lucky your first gymnastics class wasn't on Yom Kippur or Rosh Hashanah. That happened here too. I don't know why people don't learn more about each other's calendars.

To answer your question, my mother did go to temple on Yom Kippur. And she fasted. Then all of us went on a hike. The day before my father had cooked a special dinner which we heated up after sundown. It's a good think this holiday doesn't come at the end of June or we'd have been eating REALLY LATE. My friend Pattie and her family came over for dinner.

The best part of school this year is that we have a teacher who really thinks we should talk to each other. Not only does she let us talk to each other, she thinks it's part of what learning is. She sets up lots and lots of activities where we talk in small groups as part of doing the school work. And we do all sorts of art and drama and music as part of our real school work.

Love,
Amber

October 24

Dear Amber,

My teacher is more like yours this year too. One of the funny things is when we get together to talk in class she asks us more questions. She's also always trying to get us to listen to each other, not just listen to her. It's fun, but it's kind of strange.

Gymnastics is great. I'll send you some pictures from our fall show. It's not really a show, just a class that parents get to come to. I'm glad I'm getting to take classes through city recreation. They don't cost much, so my parents think it's fine if I take more than one. The problem is lots of them are on Saturday mornings. I noticed they don't offer any on Sunday mornings. Do you think they think people might go to church on Sunday mornings and they don't know that some Jewish people go to temple on Saturday morning? I've noticed this funny thing about my friends and sleep-over parties too. Usually they're on Friday nights. I think maybe they think if they did them on Saturday night it would be a problem for people who go to church on Sunday. But my parents really like us to be home on Friday evenings when we light candles for the Sabbath. And once a month our temple has a special service for children so they like us to go to that.

I've been reading all the *All of a Kind Family* books. Have you read those? I love them. I went to the library and asked the librarian to help me find books about Jewish kids. There are hardly any. I love reading about Black kids and Asian American kids and I love reading books that have Spanish and English in them, but I wish there were more books about kids like me.

I just read *Go Free or Die*. It's about Harriet Tubman. I'm making a strip of paper, it's kind of like a mural, about the Underground Railroad. It's watercolors. I'll get my mother to take a photo of it for you when I'm done.

Guess what, this year I am going to have a Famous Women party for my birthday! Harriet Tubman will be one of the famous women. You don't think you could come, do you? Last year I did Antarctica and we made penguins. I'm sorry you missed that.

Love,
Aliza

November 2

Dear Aliza,

I really like Harriet Tubman too. When we were in Maryland we got to go see a house that was a stop on the Underground Railroad. It's exciting for me to think about African American people and white people working together to help get African American people free. I also get so scared and so sad when I think that my father's ancestors were slaves.

Kind of speaking of that, my grandmother, not Savta but my father's mother, gave me Isabella for my birthday. I can't believe it. It's such a big present. But the only thing I don't like is that in the stories she starts out as a slave. I wanted her to be someone I would have wanted to be, not someone I just feel sad about. When I play with her with my friends we pretend she was a northern free black kid, not a slave. Then she's great. Do you think your mother would make me some clothes for her? She does all that great sewing.

I'm still thinking about the problem about Jewish holidays and schedules. We had a problem in our town about the primary election. I don't quite understand what a primary election is, but it comes before the regular election. For some reason I don't understand, they say elections always have to be on Tuesdays. The day they picked for the primary turned out to be the eve of Yom Kippur. A lot of Jews said that they wouldn't be able to get from work to the voting places and home by sundown. They tried to get the date changed, but too many people said moving it one week earlier or later wouldn't work and that they should just vote by mail. That doesn't seem right to me.

I've started ice skating this year. I'm sending you a picture of me skating. I'm not very good yet, but I like it. And my father really likes going skating with me and my friends.

Love,
Amber

December 4

Dear Amber,

My mother's excited to make you some clothes for Isabella. She loves to make doll clothes and she says it would be a nice change from giving you books all the time. Nana's giving me Victoria for my birthday. I really wanted a Jewish doll, but they don't have one. I wrote to the company telling them that I didn't like it that all the dolls celebrate Christmas and that I thought they should have a Jewish doll. I even suggested that they do one of a girl whose family had just come over from Russia. They sent me back a postcard saying "that's a popular request." I thought that was really dumb. If it's such a popular request why don't they just have one. I wrote them back again and told them I thought that was a good reason to make one, but their answer that time wasn't much better. They just said I should know that they "are committed" to making dolls from different times in U.S. history and from different backgrounds. But they didn't tell me at all if they're planning a Jewish doll.

There's Christmas everywhere around here. Every magazine and catalogue has stuff about Christmas. That's all the music you hear in stores. All the cities have up Christmas decorations on the streets. Even the White House has a Christmas tree on its lawn. What if we had a Jewish president? Almost all the books I really like have Christmas in them.

I don't like it that much when they try to make a big deal about Chanukah too. Chanukah isn't even an important Jewish holiday. It feels like they're just trying to make up for Christmas. I'd much rather they do more stuff about Rosh Hashanah or Passover.

We do special projects for each night of Chanukah and I like that. One night we make dip candles—I did this problem to figure out how many you need for all the nights of Chanukah. And another night we each make a menorah to give someone as a present. One afternoon we make Chanukah cookies and give them to our neighbors. One night we play dreidel. That way it feels like we're not competing with Christmas.

My parents say we really might come down for February vacation. Do you really have room for all of us?

Love,
Aliza

December 15

Dear Aliza,

My mom really liked your family's idea for Chanukah. So we're doing that this year. We're making our menorahs out of fimo. I think they'll be great. This is a time when I really like being two religions. I get to do lots of special projects from both. Do you know the book *Elijah's Angel*? It's one of my favorites. If you read it you'll see why.

The most exciting part is that I'm finally getting to sing in "Black Nativity." Its tons of work but it's so exciting. I really like to be on stage. I can tell people about it and they're surprised. And it's fun to dance and sing. It makes it hard to get my homework done and my parents are really strict about that. But it's worth it.

My school is trying to be better about Christmas. We're not doing worksheets with Christmas trees and the little kids aren't writing letters to Santa. We've been learning about winter solstice and holidays to do with light all over the world, or at least parts of the world that are dark now. But I know what you mean. Every time we go out anywhere there's Christmas. And it's not your holiday at all.

Guess what. I figured out this really great way to do long division. I did it with my friend Pattie and this other kid in our class, Erik. It's so much better than the way our parents do it. They have this really long way that doesn't make any sense.

If you and Sara sleep in sleeping bags on the floor of my room and your parents don't mind sleeping on the sofa bed, then we have room for all of you to visit. My parents think it's a great idea.

Love,
Amber

155

SARITA—LONG CHARACTER DESCRIPTION

Sarita is an African American girl, 12 years old, in 6th grade. She is in an advanced class at one of her city's elementary schools. Students start these classes in 4th grade, based on their 3rd grade scores on standardized tests. Both in school and at home, Sarita speak Black English. She is proud of this version of English, loving the richness and power of the language and loving how well it conveys her thoughts and feelings.

Sarita knows standard English and believes she has the choice to use it in situations where she thinks her needs would be better met. She's willing to use it in school for formal school papers, to most guest speakers, in letters that go to the outside world, and when they are role playing job interviews. She doesn't think school is one of the places she should have to do this all the time. She wants to be able to write her journal in Black English. She wants to be able to speak in Black English in discussions in her classroom. Her teacher disagrees. He emphasizes that to "get ahead" in our country you need to speak and write standard English and that an advanced class is a place where all students should do so all the time they are at school.

In Sarita's class students keep journals about books they are reading in reading groups. Sarita writes hers in Black English. Her teacher writes wonderful comments about what she says, but gives her a B on the journal because of what he calls, "all the grammar mistakes." Since the journal counts as 1/3 of the reading grade this will mean Sarita won't get the A in reading she thinks she deserves.

SARITA—SHORT CHARACTER DESCRIPTION

Sarita is an African American girl, 12 years old, in 6th grade. She is in an advanced class at one of her city's elementary schools. Students start these classes in 4th grade, based on their 3rd grade scores on standardized tests. Both in school and at home, Sarita speaks Black English. She is proud of this version of English, loving the richness and power of the language and loving how well it conveys her thoughts and feelings. Sarita knows standard English and believes she has the choice to use it in situations where she thinks her needs would be better met. She's willing to use it in school for some formal school work, but wants to use Black English for other work. Her teacher disagrees. He emphasizes that to "get ahead" in our country you need to speak and write standard English and that an advanced class is a place where all students should do so all the time they are at school.

The conversation will be between Sarita, Phoebe, Josh and Manuel.

BING—LONG CHARACTER DESCRIPTION

Bing is a fourth grader in a suburban elementary school. He speaks his native Chinese fluently and speaks English well, though with a Chinese accent and some non-standard grammar. His English vocabulary is not as large as many of his native English speaking classmates. He is proud of his ability to speak two such different languages. He attends Chinese school on weekends and is learning to read and write Chinese.

His teacher heavily corrects all Bing's written work in red pen and constantly corrects Bing's grammar, vocabulary and accent in class. His classmates have adopted the same pattern. Bing wishes his teacher and classmates acknowledged and appreciated his bilingual strengths rather than being critical of his mistakes in English grammar, vocabulary and pronunciation. When he looks at the papers he gets back, he is distressed to find so much emphasis on the mistakes he has made rather than on the content he has written about. He wants to know what his teachers think of what he has written, not just of the mistakes he has made. He also wishes there was somewhere in school where the fact that he is bilingual would be seen as an asset, as something special and important about him. He wants other students to listen to his good ideas in games and appreciate how well he draws and figures things out.

When students in his class were selected to work with a visiting poet-in-residence Bing was not selected. His teacher said that was because his English was not strong enough. Bing would love the opportunity to work with the poet and believes that his understanding of two languages helps him have a better feel about using language and could be a real help in learning to write poetry.

BING—SHORT CHARACTER DESCRIPTION

Bing is a fourth grader in a suburban elementary school. He speaks his native Chinese fluently and speaks English well though with a Chinese accent and some non-standard grammar. His English vocabulary is not as large as many of his native English speaking classmates. He is proud of his ability to speak two such different languages. He attends Chinese school on weekends and is learning to read and write Chinese. His teacher heavily corrects all Bing's written work in red pen and constantly corrects Bing's grammar, vocabulary and accent in class. Bing wishes his teacher acknowledged and appreciated his bilingual strengths rather than being critical of his mistakes in English. He wants more emphasis on his content not his grammar. He also wishes there was somewhere in school where the fact that he is bilingual would be seen as an asset, as something special and important about him. He wants other students to listen to his good ideas in games and appreciate how well he draws and figures things out.

The conversation will be between Bing, David, Samantha and Maria.

ILILANI—LONG CHARACTER DESCRIPTION

Ililani and Luka are two children from Hawaii, now in a 4th grade in a school in Portland, Oregon where there are very few Hawaiian children and no Hawaiian teachers. In their Hawaiian culture children often tell stories collaboratively, feeding off of and building on each other's routines. While this may look like interrupting to those not familiar with this style, they see it as helping each other and working together. When they do this in the classroom their teacher tells them that they need to develop more independent skills and learn to tell stories on their own. They aren't interested in this as they think that the best stories are ones told together as a partnership.

During Meeting Time in their classroom Ililani and Luka often choose to tell stories together. Their teacher discourages this, telling them that Meeting Time is a time for individual sharing. She wants them to develop skills in telling a story straight through, on their own, from beginning to end. Both girls think this is silly. They imagine they could do that if they wanted to, but they see no need for it. They know their classmates love their collaboratively told stories. Whenever they are telling these the classroom is silent and everyone is paying attention to them.

The school is planning their spring performance for parents and the community. One section of it will be story telling. Ililani and Luka want to enter together to tell a story in their informal and collaborative style. The teacher says that the form only has a space for one child to tell at a time and that that is the way the performance is designed. She says they may not enter their names unless they plan to tell separately.

ILILANI—SHORT CHARACTER DESCRIPTION

Ililani and Luka are two children from Hawaii, now in a 4th grade in a school in Portland, Oregon where there are very few Hawaiian children and no Hawaiian teachers. In their Hawaiian culture children often tell stories collaboratively, feeding off of and building on each other's routines. When they do this in the classroom their teacher tells them that they need to develop more independent skills and learn to tell stories on their own. They aren't interested in this as they think that the best stories are ones told together as a partnership. During Meeting Time in their classroom Ililani and Luka often choose to tell stories together. They imagine they could learn to tell on their own if they wanted to, but they see no need for it.

Conversation between Ililani, Luka, Sophia and Chen.

Chapter

7

Discrimination: Prices and Choices

Reprinted with special permission of North America Syndicate

Our lives, and the lives of our students, are very much influenced by the prejudice, stereotyping and discrimination described in previous chapters, whether we are privileged or disadvantaged by them. Yet few young people or adults have had opportunities to reflect on some of the underlying dynamics of discrimination that play themselves out in our daily lives and in the life of our nation. We live with the effects of these dynamics but seldom have been provided conceptual tools for stepping out of our lived experience to analyze and better understand them. Activities in Chapter Seven offer these opportunities.

Lessons in Section A, "Unequal Resources = Unequal Results," aim to help students examine how institutional discrimination produces inequality in both resources and opportunities for certain groups of people and how it, therefore, supports the success and achievement of other groups. Put simply, effects of the "isms" deny particular groups of people resources, thus contributing to unequal life-outcomes.

The powerful effect of institutional and cultural discrimination on opportunities for equality challenges the assumptions underlying competitive individualism—that "you can make it if you try," and that "everyone has an equal opportunity." The lessons in this section enable students to examine these assumptions critically. They also teach students to recognize the process of *"blaming the victim."* When people are denied equal resources through institutional discrimination, they are often blamed for their situations or their lack of success. Activities will help students ask if the cause of inequality is in a *system* of institutional discrimination that distributes resources, opportunities, and power unequally—rather than in the deficiencies of *individuals.*

These ideas are sometimes difficult even for adults to understand, but the experiential nature of some of these activities will help students *feel* what it's like to be expected to achieve without equal resources and opportunities. Then, through the discussion ques-

tions, *you* can encourage them to make the connections to the effects of the "isms" on groups of people in society. More information about institutional discrimination is found in the boxes throughout this chapter and in the resources listed in the Bibliography. They provide data and examples to share with your students. Take plenty of time with the discussion questions, for making the connections between their classroom activities and the dynamics of institutional discrimination in society is a crucial element in student learning.

"Connections to Others," Section B, is comprised of lessons in which students learn to examine how the privileges of some individuals and groups are directly connected to the denial of those privileges to others. It is again through your role in assisting students to tie experiential activities to theirs and others' lives that these new ideas become meaningful. Use examples to highlight the connections between the factors that create more privileges for some people than others. For example, if a man stands to gain and woman to lose through sexist practices in the workplace, there is a connection between the man's higher status and the woman's lower position. One's benefit is *due,* in part, to the other's loss. Once aware of these connections, help yourself and your students avoid guilt, for guilt is immobilizing. Rather encourage responsibility which fosters change.

Lessons will help students experience and understand the *choices* that privileged individuals or groups have in creating change. Often those with privilege—whether it be white skin, male gender, or middle-class status—tend to deny the power they have, and ignore choices that can foster greater equality by sharing resources, decision-making, and opportunities. If your students have relatively few privileges—if they are low-income students of color, for example—the activities in this chapter are still important for several reasons. While students may not have some privileges, they often have others that they can examine—the privilege of being male or lighter-skinned or able-bodied, for example.

It is these complexities of oppression that lessons in Section C help students explore. Students are introduced to the idea that their social identity is multi-faceted—and includes race, gender, age, class background, religion, among others. Because of this, they may receive privileges because of some aspects of their social identity and be discriminated against because of others. In addition, many students with few privileges blame themselves for their situation rather than understanding how social inequality has limited many of their choices. This often causes them to believe the stereotypes and myths prevalent in society about themselves or their group.

An example of such "internalized oppression" is black students who want to go to schools with predominantly white teachers because they believe that white teachers are better. This dynamic is common in adults as well. For example, many times women prefer to use the services of a male plumber, auto mechanic or carpenter because they believe that women aren't as competent in these trades. These activities can help students better understand the powerful, and sometimes subtle, effects of institutional discrimination and can contribute to changing their perceptions of themselves and the world.

Other intricacies regarding the dynamics of oppression are addressed in Section C. Students explore lateral oppression, the way some people who have been discriminated against because of one form of diversity can turn around and discriminate against others different from themselves. They examine the difference between types of discrimination—individual and institutional, intentional and inadvertent.

In the three final lessons in this section students explore the differences in experiences of people facing discrimination. They examine the differences between the impact on people of ongoing discrimination compared to occasional bias, as well as the difference between discrimination and prejudice. They explore how the lives of people experiencing the same form of discrimination can be very different. Finally they examine the effects of racism on groups of people who have suffered racism over time and groups without such a history.

As you work with students on these issues, you too will be learning to analyze the complex dynamics of discrimination in our society. It is encouraging to know, though, that young people can understand these complexities. If you have worked with students to build the groundwork by sequentially doing selected lessons in previous chapters and talked with them about issues of equity as they arise in the life of the classroom and school, many will be ready for these lessons. They can understand what appear to be complicated ideas because these dynamics are often playing themselves out in the fabric of their daily lives.

Some activities in this chapter are "rigged," in that some students are given advantages and others are not without your making this inequality explicit. The affective learning about inequality that is generated by these experiences can be very meaningful and powerful. Some teachers, however, feel uncomfortable "setting up" students in this way. Since lessons differ in degree of privilege given or withheld, your choice of lessons will depend on your feelings on this issue and your group of students. Also, if your students have difficulty handling emotionally charged situations, or if you are uncomfortable processing them, choose lessons with extra care.

In sum, activities will enable students to see their options, not only to share resources, but to make changes so that privilege becomes something that's shared. They will explore the benefits of equality to *all* people. Only when adults and students alike step back and look at unexamined choices and their consequences, can they make decisions from an "unblinded" perspective. At this point alternatives that support equality become both more conceivable and more possible.

It is also important to talk with students about what is within their power to change, and those bigger changes that need collective, organized adult efforts. These activities will enable students to see their options and make age-appropriate changes, realizing that their efforts improve the lives of others and result in more equity. While making a contribution to social change, their actions will not change society. For example, pooling book club order money and then giving each child in the class the opportunity to order a fair share of books shares privilege and gives better access to reading materials to a range of children in this class for this year. It does not change the basic inequitable distribution of resources in this country.

Students can be encouraged and helped to make important classroom and community changes and to feel good about them. They also need to realize that these changes won't in themselves bring about equal access for all. In this way students will not feel guilty, discouraged, or disempowered for not being successful at creating major social changes. They will have, however, developed the consciousness necessary to see what must be changed and taken practical steps toward those ends.

Martin Luther King on Genuine Equality

We find ourselves in a new era of our struggle for genuine equality and it is much more difficult because it is much easier to integrate lunch counters than it is to eradicate slums. It is easier to guarantee the right to vote than it is to create jobs or guarantee an annual income.

State of the Movement
Nation Magazine, March , 1968

Section A   **Unequal Resources = Unequal Results**

A LITTLE PRAISE GOES A LONG WAY

OBJECTIVES   To show students the effects of praise and support on their own and others' achievements. To help students understand how social institutions give support and praise to some groups of people more than to others, and how this affects achievement in society.

MATERIALS   Copies of "Worksheet: Praise Matters," p. 195.

IMPLEMENTATION Decide whether you want to let the children know what you are doing in this lesson. To let them know has the advantage of not "tricking" them. On the other hand, telling them makes the lesson less effective.

On a particular day, praise and support half the students for anything they do that is remotely good or correct and ignore all their wrong answers or unacceptable behavior. Set high expectations and encourage them to succeed. On the same day, with the rest of the class, praise nothing and criticize anything that is wrong. Set very low expectations for this group. Do this throughout the day in all your academic areas and interpersonal interactions.

Stop at least an hour before the end of school. Tell students what you've been doing. Discuss feelings briefly. Ask students to fill out the Worksheet. Discuss the day's experience and the Worksheet as a class.

DISCUSSION
1. Discuss the Worksheet responses.
2. Compare the feelings of those in each group.
3. How did you do in your schoolwork? Look at the work you did today, how quickly you worked, how many mistakes you made. Did you do better or worse than usual? Why?
4. When you are told you are doing well with something, how does that affect you?
5. Give an example of a time when someone expected you to do well and that made a difference in how you did. Give an example of a time when someone expected you to do poorly and that changed your performance.

Tell students that some institutions—like families, the media, places of employment—praise and support some people more than others. Sometime different *expectations* are set up for different groups of people. High expectations of a person or group tend to encourage success. If a person in authority or an institution, however, has low expectations, that tends to discourage success.

6. Ask students what would happen in the following cases:
   a. If a teacher expects boys in high school to do well in chemistry, and girls not as well, what might happen?
   b. If a principal gives a lot of praise and support to black students who do well on the basketball team, but less to them when they show improvement on a test score, what might happen?
   c. *Fact:* Latino/as make up 2.6% of full time newspaper employers in the U.S. (1992). How does this lack of support affect Latino/as' feelings about being able to achieve in journalism?
   d. *Fact:* Women hold 10% percent of all seats in the U.S. Senate (1997). What does this lack of institutional support do to women's feeling about achieving in government?
   e. *Fact:* Thirty-six percent of black teenagers who want jobs can't find them compared to 15% for white teenagers (1995). How might society's lack of support for black teenage employment affect their feelings about achieving in work?
7. What other examples can you think of of institutions that support some people more than others?

Explain to the students that, like individuals, *institutions* can praise, support, set high expectations by their practices and procedures. The *result* of this support or lack of support on people is similar to what they felt in this exercise.

GOING FURTHER Make graphs or charts of students' normal performance compared to the performance of the two groups during this day. Put these up on a bulletin board as a reminder.

> ### *Is Ability Grouping Fair? Does It Work?*
> The effects of tracking on student outcomes have been widely investigated, and the bulk of this work *does not* support commonly-held beliefs that tracking increases student learning. Nor does the evidence support tracking as a way to improve students' attitudes about themselves or about schooling. Although existing tracking systems *appear* to provide advantages for students who are placed in the top tracks, the literature suggests that students at all ability levels can achieve at least as well in heterogeneous classrooms. Students who are not in top tracks . . . suffer clear and consistent dis-advantages from tracking.
>
> Jeannie Oakes, "Keeping Track: The Policy and Practices of Curriculum Inequality" in *The Challenge of Detracking*, J. Bellanca and E. Schwartz, 1993

VALUES AUCTION*

OBJECTIVES
To enable students to clarify values that are important to them.
To help students understand how people's relative degree of economic privilege affects their ability to acquire things they value.

MATERIALS
Copies of "Worksheet: Values Auction," p. 196; play money; one pair of dice for each group of four.

IMPLEMENTATION
This activity is designed for a class of twenty-two or fewer students. If your numbers are greater, add to the Worksheet, still leaving two blank spaces. Tell students that they will have an opportunity to decide what values are important to them in their lives. Pass out the Worksheet and ask them to rank the values from most important to least important. If this is too difficult for your students, have them check five or six most important and underline the five or six least important. If they wish, they may add one or two items that are important to them but are not on the list.

Then divide students into groups of three or four and ask them to discuss their lists with each other. This gives them an opportunity to affirm their values and hear others' points of view. (For more on values clarification, see *Values Clarification: A Handbook of Practical Strategies*, by Sidney Simon *et al.*)

Distribute money. Each student begins with $100. Give a pair of dice to each group. Each student rolls the dice to determine how many more dollars she gets—one dot equals $10. Those who roll a seven or more are entitled to roll one extra die as "inheritance."

Now the auction begins. Ask students who know about auctions to explain the procedure to others. One student is appointed banker to collect the money during the auction. You are the auctioneer. Auction off the list, writing on the board the name of the highest bidder and the amount bid for each item. Keep the pace brisk and use typical auction terms, such as "Going once, going twice, sold for . . . ."

DISCUSSION
1. Did you get what you wanted at the auction? Some, none? Why?
2. What would you bid higher for next time?
3. How did you feel during the auction? How do you feel now? (At this point feelings about the unequal amounts of money will surface. Be sure to allow adequate time for students to share feelings of frustration or anger.)

---

*Adapted from *A Handbook of Personal Growth Actvities for Classroom Use*, by R. and I. Hawley.

4. How did the amount of money you had affect your ability to get the items you valued most?

5. How did the amount of money you had affect your willingness to take a risk?

6. In life, how does the amount of money or resources a group has affect their ability to get things they value most? Give examples. Some might be:

   a. In order to become a great athlete, expensive training is often necessary. This is also true for music and dance.

   b. The more financial resources you have, the more opportunity you have to get preventive health care and quality medical care when you are sick.

   c. The more financial resources a person has to get needed education or training for a job, the more opportunity she has both for choice of job and success.

7. How was the throw of the "inheritance" die like real life? How does the privilege of inheritance affect chances to get what you value?

Now tell students they may use their remaining money to purchase items that they have written in the blank spaces. Have students decide the worth of those items compared to the price of other things they bid for and got. Ask them to share a few of these items with the group. Finally, students share some "I learned" statements from this experience.

Assumptions About Equality

For some people, equality means that people are equally free to act, or to take advantage of what America has to offer. Yet this definition does not take into account people's ability to do so. For example, Jill Smoe, worker, and David Rockefeller are equally *free* to open a bank, but are they equally *able?*

Is equality possible as long as there is a disparity in wealth that allows some people access to opportunities others don't have?

BLAMING THE VICTIM

OBJECTIVES

To allow students to experience the frustration and injustice of a situation where some have an unfair advantage.

To help students draw parallels between these classroom experiences and our society, where some people are born with more advantages and privilege than others.

To help students learn the meaning of "blaming the victim."

To enable students to understand that expecting everyone to reach the same goals, either in this activity or society, and judging them by whether they have reached them is unfair when opportunities are unequal.

MATERIALS

Materials for students to make mobiles. In all cases dowels; coat hangers; eighteen gauge wire; wire cutters; yarn; scissors; rulers; markers; hole punch; glue; tape; and thread. If possible get industrial recycled scraps—e.g., colored foam shapes; tubes; cardboard caps; rubber disks—from a teacher resource center or children's museum. If this is not available; gather other sorts of items for the mobiles—e.g., shells; pine cones; construction paper; glossy and tissue paper.

IMPLEMENTATION

This lesson enables students to experientially understand the concept of blaming the victim. The learning can be very powerful. You are asked to role-play and to blame or criticize students who don't do well, even though they were given fewer resources. If you feel that the negative effect of such blaming, albeit temporary, will outweigh the positive learning, you may choose not to teach this lesson.

> ### Examples of Blaming the Victim
>
> The generic process of "blaming the victim" is applied to almost every American problem. The miserable health care of the poor is explained away on the grounds that the victim has poor motivation and lacks health information. The problems of slum housing are traced to the characteristics of tenants who are labeled as "Southern rural migrants" not yet "acculturated" to life in the big city. . . . From such a viewpoint, the obvious fact that poverty is primarily an absence of money is easily overlooked or set aside.
>
> From *Blaming the Victim*, by William Ryan
>
> People out of work are sometimes blamed for being lazy, not ambitious, or willing to take a handout when, in fact, there are not enough jobs for all Americans and the U.S. economy depends on a steady rate of unemployment. Women are sometimes blamed for not being able to fix mechanical things. Yet girls haven't been taught trades or mechanical skills. Until recently they weren't allowed to take shop in school, and women are still discriminated against in many trades.

Divide students into five groups. Explain that each groups is expected to make a mobile. These will be displayed. Use a topic from one of your subject matter areas as the theme for the mobile. Groups may only use the supplies they are given: they do not have to use all of them, but they may not use anything else. Distribute supplies as follows.

Group One—One coat hanger, two sheets of green construction paper, one spool of thread.

Group Two—Three coat hangers, two dowel rods, thread, assorted colors of construction paper, assorted colors of yarn.

Group Three—Three coat hangers, three dowel rods, spool of wire, scissors, glue, thread, wire cutters, assorted construction and tissue paper, several pieces of recycled industrial material, if available.

Group Four—Three coat hangers, three dowel rods, wire, crayons, wire-cutters, and a selection of all materials.

Group Five—A plentiful supply of all materials.

You may create more groups if you have a large class. Give each group 30 to 45 minutes to create the mobile. During that time, take notes on group process and student comments. If students complain about the way items were distributed, be very matter-of-fact. Say something like, "That's the way life is. There will be no changes."

As they work, praise the groups with the most resources for their creative, decorative work, as pertinent. Where appropriate, blame groups given few resources for their lack of initiative, creativity, etc. . . e.g., "Your mobile seems sparse. Just put more effort into your work; it's not what you have, but how hard you try."

After the activity is complete, and before discussion, have students write briefly about how they felt during the project. Then have groups show their mobiles. Blame groups with fewer resources for not having a complete mobile and for their lack of initiative, or whatever makes sense given what those groups produced. Praise the groups with more resources for their artistic, complete work, or again, whatever makes sense given your situation.

DISCUSSION Share with your students some of the comments you undoubtedly heard them making as they were working—about how the activity was set up and your behavior during the activity. Then explain that you were role-playing and you *really* don't blame those students with sparse mobiles. You wanted, however, for them to feel how it feels to be blamed for not achieving when you have an unfair dis-advantage and *conditions* aren't equal. (Save notes from this activity for use in Chapter 11.)

1. How did you feel while doing this project? (Give each student a chance for a short response.)
2. How did you feel when you looked over at the other groups?
3. How did you feel if you were given an advantage? A handicap?
4. How did it feel when I blamed some of you for your failure? Did you deserve it? Did those given more resources deserve their praise?
5. Why do you think I set up the project this way?
6. How would you feel if we had a contest and judged the mobiles? How about if we displayed them in the hallway with your names on them? How would it be if we gave prizes for the best mobiles?
7. Think of a situation in school or our community where some people start off with a greater advantage than other people. Why does this happen? How do different people feel?
8. What's a situation where people start out with fewer resources, money or power, like some of you started out with fewer materials today? How does that affect what they can do for themselves? How do they get blamed for their "failure"?
9. What happens if we expect everyone to be able to do well, even though they don't have the same amount of resources, money or power? What happens if they get judged that way—the way we might judge you on these mobiles?

Is Equality Always Fair?

In this context you can talk with students about the difference between equality and equity. Often when resources are equal the situation still isn't *fair*. For example, if someone in the class had a physical disability, even if she got equal resources she might need special tools or supplies in order to contribute to the task. Fairness isn't sameness. To promote equity, we need to think about individual needs.

You might discuss with your class what would be a fair distribution of resources given different talents in art, creative propensities and physical abilities/disabilities among the students in your room. Discuss equity as it emerges again as an issue in your class or in discussions about social issues and approaches for dealing with discrimination.

Explain that in life people with advantages often blame those with dis-advantages for their problem. This is called "blaming the victim." *People,* rather than unequal *situations,* are labeled at fault. Remind students, "I blamed the victim in this activity. What did you learn from this?"

Discuss with students how some people and groups in society think they've succeeded "on their own." They believe that everybody has a chance to succeed if they just try hard enough. Explain that such a viewpoint doesn't take into consideration inequalities and discrimination in society. These are like hurdles in a race. While everyone has personal hurdles, like family trouble, some people and groups face the additional hurdles that societal discrimination creates. Refer to the following box, "The Hurdles of Life."

FOLLOW-UP "Removing Those Hurdles," p. 340.

Case Studies—The Hurdles of Life

While life is much more complex than the relatively simplistic case studies below, they demonstrate how the access to different opportunities and various discriminatory, institutional barriers make accomplishments in life easier for some people and harder for others.

Case Study A: Poor, Latina female. This child's mother was undernourished during pregnancy. This child was born weak and had life-long health problems (hurdle 1). Because Spanish was spoken at home and lessons were only taught in English at school, she had academic difficulty in the early grades (hurdle 2). Facing discrimination in employment, her father was often out of work and her mother could only find low-paying factory work. She therefore had to work evenings and weekends to help support her family (hurdle 3). Since her counselor believed a female doesn't need a professional career, she was placed in a vocational track in high school. She was told she wasn't college material (hurdle 4).

Case Study B: White, middle-class male. This child's mother could afford quality health care during pregnancy. This child was born healthy. School lessons were taught in his native tongue and his culture was reflected in the norms and materials of the school. He had difficulty reading and received tutoring (small hurdle). His father and mother worked to support the family and the student worked on Saturday to have spending money. He broke his leg playing football and missed a month of his junior year (small hurdle). His counselor tracked him into a college prepatory program and provided financial aid information. He got into a good college.

Reprinted with permission of Kirk Andersen

ASSIGNMENT: RESEARCH PAPER

OBJECTIVES
To enable students to understand experientially the feelings and options of people with greater or lesser degrees of privilege in society.

To expand students' views of the choices for change that various groups have available to them.

To reinforce the understanding that expecting everyone to reach the same goals in our society, and judging them by whether they have reached those goals, is unfair when opportunities are unequal.

MATERIALS
Reference materials for a topic of your choice relevant to your classroom curriculum. (Pick a topic where there's not a great disparity in the knowledge students have.) Encyclopedias; library books; newspapers; magazines; name-tags; play money; paper; pencils.

IMPLEMENTATION   This is an experiential activity that can catalyze strong feelings and significant learning. Read it over carefully. If you choose to do it, allow plenty of time for processing questions. They are crucial!

This is set up for a classroom of 25 students, so modify numbers accordingly. Assign the following roles and distribute name-tags and play money (students pin on name tags and keep money hidden): one police officer; two storekeepers; one welfare worker (ten 50¢ slips); one organizer; one very wealthy citizen ($20); one upper-income citizen ($15); one upper-middle-income citizen ($12); two middle-income citizens ($10 each); four lower-middle-income citizens ($6 each); four lower-income citizens ($3 each); six totally impoverished citizens (nothing).

Tell the whole class about the various roles and what people can do in those roles. Give the storekeepers the supplies necessary for preparing the research paper: all the reference materials, books, paper, writing and drawing supplies. The students playing citizens are told that they must produce research reports on the topic you have chosen. They may use only materials they obtain from the storekeepers. They may get funds in any way they can. They will have two class periods to work.

Provide guidelines for storekeepers—for example, paper, 25¢; pencils, 25¢; use of a book for fifteen minutes, $1. Storekeepers may overcharge, sell damaged merchandise, bargain, and so on. They can mistreat the poor. They can change prices at will. They can use the police officer to collect IOU's and have citizens jailed.

The police officer patrols the area, keeps a special eye on the poor and enforces "law and order" as need be. He watches for cheating and stealing and may take sides. The welfare worker can give out fifty-cent pieces to help the poor, and can also require them to fill out long forms and wait for long periods of time. The organizer attempts to unite the poor.

Take notes of what happens, what is said, how action changes. If you have use of a video-tape camera, this is a good activity to tape. Continually stress the importance of completing the assignment. Keep reminding people they will be graded. (They will not be, of course.) As the activity is going on, praise the achievers with statements like "Oh, what fine work; I know how intelligent you are," and blame the low achievers with statements like, "If you're not doing well, you aren't trying hard," or, "Well, I didn't expect much of you slow people anyway."

At the end of the allotted times, collect papers and grade as though everyone had an equal chance.

DISCUSSION   1. How did you feel during this activity? How did you feel toward people in other roles?
2. How do you feel about your research papers? How do you think the grade you'll get is connected to the resources you had?
3. How would you feel if someone said, "There are certain people here who are less intelligent than others, which we certainly can see by the work they've produced"?
4. How did I "blame the victim"? What did that feel like?
5. In what ways was this like real life? Unlike? Give examples.
6. How did the "money" you got affect what you produced in this assignment? How did you feel about that?
7. How does the money different families have affect what they can do with their lives?
8. What did the poor people in our class do to gain more money and thus more supplies? How did that work?
9. What kinds of things can less privileged people do in life to get more of what they need? What happens when they do these things? (Note: You may add to students' comments and mention organizing, educating and boycotts. Lessons in upcoming sections focus on strategies for change.)
10. What did the privileged people in the activity do? What can such people in this country do?
11. How do policies of institutions in our country—schools, government, businesses—support this unfair system? (See box on following page for examples.)

FOLLOW-UP   "Using Privilege for Change," p. 286.
            An excellent example of the value of experiential learning is shown in the film, *Eye of the Storm*. Students learn about racism when they are discriminated against according to eye-color. Show it to your students.

Institutional Policies → Inequalities

Schools are funded in large part through local property taxes. Wealthy communities have more money to put into education, so students have more resources and special programs. Less money is spent on students in poorer districts. Sometimes it is said that poorer students are "less intelligent" and just don't do as well in school. Is it their "innate intelligence"? Remember without equal resources we can't expect equal results.
            See *Savage Inequalities: Children in America's Schools* by Jonathan Kozol and *There Are No Children Here* by Alex Kotlowitz.

IS "THE SAME" ALWAYS "FAIR"?

OBJECTIVES   To understand the difference between equality and equity and that equitable situations are not necessarily equal.
            To empathize with the feelings, and understand the situations, of people affected by inequities rooted in personal differences or institutional discrimination.
            To practice developing creative, fair approaches to situations in which people's needs are not the same.

MATERIALS   "Worksheets: Is 'The Same' Always 'Fair'?"—A, B, C, pp. 197–199.

IMPLEMENTATION   Talk with students about the way in which we often equate being "fair" with being "equal" or "the same." (*The American College Dictionary* defines equality as "the state of being equal; correspondence in quantity, value, rank ability," and equity as "that which is fair and just.")
            The Ramirez family got a pizza. Mr. Ramirez says he's going to be "fair" and give the same amount of pizza to each child—two pieces to 30-pound, 3-year-old Jose, and two pieces to 110 pound, 13-year-old Miguel. Ask the children if this is fair—why or why not. Is "the same" fair? Then ask each student to write another example from her own life on a file card. Share these examples. Ask the students to watch for examples in our classroom where fair is not equal. Tell them to keep their data in a notebook because they will share their findings periodically with a partner during the week.
            Tell students they will be working with a partner on a worksheet about fairness. They will read about a situation involving two students and then each will write an interior monologue for one character. An interior monologue is the imagined thoughts and feelings of a person. It answers the question, "How might this person experience this situation?" Tell students after they write their interior monologues they will share them with their partners. They will go on to reflect on what they heard and rethink the situation.
            Divide students into heterogeneous partners and distribute worksheets so some pairs are working on A, some on B and some on C. Tell students each member of the pair must be ready to report on the pair's responses to the questions once the class reconvenes. When pairs have completed their writing and discussions come together as a class. Sit in a circle if possible. Take each situation separately; for example begin with Lynne and Paul.

DISCUSSION Tell students that, as a class, we will repeat the process they did in pairs for each situation. Our final responses may be similar to, or different from, our original, pair-originated responses once we hear a variety of interior monologues.

1. Ask a student to read the situation in Worksheet A.
2. Ask the students who wrote interior monologues for the same character to read them. "What have we learned about the feelings and experiences of this person?"
3. Repeat for the second character.
4. Were there any thoughts, feelings or experiences that the students had in common; if so, what?
5. Has hearing the interior monologues affected your thoughts or feelings about the situation or characters? If so, how?
6. Ask someone from each partnership to share how they decided to change the situation to make it more satisfying to each, and also fair. Discuss these resolutions. What is fair? Does fair mean the same?
7. Repeat the above for Worksheets B and C.
8. After completing discussion of situations B and C ask students what they've learned about the relationship between fairness and being the same. Discuss ways they can relate this to situations in their own lives.

For more ideas for using interior monologues see Linda Christenson's work in "Rethinking Our Classrooms."

Consider Equity Through Metaphor

In his book, *From the Grassroots*, Manning Marable offers the following parable:

A white man and a black man are running a race. Right before it starts, the black man is shackled so that when the race begins the white man runs while the black man cannot move. When a black spectator from the stands undoes his shackles, the black man is able to run, but the black spectator is arrested by officials for "interrupting a sporting event." Although late and injured, the black runner almost catches up.

The black runner then calls for another contest in which the white man would be shackled through a brief portion of the race. The black man explains that this is the only way a race could be fair since he was injured from the shackles during the first race. The officials decline this solution saying that "in the interest of fairness" the race will be run again, with each man starting without shackles at the same time.

What different definitions of fairness are the black man and officials using? Think about who are moral agents in the story, when you have played the various roles in the story in your own lives, and ways in which the parable reflects current inequalities.

EQUAL OPPORTUNITY?

OBJECTIVES   To have students realize that providing "the same" school opportunities to all students doesn't necessarily mean providing equitable opportunities.
To have students better understand the impact of socio-economic class on school achievement.

MATERIALS   Paper and pencil; copies of "Worksheet: Equal Opportunity?" p. 200, one for each student.

IMPLEMENTATION   *Step One:* Divide students into groups of three. Students read "Worksheet: Equal Opportunity?" to themselves. Each group discusses the scenarios to be sure that all group members understand what was written.
Step Two: In groups, students draw two Venn diagrams. They label one diagram ELISSA and the other TANYA. They label one circle in each diagram Advantages, and the other Dis-advantages. (See below.) Students work together on each Venn diagram, to decide on all the advantages and dis-advantages that each girl has in her life in terms of what might help her succeed in school.

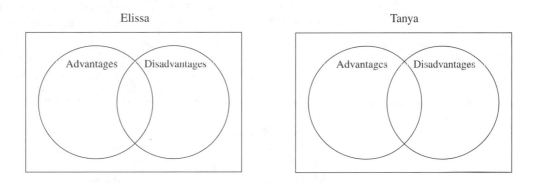

Step Three: In their groups, students discuss what changes could happen that would give both of these girls, and all their classmates, the best opportunities they could have to succeed in school. Follow this with a whole group discussion.

DISCUSSION #1   1. How could Elissa and Tanya better help each other?
2. How could their friends help?
3. How could their teacher help?
4. How could the structure of the school help?

IMPLEMENTATION   *Step Four:* In groups, students write a proposal for one change they think might be particularly important in order to make opportunities for success more available for all the students in Elissa and Tanya's school. For example this change might just be something done by a group of friends or it might involve a plan by a group of friends with the school then agreeing to make some changes.
Step Five: Have each group share their change proposal with the whole class.

DISCUSSION #2   1. In what ways are Elissa and Tanya's situations similar to each other?
2. What are some important differences in their situations?
3. In what ways do Elissa and Tanya have equal opportunities in school?
4. In what ways are their opportunities unequal?
5. How is Elissa and Tanya's situation relevant for your classroom and your school?
6. Given what you have learned in this lesson, if you heard someone say, "Tanya and Elissa have equal opportunities, Tanya must just not be as smart or work as hard," what would you say?

7. Are there changes you might want to work on in your school to have greater equity for all students? If so, how would you begin?

Section B   Connections to Others

TEAM SPIRIT

OBJECTIVES   To learn about Charles Drew, an African American doctor, who made important contributions to the preservation of blood.

To help students see how the privileges white people get are often tied to the denial of those privileges to blacks.

To see what choices white people have to share privileges.

MATERIALS   Copies of "Worksheet: Team Spirit #1," p. 201, and "Worksheet: Team Spirit #2" p. 202,—one of each of these for each group of four students. If possible, one or more copies of *Charles Drew* by Robyn Mahone-Lonesome for referral and further information.

IMPLEMENTATION   In the first part of this lesson students will learn about the life of Charles Drew. In the second part they will use this information to examine issues around privilege, the choices people have in using their own privilege and the effects these choices have on the denial of privilege to others.

Step One: If possible read aloud to students from Robyn Mahone-Lonesome's biography listed above. Or make this biography available to students. Divide students into groups of four. Give each group one copy of "Worksheet: Team Spirit #1." Students should cut the Worksheet on the lines so each student has one section to read. After reading, students share their information with the other members of their small group.

Step Two: Each small group works collaboratively to read and answer the questions on "Worksheet: Team Spirit #2." Then go on to the whole class discussion.

DISCUSSION
1. Discuss questions on "Worksheet: Team Spirit #2."
2. By accepting their privilege, how did white team members reinforce the system that denies privilege to blacks?
3. How does their acceptance of this privilege help perpetuate the system that gives privilege to some and denies it to others?
4. What choices did the white team members have in this situation?
5. How might it have been different if the white team members, or some of the white team members, had made different choices?
6. In what ways would those differences have affected Charles? affected other African Americans? affected the white members of his team?

Correcting Historical Inaccuracies

There are controversial issues that arise in biographies of Charles Drew. Dr. Drew died from injuries from a car accident. Afterwards a rumor began that he bled to death because a *whites only* hospital refused to admit him because he was black. Today there are clear reports from the black doctors who were with Dr. Drew when he died, that this is not true. Racism has caused, and still causes, many deaths in America. But Dr. Drew received quality medical care and still could not be saved.

A Wall of Separation

Little by little, year by year, a wall of separation is constructed in the child's mind to offer self-protection in the face of realistic guilt at unearned privilege and inherited excess. Poor people exist—so also do the rich—but there are no identifiable connections. One side does not live well *because* another side must live in pain and fear. It is a matter, rather of two things that happen to occur at the same time; side by side. The slumlord's daughter, therefore, is not forced to be unsettled, and still less tormented by the fact that there are black and Puerto Rican families two miles distant who must pay the rent to make her luxuries conceivable . . .

To believe in victims is to believe, as well, in victimizers. It is to be forced to come into the presence of the whole idea that there must be *oppressors* in the world for there to be *oppressed.* It is to be forced, as well, to feel, and understand, that bad results too often have bad causes, that evil acts don't just "occur"—like mushrooms after rain—but have most often been initiated by the will of those who stand to profit from them.

From *The Night Is Dark* and *I'm Far from Home,* by Jonathan Kozol

---

PAY DAY

OBJECTIVES To give students the opportunity to distribute (imaginary) financial resources.

To help students understand that, with limited resources, some people have more means, others have less.

To help students see that there is a connection between the privilege of some and the lack of privileges of others.

MATERIALS Paper; pencils; local newspapers; social studies texts about communities; chart paper; markers.

IMPLEMENTATION Explain to students that, in groups, they will divide up a pretend sum of money to pay town workers. Brainstorm to come up with a list of the kinds of workers needed by a town. Keep the number of workers manageable—about 20.

Divide into groups of four students. Then tell each group that they are the town managers and have $600,000 for town salaries. They must distribute the money so that all the workers are paid. They should be able to explain the criteria by which they decided how much each person was paid.

After groups have finished, they copy their job and salary schedules on chart paper and post them in the front of the room. Go on to discuss these questions.

DISCUSSION 1. How did you decide what to pay workers? What criteria did you use?
2. Did any group decide to pay everyone the same? Why? What would happen if you did? Did the type of job matter? The amount of education? Responsibility? The appeal of the job?
3. Did you base your decisions on what you think really happens in a town, or on what you think should happen? Why?
4. Do you think people's needs—the number of children, illnesses in the family, and so forth—should be taken into consideration in deciding salaries? Explain.
5. In a community, or society, there are limited resources, just as in your town. What are your feelings about the fact that some people get paid much more than others? Why?
6. What choices do people who get more resources have?
7. What other ways can you think of to divide the resources that might be more fair?

Explain to the students that in any city (or nation), when some people get more, others *automatically* get less. Explain how privileged and "not-so-privileged" people are therefore *connected* to each other. One's fate affects the other's.

Sharing the Work for Equity

At George School, a Society of Friends (Quaker) boarding and day school in Buck's County, PA, all of the students have on-campus jobs. They work in the kitchen, sweep hallways, and do office work. No one receives payment for this work. The money that the school saves goes into a fund which then gives full tuition scholarships to 5 or 6 day students. Contrast this to the more typical college system where students with financial need do on-campus work which then gives them needed money for tuition and room and board. In that system those students have less time to take classes, study, and be with friends than students whose families have enough money to pay for all their expenses. This puts them at a dis-advantage academically and socially. It also means that they are publicly identified as financially needy. In the system at George School everyone shares in the work and those who need the financial help receive it.

Pay Day at Ben and Jerry's

Since its founding in 1978 in a renovated gas station through 1993 when it had $140 million in revenue, Ben and Jerry's Homemade Ice Cream ran on the seven-to-one compensation principle. That plan held that no employee could make more than seven times the lowest salary at the company. If the lowest paid worker made $20,000 the CEO made $140,000. Ben and Jerry's also donates 7.5 percent of pretax earnings to causes that have included world peace, children's issues and the campaign against bovine growth hormone.

ICE CREAM SUNDAES, APPLES, OR RAISINS

OBJECTIVES To give students an experiential sense of how resources (in this case, foods) are divided among classes of people.
To help students understand the feelings of those at various economic levels, and the options open to them.
To help students understand the economic interdependence of all groups of people.
To enable students to see how the privilege of some classes of people is connected to the lack of privilege of others.

MATERIALS Ice cream, toppings and nuts for sundaes for two students; one apple each for 26 students, and one raisin each for seven students; fancy table cloth; two fancy cloth napkins; 26 plain paper napkins. (This is a set up for 35 students. If you have a different number, keep the proportions the same—5% ice cream sundaes, 75% apples, 20% raisins. These figures are for food distribution in the United States, not the world. Divide students randomly unless certain students would not be able to handle certain roles.)

IMPLEMENTATION Set this up at a time when your students are out of the room. Create as gracious a setting as possible for two students. For example, a fancy table cloth, flowers, comfortable chairs—whatever gives the feeling of elegance. For another 26 students set up chairs in a circle or seats in a carpeted area. For the other seven students block off a bare floor area.

Begin with all students sitting in a group. Then call for the two students who will be sitting in the elegant setting and will receive ice cream sundaes. Read them "Privileged Citizen" from the Information Sheet below being sure that everyone else can hear. Escort them to their setting. Seat them. Serve them their elaborate sundaes. Then call up the apple group and read them "The Middle-Class Citizen," again being sure that all in the class can hear this. Seat them in their regular classroom seats. Serve them an apple each. Call up the raisin group reading "Poor Citizen" to them so all the class can hear. Direct them to the bare floor. Give them a plain container containing *one* raisin each.

Allow students to eat. Poor students must stay within their floor area. Middle-class students may go wherever they want. Note what students do and say. Allow activity to go on until students become restless or potentially disruptive. Then gather for discussion. Be sure to talk about the feelings, so that students don't retaliate against those who had the sundaes.

DISCUSSION

1. How did you feel about *where* you were sent and what you received for your snack? How did you feel as the activity went on?
2. What did you do? Was there anything else you wanted to do, but didn't do? Why didn't you do it?
3. What guesses were you making about the feelings of the people in the other two groups? How do those compare with what you just heard about their feelings?
4. What do you think you *might* have tried to do if you had been in one of the other groups? Why might you actually have done, or not have done that?
5. (If students with sundaes didn't share, ask this.) What benefits might there have been for members of each group if the sundae group had chosen to share?
6. How do the three groups in this activity compare to groups of people in our country?
7. In what ways do people in our country share between groups? In what ways do they not share?
8. In the United States, what connections are there between people who have plenty of food and people who are hungry?
9. (Define *interdependent* for the students.) How are all people in the United States interdependent? What responsibilities does this give to each of us?
10. In what ways could all citizens of the United States benefit from a more fair distribution of food and other resources?

Information Sheet

Privileged Citizen
You are a privileged citizen of this country. Welcome. Your group makes up 5 percent of the nation's population. You have almost unlimited enjoyment of the nation's goods. You enjoy good health care, wide choices for education, and many other opportunities.

Middle-Class Citizen
You are a middle-class citizen of this nation. Your group makes up 75 percent of the nation's people. You have education, adequate health care, and enough food to live.

Poor Citizen
You are a poor citizen of the United States. You are part of 20 percent of the nation's population. Your health care is poor and you don't have enough food. You don't get to travel. You have to be creative and resourceful if you are to get by.

The data used for this activity is about the United States. Economic class lines cannot be absolutely defined so these numbers are somewhat subjective depending on the exact criteria you use. Even given this, changes in criteria would still leave the middle class group the largest and the poor group continuing to grow.

Benefits of Equality to All

Throughout this section, help students explore the potential benefits that would come to *all* by distributing resources and opportunities based on equality.

For example: White team members might have benefited by acting against racism and keeping Charles Drew on their team. Sundae eaters might have felt better about themselves, and avoided anger, resentment and hard feelings, by sharing.

Most of us feel better about ourselves when we *act* on our beliefs. When we say we believe in equality but don't act, we often feel guilty or compromised. These feelings don't help us change things. Sharing power and redistributing opportunity also lessens tension, anger and hostility between those with more and those with less. Help students see these benefits for themselves, even when they have more resources, in working for equality.

UP AND OVER WE GO

OBJECTIVES
To have students examine the choices those with privileges have to see or not to see their connectedness to others, both in the activity and in society.

To help students examine the choices those with privileges have to use or not to use the benefit of those privileges to create change, both in this activity and in society.

To have students understand the advantages of cooperative work.

MATERIALS
This is an excellent activity to use with your students if you attend a recreational center for cooperative outdoor challenges. A nine foot wall is needed for the activity.

IMPLEMENTATION
Divide students into clusters of about six to ten. Have three clusters in all. One cluster should be the tallest third of the students, one cluster the shortest third and one cluster the "middles." (If you have fewer than eighteen students, have only two groups—a tall one and a short one. With more than thirty students, make more groups, using height distinctions.)

Have students gather in clusters. Tell them "Your task is to get everyone in the group over the wall. You may not use any props that you don't now have on you." Spot carefully for safety. Don't suggest cooperation but allow it within a group or between groups, if they think of it. Give each group a turn, encouraging the others to observe carefully.

If you have a student with a physical disability or one who is very heavy, you can modify the directions. The task can be to have everyone have a role in getting all group members who are physically able to get over, over the wall. The students not physically able to get over can take part in the planning, give encouragement, support someone else in getting over and so forth.

DISCUSSION

1. How did you feel when you saw how the students were divided?
2. How did your group "solve" the task? How well did you work together to reach a decision and to carry it out?
3. How did you feel about the other groups? Was the task easier or harder for them? Why? How much of that depended on their heights and how much on the way they did the task?
4. What are some times when a size difference makes a difference in how you can do a task? An age difference? A gender difference? A race difference? What are some things you can do to make that difference less of a problem?
5. I said, "The task is to get everyone in the group over the wall." How did you define "group"? You had a *choice* to think of "group" as a small group or as the whole class. Why did you make the choice you did?
6. In this activity being tall was a privilege that made the task easier. The tall group had a *choice* to use the privilege for themselves or to share the benefits with others. What did the tall group do with the benefits that their privilege gave them?
7. Did the members of the tall group "earn" their privilege?
8. What are examples in society of individuals and groups who have privileges that make doing certain tasks, or getting ahead in society, easier for them?

Privilege

Some privileges we're born with. One example is being born white. That's a privilege in the United States today because whites don't have to face institutional and cultural racism like people of color do.

Other privileges come from circumstances we're born into—like the resources our family has or the amount of money our community spends on education, recreation or health care. These circumstances are privileges because they give some people, more than others, opportunities to develop skills and abilities to their fullest potentials.

People's social identities, of course, are very complex. A person may have privilege in one area of her life—e.g., as a white person, but not in another—e.g., as a woman, lesbian or disabled person. For example a middle class, white girl may have advantages in her racial and class status, but if she's being sexually abused, her suffering is great. With an understanding of these complexities we can better work for change.

In areas where people have privilege, they can try to change the "rules of the game," so that *all* people have equal access to resources and opportunities. For example, men who work in predominantly male jobs, like plumbers or electricians, can encourage their unions to change their union practices or training programs to include more women in their profession. Such actions get at the *causes* of inequality.

In the wall activity, our lives, or society look to find out *why* inequality exists—why some people have more opportunities than others—and work together with others to change the causes.

9. In what ways can groups with privilege in society choose to share the benefit of those privileges with others?
10. How could the wall activity have been more fair?
11. Did anybody think of changing the members of the teams, or asking me if the teams could be mixed more equally? Why or why not?

CAN I GET IN?

OBJECTIVES   To experience being part of a dominant group, or being excluded.
To learn some options people in a majority group have for including or excluding those in the minority.

IMPLEMENTATION   Tell students you will be doing an activity in which all but one volunteer will hold hands and form a circle. Form the circle. When everyone is ready, tell the volunteer—who is on the outside—to try to get in.

Many things can happen. Usually people in the circle form a tight bond. Outsiders often try to squeeze in between people, go under legs, and on occasion try to convince someone to let them in. Sometimes outsiders try to force their way in. If anyone gets too rough, or the outsider gets too frustrated, call a halt. The activity usually ends when the outsider either gets in or gives up.

DISCUSSION
1. Outsider, how do you feel now?
2. How did it feel being on the outside of the circle?
3. How did it feel being on the inside of the circle?
4. What strategies did the outsider use to try to get into the circle?
5. Did any of the insiders feel bad for the outsider? How, if at all, did you act on those feelings? What did you tell yourself that convinced you to keep the outsider out?
6. Did the people in the circle talk to each other? If so, about what? If not, why not?

Now let's compare what happened in the activity to what happens in society.

7. What are some groups of people in society that are the more powerful groups? Which groups are on the outside?
8. In society the circle might represent access to power, privileges, jobs, money, and so on. How are some of the strategies the outsider used (or might have used) like the strategies people in less powerful positions in society use to try to get opportunities?

Strategies to Gain Equality

In this activity, the outsider could have: asked politely; used an assertive strategy like giving the group a "talking to" or crawling between legs; been creative—for example, tickled; or used force—for example, tried to break the insiders' hands apart.

There are many societal comparisons. If a girl wanted to be in an all boys' baseball league she might use a variety of approaches to get in: ask; petition; get so good "they" wanted her; stage a sit-in on the baseball field.

During the civil rights movement in this country, black people originally asked for equal rights and later used assertive tactics, including mass marches and strategies like freedom rides, to gain national publicity.

In your class, you can ask students to brainstorm comparable situations and strategies.

---

9. Let's focus on the majority of people—those on the inside of the circle: How do people with power and privilege in society keep that power and privilege from others? What do they do? What arguments do they use? How is this like what you did in this activity?

How People Hold Onto Power

In this activity people might have thought to themselves: "I like being on the inside, it feels good"; "Everybody else is keeping the outsider out, I'd better not be different"; "The outsider might feel bad, but it's only a game."

Take the societal examples cited above. The boys on the baseball team might say: "Girls aren't as good as boys, so they can't play"; "If I want girls to play, my friends will call me a 'girl-lover' or 'sissy'"; "Girls might feel bad, but it's only a game."

During the civil rights movement, white people might have thought or said: "If blacks get some rights, I'll lose mine"; "I support equal rights, but I don't want to get involved"; "If I actively support civil rights I might lose my friends."

---

10. What other choices did you have in the activity for including the outsider? What choices do people in powerful positions in society have for including those with less power?

Equal Resources, More Equal Results

Use your classroom as the setting for putting the "equal resources" maxim into practice. Think of any resource that might not get distributed to children equally. With students, develop a creative way to make things fairer.

For example, because of their class-background, some children are able to order more reading books from the book clubs than others. Talk with the class about setting a class goal—for example, everyone ordering at least three books. Then devise a creative way for raising money or gathering resources.

If your school is in an economically diverse neighborhood, a car-wash, bake-sale, or raffle could be effective. Many local businesses donate items for raffles in exchange for publicity. Students have fun with such a project, and all have more equal resources with which to order books!

Ms Meg   **by bulbul**

IF MEN HAD THE BABIES CHILD CARE WOULD BE FUNDED
....LIKE THE PENTAGON IS FUNDED!

Section C   The Complexities of Oppression

THE FILTER OF OPPRESSION

OBJECTIVES   To consider how different aspects of an individual's social identity can be a source of advantage or dis-advantage.

To examine similarities in the ways that different forms of oppression can influence access to resources and power by members of various social groups.

To think about the complexity of the influences of various forms of oppression and privilege on our lives.

MATERIALS   "Worksheet: The Filter of Oppression," p. 203, one per student, and also ideally a large "Filter of Oppression" chart for your room depicting what is on that Worksheet. "Worksheet: Clues for Understanding the Filter of Oppression," p. 204, cut up (optional). Students will either use:

a. A social identity flower. If students still have flowers from the lesson, "We Are Each of Many Traits," use those. Otherwise, make a flower model out of construction paper that has 8 petals that are flexible so that each one can remain straight out or can droop. Have materials available so each student can make a similar flower.

or

b. A "Worksheet: Our Social Identities: Advantages and Dis-advantages"—1 per student. Make this worksheet by typing the following, leaving space for students to write.

Think of two aspects of your own social identity you would like to explore. If possible, choose one aspect in which you have been dis-advantaged because of it and one in which you have had advantages. Choose examples that are typical—they happen often or are a pattern.

1. One aspect of my social identity is _____
  a. One way I experience dis-advantage is . . . .
  b. Despite the dis-advantage, one source of strength is . . . .
2. One aspect of my social identity is _____
  One way I experience advantage is . . . .

IMPLEMENTATION

Part I *Thinking Metaphorically*

Review the section of Chapter 2 on Social Justice Education in preparation for this lesson. With students make a list on the board of the various aspects of people's lives that are sources of diversity. You can remind them of the Social Identity Flower that they drew in "We Are Each of Many Traits" (Chapter 5, p. 83). When students have finished, ask questions to elicit any of the following that haven't been suggested: race, gender, class, age, physical/mental/emotional ability, sexual orientation, religion, and language.

Pass out "Worksheet: The Filter of Oppression," one per student. Explain that they will explore aspects of people's social identity depicted metaphorically on the flower on the Worksheet. Modify for your class, as needed. For example, if in your class ethnicity is a source of oppression in students' lives, include it.

Discuss the Filter of Oppression diagram with your students. If you feel that they are capable of exploring the metaphor themselves on their own first, follow the following procedure.

Divide students into fours and give each group member a copy of the Filter of Oppression diagram and a clue from "Clues for Understanding the Filter of Oppression." Have them share their clues with each other. They work together to put their understanding of the diagram in their own words. When returned to the whole class for discussion, ask them to share what meaning they made of the diagram.

DISCUSSION 1

Ask students to draw on what they have learned from other lessons from *Open Minds to Equality* as well as their own experience for this discussion.

1. Discuss one form of oppression in detail and then several others more briefly. For example:
   a. What are some ways people who have English as a second language are discriminated against because of linguicism? Despite this, what are some sources of their strength?
   b. What are some ways people who have English as a first language receive advantages because of linguicism?

2. After discussing a few more examples of forms of oppression ask students:
   a. What are some similarities in the ways discrimination is experienced by members of various dis-advantaged social groups? What are some differences?
   b. What are some similarities in the ways privilege is maintained by members of different advantaged social groups? What are some differences?

If students have difficulty understanding that some social groups have greater advantages than others:

   a. Review, or go back and do more, lessons on "the isms" in Chapter 6 and lessons on institutional discrimination in Chapter 7.
   b. Jump ahead to Chapter 9, "Discrimination: Has It Helped or Hindered Me?" and show the Primetime videos recommended for that lesson on the effects of institutional racism and sexism on people's lives today.

Part 2 *Exploring Aspects of Our Social Identities*

Discuss with students that each of our own social identities has many parts, and most of us are advantaged in some aspects of our social identity and dis-advantaged in others. Also, any aspect of our social identity may not be cut and dry. For example, a student may be of mixed race, with one white parent and one parent of color. Encourage students to be flexible; the point is not to box ourselves or others into categories, but rather to start to think as clearly as possible about our lives.

Ask students who experience dis-advantages because of an aspect of their social identity to also try to identify a positive facet of that aspect of their social identity. For example, a Jewish student might talk about her appreciation of the history of her people and their traditions. She might gain confidence from the positive stereotype that members of her group are intelligent.

If you are comfortable, share aspects of your social identity with students. Make a flower out of construction paper with petals, one for each aspect of your social identity that you want to share. Build the petal to stand straight out, if you gain privileges in our society in that area of your social identity, or make a petal droop if you face discrimination because of it. Share your flower with the class.

If you are uncomfortable sharing aspects of your own identity make a hypothetical student and make a flower for him. An example could be a ten year old, African American youth, Terrence, who has faced dis-advantages because of his race and age, but advantage because of his gender. For example, he has been excluded from parties because of his race. He doesn't have a chance to make many decisions in his home or school because his parents and teachers think he's "too young." Yet he and his friends always get the basketball court at recess because that's boys' turf. On his flower the gender petal would be straight out, while the age and race petals dropping. Yet because his family has taught him to be proud of his African American heritage, the sepal under the race petal lifts the race petal up.

The Authors' Social Identity Flowers

Nancy

If I were to make my Social Identity Flower most of my petals would be straight out. My gender petal would initially be drooping. Yet because of the strength I have received from other women and the women's movement to struggle against discrimination, the sepal under my gender petal would prop up the gender petal somewhat. My class petal would be slightly limp because I grew up in a lower middle class family where periodic unemployment made money a big worry. Now I am middle class. I would realize in looking at my flower that I received many privileges being who I am in our society.

Ellen

If I were to make my Social Identity Flower most of my petals would be straight out. My gender petal might be limp but not dropping. From a societal view being female does not give a person privilege but, in my own experiences, I often received many advantages from gender. For example I had much more freedom of what to wear than did my brother. I was supported in establishing open and caring relationships with friends. My class petal might be wiggly as I had the class advantage of parents with advanced education but not the extra money that often goes with that. My religion petal might have a bend. Growing up Jewish I experienced societal religious prejudice and grew up out of the mainstream of U.S. culture. But I benefited from the stereotype of Jewish children being smart in school. In other areas I have clearly and consistently received privilege in our society.

Tell students that they will now have an opportunity to chose several aspects of their own social identity to think about. Divide students into heterogeneous pairs. Either have students make their own Social Identity Flowers or use the "Worksheet: Our Social Identities: Advantages and Dis-advantages." Ask them to be ready to discuss at least two aspects of their own social identity and as many more as they wish. When finished with flowers or Worksheets, ask students to share with a partner. Then come together for class discussion.

DISCUSSION 2

1. What are aspects of your social identity that have been the source of dis-advantages? What's an example of that?
2. What are examples of aspects of your social identity from which you've gained advantages? What are some examples?
3. Are there some aspects of your social identity that have given you both advantages and dis-advantages? If so, what are some examples?
4. Was it harder to think of aspects of your social identity that brought advantages or dis-advantages? Why do you think that was so?

5. What aspects of your social identity that have been the sources of dis-advantages have also brought you benefits? What are some of those strengths or benefits?

6. What did you learn from listening to your partner describe aspects of her social identity? What similarities or differences were there with you and your partner?

7. The effects of privilege and oppression on our lives are often complex and multi-faceted. What are some ways this is so?

8. a. What might be an effect on people who are dis-advantaged by many aspects of their social identities? How might they feel about themselves? How might they see the world?

   b. Why might this have one effect on some people and a different effect on others? What might contribute to that? (Remind students, if necessary, how easy it is for people in privileged groups to see those with multiple dis-advantages as only oppressed and not acknowledge the strength, resilience, and abilities that people have developed despite burdens of inequality.)

9. a. What might be the effect on those people who are advantaged by most aspects of their social identities? How might they feel about themselves? How might they see the world?

   b. Why might this have one effect on some people and a different effect on others? What might contribute to that?

10. What might happen to flowers if people worked to remove the Filter of Oppression? How would the diagram change if the filter was removed?

11. How can we begin to remove the filter in our classroom and school?

Teacher Resources

Much of the theory base for the ideas in this lesson was developed by faculty and graduate students at the School of Education, University of Massachusetts, Amherst, Mass. See *Teaching for Diversity and Social Justice* by Maurianne Adams, Lee Bell and Patricia Griffin for theoretical background and teaching designs to use with adults on these same issues and dynamics.

Also see Peggy McIntosh's piece on recognizing white privilege, "White Privilege: Unpacking the Invisible Backpack" in *Women: Images and Realities, A Multicultural Anthology* by Amy Kesselman, Lily McNair, and Nancy Schniedewind.

FOLLOW-UP   "Using Privilege for Change" in Chapter 10 and "Sharing Privilege: Everybody Gains" in Chapter 11 are valuable follow-ups to this lesson.

BELIEVING THE MYTHS?

OBJECTIVES   To help students begin to understand internalized oppression—how people who experience institutional discrimination can come to believe the stereotypes and myths about themselves.

To have students think about ways to respond to internalized oppression in themselves and others.

To help students consider how people would act differently if they didn't internalize so many socially-reinforced stereotypes and myths.

MATERIALS   "Worksheet: Believing the Myths—Lamar's Survey," p. 205, and "Worksheet: Believing the Myths—Survey Quotations," p. 206, cut in strips, "Worksheet: Believing the Myths—Lamar's Analysis," p. 207 (optional).

IMPLEMENTATION   Divide students into groups of 3, with a person a, b, and c. Explain that they will be learning more about how the institutional discrimination they've been studying about affects people's beliefs about themselves. In groups, ask them to share responsibility for reading "Worksheet: Lamar's Survey." After they've done that as a class, discuss with them the idea of internalized oppression. Be sure to warn students not to blame people for internalizing oppression: the power of institutional and cultural discrimination often keeps people from seeing any alternatives to the prevailing myths and stereotypes.

Make the Reading Accessible

When the reading in a lesson might be a problem for your students, make adaptations so the process of reading doesn't impede their understanding of the concepts. For example, you can read aloud to the class material that is hard for your students and then have them read it again in small groups. Or divide them into cooperatively structured groups and give the role of reader/interpreter to someone who can both read the passage and answer any questions about its meaning. Or, when something students have to read for a lesson is too difficult, reword it to make it accessible to them.

Distribute quotations 1 and 2 to person a, 3 and 4 to person b, and 5 and 6 to person c. Each student is to:

1. Examine each quote and try to find why Lamar thought it was an example of internalized oppression.
2. Try to decide what stereotype(s) or myth(s) the young person might have believed about himself or members of his group.
3. If the person hadn't believed the myth, what might she have done instead?

For example, Lamar's uncle felt he wouldn't want to live in the neighborhood if there were too many blacks. The stereotype he might have believed is that white neighborhoods are better or that too many black people spoil a neighborhood or that white people are somehow superior to blacks. Any of these myths might influence his decision to move. If he hadn't believed the myths he might not have wanted to move.

Have each student first think about the two quotations she is responsible for. After several minutes ask person a to share her responses to the questions. After she does that, others can discuss those ideas and/or suggest new ones. Continue with person b and c.

If students are having trouble with these questions, you can give them "Worksheet: Lamar's Analysis" and ask them to compare their ideas to Lamar's. Then come together as a class for discussion.

DISCUSSION   For each quotation discuss the following:

1. What stereotypes or myths reinforced in our culture might the person have believed about himself or group?
2. How would the person have acted differently if he didn't believe the myth?
3. If you read "Lamar's Analysis," to what extent do you agree, disagree, with his ideas?
4. Have you noticed any examples like these in your life? If so, which? Now that you have greater awareness, look for examples and raise them in class as you discover them.

Then broaden the discussion:

5. When have you seen young people or adults believe other oppressive ideas about themselves or members of their group? How have they acted on those beliefs?
6. What can we do when we notice ourselves doing that? When we see it in others?

Talk with students about the idea of conscious choices. Sometimes when people become aware of how they've internalized a stereotype they still might *choose* to act in a similar way. For example, after Chantelle realizes that the idea that straight hair is the only "good hair" is a racist stereotype, she still may choose to straighten her hair because she's ready for a change in how she looks. While internalizing a stereotype is not a conscious choice in the first place, with new awareness students have the power to address it intentionally.

Discuss with students the way oppressions overlap in life. For example, Rodney might be in the resource room not only because he learns differently, but because he's black or poor. Students of color and low-income children are disproportionately referred to special education. Ask students and teachers to look for these overlaps. Also look for the ways the school or other institutions perpetuate these myths and stereotypes and how people can work together to change those. For example, maybe the staff in Marla's school doesn't talk with students about sexual harassment; they could be encouraged to do so and request outside resource people to help as needed.

7. How could those people benefiting from the myths internalize a sense of false superiority? Try to answer that for each of the survey situations. (See box below for ideas.)

False Superiority

- If boys believe the myth that boys' ideas in science are better than girls', they might feel they have the right to have girls accept their ideas.
- If white girls or light-skinned girls of color believe that lighter skin makes a girl prettier, they might believe that they are more beautiful than dark-skinned girls.
- If students whose native language is English believe that English is the best language, they might believe that they are smarter than students with other first languages because they speak English.
- If students who don't go to the resource room believe that anyone who goes to the resource room is stupid, they may believe that they are smart.

GOING FURTHER
a. Ask students to keep watching for examples of internalized oppression and discuss them in class as they come up.
b. Read stories and books that deal with ways young people who have stopped internalizing negative myths and stereotypes about themselves that are perpetuated by institutions in our society. Some examples include: *Thank You Dr. Martin Luther King* by Eleanor Tate, and for younger students, *Amazing Grace* by Mary Hoffman.
c. Music often can reach young people in ways words don't. Bob Blue's excellent tape, "*Starting Small*," includes several songs that contribute to multicultural understanding. (See Media section of the Bibliography.) Young people who understand how institutional discrimination affects them are much less likely to internalize oppressive ideas and values about themselves. Use "My Landlord" from "*Starting Small*" with your students to help them empathize with a young person affected by classism, explore her consciousness about it, as well as her determination to resist its effects in the future.

What about Blacks Calling Each Other "Nigger"?

Below two African American psychologists share their views about black young people calling each other "nigger."

1. In his book, *Raising Black Children*, Dr. Alvin Poussant responds to a first-grade teacher who wonders what to do when young children call each other "black nigger" when they are angry.

In young children such expressions are not always an indication of a deep-seated negative feeling about being black. Sometimes children have simply heard the words used elsewhere and are just repeating them. You can often end such name-calling by saying something like this, "Black people who feel good about themselves do not call each other names."

2. Dr. George Roberts of the Centers for Disease Control helps us think about the broader implications of the use of the term.

Use of the term "nigger" once was so common in American speech that African Americans began using it as a way of describing each other. Its use has since evolved within African American culture from its early hostile meaning to more recent character-izations of friends and romantic partners (e.g., "that's my nigger"). Some within African American communities reject the term outright, and decry it as an example of internaliz-ing White Americans' negative stereotypes of Blacks. Still, others argue that the term has been transformed through the act of negating oppression into more positive meanings. Both are probably correct in their understanding of the social psychology surrounding use of this term in African American communities.

Regardless of the intent and the underlying motivations related to its use, "nigger" is a word that is somewhat archaic and historically inappropriate. No matter how we try to forget its historical impact on two conflicting cultures, it continues to serve as a reminder of racism, discrimination, and countless acts of brutality.

It has no place in the schools except as a teaching tool in the understanding of racial prejudice and discrimination. Because of its largely negative connotations, the term can-not provide the basis for self-esteem development in children, especially those that are African American.

PUT IT ON OTHERS?

OBJECTIVES
To help students understand the effects of institutional discrimination on people's personal behaviors.
To help students recognize examples of lateral discrimination around them and in their own lives.
To think about alternative ways to deal with the pain of discrimination.

MATERIALS
"Worksheets: Put It on Others? Situation Cards," p. 208, cut up. Make Hunch Cards and give a different card to each person in groups of 3. (See Implementation for card content.)

IMPLEMENTATION
People who have experienced personal and institutional discrimination on a consistent basis over time are affected in deep and ongoing ways. One effect is the way some people who have been discriminated against because of one form of diversity can turn around and dis-criminate against others who are different from themselves. This lesson will help students understand such lateral discrimination.

Divide students into heterogeneous groups of three. Pass out a different Situation Card to each group member. Each reads it silently and then reads her card out loud to the others. Next ask students to talk about: 1) How they feel about the situations; and 2) What the situations have in common with each other. Come together as a class and discuss the responses to those questions.

Also ask them to begin to think about examples in their lives in which young people or adults, who themselves have been discriminated against, discriminate against other people who are different in yet another way. You might give an example from your own life.

Then tell students to return to their groups of three to begin to think about a big question. *Why* do people who are discriminated against sometimes turn around and discriminate against others? Ask each student to write a few ideas. Then have them share their written ideas with each other one at a time, and then discuss them as a group.

Tell them that students in other schools have thought about this question too. Pass out a "Hunch" card to each group member.

Ellis

   I think that when someone put us down we get lousy feelings. This really hurts inside. We want to get the hurt out so we lash out at other people. We want to turn those bad feelings out and put them on others.

Laura

   I don't think kids even think about the connections between being discriminated against because of one thing and then discriminating against others because of a different thing. We just don't even think about it. Or some kids think one kind of discrimination is bad, like racism, but another kind doesn't matter, like sexism or heterosexism.

Paul

   I think kids want to try to hide the way they are different so people won't tease them. So if they are loud and making fun of someone else there will be less chance of being picked on for being who they are. For example, if I'm busy making fun of you because you're a girl, people won't notice so much that I'm poor and tease me about that.

These are ideas from students in a fourth grade class in New York state. After each student reads the card to himself, ask each to read it to their group members. Ask them to discuss how their ideas are similar or dissimilar to the ideas of the New York students.

DISCUSSION
1. What ideas did you come up with for why some people who are discriminated against also can discriminate against others who might be different in another way?
2. How are your ideas similar to, or dissimilar from, the New York students?
3. What examples can you think of in your own life or other people's lives that support your ideas?
4. What can we do to help ourselves and others change the way we discriminate against others in these situations?
5. What can adults do to help us? How can we ask for that help?

IT TAKES A VILLAGE*

OBJECTIVES To better understand heterosexism and the impact it has on all people whatever their sexual orientation.

To learn how individuals and institutions reinforce discrimination, sometimes consciously, sometimes inadvertently.

To understand how homophobia affects the lives of people.

MATERIALS Paper and pencils; poster board; markers; (optional paints, tissue paper, scissors, glue); 1 copy of "Worksheet Story: It Takes a Village," p. 209, for each student; 1 copy of "Worksheet Chart: It Takes a Village," p. 210, for each group of 3 children. If possible a copy of the "It Takes a Village" poster, available from Syracuse Cultural Workers and one copy of the book *It Takes a Village,* by Jane Cowen-Fletcher. If you have the poster, put it in the front of your room.

IMPLEMENTATION Review with students to be sure that they know about lesbians as women who love women and may have them as partners, and gay men as men who love men and have them as partners. (Be sure to have done lessons introducing students to prejudice/stereotypes based on sexual orientation and heterosexism before doing this lesson.)

Be sure students understand the terms *individual discrimination* and *institutional discrimination. Individual discrimination* means that individual people act in ways that discriminate against certain groups of people. In *individual discrimination* it is not established policies that cause this behavior, but rather individual actions. *Institutional discrimination* means that the laws or policies of *institutions* oppress people of certain groups. These *institutions* include, among others: schools, health services, government agencies and the legal system. (Review "What Are They—The 'Isms'," p. 118, if needed.) Before beginning this lesson in groups, students may want to brainstorm on criteria to use to sort items between these forms of discrimination. We suggest you post these definitions and the criteria on newsprint sheets which are available to the students throughout this lesson. For example, "Is there a law that says this is the way it is?" or "Could an individual change the way she acts and thus change the experience for a lesbian or gay family in this particular situation?"

Also be sure that children understand the difference between *inadvertent* discrimination and *intentional* discrimination. Inadvertent discrimination is not done on purpose while intentional is on purpose. A way to think about the difference between these is that once an issue is raised and called to people's attention and they still continue to act in the same discriminatory way, this now switches from *inadvertent* discrimination to *intentional.* Again you may want to post these definitions for easy referral throughout this lesson.

Read the worksheet story aloud to the class. Clarify any confusing issues. Divide students into groups of three. Give each group one copy of the worksheet chart. Students work in groups to categorize all items on the worksheet. In their groups they then brainstorm additional items and categorize those. Have the class come back together to share the results of their categorizing. Create a class chart showing institutional and individual discrimination. Discuss questions below.

Children return to their small groups to each make a poster entitled "It Takes a Village" showing a village of people of different races, sexual orientations, etc. all participating in the lives of the children of the village. This is a village where there is no

---

*This lesson is based on Ellen's daughters' godmothers. I had to change the names because even today, in 1997, it is not safe to be this out. The names I chose were my godmothers, a lesbian couple who would likely have loved to adopt a child but, 50 years ago, could not do so. So this lesson reminds me both of the progress we have made and the progress we have not yet made.

individual or institutional discrimination against any people or groups of people and where all people support and affirm each other.

DISCUSSION

1. How might institutional discrimination hurt Toni and other children with lesbian or gay parents?
2. How might individual discrimination hurt Toni and other children with lesbian or gay parents?
3. What items did you think were intentional discrimination where institutions or individuals knew they were discriminating and chose to continue to do this? What causes people to make these decisions?
4. What items did you think were inadvertent discrimination where institutions or individuals didn't think about the issue of heterosexism and didn't realize that, by their actions, some groups of people were being hurt? What causes people not to realize this?
5. What can we do to fight the effects of this discrimination?

Addressing Homophobia in School

A Boston public school assistant principal, in responding to a new teacher's question about third grade children calling each other "faggot" and "queer" said, "Homophobia is an issue to be addressed in the same way we address racism and sexism. We must respond to children's homophobic comments and behaviors as we would to racist name-calling, as clearly and as strongly. We can incorporate work about homophobia in the same way we work on racism, sexism, and classism, in multiple aspects of our curriculum."

Recommended Resources on Heterosexism and Homophobia

Debra Chasnoff at Women's Educational Media has produced a film for adults, "Its Elementary" on teaching about heterosexism and homophobia in elementary schools. She is producing a set of four videos, CD-ROM programs and a curriculum for elementary schools. These show a full range of family life styles, portray schools where teachers are discussing these issues with young children, examine name-calling, and focus on current and historical gay and lesbian figures.

A good source of support, information, curriculum and advocacy is PFLAG. Useful resource books for teachers include *One Teacher in Ten* by Kevin Jennings, and *Twenty-First Century Challenge: Lesbian and Gays in Education* and *Open Lives, Safe Schools* by Donovan Walling.

Two recommended books for upper elementary school children are *Living in Secret* by Christina Salat and *Am I Blue?* edited by Marion Dane Bauer.

DIFFERENT KINDS OF BIAS: DIFFERENT EXPERIENCES

OBJECTIVES

To have students realize that empathizing with someone who has been the victim of discrimination is not just thinking about how the experience would be for them, but understanding how it may be for the victim.

To help students think about the differences in the impact of the experience of ongoing bias compared to occasional bias.

To help students think about the differences in the experience of bias based in discrimination compared to that of prejudice.

To have students understand that how people perceive and react to incidents of bias is often related to the degree of privilege and power they have in society.

MATERIALS   One copy of "Worksheet: Let Me Tell You About My Experience," p. 211. Type a "Worksheet: Different Kinds of Bias: Different Experiences" and make three copies for each group of three students; one large copy of this worksheet on newsprint. List these questions on the worksheet with space in-between for student writing.

1. Describe the bias in the incident.
2. Was experiencing bias for this characteristic a common occurrence for the main character(s)?
3. What aspect of the social identity of the main character(s), if any, would usually give her advantages in our society?
4. What aspect of the social identity of the main character(s), if any, would make her dis-advantaged in our society and a target of discrimination?

IMPLEMENTATION   This lesson is designed as a follow-up to "What Are They?—Prejudice and Stereotypes," p. 103 and "The Filter of Oppression," p. 180. Discuss with students how people experience bias differently. If possible use some student-generated examples from the earlier lessons in discussing this. Most times people experience discrimination for a characteristic for which they are dis-advantaged in society, like being gay. Sometimes those who are privileged experience prejudice because of an aspect of their social identity, like being white or being male, that usually gives them advantages. Use ideas from the box below in your discussion in ways appropriate to your students.

After a general discussion on this issue, work as a whole class on the first scenario on "Let Me Tell You About My Experience." Have one student read this aloud. Then discuss the scenario and complete the newsprint worksheet together.

After this, divide students into groups of three. Give each group one copy of "Let Me Tell You About My Experience" and three copies of "Worksheet: Different Kinds of Bias, Different Experiences." After groups have completed the worksheets, come back together for a whole class discussion.

DISCUSSION   1. Discuss the questions on the worksheet.
2. a. In what important ways did all of these children have *similar* experiences?
   b. In what important ways were these experiences *different* from each other?
3. What impact does our own experience of bias have on how we can understand others' experiences with this?
4. a. Think back to a time you have been a victim of bias. What aspect of your social identity was the basis for this bias?
   b. How typical is this type of incident for you?
   c. Does that aspect of your social identity give you advantages or dis-advantages in our society? Was this an example of discrimination or prejudice?
5. How can we help ourselves and others
   a. understand and remember the difference between occasional and on-going bias?
   b. tell the difference between discrimination and prejudice?

Subtle Distinctions in Experiencing Bias

In order to achieve greater understanding, acceptance and equity in our country, we need to be able to empathize with those who have had a range of experiences, some similar to ours and some different. One problem that often arises here is understanding what it means to "walk a mile in someone else's moccasins." The experience of being a victim of bias is a different experience depending on a range of circumstances. To say, "I know what it's like to be called a name" isn't necessarily accurate since *what it's like* depends on the context and the degree of power and privilege we have. There is a difference between experiencing ongoing discrimination because of an aspect of our social identity for which we are dis-advantaged in society and experiencing periodic prejudice or stereotyping for an aspect of our social identity that usually gives us advantages. (See Filter of Oppression Chart, p. 27.)

If we look at a person's race, for example, he is either white, and thus privileged in our society today, or a person of color, and thus dis-advantaged. A person of color, given the racism in our society, typically experiences discrimination on an ongoing basis.

Sometimes a white person can be the target of racial prejudice or stereotyping, e.g., harassed for being white by people of color. This is most appropriately called prejudice and is different from discrimination because white people are privileged in our society because of their race and hold power because of it. Racial prejudice, while painful, is different from ongoing discrimination.

Given the diversity of each of our social identities, some of us typically experience discrimination for those aspects of our social identities for which we are dis-advantaged in our society. We may also experience less frequent occurrences of prejudice because of those aspects of our social identities that give us privilege. Understanding the subtle, but significant, *differences* in these experiences is necessary if we are to *truly* empathize, rather than think we are understanding by using only *our* experiences as the model.

MANY VOICES

OBJECTIVES   To understand how the lives of people experiencing the same form of discrimination can be very different.

To learn to avoid generalizing about people who experience the same form of discrimination.

To understand the diversity in the lives of lesbian and gay people and their families.

MATERIALS   Large poster board size definitions of *heterosexism* and *homophobia* from "Females and Males: How We're 'Supposed' To Be?" p. 111; (be sure to do that lesson first), copies of "Worksheet: Hear the Voices," p. 212, one per student. Type "Worksheet: What Do We Understand? copy one per group of three. (See Implementation for questions.)

IMPLEMENTATION   Post definitions of heterosexism and homophobia from "Females and Males: How We're 'Supposed' To Be?" Discuss these with students. Then divide students into groups of three. Give each student one copy of "Worksheet: Hear the Voices." Students work in groups to read the people descriptions. Give each group one of "Worksheet: What Do We Understand?" on which they answer the following questions.

1. What, if anything, do all these speakers have in common? Explain.
2. Geoff and Jamila are the two teenagers in this set of speakers. In what ways are their experiences similar to each other? In what ways are they different?

3. Della and Mike are the two parents in this set. In what ways are their experiences similar to each other? In what ways are they different?
4. Ethan and Emma are the two elementary school age children in this lesson. In what ways are their experiences similar to each other? In what ways are they different?
5. How do these people deal with the discrimination they face? How do they feel and what strategies do they use?
6. What would you like to ask each of these speakers in order to help you better understand heterosexism and homophobia?

DISCUSSION

1. Discuss worksheet questions together.
2. From this lesson what did you learn about the range of experiences of being lesbian or gay, or being the child of lesbian or gay parents?
3. Did this learning challenge any of your beliefs about the lives of lesbian and gay people? If so, in what ways?
4. What different examples can you think of where other groups of people that suffer the same form of discrimination also have varied lives and experiences?
5. What did you learn about discrimination based on sexual orientation? Did this learning challenge any of the stereotypes you have heard?
6. What did you learn about different responses to this discrimination?
7. Do you know anyone in your school or community who has suffered because of heterosexism and homophobia? What has been done to address this? What more could be done?

A LEGACY OF RACISM

OBJECTIVES

To help students understand the different experiences and effects of racism on groups of people who have suffered racism over time compared to groups without such a history.

To help students understand, through families' stories, the legacy of 250 years of racial oppression on African American people.

To have students understand the difference between the experience of African Americans and recent immigrants of color.

MATERIALS

A copy of the following books: *Nettie's Trip South* by Ann Turner, *Pink and Say* by Patricia Polacco, and *The Friendship* by Mildred Taylor. These are three excellent books. If they aren't in a school library in your district, they are well worth ordering. The first two are picture books geared for upper elementary students, with powerful content for this age group. The last is a longer story with pen and ink drawings.

IMPLEMENTATION

Tell students they'll be considering some of the differences between different racial groups who have come to the United States. Ask them to consider this scenario.

You overhear one white student talking to another white student. "The students who came to our school from Cambodia three years ago are really fitting in and doing well in school now. African Americans have been here 250 years. Why aren't they integrated and doing better by now?"

Ask students to think about some of the differences between the experiences of African Americans and other people of color who have immigrated here more recently. They will likely point to the similarity that both face racial discrimination today. They

---

*While this particular lesson focuses on African Americans, Native Americans have suffered similar, long-term, historical legacies of racial oppression in the U.S.

might point to these differences, among others: 1) African Americans were brought to the U.S. involuntarily as slaves while most recent immigrants came voluntarily; 2) African Americans suffered racial oppression for 250 years while recent immigrants of color have no historical legacy of racial oppression in the U.S.

After they have discussed this, tell them that by using literature for young people, they will further understand one of the differences: the legacy of racial oppression of African Americans in the U.S.

Introduce the literature by explaining that each of the stories they will hear has come from the author's own family history. *Nettie's Trip South* was inspired by Ann Turner's great-grandmother's diary of her trip South taken in 1859 when she was a young woman. There she witnessed a slave auction and returned home a committed abolitionist. Patricia Polacco's great great grandfather, Sheldon Russell Curtis, passed down through the generations the story told in *Pink and Say*. Mildred Taylor's, *The Friendship,* is based on a story her father told about his life in the segregated South.

The extent of historical context you may want to provide will depend on the needs of your students. These books will make the most sense to students if they have some knowledge about slavery, the Civil War, and segregation in the South. Explain that *Nettie's Trip South* describes slavery, endured by many blacks in the U.S. for 100 years before the Civil War. *Pink and Say* takes place during the Civil War. *The Friendship* takes place in the South in the 1930s. Tell students they will be looking for the ways in which racism affected African Americans in these different periods in U.S. history. These are just three examples of an ongoing history of racial oppression.

It will take several days to read these books out loud to your class. All are very powerful stories that stand on their own and have much in common with the others. While *Nettie's Trip South* and *Pink and Say* can easily be read in one sitting, you may choose to read *The Friendship* over two or three days.

Ask students to recall discussions your class has had about discrimination and oppression and think about the difference in what the words mean to them. If they consult a dictionary they will find something like the following:
- discrimination—to make a distinction in favor of or against a person
- oppression—the exercise of authority in a burdensome, cruel, or unjust manner

Discuss with them the force of a system of oppression, and how power is used to keep one group of people subordinate to another group of people, in this case, African Americans subordinate to whites. Ask them to listen for ways this system was maintained as they listen to the stories.

DISCUSSION After reading each book, ask students the following questions.

1. What were ways in which racial oppression toward African Americans was manifested in the story?
2. How did that oppression affect African Americans?
3. What were examples of humanity, hope, and resistance in the face of oppression?

After reading and discussing all three stories with students, discuss the following questions.

Oppression is maintained by keeping the subordinate group powerless and dehumanized.

4. What were some of the ways whites kept African Americans powerless in each of the stories?
5. What were some of the similarities in the ways African Americans were kept oppressed in all three stories?
6. What are the similarities and differences in the ways characters in the stories showed humanity and integrity in the face of oppression?
7. What kind of effect might this history of racial oppression—that still continues in different ways—have on African Americans over generations?

8. People from what other groups have experienced such a history of racial oppression in the U.S.? How has this affected them?

9. How might you respond to the white student quoted at the beginning of this lesson?

Picture Books for Older Readers

Picture books for older children have become increasingly popular in recent years. Below are some suggestions of ones you may want to consider if you teach upper elementary students or even middle school.

In addition to *Pink and Say,* Patricia Polacco has written and illustrated many other books appropriate for upper grades. These include *Mrs. Katz and Tush* about a friendship between an elderly Jewish woman and a young African American boy, and *Chicken Sunday* about the growing relationship between a Holocaust survivor and a racially and culturally mixed group of children. *Grandfather's Journey,* by Allen Say, tells the story of three generations of a family raised partly in Japan and partly in the U.S. and their love for both lands. *The Christmas Menorahs: How a Town Fought Hate,* by Janice Cohn, tells the true story of how elementary school students acted together to fight anti-Semitism.

1. Which group were you in_____?

   praised, criticized

2. How did you feel when you came to school this morning?

3. How did you feel in the middle of the morning?

4. How did you feel at lunchtime?

5. How did you feel in the middle of the afternoon?

6. How did you feel right before our end-of-day discussion?

7. How did you do in each subject compared to how you usually do?

   Math _____   Reading _____

   Language Arts_____   Social Studies_____

   Science_____   Others _____

8. What do you think happens to students who never get praised or supported by adults? What could be done to change this?

9. What do you think happens to groups of people in society who get more criticism than praise for characteristics they can't control—like their skin color?

your order	item
_____	1. great athletic ability
_____	2. ability to make a few close friends
_____	3. happy family life
_____	4. ability to lead others
_____	5. artistic skills and success
_____	6. love of learning
_____	7. good health
_____	8. chances for adventure
_____	9. lots of money
_____	10. ability to do very well in school
_____	11. success in the job of your choice
_____	12. good looks
_____	13. power over things—fix cars, computers, build houses
_____	14. being important
_____	15. musical talent
_____	16. ability to bounce back
_____	17. ability to give love to others
_____	18. ability to help other people
_____	19. ability to make many friends
_____	20. success at changing the world to make it a better place
_____	21. parents who trust you
_____	22. chance to travel wherever you want
_____	23. _____
_____	24. _____

Lynne is a fourth grader who has a physical disability that effects her school work. She is paralyzed on one side of her body. Writing is slow for her and she gets tired while writing. She also has trouble focusing her ideas. She has an aide come into the classroom and help her during writers' workshop.

Paul is in Lynne's fourth grade class. Writing is hard for Paul and he really has to work at it. Today Paul was having a particularly tough time with his writing. He looked over and saw Lynne getting help from her aide. Paul raised his voice so everyone could hear and said, "It's no fair Lynne gets an aide. That's favoritism!"

1. Interior Monologues

   Person A—Get into Lynne's shoes. On a separate piece of paper write an interior monologue that Lynne might have when she hears Paul.
   Person B—Get into Paul's shoes. On a separate piece of paper write an interior monologue that Paul might have when he sees the aide helping Lynne.

2. Listening and Reflecting

   Read your interior monologues to each other.

   Discuss:
   • Are there any thoughts, feelings or experiences that you have in common? If so, what ones?
   • How have your thoughts and feelings changed, if they have, now that you've heard each other?

3. Rethinking the Situation

   Talk together about how this situation could be made satisfying for everyone and also fair.

   What did you come up with?

   How is your resolution fair?

   Does each person get the *same* thing?

Mourka is a very able reader. She reads difficult material quickly and understands it well.

Reading is the subject Taeme has the most trouble with in school. She must read very slowly in order to understand the meaning of what she reads. If she reads a little at a time and reads carefully, she can understand her work.

Mourka and Taeme are working together with two other students in a cooperative learning group. Each student is assigned a different part of a story and each must report on their part to the group. The group will be responsible for understanding the whole story.

The teacher came to their group and assigned Mourka 8 pages. When Mourka noticed the teacher gave Taeme 2 pages she complained to the teacher. "That's not fair. Everyone should get the same number of pages."

1. Interior Monologues

    Person A—Get into Mourka's shoes. On a separate piece of paper write an interior
       monologue that Mourka might have when she sees Taeme get 2 pages to read.
    Person B—Get into Taeme's shoes. On a separate piece of paper write an interior
       monologue that Taeme might have when she hears Mourka complain about her getting
       only 2 pages to read.

2. Listening and Reflecting

    Read your interior monologues to each other

    Discuss:
    • Are there any thoughts, feelings or experiences that you have in common? If so, what
       ones?
    • How have your thoughts and feelings changed, if they have, now that you've heard each
       other?

3. Rethinking the Situation

    Talk together about how this situation could be made satisfying for everyone and also fair.

    What did you come up with?

    How is your resolution fair?

    Does each person get the *same* thing?

Christopher is in fifth grade at Kiley School, a predominantly white middle school in a suburb of a large city. He does well in school and enjoys the academic and extracurricular programs. He's in sports, the newspaper club, and a special program for gifted students.

Trevor just entered Kiley School this year. Before Trevor went to elementary school in the city. There much less money is spent per child on education than is spent in the suburbs. Since the quality of his education was not up to that at Kiley, he is behind in several subjects. Therefore Trevor participates in a special program where he gets tutoring in math and writing.

Christopher resents the special program Trevor goes to. He'd like to get some special tutoring himself to help him become the best writer on the school newspaper. One day when his classmate, Trevor, is leaving for tutoring he says, "It's not fair that Trevor gets special tutors. I've never had them in this school".

1. Interior Monologues

   Person A—Get into Christopher's shoes. On a separate piece of paper write an interior monologue that Chris might have when he sees Trevor leaving for tutoring.
   Person B—Get into Trevor's shoes. On a separate piece of paper write an interior monologue that Trevor might have when he hears Christopher's comments.

2. Listening and Reflecting

   Read your interior monologues to each other

   Discuss:
   • Are there thoughts, feelings, or experiences that you have in common? If so, what ones?
   • How have your thoughts and feelings changed, if they have, now that you've heard each other?

3. Rethinking the Situation

   Talk together about how this situation could be made satisfying for everyone and also fair.

   What did you come up with?

   How is it fair?

   Does each person get the *same* thing?

Elissa and Tanya are best friends in the seventh grade. They attend the same K–8 community school and live around the corner from each other. Often they do homework together. When Elissa and Tanya do projects together outside of school, they find they learn at equal rates. They are both quick learners with good concentration and lots of energy, and they are both good teachers once they know how to do something. While some things are sometimes a little easier for one of them than for the other, they have both done well at learning to sew and to skate, and in piloting a new math curriculum on numbers systems from other cultures. In school Elissa gets almost all As. Tanya gets Bs and Cs. Usually their classes study the same topics in each subject, but Elissa's section does harder work in each topic.

Elissa's story: Elissa is the oldest of three children. She has never met her father; he pays no child support. Elissa's extended family has always been very involved in her life and her schoolwork. Her mother and stepfather are both scientists. Her mother has two master's degrees and her stepfather has a doctorate. When Elissa's parents go into the school to talk about what they want for Elissa, the school treats them respectfully as a white, very well educated, two parent household. They are better educated than most of the school staff and were always very successful in school themselves. Elissa's household owns a set of encyclopedias, several atlases, many dictionaries, hundreds of books, and a computer. Elissa's stepfather works from 8 AM–5 PM most days, often bringing home reading or writing to do at night. Her mother works three evening or weekend shifts a week, each eight hours long. She does not bring work home. Elissa has no regular responsibility for care for her younger siblings. When she does do child care for them, she gets paid. After school Elissa sometimes has dance or violin lessons, does homework at home or at the library, or hangs out with her friends.

Tanya's story: Tanya is the older of two children. Her father lives in Ohio and does not pay child support, nor see her. Her mother's sisters and her mother's father visit often, although not owning cars, they find it hard to come to school events, especially in the evenings. Her mother has graduated from high school and works as a bank teller. When Tanya's mother goes into the school to talk about what she wants for Tanya, the school sees her as a black single parent. Tanya's mother, Sharon, was never very comfortable in school herself and doesn't know how to lobby for her daughters. For the last three years Tanya has been fully responsible for after-school and Saturday care for her younger sister, Nancy, who is now in second grade. When Sharon gets home from work she is the only adult available to do housecleaning, laundry and cooking. She cares that her daughters are clean and neat and appear well taken care of. Tanya's house has very few books and other school supplies. On her salary, Tanya's mother works very hard to earn enough to pay for rent, food and other necessities for her daughters. Tanya can do her homework at the library, but she must bring Nancy along. The librarians don't mind if they work in the children's room, but now that Tanya is in seventh grade she finds she often needs books that are in the young adult or adult sections or in reference. The librarians give her a hard time when she brings Nancy to these areas.

Charles Drew was born in 1904 in Washington, D.C. to middle class parents. His ancestors were African American, Scottish, English and Native American. His family's ties were in the African American community, particularly to their local Baptist Church. Charles was the oldest of five children. Although his parents were not poor, they did believe in all the children helping the family out by earning money. Charles worked selling newspapers and, when he was older, doing construction.

Charles attended segregated schools in Washington, D.C. His high school, Dunbar High, had more of its graduates go on to college than any other high school in Washington. While at Dunbar High, Charles was an excellent student, but an even more devoted athlete. He played football, basketball, track and baseball. He won awards for Best Athlete, Most Popular, and Student Who Has Done the Most for the School.

— — — — — — — — — — — — — — — — — — cut— — — — — — — — — — — — — — — — — — — —

Charles attended Amherst College. While more focused on studying than he was in high school, he was still passionately committed to sports, earning many awards for both football and track. In one football game he was tackled and seriously injured by the cleats of an opposing player's shoe. While recovering in the hospital, Charles' interest in medicine became stronger. His friendship with a 16 year old fan increased his interest in how the body works and in the importance of good medical care. Charles planned to attend Howard Medical College, one of the two major black medical schools in the country. First he took a year off to live at home and save money. When it came time to go to medical school, Howard Medical College did not accept him as he was missing a few credits. Instead Charles attended McGill University in Montreal, Canada. Here he continued in sports, but with a much greater emphasis on his academic work.

— — — — — — — — — — — — — — — — — — cut— — — — — — — — — — — — — — — — — — — —

While in medical school, Charles became more aware of the problems with blood donations. Blood could not be preserved. Fresh blood could only be saved several days. Many people died because of the lack of the right blood match when it was needed. Seeing the need for better blood preservation, Charles Drew made this his career goal. He began to do research in this area. Dr. Drew also trained to become a surgeon and became very good at this. At this time his father died and Dr. Drew returned to live near his family in Washington, D.C. He worked at Freedmen's Hospital, a local black hospital, while also teaching courses at Howard Medical College. Dr. Drew later moved to New York City to continue his own training and to work more on setting up a Blood Bank.

— — — — — — — — — — — — — — — — — — cut— — — — — — — — — — — — — — — — — — — —

During World War II, Dr. Drew was asked to manage blood donations for England. He was chosen because of his excellent skills at management and as a leading authority in the U.S. on blood banks. However, many Americans did not want him to have the job because he was black. He got the job and, with his understanding of the latest knowledge about blood donations, was able to help save many soldiers' lives.

Dr. Drew went on to train many black doctors as surgeons. He fought the American Medical Association which was not welcoming of black doctors. The AMA finally ended their discrimination against black members 21 years after Dr. Drew first started working on the issue.

Then one day the track team went to Brown University for an important meet.

After the game the coach talked to Charlie and the other black members of the team. He said that blacks weren't allowed in the Narragansett Hotel, where the team was going to eat dinner.

"But then where is the team going to eat?" asked Charlie.

"Why don't you boys eat in a cafeteria?" answered the coach. "The rest of us will go to the hotel."

"A team is supposed to stick together," snapped Charlie, but the coach just walked away.

Late that night the team returned to Amherst College. Charlie shut himself up in his room to think.

When I score points for the team, everyone cheers, he told himself. But when the game is over, I'm just another Negro. I don't want to be an athlete anymore, Charlie decided.

From *Charles Drew*, by Roland Bertol, p. 10.

1. Cite two examples of racism in this account.

2. How did the coach's racism harm Charles and the other black team members? How was it harmful for the whole team?

3. How was the privilege that the white team members had tied to the denial of privilege to the black members?

4. List three things the white team members could have done.

5. What might you have done? Why?

6. What benefits would the white athletes have received if they had acted against racism?

Filter of Oppression

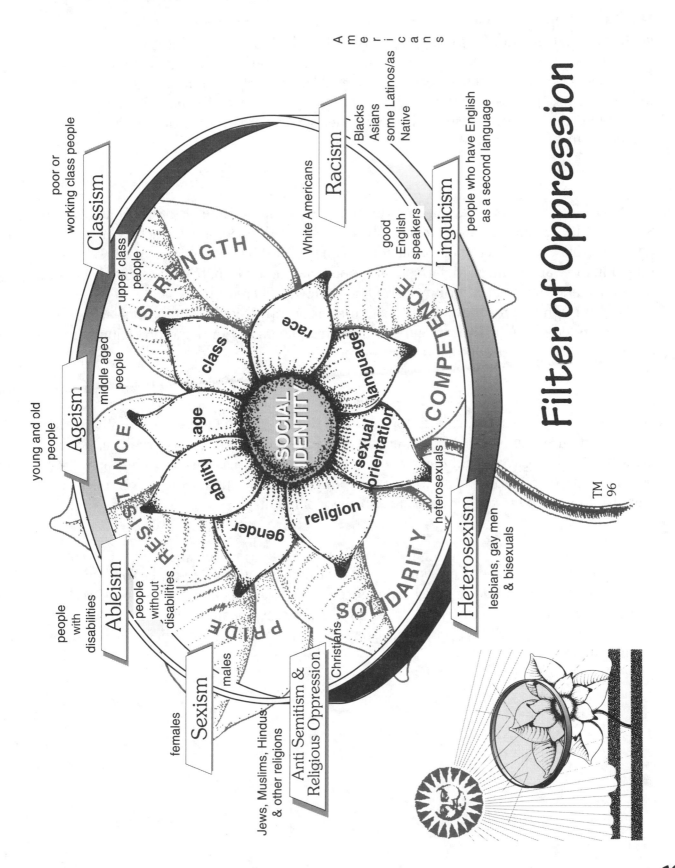

Americans

Racism
- Blacks
- Asians
- some Latinos/as
- Native
- White Americans

Linguicism
- people who have English as a second language
- good English speakers

Classism
- poor or working class people
- upper class people

Ageism
- young and old people
- middle aged people

Ableism
- people with disabilities
- people without disabilities

Sexism
- females
- males

Anti Semitism & Religious Oppression
- Jews, Muslims, Hindus & other religions
- Christians

Heterosexism
- heterosexuals
- lesbians, gay men & bisexuals

SOCIAL IDENTITY

race · class · age · ability · gender · religion · sexual orientation · language

STRENGTH · COMPETENCE · SOLIDARITY · PRIDE · RESISTANCE

TM 96

1. The Filter of Oppression in the diagram represents a filter around a plant that either lets sun and rain filter through to certain petals on the plant or keeps it out.

   In our society the Filter of Oppression is a combination of various isms that provides resources and power to advantaged groups and keeps them from dis-advantaged groups. In the Filter of Oppression diagram, dominant groups are inside the filter, having received advantages because of the isms. Dis-advantaged groups are on the outside having been denied them.

2. The Social Identity Flower can also represent an individual with petals representing various aspects of that person's social identity. The Filter of Oppression affects each petal in a different way. One aspect of his social identity may afford him advantages while others may bring dis-advantages. Metaphorically, one petal can be firm, having received sun and rain, while another petal is droopy if sun and rain were filtered out.

   Even though in a real flower, petals are firm or droopy together, in this Social Identity Flower some petals may be firm and straight, while others are limp and drooping because of the degree of power and resources they receive.

3. Each person in life—each flower—is complex and will usually be different from others even if they share a similar social group membership. For example two people may get similar privileges for being white, but have very different situations in life because they are of a different gender, religion and so forth. Even though both race petals on their Social Identity Flower are firm, other petals may be very different.

4. Even though people may be dis-advantaged in society because of an aspect of their social identity, at the same time, they may experience positive benefits from it. An oppressed person or group may develop pride, strong group identity, meaningful traditions/culture and strength from resisting oppression. The sepals, representing these benefits, can boost a sagging petal.

BACKGROUND

Lamar is a sixth grade student whose class had been studying a lot about all kinds of discrimination. When his uncle came to visit a few weeks ago Lamar got very confused by something he said. He announced that he was moving his family to a new neighborhood because they were too many blacks moving into his. Lamar couldn't understand that because his uncle is black.

Lamar talked to his teacher about what his uncle said. Mr. Lewis, also a black man, explained that sometimes people who are exposed to lots of stereotyped messages about their social group through society's institutions—like the media and schools—come to believe the myths. He said he's heard other blacks say things that suggest that they believe that white people are somehow better than blacks.

Mr. Lewis explained that this is called internalized oppression. People take into their minds ideas that keep them feeling inferior to others, even though these ideas aren't usually true. Lamar wanted to learn more about this so Mr. Lewis suggested that he do a survey and then share it with the whole class.

Lamar listened to the conversations of friends, classmates and relatives over the next week. He wrote down examples of what he thought was internalized oppression. Work on the quotations that Lamar noted. Your teacher will give them to you.

1. Sarah

"I had a good idea for our group science project today. I explained it to my group members. Next Ken gave his idea. His idea was interesting, but I thought mine was more creative and exciting. My group members just discussed his idea, and not mine, and decided to take his idea for our project. I guess Ken's idea is really better."

— cut— —

2. Chantelle

"I'm so happy. My mother's going to let me get my hair straightened tomorrow. She admitted that I wasn't born with "good hair"—hair that's soft and wavy. Mine is so kinky and rough, like lots of other black people's hair. I'll look so much better after tomorrow."

— cut— —

3. Rodney

"I got in trouble today when I went to Ms. Wang's resource room for reading. Whenever I make a mistake I say to myself, "you stupid jerk." Whenever Todd messes up I call him "doofus." I did that three times today. Ms. Wang got really annoyed and assigned me extra homework."

— cut— —

4. Sonia

"I'm so jealous of my sister. We're both Puerto Rican but she was born with much lighter skin than mine. She looks white! She's so pretty."

— cut— —

5. Marla

"At recess Paul ran by me and tapped me on my rear with a stick. At first I felt mad. Then I thought that maybe he likes me and that's his way of telling me. I guess I shouldn't mind."

— cut— —

6. Carlos

"I went to my guidance counselor, Mr. Molina, to be interviewed to be an assistant in the kindergarten after-school program. He's bilingual. I really wanted to speak to him in Spanish because I can explain myself better, but I was afraid he'd think I wasn't smart. I talked to him in English. I hope I get chosen!"

— cut— —

7. Peter

"I'm sorry for getting mad at you, John, when you cancelled out on the ride to the soccer game with me and my uncle. Other people, too, have been afraid to ride with my uncle because he's gay. I guess I can understand."

Sarah

a. Sarah might believe a sexist stereotype. She might believe that boys' ideas in science are better than those of girls.

b. If Sarah hadn't believed the myth, she might have encouraged the group to give serious consideration to her idea as well as to Ken's.

Chantelle

a. Chantelle might believe that her hair is not attractive or as good as soft, wavy hair. She might believe that the more hair is like many white people's hair, and the less it is like many black people's hair, the better it is.

b. If Chantelle didn't believe those myths she might have left her hair the way it was naturally and not get it straightened. She might feel attractive and proud as a young black woman for being who she is and not compare herself to a white image of beauty.

Rodney

a. Rodney might believe that because he goes to a resource room for help with reading that he is "stupid." He might believe that about anybody who goes to the resource room.

b. If Rodney didn't believe those myths he might not put himself and other students down whenever they made a mistake. He might understand that people have all kinds of minds and learn in different ways at different rates. He might know that lots of very intelligent, capable people learn differently from most.

Sonia

a. Sonia might believe that having lighter skin makes a person better or prettier than having darker skin.

b. If Sonia didn't believe this she might not be jealous of her sister and might feel better about her skin.

Marla

a. Marla might believe that it's okay for boys to touch parts of girls' bodies without consent. She might believe that if boys treat girls like their property, it's just part of flirting.

b. If Marla didn't believe this, she might tell Paul that when he taps her rear, she doesn't feel respected. She might tell him to stop.

Carlos

a. Carlos might believe that English is a better language than Spanish and to look smart a person should use English.

b. If Carlos didn't believe that he might feel comfortable speaking in Spanish with anyone who understood Spanish. He might feel that being bilingual is an asset and not a problem.

Peter

a. Peter might believe a heterosexist stereotype. He might believe that it's not safe to be with people who are gay.

b. If Peter hadn't believed that myth he might have worked harder to explain to John that he'd be safe with his uncle and that gay people are as safe to be with as other people.

A. Lani and Rosa

Lani moved from China to the U.S. two years ago. She lives in a city where there is a small, but growing, population of Chinese people. She has had trouble making friends not only because she is learning English, but because other young people never invite her to do anything with them outside of school. She feels that she's being excluded by other students. She hangs out with a few other Chinese students who all take the same bus to school.

Ten years ago Rosa's parents emigrated from Mexico. Rosa likes being in the U.S. except for the fact that members of her family have trouble finding permanent work. Even when Rosa applies for babysitting jobs, an Anglo (white, European) student usually gets the position instead.

Lani and Rosa ride the same school bus. The bus is overcrowded and some students have to sit three in a seat. Groups of students push to get on first to save a seat just for two. When students don't get the seats they want they start calling other groups of students names. Lani and her friends call the Chicano/a students "tortilla heads" and Rosa and her friends call the Chinese American students "slit eyes." The name-calling has been getting worse.

— — — — — — — — — — — — — — — — — — cut— —

B. Richie

Richie is proud of his European American heritage. His father's parents came from Ireland and his mother's from Poland. What he doesn't like is being discriminated against for being poor. His Dad is disabled and stays home and his mother works in a nursery school. Other young people make fun of him because his family lives in public housing and uses food stamps.

At least Richie likes school. He likes playing basketball at recess best of all. Richie's a great player who loves to win. He has a group of boys he likes to play with who are also terrific players. When girls ask to play, though, he refuses to let them play and says things like, "girls will mess up," "girls are lousy players." When a boy who's not so skilled in basketball plays and makes a mistake he hollers, "get it together you faggot."

— — — — — — — — — — — — — — — — — — cut— —

C. Ella

Ella is Jewish. She is able to talk openly about her family's experience as Jews. She explained to her class how her family was kept out of a tennis club because they were Jewish. Her uncle's family had a swastika painted on the sidewalk in front of their house. A few times Ella herself has been called names because she's Jewish.

Ella and her friends are entering the talent show at their camp. They are planning a comedy routine. They have some jokes in the routine that make fun of Italian, Polish and Irish people. These jokes always get lots of laughs. The girls are looking forward to being a big hit!

For many years, Lena and Mary wanted a baby. They often took care of their friends' children, doing projects, taking them on excursions and having them visit on special overnights. They belonged to children's museums and farms and would go to those themselves because they genuinely enjoyed these sorts of activities.

Since they were both women they were not able to physically have a child together. They couldn't apply together to adopt a child because there is so much discrimination against lesbian and gay couples. So they decided that Mary would apply on her own, as a single mother, with Lena as her roommate rather than as her partner. They had many friends who were happy to write letters saying what a good mother they thought Mary would be.

Nine months after they started this process, they received a phone call. An adoption agency had a baby for Mary. That was faster than they expected and they were thrilled. They flew down to Florida to get the baby.

When Lena and Mary arrived with Toni at the airport in Chicago they were welcomed by a whole community of their friends. One of their welcome presents was the poster "It Takes a Village" from the African proverb "It Takes a Village to Raise a Child." Their friends were delighted to be the village to help raise this child.

Toni has been adopted into a loving family, part of a loving extended family and loving community. She is fortunate to have parents who love each other, who truly wanted her and are well able to take good care of her.

But Toni will have to face discrimination because of heterosexism in this country. Some of this will be because of institutional discrimination. Institutional discrimination means that there are laws and policies that make life not fair for some groups of people. So even though Mary and Lena and Toni are a family they won't be able to get family health insurance. Mary will be able to have Toni on a family policy, but they will have to pay for a separate individual policy for Lena, costing them over $1000 more a year than if they could have the kind of family medical insurance that families with a mother and father and child can have.

Some of the discrimination will be because of individual discrimination. Some families may not let Toni's friends go over to her house to play because she has two mommies instead of a mommy and daddy. Some of it will be intentional (on purpose) and some of it will be inadvertent (people not realizing what they are doing). For example when her mothers go to enroll her in nursery school the form will say, "Mother's name _____", "Father's name _____." The school may be willing to change these forms once they understand why this is a problem, or they may not. Her mothers will find it hard to find many children's books with stories about families like theirs. Family puppet sets will come with one mommy, one daddy, and a child or children. Toni's family will need to buy two sets if they want Toni to be able to have a family like theirs.

Toni's village of family and friends will work hard to help raise Toni in a supportive, loving and accepting way. They will work hard to end this discrimination for Toni and for children in all sorts of different family situations.

What sorts of discrimination will Toni face? Sort by institutional, individual, inadvertent, intentional. Each example will have checks in more than one column. Add more examples in the space at the bottom of the chart.

Example	Institutional	Individual	Intentional	Inadvertent
nursery school forms with spaces labeled mother and father				
plastic play families, block people, family puppet sets that all have a mother and a father				
stories and pictures in children's books that are almost all heterosexual families				
pictures in children's puzzles that are almost all heterosexual families				
only possible for one mother to do the original adoption				
in order for Lena to adopt Toni, they'll have to make a legal challenge that will take time, cost money, and make the their lives public				
often have to "explain" their family situation				
can't get family medical coverage, need to pay for family insurance for Mary and Toni and pay for separate individual insurance for Lena				
can't file an income tax return as a family				
some parents of Toni's friends may object to their visiting at her house				
Toni may not be able to talk openly about her family in many places				
are afraid to read lesbian newspapers and magazines in public places				
may not have a full relationship with their extended families				
Lena and Mary not considered "immediate family" with each other if the other is sick in hospital; Lena not considered Toni's "family"			.	
If either Lena or Mary die, the other will not receive her partner's social security or pension				
If Lena and Mary separate or if Mary dies, Lena will not automatically get custody of Toni				

Roderick is a fifth grade African-American boy. He does very well in school with a special interest in math and science. His teacher, Ms. Johnson, has started an after school "Girls' Math Club." She got a special grant to do this as a way to encourage girls to continue to be interested in, and do well in, mathematics. By middle school girls do not get as high math grades as boys and do not score as well on standardized tests. By high school girls take less math and thus are not as well prepared for college math courses.

In the "Girls Math Club" they do interesting kinds of math problems, more interesting than what they get to do in the classroom. They work in pairs and small groups rather than working on their own. Some of the work they do is pre-algebra so they'll be more ready for the special algebra classes available in seventh grade. The Club meets two days after school for an hour and a half each time.

When Roderick tried to get into the "Girls Math Club" Ms. Johnson told him that it was only for girls. She explained that, by 5th or 6th grades, many girls become uncomfortable taking risks in math class with boys in the room. It helps to have a safe place where they can get extra time to experiment in mathematics.

— cut —

Adam is a sixth grade white boy. He loves playing basketball. He and his friends play during recess and sometimes after school unless the gym is being used for other groups. He and his stepfather often play at the local Y.

After he gets home from school Adam often rides his bike around town. He has noticed that there are several courts where it is pretty easy to get into a pick-up basketball game. He thinks this would be a great way to get in more basketball time.

One afternoon Adam decides to try to get into one of these games. He locks up his bike and goes up the kids playing. They're all black. He asks to join in. One of them says, "We don't want any white kids here." Another says, "Go play with your own kind."

Adam is shocked. He is a pretty good basketball player and he thinks the other kids would have fun playing with him if they gave it a try. He has never had anyone turn him away before because of this skin color.

— cut —

A group of fifth grade girls go to the bead store to get supplies for projects they are doing. Sheena and Keiana, are both black, Zoe is white, and Leah is Korean American. They wander around looking for their favorite kinds of beads and pointing out really special ones to each other.

After a while Sheena and Keiana are looking at the glass beads and Zoe and Leah are looking at the ceramic painted ones. Sheena and Keiana realize that one of the store owners moves from behind the counter and watches them as they look through the beads. The other two owners continue what they were doing, no one watches Leah and Zoe.

The girls buy some beads and start walking home. Leah asks Sheena why she and Keiana were being watched. Sheena explains that it happens a lot, that store keepers think that black kids are going to steal from them. Keiana agrees that that's what happens and tells them how much she hates it. Leah and Zoe are both totally surprised.

— cut —

Olivia is a white fourth grade girl. She has spina bifida, a birth defect that means she's paralyzed from the waist down. She walks with crutches. She wants to be in a play that a group of fourth and fifth graders wrote. They've organized try-outs and posted signs around school.

When Olivia gets to the try-outs the two kids who are running these say to her, "How are you going to walk around the stage with those crutches?" "There aren't any parts in our play for people on crutches!" They tell her she can't try-out. Olivia knows she's good at acting and singing. This isn't the first time she's been rejected for being physically disabled, but she knows she could do a part fine if they'd just give her a chance.

My name is **Della.** I have two sons. For many years I was married. I loved my husband and sons but, as the years went on, I became more and more sure that I was a lesbian. When our sons were eight and ten their father and I got divorced. I have been raising the boys mostly myself. They spend many weekends with their father. I live alone with my sons but now I'm involved with another woman. She has two kids too. Often we get together and do things as a large family. We like to go to concerts and ball games and to have giant cookouts with foods we all make ourselves. Soon we are buying a house and moving in together. I know that I am a good parent for my sons. But my ex-husband worries about my influence on them and wants the boys to live with him. I feel lucky that the boys are old enough to make their own choice to live with me so the court can't take them from me.

My name is **Mike.** I always wanted to have children. I wasn't involved with a woman so I couldn't have them by being married. Instead I adopted three boys. Later I came to understand that the reason I never had any long relationships with women was because I am gay. Now my partner and I are both fathers to my boys. When I got kids I learned how to sew and my cooking got much better. I also really like playing soccer with my sons. I can't talk openly with my sons' friends or their families about my relationship with Jeff because my sons might then be rejected by other families.

My name is **Ethan.** I'm ten. When I was 3 my parents got divorced. My mother got involved with another woman. They have both been my mothers ever since. I see my father once or twice a week, but most of the time it is my mothers who take care of me. Sometimes people ask me if I get teased in school. Sometimes I do and I think that's not fair. I know it's because kids just don't understand that poeple who are gay are regular people. I try to help them understand that. Mostly though I hang out with my friends, go to the movies, skateboard and draw. I feel very lucky that I live in a city where there is lots of support for lesbian and gay families and lots of education about homophobia in the schools.

My name is **Geoff.** I'm 15. I guess maybe I've always thought I was gay. I'm pretty athletic and I love rock climbing and swimming. I've always been into music and writing too. Lots of my friends are girls, but when the other boys started talking about being interested in girls as girlfriends, I couldn't really understand what they meant. I go to a gay and lesbian support group at my high school. It helps a lot! But I always have to be careful who I talk with. I think about how different I am every time I go to a movie, read a book, or look at a magazine.

My name is **Emma.** I'm nine. My mothers Hope and Marta say they always knew they wanted children. Sometimes we do things all together as a family, like go hiking or roller skating. Sometimes I do things with just one of my mothers, like Hope and I really like to sing and Marta and I really like to make things out of wood. I don't worry much that they're lesbians. In some ways it's expensive. Like Hope and I have medical insurance and Marta has to have separate insurance because the government says we're not "a family." And Marta doesn't count as my mom for legal stuff.

My name is **Jamila.** I'm 16. I don't know yet if I'm straight of a lesbian. I've been reading a lot of books and talking to people. Sometimes I go to groups for lesbian and gay teenagers. People there help me think about myself and never put pressure on me to make any big statements. I don't really think I need to figure this out yet. I think I can spend time with all sorts of people and try to really understand myself. I know that if I am a lesbian it's going to be much harder to be open about my life.

Chapter

8

Investigating Your Environment

Through the activities in the three previous chapters, students have had the opportunity to empathize with people experiencing discrimination and to explore how and why inequality based on difference exists. Students are now ready to take a closer look at the context of their own lives.

Chapters 8 and 9 contain activities in which students examine their environment for personal and institutional discrimination. In this chapter, they explore their classroom, school and home. In the next, they examine the media and their community, and then assess how their environment has affected them.

The intent of the activities is to educate students, and those with whom they come in contact while doing these tasks, and not to judge. Students investigate their environment, not for purposes of "putting down" people or finding fault with institutions, but to discover examples of inequality. Only when people become aware of discrimination, can changes happen. Reinforce the educational purpose of these activities constantly, so all involved perceive them as the learning experiences they are.

Until recently, for example, in much institutional literature the term handicapped person was found. Many people have since learned that "handicapped" comes from the practice of beggars who held "cap in hand" to solicit charity, and the word reflects the dependent position in which society places people with disabilities. The preferred term now is "person with a disability." By referring to the individual first, then to the disability, the full sense of personhood is conveyed, suggesting also that the person is more similar to everyone else than dissimilar. With this awareness, terminology is changing to better value diversity.

It's important to reiterate that all of us have, or do, discriminate, albeit often unintentionally. We can do so by following habitual institutional norms. For example, teachers often line children up in boys and girls lines, a practice which reinforces the differences between males and females. Sometimes just reading notices to students as they are printed reinforces discrimination. Reading, for example, "Dance class will be held at 3:30 in the gym; girls should adjust their after-school schedules accordingly," reinforces not only sexist norms, but heterosexist ones as well. It's easy for young people to harass boys who take dance as "sissies" and "faggots" if the school reinforces strict gender-based roles for males and females.

Encourage learning rather than guilt when students and teachers find examples of discrimination close to home. When, for example, a teacher discovered that she had been using literature that perpetuated biases about poor and working class people, initially she felt guilty. With encouragement, she reframed that discovery as a positive learning experience, enabling her to work to modify the literature she taught to make it nonstereotypical.

Point out also, that some institutional discrimination is intentional and serves to keep opportunities and power in the hands of some persons and groups and away from others. For example, after a class discussion about sexism in school, one fourth grade class realized that boys assumed that the playground basketball court was "theirs" and that they had the "right" to decide if girls could play on it with them. Even after this discussion, however, the boys wanted to continue to control who played on the court. Since this practice gave girls more limited opportunities to play basketball, the teacher had to step in to insist that students devise a system for using the basketball court that would be fair to all. Intentional or unintentional, stereotyping and institutional discrimination reinforce inequality.

Some of the students' investigation involves interviewing parents, teachers, and community members. Let these persons know the educational purpose of the activities, so as to alleviate potential misunderstanding. Stress with students the importance of dialogue and nonjudgmental listening. When appropriate, students can share results of these activities with interested persons to heighten their awareness of inequality. Use your judgment about what's workable for your community and school.

Before implementing some of the lessons in section A—"Exploring Your Classroom and School"—tell staff members in your building well in advance about your students' upcoming projects. You might give your endeavor a name, such as "Diversity Awareness." Enlist their support in a schoolwide effort to become more aware of stereotypes, omissions and isms in the school.

Share some examples of ways you've become aware of how things you had done in the past were discriminatory and how you've changed. Share some of the excitement of those changes. Engage your colleagues in discussion of some of the points above, as you will with your students.

Ask staff members who prefer that your students not engage them in any of the "Diversity Awareness" activities to let you know. Encouraging others who might want to collaborate with you and your students to do so is a particularly effective way to inform and involve interested colleagues. In these ways you can make the effort to pinpoint and change discrimination in your school as nonthreatening and collaborative as possible.

Many forms of diversity are covered in the activities in this chapter. Given your school, there may be some that you want to focus on more, or in some cases, others that you may not choose to give attention to. Modify the activities accordingly. Whenever possible, however, address all forms of diversity covered in this book. When approached in a nonthreatening, educational way, even those forms of diversity most difficult to explore in your school can often become the basis for productive dialogue and constructive change.

By completing activities in this chapter, students will undoubtedly discover many examples of discrimination that they may want to address further. Action projects that are follow-ups to Chapter 8 and 9 activities are included in Chapters 10 and 11. In cases where students are particularly eager to take action, move ahead to those follow-up activities now while student interest and motivation is peaked.

Bias in Textbooks

Christine Sleeter and Carl Grant completed a very comprehensive study of bias in textbooks, "Race, Class, Gender, and Disability in Current Textbooks," that was published in 1991. In analyzing texts in mathematics, science, social studies and reading/language arts they found that while there have been improvements in the way human diversity is presented in textbooks, biased patterns still remain. While some brief highlights of the authors' findings follow, a full reading of their study is very worthwhile.

"Whites consistently dominate textbooks, although their margin of dominance varies widely. . . . While books have successfully addressed gender issues mainly by eliminating most sexist language, students gain little sense of the history or culture of women, and learn very little about sexism or current issues involving gender . . . Social class is not treated in books much at all. The great majority of people and situations presented are middle class or involve at least a modest level of financial status . . . Disability is ignored as well."

The Politics of the Textbook
by Michael Apple and Linda Christian-Smith

Section A   Exploring Your Classroom and School

STOP AND LOOK CAREFULLY

OBJECTIVE   To have students look more critically at school bulletin boards for stereotypes, omissions, and "isms."

MATERIALS   A chance to roam around the school; paper and pencils.

IMPLEMENTATION   Divide students into small heterogeneous groups. Each group takes an area of the school and notes hallway bulletin boards and those in classrooms, if permission can be secured from teachers. It is helpful to have each bulletin board seen by two groups for comparison.

First, brainstorm as a group for things to note that would indicate the degree of diversity on bulletin boards. Make a list. Examples might be: (1) number of men and number of women; (2) roles and occupations of men and women; (3) number of people of color compared to white people, and their roles; (4) the ages of people and what they are doing; (5) family and job situations and what these reflect in terms of class; (6) number of people cooperating compared to those competing, or achieving individually; (7) number of people with disabilities compared to those without disabilities; (8) types of families; (9) variety of religions; and (10) variety of languages.

When the groups come back they prepare a presentation for the class. The teacher, or a student recorder, tallies the results. (Save the information for use in lessons in Chapter 11.)

DISCUSSION

1. Was there a difference in how frequently women and men were portrayed and the roles they were in?
2. What was the representation of different racial groups?
3. How were elderly people portrayed, compared to younger people?
4. What was the difference in numbers of people cooperating, compared to those competing or achieving individually?
5. Were bulletin boards geared to certain social and economic groups? If so, how?
6. When companies produce bulletin board materials with omissions, stereotypes, and "isms," what does this do to students' thinking and view of the world?
7. Number of people with disabilities compared to those without disabilities.
8. Number of traditional families compared to alternative family structures, including those with parents who might be lesbian or gay.
9. When religion is apparent or relevant, the number of various religions portrayed.
10. The number of bulletin boards in English, compared to those in other languages spoken by students in the school.

GOING FURTHER

Have students prepare a bulletin board that counters some of the stereotypes and omissions commonly found. Have students prepare a helpful and nonjudgmental critique of bulletin boards and circulate it to interested teachers.

FOLLOW-UP

"Let Me Tell You What I Think," p. 333.

WHY ARE WE OFF FROM SCHOOL TODAY?

OBJECTIVES

To have students understand how cultural discrimination can be institutionalized through school holidays.
To have students understand how this affects their thinking, learning and experiences.
To expose students to new information about important people and events whose history is not commonly taught in schools.

MATERIALS

Papers; pencils; rulers; and your school calendar. Also calendars from a variety of groups such as: women's; Hispanics; African Americans; Black Caribbeans; gays and lesbians; Asian Americans and non-Christian religious groups. These include: *Carry It on Peace Calendar* from the Syracuse Cultural Workers; *I Too Sing America* from Savanna Books; *Asian/Pacific American Calendar* from Asian Americans United, *Orthodox Union Calendar/Diary* from the Orthodox Union; *Ethnic Cultures of American Calendar* from Education Extension Systems; *Multicultural Resource Calendar* from Amherst Education Publishing; *UNICEF Wall Calendar* from UNICEF and *Mosques around the World Calendar* from the New England Islam Center. Islamic calendars may be hard to find. Muslim fasts, feasts and holy days are set by observation of the moon and thus are not set until soon before the important dates. It is thus difficult to get information enough ahead to create calendars in advance.

IMPLEMENTATION

Students meet in small groups to go through the school calendar to list all the holidays. They add any holidays that are not vacation days, but are celebrated at school. Then each group labels every item on its list as to the race and gender of the person being commemorated or the culture being affirmed.

Create a class average for each of these categories. Then, as a class, create a bar or circle graph with the following categories: white; black; Asian American; Latino/a; Native

American; Christian; other religions. For each race or religious group create space to separate "male" and "female." See examples below.

Divide students into groups. Distribute alternative calendars. Students list additional holidays they think should be celebrated in schools that would commemorate the lives of a more diverse range of Americans. They can use information from these calendars plus any other information they have. Have each group create a bar graph showing the distribution, by race and gender, of their revised calendars.

Depending on your class you may also focus students' attention on investigating whether holidays commemorate work of individual people or work of groups of people. For example July 4 looks at the work of a group, but Martin Luther King Day is focused on an individual.

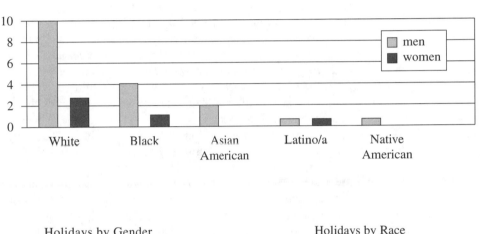

Holidays by Race and Gender

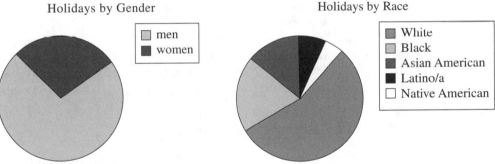

Holidays by Gender   Holidays by Race

Examples of possible graphs. These should be done for whatever traits your class is examining.

DISCUSSION
1. What groups of people are recognized in our schools? Why? Who makes the decisions about this?
2. What groups get neglected? Why? What does this tell you about what you are being taught?
3. How do you feel about this if you are a member of a group being acknowledged frequently? How about if you are part of one of the neglected groups?
4. In what ways is this damaging for all students?

FOLLOW-UP See "Calendars" page 318, for a lesson in which students create new school calendars with more inclusive holidays. These can be done as a fund-raiser or distributed for free.

OUR TEXTBOOKS: ARE THEY FAIR?

OBJECTIVES   To have students examine their textbooks for racism, sexism, classism, ageism, competitive individualism and other forms of discrimination.
To see how texts influence students' expectations of certain groups of people and of themselves.

MATERIALS   Texts you currently use (and for a longer project, others your school or district uses) in social studies, science, math and/or reading. (For a lesson on analyzing fiction, look at "Read Me a Story," p. 226.)

IMPLEMENTATION   Textbooks are one of the most powerful reinforcers of equality or inequality. If students learn to examine their texts for the "isms" they will have developed an important critical skill that they can use again and again. If you must use texts that are not ideal, students can nevertheless sharpen their critical thinking by analyzing them for inequality.

Check curriculum or school library for *Guidelines for Selecting Bias-Free Textbooks and Story Books* and *Stereotypes, Distortions, and Omissions in U.S. History Textbooks* from the Council on Interracial Books for Children. While now out of print, some old copies are still available. These are excellent resources that will provide background for this and upcoming lessons.

There are various options for implementing this activity, depending on the amount of time you allot. For all options, divide students into heterogeneous groups of four. In all cases, when groups are finished have them report their findings to the whole class and follow this with discussion. You or your students can make checklists with the specific items that students should look for while analyzing texts. Do this once you have decided on the subject area (science, math, social studies, reading) and *category* (race, gender, class, age, competitive individualism or other forms of discrimination). (Save all your information for lessons in Chapter 11.)

Options for Organizing the Lesson
1. Choose one subject area and one category. Each group analyzes the same text.
2. Choose one subject area. Each group analyzes the same book for a different category.
3. Choose one category. The groups analyze books from different subject areas.

Timing   For a *short-term project* have students

1. Analyze illustrations. Who is portrayed? Are the portrayals culturally authentic?
2. Examine content. Choose a small section of a book to examine (for example, math problems on pages 21–35), or use a portion of a text students have studied that year (for example, science text, chapters 1 to 4).
3. Record findings orally, in charts, graphs, or reports.

For a *longer-term project* have students

1. Analyze whole texts used in your classroom.
2. Compare different texts used in your school or district.
3. Write comprehensive reports on their findings and distribute them to other classes.

Categories   Suggestions for focus

1. *Racism*
   a. How many white people compared to people of color are presented?
   b. What specific racial groups are presented?

   c. Is there a difference in the roles people of different races play? e.g., Do people of color have less responsibility than whites?

2. *Sexism*
   a. How many males compared to females are presented?
   b. Are there differences in the roles they play? e.g., Are females helping and men acting?

3. *Classism*
   a. How many people are middle-class or wealthier compared to people who are poor or working-class?
   b. Are there differences in how people from different classes are presented? e.g., Are poor or working people shown as less important in the world than people of the middle class or above?

4. *Ageism*
   a. How many older people, compared to others, are presented?
   b. Are there differences in how older people are depicted? e.g., Are older persons more sick, forgetful, and in passive roles?

5. *Competitive Individualism*
   a. How many people do things individually compared to working together?
   b. Are successful people or leaders those who made it on their own, or those who work with, and for, others?

6. *Ableism*
   a. How many people with physical or mental disabilities, compared to others, are presented?
   b. Is there a difference in the way people with disabilities are presented? e.g., Are they passive, or actively engaging in activities and/or taking leadership roles?

7. *Heterosexism*
   (Most readily analyzed in reading and social studies texts.)
   a. How many lesbians and gay men or people in families with two caregivers of the same gender are portrayed?
   b. If they are presented, in what roles? e.g., In athletics, or also care-giving roles?

8. *Anti-Semitism*
   (Most readily analyzed in reading and social studies.)
   a. How many Jews are represented compared to Christians?
   b. Are there differences in the roles they play?
   c. How many people can you find whose religion isn't stated, but that you can recognize by customs, lifestyle, or holidays? Which religions are most represented?

9. *Linguicism*
   a. How many people who speak English as a second language are represented compared to native English speakers?
   b. Are there differences in how people with language differences are depicted? e.g., Are they being helped, rather than helping? For those who are bilingual/becoming bilingual, is their bilingualism a detriment or an asset?

Subject Areas   Suggestions for focus

1. Science. Look especially at pictures; examine scientists who are chosen as role models.
2. Math. Examine word problems and pictures. Look at how math is done in different cultures.
3. Social Studies. Look at the contributions of different groups of people; examine the perspective from which the subject is presented; look for omissions, distortions. Are the struggles of each group's fight for civil rights/equality presented?
4. Reading. Analyze the story line and characterization.

DISCUSSION 1. What did each group find from their study?
2. What stereotypes or "isms" were present?
3. Who was omitted?
4. How does that textbook tell students about which groups of people are leaders and achievers?
5. What influence could these textbooks have on students?
6. What can we do about textbooks that aren't fair?

FOLLOW-UP "Find That Class(ic) Bias," p. 220; "Read Me A Story," p. 226; "Textbook Alert," p. 328; "Finding Better Books," p. 329; "And We Wrote Them Ourselves," p. 330; "Change That Class(ic) Bias," p. 331. Write to the "Center for Understanding Aging" for materials for analyzing books for ageism. They include "Analysis Kit for Teachers and Librarians" and "Images of Aging in Literature for the Middle Grades: An Annotated Booklist."

FIND THAT CLASS(IC) BIAS

OBJECTIVES To learn to pinpoint examples of class bias in reading books.
To see how reading books influences students' viewpoints about class.

MATERIALS Reading books at reading level; copies of "Worksheet: Class Viewpoint," p. 228.

IMPLEMENTATION Because class is an unfamiliar concept to most students, this lesson gives them a chance to analyze their books for this factor alone.

Remind students that because of the different amounts of money that people have inherited or earned, they have various degrees of choice available to them. People's treatment of each other may be affected by class differences. As a reminder, you might distinguish between people who have more than they need to live on—sometimes called upper- or upper-middle-class; people who have enough money to live on—sometimes called middle-class; people who don't have enough money to live adequately—sometimes called lower-class; and people who are barely surviving . . . people in poverty. Stress that it is usually not a family's responsibility, but rather the result of a combination of circumstances, including discrimination, that determines class status.

Choose a number of story books that are easy for your students to read. Pick ones that are typically read and try not to think about class issues as you chose them, although you may consciously want to include one book in each group's pile that you know is free of class bias and/or authentically represents poor/working class people. Divide students into heterogeneous groups of three or four and give each group a pile of books. (See suggestions in Bibliography for books without class bias.) Have students pick one book and analyze it together using the questions on the Worksheet. Once they get the idea, have them each analyze other books and answer the questions for each Worksheet. When completed, the group makes a composite Worksheet that represents its total findings. (Save this information for lessons in Chapter 11.)

DISCUSSION 1. What classes of people are most stories written about?
2. How did you decide which classes families or people were from?
3. What kinds of concerns and problems do people or families from different class backgrounds have, according to each author?
4. How are upper-class, middle-class, lower-class and poor persons or families described by the authors? What are their opinions about them? How can you tell? How are these the same or different from yours?
5. If you were a middle-class student, how would you feel reading these books? a lower-income or poor student? an upper-class student?

Reading across Class Lines

The following books are some that do well in addressing socio-economic class in direct and helpful ways. For primary grade readers: *Tight Times* by Barbara Shook Hazen and *Grandmama's Joy* by Eloise Greenfield. For middle and upper elementary readers: *Fly Away Home* by Eve Bunting; *All Joseph Wanted* by Ruth Radin; *The Bear's House* by Marilyn Sachs and *Scooter* by Vera Williams. For middle school readers: *Crazy Lady* by Leslie Conly; *Homecoming* (and others in this series) by Cynthia Voight and *Make Lemonade* by Virginia Wolff.

WHO'S WHO IN OUR SCHOOL. . . .

OBJECTIVE To have students understand how sexism and racism are reflected in the division of labor in their school.

MATERIALS Paper; pencils; graph paper; markers or crayons.

IMPLEMENTATION Divide students into groups of four or five. Each group should be assigned a different category of school personnel to count. Categories can include: teachers, custodians, secretaries, cafeteria workers, administrators. Each group counts the number of people in its area by gender and race.

When the groups return, add the totals to find how many staff you are considering. If your students can handle percentages, have each group figure the percentage of men, women, whites, and personnel of color within each category. Then calculate these in terms of the total staff. Graph. Compare to the pupil population. For younger students use picture graphs. Come together as a class. Each group shares its findings.

DISCUSSION
1. In what areas did you find racial balance? Gender balance? What areas were very unbalanced by race or gender?
2. Brainstorm on reasons for these differences.
3. Compare the ratio of black and white teachers to black and white pupils. What reasons can you find if these are not proportionate?
4. Does the assignment of various jobs in our school reflect racism and sexism? If so, how?

GOING FURTHER Your district's administration or affirmative action office should have district-wide figures for school-system personnel in all jobs by race and gender and the salary range in each job category. Try to obtain these, simplify information, and distribute to students. Have students compare the numbers of men and women, people of color and whites, in jobs throughout the district. Have them compare salaries. Discuss the ways, if any, that the school system reinforces racism and sexism.

Women in Educational Leadership

- Only 14.5 percent of the nation's high school principals are women.
- Women represent 10.2 percent of school superintendents.

National Association of Secondary School Principals, 1994

. . . AND HOW DO THEY FEEL ABOUT IT?

OBJECTIVE   To better understand how racism and sexism may have affected opportunities for, and choices of, jobs.

MATERIALS   Paper and pencils.

IMPLEMENTATION   Review interviewing skills with students (pp. 64–5). Then divide students into pairs. Each pair interviews one, or more than one, member of the school staff, as time permits. Try to see that all staff categories are covered and that you have a representative sample of the staff.

Students will want to explain to the people they interview that they are doing a project about people's jobs. They are particularly interested in how people came to have their jobs and how their gender or race affected their job opportunities. You may also want to first talk to the adults being interviewed to make sure they are comfortable with this process. Here are some possible questions:

1. Do you like being a _____?
2. Did you plan to be a _____ as a child? At what point did you make the decision to be a _____?
3. What did your parents do?
4. Did your parents or teachers influence your expectations of future jobs? If so, how?
5. Did your race affect your job opportunities or job choice? If so, how?
6. Did your gender affect your job opportunities or job choice? If so, how?
7. Do you think your job opportunities would have been different if you were the opposite gender? Another race? If so, how?
8. If you could be anything at all now, what would you choose to be? Why?
9. What do you like about your job? What don't you like?

Have students write up their interviews. Post these on a bulletin board and have students read all interviews. Then have students work in small groups to answer some of the following questions:

1. Did racism influence people's job opportunities? If so, how?
2. Did sexism influence people's job opportunities? If so, how?
3. Employees with which types of jobs are most satisfied? What do they like? Employees with which types of jobs are most dissatisfied? What are their reasons?

DISCUSSION   Come together as a class and discuss the four questions above.

GOING FURTHER   Have students do the same interview with their parents or community people in various occupations. Write these up for the bulletin board display.

LISTEN CAREFULLY

OBJECTIVES   To encourage awareness of the subtle ways in which teachers, other school personnel, parents, and students perpetuate stereotypes and expectations based on race, gender, class, age and individualism.
To understand the impact of these "isms."

MATERIALS   Paper and pencils.

IMPLEMENTATION

Explain to students that in this lesson they will become field-researchers, people who gather information through observation. Secure permission from teachers, secretaries, recess aides, parents and so forth for students to listen to their conversations. Explain that the purpose is to learn how people, often *unintentionally*, may reinforce stereotypes. Explain that students will be happy to share their findings with them if they wish.

Explain to students that many adults and children reinforce unfair expectations based on race, gender, class, and age in their daily conversation. Their ability to notice this can help them do it less themselves, and view it more analytically when others do so.

Have students work in pairs over a couple of days. Tell them to listen to adults and other students. They might stand with paper and pencils in the back of classrooms, in the office, outside on steps for recess, at home, in the park, and so on. They should note all remarks that might have to do with someone's gender, age, class, race. Give some examples: "Big boys don't cry when they're hurt"; "Nice little girls don't make so much noise"; "She's so pokey, just like an old lady"; "You're acting like a bunch of wild Indians"; "They behave like wild animals." Also ask students to listen for examples of "me-first" statements: "Ha, ha, I beat you"; "Don't help Tom, do your own work"; "What. You don't have a ten-speed?" "If people work hard, they'll get ahead in this country—anyone can make it."

Have students relist these by age, class, gender, and race. Have them share their findings with the large group.

"FIREFIGHTER"

DISCUSSION

1. Using the students' findings, come up with a list of expectations people have for each race, gender, class, or age.
2. What examples of "me-first" statements did you find?
3. What were your emotional reactions to the comments you heard?
4. Which remarks were said most often? Can you think why?
5. What do these expectations and stereotypes teach us about white people and people of color, females and males, older people and younger people, middle-class people and lower-class people, competition and cooperation?
6. Where do people learn these expectations? In what ways are you learning them? Can you do anything about that?

GOING FURTHER

Depending on the situation, the students may want to share their findings with the people to whom they listened.

If parents agree, the students can take one kind of expectation and remind them every time they unconsciously say it. They can ask if parents are willing to change that expectation to something that will leave more choices open.

Students can be aware of what they say to younger brothers and sisters. Are they teaching them some of these same things? How can they change that?

ME OR WE

OBJECTIVE

To give students practice finding examples of competitive individualism in their environment.

MATERIALS

Chart paper; magic markers; paper; pencils.

IMPLEMENTATION

Review the definition of individualism with the students. Post the beginnings of a large chart with two headings: "Me First" and "Cooperation." This poster will describe individualistic behavior as contrasted to cooperative behavior. List several items yourself and then ask students to suggest more. For example:

Me First

Trying to beat or do better than other people.
Keeping information or ideas to self.
Putting a person down.

Cooperation

Helping others to learn things.
Sharing information and ideas.
Telling someone something positive
    about herself.

Divide students into heterogeneous pairs. Each pair makes a small chart with the two headings. They work together to observe behavior in all areas of the school. As they see examples of "me first" behavior and cooperative behavior, they add these examples to their charts. Give a few examples to get people started:

- A group of kids on the playground wouldn't let another play kickball because he wasn't "good enough."
- Janie helped Yvonne catch up with the work she missed when she was out sick.

After a couple of days of observation discuss the findings. In the discussion don't allow students to "blame" others. You can keep the reporting objective by not using people's names and only describing behavior.

DISCUSSION

1. What examples of "me first" behavior did you find in our school?
2. How do you feel when you give "me first" statements or act in "me first" ways? How do you feel when you're on the receiving end of those statements and behaviors?
3. What are examples of cooperative behavior that you found?
4. How do you feel when you cooperate and share?
5. Why do we get into "me first" behaviors and statements? How can we change some of these behaviors to cooperative behaviors in our school?

Section B   *What about Your Home?*

BUT I'D RATHER TAKE OUT THE GARBAGE

OBJECTIVES

To encourage students to look carefully at how home chores for both adults and children are allotted.
To have them understand why these are allotted as they are, and the different options that are available.

IMPLEMENTATION

As a class, students brainstorm on the chores they do at home. List these on the board by gender. Is there a pattern? Discuss. Then they brainstorm on what chores adults do at home. Identify those chores by gender, too. Discuss. Students rank each chore, on a scale of one to five, according to how much they like or don't like doing it. They pick, from the entire list, which chores they would prefer. How do these compare to the actual chores done? How much of the difference (if there is one) is because chores are assigned on some basis other than appeal?

Now students go home and discuss with their parent or parents why they have been assigned certain chores. If they live with two parents, they ask why the parents have split their home chores the way they have.

DISCUSSION

1. Does gender determine what chores children do? What adults do?
2. Did people like their own chores best, or would they prefer others? Would they prefer more variety in what they do?

3. Are gender roles more of a factor in adult chores or children's chores?
4. Why have adults decided to split chores in certain ways?
5. How did adults learn these distinctions? Are they satisfied? What happens when there is a single parent in the home? Two other adults not of different genders, like a parent and grandparent or two parents of the same gender?
6. Are chores consistent among families? Do most have the same patterns?
7. What, besides the home, reinforces who does certain chores? (For example, roles on TV shows, in stories, in magazine advertisements.)

GOING FURTHER Have the family sit down and decide what chores each member would like best. Try those for a week. Reevaluate and make necessary changes.

Have all the girls go home and ask if they can do traditionally male jobs, and the boys do female jobs. How did adults react? If they agreed and the students tried it, how did it go?

Have students who live with two parents of opposite genders ask if their parents would switch traditional chores. How did they react to the idea? If they did it, how did they react to the experiment?

FOLLOW-UP "Job Sharing or Who's the Cook Tonight?" p. 280.

PRESENTS I'VE RECEIVED

OBJECTIVE To help students understand the effects of family expectations about gender roles and competition, as shown in gifts.

IMPLEMENTATION Ask students if they can remember what kind of presents they've been given for their birthdays or other holidays. Have them make a list down the side of a piece of paper beginning with baby, one year old, two year old and continuing until their current age. Next to each they list two or three presents. If they don't remember they can take the worksheet home and interview a parent or other adult.

DISCUSSION
1. What kinds of presents have you been given?
2. Group them into types—"board games," "sports," "home-making toys," "war toys," "crafts," and so forth.
3. How do these compare to presents that have been given to your brothers or sisters?
4. Can you tell what kind of interests your family expects you to have?
5. Do they reinforce, or challenge, traditional expectations for you as a girl or boy?
6. What would you have liked to have been given that was different from what you were given? In what ways might that have changed the way you are?
7. How do adults' sex-role expectations influence their children?
8. In how many of the games do you have to compete to win? In how many do you have to cooperate to win?
9. What do games teach us about winning?

Class Differences, Hurt Feelings

Be sensitive to the potential bad feelings that could emerge from class differences in doing this lesson. If students come from a variety of class backgrounds, why not have students write down small presents rather than "big" (expensive) presents, like bikes. In this way children whose families can't afford expensive presents won't feel bad.

READ ME A STORY

OBJECTIVES   To make students and parents alert to racism, sexism, classism, individualism and ageism in the books they read at home.

To have them understand the effects their reading has on the way they view the world.

MATERIALS   Books at home; copies of "Worksheet: Review on Books," 1 *or* 2, pp. 229–30.

IMPLEMENTATION   Explain to students that this is an activity they can do with their parents. Parents and students can work together to look at the personal or library books that the students have at home. Fairy tales and nursery rhymes are particularly good. Discuss how what we read is enjoyable, and also has an effect in terms of how we think.

Introduce the lesson with a brief review of stereotypes of various groups of people. Choose the Worksheet that you feel will be more effective. Go over the Worksheet and answer any questions the students may have. You may decide to have students and parents focus only on some forms of discrimination. In that case, edit the Worksheet accordingly.

If you choose Worksheet 2, you may also ask students to look at religion and/or sexual orientation. These aspects of characters' social identities are often not made explicit. When it is clear, you may ask students to note the representation of: 1. Christians, Jews, or people of other religions; and/or 2. heterosexuals or homosexuals/bisexuals, in relationship to the questions on the worksheet. When religion or sexual orientation isn't made clear, you can ask students to think about what assumptions they make about those aspects of the characters' social identities.

5/92
Name of book: *The Star Maiden*
3/4 Critical Evaluation:

	YES	NO
1. Do all people of color look the same?	X	
2. Is the book historically accurate?		X
3. Is it sexist?		X
4. Are people's customs made fun of or exaggerated?		X
5. Are Native peoples described respectfully?	X	
6. Do Native peoples: —all wear feathers?		X
—all live in teepees (wigwams, etc.)?	X	
—all speak oddly?		X
7. Would you be embarrassed if you were Native American and read this book?		X

Children Critique Library Books

The children in a 3rd/4th grade at Cambridge Friends School in Cambridge, MA created a *Critical Reading Evaluation* form to go inside library books. They created a list of questions which was then copied and made available to readers. Now, when a child reads a library book, he can fill in the form on the left and glue it into the front cover of the book. Other children then have some questions to think critically about when they read the book.

The sample on the left can give you an idea of how to do this with your students. They would need to create their own questions based on their own thinking and learning. Some lessons that will help them think about these issues are "Our Textbooks: Are They Fair?"; "Find That Class(ic) Bias"; "Read Me a Story."

DISCUSSION

1. Go over each question on the checklist with students and discuss what they found. Then generalize from the findings.
2. What are the similarities in the books' presentations of: people of color and whites; females and males; upper, middle and lower-class persons; older persons and adults or children; and people with disabilities and people without disabilities.
3. If the religion and/or sexual orientation of characters was made clear, ask students some of the following questions accordingly. If religion and/or sexual orientation wasn't clear, ask students what they assumed about those aspects of the characters' social identities.
4. What stereotypes were most common?
5. What groups of people were omitted, or appeared very seldom?
6. What did these books teach us about whose values and ideas are right?
7. Which students would feel best about themselves by reading these books?
8. Did these books encourage competitive individualism or cooperation? Give examples. How can this influence our behavior?
9. List the books that showed none or few of these problems. In what ways did these books help fight stereotypes?
10. List some of the books with many of the problems. Give examples from the books of each of these problems.
11. How did your parents feel about doing this?

GOING FURTHER

Using the same system, work in small groups and consider three story books from the school library.

FOLLOW-UP

"Finding Better Books," p. 329.

Bring a Critical Eye to the Portrayal of People with Disabilities

Both you and your students can learn to evaluate written material and media presentations for their portrayal of people with disabilities. Here are some things to look for.

1. Are people with disabilities seen as objects of pity?
2. Are people with disabilities seen as victims of violence? (There is some reality to this, however, when people with disabilities are consistently portrayed in this way, an image of complete helplessness is reinforced.)
3. Does an evil aura surround a character with a disability? The many examples of villains with disabilities in children's literature and media portrayals creates a connection between disability and wickedness. (E.g., Rumpelstiltskin, Dr. Strangelove)
4. Are people with disabilities portrayed as super-heros? Do characters display exceptional qualities which enable her to function well?

For further information and ideas on this topic see *Educating for a Just Society* by Kathleen McGinnis from which some of this material has been adapted.

Worksheet: Class Viewpoint

Name of story	1a.	b.	c.	2	3	4	5

1a. How many people or families were upper class?

b. How many people or families were middle class?

c. How many people or families were lower class or poor?

2. Pick the 2 or 3 most important characters. What class background were they?

3. What information in the story did you use to decide on class background?

4. Choose one adjective to describe each of the 2 or 3 main characters, from the author's point of view.

5. Choose an adjective to describe each of the 2 or 3 main characters, from your point of view.

Title _____

Author_____

Checkers _____

1. *Illustrations.* Are people of color shown? If so, in varied roles or stereotypic ones? Are people of color and white people, males and females, middle-class and lower-class people included? In what proportion? Are people with disabilities represented? Are they represented positively or negatively?

2. *Story Line.* Do people succeed through competition or cooperation? Do they work for goals for themselves or to change situations to help many people?

3. *Life Styles.* Are people of different races, religions, and classes shown? Is everyone judged by white, middle-class standards? If not, how are people judged? Are people of different sexual orientations included? Are those with disabilities represented?

4. *Relationships.* Who has power? What genders are they? What races? What classes? How are families shown? Are all ethnic groups shown with the same family patterns? Are all families the standard nuclear family or are alternatives shown?

5. *Heroes.* Are the standards the same for men and women? For different races? For different classes of people? Who takes leadership and makes decisions?

6. *Loaded Words.* Are there insulting words for certain groups of people? If so, do these words label certain groups in stereotypic ways?

7. *Older People.* Are they in the story? If so, are they shown in varied ways or stereotypic ones?

Title _____   Name of Checker(s) _____

Author _____

	Race					Gender		Age			Class			Ability	
	Latino/a	Asian American	Native American	White	African American	Male	Female	Children	Adults under 65	Older People	Poor or Lower-class	Middle-class	Upper-class	People with Disabilities	People without Disabilities
1. Write the number of people in illustrations.															
2. Write the number of people in each category present in the story.															
3. Check any people who are stereotyped in pictures. Give a word that describes that stereotype.															
4. Check any people who are stereotyped in the story.															
5. Check those people who give leadership, solve problems, make decisions.															
6. Check those people whose values/ideas are presented as right.															
7. Whose positive self–image would this story reinforce?															
8. Do main characters work for goals for themselves, or work to change situations to benefit many people? Give example(s).															

9. Other Comments.

More Environmental Influences and Their Effects

As students become more aware of examples of inequality in their environment, they pose more critical questions about what they see on a daily basis. In Section A and B of this chapter students have an opportunity to examine both the media and their community for messages that influence their assumptions, beliefs, and behaviors.

As in Chapter 8, they use active investigation and data-gathering techniques to examine inequalities in situations they know, like the family and school. In Section C, students examine how the bias they found may have affected *them*.

It is important to reiterate that persons they live with and learn from—teachers, parents, friends—haven't necessarily tried to limit their experiences. Instead, it's by living in biased institutions that we come to see the world in a particular way, and believe that way is the right way. Through the activities in the final section of this chapter, students can come to understand how *their own* lives may have been affected by such inequality. They may then want to create alternatives. Some lessons in Chapter 9 include ideas for small changes. In this way students become introduced to the kind of changes they can make. Also, activities in Chapter 10 offer students examples of changes others have made that contribute to equity. Chapter 11 is totally comprised of lessons in which students take action to change the inequalities they discover. In many of those lessons students use their findings from these activities in Chapter 9 as the basis for their action.

Stereotype Vulnerability

The very powerful effects that stereotypes can have on students is documented in the research of social psychologist Claude Steele. Steele found that when college students concentrate on a scholastic task in which they risk confirming the group's negative stereotype, the burden and anxiety this puts on them can be enough to drag down their performance. He calls this burden "stereotype vulnerability."

Stereotype Vulnerability (cont.)

When black college students were given a test and told that they were just solving problems, they did as well as white students with similar abilities. However when these same students were told it was a test of their verbal abilities and limitations, the black students performed worse than students of any other race. White students performed as well as they had before.

Steele does not believe that students accept the stereotype, but have to contend with the whisper of inferiority at a time when they must be very focused. In trying not to give credence to the stereotype, students may redouble their efforts, only to work too quickly or inefficiently.

The cues that can spark the vulnerability can be subtle—like making students mark down their race before the test begins or suggesting that the test can measure ability. Stereotype vulnerability can similarly negatively affect women who believe a given math test shows gender differences.

Because black students, and women, are devalued in classrooms and society, they fear their performances will confirm the broader racial, or gender-based, inferiority they are suspected of. To challenge this dynamic, schools must become places that see the value and promise in black and female students. The culture of the school must challenge the validity of any prevailing societal stereotypes.

New York Times Magazine, 9/17/95
Atlantic Monthly, 4/92

BLACK LIES AND WHITE LIES

OBJECTIVE   To help students understand how connotations in our language perpetuate racism.

MATERIALS   Dictionaries; paper; pencils; chart paper; markers.

IMPLEMENTATION   Tell students they will work on an activity to examine language. Teach the term "connotation." Divide students into groups of four. Give each group a large sheet of paper. They list all the words or phrases they can think of that have the word "white" or "black" in them. For example, "black lies," "black eye," "white as snow." After ten minutes the groups mark their lists as follows: "+" for a phrase with a positive connotation, "−" for one with a negative connotations, and "0" for one with a neutral connotation. Groups then look up the words "white" and "black" in their dictionaries and write down the definitions. It is helpful if different groups have different publishers' dictionaries. Use dictionaries as advanced as they can handle.

The class joins together. Appoint a recorder to stand at the front of the room. Starting with "black," each group calls out a word or phrase with "black" in it. Record these along with the markings of "+," "−", and "0." Go around in turns until all the groups have their ideas listed. Then do the same for "white." Similarly, list dictionary definitions. (Save these lists for lesson in Chapter 10.)

DISCUSSION
1. How many "black" words have positive connotations? How about "white" words? How many of each have negative connotations?
2. What reactions do you have as you look at this list?
3. How might black people feel hearing these words and phrases all the time? How about white people?
4. Many of our ideas are formed through language. Our feelings about ourselves often come from words we hear. What does our language imply about white people? about black people?

GOING FURTHER
The Black Snowman by Phil Mendez is a beautifully illustrated and controversial picture book that addresses these issues. It addresses use of the word *dark* in a pejorative sense as well as many examples of *black* and *white* in negative and positive ways. The focus then moves to a highly positive image of black and blackness.

Students may want to investigate color images in fairy tales, for example the color of clothing worn by different characters and the color of horses ridden. They can compare and contrast these across cultures.

FOLLOW-UP
"Say It So They'll Hear It," p. 314, "New Words Help Us," p. 325.

Word Choice Challenges Racism

While word meanings don't change, students and teachers can be careful not to reinforce positive views of white and negative ones of black in their choice of words.

For example, don't create a hero named Colonel White and a villain named Captain Black, as a popular TV show did. When you put on a play, dress the forces of good in black and those of evil in white—or avoid color symbolism entirely. Raise others' consciousness!

ARE THEY ADVERTISING MORE THAN THE PRODUCT?

OBJECTIVE
To help students understand how advertising reinforces racism, sexism, classism, and ageism and other forms of discrimination.

MATERIALS
Access to television; props as necessary.

IMPLEMENTATION
Step One. Divide students into groups of two to four. Each group picks several television advertisements that some members are familiar with. Students tell the teacher so as to avoid repeats. The students then go home, and when possible, watch or tape these advertisements.

Several days later, any tapes are shown in class to other group members. The groups act out their advertisements. After the presentations, the class as a whole discusses the following questions.

DISCUSSION
1. How was each person in the advertisement portrayed?
2. How do these portrayals teach us to see men and women, old people and those who are younger, people of color and white people, and middle-class and poor people in certain ways?
3. a. How do these products teach us to see—or not to see—people with mental and physical disabilities and people without disabilities?
   b. How do they teach us to see—or not see—people of different sexual orientations?

c. How do they teach us to see—or not see—people of various religions?
4. Were the advertisements meant to be funny? Were they funny? Why or why not?
5. How did you feel about the advertisements?

Step Two. Now divide students into groups. Have each group look at one of the following areas: racism, sexism, classism, ageism, ableism, heterosexism, and anti-Semitism or other types of religious discrimination. Ask everyone to watch for examples of individualism.

Have students who watch TV watch for at least one-half hour a night for a week. Have students think about what audiences the advertisements are geared for. Students make notes on each commercial they watch according to the following guidelines:

Racism. Number of whites, blacks, Latino/as, Native Americans, Asian Americans? What is each person doing or saying? What are they advertising?

Sexism. Number of men, women? What is each person doing or saying? What are they advertising?

Ageism. Number of people who look over sixty-five? What is each person doing or saying? What are they advertising?

Classism. Number of wealthy people? middle-class people? Number of lower-class or poor people? What are they advertising?

Individualism. Number of people competing, or wanting to have the "best" of something? Number of people cooperating, sharing, and working together? Give examples.

Ableism. Number of people without disabilities? Number of people with physical or mental disabilities? What are they doing? What are they advertising?

Heterosexism. Number of people who appear to be heterosexual? Number of people who appear to be homosexual or bisexual? What are they doing? What are they advertising?

Anti-Semitism or other form of religious discrimination. Number of people who one could assume are Christian (e.g., celebrating Christmas, Easter, etc.)? Number of people who are Jewish? Number of people of other religious faiths, such as Moslem or Hindu. What are they doing? What are they advertising?

After a week of observing, groups compile their findings.

Jumping Around?

Are you, like many teachers, one who loves to "jump around" when using resource books? We encourage you to restrain yourself! Concepts build upon each other. Are you moving sequentially through chapters and chapter sections? While it's not necessary to teach each lesson in each chapter section, it *is* important to move from one section to the next in order to teach at least one or two lessons. Build concepts sequentially!

DISCUSSION

1. What was the number of _____ compared to _____ in the advertisements? (For example, middle-class compared to lower-class people.)
2. What aspects of peoples' social identities were hard to determine? When it wasn't clear, how did you decide, if you did?—e.g., for sexual orientation. What assumptions did you make?
3. How would you feel as a _____ watching these advertisements? (For example, person of color, white person, low-income person, middle-class person.)
4. How might you feel over a long period of time seeing these advertisements again and again?

5. How do advertising companies use TV to reinforce stereotypes based on race, gender, class, age, sexual orientation, physical or mental ability and religion?
6. How many people were competing or wanting the "best" of something? How many were cooperating? Give examples.
7. How does advertising affect our view of cooperation and competition?

GOING FURTHER   Encourage students to talk with their parents about these issues when they watch TV together.

FOLLOW-UP   "TV Turnabouts," p. 332.

2,555 HOURS A YEAR

OBJECTIVES   To encourage critical watching of television so that students think about in what ways it reflects the real world and in what ways it distorts the real world.
To have students notice both omissions and commissions in what is shown on television.
To have students understand how television perpetuates discrimination.

MATERIALS   Copies of "Worksheet: 2,555 Hours a Year," p. 256—one per student.

IMPLEMENTATION   (1) For a week have students keep track of how much time they spend watching television and how much time they spend in each of their other activities (e.g., classes, homework, sports, lessons, reading . . .). Have them create graphs of these results.

(2) Give out worksheets and review the terminology. Have students decide who will watch which television programs. They may want to have two or more children watch the same program for comparison, or have each child watch a different program to get as much variety as possible. Talk with children about the choices of shows and networks they regularly watch. If these have less variety than the possible programs that exist for their age group, you may want to encourage them to watch programs and networks not part of their regular viewing habits. For children who don't watch television, check with their parents about whether it is appropriate for them to watch a program at a friend's house or create an alternative assignment for them.

(3) After they have all had a chance to watch their program and complete the worksheet, divide students into groups of three or four. Each group goes through the worksheets, looking for patterns and commonalities, and prepares a short presentation which it shares with the class.

Who Teaches Children about Life?

"A child today is born into a home in which television is on an average of seven hours a day. For the first time in human history, most of the stories about people, life and values are told not by parents, schools, churches, or others in the community who have something to tell, but by a group of distant conglomerates that have something to sell."

George Gerbner, The Annenberg School for Communication, University of Pennsylvania, 1993

DISCUSSION

We can do it —
TOGETHER !!!

1. What did you learn about TV families' economic situations? How does that compare to what you know about what is actually true in the U.S.? Why is it different?
2. What did you learn about people of different races and ethnicities on TV? How are they portrayed?
3. What characteristics did old people have? In what ways are they realistic or not?
4. What are the roles and qualities of women and men on the shows? How are they realistic or stereotypic?
5. What did you notice about the way people with mental or physical disabilities are portrayed?
6. What were the characteristics of people of various religious backgrounds, if you were able to determine this?
7. If there were any lesbian or gay male characters shown, what did you notice about how they were portrayed?
8. What are the goals of the main characters? Are they for themselves, for others, or both? If they are "heroes" what does TV teach us about the qualities of a hero?
9. How do people in TV families solve their problems? How does your family solve its problems? If there are differences, make some guesses about why.
10. How do TV programs influence the way people think about themselves? If a person is less well-off than TV families, how might it make her feel? How about if she is equally well off? How might an Asian American feel if his race is never shown in TV shows? How might that make white people feel?
11. As you watch TV, keep alert. Do you see stereotypes and omissions of people of different races, genders, classes, ages, abilities, religions, sexual orientation. Is this related to the TV channels you watch? What can you do to not make these stereotypes part of your thinking?

Who's on Television; What Are They Doing?

- There is no overlap between the top 10 occupations in the U.S. and the top 10 occupations shown on television.
- The most negatively valued characters on television , with more members of their group being villains than heroes, are the mentally ill.
- Americans spend one-third of their freely disposable time watching television. This is **more than** the next ten highest ranked leisure time activities put together.
- Women have 45.5% of the roles in daytime serials, 55.3% in game shows, 27.8% in the news, and 23.4% in children's programs.
- Visibly old people are rarely seen on television. They are nonexistent on the Fox network, 1% on other network daytime series, and 3% in other programming.
- The U.S. census classifies more than 13% of Americans as poor, in television they represent 1.3% of all characters and only 0.6% (fewer than 1 in 100) of characters in children's programming.
- Women are in the news as government officials and business people nearly ten times as often as they are in for crime. The same ratio for men is 8.2 times, for Latino/as is 5 times and for African Americans is 1.7 times.
- For each woman in crime news there are 2.6 in business news, for each man in crime news there are 1.7 in business news. Latinos are represented equally in business news and crime news. For each African American in business news there are 6 in crime news.
- For every elderly male villain on television there are 13 male heroes of the same age. For elderly women there are *the same number* of heroines as villains. The proportion of elderly women as villains is eight times that of elderly men.

George Gerbner, The Annenberg School for Communication, University of Pennsylvania, 1993

	Major networks prime time	Fox network prime time	Cable prime time	Major networks daytime serials	Major networks children's programs	Cable children's programs
Major Characters on Television						
Women	35.1%	29.2%	26.4%	48.6%	18.4%	30.2%
Elderly	2.1%	0%	0.7%	0%	1.6%	0%
All characters of color	11.3%	33.3%	6.8%	5.3%	4%	2.2%
Blacks	9.8%	33.3%	4.4%	3.9%	2.4%	2.2%
Latino/as	0.7%	0%	1.2%	1.9%	0.2%	0%
Asian Americans	0.4%	0%	0%	0.5%	0%	0%
Native Americans	0.3%	0%	0.5%	0%	0.2%	0%

George Gerbner, The Annenberg School for Communication, University of Pennsylvania, 1993

SELL, SELL, SELL, BUY, BUY, BUY

OBJECTIVE   To increase students' awareness of the messages in magazine and newspaper advertisements, how these influence them, and why they are the way they are.

MATERIALS   Magazines; newspapers; construction paper; scissors; glue; pencils; paper.

IMPLEMENTATION   The day before this lesson, ask students to bring a magazine to class. Bring some yourself as well. Explain to the class that, since people buy products at least partly according to what they see advertised, advertisements influence many of our choices. Many advertisements are sexist, racist, ageist, classist, heterosexist or ableist. Some are obviously so. Others are so by omission—for example, only young people are shown using certain products; only middle-class homes and neighborhoods are pictured; black athletes are featured more than blacks in other professions.

Students work individually or in small groups. Everyone gets several magazines or newspapers, scissors, glue, and construction paper. Some groups cut advertisements out which reinforce a particular stereotype, mount these on paper, and label their posters "What Kind of Stereotyping?" Other groups make posters, "Who's Missing Here," to point out typical omissions. When done, display these around the room. (Save for lessons in Chapter 11.)

Also point out to students that what they see in magazines may reflect the particular community they live in and what magazines are sold there. For example, there are many magazines featuring black people that aren't sold in white neighborhoods. Help students become conscious of how the selection of magazines used for this activity will effect their findings.

DISCUSSION   1. Did you find more advertisements that were racist, sexist, ageist, classist, heterosexist or ableist? Try to think of reasons why. Talk to adults of different ages to see if this has changed in their lifetimes.

2. How do you feel when you read an advertisement in which you are a member of the group omitted or stereotyped? How about when you are in the group validated?
3. How do you feel when different aspects of your social identity are both stereotyped and validated in the same ad?
4. Why would advertisers make advertisements which stereotype women (or any other group)? Where do they get the idea? How does it serve them?
5. How would you feel if you couldn't afford most products advertised? How do advertisers teach us it's "normal" to want all these products? How does this serve them?
6. How might things change if advertisers changed their policies? Think of as many differences as you can in what people would value, would buy, and would do.
7. How did the selection of magazines available to you affect your findings?

GOING FURTHER   Prepare a display for a school showcase or bulletin board about what was learned. Or prepare an audio-visual presentation—a video tape or slide tape. Ask questions on the tape. Take it to other classes.

FOLLOW-UP   "Let Me Tell You What I Think," p. 333.

DADDY, HOW COME BOYS GROW UP TO BE MEN AND GIRLS GROW UP TO BE GIRLS?

FAIRNESS IN REPORTING?

OBJECTIVE   To encourage students to develop a critical awareness about biases in media reporting of current events and social issues related to issues of equality.

MATERIALS   "Worksheet A: Working for Change at Tyler School," p. 257, (one per group); "Worksheet B: News Report on Tyler School," p. 258, (one per group); "Worksheet C: Criteria for Analyzing News Reports," p. 259, (one per student).

IMPLEMENTATION   Explain to students that through this lesson they will learn more about how to discover bias in reporting. They will first examine a situation related to inequality based in ageism. Then they will examine current news reports on TV and in the print media.

Part A   Divide students into groups of four. Pass out "Worksheet A: Working for Change at Tyler School." Have students read it aloud, taking turns with paragraphs. Ask them to raise any questions or share any reactions to the situation for a couple of minutes. Then pass out "Worksheet B: News Report on Tyler School" and ask them to take turns reading it out loud. Explain that this represents an exaggerated example of bias.

When finished, group members each take a couple of minutes to respond in writing to the following questions.

1. What is your initial feeling about the news article just read? Why do you feel that way?
2. To what extent do you feel the article was biased? Jot down some reasons or examples.

Have students take turns reading aloud their written work to their group members. Ask them not to discuss their ideas until all responses have been read; then they talk together and respond to each others' ideas. Hold an all-class discussion about their responses to the questions. Discuss a third question as well:

3. Why might an article be biased? In whose interest is it to be so? How might you determine if the bias is intentional or unintentional?

Next tell students to work in their groups to think about what criteria they would use to assess any news report on TV or in the newspaper related to an issue about diversity/inequality. Elicit an example first, so students know they are on the right track. A recorder writes them down. After about 5 minutes come together as a class and each group shares its criteria. Use these to develop a class list of criteria. (If you anticipate that students will have difficulty with this, distribute Worksheet C and discuss it.)

Pass out Worksheet C: "Criteria for Analyzing News Reports." Go over the criteria together, ask for examples, and answer questions. Ask students to compare this to their class list. Check on the Worksheet items they had on their list. What did they have that's not on the list? Add those to the bottom or back of the worksheet. What's on the list they didn't think of? Ask students to apply any of the criteria they haven't already discussed to the "News Report from Tyler School."

Part B   Tell students they will now apply "Criteria for Analyzing News Reports Related to Inequality," with their criteria added, to current events. Brainstorm current issues in the news that have to do with issues of equality based on race, gender, class, religion, age, sexual orientation, language, ability or other. Remind students that what is presented in the mainstream media as issues are not inclusive. Ask them to think about issues that are omitted as well.

1. The class could choose one issue and each group can analyze a different media report—e.g., 3 groups look at 3 different TV networks and another 3 look at 3 different newspapers, for example.
2. Each group could take a different issue so many issues are represented. Each group member could analyze a different media source.

Help students to seek out a wide range of media sources. For example they can watch a mainstream TV station, public television, and a local station, if relevant. In addition to mainstream newspapers and news journals help them find news journals with a critical, progressive perspective. ("In These Times," "EXTRA," the journal of the organization Fairness and Accuracy in Reporting, would be accessible to good readers. See Bibliography for details.) Students can seek out media produced by and for various social groups representing different races, genders etc. On local issues, students can interview people in the community.

After group members have used the criteria to analyze their issue, they compile their findings within the group and present it in a short written and oral presentation. After listening to each others' findings, students think about all the data compiled by the class and draw some conclusions.

DISCUSSION

1. In what ways did you find the reporting on your issue fair? What are some examples?
2. To what extent was it biased? How?
3. What did you find in analyzing who was interviewed? (Worksheet questions 1–3.) Did that differ with different stations or print media? If so, how?
4. What did you find was focused on and what was omitted? (Worksheet questions 4–7.) Did that differ with different sources?
5. What did you find in looking at the reporting? (Worksheet questions 8–11.) Discuss similarities and differences in what you found.
6. To the extent that you found bias or omissions, who benefited from that? Who was hurt?
7. What are some important things you've learned from doing this project on learning to critically analyze the media? How will this affect you now and in the future?

Have students share their findings with others through a hall bulletin board, presentations to other classes and so forth. Encourage them to write letters to media sources that were found to be biased and ask for greater fairness in reporting. Discuss with students how the changes needed to create truly fair and accurate media are substantial. Share your hope they won't feel discouraged if their efforts don't produce the changes they'd like.

GOING FURTHER

Have students use "Criteria for News Reports Related to Issues of Inequality" as they continue to talk about current events and issues of inequality throughout the school year.

Fairness and Accuracy in Reporting

FAIR, a national media watch group offers well-documented criticism to try to correct bias and imbalance in the media. It focuses on the media's insensitivity to women, labor, and people of color among others.

In 1992 in an article in its bimonthly journal, EXTRA, Mark Schubb brought a critical perspective to Los Angeles TV coverage of the upheaval after the Rodney King verdict. Among the items he noted were:

- While the media emphasized the theme of black-on-white violence, the vast majority of victims weren't white. Of reported deaths, 25 were African American, 19 Latino and 10 Anglo.
- When arson and violence stopped, so did live coverage. A massive rally for peace and unity attended by 100,000 people, unlike looting, was not deemed worthy of live coverage by most stations.
- News reports didn't cover the forces behind the upheaval—years of police abuse, slashed social programs and community services, economic blight. There was an absence of discussions of racism.

EXTRA, July/August 1992

LISTENING TO THE LYRICS

OBJECTIVES

To help students analyze lyrics in popular music and see how some of these songs reinforce stereotypes.

To have students recognize how they can be affected by these lyrics even if on an unconscious level.

MATERIALS   Tapes and/or CDs of popular music; transcripts of the words to these songs; paper; pencils; poster board; markers; a poster with the "Song Guidelines" listed below.

IMPLEMENTATION   Explain to students that they will be thinking about and analyzing the words to popular songs in order to better understand ways these may reinforce stereotypes around race, gender, age, class and sexual orientation. Make a large copy and post the chart below.

Song Guidelines

1. Describe the gender roles in your song.
2. Analyze your song for any stereotypes about gender or any sexism in it.
3. Is your song about people of a specific race? How can you tell?
4. Analyze your song for any stereotypes about race or any racism in it.
5. Does your song relate in any way to age, sexual orientation, class, disability, language or religion? If so, explain how and analyze the song for any stereotypes or "isms."

Ask each student to bring in a tape, a CD and/or a transcript of the words to a current popular song that he likes. Have each student briefly describe his selection. Then have students choose partners with the same song or songs with similar themes. Partners design a poster that includes: (1) the words to their song or songs; (2) any relevant illustrations they wish to draw; (3) an analysis of the song(s) that answer the questions on the "Song Guidelines." Students put up their posters. Allow time for students to read each other's posters before having a class discussion.

The results of this activity will depend heavily on the songs your students choose. If there is not much variety in these you will want to bring in some other songs to give the students a more rounded picture of current music. Depending on the composition of your class this may involve finding music from ethnicities, races and cultures not represented by your students.

DISCUSSION
1. What did you learn about the lyrics to popular songs today?
2. How did you feel about this? Did anything surprise you? If so, in what ways?
3. Were there any trends you noticed that were true for a number of the songs? Explain these.
4. Why do you think songwriters write the lyrics they do? How could you better understand why they do this?
5. If you thought some of the lyrics you heard and read were offensive to some groups of people, what can you do about this?

GOING FURTHER
1. Invite a songwriter to class to talk with you about the process of writing and marketing songs.
2. As a class write some songs that counter common stereotypes in popular songs. Perform these for a school assembly.
3. Do some research on songs from other countries. How do these compare to current songs in the U.S.?
4. Do some research about U.S. songs historically. How have lyrics changed?

MEDIA STATISTICS: IS IT THE WHOLE STORY?

OBJECTIVES   To help students learn to read statistics critically.
To help students realize that data are not objective.

To help students understand that writers make choices about what statistics they use and how they present them in order to make the arguments they want to make.

MATERIALS   One copy of each of the "Worksheets—Graphing Data #1, 2, 3," pp. 260–262, and "Arguing with the Data"—for each group of three students; enlarged graphs to post; graph paper; pencils; markers; compasses; and rulers. Make "Worksheet: Arguing with the Data" by typing the Argument 1 and Argument 2 on the top and middle of a page, respectively. (See Implementation, Step 2.)

IMPLEMENTATION   Information for this lesson comes from *Don't Believe the Hype: Fighting Cultural Misinformation about African-Americans* by Farai Chideya. For each of its sections—including family, welfare, home, education, sports, business, arts and health—the author gives data and helps the reader look at how they might be analyzed.

Step One: Tell students that people who work with statistics have to chose what data they want to use. Then they choose how to present them. Both the choice of data and the choice of presentation have a large impact on how readers interpret the data and what they believe from them. In this lesson students learn how to analyze data accurately.

Explain to students what welfare is. Welfare is tax money our society uses to assist people who are temporarily unable to support themselves. Often this money is needed by single mothers with pre-school age children or people who are mentally or physically disabled.

We used data about welfare for this lesson because our society has many misconceptions and stereotypes about people on welfare. This lesson is designed to help students think about how this particular issue is related to racism and classism in our society. It also raises questions about equity issues that arise in a society with such unequal distribution of resources.

Welfare provides *very little* money for people. For example, the average income for a family on welfare is less than half of the poverty level. Most people are not on welfare for very long; the average length of time to receive this assistance is less than two years. Welfare is not a very big piece of the U.S. budget, in fact it is less than 1% of the total budget.

Tell students that, as a class, they will be looking at several graphs about who's on welfare. One way to look at this data is to think of *the whole* as being everyone on welfare. Then the question is, "Looking at all the people on welfare, what percent is of each race." Graph A on Worksheet #2 shows us this information.

Another way to look at the data is to think about a particular race as *the* whole and then look at "of all the people of that race, what percent are on welfare." Graphs B and C on Worksheet #2 and Graphs D through G on Worksheet #3 all present this information.

Sometimes it is the style of graph that gives a particular impression. Graphs B and C both take four different races and look at what percent *of each group* is on welfare. In Graph B you first see columns of who is on welfare and then the columns of who is not on welfare. Graph C has the same information but is visually different because you look at each racial group and see what percent of people are on welfare and what percent are not for each group.

Graphs D through G take each group separately and look at what percent of the group is on welfare and what percent is not. Take time to read and discuss all of these graphs before you go on to the next step.

Step Two: Divide students into groups of three. Direct students to look at the data in the data table on "Worksheet: Graphing the Data #1" and at the sets of statements that follow this table. All of these statements are true. The first set comes directly from the table. The second set is additional information about who's on welfare. Students read and discuss these statements.

Pass out "Worksheet: Arguing with the Data" that includes these two arguments:

Argument 1:

We don't have much of a problem with people being on welfare in this country. Not very many families are on welfare. The differences between races are minor and insignificant given that such a small percentage of American families are on welfare at all and given that people rarely stay on welfare very long.

Argument 2:

We have a big problem in this country with black and Hispanic families being on welfare. They are MUCH more likely to be on welfare than white or Asian families. Families on welfare have young parents who should be out working.

They read the two arguments. For each argument students choose which statements and which graph or graphs could be used to best support the argument.

DISCUSSION

1. In this lesson what did you learn about who is on welfare?
2. In what ways was this information confusing? In what ways was it clear?
3. How is some of what you learned about welfare related to racism and classism in our society?
4. What did you learn about how statistics can be used and misused?
5. When you are reading reports with statistical information what do you need to think about?
6. Why do people choose to use statistics in the ways they do?

Section B   _Look at Your Community_

PLEASE BUY ME ONE

OBJECTIVES   To help students understand how producers of toys and games influence their ideas about what is appropriate, and thus influence their purchases.
To help them learn how racism, sexism and ableism can be perpetuated by game companies.

MATERIALS   Paper and pencils; access to stores; copies of "Worksheet: Inventory of Games and Toys," p. 263.

IMPLEMENTATION   Explain to students that most games available in large stores are produced by major companies whose goal is to sell their products. Tell students they will research the illustrations on the boxes of games and toys that they or their siblings have or those at a local store. They should describe the cover pictures as to the race, gender and physical ability of the people depicted.

For homework each student completes the Worksheet. If they can get to a store, they work in pairs or groups of three. If not, they should examine games and toys in their homes.

After the Worksheets are done, a class tally is made. Make a large copy of the Worksheet on chart paper and list all the games investigated—don't repeat any. The class as a whole can create circle graphs, one each for race, gender, and ability. Interview answers are written in narrative form. (Save work for follow up lesson in Chapter 11.)

DISCUSSION
1. What are your reactions to our survey? Was it what you expected? If you were surprised, in what ways were you surprised?
2. What types of toys and games have primarily girls on the packages? What do these teach us about what girls are "supposed" to do?
3. Which ones have primarily boys? What do these teach us?
4. How did your parent(s) react? How did people in stores react?
5. What toys or games had children with disabilities on the packages? What were they doing?
6. What changes need to be made in toy and game boxes? Think of reasons why these changes are important. Why are they likely to happen? Why unlikely?

GOING FURTHER   Students can repeat this for games found at community centers, libraries, etc. Or have students look at products for adults. What are the race and gender roles on these packages?

Have students tell their parents or other adults what the class discovered, and ask them their feelings.

FOLLOW UP   "Let Me Tell You What I Think," p. 333; "We Can Design Them Ourselves," p. 335.

Making Pie Graphs

It is often difficult for children to understand pie graphs (circle graphs) if they do not yet know about percentages or about measuring angles with a protractor. This is a simple method to have children both construct and create meaning from pie graphs.

Start with a classroom survey like the number of siblings each child has. Have children line up so all the only children are next to each other, then all the children with one sibling, all with two siblings, etc. Now have children form their line into a circle. Place jump ropes on the floor between each section, with each jump rope being a radius of the circle reaching from the circumference to the center. This gives you a "live" pie graph of siblings.

Now take a one inch high strip of one inch graph paper. Make it as many inches long as children in the class. Pick a color for each category. Use each to color all the squares for a category sequentially on the strip. Continue with all the categories until the whole strip is colored. The strip can be turned into a pie graph by joining its ends together with tape. Place the circle on a piece of newsprint and draw radii from the center of the circle to the edges of each sibling category. Be sure to outline the circle on the paper, as well.

These methods show children that the size of the wedge of "pie" is directly related to the amount of circumference of the circle used. And that the portion of the circumference is the number of items in that category.

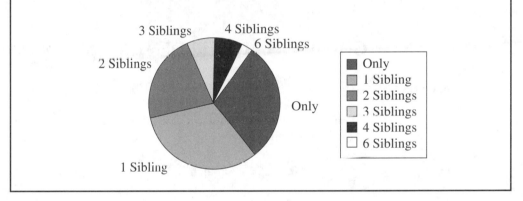

A FIREFIGHTER, NOT A FIREMAN

OBJECTIVES
To increase student awareness of the sexism of many of the occupational terms in our language.
To have them notice how these influence our images of people in these roles and the expectations they set for themselves.

MATERIALS
Chart paper and markers; children's books and magazines.

IMPLEMENTATION
Discuss sexism in occupational terms with the whole class. Give examples of a sexist and a nonsexist term, for example, fireman, firefighter.

Divide students into groups. Groups list on chart paper as many occupation terms as they can think of. They list both the traditional term and the newer, nonsexist one, if they can think of both. Occupation terms which are not sex-role-based are listed on a separate page. Students can look in books and magazines for ideas. Examples of old job titles include mailman, garbage man, housewife, and chairman. Alternatives are mail carrier, garbage collector, homemaker, and chairperson.

Join together, post the lists, and discuss their findings. (Save student work for follow-up lesson in Chapter 11.)

DISCUSSION
1. When you think of a _____, do you think of a woman or a man or both? (Use a sexist term.) Why? Discuss several terms.
2. What happens when you think of a _____? (Use a nonsexist term here.) Discuss several terms.
3. How has our language affected people's thinking about what they can be? How has it affected you?

GOING FURTHER
Students can use these new words as spelling words, or perhaps as part of an assignment for a story in language arts. Older, or more advanced students, may want to look for these words in other languages. Are they gender-role based? In what languages? How can we learn more about a culture through its language?

Students may also find it interesting to investigate the etymology of these words. Learning about the historical roots of the words can also give them more cultural understanding.

FOLLOW-UP
"Let Me Tell You What I Think," p. 333.

GUESS WHAT, OUR DENTIST IS A WOMAN!

OBJECTIVES
To have students recognize how the division of labor in community jobs can reinforce race, gender, and other forms of bias.
To encourage them to think critically about these roles and be aware of the institutional discrimination involved.

MATERIALS
Copies of "Worksheet: Neighborhood Tally," p. 264; paper; pencils.

IMPLEMENTATION
Give each student a copy of the Worksheet and go over it together. In the last two columns add any other social groups affected by discrimination that are important to examine in your community context.

Explain that we may make assumptions based on the people we see doing certain jobs. For example, if every time we have our teeth examined we are treated by a man, we may begin to think of dentists as men. Students take the Worksheet home to fill out.

After students return with completed sheets, make a class tally. Individual tally sheets can be posted, and copies of interviews can be rewritten carefully and posted on bulletin boards.

DISCUSSION
1. What percentage of the people on your tally sheet were white? People of color? What percentage were female? Male?
2. Were you surprised by these results? If so, why? What had you expected?
3. If you are used to people in certain jobs being a certain race or gender, how does that influence your thinking about those jobs, and what you can be?
4. How are opportunities for jobs influenced by racism and sexism? What can be done about this?
5. Are institutional sexism and racism evident in your community? How? What can be done about this?
6. If you looked at other social groups affected by discrimination what did you find from your tally?

7. How much do you think the findings in this survey are dependent on the composition of our community? How would the findings be different in other communities? Which ones? Why?

GOING FURTHER Invite speakers of different occupations to your classroom. Try for a wide range of occupations. Try for people in jobs not traditional to their gender or race. Encourage students to ask questions about how sexism and racism influenced these people's job opportunities.

Students may also find it interesting to compare job opportunities by gender in this country historically. For example, in 1996, 43% of law students in this country are female compared to 7% in 1972! Or they may find it interesting to do this across cultures. In the U.S. 23% of doctors are female compared to Russian where 66% of doctors are women. What other occupations seem to be based on country and culture? What can we learn from this?

THE MESSAGE IN THE PACKAGE

OBJECTIVES To better understand how the packaging of products may influence buying and how this helps perpetuate stereotypes.

To understand how images of some people (whites, middle-class, able-bodied, young) in advertising reinforce a positive self-concept and sense of being "normal."

To see how the paucity of images of some people (people of color, working-class or poor, disabled, older) reinforces feelings of lack of power.

MATERIALS Access to supermarket; paper and pencils; large bags for collecting items. Type a "Worksheet: Supermarket," and make 1 copy per student. (See Implementation below.)

IMPLEMENTATION Brainstorm as a class on the types of food, toiletries, and so on that are sold prepacked in illustrated containers—cookies, cereals, syrups, shampoo, canned juices, frozen desserts, and so on. List these on the board. Have students volunteer to take a category or two, depending on how many you list.

Give students a copy of "Worksheet: Supermarket" with the following items on it.

Number of products observed _____
Numbers of:
- *Gender*: men _____   women _____
- *Race:*   whites _____   blacks _____   Latino/as _____
  Native Americans _____   Asian Americans _____
- *Class*:   middle-class _____   working-class or poor _____   upper-class _____
  (if possible to determine)
- *Age*:   adults over 65 _____   adults under 65 _____   children _____
- *Ability*:   able-bodied people _____   people with disabilities _____

What were people doing?
What kinds of jobs did people seem to have?
What stereotypes did you find, if any?

Each child takes a copy of the Worksheet to the supermarket and takes notes of what illustrations are on the packages. If these are products that the family buys, empty containers can be brought to class.

Students work in small groups to note and compare findings and make a group report. Discuss the project with the whole class.

Be sure to discuss with students how the community they live in may affect their results; help them avoid generalizations based on their results. For example, while there are many products with black people on them, they are typically sold in neighborhoods with a sizable black population. The fact that some students in primarily white neighborhoods may not know about them further testifies to how the packaging of products can shape our view of the world. (Save packages and students' work for "Sharing Results" in Chapter 11.)

DISCUSSION
1. What kinds of products have only males on the package? Which have only females? What messages is the advertiser giving you?
2. What products use pictures of people of color? Which use white people? Why do you think they do? If you were a person of color how would this make you feel? If you were white?
3. What was the range of class backgrounds of people on the packages, if you could tell? Who was absent?
4. What products show older people, adults, or children? What is the message the advertiser is giving?
5. Does the gender, race, age or class of the person in the illustration make a difference to you in considering buying a product? If so, how?
6. What subtle messages do we receive from advertising about ourselves? About others?
7. What projects have people with disabilities on them? What message is being given?
8. How does the area you live in influence your findings? How might it be different elsewhere? Why?

GOING FURTHER
Have students do a similar study of catalogues that come into the home. Have them report their findings to the class.

FOLLOW UP
"Sharing Results," p. 334.

ON THE HORNS OF A DILEMMA

OBJECTIVES
To make students more aware of how classism, sexism, ageism, and racism influence people's expectations of others.
To understand how these affect opportunities in life.

MATERIALS
Copies of "Worksheet: On the Horns of a Dilemma," p. 265 (one story with two parts for each student pair); paper and pencils.

IMPLEMENTATION
Divide students into pairs. Each pair interviews one adult in the school—other teachers, secretaries, aides, custodians, administrators. (Get permission first.) In addition, each pair interviews at least two other students, and each student interviews at least one adult at home.

Each pair takes one of the four stories, with its two parts. (Be sure the four stories are divided among all students in class.) Students tell half of their interviewees just story a and the other half just story b. They write down a summary of each response and the reasoning. After the interviewing, students form small groups and tally the responses to story a and those to b. Through discussion, students will learn responses to all stories.

DISCUSSION
Discuss each story set separately.
1. What solutions did people give for each dilemma?
2. What reasons did they give for their solutions?
3. Did Beena's and Sean's gender affect what people thought should happen to them? If so, how? Is this fair? (Similarly: Julia's and Hillary's races; Louise's and Lucy's ages; Adam's and Aaron's class backgrounds.)
4. How can the "isms" affect people's expectations of others?
5. How do those expectations adults hold affect your views of the world? How comfortable are you with this?

Section C   *How Has This Affected Me?*

MORE TO IT THAN JUST CALCULATING

OBJECTIVES   To enable students to see how racism, sexism, classism, ageism, and other forms of inequality can influence their thinking and perceptions.
To encourage them to see how omitting people is a way to reinforce these "isms."

MATERIALS   Paper; pencils.

IMPLEMENTATION   Divide students into pairs or groups of three. Direct the students to work in their groups to write five word problems to give to another group to solve. Tell them to write problems that have characters *doing things*. Groups then trade and solve the problems they receive.

Come back together as a class and discuss the mathematical solutions for these problems. Then explain to students that they will soon be going back to their small groups to analyze the problems they received for the "isms" and for inclusiveness.

In order to help them understand this, use the problems in the box below as samples. For example, in the first problem, there is an African American girl doing a cooking project for an African American holiday. Typically African American holidays are not included in our math textbooks. She is cooking with her grandfather, countering a sexist stereotype about who cooks. In the second problem there is a low-income single parent family, purposely of indeterminate ethnicity. This problem reinforces cooperation by having the whole family work together to achieve a mutual goal.

Students discuss the third example problem as a whole class and then return to their small groups to discuss the problems they received and answer the following questions: (1) How diverse are the settings? The characters? (2) What people are doing? —do they conform to traditional gender roles? (3) Can you tell anything about the race, ethnicity or class of the people involved? What about ability, language, religion or age? (4) Do the problems deal with the experiences a variety of people—or just certain groups of people?

Examples of Math Problems That Reinforce Equality

1. Tabitha and her grandfather were baking cookies for a Kwanzaa supper. If they made five dozen peanut butter-banana cookies and one and a half dozen gingerbread-chocolate chip cookies and Tabitha's younger brother Malcolm and their dog Kuumba ate eighteen cookies, how many cookies did they take to the church supper?

2. Jimmy and Erica were working with their mother to move into a new apartment. The apartment was on the fifth floor. They counted the steps each time they carried boxes up. They didn't bother counting going down because it was too much fun to run and jump and see how many steps they could skip. If they each made thirteen trips and altogether each went up 1,495 steps, how many steps is it up to the fifth floor?

3. Meiko wanted to make her friend Kenji a present. She decided he would like a lamp. She went to a few stores to ask prices for materials. She found out the wood for the base would cost $5.65. The electrical parts would cost $3.89. She found an old frame at a yard sale for 75¢. She wanted to macramé a new one and the cord for that would cost $1.80. She had saved $14. Did she have enough? If not, how much more did she need? If yes, how much did she have left over?

DISCUSSION
1. Share responses to the questions.
2. What groups, if any, were stereotyped in our problems?
3. What groups, if any, were omitted?
4. Why did we omit the people we did?
5. What does this teach us about the effect of the "isms" on our view of the world?

GOING FURTHER   Have original groups rewrite their problems so that they include a variety of people in positive, nonstereotyped roles.

UNFINISHED ADVENTURES

OBJECTIVE   To see how racism, sexism, and ageism affect expectations of people's behavior.

MATERIALS   Copies of "Worksheet: Unfinished Adventures," p. 266, printed as 2 worksheets. Extra writing paper; pencils; "Worksheet: Picture Cards," cut for each story, p. 267; drawing paper and crayons (alternative).

IMPLEMENTATION   Give each student a copy of "Worksheet: A Sunday Surprise." Read it aloud, holding up the Picture Card. (The card has been drawn to clearly show the race of the family, but *not* to show any defined sex roles.) When you finish, the students continue the story by following the directions on the top of the page. (Alternatively, have students draw the conclusion of the story and explain their drawings.) Another day do "Worksheet: A Moving Day" in the same manner.

Either read aloud a number of the students' conclusions to the stories, or pass them around the room and give students time to read them to themselves. Then join together for discussion.

DISCUSSION
1. How did the men in your stories act? Were most of them scared? Calm? Helpful? Bossy? Efficient? Comforting? Decisive? Were there many exceptions to what the majority of you wrote? How close is this to the stereotype of how men should be?
2. How did the women in the stories act? Were most of them scared? Calm? Helpful? Bossy? Efficient? Comforting? Decisive? Were there many exceptions to this? How close is this to the stereotype of how women should be?
3. Did it matter whether the characters in the story were white or people of color? Did that affect how you decided how they should act?
4. Now think about the children in your stories. Was it important that they were young, or did it matter more whether they were girls or boys? Children of color? White?
5. Think about the grandmother. Did she act differently because she was older?
6. Who took the leader's role in each story? An adult or a child? A man or a woman? Was it different for people of color and white people?
7. How does racism, sexism, and ageism influence the way we think people act? How can we make our assumptions more fair and realistic?

Watch Assumptions about Families

As teachers it's important to think about our own assumptions about what a normative family is. Preface questions about families carefully. Perhaps some children live in foster homes, live with one parent and a same-sex partner, or with a grandparent, among many other situations. Only about 30% of the children in this country live in traditional nuclear families. Help all children feel okay about a range of living situations.

WHAT IF IT HURTS?

OBJECTIVES To examine ways that males and females are conditioned to react to hurt.
To think about what this does to people.

IMPLEMENTATION Discuss with the whole class that there are very different ways people react when they are hurt—either physically or emotionally. Explain that they will do several role-plays to help them examine this. (Use "Role-Play Guidelines and Techniques," p. 70, to refresh memories.)

Role-Play One. Four girls are playing soccer. One accidentally kicks another in the ankle instead of kicking the ball. She kicks her very hard.

Role-Play Two. Same as above, but have four boys.

Role-Play Three. Same as above but have a boy kick a girl; the other two players can be either gender.

Role-Play Four. Same as Three, but have a girl kick a boy.

Role-Play Five. Jacob is having a party. He puts invitations on all the desks except Wilbur's. Role-play is at recess with Wilbur, Rodney and Buffy.

Role-Play Six. Do the above with Tamayia having a party and not inviting Penelope.

Role-Play Seven. Three girls are at the water fountain. Sumi pushes Yolanda roughly out of the way because she wants a drink first. Yolanda's friend, Bessie, is there, too.

Role-Play Eight. Same as above, but with Leroy, Josh, and Xavier.

Role-Play Nine. Same as above but with Chris, Terry, and Pat. (That's right, those names are androgynous.)

DISCUSSION
1. The first four role-plays were about being hurt physically, by mistake. The next two were about being hurt emotionally. The last three were about being hurt physically, when someone meant to hurt. Which was the most real to you? Which was the least real? Explain your answers.
2. In which role-plays do people cry? Why? Why didn't they cry in the others? Was crying related to how badly someone was hurt? If not, what was it related to?
3. In which role-plays did people react by hurting back? Why? Discuss whether that was what would really happen. What makes people decide whether or not to fight back? Was there a difference between males and females?
4. Did anyone have any strategies for making the people in the situation less angry? If so, what? Were these more common among boys or girls, or didn't that matter?
5. What have we learned from these activities about how boys are expected to react to hurt in our society? Girls? What alternatives do you have?

GOING FURTHER Ask the students to keep a record of actual times when people get hurt. You can set up a shoe box with slips of paper by it. They could fill these out for themselves or others, anonymously. Go through the box every few days for a while and discuss how a situation was handled. Use it as a chance for the students to find sex-role related behavior and see if they can become more open to a variety of reactions.

WHAT I WANT TO BE

OBJECTIVE To help children see in what ways their future occupational aspirations are influenced by racism, sexism, and classism.

MATERIALS   For Option One: lined chart paper and magic markers.
For Option Two: thin cardboard; assorted fabrics; scissors; glue.

IMPLEMENTATION   Students complete the sentence, "When I'm an adult I want to be a . . . ." Then the boys complete the sentence, "If I were a girl, I would want to be a . . . ." The girls complete the sentence, "If I were a boy, I would want to be a . . . ." Then the white students can complete the sentence, "If I were a person of color I would want to be a . . . ." And the students of color complete the sentence, "If I were white, I would want to be a . . . ." All students then complete the following sentences: "If my family had an adequate amount of money, I would hope to be a . . . ." and "If my family had very little money, I would hope to be a . . . ."

For Option one, students print their sentences on chart paper which then can be posted for the discussion. For Option Two, they cut out cardboard portraits of themselves doing whatever it is they have chosen. They can then clothe these figures. They do the same for one of the three alternatives—being the opposite sex, being a different race, or from a different class background.

DISCUSSION
1. What did you say that you want to be when you grow up? Tell us about that.
2. Did you change your choice when you pretended to change gender? Race? Why or why not?
3. Did you choose something that others usually expect people of your gender and race to be?
4. What kinds of hopes and jobs did you list for a middle-class family? A low-income family? Why? What similarities and differences are there?
5. How does what class our family is from influence our hopes for ourselves? What can we do to change it?
6. How do racism, sexism, and classism influence what we think we can do or become?
7. What are some occupations that people usually don't expect someone of your race, gender, or class to asprire to? Would you like to be that? If so, how can you make that happen?

PUT-DOWNS

OBJECTIVES   To develop sensitivity to stereotyped put-downs, understand their sources and their effect on both people involved.
To see how they reinforce racism, sexism, classism, ageism, and individualism.

MATERIALS   Chart paper and markers.

IMPLEMENTATION   Start this as a group project. Ask students to think of put-downs they hear that stereotype people. Brainstorm either as a whole class or in small groups. Here are some examples, if you need them to get going.

"You faggot," "Retard," "Indian-giver," "You're a sissy," "Dumb nigger," "You're just a baby, I won't play with you," "That's for girls only," "Dumbie," "He's worn that same sweater for four days, I'm not going to sit next to him," "Four-eyes."

Be very insistent that students understand that these put-downs do reinforce stereotypes. This activity hits very close to home, and many times students will deny the power of these put-downs with statements like, "Everyone says that, it doesn't mean anything."

Help students see that by using such language, no matter how it is intended or what is "accepted," they are still using race, class, sex, or age to put someone down. Even if, for example, black students call each other "nigger," they are accepting and reinforcing a negative, powerless image of themselves and other black people. (See box on p. 186.)

For this reason it's crucial for you to insist on "no put-downs" in a classroom based on equality.

DISCUSSION

1. How does (put-down) reinforce a (racist, sexist, etc.) stereotype? How do put-downs reinforce "me-first" thinking?
2. How do you feel when you say one of these to someone? How do you feel when someone says it to you?
3. Where do you learn these phrases?
4. Why do people say things like this?
5. What other ways can we express the same emotions?
6. How comfortable are you about reinforcing stereotypes and the "isms" in this way? What do you want to do about it?

Dealing with Put-Downs of Homosexuality

The terms "faggot," "sissy," "dyke" are commonly used as put-downs and thereby reinforce strict gender-defined behavior and norms. What boy will dare be gentle if he risks the label "faggot"! Furthermore they perpetuate negative images of lesbians and gay men.

Talk to students about how these put-downs hurt people. Remind them it's okay for boys to be sensitive and girls strong. Discuss how these put-downs enforce homophobia. Explain that their expression of friendship and affection toward people they care about—no matter what their gender—is part of being human.

DISCRIMINATION: HAS IT HELPED OR HINDERED ME?

OBJECTIVE

To enable students to investigate the ways in which they may be privileged or disadvantaged in various life situations because of their race, gender or other aspect of their social identity.

MATERIALS

For Part A order videos of segments of two Prime Time shows, "True Colors" and "The Fairer Sex" (see Media section of the Bibliography for sources). If you can't get both, get one, though using both is preferable. If it is impossible to get the videos, you could do Part B of this lesson alone, although the context will be missing.

IMPLEMENTATION

It is often difficult for people to realize the ways in which membership in advantaged social groups has given them privileges in their lives. Sometimes people denied advantages because of their social group membership don't recognize the degree to which their lives have been negatively affected by institutional discrimination. This lesson gives young people a chance to develop experiments for exploring the effects of race and gender on opportunities in their own lives.

This lesson can be a powerful learning experience for students, and at the same time, there is an element of setting up people who are involved in the experiments. Think through the implications of the lesson to make sure you are comfortable with it.

Part A

As background to this activity try to order segments of two Prime Time shows that focus on institutional discrimination: one on racism (True Colors) and the other sexism (The Fairer Sex) which are twenty minutes each. In each, two discrimination testers of equal qualifications are sent into a mid-western city for two weeks to try to get settled—to find an apartment, a job, car and so forth. The shows document the ways in which the white and black persons in the one test, and male and female in the other were treated similarly and differently. They are very powerful, highly recommended documentaries.

Review with students some of what they learned about institutional discrimination from the lessons in Chapter 7. Discuss with them the degree to which they believe being a person of color or being female affects people's opportunities in today's world. Show one of the videos, discuss it, and then show the other.

DISCUSSION   (Use these discussion questions first for one show and then the other.)

1. What are your feelings seeing this experiment? What makes you feel the way you do?
2. How did the discrimination-testers feel about their experiences doing this experiment? Why?
3. Why is it often difficult for people advantaged by the existence of discrimination (white people in the case of race discrimination, or males in the case of gender discrimination) to recognize their privileges? What might help them see that?
4. Some people argue that blacks and whites, males and females have equal opportunity in our society. Having seen these experiments, how would you respond to them?

Part B   Talk with students about their becoming discrimination-testers to determine how they are treated similarly and/or differently from someone of a different race or gender background (or other aspects of their social identities). Ask students to think about the kinds of experiments they could plan and implement in their community. Either help students refine some of their ideas, or use the plans below. Talk with students about how the results of the experiments will vary depending on the composition of the community and neighborhood in which the experiments are done.

Experiment 1   Students of different racial backgrounds go into a store. Either they, or another student observer, record how quickly store personnel wait on each young person. Who gets waited on first? Is the tone of voice or approach to the young persons different? In either case do store personnel follow either tester around the store as he browses. Record data and repeat for several stores.

Experiment 2   Consider using this experiment if there are jobs for young people advertised in your community and if students are willing to take the jobs if offered them. Plan for pairs of students *with the same qualifications for the job* but different in race, or different in gender, to answer the ad. Who gets an interview? Who gets a job? Record data and repeat for several ads. Also have students write down anything about the job or community that may be relevant for analyzing the data later—e.g., racial composition of the community, type of job.

If your students are too young to qualify for these jobs, perhaps they could work in a pair with an older sibling or friend. The younger person could be the data collector and the older one the experimenter.

Experiment 3   Put an ad in the paper offering to do work—e.g., child care, yard work, typing, errands, etc. Make this work students are really willing to do. Make up a title for your job service—e.g., Youth at Work—and use a student's phone number. When calls come in, describe two young people who are available for the job. Have pairs with the same qualifications, but different in either race for one experiment or gender for another. Try to make the descriptions such that the caller can identify the racial background of the students. They could use one name that may be common for a Latino (Jose) or African American (Jamal), for example, and one that is not easily identified with any racial group. Record data on who is asked for an interview and on who is offered the work. Repeat for other ads.

DISCUSSION

1. How did you feel if you were a participant in these experiments? Why? What did you learn from them?
2. How do any of you feel about the results of these experiments? Why do you feel that way?
3. What were the differences, if any, in the ways people responded to young people of different racial backgrounds? How did that relate to the composition of the community?
4. What were the differences, if any, in the ways people responded to students of different genders?
5. Did any racial group or gender group have advantages in getting a job, making a sale, getting respect in a store etc.? What were the factors in giving the advantages? What factors brought the dis-advantages?
6. What have you learned about any advantages or dis-advantages people may face in their lives because of institutional discrimination? What can be done about that?
7. What might students who have had different life experiences than you have, learn from participating in this type of an experiment?

In recording and discussing these experiments, have students give respondents numbers and not names, to preserve confidentiality. If you live in a small community or if students knew the respondents, you might discuss how comfortable they would be sharing the results of the surveys with the respondents in a way that would raise their awareness, rather than be critical. This may or may not be appropriate, depending on your situation.

GOING FURTHER

Students may wish to test for discrimination based on other aspects of social group identity. Support them in designing and carrying out similar experiments.

1. Name of TV program:

2. What socio-economic class (poor, working-class, middle-class, wealthy) are the people in the show?
   Describe the qualities of the characters:

3. What races or ethnicities are people in the show?
   Describe the qualities of the characters:

4. What roles do females and males play in the show?
   Describe the qualities of the women and men:

5. What roles do older people play in the show?
   Describe their qualities:

6. What roles do people with physical or mental disabilities or people with learning problems play in the show?
   Describe their qualities:

7. Were you able to determine the religious backgrounds of people in the show?
   If so, describe the qualities of these characters:

8. What roles do heterosexuals, lesbians and/or gay men have in the show?
   Describe their qualities:

9. What problem is presented? How do people handle it?

10. What are the goals of the main characters? To get ahead, be best, be "heroes"? Or to work together to make changes for lots of people?

At the beginning of the year, the peer leaders at Tyler School had taken a student survey about changes needed in the school.

- Students wanted more variety in the lunch menu, including meals that vegetarians and student with religious restrictions could eat.
- They only had 15 minutes for recess and felt that was too short.
- The only after-school program was sports. They wanted a greater variety of programs that all student could participate in together, like drama, video production, peer mediation and community service.

The peer leaders had met with the principal about these changes. Although she said they were good ideas, no changes were ever made. The peer leaders went back to the principal and asked that a School Council be formed to work on these and other problems. It would be comprised of students, teachers, parents, and the principal. The students wanted everyone to participate in solving problems that affected the school.

The principal told the students it was up to the adults in the school to make decisions. Many students were angry about the ageist belief that students couldn't be responsible. Some teachers agreed that a School Council would be a good idea, but they were unsuccessful in convincing the principal of that. Other teachers agreed with the principal.

Students wrote letters to the School Board and Superintendent of Schools about their concerns and idea for a School Council. The Superintendent wrote back that they should take up their concerns with the principal. No one from the School Board ever answered their letters.

Very frustrated by the lack of response to many efforts to be heard, students planned a protest to call attention to their concerns. One day after school was dismissed, and before getting on their buses, about 70 students gathered for five minutes in front of the school with signs that said things like "Students Want A Voice," "Students ARE Responsible." A few peer leaders spoke about the students' suggestions for changes. The following article appeared in the local newspaper the next day.

STUDENTS DISRUPT TYLER SCHOOL

Yesterday students upset the usual orderly dismissal at Tyler School in Elmsville with an unauthorized demonstration. Carrying picket signs they refused to get on their busses until they listened to several student speeches complaining about conditions at the school.

"The students certainly did not have permission to demonstrate," Superintendent Ralph Mudge said. "I was shocked and dismayed by the report of their behavior."

Ms. Viola Perkins, principal, said that students had brought a few concerns to her, and she had been working hard to find solutions. "Change takes time. I wish they had come to me before taking to the streets."

Those teachers interviewed felt that students wanted more decision-making power than they should have at their age. "They want to make decisions that are really for staff," said physical education teacher Rosa Hernandez. "They don't understand that responsibility comes with age."

The young people who demonstrated were 14 or under and few seemed to have permission from their parents for this action. School officials are wondering if they've given young people so much license that they now think they have the right to be in control.

"I just wish the students had presented their concerns at a School Board meeting," said School Board Chairperson, Charles (Bud) Lightner. "Young people turn to sensationalism so easily these days."

The Superintendent and School Board members will meet tonight to decide how to deal with the disruptive students. The meeting will be held in the Board room at 7:30.

Select whatever criteria are relevant to the issue studied

A. WHO IS INTERVIEWED?

1. Members of what social groups were interviewed? Examine any of the following relevant to the issue: race, gender, age, class background, religion, sexual orientation, first language, ability.

2. To what extent were the voices of those affected by inequality—e.g., racism, sexism, ageism—heard?

3. What percentage of people interviewed were "official voices"—e.g., heads of institutions, government officials, business—and what percent were "voices of people"—e.g., leaders/members of community groups, local citizens, young persons?

B. WHAT IS FOCUSED ON? WHAT IS OMITTED?

4. To what extent were a wide range of points of view presented?

5. To what degree were critical questions asked, questions like:

   • what are the root causes of this problem?
   • who benefits by this situation?
   • who loses out?
   • what are alternative perspectives or solutions that haven't been suggested or tried?
   • how can we make this situation more fair?

6. Is racism, sexism, ageism, or whatever inequality is relevant, discussed?

7. What types of change efforts were highlighted—sensational/violent or ones that were not sensational/non-violent?

C. THE REPORTING

8. To what degree was there in-depth coverage of issues compared to a series of "sound bites"?

9. Were stereotypes present or reinforced? If so, which ones?

10. To what extent was language biased or fair?

11. From what perspective was the story framed? Was there a "media spin" to it, and if so, what was it?

D. OTHER

Ethnicity of family receiving welfare	% of people on welfare who are of this group	% of this group on welfare	number of families from this group on welfare
black	39%	5.7%	1,706.136
white (non–Hispanic)	38%	.1%	1,662,389
Hispanic	17%	3.3%	743,700
Asian American	3%	1.8%	131,241

Statements from the table above:

- There are about the same number of black families and white families on welfare.
- Black families are 57 times more likely to be on welfare than white families.
- Hispanic families are 33 times more likely to be on welfare than white families.
- Asian American families are about half as likely to be on welfare as Hispanic families.
- More than 94% of blacks are NOT on welfare.
- 16 out of 17 black families are NOT on welfare.

Here are some more statistics to use in making and supporting your arguments:

- The average family on welfare consists of a woman and her two young children.
- Over 40% of families receiving aid for dependent children have only one child.
- Between 3% and 4% of families on welfare have 5 or more children.
- Over 60% of children who receive welfare are five years old or less.
- Over 66% of the women on welfare are between 20 and 34 years old.
- Less than 9% of women on welfare are under 20 years old.
- Less than 2% of women on welfare are under 18 years old.
- Families receiving welfare have been on assistance for an average of 22 months.
- Only 20% of the families on welfare have been on welfare for more than 5 years.
- The average welfare payment for a family of three is $388 per month. This comes out to less than half of the poverty level in this country which is $10,860 a year.
- The average family income for a family of three (all types of benefits plus any earned income) is $456 a month, up to half of the poverty level.
- Less than 10% of those receiving welfare live in public housing.
- There are over 2 million poor black families in the U.S. and over 5 million poor white families.
- The typical benefit for a family receiving welfare is $3500 per year.
- Less than 1% of the U.S. Government budget goes to welfare, 20% goes to Social Security.

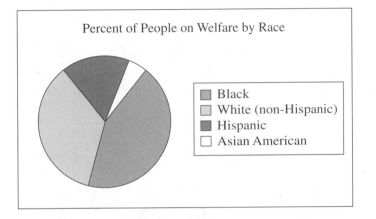

Percent of People on Welfare by Race

- Black
- White (non-Hispanic)
- Hispanic
- Asian American

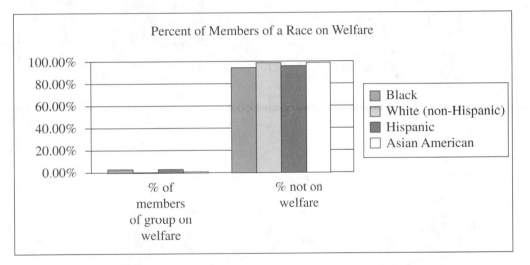

Percent of Members of a Race on Welfare

- Black
- White (non-Hispanic)
- Hispanic
- Asian American

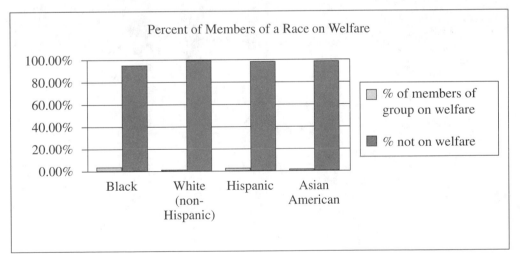

Percent of Members of a Race on Welfare

- % of members of group on welfare
- % not on welfare

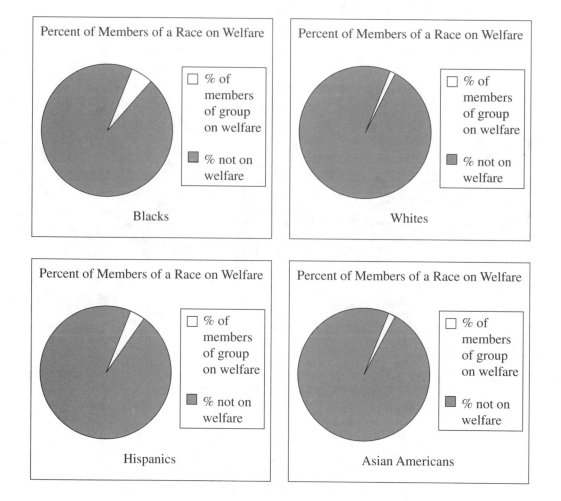

Percent of Members of a Race on Welfare

☐ % of members of group on welfare

■ % not on welfare

Blacks

Percent of Members of a Race on Welfare

☐ % of members of group on welfare

■ % not on welfare

Whites

Percent of Members of a Race on Welfare

☐ % of members of group on welfare

■ % not on welfare

Hispanics

Percent of Members of a Race on Welfare

☐ % of members of group on welfare

■ % not on welfare

Asian Americans

Name of store _____
    or
Name of your family _____

1. List three young children's toys. Next to each, list the genders and races of the children depicted on the package. What are they doing?

2. List young children's toys whose packages mix races and genders.

3. List three board games. Note race and gender of children on packages.

4. List games whose packages mix races and genders.

5. List three toys for older children. Note races and genders of children on packages. What are they doing?

6. List toys for older children whose packages mix races and genders.

7. Which packages of toys and board games included children with disabilities? How many did not?

8. If you are in a store, talk with three people shopping there. Share your findings with each. Describe these people and their reactions. If you do this at home, share your findings with an adult there. Describe that person's reactions. Act similarly at a library, community center, etc.

	black	white	Latino/a	Asian American	Native American	female	male
1. I am							
2. My neighborhood is							
3. My school is							
4. My friends are							
5. People who come to my house are							
6. My teacher is							
7. Our principal is							
8. The doctor I visited last was							
9. The dentist I visited last was							
10. We shop at a store run by							
11. The cashiers are							
12. Our mayor is							
13. Our town council is mostly							
14. The bank manager is							
15. Most police officers are							
16. Our mail carrier is							
17. Our repair people are							

Now interview one of these people about how s/he got the job and how s/he feels about it. Ask how racism and/or sexism might affect others trying to move into that job.

Story 1a: Beena is an excellent speed skater who wants to train for the Olympics. Her family lives 85 miles from the nearest large rink with an expert coach. Her father works in a shoe factory and her mother at the telephone company. If they go on living where they are, transporting Beena would be expensive and mean hard shifts in their work schedules. If they move near the rink and coach, they will need new jobs there. If they do neither of those, Beena will never become a well-trained speed skater. What should they do?

Story 1b: Sean is an excellent speed skater who wants to train for the Olympics. His family lives 85 miles from the nearest large rink with an expert coach. His father works in a shoe factory and his mother at the telephone company. If they go on living where they are, transporting Sean would be expensive and mean hard shifts in their work schedules. If they move near the rink and coach, they will need new jobs there. If they do neither of those, Sean will never become a well-trained speed skater. What should they do?

Story 2a: Julia's family is thinking of moving from their Puerto Rican neighborhood to a new neighborhood. The new neighborhood and school would be part Puerto Rican, part black and part white. Julia is happy in her school and is getting good grades. Julia's mother wants to move so she will be closer to work. Should Julia object?

Story 2b: Hillary's family is thinking of moving from their all white neighborhood to a new neighborhood. The new neighborhood and school would be part Puerto Rican, part black and part white. Hillary is happy in her school and is getting good grades. Hillary's mother wants to move so she will be closer to work. Should Hillary object?

Story 3a: Maia and Jordana's parents just died in a car accident. Their 75 year old grandmother, Louise, has offered to have them live with her. They have only met her once since she lives 2,000 miles away and their parents didn't like to travel. They are worried about leaving all their friends. They will be put in a foster home in their town if they don't go. What should they do?

Story 3b: Maia and Jordana's parents just died in a car accident. Their mother's 35 year old sister, Lucy, has offered to have them live with her. They have only met her once since she lives 2,000 miles away and their parents didn't like to travel. They are worried about leaving all their friends. They will be put in a foster home in their town if they don't go. What should they do?

Story 4a: Adam hasn't been doing his homework. His teacher must decide today if he should count Adam's homework as part of his quarter grade or give him another chance to improve. His teacher knows Adam's family is poor and Adam's mother never graduated from high school. Adam is very busy after school doing odd jobs in order to earn money to help support his family. What should the teacher do?

Story 4b: Aaron hasn't been doing his homework. His teacher must decide today if he should count Aaron's homework as part of his quarter grade or give him another chance to improve. His teacher knows Aaron comes from a well-educated family. His father is a doctor and his mother is a teacher. Aaron is very busy with many after school activities. What should the teacher do?

Finish the story by explaining what each member of the family did and how each felt.

A SUNDAY SURPRISE

The Grinch family—Becky, Neal, Mr. Grinch and Grandmother Grinch—was going on a Sunday trip. They'd packed a picnic lunch. While they were in the car, Becky and Neal played Dictionary Fictionary with their father and grandmother. Often they would stop and all get out of the car. They took photos or sketched pictures. They also played catch and Frisbee.

They had been driving for an hour when the sky started to get dark. They listened to the radio. Tornado warnings! What could they do? Just then they saw a tree fly by.

"Help, help! I'm scared!" shouted . . .

Finish the story by explaining what each member of the family did and how each felt.

A MOVING DAY

The Garner family was moving. For ten years they had lived in the city. The younger two children, Barry and Katie, had never lived anywhere else. Kristine and Jon, who were older, hardly remembered the country home they had lived in as babies. Their mother and stepfather had grown up on farms and were eager to move out of the city.

It took them weeks to pack. They had rented a truck. After driving for seven hours, everyone was tired. However, not wanting to leave their belongings in the truck, they spent several more hours carrying all 131 boxes into the house. Finally they had a supper of peanut butter and tomato sandwiches and all fell asleep.

About 3 AM Barry and Kristine woke up. They heard a knocking at the door. It got louder. It changed to banging and thumping. Then . . .

THE GRINCHES

THE GARNER FAMILY

Chapter

10

Things Can Be Different

With courage and creativity, young people and adults alike have confronted inequality and created significant changes. This chapter offers students examples of these efforts. People have more energy and commitment to make changes when they know that things can be different. When we see that more equal personal and societal relations aren't "pie-in-the-sky" fantasies, but can and do exist in the real world, this provides motivation for change. Some lessons describe actions of young people their age, offering students the knowledge that they too can make a difference. It is important for both teachers and students to affirm these small, but significant changes.

In the first group of activities, *People Making Change: From Then to Now*, students learn about individuals who have struggled for equality both in the past and present. They examine the varied strategies for change and think about ways they can be applied today.

Creating Alternatives: Envisioning the Future contains lessons with concrete examples of egalitarian living, working, or learning situations. From job-sharing in the home to equal access to medical education, these lessons give students practical examples of the creation of more equality in various institutions. They are encouraged to discuss the application of the various approaches to their communities.

A vision of a just and equal society is essential if people are to maintain the courage and perseverance necessary for what is a long process of social change. Students too, need to have a vision of *what can be*. Some lessons, therefore, include an image of a very different, and more equal, society. Especially since that society won't appear tomorrow, it's important that students can envision and hold on to a picture of a more equal future!

Benefits to One and All

Anthropologist Ruth Benedict discovered in comparing many different societies, that aggression is lowest in those social orders in which "the individual by the same act and at the same time serves his own advantage and that of the group." That is, some societies are organized so that the group values and rewards the individual for doing what benefits the group. For example, in one traditional Eskimo society, a man proved his prowess by hunting and bringing back seals, which were then distributed equally to all members of the group for food. Thus the society benefited from the same act that benefited the individual.

From Developing Effective Classroom Groups by Gene Stanford

<u>Section A</u>   <u>*People Making Changes: From Then to Now*</u>

"HERE'S WHAT SOME PEOPLE DID"

OBJECTIVES   To give students information about people and groups of people in history who have brought about change.
To give students a realistic idea of the problems and satisfactions of fostering change.
To get students excited about the possibilities for change.
To give students an historical perspective of how long groups have had to work to bring about change.

MATERIALS   A collection of library books about individuals and groups who have brought about change (see Bibliography under headings, "Biography for Young People" and "Biography Collections for Young People"); "Task Cards: People and Change," p. 289.

IMPLEMENTATION   Discuss with students how long it can take to bring about change. Groups of people often work collaboratively over many years to cause important historical changes. For example, it took 72 years from when women first publicly declared wanting the right to vote until they received this right nationally. In this case only a single woman who attended the first convention was alive when this right was won.

Ask each student to pick and read a book from your selection or a book she checks with you. Then students choose and complete one or more of the task cards. Students can do this lesson individually, or in small groups if they read the same book. Share in groups, with the whole class, or via a bulletin board.

DISCUSSION   1. What are some feelings you have about the person or people you read about?
2. How did the person or people in your book bring about change?
3. What obstacles did that person or people face?
4. What satisfaction did that person or people get?
5. What kinds of support did that person or people get? What kept them willing to work on the struggle for as long as they worked?
6. What difference did that person or people make in the world?

SOJOURNER TRUTH PUPPET SHOW

OBJECTIVES
To give students a role-model of a black woman who challenged the racism and sexism of her day.

To give students the opportunity to work cooperatively and creatively to design a product they can share with their peers.

MATERIALS
One or more copies of *Sojourner Truth: Ain't I a Woman?* by Patricia and Fred McKissack (3rd–7th grade level). Lined paper; large newsprint; pencils; scrap paper of all sorts; felt; embroidery thread; yarn; socks (brown, black, tan); stuffing; needles; thread; cardboard.

IMPLEMENTATION
Students will need to make at least five puppets, and can make up to ten. Decide size of student groups. Each group makes one or more puppet(s). Make Sojourner Truth in three outfits—as Belle, the slave child; as Belle the free woman worker and mother; and as Sojourner Truth, the preacher. Make at least one slave owner, and at least one of the people who later helped her. When possible, make Sojourner's son, whose freedom she won in court; slave owners in two stages of her life; women associates in the suffrage movement; Lincoln. Students work cooperatively to make the puppets.

Make a puppet stage—a large box, the type appliances are shipped in, serves well. Cut out an open area. When students kneel down and hold their puppets up, the bottoms of the outfits should be level with the lower part of the opening.

Before students write scripts, see that your entire class becomes familiar with the story of Sojourner Truth. Use some of your read-aloud time or social studies class time to read from the book listed above, or use the book with reading groups.

As a class, brainstorm on the scenes needed and list them on the blackboard. Then students work in groups of three or four to write the scripts. Groups which finish their scripts, and edit them with you, can make more puppets if these are needed. Make one cast of puppets first, however, since this provides motivation for the academic work, script writing.

Small groups switch scripts and critique each others'. Gather as a class and read scripts aloud. Make changes when appropriate. Students rehearse in small groups, then perform before the class. Send invitations to parents to come to a performance. Make arrangements with other classes to see your show. Have discussions with the visiting classes.

DISCUSSION
1. How did you decide which incidents in Sojourner Truth's life were particularly important? Give a reason for each incident you chose.
2. How did Sojourner Truth work with others to make changes? Give examples.
3. What strengths did she have as a person that made this possible? How can you work on developing these strengths?
4. In what ways did you like making a puppet with other classmates as compared to doing so on your own? In what ways did you dislike that?

Ain't I a Woman?

The man over there say that women need to be helped into carriages and lifted over ditches, and to have the best place everywhere. Nobody ever helps me into carriages or over puddles or give me the best place . . . and ain't I a woman? Look at my arm! I have ploughed and planted and gathered into barns, and no man could head me—and ain't I a woman? I could work as much and eat as much as a man—when I could get it—and bear the lash as well . . . and ain't I a woman? I have borne thirteen children, and seen most of 'em sold into slav'ry, and when I cried out with my mother's grief, none but Jesus heard me . . . and ain't I a woman?

Sojourner Truth, 1851

STOP! DON'T TAKE IT FOR GRANTED

OBJECTIVES   To teach children about the life of a black man who invented several items that improved the public safety.

To learn that individuals can make changes that improve many people's lives through their work.

MATERIALS   Copies of "Worksheet: Garrett Morgan," p. 290; "Task Cards: Garrett Morgan," p. 291, one card per group; paper; pencils.

IMPLEMENTATION   Divide students into heterogeneous groups of three or four. Each group reads aloud the Worksheet. Answer any questions on information or vocabulary. Then either have each group pick one of the task cards, or assign them.

After the work is completed, gather together as a class and have groups share their work. Make a display, if you like.

DISCUSSION   1. What impresses you about Garrett Morgan's life? Why?
2. What surprises you? Why?
3. We tend to forget that every useful invention was thought up by *someone(s)*. Why does that forgetting happen? Is there anything bad about that? If so what could we do differently?
4. Can you think of other people of color or women who have improved the conditions of life for all through their work?

ALONE AND TOGETHER

OBJECTIVES   To learn about the role of Rosa Parks and others involved in the Montgomery bus boycott.

To understand the power one person can have in fostering change.

To understand a variety of strategies people can use together to bring about equality.

MATERIALS   Copies of "Worksheet: I Am Only One Person," p. 292; a copy of *Rosa Parks* by Eloise Greenfield, more if possible; copies of "Worksheet: Question Cards—Rosa Parks," p. 293, one set for each group.

IMPLEMENTATION   *Part One.* Tell students they are going to study what people, both alone and together, can do to foster equality. Explain that you will begin with a poem about what one woman did to challenge discrimination. Ask students what they know about Rosa Parks.

Then provide students the context for the poem that follows. While Rosa Parks did have the courage to act alone, she was involved in organizations working for civil rights in Montgomery that planned the challenge of the bus companies' discriminatory treatment of African Americans. Next distribute a copy of the poem to each student. While you read it, have them follow along, or do a reading in unison.

DISCUSSION   1. Who was Rosa Parks?
2. What did she do?
3. Why was what she did so important?

4. Have you ever said to yourself something like, "I am only one person, what can one person do?" If so, when?

5. What does the account of Rosa Parks teach us?

Tell students they will now learn more about Rosa Parks and the beginning of the Civil Rights Movement.

Part Two. Divide students into heterogeneous groups of four. They will use the "jigsaw method" to learn more about Rosa Parks. Each person in a group will get part of the story of Rosa Parks. Each person will tell part of the story to the others, and will answer questions, so each must study carefully.

If you can get multiple copies of the book *Rosa Parks*, give one copy to each group. Otherwise, write a synopsis of the book for the students. Divide the account into four parts, so that each student has a part of the account to read. Divide amount of reading unevenly if skill levels vary greatly. Once students have read their material, they teach the others in their group. You may wish to distribute question cards at this time, if you want students to be selective in what they teach each other. Each student "teacher" should check to be confident that the others in the group understand the material.

Copy the questions (p. 293) on 3 × 5 cards, having one deck for each group. Students shuffle the deck and draw cards until all are taken. The students write their questions, followed by the answers, on their papers.

Next, students take turns reading one of their questions and the answer to the group. Group members should discuss the answer and try to reach agreement about the correct answer. Continue around the group until all questions are read. Then students make whatever changes are needed on their papers. The answers are handed in and the group is evaluated as a whole on its responses.

DISCUSSION

1. What are some feelings you think Rosa Parks might have had in fighting for her rights?

2. How did Rosa Parks give other people courage?

3. A "boycott" is a strategy for change. People collectively refuse to use or buy a certain service or product in order to put pressure on a business or group to change its discriminatory policies. Can you think of a recent boycott?

4. Civil disobedience is strategy for change. It is an organized, non-violent action to oppose a law or policy that a group of people believe to be morally unjust. Those practicing civil disobedience accept the consequences for their actions. Rosa Parks used that strategy in 1955. Can you think of more recent examples?

5. Do you think boycotts and civil disobedience are effective strategies for change? In what ways are they effective? Ineffective?

6. How is the account of Rosa Parks an example of people working alone and together to bring about equality?

Boycotts

The United Farmworkers Union in the 1960s and early 1970s used a very successful national boycott of non-union grapes and lettuce to win contracts from California growers. In the 1980s boycotts of U.S. companies that invested in South Africa brought about divestments which contributed to governmental changes that ended apartheid.

Civil Disobedience

In the 1980s people who opposed nuclear power had practiced civil disobedience by sitting in at nuclear power plants. They refused to obey policy officers' orders to move. They believed the dangers of nuclear power threatened the lives of thousands of people.

In the 1980s many U.S. citizens practiced civil disobedience as part of the Sanctuary Movement. People helped immigrants from El Salvador and Guatemala, who would be killed by repressive regimes if they were returned home, by giving them refuge/sanctuary in churches and homes in the U.S. Since the Immigration and Naturalization Service classified them as economic, rather than political, refugees, Sanctuary workers were breaking a law in aiding them.

See *The Power of the People: Active Nonviolence in the United States* edited by Robert Cooney and Helen Michalowski for an excellent historical overview of examples of nonviolent movements for change in the U.S. Powerful pictures augment the text.

CHICANAS STRIKE AT FARAH*

OBJECTIVES To learn about issues involved in the strike of Chicana garment workers in the Southwest. To examine the strike as a strategy for change.

MATERIALS Copies of "Worksheet: Chicanas Strike at Farah*," pp. 295; dictionaries. Type a "Worksheet: Questions to Consider" (see Implementation).

IMPLEMENTATION Ask students what they know about strikes, another strategy that can be used to bring about equality. Explain that they will read about a strike by Chicana garment workers in the Southwest, and then think about strikes as a tool for change. Remind them to think about the dollar amounts from a historical perspective.

Students may work individually or in groups to read "Worksheet: Chicanas Strike at Farah." Then distribute "Worksheet: Questions to Consider" which lists these questions:

1. List three reasons why the Farah workers went on strike.
2a. Cite an example of sexism.
  b. Cite an example of racism.
3. Explain why the Farah Company wanted to run non-union plants.
4. How did the strike change the role of the Chicanas?

After students have completed the Worksheets, join together as a large group and discuss the answers. Then go on with the following discussion questions.

DISCUSSION 1. In the case of the Farah workers, what were the advantages in using the strike as a strategy to bring about more fair working conditions? What were the disadvantages?
2. Can you think of other times when the strike was/is used as a method for bringing about equality?

---

*Summarized from "La Chicana Curriculum" by Susan Groves and Clementine Duran, Berkeley, California Public Schools.

3. What are the advantages of using strikes? the disadvantages?
4. There have been student strikes in many schools and colleges. For what issues do you believe it is appropriate for students to strike?

GOING FURTHER   Students can read further about strikes in American history in Milton Meltzer's, *Bread and Roses: The Struggle of American Labor*. A useful curriculum for teachers is *The Power in Our Hands: A Curriculum on the History of Work and Workers in the United States* by Bill Bigelow and Norm Diamond. While geared for high school, there are ideas and lessons that are can be adapted to lower grades.

Assign students to read the local newspaper, listen to local radio and television programs, and talk to their friends and relatives to find out if there is currently a strike in their community. If so, assign some students to try to interview workers who are striking. Assign others to try to talk with the management, or at least learn the management's point of view from local papers. Have both groups report the issues to class.

AFFIRMATIVE ACTION BEFORE AND AFTER

OBJECTIVES   To have students learn about a concrete example where providing equal access and resources produced more equal results.
To examine affirmative action policies as one way to change institutional discrimination.
To see how the results of such affirmative action changes affect individual women.

MATERIALS   Five copies of "Longshore Workers Interview," p. 295; copies of "Worksheet: Sabra's Letter," p. 296; two or three copies of "Task Cards: Affirmative Action," p. 297; paper and pencils.

IMPLEMENTATION   Introduce this lesson by reiterating that people and social institutions sometimes blame the victims for their problems. Remind them of what they learned in Chapter 7: that only with equal resources and opportunities can we expect more equal results. This lesson shows how changing institutional discrimination brought greater job equity to women workers.

Step One. Get together with a group of five students during a free period of time. Think about giving some students who aren't typically leaders a chance to take a leadership role. Review the "Longshore Workers Interview," so that they are sure of all the words and meanings; have them practice so that they can read it aloud to the class as a play.

Present this interview to the whole class. Check that the words were understood. Remind them that the amount paid longshore workers was high in 1979 and to consider dollar amounts in a historical perspective. Then discuss the first set of questions.

DISCUSSION
1. Why did women want longshore work? What was the major benefit?
2. Why didn't the employers want to hire women? Try to think of at least several reasons.
3. In what way did the National Organization for Women help these women?
4. How was what the women did an example of anti-racism, as well as of fighting gender discrimination?
5. Why were women given heavy physical labor jobs in factories during World War II? Why were these taken away from them after the war?
6. What is affirmative action?

Step Two. Hand out "Worksheet: Sabra's Letter" to all students. Before they start reading go over vocabulary. You may need to answer some questions as they read.

Divide students into heterogeneous pairs. Each pair chooses one of the Task Cards, and completes the work. After all pairs have finished, get back together as a group. Have each pair share its results with the whole class. Then go on to discussion questions, below. Task Cards 2 and 3 may require prior research.

An excellent resource for student research is *Think about Racism* by Linda Mizell which has a section on affirmative action.

Affirmative Action: Then and Now

Affirmative actions policies were instituted from the late 1960s through the 1970s as remedies for ongoing discrimination against women and people of color. The point of affirmative action was to tackle the effects of historic patterns of institutional, and sometimes unintentional, discrimination. At that time many Americans agreed that such discrimination existed and was a social problem.

Since 1980 government policies have increasingly supported the economic situation of the wealthy and hurt middle class, working class and poor Americans. Rather than target corporate and political advocates of the wealthy, many Americans blamed women, people of color and affirmative action for their worsening economic status.

Having used lessons in this book, you and your students are aware that ongoing institutional and cultural discrimination based on race and gender is still a major problem in the U.S. Accounts like the one in this lesson happen today. In discussing affirmative action it is important to continually document this reality with studies, news stories and personal accounts. *At the same time* discuss the changes needed, like a truly progressive tax structure, that would bring greater economic equality to the majority of the American people of all races and genders.

A study by researchers Allison Konrad and Frank Linnehan of Temple University found affirmation action employment policies to be the best way to correct many workplace inequities. A company's use of affirmative action policies was strongly linked to the rank of the highest ranking woman in the organization and to the percentage of people of color in management.

Data from *Academy of Management Journal,* June, 1995

DISCUSSION
1. In what ways has affirmative action helped Sabra find a job that is good for her?
2. Why do you think it had been harder for Sabra's friend, Jaconda, to support herself and her family than it would have been if Jaconda's husband had earned the family money and Jaconda had done the child care?

3. The unions might not have had the training program if it were not for affirmative action. Why?
4. How might affirmative action change the job distribution in your school?
5. How might it affect jobs in your community? Give some specific examples.
6. What are some reasons for having affirmative action as a program, rather than just letting people apply for whatever jobs they want?

Human Need before Profit

It's important to remember that affirmative action is one needed step for providing women and people of color fair access to jobs. What will guarantee full equity in jobs, however, is *full* employment and anti-discriminatory job training for *all* Americans. Such a goal necessitates basic changes in our economic system that will put human need before profit.

SPEAKING OUT AGAINST BIAS IN SCHOOL

OBJECTIVES
To learn about two elementary school students who spoke out against homophobia in their elementary school.
To consider the difficulties and benefits of educating others about the effects of bias.
To think about homophobia in your school and ways to change it.

MATERIALS
"Worksheet: Script—Interview with Julia Vanderham," pp. 298–299.

IMPLEMENTATION
Tell students that they will learn about the actual experience of two fifth grade girls who faced homophobia in their elementary school. To do this, they will take turns taking the roles of ten-year-old Julia Vanderham and an interviewer. Talk with students about the importance of being attentive and respectful during the reading. Tell students that when the interview is over they may be asked to respond to questions based on what they learned in the interview.

If possible, have your class sit in a circle. Have two copies of the "Interview with Julia Vanderham" available. Give one copy to a good reader who can read the role of Julia seriously and well. Give the other to a student in the circle. That student reads a question out loud and Julia answers. Then the questioner passes the interview sheet to the person to the right who reads the next question and Julia replies. Continue around the circle until the interview is finished.

Divide students into predetermined pairs. Try to put in each pair at least one student who can thoughtfully discuss these issues. Explain to students that you will ask them a series of questions. Have them number their paper from 1–9 alternating lines. First they will have one minute to think quietly about their response to the first question and jot down a few words to remind them of their thinking. Next partners will have two minutes to share their responses with each other. Then you will call on any person to share with the class what their pair came up with. After calling on several pairs, open the questions up for general discussion.

DISCUSSION
1. What were some of the feelings of Julia and Rose during this experience?
2. What gave them the encouragement and strength to go ahead with their plan?
3. How did their expectations of what might happen compare with what actually happened?
4. What interested or surprised you about this interview?
5. Julia and Rose were discriminated against and they took action to deal with it. What is difficult about taking action against discrimination when you are the target? What is positive about doing this?

6. What did you learn about dealing with discrimination from this interview? How can it help you deal with discrimination you might face?
7. How can other people support those speaking out about discrimination?
8. Are put-downs and jokes about lesbians and gays common in your school? If so, how could you work together to change that?
9. What's one question you have about any homophobia you see in your school? (When pairs share, ask them to discuss possible responses.)

GOING FURTHER   If students come up with ideas for changing homophobia they see in their school, discuss them further. Through a community meeting or committee work support them in acting upon an idea.

Children of Lesbians and Gays Speak Out

Julia Vanderham appears in an excellent video, "Both My Moms' Names Are Judy: Children of Lesbians and Gays Speak Out." Elementary-aged children share their feelings about how teasing and classroom silence about lesbians and gay men affects them and they discuss what they would like to see changed. This is excellent for staff development. Depending on your classroom context, you may wish to use it with your students as well as a follow up to this lesson. See the "Media" section of the Bibliography for ordering information.

TAKING A STAND

OBJECTIVES   To learn about examples of young people today who have taken a stand against discrimination.
To consider how people who aren't the subject of discrimination can be allies to those who are.

MATERIALS   For this lesson you'll need the book, *It's Our World Too: Stories of Young People Who Are Making a Difference*, by Phillip Hoose. If possible, order it yourself for it's an excellent book to have in your classroom. Also ask your librarian to order it and request it on interlibrary loan, since it's ideal to have 3 copies. Type a "Worksheet: Taking a Stand," and make one copy per student. (See Implementation Part 2 for the questions.)

IMPLEMENTATION   Ask students about ways they, or other young people they know of, have taken a stand against discrimination. Ask them what young people they can think of who have fought for justice throughout history. If they have trouble thinking of examples, ask them why they think that is so. Tell them they'll be learning some about this history, as well as examples of young people today who are taking a stand.

Ask students for examples of people, young or older, who weren't the victims of discrimination but who have acted against discrimination. After this discussion, explain that such a person is sometimes called an "ally." For example, if a Jewish student was the target of a joke and a Christian student spoke up and said, "That joke offends me. Please stop telling jokes that stereotype people," that student would be acting as an ally. Tell students they'll discover ways young people have been allies to each other in this lesson.

Part 1   Choose 5 students in your class who thrive on harder and more challenging work. Assign them the introductory chapter of *It's Our World Too*, "Young Activists Who Went before You." Ask them to read the chapter and to be prepared to report to the class as an introduction to this lesson.

Ask each one to focus on one of the following:

1. young girls in the mills in the 1830s—classism
2. Underground Railroad—racism
3. the "newsies" (newsboys) in 1899—classism
4. Central High integration—racism
5. children in Birmingham protests—racism

Each reports on the historical context, the situation of discrimination, and how the young activists organized for change. The five students work together to organize their presentation, "Young Activists Who Went before You," into a coherent whole. Encourage creative formats like skits, songs, and so forth. They present them to the class.

Part 2 This lesson is planned for 6 groups of 4. Adapt accordingly to your class size. Divide students into heterogeneous groups of 4. Assign two groups to read about each of the following young people in *It's Our World Too.*

1. Neto Villereal and Andy Percifield—two high school students, one Chicano and one white, work as allies to fight racism among fans at football games.
2. Sarah Rosen—with female and male classmates Sarah organizes to oppose a sexist event in her 6th grade.
3. John DeMarco—a 13 year old white boy takes big risks to stand up to a racist incident in his neighborhood.

Students who are working on the same young person join together and take turns reading. After reading the account of the young person each group of 4 is responsible for the questions on the "Worksheet: Taking a Stand." The questions are:

1. What was the discriminatory situation that the young person you read about was fighting against?
2. When the young person was deciding whether to take a stand, what feelings did s/he have? What did s/he have to lose? What were the benefits of acting? How did s/he decide?
3. Who were allies to the young person(s) protesting discrimination? How and why did the allies get involved?
4. In what way did the young person/people take a stand against discrimination? In what ways was each approach effective, if it was?
5. How did the student(s) feel after taking their action? How had they changed? Would they act against discrimination again?

Students number themselves 1, 2, 3, 4. Each is responsible for the question on the worksheet indicated below. Have students go over all the questions on the worksheet to clarify their meanings. (One question may be omitted if it doesn't pertain to a particular account.)

Neto and Andy—1-1, 2-2, 3-3, 4-4 (person #1 does question #1 etc.)
Sarah—1-1, 2-3, 3-4, 4-5
John—1-1, 2-2, 3-4, 4-5

Students take 10 minutes to write a response to their question on their worksheet. If in doubt, they may refer back to the book or confer with the student with the same number from the other group doing her young person.

Then students share their responses in their group one at a time. If someone in a group disagrees with the group members' response, the group discusses it and may suggest a change. Tell students each will be responsible for reporting on any one of the worksheet questions to the whole class, so make sure everyone in their group is prepared. Students hand in set of 4 worksheets from their group, each one with one question answered. All come together for discussion.

DISCUSSION   One at a time, focus on each young person students read about. Ask any of the eight students who read about that person to respond to question #1 of the Worksheet, and continue accordingly for each question. After all have been reported on, discuss similarities and differences in the accounts. Then open to broader discussion.

1. How did you feel about what these young people did? Why?
2a. What were these young people's feelings about deciding to take a stand against discrimination?
  b. How have you felt when you've been in a comparable situation, if you have?
  c. What are possible losses, benefits? Were there losses, benefits, or both in your situation?
3a. How and why did allies become involved, if they did?
  b. What are some of the risks to us of being an ally in our lives?
  c. What are some of the benefits of doing this?
4. What made these actions to fight discrimination successful? What strategies have worked for us or other people we know?
5. What other steps, if any, would be important to take to continue to deal with discrimination in these situations?
6. Before doing this lesson, what had you learned about young people fighting discrimination either in your history books or from the mainstream media? How might it affect young people to know this history and these examples?

GOING FURTHER   The last section in *It's Our World Too* is "A Handbook for Young Activists" and includes practical steps for creating change. Help students find out about young people in your area working together to fight discrimination or pinpoint issues that need addressing. Support your students in using the "Handbook for Young Activists" to take on an issue they care about.

Other Resources for Young Activists

Freedom's Children: Young Civil Rights Activists Tell Their Own Stories, Ellen Levine
Kids With Courage: True Stories about Young People Who Are Making a Difference, Barbara Lewis
Changing Our World: A Handbook for Young Activists, Paul Fleisher

---

Researching Unsung Allies

Remind students that creating change is a collaborative effort that takes the effort of many people, often people living lives like our own. Have students work in groups to do research on the collaborative work of allies in making change. You may need to help them find resources. Otherwise assign this task to a small group of committed students with good research skills. They can share their findings with the class.

For example, they can research:
1. White people active on the Underground Railroad before the Civil War;
2. Men who worked for women's right to the vote;
3. Whites active in the Civil Rights Movement; or
4. U.S. citizens involved in the Sanctuary Movement, among others.

<u>Section B</u>   <u>Creating Alternatives: Envisioning the Future</u>

JOB-SHARING, OR WHO'S THE COOK TONIGHT?

OBJECTIVES   To learn about one example of a way of allocating household jobs that is not sexist or ageist.
To consider implications of this system.

MATERIALS   Copies of "Worksheet: Job-Sharing," p. 302.

IMPLEMENTATION   Divide students into trios and have them quietly read the Worksheet to each other. One takes the role of Dave, another Noelle, and a third the interviewer.

When they've finished reading, divide into pairs. Students write down three questions they want to ask their partners regarding that person's feelings, thoughts, or questions about the job-sharing plan. (The questions and responses will be handed in at the end of the lesson.) Students then interview their partners and summarize their partners' responses in writing. (You may want to review skills for summarizing material.)

DISCUSSION

1. What are your feelings about the Porter family job-sharing plan?
2. What do you see as the strengths and weaknesses?
3. In what ways is this an anti-sexist plan?
4. What do the males gain by cooking, that people used to think of as "women's work"?
5. In what ways is this an anti-ageist plan?
6. In what ways could a job-sharing plan work for your family? What issues might arise?

Explain that sometimes people argue that equality is a good idea, but it can't be put into practice. Tell students that in fact there are many examples of equality that *do* work. This is one example that has worked very well in a family situation.

GOING FURTHER   Have students talk about job sharing with their families. If families devise equal job-sharing plans, have them report family responses to the class.

INUIT*

OBJECTIVES
To have students learn about a culture in American society that has traditionally been without class distinction and discrimination, and where cooperation is a norm.

To encourage students to think about how their lives would be different in a more cooperative culture and what they could do to achieve that.

MATERIALS
Copies of "Worksheet: Inuit," p. 301; one or more books from Bibliography on Alaskan Eskimos; other resource books or encyclopedias on Alaskan Eskimos, chart paper and markers.

IMPLEMENTATION
Step One. Hand out copies of the Worksheet to students. Divide into heterogeneous groups of three or four. Have students read the passage aloud to other group members. Encourage students to help each other with difficult words, offer your help if necessary. Each group then writes down some questions they have about traditional Eskimo life. Get together as a class and, using information from books and/or encyclopedias, have students find and share answers to as many of these questions as they can. In some cases they may find conflicting answers depending on how an author is defining "traditional" and depending on the overall point of view of the author. This can give your class a good opportunity to discuss how this kind of information is sometimes subjective and that as readers they need to discuss and sort out these conflicts and determine what they can learn from them.

Put up two large sheets of chart paper. Title them "Inuit." Students brainstorm on the advantages of cooperation and lack of class distinction for Alaskan Eskimos. List these. Then students brainstorm on problems students believe traditional Alaskan Eskimos would have if they lived in a more competitive society. List these and leave these lists up.

Step Two. Put up two more sheets of chart paper. Title them "Our Culture." Discuss with your students if they think they are all currently part of the same culture and could list characteristics of this culture. If so proceed with a single list. If not, create multiple "Our Culture" lists, labeling each for the particular culture it represents. Again brainstorm, this time on the advantages of cooperation in our culture or cultures, and on the problems caused by competition and classism. Use the discussion questions to compare these lists.

Step Three. Brainstorm on situations in your community and school which are now competitive or classist. List these with enough description so students will remember what was said. Get enough workable situations so there will be one for every group of three or four students.

Each group discusses what is competitive or classist about its situation and what problems that causes. Then groups take the perspective of people in a cooperative, non-classist culture and think of ways to handle the situation. Each group shares its ideas with the whole class. Encourage suggestions and revisions. Then each group designs a skit to demonstrate the current competitive or classist way the situation is handled and its new cooperative way.

Present skits to other classes, first explaining about the cooperative nature of the traditional Alaskan Eskimo way of life. Follow by discussion questions.

DISCUSSION
1. Give examples of the cooperative basis of traditional Alaskan Eskimo culture.
2. Why did traditional Alaskan Eskimo culture not have the same class structure that we do?
3. In terms of cooperation and lack of classism, what would you like about the Eskimo way of life? What would you not like? Why?
4. What might a traditional Alaskan Eskimo child say about your competitive way of life if she were to visit your family and school?

---

*Eskimos, like many indigenous peoples, name themselves with the word in their own language meaning "the real people."

5. Why might it be harder for you to do things more cooperatively in your family, school or community than it is for a traditional Alaskan Eskimo child to do in his? What can you do to make it easier?

THE CHILDREN'S PLACE

OBJECTIVES To learn about an example of an employer-sponsored day-care center.
To consider how availability of quality day-care can change institutional sexism.

MATERIALS Copies of "Worksheet: Children's Place," p. 302.

IMPLEMENTATION *Day One.* Begin with this five-minute discussion and homework assignment. Ask students to share what they remember about the lesson, "Who Will Take Care of Jamil?" p. 121–122. Tell them they will now read about a day-care center that is sponsored by the workers' employer.

Pass out the Worksheet. For homework have students read the information about this New York State-sponsored day-care center. Have them interview two working parents with young children concerning their opinions about the Children's Place.

Day Two. Ask students to get out the Worksheet and come together for discussion.

DISCUSSION
1. How do you feel about the Children's Place? What makes you feel the way you do?
2. How did the persons you interviewed feel about the Children's Place? Did they want to have such a day-care center at their place of work? Why or why not?
3. Think back to the lesson, "Who Will Take Care of Jamil?" How would the Children's Place help Marva and Tyrone Williams? How could it help other adults who are parents?
4. How do employers gain by providing day-care at their places of work?
5. Name at least two ways day-care centers at peoples' places of work help change sexism in society.

GOING FURTHER Write to major employers in your area. Describe the Children's Place and ask if they would start such a program. Discuss their responses. Call or write representatives of parents' groups or women's groups in your community. Tell them about the Children's Place. Ask them if they would be willing to advocate for such a center in your community. Discuss their responses.

Take away our child care centers, will ya! We'll lower your expectations.

YES, YOU CAN BE A DOCTOR

OBJECTIVES   To show students an economic system different from our own, which better meets the needs of citizens of different ages, races, and classes.
To encourage students to compare this system to that of the United States and to hypothesize what its effects might be in this country.

MATERIALS   Copies of "Worksheet: Asmund and Kirsten's Letter," p. 303; paper, pencils; possibly stationery; stamps; photographs and addresses.

IMPLEMENTATION   Explain to students that not all countries have the same economic system as the United States does. Some countries have more government programs to help people and some have fewer. The example in this lesson comes from Norway, a Scandinavian country. If you have not studied Norway in school, you may want to give students background information.

Divide students into pairs. Give each pair two copies of the Worksheet. Answer any questions about vocabulary or content. Each pair writes an answer to Asmund and Kirsten. They give their reactions to what the Norwegian students have said about Norway, and they explain how the medical system works in this country. If they have done "Letter from Sally" (p. 120), ask them to remember what they learned. If not, review it yourself.

Many more people want to be doctors than go to medical school in the U.S. Many of these can't afford the $165,000 (1994) needed for training; for others, there aren't enough places in medical schools. Most people who become doctors go into private practice in areas where they want to live rather than give service to the country in areas where they are needed. Have students get up-to-date information on current costs of medical training and medical care in the U.S. today.

Students proofread and correct their answers, then trade off with two other groups so everyone has read three letters. Post letters on a bulletin board so students see even more reactions.

DISCUSSION   1. What did you think of what Kirsten and Asmund had to say about medical training in Norway? In what ways would you like to see that system in this country? In what ways would you not like that?
2. What are some advantages and disadvantages in the Norwegian medical system as compared to the American one? If we had that system here what positive changes would it mean in our medical care? In chances to become a doctor?
3. State how the structure of medical training in Norway is an example of providing equality for people of all classes. Think back to the lesson, "Letter from Sally." Compare this to Sally's situation.

GOING FURTHER   Your class might enjoy writing to pen-pals in other countries, especially ones with different economic or political systems.

Medical Training and Care in the U.S.

1. Access to medical training depends very much on a person's class background. For example 67% of white medical students come from families where the parental income is $50,000 or more.
2. People of color are still underrepresented in medicine. For example, 12% of the U.S. population is black, yet only 3.6% of physicians are black.

Association of American Medical Colleges, 1994

Groups with Power Gain by Changing the "Isms"!

Examples from some lessons:
• *Job Sharing, or Who's the Cook Tonight.* In learning to cook, males gain a skill that is not only valuable in itself but provides them with a greater capacity to be self–sufficient.
• *The Children's Place.* By providing day-care, employers gain more contented motivated employees who can concentrate on their work, with fewer worries about their children.
• *Yes, You Can Be A Doctor.* By providing more equal access to medical training, the U.S. health care system would get the best people to become doctors, without regard to class background. Doctors from lower-class backgrounds might be more understanding of health issues of people living in poverty.

YOUTH AND AGE IN ACTION

OBJECTIVES To have students learn about the Gray Panthers, an activist group dedicated to securing equality, particularly for older Americans.
To learn about a different vision of what society could be.

MATERIALS Copies of "Worksheets: Gray Panthers (1)," p. 304 and "Worksheet: Gray Panthers (2)," p. 305, one set per group; dictionaries.

IMPLEMENTATION Tell students they will be studying ways older people in our communities are active in creating changes.

Step One. Divide students into heterogeneous groups of four and give several dictionaries to each group. Cut up pages of Worksheet (1) and give each person in each group at least one "news item." Give two to students who can handle them.

Tell students to imagine that they are all coming from different parts of the country and are meeting for the first time. They have all read a short news item about the organization, the Gray Panthers, in their hometown newspapers before they came.

Students look up italicized vocabulary words and write down the definitions. Then each summarizes to the whole group what she has learned about the Gray Panthers from her news item. Based on everyone's information, the group writes a short article. "The Gray Panthers: Who They Are and What They Do." Encourage students to summarize what they've learned. Ask them to use at least four new vocabulary words in their article. Share articles with the whole class.

Step Two. Cut Worksheet (2) into sections, and distribute to the groups. Explain to students that the Gray Panther founders had a vision of a new society. Tell them if they compile all the information they have just been given, they will get a picture of that society. Students read their own pieces of information, look up any new vocabulary words, and then summarize to each other.

Next, the group writes a cooperative story about a person who lives in the new society, as the Gray Panthers would like it. The story describes a typical day in that person's life. It should tell how the person contributes to or is affected by jobs, health care, and so on. At least four new vocabulary words should be used. When stories are completed, students read them to the class.

DISCUSSION

1. How do you think the older people in the story you wrote about feel about themselves? About being older?
2. How would you compare their feelings to those of older persons today?
3. How does the society the Gray Panthers want compare to ours today?
4. What are your feelings and opinions about the society the Gray Panthers foresee?
5. Think back to the lesson "Health or Home" p. 122, and remember the situation of Ted and Juanita Lund. How would they feel about the society the Gray Panthers want?

For Homework. Describe the society the Gray Panthers foresee to an older person you know. Write down that person's opinions about it.

Look through newspapers and magazines and talk with parents, relatives and friends. Bring in information about older people who are acting for change in your community.

Step Three (several days later). Choose one or two elders who are active in working for changes in your community and invite them to speak with your class.

The day before, students generate questions to ask. Examples: How are you working for change in our community? How is it different being an older person working for change? How do you deal with any discrimination against older persons that you face? What kinds of changes do you feel need to be made to make life for older people in America more equal? We learned about the Gray Panthers—how do you feel about their ideas? What groups or organizations are working on behalf of older people in our community? How do you think younger people can work together with older people to bring changes? What projects could we get involved with in our community now?

The Gray Panthers

Gray Panthers is a non-profit advocacy organization that works for a more humane society. We are people of all ages who believe in a peaceful world order through international cooperation, a comprehensive national health system accessible to all, and government support of affordable housing. We work for economic justice for persons of all ages and oppose ageism, racism, and sexism which stereotype and stigmatize.

GOING FURTHER   Obtain the film, "Wrinkled Radical," a 30 minute documentary about Maggie Kuhn and the Gray Panthers. Help students get involved with a community project that your visitor suggested. If appropriate, make it a school project.

A CLASSROOM FOR ALL OF US

OBJECTIVES   To have students learn about an inclusive classroom that includes students with a wide range of abilities and difficulties.

To have students better understand how, by working together and helping each other ALL students can learn better in an inclusive classroom.

MATERIALS   One set of "Worksheets: Voices from a Classroom for All of Us," pp. 306–307, for each group of three students; paper and pencils.

IMPLEMENTATION   *Step One.* Explain to students that this lesson is about a real third grade classroom in a school that, several years ago, started an inclusion program. About 10% of the students in the school would be in self-contained special education classes if it were not for this school. These children have a range of difficulties. They have cerebral palsy, hearing and vision impairment, developmental delays and emotional problems. The school began taking these children in kindergarten and is committed to keeping them until they graduate after sixth grade.

Step Two. Divide students into groups of three. If your class has studied newspapers, this lesson lends itself well to newspaper writing. Assign each group one of the following styles of newspaper writing: News article, editorial, letter to the editor, advice column. If you have eight groups you will be able to assign each style to two groups. (If students are not familiar with newspaper writing, pick one newspaper style to introduce and teach students about that type of writing. Then have all groups do that.) Give each group one set of "Worksheets: Voices from a Classroom for All of Us." Direct students to take turns, in their groups of three, reading these voices aloud.

Step Three. When groups have finished reading they use the information they learned to write a newspaper piece in their assigned style. They then meet with another group to do peer editing.

Step Four. Gather the class together as a whole. Have each group read their newspaper piece aloud. Discuss the questions below.

DISCUSSION   1. After reading these many voices, how do you feel about inclusion classes?
2. What do you see as the advantages for special education students in this model? For other students?
3. What do you see as the disadvantages?
4. What was it like to do the kind of newspaper writing you did for this lesson? In what ways was it easy or hard to write "just the facts?" In what ways was it easy or hard to write opinions with convincing arguments?
5. If you could question of any of the speakers in this lesson, what would you ask?
6. Does your school have any inclusion classrooms? Why or why not?

Achievers and Their Disabilities

a. He did not speak until age three. He was so quiet and defiant in school that his teachers suspected he might be mentally retarded. In adult life he wrote four papers which revolutionized modern physics. Albert Einstein–(Learning Disability)

b. She survived a high fever as a baby. As a result she was both hearing impaired and visually impaired. She became a writer and lecturer. Helen Keller (Hearing and Vision Impairment)

c. He grew up in the city of Detroit. A teacher took special interest in this young, blind student. He is now recognized as a famous rock and roll singer. Stevie Wonder (Vision Impairment)

d. He was considered "defective" at birth because his head was so abnormally large. The village doctor thought he might have brain fever. He did not learn to read until age 12. Thomas Edison (Learning Disability and Hearing Impairment)

From "Educating for a Just Society," Kathleen McGinnis et al.

USING PRIVILEGE FOR CHANGE

OBJECTIVES   To have students learn about how people can use their privilege to create changes.
To have students think of ways they can use the privilege they have to create changes.

MATERIALS   Copies of "Worksheet: Using Privilege for Change," pp. 308–310, one per group.

IMPLEMENTATION   Introduce the lesson by reminding children of the definition of the word "privilege." Explain that a privilege is a special advantage, benefit, or bonus that some people or groups of people have. People don't always earn privileges; often they are born with them.

Have children think of some privileges they have in school, their family, or community. For example, because some may be older than their siblings they may have certain bedtime privileges that others don't. Explain that some groups of people often have more privileges because society gives those groups more chances and opportunities than others. For example, white people's skin-color is often a privilege because it keeps them from facing the racism black people face.

Divide students into groups of four and give one personal account from the worksheet to each student. Distribute them in such a way that all the personal accounts are used.

Each person first reads her account to herself and then to her group. Each is an example of a person who had a privilege and used it to help create change. Some readings are harder than others, so distribute sections accordingly. Encourage students to ask each other the definition of words they don't know or ideas they don't understand.

After students have read the accounts aloud, have them discuss the similarities and differences in the ways the persons they read about used privilege for change. Then have them brainstorm ways they could use the privileges they have to act for change. Even if your students have few privileges, help them consider ones they do have, perhaps gender, language, lack of physical disability and so forth. They can think back to the position of the petals of the flower they made in the lesson, "Filter of Oppression" (pg. 180), for reminders. Come together as a class to discuss the accounts and share ideas.

DISCUSSION
1. What did the people in the stories gain from using their privilege for change? (Discuss each separately.)
2. What did other people gain by their actions?
3. What are some ideas you came up with to use your privileges for change?
4. How can you help each other put some of those ideas into practice?
5. Let's plan a time when people report back to the class and tell us what happened.

Students Using Privilege for Change

1. Students who can walk have the privilege of mobility. Some decided to change the rules of their recess games so that a wheel-chair-bound student could join them in play.
2. In a certain class, skin-color privilege kept white students out of trouble. When there was a conversation going on when there shouldn't have been, the teacher tended to blame the Puerto Rican students rather than the white students. To change that, some white students spoke up and were honest when they were the ones talking.
3. In some families, male privilege allows boys to avoid cooking, doing dishes, and helping with the younger children. Some boys decided to split those responsibilities so everyone would be doing their fair share of housework.

Pretend you could spend a day with the main person or the group from your book. Describe that day. What would you ask? What answers might you get? What would you do together? How would you feel about it?

Suppose a main person in your book, or a representative from the group, came to your school. What would he or she like? Dislike? Try to change? Give specific reasons for your answers, using examples from these people's lives.

Take one scene from the book. Write what you think the person or people involved were thinking and feeling. Pick a scene where the author doesn't tell this.

Write a correspondence between yourself and a main person in your book. Write at least four letters.

At the top of a page write the name of the person or group described in your book. Divide the page in half. On one half, list at least five obstacles the person or group had to overcome. On the other, list the strengths the person or group had and the support s/he or they received.

What do you and a main person in the book have in common? List some words that describe both of you. List some skills you both have. List some problems you both have. List some differences. List some ways you would like to be more like that person.

Write a radio announcement that would take two minutes for the announcer to read, that tells people why they should read this book and what it will tell them about change.

Garrett Morgan was a black man born in Kentucky or Tennessee in 1875. As is often the case for people of color at that time, historical records are incomplete, so different resource books give different information.

In 1901, Garrett Morgan created his first invention—a safety belt-cover for sewing machines. At that time, sewing machine belts were in the open and dangerous to people's hands.

Garrett Morgan continued to invent equipment to make people's lives more safe. In 1914, he invented a breathing helmet for rescuers who were entering areas filled with smoke or gas. Two years later he demonstrated the importance of this in rescuing trapped workers in a smoke-filled tunnel under Lake Erie. He received a Gold Medal for that from the City of Cleveland. People were impressed and, at first, his invention sold rapidly. Then it became known that the helmet was invented by a black man. People were so prejudiced that, even though it saved lives, they wouldn't use it.

Garrett Morgan continued to invent more safety items. In 1923 he invented the automatic traffic light. Today we take this for granted. Yet when he introduced the idea, traffic lights did not seem valuable to people. He couldn't sell his idea. Finally, years later, General Electric bought his idea and paid him $40,000 for it. ($40,000 sounds like quite a lot of money, but it doesn't sound as much when you realize that in 1981 a single traffic light cost $2,500.)

Call your city traffic department and ask about the cost of various types of traffic lights. If you live in a town with no traffic lights, call a nearby city. Then calculate the cost of any traffic lights between where you live and the school. Calculate how many traffic lights could be bought for the amount that G.E. paid Garrett Morgan.

In pairs, stand on a street corner where there is a traffic light. Using the skills you have learned about interviewing, ask passersby if they know who invented the traffic light. Record reactions. Do so until you have talked to at least ten people.

Interview five adults you know about the importance of traffic lights. Ask them if they have ever stopped to think about what would be different if we didn't have traffic lights.

Look up information about another inventor who was a woman and/or a person of color. Write a description of the person's life and invention(s). Send it to your school or town paper.

Write an article for your school newspaper or a letter to your town newspaper about the advantages and importance of Garrett Morgan's safety inventions.

Write a newspaper article that might have appeared in 1923 when people first saw a traffic light and didn't realize how important it would turn out to be. Write a letter back to the newspaper from someone who was better at imagining the future, explaining why it would be helpful.

It is 1918. Write a letter to the newspaper complaining about people not using the safety breathing helmet just because it was invented by a black man. Explain why you think people are making a bad choice.

I am only one person.
What can one person do?

Rosa Parks
Was just one person.
She said one word.
She said it on December 1, 1955.

One person
Said
One word.
She said it on a bus.
She said it to the bus driver.
On the Cleveland Street Bus
In Montgomery.

The bus driver said,
'Stand up, Nigger woman,
And give up your seat
To that white man!'

Rosa Parks,
One person
Said one word.
The word was 'No!'

One woman
Said one word
And a nation
blushed!

One woman
Said one word
And a world talked!

One woman
Said one word
And the Supreme Court
Acted!

One woman
Said one word
And the buses were
Desegregated.

I am only one person.
What can one person do?

They put her in jail,
Because she didn't 'know her place,'
Because she didn't 'stay in her place,'
Because she was an 'uppity Nigger.'

It was a Thursday
When she said
That One Word.

On Monday morning
The buses ran.
The Negroes walked.
Each white man had two seats.
Empty seats.
Symbols of a people,
Moved to walk,
Moved to march
Moved to act
By the sound of
One woman's
One word,
'No!'

One woman
Said one word
And 17,000 people
Walked.

Author unknown

1. What did the Ku Klux Klan do to black people in the South?

2. How were black people and white people treated differently in the South?

3. What did Rosa Parks learn from her mother?

4. What is the NAACP and what did it do?

5. What was the Montgomery Voters League and what did it do?

6. What did black people have to do when they rode the bus?

7. What did Rosa do that got her arrested?

8. What did black people decide to do to protest the bus company policy?

9. How were leaflets used in organizing people?

10. How were the churches used in organizing people?

11. After Rosa was arrested what happened to her at her job?

12. What was the Montgomery Improvement Association and what did it do?

13. How long did black people have to walk before the end of the Montgomery bus boycott?

14. What is the Supreme Court and what did it decide?

15. Why is Rosa Parks called the Mother of the Civil Rights Movement?

In May of 1972, 4,000 Chicana factory workers went on strike. A strike is when a group of people refuses to work until certain conditions are met. These people worked for the Farah Company, which makes men's and boys' pants.

They had many good reasons for striking:

1. They made very little money. They got $70 a week. In 1972, the average worker in the U.S. got $150.
2. The factory didn't want to pay pensions to people when they got too old to work and had to retire. So workers were fired when they got older.
3. Almost every worker was Chicana, but none of the supervisors were Chicana.
4. Most of the workers were women, but none of the supervisors were women.
5. When a woman left to have a baby, the factory would not save her job for her.
6. If they gave women their jobs back after having babies, they were paid much less than before they left.
7. The factory used a "speed-up" system. That means that they kept wanting people to do more work each day in the same amount of time. The very fastest workers got the most money.

There was so much that was bad about working for Farah that the workers wanted a union. A union is like a club for people who work at the same place. They have meetings about what is bad for them about working at a place and organize to get that changed. Many of the workers at the Farah factory met to talk about setting up a union.

Some people working with the bosses at the factory took pictures at the meeting. The next day, some of the workers who had been at the meeting were fired. More workers got mad. They went on strike. Workers in other Farah factories got angry too and went on strike.

Here is what Virgie Delgado, one of the workers said:

But I had to think about it before I walked out, because there are nine kids in my family, and me and my sisters work at Farah to support our family. I had to go home and tell my Mom what I was going to do. She said to do what I thought was right.

The next morning I got my girlfriends together and said we were going to walk out. I got all their purses.

We started in the very back and started calling to the other workers to walk out with us. My legs were shaking the whole time. We were really scared because we didn't know what was going to happen. My three sisters joined us. All these people followed us. By the time we got to the front door I looked back and saw 150 people behind me.

The strike lasted for a year and a half. During that time the workers didn't get paid any money. That was very hard on them. But the factory was losing a lot of money. Finally, the bosses said they would agree to some of the workers' demands. The workers got better pay and better working conditions.

Most of the strikers were Chicanas, Mexican-American women. They had not had practice working with a union before. They worked hard and became good at organizing. They went on trips to speak about the union. The men had to learn to let the women do this kind of work. They got better at understanding that. They knew that the work that the women were doing would help everyone. Julia Aquilar, who was a worker, said:

We women are much more on the go now than before. Because we were women, we were staying behind. Now, we just bring our children to meetings, and we bring them to the picket lines. Sometimes they ask, "Are we going to the picket today, Mommy?"

When all working people work together, they get better lives.

Interviewer: The year is 1979. We are going to meet with some women today who have fought to be longshore workers, people who load cargo on boats in New York harbor. Why did you have to fight for these jobs?

Jane Silver: No women have yet been accepted as dock workers in this area.

Interviewer: Why do women want such strenuous work?

Mary Baffi: Let me explain. I'm a divorced mother of three children. I've been working for the minimum wage at the telephone company. It's almost impossible to provide for my children on a salary of $6,000 a year. I need a better-paying job.

Interviewer: How much can you make working on the docks?

Mary: We will be able to make between $18,000 and $22,000 a year.

Interviewer: Tell us what happened when you went to apply for the jobs.

Jackie O'Shaughnessy: There were six of us who went, three black women, one Hispanic woman and two white women. Three representatives of the National Organization of Women went with us. We said we wanted to apply for the job of cargo checkers and were told there were no applications available.

Debra Brown: We asked what companies were hiring pier guards and warehouse men. The clerk at the Waterfront Commission told us he couldn't give us their names.

Jackie: When we were leaving a male employee called out, "Hey Al, you should have asked one of them for a date."

Debra: It was after this that we filed discrimination charges and began a lawsuit against the Waterfront Commission.

Interviewer: Why is this effort so important?

Jane: Many women coming to our Job Development Program are on welfare or are below the poverty level. If women can get these jobs, they will be able to get off welfare.

Jackie: Also we're excited because we're a group of black, white and Hispanic women working together. Once we get working on the docks, we'll have to support and help each other, since some men don't want us on the docks. We know we can do it!

Interviewer: How do you know you women can do heavy physical labor? Aren't you too weak?

Debra: I'd like to remind you of your American history. During World War II when the men were in Europe fighting, women worked in the factories making tanks, planes, and battleships. They worked at the blast furnaces. They riveted huge metal work. They loaded cargo on and off ships. Women have proven that they have the strength.

Interviewer: What does all this have to do with affirmative action?

Jane: Affirmative action means that employers must take steps to try to hire women and people of color for jobs for which they are qualified. In many cases, women and people of color have been kept out of these jobs because of discrimination.

Debra: We're fighting for affirmative action for longshore workers on the docks. We're fighting together for a better chance.

Adapted from "Rocking the Docks: Women on the Waterfront" by Constance Pohl.

Dear Ellen,

Remember how I've been wanting to learn a trade? I needed to be able to do my music and also earn a living. I've found a solution! The trade unions in this area needed to have more women in order to meet federal laws. They decided they wanted to train women so that the jobs would be done the way the unions wanted.

I got into a training program in Lowell, Massachusetts. There were thirty women in my group. Only a few of them were married. More than half had children they were supporting. Most of them had been doing factory work before they got into this program. Factory work doesn't pay very well. These women thought that construction would be more interesting and it pays much more.

We spent the first three weeks with a chance to decide what we wanted to learn. We did carpentry for one week, masonry for another, and painting for another. I was very lucky that we had a woman counselor who did lots to help us decide which we liked best. I decided on painting. Carpentry was much too noisy. I knew I couldn't stand it. I did best being a "bricky" (that's working in masonry) but I knew that the bad weather wouldn't be good for me and I didn't want to be on my knees so much. I know now I made the right choice. There are some bad things, like the dust from sanding, but there's lots that I like about painting.

We had fifteen weeks of training in our fields. Then we became apprentices. As an apprentice, you earn less than what a journeyperson earns. Journeypersons are the regular trained workers. In painting we work as apprentices for about three years; the brickies and carpenters spend four years as apprentices. The first year you earn about half of a journeyperson's salary. Then every six months or so you go up. If you learn fast and you're lucky, your pay goes up faster.

You've probably heard that apprentices get all the worst jobs. That's true. But still, even at the beginning, there's more independence than working in a factory. We all feel like we have real skills and that makes us feel better about ourselves. Sometimes it's scary, like when I was walking on a plank at least forty-five feet up in the air and it slipped. Sometimes it's very good, like now I'm getting the right wrist movements and can really do the things I've been watching the experienced painters do. There's a real rhythm to taping, sanding, and painting. The best part is that I can sing while I work. I love how strong my body has become.

You'd be interested in my friend Jaconda. She was one of the few married women and has two kids. Her husband would much rather stay home with the children. She needed to find a job that would support all of them. She became a mason and now they've all moved to Maine where she's working.

Love,
Sabra

1. Write an article for your school newspaper about women becoming longshore workers.

_____

2. Write a letter to the editor of your school newspaper describing affirmative action and explaining exactly why you think it should be the law.

_____

3. Write a dinner-table conversation in your household with you doing your best to argue for affirmative action. Use both the interview and the letter for information in support of what you say. Have your family members say what you think they actually would say.

_____

4. Write a letter to Sabra asking her questions about her job and about women in construction work.

_____

5. Write a list of at least five reasons why working as a painter is a good choice for Sabra.

_____

6. Pick a job that you would like as an adult that is usually not associated with your gender. Write down as many reasons as you can why you would enjoy and do well in that job. Write down as many reasons as you can why an employer should hire you.

_____

7. Pick an area in your school where most, or all, of the workers are of the same gender, race, or age. Write down why the school should go out of its way to hire workers of different genders, ages, or races. How would that benefit the people hired? The school? The community?

_____

8. Pick an area in your community where most, or all, of the workers are of the same gender, race, or age. Write down why the employer should go out of his way to hire workers of different genders, ages, or races. How would that benefit the people hired? The employer? The community?

_____

9. Make a list of reasons present employees in a job might be against affirmative action. Why might they want to keep things the way they are? Then give some ideas of what could be done to meet those concerns.

1. What was the situation in your school that prompted your action?

For the last two years of my going to Buena Vista (fourth and fifth grade) there was a lot of putting down of gay people and of putting down kids with gay slurs such as "gaybob." Also there was a lot of "Oh, that's so gay!" Gay was bad and bad was gay.

My friend, whose mother is also a lesbian, and I were walking down the hall one day in fifth grade when a boy came up to us and said, "Rose,* your mom's gay, huh? She's a *lesbian*." She said that he was right and asked him where he had found out. It wasn't a big secret that either of our parents were gay at that time, but she still wondered. He told her that he had heard it from a boy named Sam. We didn't say anything about it for the rest of the day, but on our way out of school, another of our friends told us that she had overheard Sam and another boy talking, and that the other boy said that we were "carrying on the tradition" by being such good friends.

2. How did you feel about this situation?

We were surprised by this because we didn't know of anyone having any problem with our parents before this. We were mad at the boys for saying what they did and we were confused because we weren't sure how to respond.

3. What idea did you come up with for dealing with this? How did you come up with it?

The idea that we came up with was to go around to the upper grade classes and talk to them about what had happened and how we felt about it. Actually, I didn't come up with the plan and neither did Rose. Her mom did. Rose called me that night after talking to her mom and told me about their idea. I thought it was a good idea and so did she, so we decided to do it. Rose's mother is part of a speaker's bureau called CUAV (Community United Against Violence), and so it was a natural thing for her to think up.

4. How did you feel about doing this before you did it?

We were scared and worried that the response wouldn't be a good one, and a little excited. It all seemed kind of like a TV show at the time. We didn't give ourselves a whole lot of time to think about it, though, since we talked to students the following afternoon. It seemed like the right thing to do.

5. What kind of support from others did you have for developing and implementing your plan?

---

*These names have been changed.

My moms thought it was a great idea. We didn't really talk it over with our friends beforehand. The principal was supportive because she said that she would go with us. She also said, though, that we would need parental permission if we were going to have an in-depth conversation about homosexuality. Looking back on it now, it seems a little strange that she would say this because the school has become a lot more supportive of the gay and lesbian families attending it.

6. Describe what you did.

At about eleven o'clock the day after the incident, we went around to the three upper grade classes (consisting of fourth and fifth graders) and said that we weren't going to say any names, but two boys had been talking about us behind our backs and that we didn't appreciate it. We said that for those of the students who didn't know, we both had lesbian parents and that if anyone had any questions, they could ask us.

7. What was hard about taking the steps you did? Was anything easier than you expected?

It was scary speaking to a group of sixty rowdy kids. We both expressed afterwards that we never would have done it if there weren't two of us. I was amazed, though, that they actually listened to us talk and that they responded positively.

8. What were the results of your actions?

People completely stopped with the put-downs, for a while at least. And there continued to be a very small amount of name-calling in the gay department. People were a lot nicer to the two of us in general, also, although the put-downs had never been toward us directly until that episode.

9. What did you learn from taking the steps you did?

What I learned was, who cares? Sure, they always *might* say something bad but if you just get up there and do it, what they *will* say will be good, in my experience.

10. What can you say to other kids who are bothered by homophobia in their school and would like to do something about it?

Listen to Nike. Just do it. Ask your principal and don't be afraid. I was in a small and not too hostile environment, but now that I've done it once, I believe that I could take on any number of kids who were five times as hostile as the kids at my elementary school. It's not as bad as you think. Once you get their attention, they will listen and they will care. Whether you're the most popular kid in the school or the least popular, it has an amazing effect that you would never expect.

Dave and Noelle Porter, their father, and stepmother have developed an equal way to share jobs in their household. They began their system about six years before this interview when Dave was eleven and Noelle was eight. As it was a success, they continued it!

Interviewer: Please tell us about your job-sharing plan.

Dave: The first step in our job-sharing plan is to get everybody to sit down together and make a list of all the jobs that need to be done each day and another list of the jobs needed to be done each week.

Noelle: Our daily chart has these jobs: cook, set the table, wash dishes, clear the table, and dry dishes.

Dave: This only applies to dinner. All of us get our own breakfast and wash our dishes. On weekends, the same applies to lunch.

Interviewer: What about the weekly jobs?

Noelle: Our weekly chart has these jobs: clean the kitchen, living room, bathroom, and dining room. Each person cleans his or her own room.

Dave: Once we list the jobs we make two charts. The weekly chart is easy, because each person gets one job. We must each do our jobs on Friday night or Saturday morning.

Noelle: We post the jobs on the refrigerator. If we forget our job, we can be sure there are people to remind us!!

Interviewer: How does the daily job chart work?

Noelle: For the daily jobs, we make a bigger chart with a column for each day of the week and rows for each job. One person chooses one job and Dave and I fill it in on the chart. Then the next person chooses, and we continue until the chart is full.

Dave: The fact that there are seven days in the week and four of us causes a small problem. One person gets the most time-consuming job—cooking—only once a week. Usually that person gets the hardest weekly job—like cleaning the kitchen.

Interviewer: How do you feel about this system?

Dave: Having a definite schedule posted allows me to make my plans around jobs I know about. I don't have to worry about someone asking me to do something at the last minute.

Noelle: The adults think the system's terrific! They don't have time to fix complicated meals, but they can often count on Dave or me to fix something special. We've become great cooks.

Interviewer: Do either of you feel angry that you have to do these jobs?

Noelle: Sometimes I go, "Yuck!" But then I remind myself that many people don't like to do jobs and this is certainly the fairest way.

Dave: I think the job-sharing system brings a feeling of equality and unity to all of us. It's a more positive experience to tell yourself you have to do something than to have some "superior" reminding you all the time. It makes me feel a lot freer, because I'm not being bossed around. The adults become people on the same level and having the same responsibilities as the kids: not more, not less.

Interviewer: What are some problems with this system?

Noelle: One cook is very messy to clean up after!

Dave: Some unfairness comes because on certain days it's more common to have company. This can usually be evened out by rotating the schedule every few months.

Interviewer: What recommendations do you give to others who might want to try a system like this?

Dave: Do it! But don't worry about copying ours exactly. Find a system that works for your family.

Interviewer: Do you have any final thoughts or feelings about job-sharing?

Noelle: Yes, kids and adults who come over notice our schedule and are very interested in it and eager to try it.

Dave: I never feel embarrassed about our job-sharing system. In fact, I'm pretty proud of my cooking ability which the responsibility has encouraged me to develop.

Both: Try job-sharing!

The Eskimos presently living in Alaska migrated there at least 10,000 and perhaps 28,000 years ago. Eskimos learned to get food, clothing, and shelter from their frozen land.

Eskimos have had to make frequent choices about how to survive. For example, with only a small supply of fat (in the form of blubber from seals and whales) they discovered they could live longer by eating it than by burning it.

Eskimos developed a cooperative lifestyle in order to survive. It was impossible for an Eskimo to hunt alone, kill game, and bring it back alone. Cooperation was necessary in order to win life from the land. Eskimos realized that they did not, and could not, control their natural world. Hard work was admired, but it was also understood that a certain amount of what happened was luck. Those who worked hard and did not hunt successfully were never looked at as though they did anything wrong.

Children learned that they must help in order to receive help and attention. Family members were dependent on each other for comfort and for survival. There was only free time for play if all those in the family first worked to see that their basic needs were met. If a man inherited a boat and already had one, he could choose which to keep for his family. The other would go to a family in need of a boat. Land was *never* owned by anyone.

Sharing is a natural way of life for Eskimos. There is no need to thank someone for shared food, or to give a gift in return. The belief is that the time will come when the receiver will be able to be the giver and that, in all, it evens out. When an Eskimo or group of Eskimos kills an animal in a hunt, the food and skins are shared with the whole community. No hunter would hoard food for his family while others in the community were hungry.

The Children's Place is a special kind of day-care center. It is a center that New York State has set up for the children of its workers.

The Children's Place is in the government office buildings in Albany, New York. Admitting children from eight weeks to four years of age allows parents to return to work soon after their child is born. Parents work close to the Children's Place. They spend lunch hours with their children and can attend to their children's illnesses. Mothers can nurse their infants at the center.

The center has had a positive effect on the government workplaces. Supervisors have not minded when parents have to leave to attend to a sick child. In fact, morale among parents and nonparents has improved since the center opened.

Molly Hardy, the director of the Children's Place, said, "Workers are also parents and New York State has shown they understood this with the opening of the center."

Interview Questions

1. How do you feel about the Children's Place?

2. Would you like to have such a day-care center at your place of work? Why or why not?

Kjære Venner,

That means "Dear Friends" in our language. We are glad you want to know more about our country. We hope you will want to write back and tell us about your country. We go to school in Bergen, Norway's third-biggest city. It is on the Atlantic coast.

Our father is a doctor and our mother is a teacher. In Norway it is not expensive to get an education. We understand that that is different in your country. Both our parents went to college and graduate school without paying any money for tuition. That is true for all Norwegians, it doesn't matter how much money your family earns—anyone can get an education. If students don't have enough money for living expenses while they are studying, the government will give them loans. After they finish their training they are expected to work for two years in areas the government assigns them to pay back their loans.

This is especially true of doctors. That is how our country gets good medical care even way out in the country, on islands far away from the coast, or way up north far away from anything.

Since doctors do this service after getting trained, we can have good medical care all over. Sometimes, though, sick people need to come into cities to specialists. When they have to do that, the government pays all their transportation. Our government really does believe that all our citizens should have good medical care and that all our doctors should help provide it. We believe that anyone who is interested enough and smart enough to be a doctor should get to be one, not just those from families with money.

When our family is on vacation, we go cross-country skiing to our mountain cabin. Some of the kids we know there come from doctor's families, but others come from families where their fathers work in the post office, or their mothers work in stores.

Tell us about medical care in your country. We look forward to hearing from you.

Beste hilsen,
Kirsten and Asmund

News Item:

The motto of the Gray Panthers is "Age and Youth in Action." The main purpose of the Gray Panthers is to fight for the rights of the *elderly*, but the Gray Panthers also struggle for a better life for everyone.

News Item:

Naomi Howard, a Gray Panther in Arizona, *testified* at a public meeting to protest constantly rising electric rates in that state.

"It's as if the Valley of the Sun has had an *epidemic* of rate increases. Low-income people are at rock-bottom now. If they have to pay more for utilities, that means they don't eat, they don't get their medicine, or they change their housing situation."

News Item:

In Austin, Texas, Gray Panthers have supported *alternative* housing and day-care for the elderly. In the "cooperative living center," a dozen older people live in a group of apartments with a recreation room in common and someone on call.

There are adult day-care centers in Austin with fees on a *sliding scale*. These centers are used by people who live with a family but can't stay alone during the day.

News Item:

The Gray Panthers have advocated for national health care for 20 years. Gray Panthers is one of the nation's leading advocates for affordable, universal health care.

In the spring of 1994 members of the Gray Panthers lobbied in Washington for a "single payer health care system" which would provide the cheapest and most extensive health care coverage for all Americans.

News Item:

The Gray Panthers fight for affordable housing for all Americans. In 1994 the Gray Panthers documented how the federal housing budget had been cut to almost nothing. They argue, "Put up more houses, and fix up the ones that are falling down. It's time for this most basic human need to become a national priority."

News Item:

Gray Panthers suceeded in introducing an intergenerational amendment to the Older Americans Act that expanded opportunities for older people to nurture and assist children in their area through volunteer programs in senior centers.

Jobs

The right to a job must become the most basic of civil rights. Otherwise *generations* will be pitted against each other for paid employment.

Service to America

In our *vision* there will be a United States Unarmed Services (USUS) which will *recruit* people of all ages to provide basic health care and to work on *conservation* projects. The USUS will be strong on equality of the *sexes* and *opposed* to any age *bias*.

Politics

Political parties will be replaced by *regional* councils. The rise of neighborhood block organizations will make *officials* far more sensitive to local citizens.

Health Care

Health care will be turned on its head, with *preventive* care and health education becoming top *priorities*. The "healthy block" will become the *cornerstone* of neighborhood organization. People will help each other with basic care for minor sickness and injuries. Health care, like employment, must be considered a basic human right.

Teaching

Older people, often discarded now, will become teachers in the Elder Training Program. Elders can settle fights, be *counselors*, advocates, and historians, telling about the past and helping with the management of children.

Family

The idea of family will grow to include two or more persons who share *resources*, goals, and values over time. *Intergenerational cooperatives* will develop, inhabited by families.

This is taken from a statement written by Gray Panther founder, Maggie Kuhn, and Tish Sommers, *Gray Panther Network*, January/February, 1981.

Caitlin's Voice:*

I like my class a lot. We all get help on some things from the teachers and other students. Here's an example. I didn't have really good handwriting and it was frustrating for me to write a story. But the teacher showed me how to write on the computer. Our teachers figure out what we each need and give the right kind of help to each kid. It's different for different kids.

Some students need more help. We're trying to teach Brian that he can't always depend on someone else to do all his work for him. We have to help Jason in a special way. He can understand what we're saying but we can't understand what he's saying. He has this special picture board. If he wants something he has a little communication book with all these pictures in it. Someone can flip up the pages and he can point to what he means. Also we're trying to help him learn to walk. He just started.

My dad's in a wheelchair. When I see people in a wheelchair first I think I should go help them, but then I think, "Hey, wait a minute, I think these people need to learn how to do things and not depend on other people to do everything." I've learned a lot about what people can do on their own. And that we all need help in some ways.

___

Caitlin's Mother's Voice:

In general I've been thrilled with Caitlin's inclusive classroom. Since Caitlin's father is in a wheelchair, I think it's great that children get comfortable with handicapped people and see that they're just regular people.

I think the most important lesson of the integrated classroom is that everyone faces life with a different combination of skills and challenges. And that everyone's worthy of respect. Being loved by the teacher isn't dependent on being "smart." This makes kids realize that there's no such thing as "average." They know that everyone doesn't need to be doing the same work at the same time. It lessens competition.

I think Caitlin's gotten more individual attention than she would have in a traditional classroom. It's natural that everyone is different and needs attention on different things. It's expected that each is working on their own level. When I was a child getting extra spelling words because I was good at spelling was a big deal. In this classroom getting something different is not a big deal.

Caitlin's teachers have been wonderful. They've been able to offer a rich enough and supportive enough environment for all different kinds of kids with different needs.

___

Nicholas' Mother's Voice:

I've been really pleased with the classroom because it is a non-competitive atmosphere. I feel that Nicholas has developed an enormous amount of compassion because part of the classroom activity is helping take care of others. He'll have different classroom jobs that involve interacting and helping, like pushing a wheelchair.

Academically what I like is that he hasn't become an arrogant kid. He doesn't talk about reading better or faster. He gets a lot of support around his strengths and a lot of support around his weaknesses. The classroom is really focused on cooperation, not competition—they don't compare and talk about being "smarter." The concept of being differently-abled was introduced in kindergarten. These children really believe that everyone can do something well.

There's a real sense of unity, comfort, security, and friendship. The teachers use everything as a way to pull the kids together, rather than a way to divide them. Parents are very involved in everything.

I know that at first parents had worried that the more advanced kids would have to function on a lower level. The teachers are good and the children have learned how to help each other, so that hasn't been a big problem.

___

*Names have been changed in this lesson.

Nicholas' Voice:

It's good to be in my classroom. I like that I have special projects to do. It's fine to have differently-abled kids in my class. Brian is sounding good. We can understand him now. Jason is smiling a lot now. In first grade they'd sometimes hit me, but that was a long time ago. When they did that, I'd tell them to stop. Jason hasn't hit anybody this year.

We have three teachers so we get enough attention. I see myself as a peacemaker. We work a lot on getting along. Peacemakers don't do mean things. They work cooperatively with everyone and talk about how to solve problems.

Jason's Father's Voice:

We think inclusion is right for Jason. Special classes still need to be available for children with even more severe needs than Jason, as they have a right to an education too. Jason is eight, the same age as the others in his class. He's multiply handicapped. He doesn't talk and doesn't walk. He's also retarded. Jason learns from the other children as much as he learns from the teacher.

We believe it is better to have more than one disabled child in a class. It helps with their self esteem when they see other children working on the same hard issues. It also allows disabled children to be in the role of helping others. There's a girl in Jason's class who has cerebral palsy herself and prides herself on what a good helper she is for Jason.

There are several reasons I think inclusion is good for the non special education children in the class. One is that most of them will grow up to be parents, and being with my boy now and helping and encouraging him helps them learn how to help. Everyone started by doing everything for Jason, but soon they realized that he needed encouragement, not doing for him. That's a lesson for all of them.

Also this type of program has to be developmental. It can't be standardized with the same work for everyone. That makes it better for all kids as the help they receive is more tailored to their needs as well. There's also an opportunity for children with less severe needs to get services because of the physical therapist, occupational therapist and speech pathologist who are involved with the room.

In society there are all types of people and all types of people should have an opportunity to learn together. Being in a separate place does not prepare anyone for the real world. The sooner everyone is exposed to real life the more sensitive they'll be.

The Teacher's Voice:

This is my second year in an inclusion classroom. This year I have a group with more special needs, but it is easier because I know more how to respond in different situations. I know more how to assess children and how to create individual plans for each lesson. When I put my lessons together, I focus on the most advanced children in whatever I am planning. Then I figure out how to make it work for the children with more special needs.

My belief in inclusion is a belief that as human beings we can come together. We have to accept and know that we all learn in different ways and they we're all differently-abled and can all help each other. Inclusion is not just an academic experience, it also provides incredibly important skills for life in how we, as human beings, relate to one another.

My class thinks about what people *can* do, not about barriers. Children learn to be compassionate, they learn they can be friends. They celebrate the successes of others; they're delighted in each others' accomplishments.

There are some conditions you have to meet to make inclusion work. You need to have physically big rooms if you have physically-challenged children. You need several teachers or assistants in each class. You can't have too many students and you have to be sure that not too many of the ones you do have have major special needs. Parents need to be informed and helped to understand why this program is good for all children.

1. Ann was a geologist who lived in New York in 1964. She knew that, in the South, black people weren't allowed to sit with white people in public buses, to use the same bathrooms, or drink from the same water fountains. Ann said to herself, "Because I'm white I get the use of the best water fountains and bathrooms. It's not fair that black people don't. I have a privilege black people don't have. I want to do something about this."

   Ann decided to become a Freedom Rider. Freedom Riders were black and white people who went on buses through parts of the South. They went into segregated bus stations and used any water fountain and toilet they wanted. They were sometimes beaten by people who wanted segregation. A few of them were beaten so badly they were crippled for life.

   The Freedom Riders made people more aware of segregation and many other Americans became angry. Their courage helped to end this type of segregation.

2. Roderick is a social worker and his wife, Vivian, is a meteorologist. They are very proud of their two year old daughter, Latisha. Roderick spends many hours in the evening helping her with dinner, bathing her, and playing with her. The only problem is when Latisha gets sick, Vivian takes time off from work. Then Roderick got to thinking, "Why should Vivian be the one who always loses a day at work when Latisha is sick? Some people think that the woman should always be the person to stay home with a sick child. That's not fair! I have a privilege women don't have. I want to do something about this."

   The next time Latisha was sick Roderick said, "Vivian, let's take turns staying home with Latisha when she's sick. I'll do it today and you can do it the next time. I know my boss won't like it, but I'll have to help him see that men can't hold on to privilege forever."

3. Theresa is 38 and the mother of a young daughter. For many years Theresa worked for a large company and earned a good salary. Gradually Theresa saw how unfair the company was. People with important jobs made a lot of money. The other workers, who worked just as hard, were paid very little. The company spent lots of money keeping a union out. Unions fight for more pay and better conditions for the low-paid workers. Theresa knew she didn't like what the company was doing.

   Theresa said to herself, "Because I'm middle-class and have an education, I can earn a good salary. It's not fair that other people can't. I have a privilege poor people don't have. I want to do something about this."

   Theresa decided to change jobs. She took a job working for a union organizing workers to get better health and safety conditions at work. She earned less money but she felt better, "I have many skills I gained because of my middle-class background. I want to put them to use to make changes so everybody can have a better life."

4. Ed works in a hospital. He loves his work because he's helping people. He works with many older people, and he has learned about many of the problems they face.

   Many of them can't find housing because they live on a "fixed income." Workers like Ed often get pay increases at their jobs. Older people get Social Security or a pension. This amount of money stays nearly the same. Many older people can't keep up with the prices that keep getting higher.

   Ed said to himself, "Because I'm working age and have a job, I can pay to live in a nice house. It's not fair that many older people can't. I have a privilege many older people don't have. I'd like to do something about this." Ed decided to convert the extra bedroom in his house to a small apartment and rent it to an older person at a price that person could pay. "I wasn't using that room. Now I'm making good use of it, and at least one older person can have a better life."

5. Arturo was a fifth grade teacher who loved his job and his school. He particularly liked the school celebrations around the holidays. Being a Christian, Arturo knew many Christmas carols and customs. His class often did splendid art work and musical programs at Christmas time.

   Arturo lived in the same town as his school. Next door to him lived the Bennett family whom he respected greatly. The family was always involved with community projects that helped people. One year Sara Bennett was in his class.

   Arturo was surprised when Sara's mother told him that Sara and her friend Rashide were uncomfortable in his class. As part of a study of religions, Mr. Davila had asked that the children share something about their religious backgrounds. Sara hadn't known what to say; her family were not members of any religious faith. Later on the playground classmates had made fun of the Hindu traditions Rashide talked about.

   Through discussions with the Bennetts, Mr. Davila realized that his privilege as a Christian had made him unaware of the feelings of people who weren't Christian. He hadn't realized how hard it was not to be part of the religious majority. He decided to use this privilege for change.

   He talked with other teachers and parents about religious diversity. He shared with them how he intends to help his students appreciate all their classmates of diverse religious backgrounds as well as those students who don't practice a religion. He changed his celebrations to ones that weren't based on any religious tradition. For example, his class had a poetry festival where all the students read their work and they celebrated their creativity with home-baked treats. He raised issues that helped other members of the school community think about how school practices affected children, whatever their religious belief or nonbelief.

---

6. Hattie and Nathaniel Johnson were proud of their 15 year old son, Reginald. Reggie was a good student and fine athlete. It was a shock to the Johnsons when their son told them he was gay. At first they were angry at Reggie. After having many discussions with him, reading books, and talking with other parents of gay youth, they realized that his sexual orientation was part of him and something that he couldn't change.

   As heterosexuals, Hattie and Nathaniel Johnson had the privilege of not facing any discrimination because of their sexual orientation. At first they wanted to keep that privilege and not admit publicly to others that their son was gay. However because Reggie told them about how he was harassed in school, they decided they wanted to use their privilege for change.

   The Johnsons became advocates for their son and other gay youth in the school and community. The joined PFLAG, Parents and Friends of Lesbian and Gay Youth, a national organization of adults that supports gay youth and confronts the homophobia they face. The Johnsons worked to make the school and community safe for gay youth. While they faced harassment from some community members, they gained respect from others. They felt strength in the fact that they were educating others to better appreciate diversity.

7. May Murray was the minister of a historic church that had a long tradition in the city. While the church had mostly white members, in recent years many Spanish-speaking immigrants from Central and South America began to attend. Everything at the church was conducted in English. Reverend Murray didn't speak Spanish.

   May's friend, Elisa, had come to this country from Columbia fifteen years ago. She explained to May how difficult it had been then to go to schools, libraries, churches and offices where only English was spoken as she was struggling to learn English. May decided to use the privilege she had as an English-speaker to create change.

   Reverend Murray met with church members and discussed the need to provide more in Spanish. While some people thought new churchgoers should "just learn English," others agreed with Rev. Murray. They decided to offer a Spanish class and an English class so members could start learning each others' language. Rev. Murray and other English-speaking church members took the Spanish class.

   A support group was set up for Spanish-speakers where issues of concern could be discussed. Reverend Murray invited others to translate parts of the Sunday morning service. Eventually she became fluent enough in Spanish to use both languages. She felt pleased that she had helped support a process that made the church more accessible to all its members.

---

8. Yong Wang was a teacher in a very well-respected elementary school. As a child, Yong learned easily and always did well in school. She loved teaching.

   Over the summer Yong tutored a little boy, Lee, who had just moved to their community. Lee was a bright boy, but had trouble keeping his thoughts focussed. He was jumpy and always moving around. Yong helped him learn through activities that kept him doing things, rather than sitting quietly for long periods of time.

   Yong was shocked to hear from Lee's parents that Lee was not going to be allowed to attend the neighborhood school she taught in. Instead the school district was sending him to a special program for students with learning disabilities. There he would only be with kids with learning problems and wouldn't have contact with all kinds of kids. Because Lee had ADHD (Attention Deficit Hyperactivity Disorder), a learning disorder that makes it hard to concentrate, he was being segregated.

   Yong decided to work to have Lee and other students like him allowed in her school. Her school had good teachers and many resources. She wanted to use these privileges to promote change. She knew teachers could work with students like Lee if they had more lessons that actively involved students, like using math manipulatives, putting on skits, making projects and so forth. She also got another adult to be in the room to support Lee and help other students. Teachers could teach students in the class how to help Lee stay involved and focussed.

   Yong formed a group of parents of children with learning difficulties, teachers, and administrators to talk about creating a more inclusive school, one where students with diverse learning styles were included. They talked with others and finally the decision was made to admit Lee and others. They would be part of a school with all kinds of learners.

We Can Make Changes

Once young people have developed a heightened awareness about inequality and ways others have made changes, they are often eager to take action themselves. That's why "We Can Make Changes" is an exciting chapter. The activities here provide chances for students to act to make a difference.

These lessons are very conducive to group projects and group action. Such collaborative efforts reinforce the idea that people working together can create changes. When students put their new-found awareness into constructive action, a sense of personal power and self-confidence develops. Emphasize to students that small changes *are* important, and that they can make a difference by taking action. Encourage cooperation, creativity, and perseverance when using these lessons.

The initial activities help students build the skills and confidence to foster change most effectively. In the section, "Making Changes at School," students not only create new products and experiences, but share their materials, skills, and new knowledge with other students. In the following two sections, students have a variety of opportunities to make books, packaging, and so on more fair and equal. Through skits, bulletin boards, and new materials, these improvements are shared with others. Finally, students reach out to have an impact on friends, family, and community.

Talk with students about ongoing projects and organizations in their community that are working for equality. Stay abreast of local issues and activities and invite members of community organizations into your classroom to talk about their efforts. Explore ways that young people can become involved.

Also remember that you are a role model for your students. It means a lot to students to see their teacher standing up for what is just. A fourth grade student wrote, "I love Ms. Cathers because she always stands up for what's fair. . . . She even tells the boys that her basketball is coed" (i.e., girls and boys will play *together* with the ball at recess). The more students see you challenging inequality, the more motivated they will be to do the same.

Support students in finding as many ways as possible to share the results of the lessons in this chapter. Visit other classes, make displays for your school and community, and write articles for the school and local newspapers. Change is contagious!

Taking Action

Paulo Freire, the well-known Brazilian educator, believes learners should use their new-found analysis to transform the world. In the school setting transforming-type activities depend on the nature of the group of students, the community, and the school system, and the courage and seniority of the teacher. My students have gone with me to marches that protested police brutality, demanded that King's birthday be made a national holiday, asked that Congress not fund the Contras, and requested nuclear disarmament. Two of my students testified before the City Council, asking that a Jobs with Peace referendum be placed on the ballot. In another instance, the students went to observe the court proceedings in the case of a police killing of an African-American man. Obviously teachers need to be involved in the community in order to know what's happening and what possibilities exist for involvement of children.

Robert Peterson, La Escuela Fratney
Milwaukee Public Schools

Section A — Gaining Confidence and Skills for Change

FACING DISCRIMINATION: FINDING COURAGE

OBJECTIVES

To use children's literature of high quality to explore alternative responses to discrimination

To consider alternative approaches for young people to deal with discrimination against themselves or a peer in their own lives.

MATERIALS

Type a "Worksheet: Facing Discrimination, Finding Courage," and make a copy for each student. (See Implementation for questions.) A copy of each of these books that describe children's varied positive responses to different forms of discrimination: *Amazing Grace*, Mary Hoffman (race and gender); *Friends from the Other Side/Amigos Del Otro Lado*, Gloria Anzaldua (a bilingual book, nationality); *Make a Wish, Molly*, Barbara Cohen (anti-Semitism) and *The Rag Coat*, Lauren Mills (class).

Before you do this lesson if they are not in your classroom or school library already, ask your librarian to order these books, if possible, or request them from interlibrary loan. All are excellent books for exploring children's experiences with, and responses to, discrimination. You may have other books you could substitute in this lesson if any one of these are inaccessible. Even though these are picture books, they are still appropriate to use with upper elementary students; they are powerful and accessible to analyze.

IMPLEMENTATION

Part 1

This jigsaw lesson is planned for six groups of four students; adjust according to your class size. Each student in the group will be responsible for a different book. Set up your groups carefully to meet the heterogeneity of your students. *Friends* is written in both English and Spanish. *Amazing Grace* is the easiest book and *Make a Wish, Molly* the longest. Also be aware of particular prejudices students might hold. While you will want to have some read a story in which they'll have to empathize with people about whom they hold prejudices, try to make sure that students without those biases are in the group as well.

Get students into their groups of four. Introduce the lesson by telling them that they will read children's literature to explore ways various characters and their friends responded to discrimination. Then they will think about responding to discrimination in their own lives. Explain that each group member will be responsible for a different book and will report on it to other group members. First, however, they will meet in groups of students reading the same book.

Temporarily break students up into Story Groups—all students reading *The Rag Coat*, for example, get together. They take turns reading the story out loud to each other so everyone gets a turn, clarifying any questions about the plot, characters, and setting as they go along.

When finished reading the story, students individually write a response to "Worksheet: Facing Discrimination: Finding Courage" which is comprised of these questions.

1. How was a young person in the story discriminated against?
2. How did s/he feel? Why?
3. Why was s/he discriminated against?
4. What were his/her responses to the discrimination?
5. How, if at all, did other young people reach out to support the person discriminated against? What about adults?
6. What could other young people have done that they didn't do? What about adults?

When students are finished, they share their responses with each other, check for understanding, and revise as needed.

Part 2   Students return to their original groups. Each briefly tells about the book he read. Each reports answers to the worksheet questions to each other. Inform students that in the large group discussion you will call on anyone to discuss any book, not just the one they read. Then the foursome takes each worksheet question one by one and discusses the similarities and differences in the stories. Then come together as a class.

DISCUSSION
1. Discuss students' responses to the questions on the worksheets; look at similarities and differences in the stories.
2. In some stories young people were discriminated against by someone different from themselves. Why might people discriminate like this?
3. In other stories people were discriminated against by someone in their same social group, although perhaps slightly better off within that group—e.g., Minna. Why might this happen?
4. If the young person discriminated against had support, where did it come from—adults, family, peers, a community? How did that effect her/his response to the discrimination?
5. Some characters gained more strength to deal with the discrimination as the story progressed. Where did the strength come from?
6. What do you think motivated another young person to become an ally, a person who speaks up for someone facing discrimination?

For homework have each student write an essay about a time they have been discriminated against because they were different. How did it feel, what did they do, what did others do, what would they have liked others to do? If you use a peer review writing program remind students of the criteria for their writing.

Part 3   The next day ask students to read their stories to each other in their groups of four. After all have read their stories, ask students to discuss the same questions that they did for the characters in the stories.

If you use a peer review writing program, have children give feedback on each other's work for a rewrite. Otherwise collect essays and come together for class discussion.

DISCUSSION

1. What kind of discrimination did you write about? What kinds of differences made you targets of prejudice? How is that similar to, or different from, characters in the stories we read?
2. What are the similarities and differences in the feelings you felt in these situations?
3. In what kinds of ways did you respond? To what degree were the responses helpful or not? Why?
4. If at least part of your response to the discrimination you faced was constructive, where did the commitment, skills, or support for that come from?
5. In what different ways did others nearby try to support you, if they did, when you were being discriminated against? How did you feel about that?
6. What would have been helpful for others to do that they didn't do?
7. What are some difficulties in being an ally to someone when they're being discriminated against? How could we lessen some of those difficulties?
8. What are some ways you've found courage to act against discrimination? How can we do that in the future?

GOING FURTHER

1. Students can read novels that depict young people standing up to discrimination. Some we recommend include: *Journey Home*, Yoshiko Uchida (racism against the Japanese Americans after WWII); *Liddy*, Katherine Paterson (class, labor organizing in Lowell, Mass. 1840's); *Maudie, Me and the Dirty Book*, Betty Miles (ageism, among other issues, contemporary); *Roll of Thunder, Hear My Cry*, Mildred Taylor (racism against African Americans 1930s)
2. Students can research the sources of the oppression that young people faced in the books in the lesson and supplemental books and how people *by working together* tried/are trying to change them. For example they could research the oppression of coal miners in Appalachia (*The Rag Coat*) or the practices of the border police (*Friends from the Other Side*) and so forth. They can then report to the class.

SAY IT SO THEY'LL HEAR IT

OBJECTIVES

To help students develop strategies for sharing their learning about stereotypes and the "isms" in a way that others will hear rather than reject.
To help students develop general skills for sharing opinions, convictions, and information in a positive way.

MATERIALS

Copies of "Worksheet: Strategies for Confronting Stereotypes and 'Isms,'" p. 343; paper and pencils; video-tape equipment, if available.

IMPLEMENTATION

Discuss with students what they have learned about stereotypes and discrimination due to gender, class, race, age, religion, sexual orientation, ability, and language. Discuss how, when we make discoveries, we often want to share our excitement with others. Explain that one of the purposes of this unit is to encourage this, since social change is brought about when we get others thinking about promoting equality. Therefore it is important to develop positive strategies for sharing what we have learned. Emphasize that though it is not our fault that we have been taught stereotypes and the "isms," it is our responsibility to unlearn some of that—which is hard and takes practice.

Tell students that although we sometimes feel frightened about addressing stereotypes and "isms," with practice we develop judgment about when and how to do this. The role-plays are meant to provide that practice!

Step One. The class brainstorms the sorts of situations in which they could confront someone who has just said or done something racist, classist, ageist, or sexist or otherwise discriminatory. Make a list on the board. If you need to get them going, give examples from your school or community. The class picks one example. Follow the guidelines on role-playing (p. 70) and act out the scene. Debrief carefully.

In the discussion of the situation, encourage students to discuss alternative ways of communicating. With students, make up a list of Communication Guidelines for such situations. Do and discuss several situations as a class.

Examples of Communication Guidelines

1. Since you want people to listen to you, don't say anything in a way that attacks or puts them down.
2. Share your learning and opinions in a way that makes someone else feel glad to be learning something new.
3. Work with the other person to develop ideas of very practical ways to change.
4. Add new ideas, rather than just criticize what's there.

Step Two. Hand out "Worksheet: Strategies for Confronting Stereotypes and 'Isms.'" Thoroughly discuss the four types of strategies listed.
1. Provide correct information.
2. State how you feel (use feeling messages).
3. Encourage a group of people to speak up together.
4. Take creative, cooperative action.

Don't give out the role-plays yet, but give concrete examples of each strategy, using other examples.

Divide students into groups and assign two groups to each of the situations on the Worksheet. Assign about two or three students to situations 1 and 2, four students to situation 3 and three students to situation 4. Have groups plan a role play to dramatize each situation, making sure each person has a part.

Students present their role plays to the class for situation #1.

DISCUSSION
1. Why is it hard for people to look at their behavior that may be biased? Why is it hard for you to have others give you feedback about your behavior?
2. What people or kinds of people do you find it easier to address in these types of situations? Why? Which are harder? Why?
3. Now that you've done the role-plays, do you have some more helpful suggestions? How does role-playing help you find these? List them with our initial Guidelines.
4. In what ways is group action easier and more effective than individual action?
5. In which type of situation is strategy most effective? Why?
6. Which strategies are you most comfortable with? Why?

FROM FEAR TO POWER

OBJECTIVES
To have students examine internal blocks to acting for change.
To learn a strategy for feeling more confidence and power in order to stand up for one's feelings and beliefs.
To experience peer support for speaking up for equality.

MATERIALS
Type a "Worksheet: Recess Fantasy," and make 1 copy per student (see Implementation for the questions); copies of "Worksheet: Power Statement Contract," p. 344.

IMPLEMENTATION   Explain to students they will be practicing a way to feel confident in challenging stereotypes and "isms." It is best to do "Say It So They'll Hear It," p. 314, first.

Tell students they will be participating in a fantasy activity. Explain that you will begin a story and they should imagine it in their minds. You will stop the story and they should finish it in their own imaginations. Answer any questions about what is going to happen.

Tell students to get in a relaxed position. Tell them not to answer the questions aloud. Direct the fantasy as follows:

> Close your eyes and try to relax as much as possible. [Wait ten seconds.] Get the thoughts of the day out of your mind. Concentrate on your breathing. Now I want you to imagine that you and a group of your friends are on their way out to recess. Who's with you? [Wait five seconds.] How are you feeling? Picture this in your mind. [Wait ten seconds.] Someone in the group mentions black people. Another person says, "I can't stand black people, they rot." [Substitute Puerto Ricans, kids from X neighborhood; gay youth and so forth—whatever is most relevant to your group of students.] Take as much time as you need to finish the fantasy in your mind. What happens next? [Wait one minute or more.] When you have finished your fantasy, slowly open your eyes.

Each student then fills out the "Worksheet: Recess Fantasy." It includes the following questions:

1. What feelings did you have at the very beginning of the story?
2. What feelings did you have when your friend made the negative comment?
3. What different ideas went through your mind when your friend made that comment?
4. In your fantasy, what did you say or do, if anything, after your friend made that comment?

With partners, they read or tell their fantasy and share Worksheet responses. Then come together for discussion.

DISCUSSION
1. First talk about each of the questions on the Worksheet.
2. Sometimes when we are trying to decide what to do, there are two different voices in our heads having a conversation. This is called an "internal dialogue." For example, if you just earned a dollar, your internal dialogue might go like this:

> Voice-in-your-head #1: Oh great, I'll buy a candy bar!
> Voice-in-your head #2: Wait, save the dollar and you can get something you really need!
> Voice #1: I'm hungry now.
> Voice #2: If I buy candy Mom will tell me I wasted my money and I'll get cavities on top of it all.

Think back to your fantasy. What was your internal dialogue when you were trying to decide what to do in response to the remark of your friend? Who can tell us about that?

3. When we are making a decision about whether we will stand up for our beliefs, one of our voices is sometimes a scared voice that gives us "Fear Messages." Let's make a list on the board of the "Fear Messages" we sometimes give ourselves. For example: "If I say something, my friends won't like me anymore." "What X said isn't right, but I'm afraid my words will get mixed up." "I should speak up, but oh well, it won't make a difference anyway." "I might get attacked and hurt; it's not worth the risk!" In many cases Fear Messages serve to keep us from finding the courage to act on our beliefs. In some schools and neighborhoods, however, they may be realistic messages that keep us out of danger.

4. Tell the students that, instead of "Fear Messages," they can give themselves "Power Statements." These are voices that give you power and remind you how important it is to stand up for what's fair. Make a list of "Power Statements" on the board. For example: "It's important to speak up for what's fair no matter what others think." "I *can* speak clearly and can get people to stop and think." "I can make a difference!"

5. What can *we* gain by speaking up for equality?

Finally, students form support pairs. They fill out a "Worksheet: Power Statement Contract" with each other and sign it. (Remind students to use the Communication Guidelines. Feeling powerful is only part of being effective.) Have a few students share their "Worksheet: Power Statement Contract" with the class. Give them encouragement. Set a date when they'll report back to their partners and the class.

Speak Up

In Germany they first came for the Communists and I didn't speak up because I wasn't a Communist. Then they came for the Jews and I didn't speak up because I wasn't a Jew. Then they came for the trade unionists and I didn't speak up because I wasn't a trade unionist. Then they came for the Catholics and I didn't speak up because I was a Protestant. Then they came for me and no one was left to speak up.

Martin Niemoller, an activist pastor in the German resistance

---

YOU HAVE TO MAKE DECISIONS

OBJECTIVES   To help students realize that frequently they are confronted with moral dilemmas concerning issues of equality.

To encourage students to look at these dilemmas in terms of what they have learned and to make conscious decisions that promote equality.

MATERIALS   Copies of "Worksheet: Rebekah's Journal," continued, p. 345–346; paper for additional entries; pencils.

IMPLEMENTATION   This follows the lesson, "A Girl on Our Team," p. 85. Do that one first. Hand out copies of the Worksheet. Students staple on additional sheets to create a notebook.

Discuss with students their sense of Rebekah from the lesson in the earlier chapter. Have them read the four new entries for this lesson. Then have each student write journal entries as follow-ups to each of these new entries. (Tell them Rebekah has been learning about sexism, racism, class bias, and age discrimination in school. She is trying to put what she learned into practice in her life.) Next, get together in small groups. Students share what they wrote and get ideas from each other.

Re-divide into heterogeneous groups of three to five students. Each group picks one worksheet entry from this lesson (be sure that each entry is picked at least once) and thinks of alternative ways of acting in the situation described—as many ways as possible. Remind them they, like Rebekah, are trying to put what they've learned about equality into practice in their lives. They should think of the possible results of their actions and decide which of their options seems most sensible and fair. Students can either share their favorite ideas or act them out for the whole class.

DISCUSSION   **1.** When you were writing journal entries, what criteria did you use for deciding what to do or say? What values were most important to you? What worried you most?

2. Which situations were easy for you? In what ways? Which situations were harder? Why?

3. What did you think others—your friends, family, or adults—could do to help you in these situations? How could you ask for that help?

4. What could you do to help others in each situation? How could you offer that help?

5. These situations involve acting or not acting on values that support equality. Think of some similar situations you find at school, in your community, or at home. List them. What can you do in each case?

6. Tell about a time when you acted on values that supported equality. How did you feel? What did you learn?

Section B   *Making Changes at School*

CALENDARS

OBJECTIVES   To encourage a multicultural appreciation of history and celebrations through learning new information.

To provide opportunities for critical decision making.

To have students share their learning with others in succinct ways by creating a group product that can be distributed more widely than the classroom.

MATERIALS   Large sheets of good-quality paper; rulers and yardsticks; pencils, paint or markers; books with information about holidays from many cultures; biographies of American women and people of color (collections works well for this); school calendars from your own and other systems; calendars from specific groups—see page 216, "Why Are We Off from School Today?" for ideas for these.

IMPLEMENTATION   Divide students into small groups. Each group takes several calendars collected from other school systems and from other specific groups. Each group also takes at least one library book with holiday information and one or more biographies. Each group lists several holidays it would like to add to the school calendar that acknowledge the contributions of diverse peoples to our cultures, history and customs. For each holiday the group writes a few clear sentences of explanation. See p. 314 for some ideas to get you going.

Groups share their selections and discuss the process and results. Questions to ask include:

(a) What criteria did your group use to choose new holidays to add to our calendar? Did you keep the same criteria the whole time or did these change as you worked?

(b) Were you able to find events to commemorate a range of Americans? What groups of people were most represented? Were there any you couldn't find? Or couldn't find much about?

(c) In what ways was it easy or hard to come to consensus on what holidays to add?

Students graph these additional choices to check for ethnicities and gender represented. They may then wish to make changes or additions. Students then begin work to create a calendar for the upcoming year. The teacher or a student can create a monthly grid, by hand, or on a computer, with the days of the week written in. Leave space for the name of the month and for students to number the month correctly. Be sure there is room for students to write in particular events.

Twelve students can be assigned one month each. They write in the name of the month, number the days, and write in the chosen holidays and other events. Another twelve students each get a month for a picture. Students may want to collaboratively decide which event to commemorate in the picture, may want to do several, or may want to leave this up to the artists. Additional students can create the cover for the calendar and pages to go at the end which give the more detailed explanations of holidays that have been added. If you have fewer than 26 students you can double up on some jobs.

Some Dates to Celebrate

January 21, 1974—Court decides school districts must provide bilingual education for all non-English speaking students
February 15, 1820—Susan B. Anthony's birthday
February 27, 1973—Occupation of Wounded Knee, SD
February (date dependent on lunar calendar)—beginning of Ramadan, Islamic Holy Month
March 8—International Women's Day (commemorates a 1908 Women's March for Suffrage in NYC)
March 30, 1870—15th amendment, African American men gain right to vote
April (date dependent on lunar calendar)—beginning of Passover (goes for 8 days)
April—Yom heShoah, Holocaust Day of Remembrance, commemorates the Warsaw ghetto uprising which was at the beginning of Passover.
April 11, 1968—Civil Rights Act becomes law
May 1—International Workers' Day, begun in 1886 with strike for 8 hour work day
May 19, 1925—Malcolm X's birthday
June 27, 1969—Gay Pride Day, anniversary of Stonewall uprising
July 2, 1946—Bill passed allowing Indians from India to become US citizens
July 19, 1848—1st women's rights convention in Seneca Falls, NY, launches US feminist movement
July 26, 1990—Americans with Disabilities Act signed into law
August 8, 1988—Japanese Americans win reparations from W.W.II internment camps
August 26, 1920—Ratification of 19th amendment, US women gain right to vote
September 8, 1965—strike of Mexican and Filipino farmworkers that leads to founding of United Farmworkers Union
September (dates dependent on lunar calendar, always 9 days apart)—Rosh Hashanah (Jewish New Year) and Yom Kippur (Jewish Day of Atonement)
October 11—National Coming Out Day
October 12—Dia de la Raza (Day of the Race)—struggle for justice by Indian/Spanish peoples of Western Hemisphere
December 1, 1955—Rosa Parks arrested, triggering Montgomery Bus Boycott
December 17, 1943—Chinese Exclusion Act repealed
December 26—first of seven days of Kwanzaa
February—Black History Month
March—Women's History Month
September—Hispanic Awareness Month
October—Native American Heritage Month; Gay and Lesbian History Month

Name of Month						
Sun	Mon	Tue	Wed	Thurs	Fri	Sat

Calendars can be bound with a GBC binding machine if your school district owns one, or sewn with yarn and punched holes. These calendars make holiday gifts as well as excellent products for classroom fund raising.

DISCUSSION
1. In what ways was it easy or hard to come to a classroom consensus on which holidays to use?
2. Are there some types of holidays you think should exist, in support of a more egalitarian world, that you didn't find? What might these be? How could we add those to our group calendar?
3. How do you want to distribute the new calendar? What people do you want to have receive it? Why?

GOING FURTHER Celebrate at least one of these new holidays in your classroom and perhaps elsewhere in the school. Suggest that students may want to celebrate it at home? Have students write up more detailed reports on some of the holidays, including suggestions for appropriate activities and reasons for celebration. Share these with others.

Helping Your Community Know about Diverse Holidays

The Arlington Advocate, a weekly community newspaper in Arlington, MA prints a "Diversity Calendar" each month listing holidays of a range of cultures. The column is prepared by Arlington Vision 2020 Diversity Task Group, a local group committed to "honoring the rich diversity in their community." They have created this column using many of the calendars referred to in the "Materials" section above. Would your newspaper be interested in such a column? Perhaps your students might want to take responsibility for this.

Who Decides on Holidays?

Students can think about how holidays become official. Thanksgiving and Martin Luther King's birthday are examples of holidays voted on by Congress. The government can also move holidays, e.g., making Washington's birthday so it is always on a Monday to create a three day weekend. There are unofficial holidays that commemorate important events such as a celebration for ratification of the 19th Amendment giving women the right to vote or birthdays of important people such as Malcolm X. Other holidays are based on religious observations of different religious groups. The government can choose, as the U.S. government has for Christmas, to make these national holidays also. Still other holidays are decided upon by groups of people. For example National Coming Out Day was chosen by lesbian and gay people. There are a number of other categories to look for that your students might find interesting. For example, Kwanzaa was created by African Americans based on African traditions.

KEEP YOUR RIGHTS*

OBJECTIVES To give students information about the Title IX law.
To help students examine their school for compliance with Title IX.
To give students strategies to use this law to bring about an anti-sexist atmosphere in their school.

MATERIALS Copies of "Worksheet: Title IX," p. 347; "Worksheet: Situation Cards" cut up, p. 348; paper and pencils.

IMPLEMENTATION *Step One.* Post a large copy of these Title IX regulations.

1. A school system must have a policy saying it does not discriminate on basis of sex. This must be printed on school mailings and in the newspaper.

---

*Material for this lesson was adapted from *A Student Guide to Title IX*, by Myra Sadker (oop).

2. A school system must have a Title IX coordinator to see that it follows the regulations.
3. A school system must have a method for people to file complaints and get answers to those.
4. A school system must do a self-evaluation about sex discrimination and make necessary changes.
5. If school systems ask for money from the federal government, they must fill out a form saying that they don't discriminate on the basis of sex.

Discuss this with the class. Make sure they understand the vocabulary and the concepts.

Divide student into groups of four. Hand out Worksheets and go over them with the groups. Answer questions. Use examples to clarify. Hand out one Situation Card to each group. Instruct each group to read its card and decide if any Title IX regulations have been violated. Each group prepares a short presentation for the class, explaining the situation and what regulations either have or haven't been followed. Correct answers are at the end of the lesson.

Step Two. The next day, ask each group to think of a way that your school system has been active in support of these regulations. Working in groups, write letters of praise to the people responsible. For example, if a guidance counselor is good about encouraging boys to be in chorus, she gets a praise letter. Or if a physical education teacher actively supports girls' participation on the intramural basketball team, he gets a praise letter.

Then have groups think of a way that the school is not actively supporting these regulations. Have them work out a strategy for taking action. They could plan to write letters, make phone calls, make visits, enlist their parents' support, and so on. If groups have trouble, give them help or brainstorm as a class.

Make a classroom poster of guidelines to follow in making complaints. The class can generate these or you can present them with the following:

1. Remember that counselors, teachers, and administrators may be well-meaning but unaware of their responsibilities, or unaware that they are behaving in a discriminatory way.
2. Call this behavior to the adult's attention in a way that is polite and shows you are knowledgeable. Be positive and helpful.
   If that doesn't work:
3. Go to the Title IX coordinator for the district. Share your concerns, with detailed information, and ask for changes.
   If that doesn't work:
4. Get help from your parents and other students and other adults. File a complaint, using the correct procedure.
   If that doesn't work:
5. File a complaint with: Director, Office for Civil Rights, U.S. Department of Education, 330 C St., S.W., Washington, D.C. 20202. Include your name, person(s) who has been discriminated against, school district name, date, and explanation of what happened.

Finally, discuss the whole lesson with the class.

DISCUSSION
1. Did you know about this regulation before doing the lesson? Why or why not?
2. What did you discover about our school district?
3. What reactions did you get to your compliment letters? To your concerns?
4. In what ways were people willing to help bring about change for gender equality? In what ways were they not?

Answers to Title IX Situation Cards: Rose—not violated; Gregg—violated; Dan—violated; Gilah—violated; Gurtney—not violated; Ming—not violated.

It's Your Right

Excellent ideas for follow-up to this lesson for older students can be found in "It's Your Right" by Joyce Kaser and Susan Shaffer, available from the Mid Atlantic Equity Consortium. Geared for high school students enrolling in a vocational course nontraditional for their sex, this resource raises some Title IX issues relevant to upper elementary and middle school students and staff as well.

Some situations that fall under Title IX include:
- a deliberate and consistent pattern of restricting the participation of one gender in class discussion
- a deliberate and consistent pattern of a teacher praising or grading those of one gender higher than another
- sexual harassment
- a counselor not informing a student of her/his rights under Title IX after s/he complains about discrimination

---

RELEARNING ABOUT NATIVE AMERICANS

OBJECTIVES
To give students some correct information about Native Americans.
To help students learn to look critically at what they are taught about Native Americans, encourage them to reject that which is discriminatory, and seek out correct information.

MATERIALS
Guidelines chart on large oaktag; books (see Bibliography).

IMPLEMENTATION
Some of the ideas in this activity and the guidelines listed below come from *Unlearning "Indian" Stereotypes*, an excellent resource now out of print. It might be available through interlibrary loan systems.

Part 1: Correcting Stereotypes
Make an oaktag chart for "Guidelines on Native Americans" and post it.

Guidelines on Native Americans

1. Don't give the idea that all Native American nations live or lived in the same manner, with the same housing, dress, customs.
2. Don't say "Mohawk Indians" which is repetitive (like "French Europeans"). Just "Mohawks" or "Navajos" is enough.
3. If talking about customs of the Cheyenne or Seneca or any specific people, say that, rather than Native Americans in general.
4. Do not use words that describe Native Americans in ways that are frightening.
5. Do not use sentences such as "Acting like a bunch of wild Indians," "Indian giver," "Sitting Indian style," "Walking Indian file."
6. Don't use an alphabet chart with "I is for Indian," if your other letters use fruits, or objects for examples.
7. Don't talk about Native Americans only in the past—they are very much a part of today's world.
8. Don't let TV stereotypes go unchallenged.
9. Don't talk about "us" and "them."

Discuss the chart with the class. Look for examples in each area. Post the pictures and stories your class did for "From Feathers to Facts," page 108. Look at these and discuss where these stereotypes come from, in what ways they can be damaging, how they are inaccurate, and what we can do to rid ourselves of them. Discuss with students how their stereotypes of Native peoples have been formed. If students have met any Native Americans discuss with them what they know about them and how they live. Often when children have met only one or two people from any group they tend to think that these people represent the entire group. Caution children to think about the variety of types of people in any other groups they know so they can remember that knowing a Native person doesn't give them information about Native Americans in general.

Many people think of Native Americans as being of all one culture and nation. Help children to see this error by comparing to Europeans. Have them think of a characteristic of a European nation—for example, tulips in Holland. Would they think of all countries of Europe as having tulips growing all around? Now compare to Native Americans. Tipis were a form of housing on the Plains, but not in other areas of the country. Not all Native Americans wore feathered headdresses. Drawing a headdress on all Indians is analogous to drawing yarmulkes on all white people. Some Omaha or Winnebago, for example, would correctly be pictured with headdresses for ceremonies, but this is not correct for all nations of Native Americans, nor for daily wear for any. Encourage students to share information with friends and relatives about these stereotypes.

Part 2: Role-Plays

Here are a few ideas for role-plays and dramatization. Develop more with your students. *Adam Norwall.* Adam Norwall, an Ojibway dressed in Native clothing and traveled by jet to Italy in 1973. When he got off the plane he said "In the name of the Indian people, I claim the right of discovery and take possession of this land." He said that since Columbus claimed to have discovered America when Indians were here, he could claim Italy.

Processing questions can include the following: How might you feel as Italian people? How might Adam Norwall have felt? How might Native Americans have felt when Columbus "discovered" America? What new ideas do you have about Native Americans because of this role-play?

The Settlers Are Landing. Have several children play Native Americans. They stand in the classroom which represents their land. The other students play the roles of white settlers. Each time a small group of them come from the hall (ocean) into the room (land), they represent another boat of settlers. When they arrive, they ask the Native Americans for some land. They agree and give up a section of the room. Other small groups of students from the hall keep coming until the Native Americans are standing in a corner of the classroom.

Discuss with children, "Should the Native Americans give up their space to these new people?" Have children take roles, some as settlers and some Native Americans. Subsequent discussion questions include the following: How did you feel as a Native American? How did you feel as a white settler? What did you learn from this activity?

"I" is for . . .

"Indian" is so frequently found under the letter "I" that one wonders if there is a lack of other words beginning with that letter. No other group is similarly treated: the "I–Indian" is never followed by a "J–Jew" or a "P–Puerto Rican." Nor is it accompanied by an "I–Italian," even though the "I" in Indian and the "I" in Italian have the same sound. Rather, the "I–Indian" coexists with objects–Igloos, Islands, Ink, etc.

From Unlearning "Indian" Stereotypes

Part 3: Research and Reading

There are some good books on Native Americans for children. (See the Bibliography.) Assign students research on topics that will correct stereotypes about Native Americans, or have them read fiction that portrays Native peoples accurately and with dignity.

Recommended Books: A Beginning

For students:

The People Shall Continue, by Simon Ortiz

Children of the Sun: Stories by and about Indian Kids, edited by Adolf and Beverly Hungry Wolf

Happily May I Walk: American Indians and Alaskan Native Today by A.B. Hirschfelder

Rising Voices: Writings of Young Native Americans edited by A.B. Hirschfelder and Beverly Sluger

Women in American Indian Society by Rayna Green

Pueblo Storyteller by Diane Hoyt-Goldsmith

For teachers:

Bury My Heart at Wounded Knee by Dee Brown

Lakota Woman by Mary Crow Dog

Native Roots: How Indians Enriched America by Jack Weatherford

---

GOING FURTHER

Have students put on a role-play for another class; make a bulletin board—Correcting Stereotypes about Native Americans—for the school; or make a book display on fair and unfair portrayals of Native Americans for the PTA book fair.

MAKING LEARNING COOPERATIVE

OBJECTIVE

To have students make cooperative learning materials that support diversity for younger children.

MATERIALS

Recycled materials; fabric; wood; oaktag; paints; and other materials to make games and toys.

IMPLEMENTATION

Introduce the lesson by telling students that one way to encourage cooperation, instead of competition, is by providing children with materials and projects that have them work together. As a class discuss what would make for good cooperative learning materials that would appeal to younger children. Create a group list of guidelines. Then have students think back about what they have learned about equity and diversity and create a second list of guidelines for materials that affirm these values.

Divide students into groups of three or four. Each group discusses possible games or toys that they could make that would *necessitate* younger children playing cooperatively in order to use these. They must also be clear about how these materials support diversity as *an inherent part of their design.*

Come back together as a class and discuss the ideas. Look for practicality, creativity, cooperation, and diversity. Give groups the opportunity to modify their designs after they receive feedback from the class.

When the projects are finished, have students bring them to a daycare center, kindergarten or younger classroom, whatever is appropriate for the materials created. Have students play with the younger children as they explore these new materials. Your students may wish to donate their materials to the daycare center or classroom.

DISCUSSION
1. What did you learn from designing these materials?
2. What aspects of your group's design process were easier? What aspects were harder?
3. Were there some design aspects that you "were stuck on"? How, if at all, did you resolve these?
4. How did the younger children react to playing with these materials?
5. What did you learn from using the materials with them?
6. How would you modify these materials if you were to make them again? Why?

GOING FURTHER
Encourage students to write an article for the local newspaper about this cooperative project.

Synergy

A society that is organized so that the individual can get ahead (accumulate wealth or power) only at the expense of the group is more likely, according to Ruth Benedict, to produce aggression. "Nonaggression occurs," she said, "not because people are unselfish and put social obligations above personal desires, but when social arrangements make the two identical." She called this quality of combining the efforts of the individual to advance the interests of the group synergy, a word which means that the combined action of a number of things produces results greater than the sum of the separate actions.

From *Developing Effective Classroom Groups*, by Gene Stanford

---

NEW WORDS HELP US

OBJECTIVES
To help students see how an egalitarian vocabulary can help them think in a more open-minded way.
To help students develop vocabularies that do not have racist, sexist, classist, ageist or homophobic connotations.
To encourage students to share their learning.

MATERIALS
Paper and pencils; dictionaries; student work saved from the lesson "Black Lies and White Lies," p. 232.

IMPLEMENTATION
First, look back at the earlier lesson. Post the lists the students made for "black" and "white" phrases. Working as a whole class, brainstorm alternative words or phrases for any of those that held positive connotations for white and negative connotations for black. For example, "white lies"—to "small or unimportant lies." If students seem to be getting the idea, have them work in small groups to continue.

In the same groups, students list words that have sexist connotations. These can be of two types—words like "mailman" or "fireman," which use gender-related words to describe all people, and words like "manmade," "manhandle." Allow about ten minutes.

Now the group thinks of one or more alternative words to the sexist ones. Get together as a class and share lists. If groups came up with sexist words but not alternatives, others in the class can help them. List all the original words and phrases and all the new alternatives on paper.

Make a cover for your newly created class dictionary. Make a copy for each student, and others to distribute to other classes in the building. If you have a school newspaper, write a synopsis of this exercise for it. Each week your class can pick one racist or sexist word and its alternative and post both on a central bulletin board.

DISCUSSION

1. What harm does it cause to use words with racist or sexist connotations?
2. How does it help to change these words? How does it change our thinking?
3. For which words was it difficult to think of alternatives? Do you have any ideas why? Why were some words easier?
4. What can you do as an individual, and what can we do as a class, to encourage use of the more egalitarian words?

Alternatives in Language

man	person, human being, people, women and men
"it's not all black and white"	"it's not one extreme or the other"
forefathers or fathers	precursors, ancestors, forebears
black deeds	evil deeds
brotherhood	unity, community
white-wash	cover-up
mankind	human kind
women's lib	women's liberation, feminist movement

A FAIR BOOK FAIR

OBJECTIVES

To have students explore examples of opportunities in school that aren't available to some children because of class discrimination.

To encourage students to examine one example for making a typical school event—the book fair—more accessible to all students, regardless of economic background.

To support students to develop and implement a plan to make such a situation in their school available to all students whatever their class background.

MATERIALS

"Worksheet: A Fair Book Fair," p. 349, cut in 4 sections.

IMPLEMENTATION

Part 1

Ask students to share some things they've learned so far about class bias from lessons in *Open Minds to Equality*. Raise key points yourself if students omit them. Ask each to take two minutes to think about examples in school they've experienced or observed in which an opportunity costs money that might make it hard for some students to participate. Ask students to jot the examples down on a piece of paper—no names necessary.

Discuss with students how difficult it often is for young people and adults to talk with others about how much money their families have. People have a range of reactions. In fact, some families believe such discussion is inappropriate. Sometimes people from low income backgrounds believe the myth that if you work hard you get ahead. They often blame themselves, as others also blame them, for not having more money rather than understanding how class discrimination limits peoples' opportunities. Sometimes low income people are angry because they understand how they are affected by an economic system that privileges the wealthy. Sometimes people with higher incomes may feel better about themselves because of their class status. Encourage students not to blame themselves or others for their situations. Our task will be to think of ways to make school more fair.

Divide students into partnerships that cross economic class lines. Ask students to share the examples they thought of with their partners. Then partners talk together and add more examples if possible. Call on any students to share an example from their partnership. Make a list of these on newsprint or the board. Tell students that sometimes there are ways to change these situations to make them more fair for everybody. Before looking at their school, they'll look at another example.

Part 2   Join partnerships together into heterogeneous groups of four. Give each student a section of the worksheet, "A Fair Book Fair." Students read to themselves, and then, in order, read out loud.

When finished, have students briefly discuss their thoughts and feelings about the book fair at Barry's school and the action plan his class came up with. If you have a book fair at your school ask them to discuss their thoughts and feelings about that.

DISCUSSION
1. What feelings might young people have when they can't get any/many books at the book fair when they want to?
2. Would they be apt to share these feelings? Why or why not?
3. Some students say "We shouldn't care that some students can't afford things. It's not our problem." Think about what we've learned about class bias. How might you answer them?
4. What are your feelings and thoughts about the action plan Barry's class came up with? Why?
5. What could be other alternatives to try to make the book fair more fair?
6. If you have a book fair in your school, discuss some of these questions in relationship to your book fair.

Share and Share Alike

In one school we know about in Somerville, Massachusetts, when an event costing money is coming up the teacher sends home a note to parents telling how much the event will cost and asks them to send what they can afford in an anonymous sealed envelop. Some send in the exact amount, some more to help support another child, and some less. If enough money isn't raised, the teacher sends home a second note asking those who can afford it to contribute more, as possible. Any extra money that comes in is saved for the next event. This system works very well and no one feels better or worse than others because of their financial status.

Part 3   Now go back to the list the class made of opportunities in school that cost money that might make it hard for some students to participate in. Examples might be things like: 1. being in the band because students must rent their musical instrument or 2. participating in field trips which students' families have to pay for. Explain to students that sometimes schools have a fund for financial aid, yet many students' parents may not want their children to accept that money because of family or cultural values.

The class picks one of its brainstormed ideas to try to make it more available to all students, just as Barry's class worked on the book fair. Suggest the following three steps for any change project.

1. Define the Problem/Gather Information
2. Study Information/Plan Action
3. Take Action/Evaluate

Given the difficulties discussed earlier about talking about money, discuss with students ways to gather information that will build trust and foster honesty. As the teacher, be acutely aware of the demographics of your classroom and set appropriate limits on what kinds of information gathering students do. For example, if exploring the band issue, the class might decide to interview students who never signed up for band and to have the interviewers be students who themselves were never in band. Or they might decide that they would get the most accurate information through anonymous surveys. You may need to advise them given your sensitivity about these issues in your school and community.

Help students organize committees to take responsibility for the different steps in the action project, just as Barry's class did. Make sure the steps are well structured with a time line so that the project can be accomplished in a focused and organized way. Help them discuss and work through the inevitable unexpected problems that come with any change effort. Provide support for them to evaluate their change project and summarize what they learned.

GOING FURTHER Community meetings are excellent forums in which students can learn to take responsibility for identifying problems and planning solutions. A fine description of guidelines for community meetings and a description of how they are used to foster student responsibility and change projects can be found in an interview with Karen Cathers, "The Cooperative Classroom: The Context for Cooperative Learning," in *Cooperative Learning*, Vol. 14, #2, winter 1994. Ms. Cathers also describes exciting action projects her students developed.

Section C *Changing Our Texts and Books*

TEXTBOOK ALERT

OBJECTIVE To give students an opportunity to carry out small action projects concerning biased textbooks.

MATERIALS Paper and pencils; textbooks analyzed in Chapter 8.

IMPLEMENTATION Remind students of their work analyzing textbooks in "Our Textbooks: Are They Fair?" p. 218. Tell students they will have a chance to take action to begin to alert people to bias in their textbooks, and to change this. There are three possible action projects. Either divide into three groups and have one group work on each, or decide on one activity for the whole class.

1. *Warning Labels.* Just as cigarettes have a warning label, "This product is dangerous to your health," so too textbooks can have a label in the front jacket, "This book requires careful thinking about the effects of . . . because." Make copies with that statement on top. For each text, students complete the label. For example, "This book requires careful thinking about the effects of sexism because women scientists are not shown," "because American Indian culture isn't represented fairly." Once students have agreed upon labels for each text, tape them in the text or make copies for texts of multiple copies. Give labels to other classes using the same texts.
2. *Equality Textbook List.* Students go over the texts they've analyzed and make a list of those texts in each subject area that either aren't biased or are least biased. Stu-

dents make an Equality Textbook List of such books and distribute to other teachers in the district.

3. *Letters to Publishers.* Students write to publishers of biased texts, explaining and asking for changes. Students write praise letters to publishers of textbooks that promote equality.

Fourth Graders Make Big Changes!

A number of years ago a fourth-grade class in Maryland did a project that brought changes to many other fourth-grade classes throughout their district. Here's what they did.

The class learned to analyze textbooks to discover examples of racism and sexism. Some students got so good at it that they took on a special project. They gathered all the fourth-grade textbooks used in the whole district and examined them for examples of race and sex bias. These students wrote a report about what they found and made copies of it. They distributed the report to all the other fourth-grade classes in the school district. Other teachers and students then learned to pinpoint materials that didn't portray women and people of color equally. That's a big change, and fourth-graders take the credit!

FINDING BETTER BOOKS

OBJECTIVE To give students experience and tools for choosing books that promote equality.

MATERIALS Use of library; paper and pencils; copies of "Worksheet: Review on Books," pp. 229–230, enough for at least four per student.

IMPLEMENTATION This lesson is a follow-up of "Read Me a Story" p. 226, which should be done first. Tell students that since they have learned to analyze books for equality, they now will try to find books that promote equality, and share that information with others. Hand out a Worksheet to each student, and have extras available.

If students have access to a library, they go in pairs or small groups and pick what they think might be books that promote equality to bring back to the classroom. Otherwise collect books yourself. (See Bibliography.) Still in pairs or groups, they check each book according to the criteria and fill out Worksheets. If students did "Read Me a Story" with their parents, encourage them to do this lesson with them as well.

Display the books, together with the Worksheets, around your classroom. Have students bring other books that promote equality to class to share. If you do book orders from paperback companies, ask students to review the books that are offered by these criteria.

As a class, prepare an annotated bibliography of egalitarian books. Give copies to your school librarian, children's librarian at the public library, other teachers or parents. Involve parents actively in this lesson if they participated in "Read Me a Story."

DISCUSSION
1. How hard was it to find books that promote equality? Did you have to look through many to find some that meet these standards? Did you have any method for picking?
2. Did you find some books that actively fight stereotypes? Were they written by the same authors? Published by the same publishers?

3. Were certain stereotypes countered better than others? If so, which ones?
4. Were there any "isms" for which you couldn't find books that were fair? If so, why do you think that is?

Source of Children's Books That Promote Equality

"Everyone's Kids Books," 23 Elliott St., Brattleboro, Vermont 05301 1-800-473-0804. Send for their newsletter that has an annotated listing of high quality, multiracial and non-sexist books, as well as books for teachers and parents. Mail-order service is very efficient and bookstore staff extremely helpful.

. . . AND WE WROTE THEM OURSELVES

OBJECTIVES   To challenge students to create stories that actively promote equality.
To give students the opportunity to share their learning with others in a way that is creative, enjoyable and constructive.

MATERIALS   Copies of "Worksheet: Book Writing—Criteria for Equality Checklist," p. 350; unlined paper; pencils; pens; markers; crayons; dental floss; large needles; cardboard; fabric; wallpaper samples; glues; scissors; papercutter; books on book-binding.

IMPLEMENTATION   Review "Read Me a Story," p. 226. If you haven't done those activities with the children, take time to do them now.

Students can do this activity independently, in pairs, or in small groups. Allow students to choose. Each student or group of students writes a story for younger children that fosters equality and cooperation. Review "Worksheet: Criteria for Equality" before students begin working. If starting from scratch is too difficult, the students can take a typical stereotypical fairytale, like Cinderella, and rewrite it according to the criteria.

After students have written their rough drafts they proofread for errors in mechanics and structure. They then exchange stories and proofread each other's stories for these errors.

Students then take their own stories back and proofread them for stereotyping, While any one story doesn't have to address *all* forms of equality in a positive way, it shouldn't be biased about any. Use "Worksheet: Book Writing—Criteria for Equality." Again they trade stories and Worksheets and proofread each other's. Collect drafts and check for errors and stereotyping. Then return to students, to copy over if needed.

Divide students into groups of eight to twelve. Have each group of students read the stories aloud. They listen to see if the stories will be interesting to younger children. Check for a well-developed plot, setting, character and good word-choice.

Look through books on book-binding. Again, students may work independently or with others. They create their books, bind them, and copy over their stories, leaving room for illustrations. Students can work in their independent work time to finish illustrating their books. When the books are finished, students will read them to younger classes. First discuss or role-play ways of answering young children who respond to the nonstereotypical nature of the books. For example, role play answering responses like, "Women can't be electricians," to find out which are most effective.

DISCUSSION

1. What were some hard parts of this project? (You may need to give examples such as "thinking of a plot," "being careful not to have any sexist words," "making it mixed culturally.")
2. What were some easy parts?
3. Did you find yourself unintentionally putting in anything that was racist, sexist, classist, ageist? How did you feel about that? What did you do about it?
4. Were you basing your stories on any real incidents in life? Why or why not? Did you base them on books you have read which are multicultural?
5. How did younger children react to your stories? Give specific examples of what they liked and didn't like.
6. How would you change your story for another time?

CHANGE THAT CLASS(IC) BIAS

OBJECTIVES

To hear and examine an example of a story that challenges class bias.
To develop a story and presentation that counters stereotypes of lower or working class people.

MATERIALS

A copy of *New Life: New Room* by June Jordan (this is in many school libraries or may be ordered on interlibrary loan); paper and pencils; materials for skits such as story boards, camera and filmstrip projector, video camera.

IMPLEMENTATION

Part One. Ask students to review what class bias is and give examples of ways lower income people are sometimes portrayed or stereotyped. If you did, "Find that Class(ic) Bias," p. 220, ask them to talk about what they remember from it.

Now ask students to think of a family with two parents and three or four children who live in a small two bedroom apartment. If your students know what a housing project is, you may want to add that to your description. Ask students to think of stereotypes some people might have of that family in that situation. List these on the board. Note: If you have low income students in your class who live in tight housing situations and others who are better off financially, you will want to think about the impact of that as you frame this lesson.

Talk with students about different reasons some authors write realistic stories about low income people affected by class discrimination. They may be writing stories based in their own lives, or writing for children who live these lives, or writing to counter negative stereotypes, or writing to help economically better off children learn about the lives of others. Often these stories point to the resourcefulness and creativity of people confronted with difficult living or working situations.

Over the next few days read *New Life: New Room* aloud to your class. As you go along, discuss the characters in the story and their various responses to their financially difficult situation. By the end of the story, be sure you have discussed many of the questions listed below.

DISCUSSION

1. Describe the Robinson family. How are they like or unlike your family?
2. Choose several adjectives that you feel best describe each of the members of the family.
3. The Robinsons are probably working class. What information is there in the story to help you know this?
4. Why did the Robinsons have to stay in their small apartment even though another child was being born?
5. What do you think should be done about the fact that there isn't enough housing for poor and low income people in the United States? What do you think should be done about homeless people having no housing?

6. How did the Robinson family use creativity and intelligence to deal with a difficult situation?
7. How have you used your creativity to deal with a situation where there wasn't enough to go around?
8. How did the Robinson family compare with the stereotypes our class listed at the beginning of this lesson?
9. How is the author of this story countering stereotypes through her work?

Part Two. Tell students that it is now their turn to develop a story that counteracts stereotypes about low income people. Divide students into groups of two to four students. First ask them to imagine a family that makes hardly enough money to live on. Then ask them to think of a problem this family might face because of unequal opportunities and resources. Finally, ask them to come up with a creative solution to this problem that is cooperative and includes people making changes in the conditions that cause their problem. Tell students they can involve more people in the solution than the original family. Remember that how you frame this assignment will depend on the economic situations of those in your classroom and whether this scenario is reality for none of your students, some of your students, or many of your students. In any case remind students to check their stories to be sure that they avoid perpetuating stereotypes of low income people.

When each group has decided on the problem and on a creative, cooperative solution, have them tell this to other groups. Other groups should be alert for stereotypes. They listen to make sure the families are shown in realistic, positive ways. Writing groups then consider this feedback in making revisions in their stories. Also have students identify the role that nonstereotypical literature plays in bringing about social change.

Part Three. According to the resources you have available, ask your class to decide if they want to present their stories in the form of skits, filmstrips, story-boards, or videos. If your class creates skits or videos, provide practice time. After that, if the class is making a video tape it. If the class is making a filmstrip they will need time to create their drawings and perhaps an audio tape to accompany these. Then have your class present the skit, or show the video or filmstrip, to other classes. Have one student explain the purpose of the presentation to the audience, specifically as it relates to countering class bias in stories. Follow the presentation with a discussion with the viewing class. If your class designs story boards, provide them with large sheets of paper for their drawings and narratives. Post these in a common space in your school with a title like "Changing That Class Bias." Include a written description of the purpose of the project.

GOING FURTHER You may want to continue to work in this area with other appropriate picture books. Ezra Jack Keats, Eloise Greenfield and Vera Williams are authors who write stories portraying low income people in positive and empowering ways. We also suggest *Wanda's Roses* by Pat Brisson, and *All Joseph Wanted* by Ruth Radin. Consult the bibliography for chapter books with a more complex look into class and classism.

Section D *Making an Impact on the Media*

TV TURNABOUTS

OBJECTIVE To help students develop a sensitivity to what is nonstereotypic advertising and to design a project accordingly.

MATERIALS Paper and pencils; possibly props and costumes.

IMPLEMENTATION

"we've got a lot in common!!!"

FDA ALL the WAY!!!

* Future Dishwashers of America

Divide students into groups of three to four. Each group brainstorms on a list of television advertisements that are discriminatory—ageist, racist, sexist, or classist and so forth—overtly or subtly.

Each group picks one of its ideas to dramatize in a new way. (Check to see that each group has picked a different advertisement.) Ask the children to create an advertisement, using the same product, but with a script that does not put down any groups of people.

Get together as a class and review what you have learned so far about stereotypes, discrimination, and the "isms." Develop guidelines for television advertisements that foster equality and are not stereotypical. Small groups may then make modifications in their scripts. After rehearsal, each group performs its advertisement for the class. Then discuss it.

Another version is to have the class brainstorm on new products that people truly need, not luxury items, as they might be advertised on TV. Instead of rehearsing these, have students volunteer to act out advertisements in an impromptu manner.

DISCUSSION

1. How easy or difficult was the process of thinking of stereotypical advertisements? Could you think of only a few? Many? Why?
2. What sorts of products seem to have advertisements that are most stereotypical? Were some advertisements bad in several of these ways?
3. How well did your group work together? Describe the process of developing ideas and deciding on them.
4. In what specific ways was it easy to come up with advertisements that fostered equality? In what ways was it hard?
5. Was it harder to re-design the advertisements for some products than others? What reasons can you give for this?
6. How hard was it to create new products? How did you feel about the products the class created?

GOING FURTHER

Students can show their advertisements to other classes or at a school assembly. They can write to advertisers and share the guidelines for unbiased advertisements with them.

LET ME TELL YOU WHAT I THINK

OBJECTIVE

To give students an opportunity to take action by communicating their learning and beliefs to those with decision-making power.

MATERIALS

Paper; pencils; envelopes; stamps; drawing paper; markers.

IMPLEMENTATION

Before doing this students should have done at least one of the following: "Sell, Sell, Sell, Buy, Buy, Buy," p. 237; "Please Buy Me One," p. 244; "A Firefighter, Not a Fireman," p. 245; "Stop and Look Carefully," p. 215. Ask students to think back and remember what they learned. Bring out their work as a reminder.

The class has the option of writing to advertisers, school product companies, toy manufacturers, or newspapers or magazines. Divide into pairs or trios with similar interests. Each group picks an advertisement, product, or word-use to which it objects.

Go over the discussion questions in the earlier lessons. Students need to be sure to explain in their letters: 1) why they found these products, advertisements, or word-uses to be discriminatory; and 2) why they find that offensive. They should include suggestions for improvements.

Once letters have been written in rough draft form, display them around the room along with the offending advertisements, products, bulletin board pictures, or newspaper articles. Everyone circulates around the room to read all letters and add ideas. Briefly discuss the letters and ideas for improvement. Then each pair or trio writes final copies, checking for proper mechanics. Stress that it is especially important to use correct grammar, spelling, and punctuation so that their letters will be taken seriously. Students may include drawings illustrating their suggestions. When writing to advertisers, students should send copies of the letters to the magazines that publish the advertisements.

DISCUSSION

1. How difficult was it to phrase your arguments in a convincing way?
2. How do you predict the advertisers or publishers to react? Why?
3. When, if at all, do you think publishers should refuse to publish advertisements that are offensive to some people? Give your reasons.
4. What do you think might change if advertisers and publishers used much less of this kind of advertisement and used more that encouraged equality?

GOING FURTHER

Write letters to advertisers and publishers who have advertisements that promote equality and compliment them on their good work.

SHARING RESULTS

OBJECTIVES

To share with others how packaging of products perpetuates stereotypes and the "isms." To give students an opportunity to display their learning in a way that will interest others and get students, teachers, and visitors thinking and questioning.

MATERIALS

Packages collected for "The Message in the Package," p. 247; file cards and/or construction paper; markers; scissors; tacks; use of a show case or, if this is not possible, a hallway bulletin board.

IMPLEMENTATION

This is a follow-up to "The Message in the Package" which must be done first. Students work together to sort the packages they collected by types. Divide students into groups so that each group has a pile of packages.

Each group writes cards that either ask questions of a person viewing the package or make points to get the viewer thinking. Give a few examples: "How would you feel if you were an American Indian and saw this package?" "How would you feel if you were Asian American and saw how small a pile we have with Asian American pictures?" "Why do you think advertisers show a woman in this pose on this package?"

After completing their cards, each group makes a mini-display of their products and cards in the front of the room. Have all the students peruse these displays. Gather as a class and discuss the cards, encouraging suggestions from everyone.

Students can now make a title banner for a display and labels for each category. Install the display in a public place. If you use a bulletin board, open packages and flatten them.

Alternatively, students can write a script for a film-strip with comments or questions about each product. This can be read aloud or played on tape as the film is projected. Put the film in the camera and, with the cover on the lens, advance about 8 frames. This is your lead off strip to thread into a projector. Now you are ready to shoot. Two filmstrip frames fit a regular slide frame. Put down your first two frames and shoot that. Get close enough so no background interferes. Then put down the next two. Continue until you have shot your whole filmstrip, leaving leader film free at the other end. Students can make a title page and picture for the beginning and a credits page for the end. When you have the film developed tell the company *not* to cut it apart for slides. When developed, run it through a filmstrip projector. Then students either write a narrative that is read aloud, or audiotape a script. A video is an alternative to the film strip.

DISCUSSION
1. What more about packaging and products did you learn while doing this? Give examples.
2. In what ways might those who look at your display or film-strip react? Why?
3. What are some ways we can get others to look with an open, questioning mind at what we have learned? What are some pitfalls to avoid?
4. Were there conflicts your group had in designing the display or film-strip? If so what, and how did you handle them?
5. What are some other ways, besides displays, that you can share your learning with others? What are the advantages and dis-advantages of these?

GOING FURTHER
Set up your display in other schools or community centers in town. Call your local newspaper. Ask the reporter if she would like to do a story on your work.

WE CAN DESIGN THEM OURSELVES

OBJECTIVES
To help students focus on the components of egalitarian illustrations on packages, and appreciate both the difficulties in designing these and the advantages of having them.
To give students the opportunity to share the broader perspectives they have gained in a practical way.
To give students the opportunity to change competitive games to cooperative ones.

MATERIALS
Game boxes from home, after-school programs or school; paper large enough to cover the box covers; drawing materials; adhesive-backed paper or laminating film.

IMPLEMENTATION
Ask students to bring in games from home. These can be complete or have missing pieces. Collect some classroom games. If you need more, used games can be bought at yard sales. Choose games with content that is not discriminatory when possible.

Step One. Students divide into groups of three or four. Each group picks one or several games. First, using scrap paper, they sketch ideas for new game box covers that aren't biased. They may need to try out many scrap paper ideas before finding one that is actively egalitarian and artistically appealing, and that would sell. They then sketch out their idea on a piece of paper which would cover the box. Remind students that they also need a design along the sides of the box, a catchy slogan somewhere on the box, a title, and the name of the manufacturer. After designs are drawn and colored in, preserve them. If laminating, do so before sticking them to the boxes. If using clear contact paper, put the new covers on the boxes first, then cover them.

This chapter encourages sharing. Therefore, display the new game covers in the library, in a showcase, or at a school or library fair. Set up the display in the community at the public library, banks, community center and so on.

Another action option is to enclose color photographs of the covers in letters to the game manufacturers. In these, students explain why they didn't like the old covers and why they feel theirs are fairer. See "Let Me Tell You What I Think," p. 333, for further guidelines for such letters.

Step Two. Most games foster competition rather than cooperation. Have students brainstorm guidelines for what makes games "really fun." Asterisk those items on this list that do *not* have to do with getting satisfaction from competition. Then, in order to address the ones that *do* have to do with competition, have students brainstorm ideas of how to make cooperative games fun when they don't have the competitive piece in them. You may want to have some games, or descriptions of games, from *Family Pastimes*, a company that produces cooperative games. (See Bibliography.)

Choose a collection of games that still have all their parts. Divide students into groups of three or four and give each group a game. Students revise the rules to make it a cooperative game—a game in which people win as a group by working together, or in which winning isn't part of the structure at all. Each group plays their own game. Have all the games available for rainy day recesses or activity periods.

DISCUSSION

1. What criteria did you use for an egalitarian game box cover design? Did you have any disagreements in your group over what was acceptable? Give examples. How did you resolve those?
2. What are some of the hard points about this kind of box cover design? How did you overcome those?
3. In what ways would these box covers sell the product better? In what ways would they hinder sales?
4. If there are some ways they might hinder sales, what arguments could you give manufacturers that these are still good changes to make?
5. How do you feel about the old box covers? the new ones? Why?
6. How would changes like this help to change the way children and adults choose games and play with them? How would those changes affect ways children see themselves and others?
7. Describe your group's process in making a competitive game into a cooperative one. What problems did you have to overcome? What steps did you take to address these? What problems do you still have to address?
8. How did you like playing your cooperative game? How were your feelings the same or different from those during a competitive game?

GOING FURTHER

This is one of many lessons from *Open Minds* that may be interesting to your local or neighborhood newspaper. Often a reporter assigned to schools will be willing to come to your classroom on request.

USING STATISTICS TO MAKE AN ARGUMENT

OBJECTIVES

To analyze and use statistics to make the points you want and to argue your points well. To analyze the media for biased use of statistics related to racism or sexism.

MATERIALS

One copy of "Worksheet: Facts on Education," p. 351, for each group of three students; paper; pencils; rulers; graph papers.

IMPLEMENTATION

This lesson is designed as a follow-up to "Analyzing Statistics" on pg. 115. You will need to have done that lesson first in order for this one to work.

The data we have chosen for this lesson, on race and education, are complex. We have chosen them because there is a great deal of conflicting data available on this topic, and these data are commonly used both by the press and by educational institutions to make whatever points people want to make, some of them to reinforce racial stereotypes. In order for your students to really understand these data, you will need to discuss and help them understand the context and some of the questions and issues involved. This will likely include having students do additional reading and research. You may also find that you have additional or alternative data on other topics that are particularly appropriate for something your class is currently studying.

In groups of three give students "Worksheet: Facts on Education." Direct them to create two possible arguments that could be made with the data, one supporting racist stereotypes and one countering them, and to create graphs for each of these. (See p. 245 for ideas on how to help students create pie graphs.) Stress that these arguments should be ones that *conflict* with each other and that each of the arguments needs to be firmly grounded in the data given. Each group shares their arguments and graphs with the class. Follow this with a class discussion.

Students bring in a newspaper article or set of articles around an issue related to racism or sexism that use statistics. They analyze the statistics for what information is missing or might be presented incompletely or in a biased way. They then find more data on this issue and write an article analyzing their findings. Finally they write to the original media source with their analysis.

DISCUSSION

1. In what ways was the "Facts on Education" information in this list clear? In what ways was it confusing? What questions came up for you as you read the list?
2. Were you able to create the two conflicting arguments with these data? What was easy or hard about this?
3. Were there pieces of data that appeared to conflict with other pieces of data? If so, what did you do to understand the data?
4. By creating the arguments and graphs yourself what did you learn about statistics? About how people use statistics? About how the media presents statistics?
5. In creating these arguments, what did you learn about how race and racism relate to education?
6. What did you learn about the way the media can use statistics to reinforce racism?

Mathematics Resources for Diverse Learners

Some of the newly published mathematics teaching materials are particularly strong in terms of an investigative approach, cooperative learning and multicultural education. A few that we particularly recommend are:
- *Number Power* published by Addison-Wesley. Grades 2–6.
- *Investigations in Number, Data and Space* by Susan Jo Russell and many others, distributed by Dale Seymour.
- *The Language of Numbers*, a unit from *Seeing and Thinking Mathematically*, developed by Education Development Center, distributed by Creative Publications. Grades 6–8.

Section E   **Reaching Out: Friends, Family, and the Community**

WON OR FUN?

OBJECTIVES   To have students learn about ways people are revising sports and games to make them cooperative.
To have students experience, and then develop, cooperative sports.

MATERIALS Red rubber ball and a net or rope, or regular volleyball equipment; equipment for the games students develop.

IMPLEMENTATION If possible get a copy of *The Cooperative Sports and Games Book* or *The Second Cooperative Sports and Games Book* by Terry Orlick. The many fine ideas provide good background for this lesson.

Ask students if any of them have played active cooperative games and to describe their experience. Tell students that across the country many people are revising traditional sports and games to make them more cooperative. Describe the following example:

> The American Youth Soccer Organization (AYSO) is dedicated to the motto "Everyone Plays." AYSO is for boys and girls, from five to eighteen years old, playing soccer, not because they're good or bad athletes, but because they want to play. AYSO is a nonprofit organization dedicated to the philosophy that everyone plays at least one half of every game on balanced teams. Some people have suggested that this philosophy promotes "mediocrity" in the level of youth soccer. Statistically this has not proven to be true. There is an almost equal percentage of highly skilled soccer players coming from competitive and cooperative-based organizations.

Step One. Students think of ways to make a game of soccer more cooperative. Here are some examples: give a point to a team that passes the ball to all the players in the course of getting the ball down the field; rotate players between teams every time out; keep team rather than individual scores (for example number of shots on goal by all forwards, number of assists); make a rule that four different players must make a goal before the team can win.

Most of these variations keep the competitive structure of soccer, but build more cooperation into the game. This is different from restructuring the games to make them purely cooperative where everyone would win or lose as a whole group. Then go to the playground or gym and play the new variation. Discuss. Play another new variation the next day. Discuss again. Continue until all alternatives have been tried.

DISCUSSION Be sure to encourage equal discussion from those who usually do well in sports and those who don't.

1. How did you like these versions of more cooperative soccer? What did you like about them? What didn't you like about them?
2. What were some feelings you had while you were playing? How are these feelings different from those you experience when you play more competitively?
3. What is the difference, if any, in your feelings about more cooperative as compared to more competitive sports, if you're a skilled player, or a less skilled player?
4. In what ways is including everyone and having fun important to you? Why? In what ways is winning important to you? Why?
5. How do you think our society as a whole would be different if people grew up playing more cooperative sports?

Step Two. Divide students into heterogeneous groups (be sure to mix males and females) and have each pick another sport or game and redesign it to make it more cooperative. Groups share their new rules with each other and choose a few to try out at recess. After, discuss their assessment of the new sports and their feelings while playing. Students teach these more cooperative sports or games to their families and neighborhood friends.

> *Another Approach for Thinking about Cooperative Alternatives*
>
> Have students use the "Seeing-Eye Glasses" technique, p. 91, to role-play solutions to problems with their friends, family and in the community. Choose situations that could be resolved either individualistically or cooperatively.
>
> Examples:
>
> 1. At recess, player A, sitting on the sidelines all game, asks player B, who has been playing the whole game, if she can substitute for her.
> 2. A has finished his homework. His sister, B, asks for help with hers. A must decide to help his sister or go play ball with his friends.
> 3. The scout leader asks scouts to discuss, in pairs, if dues can be levied on a sliding scale to allow more low-income people to join the troop.
>
> Students role-play the situation in pairs, first with "me-first" glasses and then "we-first" glasses. Discuss how sharing the "we-first" glasses strategy with family, friends, and community members might help resolve problems of inequality.

SHARING PRIVILEGE: EVERYBODY GAINS!

OBJECTIVES To explore the ways that people with privilege can benefit by sharing those privileges or by changing unfair situations to make them more equitable.

To think about ways young people can share what aspects of privilege they have and what they could gain from that.

MATERIALS "Worksheet: Sharing Privilege—Everybody Gains!," p. 352, situations cut into strips, "Worksheet: Sharing Privilege—Some Ideas," p. 353, cut in strips (optional, if needed).

IMPLEMENTATION Talk with students about the ways in which people often avoid making a situation more fair because they fear giving up an advantage they have. For example, some students didn't want students with disabilities in their school because they were afraid of losing the attention and time of teachers who would give so much to the new students.

Discuss with students the benefits of sharing our privilege that we often don't think about. For example these students later decided that they benefited from being in a class with physically challenged students. They lost their fear of people with physical disabilities. They learned a lot about disabilities and became more sensitive to the problems people with disabilities face. They were proud of the creative ways they devised to work with the new students. Also they made friends. In this lesson we will think about these sorts of benefits in different situations.

Review with students what they learned in "Filter of Oppression" in Chapter 7 and "Using Privilege for Change" in Chapter 10. If you haven't done them, do them now. Even if your students come from the least privileged groups in society, ask them to think about a way they have privilege in some situations. Remind them of the many aspects of their social identities (see p. 83). Help students having trouble identifying an area of privilege.

Divide students into partners within heterogeneous groups of four, considering students' relative degree of privileges. Give each pair a couple of situation strips; give the other pair the same. Distribute strips similarly to other groups.

Have students work for five minutes with their partners. Each reads one situation strip out loud and tries to respond to the questions. Then partners talk together. Partner two does the same for his situation strip. If they're having a lot of trouble with the concepts, give them a copy of the relevant strips from "Worksheet: Sharing Privilege—Everybody Gains!"

After about five minutes all four group members convene to share their responses to each situation. After discussion they decide on a thoughtful and creative response to both issues: 1) how the young person(s) could use their privilege for change and 2) how the young person(s) could benefit from that. Then come together for class discussion.

DISCUSSION

1. Call on various students to share a situation they addressed, how the young person(s) used privilege for change, and how they could benefit. Others who dealt with the same scenario can share their ideas. Continue until all situations have been discussed.
2. How hard was it to come up with ideas for using privilege for change. Why might that be?
3. What are some of the benefits to people sharing privilege that are common to many situations? Which ones are extrinsic/tangible benefits? Which are intrinsic/feelings about ourselves?
4. In our school and outside school what situations are there in which sharing privilege might give us a benefit we hadn't thought about? How could we go about sharing privilege in those situations? How can we support each other in doing that?

REMOVING THOSE HURDLES

OBJECTIVES

To give students an opportunity to investigate barriers to equality in their community.
To learn a process for cooperatively confronting a barrier to equality.
To develop a collective action project to deal with one of those hurdles.

MATERIALS

Copies of "Worksheet: Community Problem-Solving," p. 354.

IMPLEMENTATION

Review with students case histories, "The Hurdles of Life" p. 167. Remind students that institutional discrimination sets up barriers or hurdles for people that makes it hard for them to achieve their goals. Review some of those hurdles. Tell students they will be using a cooperative process to pinpoint and attempt to solve a community problem. Go over the Worksheet together.

Divide students into groups of about four. Have each group pick a group of people in society that often faces special hurdles—women, people of color, older people, low-income people, lesbians, gay men, people with disabilities, people who speak English as a second language, Jews and so on. Assign one such group to each student group.

Step One. For the next few days, students will conduct interviews with members of the population their group is focusing on. (Review the lessons on interviewing, pp. 64–65.) They will ask members of that group.

1. What are strengths you and other members of your social group have as individuals and a group that you take pride in?
2. What barriers do you and other members of your social group face that hinder you from gaining equality in our community?

Each student interviews at least two persons and brings a written summary to class.

Alternatively (or additionally), invite a member of each population group to class where students can interview that person together. For example, a member of a welfare rights group might represent low-income persons, or a member of a Hmong civic association represent that cultural group.

After interviews are completed, students work together in their group to identify the strengths and hurdles mentioned most often. As a class, list the strengths and hurdles, by population group, on the board. The class picks one problem area that they want to work on further.

DISCUSSION

1. What are the commonalities in the strengths mentioned by members of the various social groups interviewed? What are the differences?
2. What are the commonalities and differences in the hurdles mentioned?

3. What relationships are there, if any, between the strengths and the hurdles?
4. Why did the class decide on the problem area that it did to work on?

Step Two. As a class, brainstorm about what to do to help lessen this hurdle. Next, students try to reach an agreement on a manageable project that they could organize or take part in, toward that end. For example, one hurdle to equality in the workplace that women, especially low-income women, face is lack of after-school child-care. Many women, therefore, can take only part-time jobs. The class might choose one of a number of alternative solutions to this problem. They might document the need, write articles and try to encourage the school system and community groups to start an after-school program. They might research all the available after-school opportunities and make a booklet "After-school Programs for Children in Our Community," to be distributed.

Cooperative Ventures at Work in Your Community

It is important that students learn that cooperative endeavors can work in daily living. If there is a food cooperative, recycling program, or any other type of cooperative project operating successfully in your community, invite members from that group to visit your class to describe their aims and processes. There may be a way that students can take part in the ongoing work of that cooperative.

NEW VILLAGE

OBJECTIVES To imagine and design social institutions in a community that would provide equality for all.
To depict these institutions in stories and art work.
To share this envisioned community with friends, family, and community members.

MATERIALS Art supplies for a large mural: mural paper; paint; markers; scissors and so on.

IMPLEMENTATION *Part One. Reviewing and Envisioning.* Tell students that they will review what they've learned about discrimination and competitive individualism in order to create a fair and just community—one that gives everybody an equal chance.

The class decides on a name for its community. Here it is named New Village. Divide students into small groups of about four. Have each group choose one institution to work on—family, school, media, business, or community groups. Make sure that each institution is being covered by at least one group. (Notice that these are the same areas covered in Chapters 8 and 9.) There may be two groups working on the same institution.

Groups make a list of the specific ways they've learned that institutions can discriminate on the bases of race, class, gender, age, ability, sexual orientation, religion, language, or competition. For example if the area is the media, the group can write, "Very few positive pictures of older people on TV." If students have reports or projects from previous lessons, they should review those for information as well.

Then students make a list of how those examples of inequality would be changed in a just society. Encourage them to be specific. For example, "Older adults will be shown in the media in nonstereotyped ways." Circulate from group to group helping students as needed. Students read the lists to the whole class. Group members ask others for additional suggestions.

DISCUSSION 1. In what specific ways was it hard or easy to think of ways to change things that supported inequality? Why?
2. How do you think you would feel living in New Village? Why?

Part Two. Writing. Students now write about their view of a just society, focusing on the institution they have chosen to work on. Students choose one or two of their group members to write a paper describing the institution—for example, "Schools in New Village," The remaining students choose to be a person of a race, religion, class, gender, sexual orientation, ability, first language, or age different from their own. Then write about a day in their lives in that institution—for example, "My Day in School in New Village."

Students within groups read their papers to each other to make sure that all papers fit together to present a consistent picture. They check each others' papers for grammar and punctuation. These papers will be posted on the bulletin board with an accompanying mural.

DISCUSSION

1. In what ways was it hard or easy to write a clear picture of your institution in New Village? Give reasons and examples.
2. How hard or easy was it to write from the point of view of a person of a different gender from yourself? Why? What did you learn?

Part Three. Class Mural. The third step of this project is to make a class mural depicting New Village. Each group plans and designs a section showing the institution they've focused on. Students often find this works more easily if they make group decisions; then each student cuts out his own buildings, trees, figures, etc. from oaktag, and covers these with fabric, construction paper, crayon or marker. Each group assembles its own section and then puts it together with others' sections. Students place their stories beneath or around the mural.

DISCUSSION

1. What were some of the decisions groups had to make in planning the mural?
2. How did you show that all people had equal opportunities in your institution?
3. Let's look at the sections of the mural. Are people who should be there missing?
4. What can we do to make our families, schools, the media, and community more like New Village?

Part Four. Sharing. Invite other classes to your room to see the mural. Class members describe how New Village depicts a just community. Answer questions other students raise. Move the mural to a bulletin board in the hall or at the entrance to the school. Students explain the mural to visitors at a PTA meeting or at parents' nights.

Display the mural in your community. The library, community center, post office, or a bank are possible locations. Write an article about the mural for your local newspaper. Invite a photographer from the paper to take a picture. Convince your friends, family, and community members that equality is possible and together *we can make changes!*

1. *Provide Correct Information*

   Situation: Your younger brother is watching a TV movie in which the army is gunning down Native Americans. He is rooting for the military and calling the Native Americans "barbarians."

   You say and/or do   *He reacts*

2. *State How You Feel* (use feeling messages)

   Situation: Your friend Robert calls Rodney a sissy because he won't play a rough game with you.

   You say and/or do   *He reacts*

3. *Encourage a Group of People to Speak Up Together*

   Situation: You notice that the crossing guard outside your school is nasty to children who recently immigrated to this country and whose second language is English. You're scared to say something to her yourself.

   You, with others, say and/or do   *She reacts*

4. *Take Creative, Cooperative Action*

   Situation: Your school's PTA is having a book fair. You know that very few books being sold are positive stories about children of color or poor children.

   You, with others, say and/or do   *People at the fair react*

1. Here's a situation where I might have to stand up for what I believe and challenge a stereotype or "ism":

2. The Fear Statements I could tell myself are:

3. The Power Statements I could tell myself, instead, are:

4. The Guidelines for Communication I'll remember when I state my feelings are:

5. I contract that I will tell myself a Power Statement next time I hear a stereotype or "ism." I'll report back to you, my partner, what I do and what happens.

Signed _____

Partner's Statement

I'll encourage you to think of your Power Statements and give you support. If you hear your Fear Statements, let me know and I'll remind you of your Power Statements. We'll talk about how things are going soon.

Signed _____

October 18

Dear Diary,

We were discussing Halloween in school today. Some of the kids think they are too old to get in costumes but I think that, secretly at least, most of us still like to do that and especially like to go trick or treating. Tammy and I were having lunch with a bunch of kids including Lester and Derek. They said they were going to dress up like "wild Indians." We didn't say much. I wondered why they hadn't outgrown that, it sounded like the two little boys I babysit for.

Later when we were at Tammy's house working on our costumes—she's going to be a computer and I'm a photocopy machine (have you ever tried to make a photocopy machine costume?)—we were talking about how those two still think of Indians in such an unfair way. Last year in school we studied a lot about all the things the white settlers learned from the Native Americans and about how the Native Americans only fought them because the settlers were taking their land.

Should we say anything to them? What should we do?

Love,
Rebekah

October 27

Dear Diary,

Halloween this year sure is giving me lots of problems. A bunch of us decided to go trick or treating together. Serena and Sherisse are coming over to meet Tammy and me and then we're going to Angela's house. We were trying to decide the best places to go then. I especially wanted to go to Mrs. Rivera's house up on Union St. When we were little kids we were always scared of her. She's old and walks with two canes and her legs look all knotted up. To make it even worse, she lives in an old house with a porch that's falling in.

One day, years ago, Scott let go of our dog, Muffin, and Muffin ran up on to Mrs. Rivera's house. Scott wouldn't go get her and I was afraid Dad would be furious if he had to do that for us, so I went. Mrs. Rivera's hard to understand, I think most of her teeth are gone, but she was really glad to see me and really friendly.

I keep wanting to go there, but I don't want to make a big deal with the other kids. They're always saying I'm such a "goody-goody." They'll make fun of me for wanting to do something kind on Halloween when it's supposed to be a holiday just for fun for kids.

Well, I guess I'll have to decide soon.

Love,
Rebekah

November 8

Dear Diary,

Dumb, dumb, dumb! Sometimes people are so dumb. Scott came home from school today all upset about something. Now that he's thirteen, he won't talk to me about stuff very much. That's dumb too, he thinks that teenage boys aren't supposed to talk about stuff when they're upset. But that wasn't what I was going to write about.

He did say a little—I guess he was too upset to hide it all. I think I'm glad he told me what was wrong, but now he won't discuss it. Some of the boys in his class have been making comments about Dad. It's not his fault that he is bringing us up alone. And he's doing a good job of it. But they were saying all these stupid things about Dad's cooking and cleaning, and going places with us when all the other grown-ups are mothers. I think they were calling him names.

Scott's just sitting in his room sulking and says I should leave him alone. I don't know what to do, but I don't want to just do nothing.

We're supposed to be getting tulip bulbs in the ground today. Maybe he'll get more talkative while we're digging into the almost frozen ground. I guess I'll stop writing and go get him.

Love and confusion,
Rebekah

November 19

Dear Diary,

Guess what, Norbert's coming to visit us over Thanksgiving. I can't wait. And Tammy's cousins who live in Alaska are coming to her house! And it looks like it might snow! And we're having tacos for dinner!

Last night while we were eating, a man came to the door with a petition for Dad to sign. They are planning to build a low-income housing project in this neighborhood and the man who came around was against that. He kept saying how property values would go down. He said it wouldn't be safe to play around the streets anymore. He said the neighborhood would get messy and dirty and noisy. He wanted Dad to sign.

After he left we talked about it. We all think that it would be good for them to build the project here. I know from stuff we've done in school that this town needs much more low-income housing. There would be families with kids there and I'd love to have more kids around. I don't think it's fair that people have all these ideas in their minds about low-income people and won't give them a chance.

I'd like to get together with some kids from school and see if we can do anything to help the project get built. I wonder if I dare do it. Some kids won't like the idea.

You should see the great pumpkin we grew for Halloween. We're going to all help make pies out of it.

Love,
Rebekah

Physical Education

1. Equal requirements.

2. Classes open to girls and boys.

3. Classes co-ed except for ability groups or contact sports.

4. Standards for success clearly stated and fair.

5. Wide range of activities.

Guidance and Counseling

1. Graduation requirements the same for both sexes in all courses.

2. Vocational courses all co-educational.

3. Descriptions and pictures include males and females in all courses.

4. Counselors avoid sex-role stereotyping.

5. Counseling provides wide range of courses and ideas for males and females.

Treatment of Students

1. Prizes and honors open to both sexes.

2. No segregated activities except Scouts and Ys.

3. Equal use of all school equipment.

4. Equal punishments for school rule violations.

Rose wanted to play tennis, which she'd never played before. When she got into her beginners' tennis class, she found that all the other students were also girls. After class, she was walking by the courts looking at the intermediate and advanced classes and found that the advanced class was all male. She complained that that was segregating by sex and wasn't fair.

Gregg was looking through booklets about jobs in his school's guidance office. He'd been planning to do the mini-course on nursing so that he could work as a volunteer nurse's aide at the local hospital. When he looked at the pictures, he realized that all the nurse's aides were female. He felt silly taking a course where he expected only girls. So he decided to take an auto mechanic workshop which didn't interest him, but where at least there'd be lots of other guys.

The principal told Dan he would be suspended from school until he cut his hair. The principal said that he could tolerate shoulder length hair in a boy, although he wasn't happy about it, but he certainly couldn't allow him into school with hair longer than that. Dan's sister, Tara, went to the same school and had hair down to her waist. Dan insisted that wasn't fair and that he should get to wear his hair however he wanted.

Gilah got pregnant while she was in high school. The assistant principal said that as soon as it became obvious that she was pregnant she couldn't come to regular classes. Gilah's parents complained saying that as long as she had a doctor's note saying she was healthy, she should get to come to school.

Gurtney wanted to join Boy Scouts, which met at her school, since she didn't like the kind of activities they did in Girl Scouts. The scout leaders and the administrators of her school both said that it was legal to separate scout troops by gender and that she couldn't join Boy Scouts.

Your school has had eleven teams for boys and only four for girls. One of the girls' teams is archery. Ming wants to be on what has been the girls' archery team since there aren't enough boys who are interested to start a boys' team. The coach says no, that there are plenty of sports for boys and she wants to keep this for girls only.

1. Background

Barry's mother was a second grade teacher. At dinner one day she told the family that one of the children in her class was in the nurse's office all afternoon. At the end of the afternoon the girl, in tears, finally told the nurse what was wrong. She had come to the nurse's office with a bad stomach ache because she was thinking about what would happen in her class that afternoon. The students would be getting the books they had ordered from the book fair. Everyone else would get several books, but she wouldn't get any because her family couldn't spare the money for books. Just the thought of it had made her sick.

2. Barry's Thoughts

Barry had never thought about the book fair much before. He had looked at the books arranged in the cafeteria on book fair day, ordered four or five books, asked his parents for the money for them and that was that. He never considered about how you would feel if you couldn't get books.

As he thought more about it he could picture other students in his class on book fair day. A few would walk in with 15 books piled high, boasting about how many books they got. Others would argue over who got the best books. One kid told the students at his table that his parents gave him $50 for books!

The more Barry thought about it the more he decided that it really wasn't fair that some kids could get 15 books and others none. Everybody in his class really liked reading books.

3. The Class' Survey

Barry's class had weekly community meetings where students and their teacher discussed plans, issues and problems. Barry put "book fair" on the list for agenda items for the next meeting.

During that week's community meeting Barry described how he had come to think the book fair wasn't fair. Other students shared their opinions. The class decided to do a survey to find out how students in the school felt about the book fair. They decided because it's hard for kids to really be honest about not being able to afford something, they would make the survey anonymous—no names would be asked for.

One committee came up with questions and wrote a survey form. 1) What do you like about the book fair? 2) What don't you like about the book fair? 3) How do you *feel* on book fair day when everyone gets their books. Why did you feel that way? 4) If you ever wanted to get more books than you could afford, how did you feel? What did you do?

Another committee distributed survey forms to one class in each grade in the school and compiled the results. For the younger grades where students couldn't write their thoughts, they interviewed a random group of students. They found that some students liked the book fair as it was. As many others either felt bad when books were distributed, or wished they could afford more books and felt disappointed about that.

4. Action Plan

At the next community meeting the survey committee reported its results. The class brainstormed ideas for making the book fair more fair so that the amount of money a family had wouldn't keep a student from getting books. The class decided on one alternative that a few teachers said they would try next year to see how it worked.

The Plan:
1. This year students would write a letter to parents explaining why they wanted to try a different approach to the book fair.

2. The class would have a fund raiser to raise money for the book fair so each student in the class could buy one book.

3. Parents would be asked to give money, as they could afford it, to a fund to buy books from the book fair for the class lending library. Then all students could take home the books and read them. They'd be able to read more new books that way than they could buying individually.

Barry and his classmates are eager to see how this plan will work.

Title:_____

Author(s): _____

Criteria	Author Check	Proofreader Check
1. Look at the female and male characters. What kinds of personalities do they have? What kinds of tasks are they doing? Are the tasks anti–sexist?		
2. Look at the ages of the people. Are there elderly people and young people? Are they doing different interesting things? Do they have the freedom to be different sorts of people?		
3. Does the book show people of different incomes? Do people of different classes take leadership and make decisions?		
4. Does the book include people of different races? Have stereotypes been avoided?		
5. Does the book include people with different physical, mental or emotional abilities? Have stereotypes been avoided?		
6. Does the book show people of different religions? If so, have stereotypes been avoided?		
7. Does the book include people from different types of families or include lesbians and gay men? If so, have stereotypes been avoided?		
8. Does the book include people whose first language is not English? If so, have stereotypes been avoided?		
9. Do people work cooperatively together? Do they make changes to promote equality?		

While any one story is unlikely to have positive examples of all forms of equality, it *is possible* to avoid bias in each area.

- 16% of public school children are black.
- Between 1973 and 1990 the high school dropout rate for blacks dropped from 22% to 13%, for whites it dropped from 12% to 9%.
- In 1992 a total of 68% of blacks 25 and over had a high school diploma.
- 92% of blacks and 93% of whites aged 16 to 17 are enrolled in school.
- Foreign students get 3/4 of their graduate tuition as scholarships, white students get less than 1/2, and black students get 1/4 of their costs paid.
- In schools that are almost all students of color, 28% of math and science classes are low track and 9% are high track.
- In schools that are almost all white, 7% of math and science classes are low track and 11% are high track.
- In 3rd grade the same percent of black children and white children test below grade level.
- By eighth grade almost twice as many black children test below grade level as white children.
- In 1980 12% of public school teachers were black, in 1992 only 8% were black.
- In 1991 there were 136,000 black males aged 18 to 24 in prison and 378,000 black males the same age in college.

Argument #1:

(Choose facts to create an argument that supports racism, write the argument, then create a graph.)

Argument #2:

(Choose facts to create an argument that counters racism, write the argument, then create a graph.)

1. Students who can walk have the privilege of mobility. In John's neighborhood a boy who uses a wheelchair can't join in the street games because the rules of the games are complicated and fast-paced. How could John and his friends who can walk and run use their privilege for change? How might they benefit?

   _____

2. In a Leora's class, skin-color privilege kept white students out of trouble. When there was a conversation going on when there shouldn't have been, the teacher tended to blame the Haitian students even when there were white students talking. How could Leora and her white friends use their privilege for change? How might they benefit?

   _____

3. In Holly's community center people who speak English, like Holly, have language privilege. Even though there are lots of people who use the community center who have just immigrated to the U.S. and who speak Spanish or Arabic, all the signs and posters in the halls are in English. How could Holly and her English-speaking friends use their privilege for change? How would they benefit?

   _____

4. In Bud's family male privilege allows Bud and his brothers to avoid cooking, cleaning and taking care of the baby. How could Bud and his brothers use their privilege for change? How would Bud and his brothers benefit?

   _____

5. Natasha enjoys religious privilege in her school. She can eat whatever the cafeteria serves, but her friends who are Jewish and Muslim often can't eat the food that's served. For example pork hot dogs are on the menu at least every ten days. No alternatives are provided. How could Natasha and other Christian students use their privilege for change? How would they benefit?

   _____

6. Leroy enjoys heterosexual privilege at his camp. He and his friends play sports there, but Mark takes dance and is hassled and called "gay" by some of the guys. How could Leroy and his friends use privilege for change? How would they benefit?

   _____

7. Yolanda and her family have class privilege in that they can afford to buy a membership in the local pool for the summer. Her best friend's family can't afford the membership fee so they can't go to the pool together. How could Yolanda, her family and friends use their privilege to change the pool's policy? How would Yolanda benefit?

   _____

8. Being in 8th grade, Meremu and her friends have age privilege at her church because 8th graders get to do the childcare for the young children. Even though it's lots of work, they get good experience. Some 6th and 7th graders really want to do it too. How could Meremu and her friends use the privilege for change? How would they benefit?

1. a. John and his friends could change the rules of some of their games to make it possible for the boy in the wheelchair to play.
   b. Possible benefits to John and his friends:
      - A greater variety of games, more creative games.
      - Satisfaction from including another person who couldn't play before.
      - New friendships.

2. a. Leora and other white students could honestly tell the teacher they were talking if the Haitian students got blamed.
   b. Possible benefits to Leora and her friends:
      - The sense of integrity that comes from being honest.
      - They could gain the respect, and possible friendship of the Haitian students who were being unfairly blamed.

3. a. Holly and her friends could make new signs and posters in three languages.
   b. Possible benefits to Holly and her friends:
      - They would learn new words in other languages.
      - They might become motivated to learn more in those languages and would have greater communication with others at the Center.

4. a. Bud and his brothers could start doing some cooking, cleaning and childcare.
   b. Possible benefits to Bud and his brothers:
      - They would be learning new life skills that could provide them know-how, self-sufficiency, and potential employment.
      - They would have fun and bond with the baby.

5. a. Natasha and her friends could start a petition asking the dietitian to plan more alternative foods that would give options to people of different faiths. Even if they had to have hot dogs, turkey hot dogs could be served.
   b. Possible benefits to Natasha and her friends:
      - Natasha and others would have more food variety themselves.
      - They would be learning more themselves, and educating others about different religions and different foods.

6. a. Leroy and his friends could start taking dance, too, knowing that lots of athletes strengthen their muscles through dance; or tell the guys hassling Mark to stop since everybody should be able to follow their interests without being stereotyped.
   b. Possible benefits to Leroy and his friends:
      - If they took dance, they might become even better athletes.
      - They might find they liked dancing.
      - If they talked to the other guys, they might feel pride in themselves for standing up to prejudice.

7. a. Yolanda, her parents, and friends could organize a petition to get a sliding scale membership for the pool so families would pay different memberships based on their incomes.
   b. Possible benefits to Yolanda and her friends:
      - All her friends would be able to have fun together at the pool.
      - They'd learn about an approach for organizing to make change.

8. a. Meremu and her friends could talk to the adults in charge of childcare to include 6th and 7th graders in the childcare program.
   b. Possible benefits to Meremu and her friends:
      - They would have extra help with the children, or they could rotate schedules so they'd get some breaks.

Step 1. Problem

What is the problem we're concerned about? _____

How is it defined by members of the group affected? _____

Step 2. What are we doing to understand the problem more fully? _____

Step 3. Proposed change

What can we do about it? _____

Is our plan possible? Why? _____

Are we committed to following through? _____

How do we know? _____

Step 4. Allies

Who can work with us? _____

What members of the group affected by the problem are we cooperating with? _____

Step 5. Activities

What are all the activities we need to do to accomplish our plan?

_____

Who will take responsibility for each activity? _____

Step 6. Evaluations (Questions to ask after every few steps)

How effective is our program solving? _____

What do we need to change before moving on? _____

Resource Section

Integrating Open Minds to Equality into Your Curriculum

Many of the lessons in *Open Minds to Equality* are written to fit easily into your standard curriculum. Some of these lessons are designed to fit into a single subject area, whereas others are interdisciplinary. Many of these lessons fit in well with an integrated thematic approach to curriculum. While we encourage you to make choices that fit with what you are teaching, we also believe it is essential to pay attention to the sequence in *Open Minds to Equality* rather than just choosing particular isolated lessons. The chapters, and sections within chapters, are designed developmentally to introduce students gradually to more complex and sophisticated ideas, while building on concepts they have already explored. In order for students to truly engage in and understand these later lessons they need to have the background of the earlier ones. In addition to the specific lessons in *Open Minds to Equality,* we offer you the suggestions below to help you take an overall look at your own curriculum with a more egalitarian perspective. In all of these, the goal is to help you help students fulfill their academic goals while also teaching for equality.

READING

Open Minds to Equality can be used well to enhance students' reading skills in a variety of areas. These include reading comprehension, vocabulary development, use of an index and table of contents and writing literary critique. Throughout these lessons there is an emphasis on reading critically. This includes analyzing stories for hidden assumptions, developing awareness of point of view and developing empathy with a range of characters both fictitious and real. Students learn about different forms of writing especially historical fiction, modern fiction and biography.

Many lessons encourage students to look at familiar words in new ways. They learn to examine words for "loaded" meanings, to understand how language influences thinking, and to use new vocabulary that is not discriminatory. Vocabulary from *Open Minds to Equality* can be used to help students apply developing skills in understanding origins of words.

We hope that *Open Minds to Equality* will help you think about how you teach your reading curriculum. The extensive bibliography of children's fiction, non-fiction, biography, poetry and legends can be of great use in selecting books from and about a diverse range of people. If you teach in a whole language classroom, or in any setting where you have the opportunity to choose your own chapter books for reading instruction, you can use this bibliography to guide your choices. Many of the lessons in *Open Minds*, while designed around particular books, can be adapted for other books that promote egalitarian values. *Open Minds to Equality* has a number of lessons suitable for reading literature aloud. If you have a read aloud time in your classroom, you can use these lessons directly, or modify them to go with other books you select.

If you have an assigned reading textbook, lessons from *Open Minds to Equality* can help you and your students to critique selected stories for their portrayal of people of different races and classes, people with different language backgrounds, people with different abilities. If you can choose stories from within these textbooks, there are lessons that will increase student awareness and help make this process one that promotes equity. If students are required to read books that we now consider "out of date," they can use lessons from *Open Minds to Equality* to help them read these critically, looking for what has changed and what still needs to change.

You can use lessons from *Open Minds to Equality* to help your students develop the necessary critical reading skills to write book reports. If these are generally a monthly assignment in your class you may want to assign students particular groups of people for each month. For example, one month all the students could read different books about Asian Americans, another month about elderly people and another month about those with disabilities. Use the bibliography to help your students select high quality nonstereotypic books for these reports.

LANGUAGE ARTS

Language arts curricula teach children skills in communicating—in speaking, listening, writing and spelling. The lessons in *Open Minds to Equality* can be adapted to fit either a whole language approach or a more traditional textbook based language arts curriculum. Teaching handwriting, spelling and English mechanics all involve choices by the teacher of what content to use for words, sentences or paragraphs. You can make the choice to have your daily content include names and activities of people from a range of cultures, languages, abilities, socio-economic classes, and lifestyles. This content can be chosen to teach children about lives of diverse Americans.

For example, if you teach handwriting by having students copy from the board, you can include quotations or poems by people who worked to make our country more equitable. You can include paragraphs about the lives of women and people of color who worked to bring about change. If you give students sentences or paragraphs to edit for punctuation and capitalization, you can make the content of these counter commonly held stereotypes.

In both spelling and vocabulary building, you can encourage appreciation of other cultures, look at words in our language that come from Native American words, or come from other cultures that are represented in the current American population. As students learn to spell these words and use them correctly, they can develop appreciation for how much we have learned from other cultures.

Open Minds to Equality has many lessons that help students develop letter writing skills. These include attention to both the convincing content of a letter and to English mechanics. Students are more willing to be careful in their writing in work that is being sent to the outside world. When they are highly invested in having the readers truly understand what they are saying, they will pay better attention to handwriting, spelling, grammar and punctuation and work harder to write prose that is convincing and easy to understand.

Many lessons in *Open Minds to Equality* help students develop interviewing and note-taking skills. Rather than learn these as isolated skills, students appreciate how useful these are for them and thus become more adept at developing questions, listening attentively to their interviewees, and taking careful notes.

Many of these activities promote skills in careful observing and listening. Students increase their awareness of the world through looking at bulletin boards, television advertisements, packaging of goods at stores, and magazines. They learn to listen more carefully for the "isms" in what people say. Students are encouraged to analyze what they hear and to understand the reasons for different viewpoints.

Creative and expository writing are the basis for many activities in *Open Minds to Equality*. These assignments can become part of your regular writing curriculum, either modified to fit in with an already structured method you use, or used as they are written here if you have more flexibility in approach.

MATH

Often teachers do not think of mathematics as lending itself to a multicultural approach as easily as reading or social studies. *Open Minds to Equality* can help you see mathematics through a multicultural lens. This can include many areas of mathematics instruction such as the wording and content of story problems, graphing, working with statistics, learning computation algorithms from many cultures and playing math games.

Perhaps you create some of your own story problems. If so, these can be consciously designed to be inclusive of a diverse range of people and their lives. You can use your students' names in scenarios that actively counter stereotypes. You can use the content of these problems to teach children information about the lives of people different from them while they are engaged in doing the mathematics.

Several lessons in *Open Minds to Equality* have students gather data and create and interpret graphs. These could be used as replacement lessons for standard textbook lessons on particular graphing skills. Or you could create an entire unit on graphing, having as one of your goals that students will learn information about equity and lack of equity in the distribution of resources in this country. *Open Minds to Equality* encourages students to read and interpret data critically and suspiciously. They learn that data are used by people to make the points they want to make and that, as citizens, we need to think about the bias of information we read and hear, analyze it, and draw our own conclusions.

Other lessons on ratio, proportion and percents have students explore these mathematical principles while helping them learn actual information about the lives of Americans today. In all these lessons, and others you create yourself, students can learn how to work with data and statistics to understand both the mathematical and societal implications.

For younger students there are calendar lessons, an integral part of most beginning mathematics curricula. These can be used in conjunction with your regular calendar lessons to have children learn more about the diverse cultures that make up our country.

In the bibliography you will find several resources for multicultural mathematics materials. Many of these have traditional games from diverse cultures that are helpful for students in patterning, sequencing, strategy, and problem solving. Playing these helps students develop better mathematical skills while also developing an appreciation for other cultures. These materials also have many ideas for using art, history and literature from diverse cultures in order to help students learn various traditional math skills.

In addition you may be interested in exploring algorithms from different cultures. If you have Caribbean immigrant families in your classroom, they may be able to teach your students a method of multi-digit subtracting that is easier for many children than our traditionally taught regrouping algorithm. Or you may have Russian immigrant children who can share their way of dividing fractions—a method which many students can understand better than the "flip and multiply" method our textbooks most often teach. Learning these algorithms, and others like them, helps children both better understand mathematics and better appreciate the mathematical sophistication of a range of cultures.

SCIENCE

In our schools today, if students learn about famous scientists, these are most often white men. *Open Minds to Equality* can inspire your students to learn more about women and people of color whose discoveries have contributed to the development of this country. One example of this is in the lesson *Stop, Don't Take It for Granted*, a lesson about Garret Morgan, an African American man who invented the traffic light. The bibliography will help you uncover important people of color and women who have made significant scientific contributions to our society. Students could do reports, oral presentations or perhaps create a book about these often neglected Americans.

There are parts of our science curriculum that may be ethnocentric without our realizing this. *Open Minds to Equality* can help you and your students develop greater sensitivity to the lenses we use when we think about science, and to broadening these lenses. For example when we teach astronomy the names and stories for the constellations we teach are the Roman and Greek ones. It is likely that most of us have grown up thinking that these simply are "the names" of these. However Native Americans had their own names and stories for constellations as did Caribbean people, Chinese people, African people and many others. Learning about these can help your students' knowledge of astronomy and their appreciation for the science, storytelling and history of diverse American people.

SOCIAL STUDIES

Open Minds to Equality ties in particularly well in the area of social studies. Elementary school social studies curricula often teach about family living, communities, and different cultures. Since American history appears as the major focus in at least one year of upper elementary and middle school social studies, all the lessons that examine our country are relevant there. For middle school students, the emphasis on local history and historical perspective ties into *Open Minds to Equality*.

For younger students to comprehend the world around them, they must understand their own immediate world. Included here are lessons on students' closest environments—their home and school. When you study families, children can do the lessons that allow them to look more clearly at some of their family patterns. As they compare these to other families', they will find both commonalities and differences and learn about alternative family structures.

Chapters Four and Five are concerned primarily with our lives and those of others. No matter what your social studies topics for the year, these can easily be incorporated. You can help students to look at their life-experience as one of many, with some advantages and some disadvantages. They can see how their life-situation was determined, in part by choices they and their families made, in part by how society sets up expectations and possibilities for them. They can look at others' lives in the same way.

A broader grasp of economics is encouraged in the book. Students look critically at television programming and advertising and compare the life-experiences there to actual ones. Examining stores, food products, and toys, students develop a greater insight into the effects of our economic system.

Critical reading is encouraged throughout *Open Minds to Equality*. As students read texts and books, they learn to recognize prejudice and stereotyping. They thus develop the important critical skill of understanding how textbooks influence their view of the world. When they do social studies reports from reference or library books, they will read more critically and write from a more objective perspective. For middle school students, research from several sources for a single report supports skills emphasized at that level.

In many schools students begin learning to write research papers in third or fourth grade. *Open Minds to Equality* can help you teach them the necessary skills and a more equitable attitude toward these. Use the bibliography to help you find historical sources that treat all Americans fairly and accurately. Through lessons in *Open Minds to Equality* students can also learn to read other sources with an eye toward who and what has been left out and with an awareness of the biases of the authors. Students can learn to understand the importance of the point of view of the author in the material that is being presented. Many lessons in *Open Minds* have students take what they have learned and present information to share with other students and the wider school community. In this way students are not only developing their research skills but gaining experience in sharing information in coherent and interesting ways.

ART

In *Open Minds to Equality*, there are frequent opportunities for students to be involved in artistic design and creation. These include developing game box covers, posters, advertisements, packaging for products and displays. In all of these students learn about visual products that are inclusive—that have people of different races, genders, classes, ages sexual orientations and abilities. Students have the opportunity to counter stereotypes as they create work that doesn't just ignore these common images, but rather work that actively shows diverse peoples in equitable ways.

Students also learn to analyze art as consumers. They learn to look more critically at the art they see in books, in packaging, around their community. Through *Open Minds to Equality* students can learn to appreciate art from a greater range of artists of all cultures. They can broaden their view of what art is and incorporate styles from diverse cultures into their own artistic work.

Annotated Bibliography

1. SOURCES OF MATERIALS

Many of the resources listed in this bibliography, including curricula and media, may be obtained from these sources.

Akwesasne Notes, Indian Time, P.O. Box 196, Rooseveltown, NY 13683-0196, (518) 358-9531. Information, books, art work of Native American peoples.

American Association of Retired Persons, 601 E Street NW, Washington, DC 20049, (202) 434-2277. Supports health-care reform and long-term independent care for the elderly.

American Association of University Women, 2401 Virginia Avenue NW, Washington, DC 20037. Source of reports and data on sexism in education.

American/Arab Anti-Discrimination Committee, 1731 Connecticut Avenue, NW, Washington, DC 20009. Helpful classroom resources, articles and curriculums.

Anti-Defamation League, 823 United Nations Plaza, New York, 10017. Provides curriculum materials to combat prejudice and improve intergroup relations.

Arte Publico Press, University of Houston, Houston, TX 77204. Literature including books for children and young adults by Mexican American, Cuban, Puerto Rican, and U.S. Latino/as.

Asian American Curriculum Project, P.O. Box 1587, 234 Main Street, San Mateo, CA 94401, (800) 874-2242. Non-profit educational organization that develops and distributes Asian American curriculum materials.

Bilingual Publications Company, 1966 Broadway, New York 10023. Books in Spanish—many about Puerto Rican and Chicano people and culture—for all grade levels.

California Newsreel, 149 Ninth Street, Suite 420, San Francisco, CA 94103, (415) 621-6196. Resource for hard-to-find film and videos made by independent filmmakers, including women, people of color, gays and lesbians and international films.

Cambridge Documentary Films, P.O. Box 385, Cambridge, MA 02139, (617) 354-3677. Resource for documentary films about social issues.

Campaign to End Homophobia, P.O. Box 438316, Chicago, IL 60643-8316. Useful workshop and teaching materials are available; write for a listing of resources.

The Center for Understanding Aging, P.O. Box 246, Southington, CT 06489. Annotated bibliographies and guidelines for choosing anti-ageist books.

Chaselle, Inc., 9645 Geerwig Lane, Columbia, MD 21046-1503. A resource for multicultural program materials; catalogue.

Children's Book Press, 1461 Ninth Ave., San Francisco, CA 94122. Source of stories and folklore of peoples of color living in North America.

Educational Equity Concepts, 114 E 32nd St., NY, NY, 10016, (212) 725-1803. Source of materials that promote equity based on gender, race and disability with particular attention to science, K–3 girls with disabilities, and early childhood education.

Educational Video Center, 55 East 25th St., NY, NY 10010. EVC produces and distributes videos directed by youth about a variety of issues, as well as develops curriculum materials and sponsors workshops about youth video production.

Educators for Social Responsibility, 23 Garden St., Cambridge, MA 02138. Publishes books and distributes videos on teaching about social issues. Provides quarterly newsletter, Forum, to members.

Everyone's Kids Books, 23 Eliot St. Brattleboro, VT 05301, (800) 473-0804. Send for their biannual newsletter that has an annotated listing of high quality multiracial and nonsexist books, as well as books for teachers and parents. Mail order service is efficient and bookstore staff extremely helpful.

Facing History and Ourselves National Foundation, Inc., 16 Hurd Road, Brookline, MA 02146, (617) 232-1595. National organization promoting the development of a more humane and informed society. Publishes a free informative newsletter; offers books, periodicals, videotapes, speakers, and a resource library.

Fairness and Accuracy in Reporting (FAIR), 130 W 25th St., NY 10001. National media watch group working to correct bias. Publishes materials documenting the media's insensitivity to women and people of color, among others.

Family Pastimes, RR 4, Perth, Ontario, Canada K7H3C6. A source of cooperative games for family and school. Catalogue available.

First Run/Icarus Films, 153 Waverly Place Sixth Floor, NY, NY 10014, (800) 876-1710. Distributor of progressive films.

The Gay, Lesbian and Straight Teachers Network (GLSTN), 122 W 26th St., Suite 10011, NY, NY 10011. Source of videos, school materials and other publications to support educators' work to confront homophobia in schools.

Gray Panthers, 1424 16th St. NW, Suite 602, Washington, DC 20036. One of the foremost advocacy groups for older people, the Gray Panthers also publishes resource material. Their newsletter is filled with information on ageism.

Hetrich-Martin Institute, 2 Astor Place, NY, NY 10003-6998, (212) 674-2400. Education and advocacy organization offering services and information for lesbian, gay, and bisexual youth. Many articles and resources available that would be useful to teachers.

Highsmith Multicultural Bookstore, W5527 Highway 106, P.O. Box 800, Fort Atkinson, WI 53538-0800, (800)

558-2110. Multicultural books and media, catalogue and mail order available.

Human Policy Press, Syracuse University, P.O. Box 127, Syracuse, NY 13210. Sources of books, materials, and posters about people with disabilities.

Indian House, Box 472, Taos, NM 87571. Records, cassettes and tapes of Native American music from many nations.

Institute for Peace and Justice, 4144 Lindell Blvd. H124, St. Louis, MO 61308. Curriculum and media dealing with racism, sexism, and peace education.

L & S Video, Inc., 45 Stornowaye, Chappaqua, NY 10514, (914) 238-9366. Distributor of multicultural artist biographies and documentaries.

Lakeshore Learning Materials, 2965 E. Dominguez St., P.O. Box 6261, Carson, CA 90749. Source of progressive educational materials.

Lesbian and Gay Parents Association, 6704 California St. #1, San Francisco, CA 94121. Sources of a video "Both My Moms Names Are Judy," a training guide, and inservice workshops for educators on overcoming homophobia in the elementary classroom.

Massachusetts Department of Education Safe Schools Program, Main St., Medford, (617) 388-3300. Resources for school personnel who want to make schools safer for gay, lesbian and bisexual students.

Mid-Atlantic Equity Consortium and the Mid-Atlantic Center, 5454 Wisconsin Ave., Suite 65, Chevy Chase, MD 20815. Source of resources and support for promoting race, sex and national origin desegregation.

The Museum of Afro-American History, Abiel Smith School, African Meeting House, 46 Joy St., Boston, MA 02114. Sources of materials on African American history; catalogue available.

National Asian American Telecommunications Association (NAATA)/Cross Current Media, 346 Ninth St., 2nd Floor, San Francisco, CA 94103, (415) 552-9550. A comprehensive, annotated resource list of films, videos and audiocassettes that promote better understanding of the Asian, South Asian, South East Asian and Pacific Islander American experiences, primarily by Asian American media makers.

National Association for Asian and Pacific American Education, 310 Eighth St., Suite 200, Oakland, CA 94607. A newsletter and various fact sheets available.

National Caucus and Center on Black Aged, Inc., 1424 K St., NW, Suite 500, Washington, DC 20005. Monographs and articles for educators. Catalogue.

National Center for Fair and Open Testing, 342 Broadway, Cambridge, MA 02139, (617) 864-4810. Source of information and resources on bias in testing and alternatives to it—books, reports, and a quarterly newsletter are all available.

National Center for Immigrant Studies, 100 Boylston Street, Suite 737, Boston, MA 02116-4610, (800) 441-7192. This organization houses the Clearing House for Immigrant Education (CHIME) which offers literature and resources relevant to the education of immigrant students.

National Coalition for Sex Equity in Education, Teddy Martin, 1 Redwood Drive, Clinton, NJ 08809, (908) 735-5045. Newsletter, yearly conferences, and institutes.

National Coalition of Education Activists, P.O. Box 405, Rosendale, NY 12472. National coalition which provides a newsletter with ideas and materials for change-oriented teaching and holds an annual conference with a focus on social justice.

National Council on the Aging, Inc., 600 Maryland Avenue, SW, West Wing 100, Washington, DC 20024. The publications catalog of this group lists innumerable resources on aging.

National Film Board of Canada, 16th Floor, 1251 Avenue of the Americas, NY, NY 10020. Distributor of progressive, independent films from a variety of underrepresented perspectives.

National Institute for Gay, Lesbian, Bisexual, and Transgender Concerns in Education, 55 Glen St., Malden, MA 02148. Resource center for schools and individuals working to create safe and supportive learning environments for gay, lesbian, bisexual and transgendered youth, teachers and families.

National Women's History Project, 7738 Bell Road, Windsor, CA 95492. The project has a variety of K–12 curriculum materials and also offers workshops and seminars.

Native American Authors Distribution Project, Greenfield Review Press, 2 Middle Grove Road, P.O. Box 308, Greenfield Center, NY 12833. Source of books by authors of Native American ancestry; children's literature and audio cassettes of American Indian storytelling are included.

Navajo Curriculum Center Press, Navajo Curriculum Center, Rough Rock Community School, Box 217, RRDS, Chinle, AZ 86503. This center was established specifically for developing curriculum materials and other major publication dealing with Navajo life, history, and culture. Many of their resources have teacher guides. Free catalog.

Network of Educators on the Americas (NECA), 1118 22nd ST. NW, Washington, DC 20037. Source of anti-racist, multicultural curricula and materials with a critical pedagogical approach; offers catalog, *Teaching for Change*.

New Day Films, 121 West 27th Street, Suite 902, NY, NY 10001, (212) 645-8201. Distributor of progressive videos.

New Seed Press, P.O. Box 9488, Berkely, CA 94709-0488, (510) 548-0585. Anti-sexist children's books.

New Society Publishers, New Society Educational Foundation, 4527 Springfield Avenue, Philadelphia, PA 19143. Publishers of social change and social action books.

New Words Bookstore, 186 Hampshire St., Cambridge, MA 02139, (800) 928-4788. Well-stocked feminist bookstore that accepts mail orders; a holiday catalogue of new and suggested books is published each fall. Monthly newsletter available.

Organization for Equal Education of the Sexes, P.O. Box 438 Dept. WA, Blue Hill, ME 04614. Posters for classrooms: multicultural education, women at work.

Parents and Families and Friends of Lesbians and Gays (PFLAG), 1101-14th St., NW, Suite 1030, Washington, DC 20005. Source of useful information about lesbian and gay issues, particularly supporting and educating families and friends; active network of local chapters.

Rabbit Ears Production, Distributed by Uni, Universal City, CA. Video production house of beautifully animated and narrated multicultural American stories, as well as international myth, legends and folktales. Available at most video stores.

Shen's Books and Supplies, 821 South First Ave., Arcadia, CA 91006, (818) 445-6958. Excellent collection of multicultural books.

The Stone Center, Wellesley College, 106 Central Street, Wellesley, MA 02181. Newsletters, papers, audio tapes, videotapes and project reports on women's issues.

Third World Newsreel, 335 West 38th St., NY, NY, (212) 947-9277. Specializing in the distribution of films by and for people of color, both inside and outside the United States.

Up and Out of Poverty Campaign, 54 Essex St., Cambridge, MA 02139. Coalition for Basic Needs. Resources on class and poverty issues.

War Registers League, 339 Lafayette St., NY, 10012. Source of information about peace and justice, with excellent information on how militarism reinforces economic inequality.

Wilmington College Peace Resource Center, Pyle Center, Box 1183, Wilmington, OH 45177. An excellent source of media, books, and curriculum related to nonviolence, the civil rights movement, and racial justice. Catalogue available.

Women's Educational Equity Act Publishing Center, Education Development Center, 55 Chapel St., Newton, MA 02158. Curriculum and in-service materials for addressing gender inequities in education. Catalogue available.

Zenger Media, Social Studies Media Services, 10200 Jefferson Blvd., Room 92, P.O. Box 802, Culver City, CA 90232-0802. Source of social studies materials, including video, "The Columbus Controversy."

2. TEACHER RESOURCES FOR PROMOTING EQUITY IN SCHOOLS

The AAUW Report: How Schools Shortchange Girls, Bailey, Susan and Wellesley College Center for Research on Women. New York, Marlowe and Co., 1995. An analysis of the subtle and blatant manifestations of sexism in schools.

Affirming Diversity: The Sociopolitical Context of Multicultural Education, Nieto, Sonia. New York, Longman, 1996. A comprehensive framework for analyzing multiple causes of school failure among students, with suggested creative intervention strategies supported by research and theory. Ten case studies give students' voice a central place.

Against Borders: Promoting Books for a Multicultural World, Rochman, Hazel. United States, ALA Books/Booklist Publications, 1993. A useful guide to developing thematic reading lists for middle and high school readers; defines multicultural as being *across* cultures.

All Kinds of Minds: A Young Student's Book about Learning Abilities and Disabilities, Levine, Mel. Cambridge, MA, Educator's Publishing Service, 1993. A very readable sourcebook for students and teachers about how our different kinds of minds effect our learning abilities, with a vision of authentic inclusion.

Analysis Kit for Teachers and Librarians, P.O. Box 246, Southington, CT 06489, Center for Understanding Aging. A useful kit of guidelines for choosing non-ageist books.

The Asian American Educational Experience: A Sourcebook for Teachers and Students, Nakanishi, Don and Tina Nishida. New York, Routledge, 1995. A comprehensive reader with a variety of essays about Asian/Pacific American education bringing together fine writers and articles addressing the educational needs of Asian Americans.

Barrios and Borderlands: Cultures of Latinos and Latinas in the United States, Heyck, Denis Lynn Daly, ed. New York, Routledge, 1994. A collection of readings and visual images for high school and middle school students about the historical and contemporary experiences of primarily Cuban, Puerto Rican and Mexican Americans.

Carry It On! A History in Song and Picture of America's Working Men and Women, Reiser, Bob and Peter Seeger. New York, Simon and Schuster, 1985. A scrapbook full of drawings, photos, and quotes as well as historical information pertaining to the 84 songs that describe the diversity of occupations and backgrounds of American workers.

The Challenge of Detracking: A Collection, Palatine, IL, Skylight Publishing, Inc., 1993. A fine collection of writings that provides research about the effects of tracking and offers alternatives to tracking and ability groupings.

Choosing to Participate: A Critical Examination of Citizenship in American History, Stoskopf, Alan L. Brookline, MA, Facing History and Ourselves, 1990. Activities and discussion of the meaning of citizenship and democracy in the United States. Contains useful bibliography and index.

Circles of Learning: Cooperation in the Classroom, Johnson, David W., Roger T. Johnson and Edythe Johnson Holubec. 7208 Cornelia Drive, Edino, MN 55435, Interaction Book Company, 1993. Valuable guide with rationale and practical strategies for structuring learning cooperatively.

Coming Out of the Classroom Closet, Harbeck, Karen. Binghamton, NY, Haworth Press. A collection of essays that encourages educators to understand and confront homophobia in the schools.

Common Bonds: Anti-Bias Teaching in a Diverse Society, Association for Childhood Education International. 11501 Georgia Ave., Wheaton, MD 20902. Useful guide for teachers creating classrooms that are inviting for all students regardless of their background.

Contemporary Art and Multicultural Education, Cahan, Susan, Zoya Kocur and the New Museum of Contemporary Art. New York, Routledge, 1996. Theoretical foundations and practical resources for art educators who want to integrate social concerns and contemporary art with classroom learning. Includes reproductions of over 50 works of contemporary paintings, sculptures and public installations; lesson plans geared to middle school students, and an extensive bibliography.

Cooperative Learning, Cooperative Lives: A Sourcebook of Learning Activities for Building a Peaceful New World. Schniedewind, Nancy and Ellen Davidson, 30 Walnut Ave., Somerville, MA 02143. Circle Books, 1987. A comprehensive introduction to cooperative learning with over 75 lessons in various disciplines that include a focus on teaching about cooperation as an idea and value.

The Cooperative Sports and Game Book, Orlick, Terry. New York, Pantheon, 1978. An excellent book full of cooperative physical activities and ways to make traditional sports more cooperative.

Creating Contexts for Second Language Acquisitions: Theory and Methods, Ramirez, Arnulfo G. Longman Publishers, 1995. An excellent practical resource book for theory and methods for teaching second languages.

Culturally Relevant Teaching, Theory into Practice, Volume 34:3, Summer 1995, (614) 292-3407. Special issue of *Theory into Practice* edited by Gloria Ladson-Billing.

The Dreamkeepers: Successful Teachers of African American Children, Ladson-Billings, Gloria. San Francisco, Jossey-Bass, 1994. Portraits of eight exemplary teachers help us learn how successful teachers of African American students teach.

Educating for a Just Society, McGinnis, Kathleen. St. Louis, MO, Institute for Peace and Justice, 1993. Activities and resources for teaching about and changing a variety of forms of oppression.

Empowerment through Multicultural Education, Sleeter, Christine. Albany, SUNY Press, 1991. A collection of essays that explore ways that multicultural education can empower teachers and students to effect educational and social change.

Equity in Physical Education, Clement, Annie and Betty Hartman. Newton, MA, Women's Educational Equity Act Program. Booklet to aid teachers in planning an equitable co-educational program.

Everyone Wins!: Cooperative Games and Activities, Luvmour, Sambhava. Philadelphia, New Society Publishers, 1990. Excellent resource for teachers developing cooperative situations, includes bibliography.

Failing at Fairness: How America's Schools Cheat Girls, Sadker, Myra and David Sadker. New York, MacMillan, 1994. An excellent resource documenting sexism in education at all levels, K–college, with a chapter also on the miseducation of boys.

Foundations of Bilingual Education and Bilingualism, Baker, Coline and Ofelia Garcia. Philadelphia, Multilingual Matters, 1993. Good background reading on bilingual education.

Freedom's Plow: Teaching in the Multicultural Classroom, Perry, Theresa and James W. Fraser. New York, Routledge, 1993. Teachers from all levels reflect on their struggles to implement anti-racist curricula and offer practice-based guidelines. Bibliographies, discographies, sample math and writing exercises, and reading lists are included.

The Friendly Classroom for a Small Planet, Prutzman, Priscilla, et al. Tucson, Zephyr Press, 1988. Handbook for teachers for enhancing classroom communication and creative conflict resolution.

Funding for Justice: Money, Equity, and the Future of Public Education, Karp, Stan, Robert Lowe, Barbara Miner, Bob Peterson. Milwaukee, *Rethinking Schools*, 1997. Issues of school finance are presented in a readable format and make a case for equitable funding to all schools.

Handbook of Research on Multicultural Education, Banks, James and Cheryl McGee Banks, eds. New York, MacMillan, 1995. Brings together scholarship, research, and theory in the field of multicultural education.

Here's to the Women: 100 Songs for and about American Women, Wenner, Hilda E. and Elizabeth Freilicher. Syracuse, Syracuse University Press, 1987. A comprehensive anthology of traditional and contemporary songs ties women's song to their culture and history; included are extensive notes, lyrics, sheet music, and chord arrangements.

Hostile Hallways: The AAUW Survey on Sexual Harassment in America's Schools, AAUW Educational Foundation. Washington, D.C., 1993. Survey on sexual harassment in America's schools.

Images of Aging in Literature in the Middle Grades, P.O. Box 246 Southington, CT 04689. Center for Understanding Aging. An annotated booklist to analyze children's books for their views on aging.

Letters to Marcia: A Teacher's Guide to Anti-Racist Education, Lee, Enid. 2909 Dundes St. West, Toronto, Ontario M6P121. Cross Cultural Communication Center, 1985. Commentary and activities that help teachers understand anti-racist education and examine their school, community relations, and student services for their anti-racist practices.

Lies My Teacher Told Me: Everything Your American History Textbook Got Wrong, Lowen, James. New York, New Press, 1995. While focussed on high school history textbooks, this analysis of inaccuracies and omissions is useful to teachers of history at lower levels as well.

Making Choices for Multicultural Education: Five Approaches to Race, Class, and Gender, Sleeter, Christine and Carl Grantt. NY, MacMillan, 1994. Description of five approaches to teaching about race, class and gender that help educators reflect on their own teaching.

The Multicolored Mirror: Cultural Substance in Literature for Children and Young Adults, Lindgren, Merri V. and Cooperative Children's Book Center, Wisconsin, Highsmith Press, 1991. This volume includes materials on cultural authenticity; authors, illustrators and publisher's perspectives; bibliographies and resource lists.

Multicultural Education: Issues and Perspectives, Banks, James and Cherry McGee. Boston, Allyn and Bacon, 1993. Theories and strategies for creating multicultural classrooms and schools.

The New Games Book, Fluegelman, Andrew. Garden City, NY, Doubleday, 1976. A resource of both cooperative and competitive games for all numbers and all ages.

Often Invisible: Counseling Gay and Lesbian Youth, Schnieder, Margaret. Guide for educators that includes background, strategies and resources.

One Teacher in 10: Gay and Lesbian Teachers Tell Their Stories, Kevin Jennings, ed. Boston, Alyson Publishers, 1994. An anthology of personal accounts of lesbian and gay teachers as they deal with homophobia in schools and in society.

Open Lives: Safe Schools, Donovan Walling. Phi Delta Kappa Education Foundation, Bloomington, IN, 1996. A collection of essays written for educators that points to the benefits to all when everyone can be open with respect to sexual orientation.

Other People's Children: Cultural Conflict in the Classroom, Delpit, Lisa. NY, New Press, 1995. A critique of the teaching practices of many white teachers that do not address the educational needs of students of color, this collection of essays also suggests ideas for ways that teachers can be better cultural translators.

The People's Voice: Puerto Rico, Dominican Republic and Cuba Culture and History (three volumes). The People's Publishing Group. Rochester, NY, (800) 822-1080, Rochester City School District, 1993. A comprehensive series of primary and secondary readings, maps, illustrations, and curriculum ideas.

Playfair: Everybody's Guide to Non-Competitive Play, Weinstein, Matt and Joel Goodman. San Luis Obispo, CA, Impact Publishers, 1980. Resource book of cooperative games.

Playing Favorites: Gifted Education and the Disruption of Community, Sapon-Shevin, Mara. Albany, NY, SUNY Press, 1994. Examination of the ways gifted education disrupts the classroom community, deskills regular classroom teachers and impairs the climate of inclusion and acceptance of difference.

Project 10 Handbook: Addressing Lesbian and Gay Issues in Our Schools, Friends of Project, 7850 Melrose Ave., Los Angeles, CA 90046. A resource guide for adults for addressing heterosexism in schools.

Promoting Self-Esteem in Young Women: A Manual for Teachers, Division of Civil Rights and Intercultural Relations. Albany, NY, University of the State of New York, State Education Department, Division of Civil Rights and Intercultural Relations, 1988. Free at this address.

Reaching Out: Interpersonal Effectiveness and Self-Actualization, Johnson, David. Englewood Cliffs, NJ, Prentice-Hall, 1992. A basic handbook of communication skills.

Reach, Touch and Teach: Student Concerns and Basic Education, Burton, Terry. NY, McGraw Hill, 1970. A basic introduction to affective teaching strategies for teachers reflecting a humanistic approach to education.

Resource Guide for Asian and Pacific American Students K–12. Lu, Janet. 310 Eighth St. Suite 280, Oakland, CA 94607, National Association for Asian and Pacific American Education. Information and lessons plans.

Rethinking Columbus, Rethinking Schools. 1001 E. Keefe Ave., Milwaukee, WI 53212. The 1992 special edition of the *Rethinking Schools* periodical contains lessons, essays, short stories, interviews, poetry, and bibliography to help teachers critically analyze the celebration of Columbus Day.

Rethinking Schools: An Agenda for Change. Levine, David, et al. NY, New Press, 1995. A volume of essays by leading reformers, including teachers, that focus on multiculturalism, curriculum, and national policy concerns, among others.

Rethinking Our Classrooms: Teaching for Equity and Justice, Bill Bigelow et al., eds. 1001 E Keefe, Milwaukee, WI 53212, 1994. A special edition of the journal *Rethinking Schools*, this is an outstanding collection of teaching ideas, classroom narratives, and hands-on examples of ways teachers can promote values of community, justice and equality.

The Second Cooperative Sports and Games Book, Orlick, Terry. NY, Pantheon, 1982. Two hundred non-competitive games for kids and adults both, offers a variety of cooperative games, many with a multicultural focus.

Secrets in Public: Sexual Harassment in Our Schools. Stein, Nan, Nancy Marshall and Linda Trup. Wellesley, MA, Center for Research on Women, Wellesley College, 1993. Responses to a 1992 survey of 4,200 girls in grades 2–12 on sexual harassment in schools.

Selling Out Our Schools: Vouchers, Markets, and the Future of Public, Lowe, Robert and Barbara Miner, Milwaukee, WI. *Rethinking Schools*, 1996. Articles by nationally known educators about how vouchers and marketplace approaches to education threaten our basic concepts of equality.

Shadow and Substance: Afro-American Experience in Contemporary Children's Fiction, Sims, Rudine. Urbana, IL. National Council of Teachers of English, 1982. A history and criticism of the African American experience in children's literature.

Student Social Class and Teacher Expectations: The Self-Fulfilling Prophecy in Ghetto Education. Ris, Ray. *Harvard Educational Review* 40:3 (1970): 411–50. A powerful study on the effects of teachers' attitudes about class on student achievement.

Symposium on Multicultural Approaches to Music Education, 1902 Association Drive, Reston, VA 22091. Music Educators National Conference Publication Sales. Series includes videos on teaching the music of the American Indian, Hispanic Americans, Asian Americans, and African Americans, with practical ideas and examples for use in the classroom.

Teaching Multicultural Literature in Grades K–8, Harris, Violet. Norwood, MA, Christopher-Gordon Publishers, 1992. Discussion and criticism of children's books about people of color as well as suggestions on how to make informed choices. Includes sources for multicultural children's literature.

Teaching Strategies for Ethnic Studies, Banks, James. Boston, Allyn and Bacon, 1991. Very thorough volume of ideas and materials for teaching about a variety of ethnic groups.

Through Indian Eyes: The Native Experience in Books for Children, Slapin, Beverly and Doris Seale. Philadelphia, New Society Publishers, 1992. Through personal recollections, poetry, art, bibliographies, over 100 book reviews, and a resource section on Native American publishers, this collection of articles discusses the impact of the stereotyping, sometimes subtle, of Native peoples and its effects on youth readers.

Title IX: A Practical Guide to Achieving Sex Equity in Education, National Coalition for Women and Girls in Education, 1616 P St. NW, Washington, DC 20036. National Coalition for Women and Girls in Education, c/o National Women's Law Center, 1988. Useful resource of strategies for achieving classroom sex equity.

Towards a Humanistic Education. Fantini, Mario and Gerald Weinstein. New York, Praeger Publishers, 1970. Combines theory and practical strategies for affective education.

Twenty-First Century Challenge: Lesbians and Gays in Education, McConnell-Celi, Sue. P.O. Box 8932, Red Bank, New Jersey 07701. Lavender Crystal Press. Explores lesbian and gay experience within the classroom setting. A few activities for students are included.

Unlearning Indian Stereotypes (oop), Council on Interracial Books for Children. Booklet and 15 min. film strip with valuable information about teaching accurate information about Native Americans to elementary students.

Values Clarification: A Handbook of Practical Strategies, Simon, Sidney, Leland Howe and Howard Kirschenbaum. New York, Values Press, 1991. Numerous values clarification activities to use with both students and adults.

Women of Hope: African Americans Who Made a Difference 330 West 42nd St., 15th Floor, NY, NY 10036, (212) 631-4565. Bread and Roses Cultural Project, Inc. Large, attractive biographical posters of 12 African American women.

Women of Hope: Latinas Abriendo Camino, Bread and Roses Distribution Center, P.O. Box 346, Kitztown, PA, 19530-0346, (800) 666-1728. Large, attractive biographical posters of 12 Latinas.

3. CURRICULUM

Anti-Bias Curriculum: Tools for Empowering Young Children, Derman-Sparks, Louise. Washington, National Association for Education of Young Children, 1989. Explores the roots of prejudice and offers guidelines for helping children recognize and reject biased behavior.

Asian American Studies Curriculum Resource Guide, Kiang, Peter. P.O. Box 630, Needham, MA 02192, Massachusetts Asian American Educators Association, 1992. Developed in Massachusetts for K–12 teachers, this guide provides activities and resources for a thematic approach to teaching about the Asian American experience.

Asian American Women, Yokota, Yolanda and Linda Wing. Berkeley, CA, Berkeley Unified School District. Available from Susan Groves at (510) 644-8839. A teaching unit on the history and experience of Asian women in this country, grades 5–8.

Bullyproof, Sjostrom, Lisa and Nan Stein. Wellesley, MA, Wellesley College Center for Research on Women, 1996. While naming bullying, like its cousin sexual harassment, an issue of social justice, the authors provide lessons for 4th and 5th graders on teasing and bullying.

Caribbean Connections Series: Overview, Puerto Rico and Jamaica, Sunshine, Catherine. Washington, D.C., NECA/EPICA, 1991. Three highly acclaimed collections of fiction, non-fiction, oral histories, interviews, poetry, drama and songs; includes a teacher's guide.

Chinese Americans Past and Present, Asian American Curriculum Project. San Mateo, CA, Japanese American Curriculum Project. A book of 20 stories for students 9–12 with activity sheets, book, and teacher guide.

Creative Conflict Solving for Kids, Schmidt, Fran and Alice Friedman. P.O. Box 191153, Miami Beach, FL 33119, Grace Contrino Abrams Peace Education Foundation, 1991. Well sequenced series of practical activities necessary to creative conflict resolution—affirmation, dealing with feelings, "fighting fair," conflict resolution strategies, and mediation.

Decisions, Decisions: Prejudice. Snyder, Tom. 80 Coolidge Hill Road, Watertown, MA 02172, (800) 342-0236. Free 45 day trial. Computer software. 1992, Apple/Mac/MD-DOS. A cooperative role-playing software package that gets groups of students learning and talking about prejudice and discrimination.

Fighting Fair: Martin Luther King for Kids, Schmidt, Fran and Alice Friedman. 2627 Biscayne Blvd. Miami, FL 33137, 1987. An excellent short curriculum that links key practices of conflict resolution for kids to the nonviolent principles of the Civil Rights movement. An excellent video is a part of the package.

Flirting or Hurting? A Teacher's Guide on Sexual Harassment in Schools for 6th through 12th Grade Students, Stein, Nancy and Lisa Sjostrom. 106 Central Street, Wellesley, MA 02181, Wellesley College for Research on Women, 1994. Activities and strategies for helping students deal with sexual harassment.

Holocaust Testimonies: Facing History and Ourselves, Elements of Time. Facing History and Ourselves. Brookline, MA, Facing History and Ourselves, 1989. Text is companion manual for Facing History videotape collection of Holocaust testimonies.

"I Am Loveable and Capable," Simon, Sidney. Hadley, MA, Values Press, 1991. Short pamphlet with the complete text of the original "I Am Loveable and Capable" story.

Investigations in Number, Data and Space, Susan Jo Russell et al. Dale Seymour, 1994. Emphasizes children inventing mathematics. Strong parental contact, cooperative learning, and in-depth mathematical understanding. Also has an English as a second language component to each lesson.

It's Your Right!, Kaser, Joyce and Susan Shaffer. Chevy Chase, MD, Mid Atlantic Equity Consortium, 1996. A handbook for students about Title IX, with a focus on high school students enrolled in courses nontraditional to their gender.

The Japanese Americans: An Inside Look, Asian American Curriculum Project. 414 E 3rd Ave., San Mateo, CA 94401, Asian American Curriculum Project. Program covers experience of Japanese Americans, issues of citizenship, racism, etc. Two film strips, cassette/record also available in Japanese.

La Chicana Curriculum, Groves, Susan and Clementine Duron. Berkeley, CA, Berkeley Unified School District. Available from Susan Groves at (510) 644-8839, Lessons and activities about Mexican American women.

The Language of Numbers, Education Development Center. Portsmouth, NH, Heinemann, 1994. For 6th and 7th grade students; has students explore and compare number systems throughout the world and times in history.

Mainstreaming for Equity: Activity and Resource Kits, New York, Educational Equity Concepts, Inc. A curriculum for all children, disabled and nondisabled, that can be integrated into language arts and social studies classes in grade K–6.

A Manual on Nonviolence and Children, Judson, Stephanie. Philadelphia, PA, Friends Peace Committee. Describes program and activities that help children resolve conflicts nonviolently.

A Map of American Indian History, 8821 N. 1st St., Phoenix, AZ 85020, Thunderbird Enterprises. Valuable resource for teaching U.S. history, locating reservations and historical sites.

Number Power, Robertson, L., et al. Addison-Wesley, 1993. Emphasizes mathematical understanding and problem solving through a clearly structured and processed cooperation learning format. Available in separate books for grades 2–6.

The Power in Our Hands: A Curriculum on the History of Work and Workers in the United States, Bigelow, Bill and Norm Diamond. New York, Monthly Review Press. While geared for high school students, ideas and lessons can be adapted to lower levels. Available from the Network of Educators on the Americas.

Teaching about Hair, Network of Educators on the Americas. 1118 22nd St. NW Washington, DC 20037. Teaching ideas, materials, stories, folktales, cultural information about all kinds of hair in one compact resource.

Teaching about Haiti, Network of Educators on the Americas. 1118 22nd Street NW, Washington, DC 20037. Factual information, folktales, and cultural information about Haiti in one compact resource.

4. MEDIA

These media selections are geared for a range of audiences. Be sure to preview to make sure they are appropriate for your students.

Adelante Mujeres, National Women's History Project. A comprehensive video on the history of Chicanas. 30 min.

American Women of Achievement video series, Schlessinger Video Productions, available from National Women's History Project. Thirty-minute videos on, for example, Jane Addams, Helen Keller, Wilma Rudolph.

Bill Cosby on Prejudice. University of Minnesota, Minneapolis, MN. Warren Schloat Productions. Video/25 min. A biting monologue by Bill Cosby that hits home regarding prejudice.

Black Americans of Achievement video series, Schlessinger Video Productions, available from National Women's History Project. Thirty-minute videos on Harriet Tubman, Sojourner Truth, Mary McLeod Bethune.

Black History, Lost, Stolen, or Strayed. Movies Unlimited, 6736 Castor Ave. Philadelphia, PA, (800) 523-0823. Video/60 min. Powerful account of how the black race has been dehumanized through the media and history.

Both My Moms' Names Are Judy. c/o 6705 California St., #1, San Francisco, CA 94121: LGPA. Video/10 min. A racially diverse group of children (ages 7–10) talk about the love they feel for their families, how teasing and the classroom silence about lesbian and gay men affect them, and how they would like their families validated in school.

Chinese Americans: Realities and Myths. Institute for Peace and Justice. St. Louis, MO. Set of four filmstrips and cassettes discuss the historic and present day realities of life for Chinese Americans.

Chinese Jump Rope. 727 O St., Lincoln, NE 68508, (800) 228-0164: Instructional Video. video/28 min./1995. Chinese jump rope, a double elastic band stretched between two players legs, is introduced clearly in all its complex variations by a grandmother and granddaughter team. The game's Chinese heritage is well discussed.

Chrysanthemums and Salt. San Francisco: NAATA. Video/26 min./1994. A powerful examination of Japanese Americans who lived in Northern California from 1872–1942.

The Columbus Controversy: Challenging How History Is Written, Culver City, CA: Zenger Media. Video/30 min. This video presents different points of view about Christopher Columbus' actions and influence; it raises questions about the legacy of racism toward Native peoples that began with Columbus' "discovery" of America.

Crystal Lee Jordan. Bloomington, IN: Indiana University AV Center. Film/video. From the perspective of a strong woman union leader, a view of the organizing struggle of blacks and whites at the J.P. Stevens Mills in the South.

Environmental Racism. New York: Third Word Newsreel. video/60 min./1990. Two thirty-minute programs: Part

I combines footage from 20 sources that document urban waste dumping, fighting for clean air and water, etc. Part II targets issues in Native American and Mexican communities.

Ethnic Notions. San Francisco, CA: California Newsreel. Video/56 min./1987. Award winning documentary that traces the evolution of deeply rooted stereotypes which have fueled anti-black prejudice for over 150 years.

Eye of the Storm. 245 Long Hill Rd., Middletown, CT 06457: Xerox. Film/video/30 min. An in-the-classroom view of a 4th grade public school teacher using the blue-eye/brown-eye experiment to effectively teach about discrimination.

Eyes on the Prize: America's Civil Rights Years. Alexandria, VA.: PBS Video. Video/60 min. Series I and II; 10 outstanding videos documenting the American civil rights movement from 1954 through the 1980s.

The Fable of He and She. University of Minnesota Media Center, Minneapolis, MN, (612) 627-4270. Video. A short animated story of men and women freeing themselves from their sex role definitions.

The Fairer Sex. 1359 Barclay Blvd. Buffalo Grove, IL 60089, (800) 537-3130: Core Vision Media. Video/20 min. This segment of an ABC Prime Time program followed two discrimination testers—one male, one female— as they moved to new city and tried to get housing, employment, buy a car, etc.

Faith Ringold, Part II: The Crown Heights Story. Chappaqua: L & S Video, Inc. Video/28 min./1995. Inspirational look at 12 cultures that have settled in Crown Heights, Brooklyn as depicted in Ringold's story quilt, combining painting, quilting, and storytelling.

Faith Ringold: The Last Story Quilt. L & S Video, Inc. Video/28 min./1992. Biography of African American artist and children's book writer who paints on quilted canvases, with frames of text and traditionally quilted fabrics.

Fannie Lou Hamer. 2 Halfmile Common, Westport, CT 06880: Rediscovery Productions. Film/10 min. A short film about the black female Civil Rights activist.

Free to Be You and Me. McGraw-Hill Films. Available in most major video stores. 40 min. Video of stories, songs, dances emphasizing human potentialities for boys and girls and women and men.

From Mott to Mulberry. New York: Third Word Newsreel. Video/30 min./1992. Humorous and poignant story of a first generation Chinese American adolescent who is torn between his mother's desire for him to find a nice Chinese girl and his desire to assimilate.

Fundi: The Story of Ella Baker. New York: First Run/Icarus Films, film/video/45 min./1986. Life story of a dynamic civil rights activist who challenged the inclusion of old, young and women in the Black Movement.

A Gang for Good. New York: First Run/Icarus Films. Video/58 min./1992. Boys from ages 6–18 in NY's Lower East Side join the Citizens of the Boy's Brotherhood Republic, where they elect their own mayor, city council, and have their own police and court systems. Founded at the turn of the century, BBR develops self-reliance and self-esteem in young boys.

The Hundred Penny Box. Chicago: Terra Nova Films. Film/video/. Award-winning film based on the children's book of the same name; a young African American boy and his warm relationship with his 100 year old great aunt are contrasted with his conflicts with his busy mother.

I Am Somebody. University of Minnesota Media Center, Minneapolis, MN, (612) 627-4270. A documentary film of the 1969 Charlestown hospital workers strike. Strikers are mainly black women fighting for civil rights and union representation.

Ida B. Wells: A Passion for Justice. New York: William Greaves Productions. Video/53 min./1991. Multi-award winning documentary presents the life story of Ida B. Wells (1862–1931); investigative journalist, social activist and champion of racial justice.

In Remembrance of Martin. Pyle Center, Box 1183, Wilmington, OH 45177: Wilmington College Peace Resource Center Film. A PBS broadcast commemorating Dr. Martin Luther King, Jr.; an excellent summary of his leadership in the civil rights movement.

Lives on the Line: Civil Disobedience in the United States. Pyle Center, Box 1183, Wilmington, OH 45177: Wilmington College Peace Resource Center. Film. Excellent history of civil disobedience in the U.S. from colonial days to the present.

Men Caring for Your Children. Cobbleskill, NY: Bonita Klemm, Early Childhood Division, SUNY Cobbleskill. Video. Celebrates a diverse group of men who have chosen careers in working with infants and young children in a variety of settings.

Men's Lives. 22D Hollywood Ave., Hohokus, NJ 07432, 201-652-6590: New Day Films. Introductory film about the socialization of men in our society.

Miguel: Up from Puerto Rico. University of Minnesota Media Center, Minneapolis, MN (612) 627-4270. Film/video/15 min./. Story of young Puerto Rican boy living in New York City who uses his knowledge of Spanish to earn money to get his father a special birthday treat.

My Brown Eyes. San Francisco: NAATA. Video/18 min./1994. A 10 year old boy, the son of Korean immigrants, rises and prepares himself for his first day in an American school. Told from a child's point of view, the problems he encounters are not what one would expect.

Not in Our Town. Brookline, Mass: Facing History and Ourselves. Video/30 min. Interviews with the people of Billings, Montana who courageously cooperated to fight hate groups that targeted other citizens because of race, religion, and sexual orientation. Excellent.

Other Women: Other Work. 662 N. Robertson Blvd., Los Angeles, CA 90069: Churchill Films. Film/20 min. Women working in traditionally male fields are interviewed and shown in their work e.g., roofer, pilot, marine, biologist, veterinarian, reporter, carpenter.

Pink Triangles. New York: Cambridge Documentary Films. Video. Documentary that explores prejudice against lesbians and gay men, its historical roots and connections with other forms of oppression.

Playing Fair: Anti Racism Scenes. New York: National Film Board of Canada. Film/15 min. each/. A series of 4 interaction dramas for 7 to 12 years olds to spark thought and discussion about the effects of racism.

Respect Is Due. New York: Third Word Newsreel. Video/10 min. 1992. Black youth discuss the ways women of African descent are portrayed in rap lyrics and music videos.

Rice and Peas. New York: First Run/Icarus Films. Video/12 min./1990. Gillian Charles, restaurant owner and chef, makes rice and peas while reminiscing about her native Trinidad and the adjustments that she has made in moving to the U.S., keeping her cultural heritage intact by introducing it to a new world.

The Right to Be a Mohawk. 22D Hollywood Ave., Hohokus, NJ 07432, 201-652-6590: New Day Films, video/. Documents the Mohawk's determination to preserve their culture.

Rosa Parks. 2747 Rutger, St. Louis, MO 63104: Institute for Peace and Justice. Filmstrip/cassette/15 min. The story of Rosa Parks.

The Safe Schools Video Project. Main St., Medford, MA 617-388-3300: Massachusetts Department of Education Safe Schools Program. Video/28 min./1996. A diverse group of teens talk about how they are making their schools safer for gay, lesbian, and bisexual students.

Starting Small: A Cassette Tape by Bob Blue. 54 Walnut Street, Apt. 213, Waltham, MA 02154,1990. Excellent tape with songs that raise issues about various kinds of diversity.

Strangers in Good Company. First Run/Icarus Films. Film/video/105 min./1990. Eight older women, stranded in the middle of nowhere after their bus breaks down, turn a crisis into a magical time. The film uses real women in a fictional setting.

True Colors. P.O. Box 2284 South Burlington, VT 05407, (800) 913-3434: Prime Time ABC News. Video/20 min./. This segment of PrimeTime News follows two discrimination testers, one black, one white, as they move to a new city and try to find housing, get a job, buy a car, etc.

Union Maids. 22D Hollywood Ave., Hohokus, NJ 07432, 201-652-6590: New Day Films. Film/video/45 min. Account of three women workers in Chicago and their history as union members—vibrant music backs up a moving film.

We Shall Overcome. San Francisco: California Newsreel. Video/58 min./1989. By tracing the source of this civil rights anthem, the diverse strands of social history become intertwined with the cultural roots of the Civil Rights movement.

Women in American History. Baldwin, NY 11520, (516) 223-4666: Educational Activities. Filmstrip. Series of six filmstrips and tapes tracing the history of women in America concluding with the current Women's movement.

Women on the March. New York National Film Board of Canada. Film/30 min. A documentary of the women's rights movement in Britain and the U.S.

Women Should Be (A Priority). New York: Global Vision. Video/6 min./1993. Grammy Award winning music video about contemporary women's rights by black female acapella group, Sweet Honey in the Rock.

Wrinkled Radical. Instructional Support Services, Indiana University, Bloomington, IN 47405. 16 mm/video. A documentary film about Maggie Kuhn, the spirited leader of the Gray Panthers.

The Writing on the Wall. 6901 Woodley Ave. Van Nuys, CA 90410, (800) 334-7830: Churchill Media. Video/45 min./1995. Based on actual events, this CBS Schoolbreak Special dramatizes the story of three teens who write anti-Semitic messages on a temple wall and on a rabbi's home.

5. PERIODICALS

Action for Better Schools, Newsletter of the National Coalition of Education Activists. P.O. Box 405, Rosendale, NY 12472. Resources and articles on multiculturalism and other current issues.

Akwesasne Notes, Indian Time, P.O. Box 196, Mohawk Nation, Rooseveltown, NY 13683-0196, (518) 358-9531. Voice of Native people throughout the Americas.

Cooperative Learning. c/o CSCP-LB 581, Concordia University, 1455 De Maisonneuve Blvd. West, Montreal, Quebec, Canada, H3G1M8. A quarterly magazine about cooperative learning with special focus issues that sometimes highlight fostering diversity.

Dollars and Sense, 1 Summer Street, Somerville, MA 02143. Provides easy to understand articles about the economy from a progressive perspective.

Equity Coalition, University of Michigan, School of Education, Program for Educational Opportunity, Ann Arbor, MI 48109. Quarterly journal for educators on all aspects of equal educational opportunity.

EXTRA, 130 West 25th St., New York, NY 10001. A bimonthly magazine documenting bias in the media. See past special issues on "Racism and the Media," and "Missing Voices: Women and the U.S. News Media."

Fair Test Examiner, National Center for Fair and Open Testing, 342 Broadway, Cambridge, MA 02139. Quarterly newsletter with reports and articles about bias in standardized testing and alternative testing structures.

Feminist Teacher, Ballantine Press, Indiana University, Bloomington, IN, 47405. Journal for teachers published three times per year with good articles for promoting gender-fair, multicultural classrooms and schools.

Gray Panther Network, 2025 Pennsylvania Ave., NW, Suite 821, Washington, DC 20006, (800) 280-5362, (202) 466-3132. Newsletter of the Gray Panthers, an elder activist network.

In These Times, 1300 W. Belmont, Chicago, IL 60657. Biweekly journal of contemporary news with a critical perspective.

Journal of American Indian Information, 415 Farmer Building, Arizona State University Tempe, AZ 85287-1311, Center for Indian Education. Journal covers different topics in the whole area of Indian education. Good background reading for teachers.

Ms, 370 Lexington Avenue, New York, 10017. Popular monthly magazines aimed at a broad audience reflecting a variety of perspectives on women.

The Nation, 72 Fifth Ave., New York, NY 10011. America's leading left/liberal weekly magazine.

"New Voices": A Newsletter from the National Center for Immigrant Students, National Coalition of Advocates for Students, 100 Boylston St., Suite 737, Boston, MA 02116. Source of information and materials about recently immigrated students.

Rethinking Schools, 1001 E Keefe, Milwaukee, WI 53212. Excellent education journal offering discussions on a wide variety of recent topics, including anti-racist education, geared for teachers.

Southern Exposure, 2000 Chapel Hill Road, Durham, NC 27701. Periodical with special attention to Southern struggles.

Teaching Tolerance, 400 Washington Ave., Montgomery, AL 36104. Free magazine published twice yearly by the Southern Poverty Law Center that focuses on multicultural and anti-bias diversity strategies for teachers.

Women's Studies Quarterly, Feminist Press, City University of New York, 311 E. 94th St., New York, NY 10128. Articles and information on women's studies and feminist curriculum for both the college level and K–12 teachers.

6. BACKGROUND READING FOR TEACHERS

Adams, Maurienne, Lee Bell and Pat Griffin, eds. *Teaching for Diversity and Social Justice*. New York, Routledge, 1997. A handbook of rationales and designs for workshops geared toward adults that foster social justice, focussing on the issues of racism, sexism, homophobia and anti-Semitism, among others.

Acuña, Rodolfo, *Occupied America: A History of Chicanos*. New York, Harper, 1988. A comprehensive history of Chicanos.

Albrecht, Lisa and Rose Brewer, eds. *Bridges of Power: Women's Multicultural Alliances*. Philadelphia, New Society Publishers, 1990. Discusses women in coalitions that include women across lines of race, class and sexual orientation.

Ada, Alma Flor and Josefina Tinagera, eds. *The Power of Two Languages: Literacy and Biliteracy for Hispanic Students*. New York, MacMillan, 1992. Collection of essays on bilingual issues, including a valuable chapter, "We Speak in Many Languages: Language Diversity and Multicultural Education," by Sonia Nieto.

Anzaldúa, Gloria, ed. *Making Face, Making Soul: Haciendo Caras, Creative and Critical Perspectives by Women of Color*. San Francisco, Aunt Lute Books, 1990. A powerful compilation of scholarly research, folk tales, personal narratives, poetry, art, and fiction that confronts and challenges the simplicity with which feminists of color are viewed.

Asian Women United of California, *Making Waves: An Anthology of Writing by and about Asian American Women*. Boston, Beacon Press, 1989. A collection of autobiographical writings, short stories, poetry, essays and photographs by and about Asian American women includes the discussion of immigration, war, work, generations, identity, discrimination and activism.

Barlett, Donald and James Steele. *America, What Went Wrong?* Kansas City, MO, Andrews and McMeel Publishers, 1992. An excellent analysis of how the government and corporate leaders have developed laws and policies to favor the privileged at the expense of everyone else.

Baxandall, Rosalyn, Linda Gordon and Susan Reverby, *America's Working Women: A Documentary History— 1600 to the Present*. New York, Vintage, 1995. Primary source materials about working women through U.S. history with very useful commentary.

Bell, Derrick, *Faces at the Bottom of the Well: The Permanence of Racism*. New York. Basic Books, 1992. Intertwining fact and fiction, Bell offers a series of short stories to support his belief that racism is a permanent part of U.S. culture and society.

Bonilla, Frank and Rebecca Morales, eds. *Latinos in a Changing U.S. Economy: A Comparative Perspective on Growing Inequality*. San Francisco, SAGE Publishers, 1993. A collection of essays on the economic contexts of Latinos and Latinas in the United States.

Boston Women's Health Collective, *The New Our Bodies, Our Selves*. New York, Simon and Schuster, 1992. A thorough, practical handbook for women providing factual information about their bodies and discussion of women's health issues.

Brown, Dee, *Bury My Heart at Wounded Knee*. New York, Bantam, 1975. A comprehensive story of the Native American perspective of American History.

Brown, Wesley and Amy Ling, eds. *Imagining America: Stories from the Promised Land*. New York, Persea Books, 1991. Following the waves of immigration from the 1930s to the present, thirty seven stories reflect immigrants' need to reconcile America's mythologized "promise" with her more complex reality.

Brown, Wesley and Amy Ling, eds. *Visions of America: Personal Narratives form the Promised Land*. New York, Persea Books, 1991. Autobiographical narratives by both well-known and unknown writers discuss what it has meant to be in America, whether as an immigrant or as a citizen, over the last one hundred years.

Bulosan, Carlos, *America Is in the Heart*. Seattle, WA, University of Washington Press, 1973. A complex and compelling autobiography of a Filipino immigrant and poet in the 1930s and 1940s.

Burke, Phyllis, *Family Values: A Lesbian Mother's Fight for Her Son*. New York, Vintage Books, 1993. The moving story of Burke's entry into motherhood, and her growing politicization when her lesbian partner bears a child by donor insemination and Burke tries to adopt him only to find that lesbians are denied the legal rights to be mothers.

Chideya, Farai, *Don't Believe the Hype: Fighting Cultural Misinformation about African-Americans.* New York, Plume Books, 1995. Written in a question/answer format, Chideya gives the reader facts and statistics to refute the stereotypes and misinformation often accepted as "truth" about the 31 million African Americans in the U.S.

Chin, Frank, et al., eds. *The Big AIIIEEEEE! The History of Chinese American and Japanese American Literature,* 1991. A literary anthology and an historical exploration and exposure of the forces that created and perpetuated the Asian American stereotype.

Cohen, Leah Hager, *Train Go Sorry: Inside a Deaf World.* Boston, Houghton Mifflin, 1994. Poignant discussion of the controversy over mainstreaming the deaf and the use of hearing aids vs. deaf cultures and communities.

Cole, Jim, *Filtering People: Understanding and Confronting Our Prejudices.* 1990. A quick read, this book shows us one person's journey through developing prejudices to understanding and beginning to deal with them. Many cartoon-like drawings and captions.

Comer, James and Alvin Poussaint, *Raising Black Children: Questions and Answers for Parents and Teachers.* NY, Penguin, 1992. With a focus on parents, this book also addresses concerns teachers have about educating black children. Written in question/answer format.

Cooney, Robert and Helen Michalowski, eds. *The Power of the People: Active Non-Violence in the United States.* Philadelphia, New Society, 1987. A resource that documents the struggles of U.S. women and men working for peace and social justice through nonviolent action. Many excellent photographs.

Cose, Ellis, *The Rage of the Privileged Class.* New York, Harper Collins. 1993. Examination of the racism middle class African Americans experience and its effects on them.

Cummins, Jim, *Empowering Minority Students.* Sacramento, California Association for Bilingual Education, 1988. Cummins presents a valuable framework for the education of linguistic minority children.

David, Deborah and Robert Brannon, *The Forty-Nine Percent Majority: The Male Sex Role.* Reading, MA, Addison-Wesley, 1976. Analysis of the effects of sexism on men.

Dew, Robb Forman, *The Family Heart: A Memoir of When Our Son Came Out.* New York, Ballantine Books, 1994. The story of a mother trying to understand the implications of her son's homosexuality; originally accepting, she continues to be challenged about what she doesn't know but comes to learn, about being gay in America.

Dog, Mary Crow, *Lakota Woman.* NY, Harper Collins, 1990. Autobiography of Mary Brace Bird, a Sioux woman who fought poverty and oppression in order to live in dignity as an American Indian. Sequel is *Ohitika Woman* (1994).

Dorris, Michael, *Native Americans: 500 Years Later.* New York, Thomas Crowell, 1975. Valuable reference of hundreds of photos of Native American life around the country today.

Drinnon, Richard, *Facing West.* Schocken, 1990. Well written account of the pattern of imperial expansion by the U.S. against the Native Americans and overseas in the Philippines and Vietnam.

Edelman, Marian Wright, *The Measure of Our Success: A Letter to My Children and Yours.* Boston, Beacon, 1992. In the form of a letter to her three sons, Edelman, founder and president of the Children's Defense Fund, has written a compelling book detailing some lessons of life to pass on to our children.

Faludi, Susan, *Backlash: The Undeclared War against American Women.* New York, Crown Publishers, 1991. A very thorough analysis of the way powerful interests and institutions have created a backlash against women's progress by blaming the women's movement.

Fernandez, José, *Conquered Peoples in America.* Fifth ed. Dubuque, Iowa, Kendall-Hunt, 1994. Provides a good overview of the social context of various conquered people in the United States, including Puerto Ricans, Native Americans, Hawaiians and Filipinos.

Folbre, Nancy and Center for Popular Economics. *The New Field Guide to the U.S. Economy.* New York, New Press, 1995. An accessible guide for the lay person that focuses on the effects of national economic policies on people's lives, with a special focus on class, inequality and equity issues.

Frackenberg, Ruth, *White Women, Race Matters: The Social Construction of Whiteness.* Minneapolis, University of Minnesota, 1993. This book helps white women look at their racial identity and examine the implications of whiteness personally and politically.

Franklin, John Hope, *From Slavery to Freedom.* New York, Alfred Knopf, 1994. A standard history of blacks in America.

Freire, Paulo, *Pedagogy of the Oppressed.* New York, Herder and Herder, 1968. A provocative book about the relationship between education and social change—the theoretical basis of Freire's work.

Fry, Gladys-Marie and in association with the Museum of American Folk Art, *Stitched From the Soul: Slave Quilts from the Ante-Bellum South.* New York, Dutton Studio Books, 1990. Well researched book on the history and significance of quilts made by slave women in the eighteenth and nineteenth centuries, many black and white and color photographs.

Gates Jr., Henry Louis, *Colored People.* New York, Vintage, 1995. A vivid coming-of-age story, Gates recounts his childhood in the mill town of Piedmont, West Virginia in the 1950s and 1960s.

Golden, Marita, *Saving Our Sons: Raising Black Children in a Turbulent World.* New York, Doubleday, 1995. Golden shares her feelings, as a mother of a teenage African American boy, the terrors by and against black male children in the United States.

Hadaad, Yvonne, ed. *Muslims in America.* New York, Oxford University Press, 1991. Good basic book on the lives and culture of Muslims in the U.S.

Haley, Alex, *The Autobiography of Malcolm X*. New York, Grove Press, 1964. Powerful, comprehensive account of the life of Malcolm X.

Hamers, Josiane and Michael Blanc, *Bilinguality and Bilingualism*. New York, Cambridge University Press, 1992. A scholarly, comprehensive treatment of bilingualism with attention to social and psychological aspects of bilinguality, such as culture, identity and power.

Hampton, Henry, Steve Fayer and Sarah Flynn, eds. *Voices of Freedom*. New York, Shocken, 1990. An oral history of the black movement for civil rights, from the 1950s to the 1980s.

Hooks, Bell, *Ain't I a Woman: Black Women and Feminism*. Boston, MA, South End Press, 1981. An examination of the impact of sexism on black women both historically and currently with a focus on black women's involvement with feminism.

Hughes, Langston and Milton Meltzer, *A Pictorial History of the Negro in America*. New York, NY, Crown Publishers, Inc. 1995. A classic. This book, originally written BEFORE the Civil Rights movement, is now historically interesting as a piece of history about history. Includes photographs and original documents with some text to carry through the story.

Hungry Wolf, Beverly. *The Ways of My Grandmothers*. New York, Morrow, 1980. Experiences of the lives of women of the Blackfoot Nation during the recent past.

Iglesias, Cesar Andreu, ed. *Memoirs of Bernardo Vega: A Contribution to the History of the Puerto Rican Community in New York*. Translated by Juan Flores. New York, Monthly Review Press, 1984. A readable autobiography of the experiences of a Puerto Rican immigrant and activist during the first half of this century.

Kadi, Joanna, *Food for Our Grandmothers*. Boston, South End Press, 1994. Groundbreaking collection by over 40 Arab American and Arab Canadian feminists whose responses to the Gulf War, misrepresentations of Arab women, racism in the women's movement and the pressures of cultural assimilation are thought-provoking reading.

Kanter, Rosabeth Moss, *Men and Women of the Corporation*. New York, Basic Books, 1993. An analysis of the dynamics of a typical corporation, with particular focus on the effects of institutional sexism.

Kesselman, Amy, Lily McNair and Nancy Schniedewind, eds. *Women: Images and Realities a Multicultural Anthology of Women in the United States*. Mt. View, CA, Mayfield, 1995. An anthology of fiction, poetry, analytical essays and narratives that reflect diverse women's live in the U.S. today.

Kivel, Paul, *Uprooting Racism: How White People Can Work for Racial Justice*. Philadelphia, New Society Press, 1996. A practical book to help white people understand the dynamics of racism in our society, both in institutions and our daily lives, and work for change.

Kogawa, Joy, *Obasan*. New York, Anchor Books, 1994. Based on the forcible relocation of Japanese Americans and Canadians during World War II, this is the story of a small girl who is sent away from her home in 1942 to live in an internment camp. The sequel *Itsuka* is of their fight to receive government compensation property that was never returned following WWII.

Kohn, Alfie, *No Contest: The Case against Competition*. Boston, Houghton Mifflin Company, 1992. Arguing that competition is inherently destructive, Kohn shows how the majority of psychological and sociological studies support this view. The antidote to competition is cooperation, and Kohn makes a strong case for making a collective commitment to restructure social institutions.

Kotlowitz, Alex, *There Are No Children Here: The Story of Two Boys Growing Up in the Other America*. New York, Anchor Books, 1991. Kotlowitz follows two brothers in a Chicago housing project, chronicling their family, their communities and their fears and hope. A powerful glimpse of urban poverty.

Kovel, Joel, *White Racism*. New York, Vintage, 1984. A complex and scholarly study focussing on the psychological roots of racism in America.

Kozol, Johnathan, *The Night Is Dark and I'm Far from Home*. Boston, Houghton Mifflin, 1990. Kozol exposes the political implications of policies and principals common to American education and asks hard questions of teachers.

Kozol, Jonathan, *Savage Inequalities: Children in America's Schools*. New York, HarperCollins, 1991. A powerful account of the extremes of wealth and poverty in America's schools.

Ladner, Joyce, *Tomorrow's Tomorrow: The Black Woman*. New York, Doubleday, 1995. A thorough study of black womanhood that challenges many established theories about the black family and women.

Lerner, Gerda. *The Black Woman in White America: A Documentary History*. New York, Vintage Books, 1992. Anthology of the life experiences of black women as recorded in primary sources throughout American history.

Lerner, Gerda, *The Female Experience: An American Documentary*. Oxford, 1992. Excellent collection of women's writings throughout U.S. history.

Lerner, Gerda, *The Woman in American History*. Menlo Park, CA, Addison-Wesley, 1971. Short, comprehensive survey of the role of women in American history.

Lim, Shirly Geok-Lin, ed. *The Forbidden Stitch: An Asian American Women's Anthology*, 1989. A collection of visual art, short stories and poetry by various Asian American women artists. An effort to dispel myths about Asian American women and express the richness and complexity of their cultures.

Lukas, J.A., *Common Ground*. New York, Vintage, 1986. A powerful story of the court ordered desegregation of the Boston, MA public schools.

Marable, Manning, *Beyond Black and White: Transforming African-American Politics*. New York, Verso, 1995. A collection of essays on the transformation of 'race' in America, written by Marable in the early 90s.

Martinez, Elizabeth, *500 Años del Pueblo Chicano: 500 Years of Chicano History*. Albuquerque, Southwest Organizing

Project, 1991. Bilingual text of valuable history and wonderful photographs.

Meier, Matt and Feliciano Rivera, *Mexican Americans, American Mexicans: From Conquistadors to Chicanos.* New York, Hill and Wang, 1993. A comprehensive historical account of the Mexican experience in the United States.

Miedzian, Myriam, *Boys Will Be Boys: Breaking the Link between Masculinity and Violence.* New York, Doubleday, 1991. Book analyzing the relationship between the values of masculinity in our culture and violence.

Moody, Ann, *Coming of Age in Mississippi.* New York, Dell, 1992. Account of this black woman's experience growing up in the deep South.

Moraga, Cherríe and Gloria Anzaldúa, eds. *This Bridge Called My Back: Writings by Radical Women of Color.* New York, Kitchen Table Press, 1981. This anthology defines feminism and activism through the eyes of lesbian women of color in the United States including poetry, prose, personal narrative, and essays.

Morgan, Robin, *Sisterhood Is Powerful.* New York, Vintage, 1970. An excellent anthology of early writings from the women's liberation movement.

Morrison, Toni. *The Bluest Eye.* New York, Penguin, 1993. A very powerful novel describing the effects of racism and sexism on a black family.

Muñoz, Carlos, *Youth, Identity and Power: The Chicano Movement.* New York, Verso, 1989. Account of the political movement of Chicano youth from the mid 1950s until the early 80s.

Neeley, Barbara, *Blanche among the Talented Tenth.* New York, St. Martin's Press, 1994. A mystery that examines a dark-skinned woman's struggle to fight internalized oppression about race while vacationing at an exclusive black-owned resort.

Oakes, Jennie, *Keeping Track: How Schools Structure Inequality.* New Haven, Yale University Press, 1986. Analysis of the system of tracking and how it reinforces inequality.

Oboler, Suzanne, *Ethnic Labels: Latino Lives.* Minnesota, University of Minnesota, 1995. This book discusses how ethnic labels affect the meaning of citizenship and struggles for full participation in the United States, with a focus on Latinos.

Olsen, Laurie, et al., eds. *The Unfinished Journey: Restructuring Schools in a Diverse Society.* Fort Mason Center, Building B, San Francisco, CA 94123. California Tomorrow, 1994. This publication documents what is happening in California to restructure schools that address the diversity of a community. Strategies for assessing a community's needs are included.

Orenstein, Peggy, *School Girls: Young Women, Self-Esteem and the Confidence Gap.* New York, Anchor Books, 1994. Orenstein spends a year observing eighth-grade girls in two Northern California middle schools. Her essays shows how identity and self-esteem are constructed, both by the teachers and the students themselves.

Paley, Vivian Gussin, *Kwanzaa and Me: A Teacher's Story.* Cambridge, Harvard University Press, 1995. Paley, through many discussions with teachers that she adapts into stories, discusses integrated multicultural classrooms from the perspectives of those who have worked and lived within them.

Parenti, Michael, *Democracy for the Few.* New York, St. Martins Press, 1994. A critical analysis of the U.S. political and economic system with an emphasis on how it reinforces inequality.

Pharr, Suzanne, *Homophobia: A Weapon of Sexism.* Little Rock, AK. Chardon Press/The Women's Project, 1988. This book links an understanding of homophobia with ways it reinforces sexism.

Pipher, Mary, *Reviving Ophelia: Saving the Selves of Adolescent Girls.* New York, Ballantine, 1994. The voices of adolescent girls tell of the effect of sexism on their lives, spirit and self-esteem.

Pons, Frank Moya, *The Dominican Republic: A National History.* New Rochelle, NY, Hispaniola Books, 1995. Good background reading for the history of the Dominican Republic.

Rafkin, Louise, *Different Daughters.* Pittsburgh, Cleis Press, 1996. Interviews with 25 mothers about their changing relationship with their lesbian daughters.

Rafkin, Louise, ed. *Different Mothers: Sons and Daughters of Lesbians Talk about Their Lives.* Pittsburgh, Cleis Press, 1990. Thirty-eight "children" (age five to forty) discuss growing up in lesbian families; peer pressure, closets, custody issues, families, sexuality, coming out, schools and friends, fathers and co-moms are some of the issues.

Reddy, Maureen T., *Crossing the Color Line: Race, Parenting and Culture.* New Jersey, Rutgers University Press, 1994. Reddy is a white feminist married to a black man; together they have two children. This book links her personal experience with her developing theories about race and gender. Many historical and scholarly references are included.

Rose, Stephen, *Social Stratification in the United States.* New York, New Press, 1992. Forty-eight page booklet and large poster bring together data on income, wealth, race and occupation to depict the U.S. social structure—in particular the disappearance of the middle class.

Rosenthal, Robert and Lenore Jacobsen, *Pygmalion in the Classroom.* New York, Irvington Publishers, 1989. Analysis of the effect of teacher expectations and the self-fulfilling prophecy effect on student learning.

Rubin, Lillian Breslow, *Worlds of Pain: Life in the Working Class Family.* New York, Basic Books, 1992. Interviews with working class women and men with clear, provocative analysis.

Ruiz, Vicki L. and Ellen Carol Dubois, eds. *Unequal Sisters: A Multicultural Reader in US Women's History,* 1990. An engaging collection of essays by Native American, African American, Euro American, Latina, lesbian, Asian American, etc., women about United States women's history.

Ryan, William, *Blaming the Victim.* New York, Vintage Press, 1976. Analysis of how white society blames the victims of racism and poverty for "their problems" rather than change its own policies.

Ryan, William, *Equality* 2. New York, Pantheon, 1982. A persuasive analysis of how inequality is institutionalized in the U.S.

Samora, Julian and Patricia Vandel Simon, *A History of the Mexican-American People*. Notre Dame Press, 1993. Offers a useful overview spanning from the arrival of the Spaniards to current events.

Santiago-Valoes, Calvin A., *"Subject People" and Colonial Discourses: Economic Transformation and Social Disorder in Puerto Rico, 1898–1947*. New York, SUNY Press, 1994. A history of the turn of the century contexts for Puerto Rican emigration to the United States.

Sennett, Richard and Johnathan Cobb, *The Hidden Injuries of Class*. New York, Vintage, 1993. Through a series of conversations the authors define a new form of class conflict in America among blue-collar workers who compare their lives to those valued by society.

Shange, Ntozake, *sassafrass, cypress & indigo*. New York, St. Martin's Press, 1982. Three colored girls, three sisters—a poet, a dancer and a dreamer—and their mama from Charleston, South Carolina grow and live their lives.

Shapiro, Andrew, *We're Number One: Where America Stands—and Falls—in the New World Order*. New York, Vintage, 1992. An excellent comparison of the United States to 19 other major industrialized nations in the areas of education, health care, the economy, crime and so forth.

Shapiro, Joseph, *No Pity: People with Disabilities Forging a New Civil Rights Movement*. New York, Random House, 1993. History of the disability rights movement in the United States.

Sherr, Lynn and Jurate Kazickas, *Susan B. Anthony Slept Here: A Guide to Women's Landmarks*. New York, Times Books, 1994. By state and by city, the authors guide us to almost two thousand landmarks pertaining to women's history in America. Biographical, historical, and architectural information are included.

Sherman, Arloc, *Wasting America's Future: The Children's Defense Fund Report on the Costs of Child Poverty*. Boston, Beacon Press, 1994. A powerful documentary of the human, social, and economic costs of child poverty in America, with a focus on the economic benefits to the nation ending child poverty.

Shorris, Earl, *Latinos: A Biography of the People*. New York, Avon, 1992. A social history of Latinos/as in the United States.

Silán, Juan Angel, *We, the Puerto Rican People: A Story of Oppression and Resistance*. New York, Monthly Review Press, 1983. Comprehensive account of colonization and struggle for liberation of Puerto Rican people.

Sklar, Holly. *Chaos or Community: Seeking Solutions, Not Scapegoats for Bad Economics*. Boston, South End Press, 1995. Accessible economic analysis of the reasons for the deterioration of the American Dream; a combination of facts, statistics and social analysis.

Skutnabb-Kongas, Jove and Jim Cummings, eds. *Minority Education: From Shame to Struggle*. Clevedon, England, Multicultural Matters, 1988. This book is particularly valuable on issues of language differences.

Smedley, Agnes, *Daughter of the Earth*. Old Westbury, NY, Feminist Press, 1987. A very powerful account of a working class woman's life from childhood to womanhood. Excellent combining of personal and political perspectives.

Smith, Anna Deavere, *Fires in the Mirror: A Performance Piece Conceived, Written and Performed by Anna Deavere Smith*. New York, Anchor Books, 1993. Tensions in a black/Jewish Brooklyn neighborhood were already high when a black Guyanese American boy was killed by a car in a rabbi's motorcade and a Jewish student was killed in the rioting aftermath.

Sojourners Resource Center, *America's Original Sin, a Study Guide to White Racism*. Box 29272, Washington, DC, 20017. Designed for use by schools, churches, and community groups.

Stalvey, Lois, *The Education of a WASP*. Madison, University of Wisconsin Press, 1989. A compelling and honest account of one woman's discovery of her racism and subsequent struggle to act upon these new learnings.

Stalvey, Lois, *Getting Ready*. New York, Bantam, 1975. Provocative account of a parent's growing awareness of white racism in education through the experiences of her family in inner city schools.

Stoltenberg, John, *Refusing to Be a Man*. New York, Dutton, 1990. A compelling examination of male sexual identity with a fully argued liberation theory for men.

Takaki, Ronald, *A Different Mirror: A History of Multicultural America*. New York, Little, Brown, 1993. Comprehensive account of the history of the many different peoples who, together, compose the United States.

Takaki, Ronald, *Strangers from a Distant Shore*. New York, Penguin, 1989. Story of Asian Americans from early republic years through tragic experiences of Japanese and Chinese immigrants.

Tannen, Deborah, *Gender and Discourse*. New York, Oxford University Press, 1994. Five essays on language and gender discuss the theoretical and empirical work that support her best-selling book, *You Just Don't Understand*, that discusses men and women's differing conversational styles.

Tatum Beverly, *Why Are All the Black Kids Sitting Together in the Cafeteria: And Other Conversations about Racial Identity*. New York, Basic Books, 1997. At the center of these conversations is an understanding of racial identity; the meaning people construct about what it is to be white or a person of color in a race-conscious society.

Thompson, Becky and Sangeeta Tyagi, eds. *Names We Call Home: Autobiography on Racial Identity*. New York, Routledge, 1996. Twenty-seven autobiographical essays from artists, educators, and activists who explore complex definitions of race identity and its implications both personally and politically.

Thompson, Becky W. and Sangeeta Tyagi, eds. *Beyond a Dream Deferred: Multicultural Education and the Politics of Excellence*. Minneapolis, Minnesota, 1993. A multidisciplinary work that consolidates progressive perspectives on multicultural education with views of students, faculty and administrators, activists and intellectuals.

Thorne, Barrie, *Gender Play: Girls and Boys in School*. New Brunswick, Rutgers University Press, 1993. Thought-provoking, insightful analysis of the complex effects of sexism on young people in schools, with a focus on power relations.

Tsuchida, Nobuya, ed. *Asian and Pacific American Experiences: Women's Perspectives*, University of Minnesota, 1982. A collection of essays and interviews by/with Asian/Pacific American women, dealing with racism and sexism within women's own ethnic communities as well as within United States macroculture.

Turner, Margery Austin, Michael Fix and Raymond Struyk, *Opportunities Denied, Opportunities Diminished: Racial Discrimination in Hiring*. Washington, D.C., Urban Institute, 1991. Contemporary study of racial discrimination in hiring.

Wagenheim, Kal, *Puerto Ricans: A Documentary History*. Princeton, NJ, Markus Wiener Publications, Inc., 1993. A good book for basic information about Puerto Rico.

Walsh, Catherine E., *Pedagogy and the Struggle for Voice: Issues of Language, Power and Schooling for Puerto Ricans*. New York, Bergin and Garvey, 1991. A good presentation of the historical context for the educational experiences of Puerto Ricans in the United States.

Walker, Alice, *In Love and Trouble: Stories of Black Women*. New York, Harcourt Brace, 1967. Anthology of powerful short stories about black women.

Walker, Rebecca. *To Be Real: Telling the Truth and Changing the Face of Feminism*, New York, Anchor Books, 1995. Strong essays written by young American feminists from diverse backgrounds cover a myriad of contemporary issues.

Weatherford, Jack. *Native Roots: How the Indians Enriched America*. New York, Crown Publishers, 1991. A rich resource describing the many ways—from farming, language, to intellectual ideas—that native people contributed to America.

West, Cornell, *Race Matters*. Boston, Beacon Press, 1993. West grapples with several contemporary controversial issues such as the new black conservatism, nihilism in the black community, black rage, the crisis of black leadership, black-Jewish relations and myths of black sexuality.

Willie, Charles, *Black and White Families: A Study in Complementarity*. Bayside, NY, General Hall, 1985. Willie analyzes patterns of similarity and difference in modes of adaptation across race and class lines. His study is grounded in 24 cases of black and white families from middle class, working class, and poor backgrounds.

Wright, Richard, *Native Son*. Originally published in 1940: New York, Harper and Row, 1992. Wright's classic and compelling novel captures the anguished emotions and sufferings of black Americans.

Wright, Richard, *Uncle Tom's Children*. Originally published in 1936: New York, Harper and Row, 1993. A superbly written short novel that graphically depicts struggles in the lives of black people. Accessible to middle school students.

Yellen, Samuel, *American Labor Struggles*. Pathfinder, 1974. Discusses the great labor conflicts of American history; 1877 railroad strikes, San Francisco general strike of 1934, etc.

Zinn, Howard, *A People's History of the United States*. HarperCollins, 1995. Provides a comprehensive alternative to traditional views of U.S. History.

Zinn, Maxine Baca and Bonnie Thorton Dill, eds. *Women of Color in U.S. Society*. Philadelphia, Temple, 1995. A collection of essays examining the convergence of race, class and gender as interlocking oppressions in the experiences of women of color.

7. FICTION FOR YOUNG PEOPLE

P-Primary E-Elementary M-Middle School

Andrews, Jan, *Very Last First Time*. New York, Atheneum, 1985. An Inuit girl walks on the bottom of the sea, gathering mussels for dinner, for the first time. (P)

Anzaldúa, Gloria, *Friends from the Other Side/Amigos del otro lado*. San Francisco, Children's Book Press, 1993. The story of Prietita, a young Mexican American girl, and Joaquín, a young boy who, with his mother has crossed the Rio Grande River into Texas in search of a new life. (E)

Bambara, Toni Cade, *Gorilla My Love*. New York, Vintage Books, 1992. A collection of fifteen short autobiographical fiction stories that take the reader inside the complexity of growing up black, both in style and content. (M)

Bannerji, Himani, *Coloured Pictures*. Toronto, Ontario, Sister Vision, 1991. Sujata, a 13 year old South Asian Canadian Sikh, and her friends confront racism in her classroom and community. (E)

Bauer, Marion Dane, ed. *Am I Blue? Coming out from the Silence*. New York, HarperTrophy, 1994. Short stories written especially for this anthology by noted young adult fiction writers about growing up gay or lesbian, or with gay or lesbian parents or friends. (M)

Beattie, Patricia, *Who Comes with Cannons?* New York, Morrow, 1992. Novel takes place during the civil war, and provides a fascinating look at the pacifism of the Quakers. (E, M)

Blanc, Esther Silverstein, *Berchick*. Volcano, CA, Volcan Press, 1990. Homesteading in Wyoming in the early 1900s, a Jewish mother develops an unusual relationship with a young horse she names Berchick. (E)

Bledsoe, Lucy Jane, *The Big Bike Race*. New York, Holiday House, 1995. Ernie wants a racing bike for his birthday, but instead his grandmother gives him a second-hand clunker. Realizing money is tight, he makes the best of it; when he meets a champion adult bike racer, he finds the courage to turn a dream into a reality. (P, E)

Block, Francesca Lia, *Baby Be-Bop*. New York, Harper-Collins, 1995. Dirk is gay, and he's known that forever, but when he falls in love with Pup and is rejected, it is his grandmother who helps him make peace with himself and the different ways people in his family have learned to love. (M)

Brisson, Pat, *Wanda's Roses*. Honesdale, PA, Boyd Mills Press, Inc., 1994. Wanda mistakes a thornbush for a rosebush in an empty lot. In the process of taking care of the "rose bush" Wanda receives help from neighbors of all ages. In the end the neighborhood gains a clean, blooming rose garden. (P)

Brooks, Bruce, *The Moves Make the Man*. New York, Harper & Row, 1984. A black boy and an emotionally disturbed white boy in North Carolina form a precarious friendship. (M)

Bunting, Eve, *Fly Away Home*. New York, Clarion Books, 1991. Andrew and his father live in an airport. Andrew tells the details of his daily life, survival strategies and his homeless family's hopes for a better life. (E)

Bunting, Eve, *How Many Days to America? A Thanksgiving Story*. New York, Clarion Books, 1988. Refugees from a Caribbean island embark on a dangerous boat trip to America where they have a special reason to celebrate Thanksgiving. (P)

Bunting, Eve, *Smoky Night*. San Diego, Harcourt Brace Jovanovich, 1995. Daniel and his mother watch with horror and amazement as their neighborhood is looted during the 1991 Los Angeles riots, and become homeless when their house burns down. After spending the night in a shelter with their Korean American grocer, they decide to try to work together. (E, M)

Buss, Fran Leeper and Daisy Cubias, *Journey of the Sparrows*. New York, Dutton, 1991. When 15 year old Maria's father is murdered by the government of El Salvador, she and her siblings join thousands of others living "illegally" in Chicago. (M)

Cameron, Ann, *The Stories Julian Tells*. New York, Pantheon Books, 1981. Six short stories about the home life of Julian and his family. (E) Other books by this author are also recommended.

Castañeda, Omar, *Abuela's Weave*. New York, Lee and Low Books, 1993. A young Guatemalan girl and her grandmother grow closer as they weave some special tapestries and then make a trip to the market in hopes of selling them.

Charlip, Remy and Burton Supress, *Harlequin and the Gift of Many Colors*. New York, Parents Magazine Press, 1973. A beautifully told and illustrated story on the value of love and cooperation. (P)

Chetin, Helen, *Angel Island Prisoner 1922*. New Seed Press, 1993. Story of a young Chinese girl, her mother and other Chinese women and children who waited on Angel Island to enter San Francisco. (E)

Cisneros, Sandra. *The House on Mango Street*. New York, Vintage Contemporaries, 1991. A deeply touching series of vignettes tell the story of a Mexican American girl's coming of age in Chicago; good for reading aloud, and available in Spanish. (M)

Clifton, Lucille, *My Friend Jacob*. New York, Harper and Row, Inc., 1980. Friendship between an 8 year old boy who is black and his friend, a retarded white teenager; strong, not sentimental. (P)

Cofer, Judy Ortiz, *An Island Like You: Stories of the Barrio*. New York, Orchard Books, 1995. Twelve stories about youth of Puerto Rican heritage and their lives in a New Jersey barrio. (E)

Cohen, Barbara, *Make a Wish, Molly*. New York, Lothrop, Lee & Shephard, 1995. Molly tries to fit in with her new classmates at the turn of the century. Invited to a party of a non-Jewish friend during Passover, Molly can eat no leavened bread, including birthday cake. Luckily, Molly's ingenious mom comes to the rescue. (E)

Cohen, Barbara, *Molly's Pilgrim*. New York, Lothrop, Lee & Shephard, 1983. A young immigrant Jewish girl, with the help of her mother, begins to feel pride in her heritage and the true meaning of Thanksgiving. (E)

Cohen-Fletcher, Jane, *It Takes a Village*, New York, Scholastic, 1994. Members of an African village help a girl take care of her little brother. (P)

Collier, James Lincoln and Christopher Collier, *With Every Drop of Blood*. New York, Bantam Doubleday, 1994. Gripping story of the friendship that develops between fourteen year old Johnny who works for the Confederate troops for money, and Cush, a young African American who joined the Union army to escape slavery. (M)

Conley, Jane Leslie, *Crazy Lady*. New York, HarperCollins, 1993. Vernon and his friends have always teased an alcoholic woman and her retarded son. Through a series of incidents he begins to develop a relationship with both and as he begins to care about Ronald, Vernon begins to understand that there is more to kids with developmental disabilities than what you can simply see. (M)

Cornwell, Anita, *The Girls of Summer*. New Seed Press, 1993. Three black sisters and their white friend integrate the Pee-Wee league with the help of a very smart Granny who was once affiliated with the Negro Leagues. (E)

Crew, Linda. *Children of the River*. New York, Delacorte Press, 1989. Compelling story of the cultural conflicts of 17 year old Cambodian American Sundara: her desire to be a "regular" American kid and traditional Cambodian values.(M)

DiSalvo-Ryan, Dyanne, *Uncle Willie and the Soup Kitchen*. New York, Morrow Junior Books, 1991. The young narrator wonders why his uncle works in a soup kitchen until one day he visits and realizes that it's a friendly place where hungry people go and are glad that it exists. (P, E)

Dooley, Norah, *Everybody Cooks Rice*. Minneapolis, Carolrhoda Books, Inc., 1991. On a mission to find her brother at dinnertime, Carrie stops at friends' houses, only to find that everyone is having rice for dinner—eight different ways! Rice recipes representing eight different ethnicities are included. (P)

Duffy, James, *Radical Red*. New York, Charles Scribner, 1993. The life of a thirteen year old Irish girl living in Albany, New York in the 1890s undergoes many changes when her mother leaves her abusive husband, and they both become involved with Susan B. Anthony and the suffragist movement. (M)

Elwin, Rosamund and Michele Paulse, *Asha's Mums*. Toronto, Ontario, Women's Press, 1990. When Asha brings back her permission slip, her teacher refuses to believe that she lives with her two moms. (P)

Estes, E., *The Hundred Dresses*. New York, Harcourt Brace Jovanovich, 1944. The classic story of a poor white girl who wears hand me down clothes of other girls in her school and wins first prize in a school drawing contest. (E)

Flourney, Valerie, *The Patchwork Quilt*. New York, Dial, 1985. Using scraps cut from the family's old clothing, Tanya helps her grandmother make a beautiful quilt that tells the story of her family's life. (E)

Fogel, Julianna, *Wesley Paul, Marathon Runner*. New York, Lippincott, 1979. Story of an Asian American boy who is a long-distance runner. (P)

Fox, Mem, *Wilfred Gordon McDonald Partridge*. New York, Kane/Miller, 1985. Boy with four names collects memorabilia in a box to take to his friend in a nursing home, who also has four names, because he hears that she is losing her memory. (P)

Gallo, Donald R., ed. *Join In: Multiethnic Short Stories by Outstanding Writers for Young Adults*. New York, Delacorte Press, 1993. In these short stories, everyday moments of being an American teenager—listening to their own music, studying for SATs, getting a driver's license, playing baseball and falling in love—reflect young adult views on friendships and prejudice. (M)

Garden, Nancy, *Annie on My Mind*. New York, Farrar, Strauss, Giroux, 1984. Liza puts aside her romantic feelings for Annie after a disaster at school, but eventually allows love to triumph over the ignorance of people. (M)

Garden, Nancy, *Lark in the Morning*. New York, Farrar, Strauss, and Giroux, 1991. Gillian, who is a lesbian and 17 years old, finds out that the thieves that broke into her family's summer home are two runaways terrified of being sent back to their abusive parents. (M)

Getz, Arthur, *Tar Beach*. New York, Dial Books, 1991. Depiction of one hot Saturday in a low income Latino and black urban neighborhood with good interconnectedness of people. (P)

Gilmore, Rachna, *Lights for Gita*. Gardiner, ME, Tilbury House, 1994. Gita can't believe it's Divali, a major Hindu holiday of light, in her new cold and gray country. She wishes she were back in India, setting off firecrackers and celebrating with her family until she learns something about filling the darkness with light from inside herself. (P, E)

Green, Bette, *The Drowning of Stephen Jones*. New York, Bantam, 1991. A high school girl is torn between her loyalty to her gay male friend and her homophobic boyfriend. (M)

Greenfield, Eloise, *Grandmama's Joy*, New York, Philomel Books. A lovely story of an African American grandmother and granddaughter. (E)

Greenfield, Eloise, *Me and Nessie*. New York, Harper & Row, 1975. Young girl outgrows her need for an imaginary friend in this story told partially in an African American dialect. Other books by this author are highly recommended. (P)

Guback, Georgia, *Luka's Quilt*. New York, Greenwillow Books, 1994. When Luka's grandmother makes her a traditional Hawaiian quilt, she and Luka disagree over the colors it should include. (P)

Guy, Rosa, *Ruby*. New York, Bantam, 1974. A classic love story between a young West Indian woman and a young African American woman in New York City. (M)

Hansen, Joyce, *The Gift Giver*. New York, Clarion, 1980. Set in a poor area of a large city, this book focuses on the friendship between a 5th grader, Doris, and a newcomer, Amir, who shares with her the strength to not always go along with the crowd. A story of survival and hope. (M)

Havill, Juanita, *Jamaica's Find*. New York, Houghton Mifflin, 1986. Jamaica brings home a stuffed dog she found in the park; when she returns the dog to the park, she finds its true owner. (P)

Havill, Juanita, *Treasure Map*. Boston, Houghton Mifflin, 1992. A young girl learns how her great, great grandmother came to the U.S. from Mexico, bringing a special treasure. (P)

Hazen, Barbara Shook, *Tight Times*. New York, Puffin Books, 1983. A young boy tries to understand why "tight times" means that he can't have a dog. When his father loses his job, he brings home a surprise. (P)

Heron, Ann and Meredith Maran, *How Would You Feel if Your Dad Was Gay?* Boston, Alyson Publications, 1991. Powerful exploration of the choices that children of gay parents make in "coming out"—letting friends know that someone they love is gay. (M)

Hinton, N. *The Long Red Scarf*, Minneapolis, MN, Carolrhoda Books, Inc. After discovering all the active, interesting women in his extended family don't knit, grandfather decides to knit a scarf for himself.

Hoffman, Mary, *Amazing Grace*. New York, Dial, 1991. Grace is told she cannot play Peter Pan in the class production because she's a girl and she's black. (P)

Hooks, William H., *Freedom's Fruit*. New York, Alfred A. Knopf, 1996. Mama Manna, a slave woman and conjurer, casts a spell on her master's grapes as a part of her plan to win freedom for her daughter Sheba and the man she loves. (P)

Hopkins, Lee Bennett, *Mama*. New York, Simon and Schuster, 1992. A young boy describes his mother's struggle to feed, clothe and protect him and his brother, sometimes stealing to do so. (E)

Hopkinson, Deborah, *Sweet Clara and the Freedom Quilt*. New York, Knopf, 1993. When 11 year old Clara is sold away from her mother, she vows to return and find her. After an elder teaches her fine stitching, she uses her intelligence and ability to visualise to create a quilt-map of the way north. Leaving the quilt behind for others to use, she escapes and finds her mother. (P, E)

Jackson, Isaac, *Somebody's New Pajamas*. New York, Dial, 1996. Jerome becomes uncomfortable with the difference between his family's small, cramped apartment and his friend Robert's spacious brownstone when he sleeps over one night and notices that Robert sleeps in pajamas, while he sleeps in his underwear. (P)

Jenness, Aylette, *Families: A Celebration of Diversity, Commitment and Love*. Boston, Houghton Mifflin, 1990. Comprehensive representation of all kinds of families including some with step relationships, divorce, gay parents, and foster siblings, among others. (E, M)

Jenness, Aylette, *Who Am I?* Cleveland, OH, Modern Curriculum Press, 1992. When David's school decides to host a Family Heritage Day, he has to think deeply about who he is—and make a number of phone calls to his Italian/Polish/Scottish/German/French grandparents. (P)

Johnson, Dolores, *Seminole Diary: Remembrances of a Slave*. New York, MacMillan, 1995. Written in diary form by a young slave whose family, in 1834, escapes from slavery and joins the Seminole, where they find safety and acceptance. (P)

Jonas, Ann, *The Quilt*. New York, Greenwillow Books, 1984. An African American child's patchwork quilt made for her by her mother and father recalls old memories and provides new adventures at bedtime. (P)

Jordan, June, *New Life: New Room*. New York, Crowell, 1975. A family must make arrangements for a new sibling; good strong problem solving in a low income city family. (P)

Jordan, Mary Kate, *Losing Uncle Tim*. New York, A. Whitman, 1989. While Uncle Tim, who has died of AIDS, is never identified as gay, it is easy to infer this, and he is depicted in a loving way. Good book for young children dealing with HIV illness or death of any kind. (P, E)

Juster, Norton, *The Phantom Tollbooth*. New York, Random House, 1961. A superb story giving the reader a whole new look at reality, choices, values. (E)

Keats, Ezra Jack, *Goggles*. New York, Collier Books, 1969. Many books by this author are also recommended, they feature young black children in central roles. (P)

Knight, Margy Burns, *Who Belongs Here? an American Story*. Gardiner, ME, Tillbury House Publishers, 1993. An account of a Cambodian immigrant to the United States, including his past life experience as well as current struggles in school, providing an excellent context for learning about the history of immigration, and speaking to current issues as well. (E)

Leaf, Munro, *The Story of Ferdinand*. New York, Viking, 1938. A simply beautiful classic story of Ferdinand, a very large bull, who is different from other bulls. By mistake he is taken to Madrid to be in a bullfight—where he sits quietly and smells flowers. (P)

Lester, Julius, *Long Journey Home*. New York, Dell, 1975. Six stories told through eyes of mother and grandmother on blacks during slavery and emancipation, struggles and sacrifice, courage, humor and sadness. (E)

Levine, Arthur, *Pearl Moskowitz's Last Stand*. New York, Tambourine Books, 1993. Pearl Moskowitz and her elderly neighbors of many different ethnicities are determined not to let the last gingko tree on their block be chopped down. They are successful in their efforts with

the tree and helping to bring their community together. (P)

Levinson, Riki, *Our Home Is the Sea*. New York, Dutton, 1988. A young Chinese boy hastens through a crowded market to his family's houseboat in Hong Kong Harbor to join his father and grandfather in fishing, the family's occupation. (E)

Levinson, Riki, *Watch the Stars Come Out*. New York, E.P. Dutton, 1985. Grandmother tells the story of her mother's journey to America by boat in the early part of this century. (E)

Levy, Marilyn, *Rumors and Whispers*. New York, Ballantine/Fawcett, 1990. One of the best books available dealing with AIDS, as well as a realistic and caring portrayal of one young man's decision to tell people he is gay. (M)

Mandelbaum, Pili, *You Be Me, I'll Be You*. Brooklyn, NY, Kane/Miller, 1990. Anna, a bi-racial child, and her father deal with self image when Anna decides she wants skin and hair like her white father. (P)

Mathis, Sharon Bell, *The Hundred Penny Box*. New York, Viking Press, 1975. Aunt Dew tells young Michael about her experiences through a box that contains a penny for each year of her life. (P, E)

Mathis, Sharon Bell, *Sidewalk Story*. New York, Viking, 1971. When her best friend's family is evicted from their apartment, a nine year old black girl decides to do something. (P)

Maury, Inez, *My Mother and I Are Growing Strong*. Stanford, CA, New Seed Press, 1979. A Latino family handles a father's being sent to prison for his response to a racist insult, and a mother and daughter's growth. (P, E)

Mazer, Anne, ed. *America Street: A Multicultural Anthology of Stories*. New York, Persea Books, 1993. Fourteen stories about young people, by Langston Hughes, Gish Gen, Grace Paley, and others. (M)

Mazer, Norma, *Mrs. Fish, Ape and Me, the Dump Queen*. New York, Avon, 1984. A friendless girl is teased because her uncle, with whom she lives, manages the town dump, but she begins a satisfying friendship with Mrs. Fish, the school custodian. (M)

McKissack, Patricia, *The Dark Thirty*. New York, Knopf, 1992. Original tales inspired by African American history that deal with justice and the conditions of life for African Americans, as well as ghosts and hauntings. (M)

McClain, Ellen Jaffe, *No Big Deal*. New York, Lodestar, 1994. When fourteen year old Janice finds out talented teacher, Mr. Padovano, is gay, she gets involved by challenging adults as well as herself and her own values. Realistic conclusion, and a strong message to stand one's ground, and not give in to popular opinion. (M)

Mendez, Phil, *The Black Snowman*. New York, Scholastic, 1989. A magical kente brings a black snowman to life and helps young African American Jacob discover the beauty of his black heritage as well as his own self worth. (E)

Merrifield, Margaret, *Come Sit by Me*. Toronto, Canada, Women's Press, 1990. An educational storybook about

AIDS and HIV infection for young children and their caregivers. (P)

Miklowitz, G., *The War between the Classes*. New York, Dell, 1986. Seventeen year old Emiko, brought up in a strict Japanese American family, is in love with blond Adam in spite of her father's expectations that she find a Japanese husband. (M)

Mills, Lauren, *The Rag Coat*. Boston, Little, Brown and Company, 1991. Minna, an Appalachian girl, proudly wears her new coat made of clothing scraps to school, where the other children laugh at her until she tells them the stories behind the scraps. (E)

Mochizuki, Ken, *Baseball Saved Us*. New York, Lee and Low, 1993. Extraordinary story is told by a boy whose life is thrown into disarray when his family is forced into an internment camp for Japanese Americans in 1942. His father is the inspiration behind a baseball field and team in the camp. Vivid paintings illustrate the story. (P, E)

Mohr, Nicholasa, *El Bronx Remembered*. Houston, Arte Publico Press, 1989. Mohr's first short stories originally published in 1973, range from comical to tragic experiences of the early Puerto Rican community in the Bronx. (M) Other novels by this author are highly recommended.

Mohr, Nicholasa, *Felita*. New York, Dial, 1979. *Going Home*. New York, Dial Press, 1986. In *Felita*, a nine-year old Puerto Rican girl and her family struggle with moving into a white community. In the sequel, she goes to Puerto Rico after the death of her Abuelita and endures further discrimination. (M)

Moss, Marissa, *In America*. New York, Dutton Children's Books, 1994. While Walter and his grandfather walk to the post office, Grandfather recounts how he decided to come to America while his brother Herschel stayed in Lithuania. (P)

Munsch, Robert and Michael Kusugak, *A Promise is a Promise*. Toronto, Annick Press, 1988. A Qallupilluit, or troll, that lives in Hudson Bay almost captures Allashua—who plays too close to the cracks in the ice—and her brothers and sisters—until her ingenious parents think of a way to trick the troll. (P)

Myers, Walter Dean, *Won't Know until I Get There*. New York, Puffin, 1988. Steve's parents decide to adopt a street-wise 13 year old "throw-away kid." When he and Steve get in trouble, they end up doing community services with a group of independent and interesting elders. (M)

Myers, Walter Dean, *The Young Landlords*. New York, Puffin, 1989. After getting involved on a neighborhood improvement project, six teenagers unwillingly become the landlords of a Harlem tenement; high adventure, good characterization, good for discussion. (M) Other novels by this author are highly recommended.

Nolan, Madeena Spray, *My Daddy Don't Got to Work*. Minneapolis, Carolrhoda Books, Inc., 1978. An urban black family deals with a father's unemployment with strength, sensitivity, and a direct dealing with emotions. (P)

O'Dell, Scott, *Island of the Blue Dolphins*. Boston, Houghton Mifflin, 1990. Nineteenth Century Indian girl grows up alone for 20 years on an island off the California coast. Excellent as anti-sexist; high adventure story. (E)

O'Dell, Scott, *My Name Is Not Angelica*. New York, Dell/Yearling, 1989. Sixteen year old Raisha and her part in the 1733 Great Slave Rebellion on the Caribbean island of St. John. (E)

Okimoto, Jean Davies, *A Place for Grace*. Seattle, Sasquatch Books, 1993. Grace isn't big enough to be a seeing eye dog, so with help from her hearing impaired friend she learns to be a hearing ear dog responding to honking cars, phones, doorbells and alarm clocks. Her friend works hard to train Grace, as her learning style does not fit with the school's standard teaching style. (P, E)

Paek, Min, *Aekyung's Dream*. San Francisco, Children's Book Press, 1988. A young Korean immigrant learns to adjust to her new life in America by heeding the words of an ancient Korean king that come to her in a dream. (P)

Paterson, Katherine, *The Great Gilly Hopkins*. New York, Crowell, 1978. An 11 year old foster child tries to cope with her feelings, as she schemes against everyone who tries to befriend her; very well written and funny with strong female roles, and is excellent on class, race, education. (E)

Paterson, Katherine, *Lyddie*. New York, Penguin, 1991. Working in the mills in Lowell, MA in the 1840s with the hope of earning enough money to reunite her family, Lyddie Worthen risks her job to organize for better working conditions. (M)

Perera, Hilda, *Kiki: A Cuban Boy's Adventure in America*. Coconut Grove, FL, The Pickering Press, Inc., 1992. In the early 1960s eight year old Kiki leaves Cuba and tries to adjust in two very different foster homes in Florida, first with a poor family in the Everglades and then with a rich family in Miami, until he is reunited with his parents. (E)

Perkins, Mitali, *The Sunita Experiment*. Boston, Joy Street Books, 1993. When Sunita's Bengali grandparents visit, her mother tries to hide her American-ness while Sunita denies her Indian-ness. One of the only young adult novels that discusses growing up South Asian in America, this story does not adequately reflect these complexities and should be taught with careful attention to the issues of identity and self-esteem. (M)

Philip, Marlene Nourbese, *Harriet's Daughter*. Toronto, Ontario, The Women's Press, 1988. Margaret, who wants to be called Harriet after brave, strong Harriet Tubman, tries to help her best friend Zulma escape from Canada and fly back to Tobago to live with her grandmother. On the way she deals with issues of immigration, exile, culture and identity, language, and generational conflicts. (M)

Picó, Fernando, *The Red Comb*. Mahwah, NJ, Troll Books, 1987. Set in nineteeth century Puerto Rico, Pedro Calderón earns money by turning in fugitive slaves—until a little girl and her neighbor outwit Pedro and help a runaway. Based on a true incident, this historical fiction deals with complex relationships between Africans and "Latinos." (P)

Polacco, Patricia, *Mrs. Katz and Tush*. New York, Bantam, 1992. A long lasting friendship develops between Larnel, a young African American, and Mrs. Katz, a lonely Jewish widow, when Larnel gives Mrs. Katz a kitten. (P) All titles by this author are highly recommended.

Polacco, Patricia, *Pink and Say*. New York, Philomel Books, 1994. Powerful picture book account of two 15 year old Union soldiers, one white and one black, as told by the family of Sheldon Curtis; the legacy of racism as well as interracial friendship is clear. Poignant story and drawings. (E, M)

Polacco, Patricia, *Tikvah Means Hope*. Justine and Duane are helping their neighbors, the Roths, build a Sukkah. As they are preparing for the holiday, the terrible Oakland fire occurs; all the houses are burned and the Roth's cat Tikvah is lost. When they return home, a miracle has occurred: the Sukkah still stands, and Tikvah is found. (P, E)

Radin, Ruth, *All Joseph Wanted*, New York, MacMillan, 1991. Eleven year old Joseph wishes his mother could learn to read since her inability to read directions or street signs has complicated their lives. (E)

Ringgold, Faith, *Aunt Harriet's Underground Railroad in the Sky*. New York, Crown Publishers, Inc., 1992. With Harriet Tubman as her guide, Cassie retraces the steps that escaping slaves took on the Underground Railroad in order to reunite with her younger brother. Based on the dreams of Harriet Tubman, and the slave custom of throwing a quilt over the roof of a house for good luck Ringgold's paintings and story are wonderful. (P)

Ringgold, Faith, *Tar Beach*. New York, Crown Press, 1991. Told by the author/illustrator, Cassie, an eight year old black girl in 1939, has a dream to be free to go anywhere she wants for the rest of her life. She and her brother make her dream come true by flying through Harlem and the streets of New York City. Based on Ringgold's painted art quilt. (P) All books by this author are recommended.

Rosen, Michael, *A School for Pompey Walker*. New York, Harcourt Brace Jovanovich, 1995. A powerful novel based on the true story of Gussie West, a slave who sold himself again and again into slavery, then escaped with the help of a white friend; he used the money from selling himself to build a school for freed black children. (E)

Ross, Rhea Beth, *The Bet's on, Lizzie Bingman*. New York, Houghton Mifflin, 1992. Fourteen year old Lizzie's bet with her older brother about women deserving equal rights starts off a summer of adventure, rare for a young lady in 1914. Funny, fast, and educational story about the limited sphere for women in the early part of the century. (E, M)

Sachs, Marilyn, *The Bear's House*. Garden City, NY, Doubleday, 1971. Explores the role of the school on an urban, white family living in poverty. (E)

Say, Allen, *Grandfather's Journey*. 1993. A Japanese American man recounts his grandfather's journey to America which he also undertakes and the feelings of being torn by a love for two different countries. (P)

Say, Allen, *A River Dream*. New York, Houghton Mifflin, 1988. Story of a young Asian American, sick in bed, dreaming about being out on the river fishing with his uncle. Illustrations are vibrant and realistic placing Asian Americans in contemporary experiences. (M)

Scott, Virginia, *Belonging*. Washington, DC, Kendall Green Productions, Galludet College Press, 1986. A 15 year old girl becomes deaf after recovering from spinal meningitis; her adjustment, the reactions of her friends and the dilemma of using only speech reading or learning to sign are explored. (M)

Shannon, George, *Unlived Affections*. New York, Harper and Row, 1989. A young man discovers his father is gay; characters are lovingly portrayed and relationships are treated respectfully. (M)

Singer, Bennett L., ed. *Growing Up Gay/Growing Up Lesbian: A Literary Anthology*. New York, The New Press, 1994. This collection of essays, short stories, poems, diary excerpts, letters, songs, excerpts from novels and autobiographies is about growing up as a lesbian or gay person. Includes experiences from a wide variety of backgrounds, races and ethnicities. (M)

Smalls-Hector, Irene, *Irene and the Big, Fine Nickel*. New York, Little, Brown and Co., 1991. The adventures of independent Irene, seven, and in heaven on the morning that she finds a nickel in the streets of 1957 Harlem, USA.

Stenek, Muriel, *I Speak English for My Mom*. Albert Whitman and Company, 1989. Lupe, a young Chicana must translate for her mom who speaks only Spanish. (P)

Tabor, Nancy Maria Grande, *Somos Un Arco Iris: We Are a Rainbow*. Watertown, MA, Charlesbridge Publishing. A picture book of paper cuts that compares the differences and similarities between people of many cultures. (P)

Tate, Eleanor E., *Thank You, Dr. Martin Luther King*. New York, Bantam Books, 1991. Through drama and supportive contact with her grandmother, fourth grader Mary Elouise learns to feel pride in being black and to develop self-confidence and a better sense of herself. (E)

Taylor, Byrd, *The Table Where Rich People Sit*. New York, Charles Scribner's Sons, 1994. A young girl, who believes her family is pretty poor, discovers that they are in fact quite rich with the things that matter in life, including being outdoors, experiencing nature, and each other. (P)

Taylor, Mildred, *Song of the Trees*. New York, Dial Press, 1973. *Roll of Thunder, Hear My Cry*. New York, Dial Press, 1976. *The Friendship*. New York, Bantam, 1987. Set in the depression, these stories show an intact black family actively defending itself and caring for each other. Powerful accounts of racism in the south from the perspective of children; the heroine is a black 9 year old girl. Other novels by this author are highly recommended. (M)

Taylor, Theodore, *The Maldonado Miracle*. New York, Avon Books, 1986. The haunting story of a 12 year old Mexican boy who illegally comes into the US to find his father. (M)

Thomas, Jane Resh, *Lights on the River*. New York, Hyperion Books for Children, 1994. Teresa, a migrant worker, misses her family in Mexico and the dignity they had there. When they move to a new farm and are shown the shabby quarters, outhouse and filthy drinking pump, she realizes that what she knows in her heart about herself is what matters most. (E)

Thomas, Ianthe, *Hi, Mrs. Mallory!* New York, Harper and Row, Inc., 1979. Story of love and caring between a black girl and an elderly white woman shows age, race and economics not necessarily preventing people's relating to each other. (P)

Treviñoh, Elizabeth Boton de, *I, Juan de Pareja*. New York, Farrar, Straus and Giroux, 1993. This historical novel tells the true story of Juan, son of an African woman and a white Spaniard, who willed him to artist Velázquez. A story of friendship between two artists, who began as master and slave, became companions, and ended as equals and friends. (M)

Turner, Ann, *Nettie's Trip South*. New York, MacMillan, 1987. Based on the actual diary of a trip south by a Northern white girl in 1859, this account depicts the realities of slavery. (E)

Uchida, Yoshiko, *A Jar of Dreams*. New York, Aladdin, 1993. *The Best Bad Thing*. Aladdin, 1986. *The Happiest Ending*. New York, Atheneum, 1985. A trilogy of novels about an 11 year old Japanese American girl. Shows the warmth and love of family in Japanese American communities. (M)

Uchida, Yoshiko, *Journey to Topaz*. New York, Scribner's, 1985. *Journey Home*. New York, Aladdin, 1992. The story of a Japanese American family who suffer humiliations when they are forced to live in an "aliens" camp in Utah after the bombing of Pearl Harbor. *Journey Home* tells the story of their struggle to adjust in California after their release from the camp. (M)

Valentine, Johnny, *The Daddy Machine*. Boston, Alyson Publications, 1992. What happens when a child wishes to have a daddy instead of two mommies? (P)

Valentine, Johnny, *The Day They Put a Tax on Rainbows and Other Stories*. Boston, Alyson Wonderland, 1992. *The Duke Who Outlawed Jelly Beans and Other Stories*. Boston, Alyson Wonderland, 1991. Original and well illustrated progressive fairy tales that incorporate imagination, action, and drama as well as lesbian and gay parents without focusing heavily on the lesbian/gay issues. (P, E)

Valentine, Johnny, *Two Moms, the Zark and Me*. Boston, Alyson Publications, 1993. A kid runs into the Zark at the zoo, who says that having two moms is not acceptable. (P)

Villanueva, Marie, *Nene and the Horrible Math Monster*. Chicago, Polychrome Books, 1993. Nene, a Filipino American girl, confronts the model minority myth that all Asians excel at math, and in doing so, overcomes her fears. (E)

Voight, Cynthia, *Homecoming*. New York, Fawcett, Jr., 1981. First of a series of novels about the four Tillerman children who, when abandoned by their mother, begin a search for their home and identity. (E, M) Other titles by this author are highly recommended.

Walter, Mildred Pitts, *Second Daughter: The Story of a Slave Girl*. New York, Scholastic, 1996. Aissa, the fictional younger sister of Mum Bett (Elizabeth Freeman), tells the true story of the slave who, in 1781, sued her owner for her freedom under the Massachusetts constitution and won. (E, M) Other titles by this author are highly recommended.

Willhoite, Michael, *Uncle What-Is-It Is Coming to Visit!!* Boston, Alyson Publications, 1993. When Igor and Tiffany find out that their gay uncle is coming to visit, they set off to ask the neighbors what "gay" means. (P, E)

Williams, Vera, *Scooter*. New York, Greenwillow, 1993. A child's silver blue scooter and her imagination help her adjust to her new home. (E) Other titles by this author are highly recommended; most are for primary students.

Williams-Garcia, Rita, *Fast Talk on a Slow Track*. New York, Dutton/Lodestar, 1992. Denzel Watson is the smartest student in his neighborhood high school, but finds it hard when he gets to Princeton; he struggles with his self-identity and the disappointment of his family. (M)

Williams-Garcia, Rita, *Like Sisters on the Homefront*. New York, Dutton/Lodestar, 1995. A funny and moving story about a pregnant teenage girl who is sent to live with her pastor uncle and his family in the south. (M)

Wolff, Virginia, *Make Lemonade*. New York, Henry, Holt and Co., 1993. In order to earn money for college, 14 year old LaVaughn babysits for a teenage mother. (M)

Wolf, Adolf Hungry and Beverly Hungry Wolf, eds. *Children of the Sun: Stories by and about Indian Kids*. New York, Morrow, 1987. Diverse collection of short stories about growing up in different parts of Native America. (E)

Woodson, Jacqueline, *The Dear One*. New York, Dell, 1993. Twelve year old Femi is furious when her mother agrees to take in the 15 year old pregnant daughter of an old friend who doesn't have the resources to support her. (M)

Woodson, Jacqueline, *From the Notebooks of Melanin Sun*. New York, Blue Sky Press, 1995. A beautiful, complex and powerful novel; thirteen year old Melanin Sun tells us, through his diary, how his life has changed since the summer his mother reveals that she has fallen in love with a women. His friends both challenge and support him. (M)

Woodson, Jacqueline, *I Didn't Mean to Tell You This*. 1994. Marie, a girl who lives in the rich African American part of town, is the only girl in the eighth grade willing to be friends with poor white Lena; Marie then finds out that her friend is being sexually abused. (M)

Woodson, Jacqueline, *Last Summer with Maizon*. New York, Dell Publishing, 1992. *Maizon at Blue Hill*. New York, Dell Publishing, 1993. *Between Madison and Palmeito*. New York, Dell Publishing, 1993. A trilogy of stories of Margaret and Maizon's friendship that is tested when Maizon is offered a scholarship to an exclusive boarding school where there are only 5 black students, and as their neighborhood begins to gentrify, and they made friends with Caroline, a white girl. (M)

Wright, Susan, *Real Sisters*. Claire's brown skin makes her look different than her light skinned older sister; when she enters a new school kids tease her and say that she and Jenny are not "real" sisters—a good look at what makes people "family" as well as a good discussion of interracial adoption. (P)

Yarbrough, Camille, *Cornrows*. New York, Coward-Mc-Cann, 1979. Past and present mingle in this discussion of hairstyles. (P, E)

Yashima, Taro, *Umbrella*. New York, Viking Press, 1958. A classic story that uses rich language and rain-like rhythm to tell of a young Japanese American girl's anticipation to use her new boots and umbrella. (P)

Yep, Laurence, *Child of the Owl*. New York, Harper, 1977. A twelve year old Casey, who knows little about her Chinese heritage, is sent to live with her grandmother in San Francisco's Chinatown. (M) Others by this author are also recommended.

8. NON-FICTION FOR YOUNG PEOPLE

P-Primary E-Elementary M-Middle School

ABC Quilts, *Kids Making Quilts for Kids*. California, the Quilt Digest Press, 1992. "At Risk" Babies Crib Quilts are passed on to children under age six who test positive to the HIV/AIDS virus, or are born with alcohol or drug related problems. (E, M)

Asian American Curriculum Project, *Japanese American Journey*. P.O. Box 367, San Mateo, CA 94401, Asian American Curriculum Project. The journey of people of Japanese ancestry in America. (M)

Ashabranner, Brent, *An Ancient Heritage: The Arab American Minority*. New York, HarperCollins, 1991. Thoughtful, balanced and provocative history of Arab Americans from the early immigrants to the 2.5 million recent arrivals. (E)

Blumberg, Rhoda, *Bloomers*. New York, Bradbury Press, 1993. The story of how that new-fashioned outfit, bloomers, helped Amelia Bloomer, Elizabeth Cady Stanton and Susan B. Anthony spread the word about women's rights. (P)

Chief Seattle, *Brother Eagle, Sister Sky: A Message from Chief Seattle*. New York, Dial Books, 1991. A Suquamish Indian Chief, Chief Seattle lived from 1790 to 1866; this illustrated book is of a speech given in response to the U.S. government attempt to buy the lands of the Pacific Northwest in the 1850s. (P, E)

Chocolate, Deborah Newton, *Kwanzaa*. Chicago, Children's Press, 1990. Positive descriptions of the African American holiday that celebrates African roots and cultural heritage and its transformation in the New World. (P)

Cohn, Janice, *The Christmas Menorahs: How a Town Fought Hate*. Morton Grove, IL, A. Whitman, 1995.

Based on real events in Billings, Montana, this narrative tells of how two children, two families and a community stood together to fight a series of anti-Semitic hate crimes against a Jewish family. (P, E)

Coleman, Penny, *Rosie the Riveter: Women Working on the Homefront in World War II*. New York, Crown Publishers, 1995. Well-illustrated documentary of the women who worked during WW II in nontraditional jobs, with good, critical text about economic, racial and gender before, and after, the war. (E, M)

Dash, Joan, *We Will Not Be Moved: The Women's Factory Strike of 1909*. 1995. Well told and illustrated story of the first strike of women workers, mostly Jewish immigrants, in a shirtwaist factory and their struggle to form a women's trade union. (E, M)

Deephaven School and Learning Lab and Margo Holen Dineen, *If They Can Do It, We Can, Too!* MN, Deaconess Press, 1995. Children from grades 1–4 write biographies about famous people who overcome learning differences similar to their own; a short autobiography of each student follows. (P)

Dwight, Laura, *We Can Do It*. New York, Checkerboard Press, 1992. In their own words and photos, a group of five young children with different disabilities talk about all the things that they can do. (P, E)

Fricke, Aaron, *Reflections of a Rock Lobster: A Story About Growing Up Gay*. Boston, Alyson Publications, 1981. Groundbreaking and controversial when it first appeared, it remains a positive example of being out at an early age; a gay teenager tells his story of letting people know he's gay, including his act of taking a male date to his senior prom. (M)

Goble, Paul, *Death of the Iron Horse*. New York, Bradbury Press, 1987. In an act of bravery and defiance against the white men encroaching on their territory in 1867, a group of young Cheyenne derail and raid a freight train. Stunningly illustrated. (E)

Goldsmith, Diane Hoyt, *Hoangh Anh: A Vietnamese American Boy*. New York, Holiday, 1992. Hoang Anh Chau's story, from his experiences as a refugee from the war through his life as an American. (P)

Green, Rayna, *Women in American Indian Society*. New York, Chelsea House, 1992. An engaging examination of the life and culture of North American Indian women. Excellent pictures. (M)

Greenfield, Eloise, *Lessie Jones Littles, Pattie Ridley, Childtimes: A Three Generation Memoir*. New York, Crowell, 1979. A beautiful book of shared memories of three generations of black women, strongly feminist and with strong family ties. (E, M)

Grimes, Nikki, *Growin'*. New York, Dial Press, 1978. Urban black families; good on race and gender roles and on acceptance of nonconformity. (E)

Hakim, Joy, *A History of US*. New York, Oxford University Press, 1994. A ten volume history of the United States that honors the diversity of Americans who have contributed to the growth of this country; written to help students understand the range of experiences of Americans of different ethnicities, races, religions and classes. (E, M)

Hamanaka, Sheila, *The Journey: Japanese Americans, Racism and Renewal*. New York, Franklin Watts, 1990. Text and photographed details of a five panel mural by Hamanaka documenting the experiences of Japanese Americans in the first half of the century, including their internment during WW II. (E, M)

Hamanaka, Sheila, *On the Wings of Peace*. New York, Clarion, 1995. Thoughtful and thought provoking book about war; primarily focusing on WW II and its repercussions, contemporary wars are also discussed. Poetry, stories, letters, essays and illustrations were donated by over 60 contributors. (E)

Hamilton, Virginia, *Many Thousands Gone: African Americans from Slavery to Freedom*. Knopf, 1988. Hamilton retells the story of slavery, from the earliest kidnappings of young Africans through the Emancipation. These fascinating stories should engage even the most reluctant reader of history. (E)

Hewett, Joan, *Hector Lives in the United States Now: The Story of a Mexican-American Child*. J.B. Lippincott, 1990. This photodocumentary traces events in the life of ten year old immigrant Hector Almaraz in the month preceding the 1988 deadline for permanent residency under the U.S. Immigration and Naturalization Services' amnesty act. (P, E)

Hirschfelder, A.B., *Happily May I Walk: American Indians and Alaska Natives Today*. New York, Scribner's 1986. An absorbing look at the lives of Native peoples in the United States today and how their present conditions came about. (E, M)

Hirschfelder, Arlene B. and Beverly R. Sluger, eds. *Rising Voices: Writings of Young Native Americans*. Riverside, NJ, MacMillan, 1993. Collection of poems and essays written by young Native Americans about family, identity, education, ritual and the harsh realities of their lives. (E, M)

Hoyt-Goldsmith, Diane, *Pueblo Storyteller*. New York, Holiday House, 1991. A young Cochiti Indian girl living in the Cochiti Pueblo near Santa Fe describes her home and family and the day-to-day life and customs of her people. (P, E)

Hu, Evaleen, *A Level Playing Field: Sports and Race*. New York, Lerner, 1995. Good resource with charts, graphs and a good bibliography that questions why silver medalist Nancy Kerrigan has more endorsements than gold medalist and world champion Kristi Yamaguchi, or whether black athletes should have to discuss social issues, etc. (E, M)

Jacobs, Francine, *The Tainos: The People Who Welcomed Columbus*. New York, G.P. Putnam's Sons, 1992. A history of how the Native people of the Greater Antilles welcomed Columbus peacefully, only to become extinguished as a people less than 50 years later. (E)

Johnson, James Weldon, *Lift Ev'ry Voice and Sing*. New York, Scholastic, 1995. A well illustrated book with the words to "Lift Every Voice and Sing," the Negro National Anthem. (P, E)

Johnston, Norma, *Remember the Ladies: The First Women's Rights Convention*. United States, Scholastic, Inc., 1995. The story of five women who in 1848 organized a convention to discuss the rights of women; events leading up to the convention and the two day proceedings and related documents are included. (E, M)

Katz, William Loren, *Black Women of the Old West*. Atheneum, 1995. Photographs and vignettes of the women who helped to settle the western frontiers; a good addition to a black history collection. (M)

Katz, William Loren, ed. *The History of Multicultura America*. 8 vols. Austin, TX, Raintree Steck-Vaughn, 1993. A history of the people often neglected in standard history textbooks with an emphasis on the fight for justice equality and democracy.

Knight, Margy Burns, *Talking Walls*. Gardiner, ME, Tilbury House, 1992. An illustrated description of walls around the world and their significance; includes the Great Wall of China, the Berlin Wall, Mahabalipuram's carved animal walls, the Mexican murals, the Vietnam Veterans Memorial, and Nelson Mandela's prison walls. There is an accompanying activity guide. (E)

Kranz, Rachel, *Straight Talk about Prejudice*. New York, Facts On File, 1992. Useful resource for students to help them examine the realities of prejudice. (P)

Kuklin, Susan, *How My Family Lives in America*. 1992. African American, Asian American and Hispanic American children describe their families' cultural traditions. (E)

Lawrence, Jacob, *The Great Migration*. New York, HarperTrophy, 1994. Illustrated and written by the great painter, Jacob Lawrence, this is a moving illustration of the black migration from the south to the north. (P, E)

Levine, Ellen, *Freedom's Children: Young Civil Rights Activists Tell Their Own Stories*. New York, G.P. Putnam, 1993. Southern blacks who were young and involved in the civil rights movement during the 50s and 60s describe their experiences. (E, M)

Lewis, Barbara, *Kids with Courage: True Stories about Young People Making a Difference*. Minneapolis, MN, Free Spirit Publishing, 1992. Real kids who fight crime, take social action, perform heroic acts, and save the environment. (M)

Lomas Garza, Carmen, *Family Pictures/Cuadros de Familia*. Emeryville, CA, Children's Book Press, 1990. Brilliant artwork illustrates the author's Chicana childhood in Texas. Details of traditional Hispanic family and community life; explanatory passages in Spanish and English. (P, E)

McKissack, Patricia C. and Frederic McKissak, *Christmas in the Big House, Christmas in the Quarters*. New York, Scholastic, 1994. A well researched history of the contrasting celebrations of a traditional Christmas in 1859 Virginia, from the perspective of the slaveholder and his household and from the slave community. Includes carols, spirituals, recipes, poetry and an extensive bibliography. (E)

Meltzer, Milton, *Bread and Roses: The Struggle for American Labor, 1865–1915*. New York, Vintage, 1967. Excellent historical overview of working peoples' struggle for economic equality during this period.

Meltzer, Milton, ed. *In Their Own Words: A History of the American Negro 1916–1966*. 2 vols. New York, Thomas Y. Crowell Co., 1967. Excellent collection of oral histories, primary documents, journal entries, etc. (E) Other titles by this author are excellent.

Meltzer, Milton, *The Jewish Americans: A History in Their Own Words*. New York, Harper Collins, 1982. Meltzer turns personal accounts into a living history of Jewish Americans from colonial times to the 1980s. (M)

Meltzer, Milton, *Starting from Home: A Winter's Beginning*. New York, Viking, 1988. Meltzer's autobiography fuses his personal story as a child of Jewish American immigrants in the 1920–39's with an account of the sociopolitical conditions at the time. (M)

Milne, Teddy, *Kids Who Have Made a Difference*. Pittenbruach Press, 1989. Empowering stories for children, about children who have taken action against trouble in the world. (E, M)

Moutoussamy-Ashe, Jeanne, *Daddy and Me: A Photo Story of Arthur Ashe and His Daughter Camera*. New York, Knopf, 1993. Ashe's young daughter discusses her father's illness, and her important job helping him to keep his morale up as he dies from AIDS. (P, E)

Murrow, Liza, *Twelve Days in August*. New York, Holiday House, 1993. Twelve days change a sixteen year old soccer player's perception of himself, his family, girls, and gays. A fascinating look at homophobia in a small town high school, and the way teens handle the situation. (M)

Myers, Walter Dean, *Now Is Your Time: The African American Struggle for Freedom*. New York, Harper Collins, 1991. A history of African Americans' fight for freedom from 1619 until the present interwoven with the author's tracing of his family history. (E)

New Mexico People and Energy Collective, *Red Ribbons for Emma*. Berkeley, CA, New Seed Press, Emma Yazzi, a Navajo grandmother and sheepherder, is a modern day hero fighting the pollution of reservation lands. (E)

Ortiz, Simon, *The People Shall Continue*. San Francisco, Children's Book Press, 1977. Simple and powerful account of the history of Native people to the present; beautifully illustrated, it is one of the best epic poems for young readers. (P)

Rosenberg, Maxine, *Living in Two Worlds*. New York, Lothrop, Lee & Shephard, 1986. Good, positive accounts of interracial families.

Ruíz, Catherine de and Dana and Richard Larios, *La Causa: The Migrant Farmworkers Story*. Austin, Raintree Steck-Vaughn, 1993. Well told story of Cesar Chavez and the United Farm Workers Union. (P)

Seltzer, Isadore, *The House I Live In: At Home in America*. New York, Macmillan Publishing Co., 1992. An illustrated introduction to the architecture of different types of homes across the United States, explaining why people built where they did and the way that they did. (E)

Sing, Bill, ed. *Asian-Pacific Americans*. Los Angeles, CA, National Conference of Christians and Jews, Asian American Journalists Association and the Association of Asian Pacific American Artists, 1989. History of Asian/Pacific Islanders in America until the present day. (M)

Sobol, Harriet Langsam, *Grandpa—A Young Man Grown Old*. New York, Coward, McCann, and Geoghegan, 1980. Parallel soliloquies by a 17 year old girl viewing her grandfather and the grandfather viewing his life. (E, M)

Souci, Robert D. San, *Kate Shelley: Bound for Legend*. Dial/Penguin, 1995. The true story of a young girl in Iowa who, when a terrible storm took out the railroad bridge near her home, walked miles in the dark to warn the railroad company. Well illustrated. (P)

Steffoff, Rebeca, *From the Land of Morning Calm: Koreans in America*. New York, Chelsea, 1995. History of Korean immigration, and the particular problems they face in rural and urban areas. (E)

Sullivan, Mary Beth, *A Show of Hands: Say It in Sign Language*. Reading, MA, Addison-Wesley, 1980. An introduction to the sign language used by many deaf and hearing impaired people. (E)

Takaki, Ronald, *From Exiles to Immigrants: The Refugees from Southeast Asia*. New York, Chelsea House, 1995. Historical information about Southeast Asian at home, and their journeys to America. (E)

Takaki, Ronald, *India in the West: South Asians in America*. New York, Chelsea, 1995. The immigration histories of Indians, Pakistanis and other South Asians. (E)

Teacher's Committee on Central America, *Wilfredo, the Story of a Boy from El Salvador (La Historia de un Nino de El Salvador)*. Los Angeles, Teacher's Committee on Central America, 1986. True story of a refugee boy from El Salvador who tells of his move to the United States; bilingual, large print. (P)

Walker, Alice, *To Hell with Dying*. New York, Harcourt Brace Jovanovich, 1988. Alice Walker tells of her lifetime friend Mr. Sweet who, often on the verge of dying, could always be revived by the loving attention that she and her brother gave him. (M)

Walker, Lou Ann, *Hand, Heart and Mind*. New York, Dial Books, 1994. A comprehensive story of the history of the education of America's deaf community. Also explores the conflict between oralism and manualism. Photo illustrations. (E)

Webb, Sheyann and Rachel West Nelson, *Selma, Lord Selma: Girlhood Memories of the Civil Rights Days*. Alabama, University of Alabama Press, 1980. An excellent account of the civil rights struggle from two children who were active in it. (E, M)

9. POETRY AND LEGENDS

Baylor, Byrd, ed. *And It Is Still That Way: Legends Told by Arizona Indian Children*. New York, Scribner's, 1976. Some of the oldest and best known Indian legends, with good respect for environment. (P) Other titles by this author are highly recommended.

Bruchac, Joseph, *Flying with the Eagle, Racing the Great Bear: Stories from Native North America*. USA, Penguin, 1995. Sixteen coming of age stories for and about boys; this is a companion to the collection by Bruchac, and Gayle Ross, *The Girl Who Married the Moon: Tales from Native North America*. USA, Penguin, 1995, that focuses on the roles of girls and women growing up in Native cultures. Other titles by this author are highly recommended. (E)

De Sauza, James, *Brother Anansi and the Cattle Ranch*. San Francisco, Children's Book Press, 1989. Folktale from the Spanish speaking Caribbean featuring the tricky Anansi, the spider. (P)

Esbensen, Barbara Juster, *The Star Maiden: An Ojibway Tale*. Boston, Little, Brown and Co., 1988. The retelling of an Ojibway legend that explains how the stars came to be water lilies. (P, E)

Feelings, Tom, *Soul Looks Back in Wonder*. New York, Dial Books, 1993. Feelings approached thirteen poets such as Maya Angelou, Askia M. Tore, Mari Evans, Langston Hughes and Walter Dean Myers to write selections to accompany his beautiful multicolored drawings of the strength, creativity and beauty of the African American heritage. (E)

Galloway, Priscilla, *Truly Grim Tales*. New York, Delacorte, 1995. Eight traditional folktales are retold from some surprising points of view—such as Jack and the Beanstalk retold from the point of view of the ogre's wife. (M)

Goble, Paul, *Star Boy*. New York, Aladdin Books, 1991. The story of how the sacred knowledge of the Sun Dance was given to the Blackfoot people. Beautifully illustrated by the author. (P) Other titles by this author are highly recommended.

Greenfield, Eloise, *Honey, I Love and Other Love Poems*. New York, Crowell, 1978. Sixteen poems on family love and friendship as experienced by an African American girl. (E)

Hallworth, G., *Cric Crac: A Collection of West Indian Stories*. Kingston, Jamaica, Heinmann Caribbean, 1990. A collection of Haitian/Creole fables. (P)

Hamilton, Virginia, *Her Stories: African American Folktales, Fairy Tales and True Tales*. New York, Scholastic, 1995. Beautifully told, lavishly illustrated tales that focus on the strengths, beauties and imaginations of African American women. (P, E, M)

Hamilton, Virginia, *The People Could Fly: American Black Folktales*. 1985. Retold folktales of animals, tricksters and the supernatural, slave narratives, fantasy escapes and the desire for freedom. (E)

Hughes, Langston, *The DreamKeeper and Other Poems*. New York, Borzoi Books, 1994. These sixty-six poems originally published in 1932 were selected by the author for young readers and include lyrical poems, songs, and blues that explore the Black experience. Inspirational, proud and uplifting, these poems celebrate hopes, dreams, aspirations, life and love. (E)

Jones, Hettie, ed. *The Trees Stand Shining*. New York, Dial, 1971. Songs, printed as poems, from many generations of Native Americans. (P, E)

Joseph, Lynn, *A Wave in Her Pocket: Stories from Trinidad*. New York, Clarion, 1991. A collection of tales written from the perspective of a young girl in Trinidad listening to a great aunt's traditional folklore stories. All are framed by family events; while some of them teach, some amuse, some scare, all delight the reader. (P, E)

Lester, Julius, *John Henry*. New York, Dial, 1995. Beautifully illustrated and well researched retelling of the African American tall tale. (P, E)

Marlo, Thomas, *Free to Be You and Me*. New York, McGraw-Hill, 1974. Poems, songs, stories and pictures about growing up with nonstereotypic sex roles. (P, E)

Morgan, Robin, *The Mer-Child: A Legend for Children and Other Adults*. New York, Feminist Press, 1991. An enchanting story of two outsiders who find a deep kinship in each other. (E)

Peña, Sylvia, ed. *Tun-ta-ca-tun: More Stories and Poems in English and Spanish for Children*. Houston, Arte Público Press, 1986. Stories and poems about immigrant Latino/a experience in America. (P, E)

Peña, Sylvia, *Kikirikí: Stories and Poems in English and Spanish for Children*. Houston, TX, Arte Público Press, 1987. A series of short stories, poems, and *adivinanzas* (riddles), some selections in Spanish, some in English; all written by Latina/Latino authors. (P, E)

Rosen, Michael, ed. *South & North and East & West: The Oxfam Anthology of Children's Stories*. Cambridge, Candlewick Press, 1992. A collection of twenty-five traditional tales from countries around the world, including Mali, Malta, Mauritania, Bangladesh and the Dominican Republic. Twenty-five outstanding illustrators are represented. (E)

Soto, Gray, *Canto Familiar*. New York, Harcourt, 1995. Poems that detail the everyday experience, particularly that of growing up Mexican American. (E)

Souci, Robert San, *Cut From the Same Cloth: American Women of Myth, Legend and Tall Tales*. New York, Philomel Books, 1993. A wide variety of groups—Native American, Mexican American, African American, Anglo American—are represented among these legendary American female heroes. (E)

Yolen, Jane, *The Ballad of the Pirate Queens*. New York, Harcourt Brace, 1995. The ballad of famous pirates Anne Bonney and Mary Reade who fought to protect their ship. Beautifully illustrated. (P, E)

10. STUDENT RESOURCE BOOKS

Changing Our World: A Handbook for Young Activists. Fleisler, Paul, PO Box 13448, Tucson, AZ 85732, Zephyr Press, 1993. A practical resource for supporting middle school students in their change efforts.

Hopscotch Around the World, Lankford, Mary D. New York, Morrow Junior Books, 1992. Eighteen different versions of the ancient game hopscotch with directions for playing. Very useful illustrations. (P, E)

It's Our World, Too! Young People Who Are Making a Difference (and how they're doing it), Hoose, Phillip. Boston, Joy Street Books, 1993. Profiles specific young people and groups of kids who are working to make the world a better place. (E, M)

The Kids' Guide to Social Action, Lewis, Barbara. Minneapolis, Free Spirit Publishers, 1992. Helps kids turn creative thinking into positive social action. (M)

Teen Voices, P.O. Box 6009, JFK Station, Boston, MA 02144, Women Express. National magazine for and about teenage girls with a multicultural focus. (M)

Think about Racism, Mizell, Linda. NY, Walker Publishing Co., 1992. A readable book for young people about racism.

Young Peacemakers Project Book, Fry-Miller, Kathleen M. Elgin, IL, Brethren Press, 1988. (E, M) Instructions for a variety of projects that promote peace and concern for the environment. (E, M)

11. BIOGRAPHY

P-Primary E-Elementary M-Middle School

Alvin Ailey, Pinkney, Andrea Davis. Hyperion Books for Children, 1993. Gay African American master dancer and choreographer who founded an international dance theatre. (E)

Young Arthur Ashe: Brave Champion, Dexter, Robin. New York, Troll Communications, 1996. (P) *Arthur Ashe: Against the Wind*, Collins, David R. New York, Dillon, 1994. (E) *Arthur Ashe and His Match with History*, Quackenbush, Robert. New York, Simon and Schuster, 1994. (M) African American tennis legend, who dedicated his life to social causes, and struggled against heart disease and AIDS.

Audre Lorde, Gomez, Jewelle. New York, Chelsea House, 1997. Black lesbian poet, activist and New York State Poet Laureate. (M)

A Boy Called Slow: The True Story of Sitting Bull, Brouchac, Joseph. New York, Philomel, 1995. A boy named Slow who became one of the greatest warriors. (P)

Brave Bessie Flying Free, Fisher, Lillian. New York, Hendric-Long, 1995. Two years before Amelia Earhart, Bessie Coleman became the first African American aviatrix to receive her flying license. (E)

Calling the Doves, Herrera, Juan Felipe. New York, Children's Press, 1995. A bilingual memoir of the Mexican American poet, son of migrant workers. (E)

Charles Drew, Mahone-Lonesome, Robyn. Danbury, CT, Grolier, 1990. African American doctor who developed modern blood plasma science. (E)

Charles Eastman, New York, Chelsea House, 1994. Sioux physician and writer. (E)

Cesar Chavez: Labor Leader, Cedeño, Maria, Brookfield, CT. Millbrook Press, 1993. Chicano migrant worker, organizer of the United Farmworkers' Union. (P)

Chris Burke: Actor, Geraghty, Helen Monsoon. New York, Chelsea Books, 1994. The first actor with Down syndrome to star in a television series. (E)

Coming Home: From the Life of Langston Hughes, Cooper, Floyd. New York, Philomel, 1993. (E) *Free to Dream: The Making of a Poet—Langston Hughes*. Osofsky, Audrey, New York, Lothrop, Lee and Shepard, 1996. (E, M) African American poet of the Harlem Rennaisance.

Dear Benjamin Banneker, Pinkney, Andrea Davis. New York, Gulliver, 1994. African American self-taught scientist and mathematician. (P)

Eleanor Roosevelt: A Life of Discovery, Freedman, Russel. Clarion, 1992. First Lady who devoted her life to working for peace and helping others. (E)

Young Frederick Douglass: The Slave Who Learned to Read, Girard, Linda Walvoord. 1994. (P) *Frederick Douglass: The Last Day of Slavery*, Miller, William. 1995. (P) *Escape from Slavery: The Boyhood of Frederick Douglass in His Own Words*, McCurdy, Michael. New York, Knopf, 1994. (E) *Frederick Douglass: In His Own Words*, Meltzer, Milton, New York, Harcourt, 1995. (M) A former slave, abolitionist, editor and agitator for black rights.

Getting the Real Story: Nellie Bly and Ida B. Wells, Davidson, Sue. Seattle, Seal Press, 1992. Two independent news reporters at the turn of the century—Bly focused on the issues of prisons, mental institutions and the poor while Wells focused on Black women, lynching, and civil rights. (E, M)

Minty: A Story of Young Harriet Tubman, Schroeder, Alan, New York, Dial Press, 1996. (P) *Go Free or Die: A Story about Harriet Tubman*, Ferris, Jeri. Minneapolis, Carolrhoda, 1988. (P, E) *Wanted Dead or Alive: The True Story of Harriet Tubman*, McGovern, Ann. New York, Scholastic, 1965. (E) *Harriet Tubman, Conductor of the Underground Railroad*, Petry, Ann. New York, Crowell, 1955. (M) Black woman born as a slave who sought freedom in the North for herself and others, using the Underground Railroad. Both the McGovern and Petry are classics.

Harriet Beecher Stowe and the Beecher Preachers, Fritz, Jean. 1994. Anti-slavery activist. (E)

A Heart in Politics: Jeanette Rankin and Patsy Mink, Davidson, Sue. Seattle, Seal Press, 1992. Rankin was the first woman to run and be elected to Congress, and Mink was the first women of color (Japanese American) to be elected to Congress. (E)

Hiawatha, Messenger of Peace, Fradin, Dennis Brindell. New York, Macmillan, 1992. Diplomatic leader who persuaded the warring Iroquios nations to construct a cooperative, constitutional relationship. (M)

I Always Wanted to Be Somebody, Gibson, Althea. New York, Noble and Noble, 1967. Autobiography of a talented African American female athlete who overcame physical difficulties to win Olympic Gold medals. Out of print, but worth obtaining. (E)

The Invisible Thread, Uchida, Yoshika. New York, Julian Messner, 1991. Japanese American young adult novel writer. (M)

Isamu Noguchi: A Sculptor's World, Noguchi, Isamu. New York, Harper and Row, 1968. Japanese American modernist sculptor. (P, E)

James Baldwin, Kenan, Randall. New York, Chelsea House, 1994. Black, gay essayist, novelist and activist. (M)

James Meredith and School Desegregation, Elish, Dan. Brookfield, CT, Millbrook, 1994. Story of Meredith's efforts to attend the then segregated University of Mississippi in 1962. (E)

Jim Abbot: Major League Pitcher, Macht, Normal L. New York, Chelsea House, 1994. Major league pitcher who was born without a right hand. (E)

Jim Thorpe, Bernotas, Bob. New York, Chelsea House, 1992. Sac and Fox athlete who won gold medals at the 1912 Olympics and became a professional football player. (E)

Kids At Work: Lewis Hine and the Crusade against Child Labor, Freedman, Russel. Clarion, 1994. Photographer who documented the problems of child labor. (E)

The Last Princess: The Story of Princess Ka'iulani of Hawai'i, Stanley, Fay. New York, Four Winds, 1991. Crown Princess of Hawai'i who tried to save her country from annexation by the United States. (E)

Lorraine Hansberry, Scheader, Catherine. Chicago, IL, Children's Press, 1978. African American playwright. (E)

The Lost Garden, Yep, Lawrence. Julian Messner, 1991. Yep writes about his own search for dignity as a Chinese American and a young adult novel writer. (M)

Louis Braille: Inventor, Bryant, Jennifer Fisher. New York, Chelsea House, 1994. Inventor of raised dot system that enabled him and other blind people to read. (E)

Malcolm X: By Any Means Necessary, Meyers, Walter Dean. Scholastic, 1993. (E) *Malcolm X: Black Rage*, Collins, David R. New York, Dillon Press, 1992. (E, M) African American social and political activist.

Margaret Sanger: "Every Child a Wanted Child", Whitelaw, Nancy. New York, Dillon, 1994. Activist for reproductive rights for women. (M)

Marian Wright Edelman: The Making of a Crusader, Siegel, Beatrice. New York, Simon, 1995. Champion of human rights for children. (E) *Martin Luther King*, Bray, Rosemary L. New York, Greenwillow, 1995. Civil rights activist. (E)

Mary Lincoln's Dressmaker: Elizabeth Keckley's Remarkable Rise from Slave to White House Confidante, Rutberg, Becky. Chicago, Walker Publishing, 1995. Slave who bought her freedom and was close friend to the president's wife despite public disapproval. (E)

Mary McLeod Bethune, Greenfield, Eloise. New York, Crowell, 1977. (P) *Mary McLeod Bethune: Teacher with a Dream*, Anderson, LaVere. New York, Chelsea Juniors, 1991. (E) African American teacher and founder of schools. (E)

Maya Angelou: Journey of the Heart. Pettit, Jayne, New York, Lodestar Books, 1996. African American civil rights activist, writer, poet and university professor. (E)

Mother Jones: One Woman's Fight for Labor, Kraft, Betsy Harvey. New York, Clarion, 1995. Activist for child laborers and miners. (E)

Nicholasa Mohr: Growing up inside the Sanctuary of My Imagination, Mohr, Nicholasa. New York, Messner, 1994. Puerto Rican writer of young adult novels. (M)

No Stone Unturned: The Life and Times of Maggie Kuhn, Kuhn, Maggie, Christine Long and Lara Quinn. NY, Ballantine, 1991. Founder and chair person of the Gray Panthers, an elder activist organization.

Paul Robeson: A Voice to Remember, McKissack, Patricia and Fredrick McKissack. Hillside, NJ, Enslow, 1992. Black singer and actor who spoke out against racism and injustice. (P)

Peace and Bread: The Story of Jane Addams, McPherson, Stephanie. Minneapolis, Carolrhoda, 1993. Wealthy woman who devoted her life to working for the poor, world peace and human rights. (E)

Pocahontas, Iannone, Catharine, New York, Chelsea, 1995. Powhatan peacemaker. (E)

Poet and Politician of Puerto Rico: Don Luis Muñoz Marin, Bernier-Grand, Carmen T. New York, Orchard, 1994. First elected governor of Puerto Rico. (E)

Ray Charles, Bell, Sharon Mathis. New York, Crowell, 1973. (P) *Ray Charles*, Ritz, David. New York, Chelsea, 1994. (E) African American musician who lost his sight when he was seven.

Roberto Clemente: Puerto Rican Baseball Great, Gilbert, Thomas. New York, Chelsea House, 1991. Puerto Rican baseball player and social activist. (E)

Ron Kovic: Anti-War Activist, Moss, Nathaniel. New York, Chelsea, 1995. Paralyzed U.S. Marine who became an anti-war activist. (E)

Rosa Parks, Greenfield, Eloise. New York, HarperCollins, 1995. Civil rights activist. (E)

Sarah Winnemucca, Kloss, Doris, Milwaukee, Raintree Publisher/Pinnacle Press, 1990. Paiute woman who fought for justice and equity for her people. (E)

Scientist with Determination, Elma Gonzalez, Verheyden-Hillard, M. Bethesda, The Equity Institute, 1985. Mexican-American woman who grew up in a family of migrant workers and went on to earn a doctorate in cellular biology and eventually head her own research laboratory. (P, E)

Sequoyah's Gift: A Portrait of the Cherokee Leader, Klausner, Janet. HarperCollins, 1993. Cherokee leader. (E)

Sojourner Truth: Ain't I a Woman?, McKissack, Patricia and Frederick McKissack. New York, Scholastic, 1993. African American feminist and abolitionist.

Steven Hawkins: Revolutionary Physicist, McDaniel, Melissa. New York, Chelsea, 1994. Physicist who has Hodgkins disease has made major contributions in his field. (E)

Stitching Stars: The Story Quilts of Harriet Powers, Lyons, Mary E. 1993, Charles Scribner's Sons, 1993. An illustrated biography of an African American quilter who, during the late 1800s, made quilts of her favorite Bible stories and folktales. (E)

Toni Morrison, Century, Douglas. New York, Chelsea, 1994. Black female novelist. (E)

Vilma Martinez, Codye, Corinn. Austin, TX, Steck-Vaughn, 1993. Bilingual biography of a Chicana lawyer who has won many civil rights cases. (E)

W.E.B. DuBois: Crusader for Peace, Cryon-Hicks, Katherine. Lowell, MA, Discovery Enterprises, 1991. Black theorist and activist of the early twentieth century. (E)

Warriors Don't Cry: A Searing Memoir of the Battle to Integrate Little Rock's Central High, Beals, Melba Pattilo. New York, Archway Paperback, abridged 1995. Autobiography of a 16 year old girl who was one of nine teenagers in 1957 to integrate Central High. (E, M)

We Flew Over the Bridge, Ringold, Faith. Bulfinch Press, 1995. African American artist and children's book author. (E)

When Justice Failed: The Fred Korematsu Story, Chin, Steven A. Ed. Alex Haley. New York, Steck-Vaughn Company, 1993. Japanese American who defied the order of internment during World War II and took his case to the U.S. Supreme Court. (E)

Wilma Mankiller: Chief of the Cherokee, Simon, Charman. Chicago, Children's Press, 1991. (P) *Wilma Mankiller*, Lazo, Caroline. New York, Dillon, 1995. (E) Cherokee activist who is currently the first woman leader of the Cherokee nation.

Zora Hurston and the Chinaberry Tree, Miller, William. New York, Lee and Low, 1994. (P) *Jump at de Sun: The Story of Zora Neale Hurston*. Porter, A. P., Minneapolis, Carolrhoda, 1992. (E) *Sorrow's Kitchen: The Life and Folklore of Zora Neale Hurston*, Lyons, Mary E. 1990. (M) Black woman ethnographer, novelist and collector of African American folklore during the Harlem Renaissance.

12. BIOGRAPHY COLLECTIONS FOR YOUNG PEOPLE

P-Primary E-Elementary M-Middle School

African-American Scientists, McKissack, Patricia and Frederick McKissack. New York, Millbrook, 1995. Good resource that pays attention to lesser known and women scientists. (E)

American Women: Their Lives in Their Words, Rappaport, Doreen. New York, Crowell, 1990. Ground-breaking collection of the oral histories of women, form the "New Word" era to the present. Includes Eleanor Roosevelt, Fannie Lou Hamer, Margaret Mead, Jane Addams as well as lesser known women. (M)

Extraordinary Asian Pacific Americans, Sinnot, Susan. Chicago, Children's Press, 1993. Comprehensive, well written sketches of over 70 Asian, South Asian, Southeast Asian and Pacific Islander Americans.

Famous Asian Americans, Morey, Janet Nomura and Wendy Dunn. New York, Cobblehill Books, 1992. Fourteen biographies including: Jose Aruego, Michael Chang, Connie Chung, Myung-Whun Chung, Wendy Lee Graham, Daniel Inouye, Maxine Hong Kingston, June Kuramoto, Haing Ngor, Dustin Nguyen, Ellison Onizuka, I.M. Pei, Samuel C.C. Ting and An Wang.

Focus: Five Women Photographers, Wolf, Sylvia, Whitman, 1994. Margaret Bourke-White, Julia Margaret Cameron, Flor Garduño, Sandy Skoglund and Lorna Simpson. (E):

Going Where I'm Coming from: Memoirs of American Youth, Anne Mazer, ed. New York, Persea Books, 1995. Fourteen autobiographical narratives of immigration from the point of view of a young person; these stories look at the process of immigrating itself as well as the issues surrounding growing up within two cultures. (M)

Great Women in the Struggle, Toyomi, Igus. Orange, NJ, Just Us Books, 1991. Book for young readers with pictures and information on 80 African American women who have contributed to the history and culture of the United States. (P)

Herstory: Women Who Changed the World, Ashby, Ruth and Deborah Gore Ohrn. New York, Viking, 1995. Sappho, Susan B. Anthony, Indira Gandhi, Wilma Mankiller plus 119 others. (M)

I Dream A World: Portraits of Black Women Who Changed America, Summers, Barbara and Photographs and interviews by Brian Lanker. New York, Stewart, Tabori and Chang, 1989. Seventy-five large photo portraits of contemporary Black women of the diaspora, from artists to activists; educators to environmentalists; poets to politicians. (M)

Inventing Ourselves: Lesbian Life Stories, Hall Carpenter Archive Lesbian Oral History Group. Routledge London, 1989. Fifteen lesbians interviewed for the Oral History Project speak of their childhoods, lovers, friends, and work, as well as lesbian social and political life from the 1930s to 1987. (M)

Is There a Woman in the House . . . or Senate?, Fireside, Bryna J. New York, Whitman, 1995. Ten portraits of political women from Jeanette Rankin in 1916 to Barbara Mikulski today. (E)

Keeping Secrets: The Girlhood Diaries of Seven Women Writers, Lyons, Mary E. New York, Holt, 1995. Seven nineteenth century writers: Louisa May Alcott, Charlotte Forten, Sarah Jane Foster, Alice Dunbar Nelson, Ida B. Wells and Charlotte Perkins Gilman. (M)

Lives of Notable Asian Americans: Art, Entertainment, Sports, Gan, Geraldine. New York, Chelsea House, 1995. E.g., Michael Chang, Zubin Mehta, Kristi Yamaguchi, Maya Lin, Isamu Noguchi, and Margaret Cho.

Lives of Notable Asian Americans: Business, Politics, Science, Ragaza, Angelo. New York, Chelsea House, 1995. E.g., Ellison Onizuka, Senator Daniel Inouye, Dr. David Ho, Josefine Cruz Natori, and Loida Nicolas Lewis.

Lives of Notable Asian Americans: Literature and Education, New York, Chelsea House, 1995. Short autobiographies on the lives of prominent women and men.

Outward Dreams: Black Inventors and Their Inventions, Haskins, Jim. New York, StarFire, 1992. A diversity of inventors, including Ben Bradley, Madame C.J. Walker, and more. (E)

A Separate Battle: Women and the Civil War, Chang, Ina. New York, Lodestar/Dutton, 1992. Louisa May Alcott,